ISSUES

OF

THE EXCHEQUER;

BEING

A COLLECTION OF PAYMENTS MADE OUT OF
HIS MAJESTY'S REVENUE,

FROM

KING HENRY III. TO KING HENRY VI. INCLUSIVE.

WITH AN APPENDIX.

EXTRACTED AND TRANSLATED FROM THE ORIGINAL ROLLS OF THE ANCIENT
PELL OFFICE, NOW REMAINING IN THE CUSTODY OF

THE RIGHT HONOURABLE SIR JOHN NEWPORT, Bart.,
COMPTROLLER-GENERAL OF HIS MAJESTY'S EXCHEQUER.

By FREDERICK DEVON,
OF THE CHAPTER-HOUSE RECORD OFFICE, POET'S CORNER,
WESTMINSTER.

LONDON:
JOHN MURRAY, 50, ALBEMARLE STREET.
1837.

LONDON:
PRINTED BY W. CLOWES AND SONS,
STAMFORD-STREET.

My Lord,

I cannot sufficiently express my gratitude for the permission that has been granted me to dedicate to your Lordship the following Work, which I regret is not more complete, that it might be less unworthy your distinguished name and patronage.

The readiness with which your Lordship was pleased to accede to my request must be attributed solely to the solicitude which you unremittingly manifest to facilitate the advancement of general literature, and of whatever may tend to promote the benefit of your country, whether in affairs of magnitude, or in those of inferior importance.

In confirmation of this opinion I need only appeal to the high office which your Lordship holds in his Majesty's Government, and to the fact that during the heat of political contest you enjoy the esteem of all parties, the confidence of your sovereign, and the admiration and respect of the nation at large.

That you may long experience the blessing of health, and the heartfelt satisfaction attendant on your laudable exertions, is the sincere wish of,

My Lord,

Your Lordship's

Most obedient

And very humble Servant,

FREDERICK DEVON.

April, 1837.

INTRODUCTION.

THE Editor, in the Introduction to his last volume of
the Pell Records, of the period of King James I., promised to furnish a selection from these Records of pa.
sages connected with history of a more rare and curious
nature, to commence with the reign of King Henry III.
He trusts, upon a careful examination of the contents of
the present volume, that it will be considered he has
redeemed his pledge.

The Records from which the following extracts are
taken, on account of their variety, authenticity, and importance, afford valuable illustrations to every branch of
our history, foreign and domestic: and it would be diffi-
cult to point out any other class of Records furnishing
so rich and exhaustless a mine of information to the
Historian, Statesman, Political Economist, Jurisconsult,
or Biographer.

The nature of these documents having in a previous
volume[1] been so fully explained, it now only remains to
proceed at once to the usual object of a Preface—to notice,

---

[1] See the Editor's Introduction to Issue Roll of Thomas de Brantingham,
44 Edward III.

b

and draw the reader's attention to, some of the more pro-
minent features in the volume before him.

HENRY III.

The earliest Roll from which any extracts are made
is a Liberate Roll of the tenth year of the reign of
King Henry III., and though the entries in the earlier
Records are generally of a more concise nature, yet they
contain numerous particulars confirmatory of many points
of general history, and illustrative of our fiscal, legal, and
municipal rights.   The first entry on the Roll above referred to furnishes evidence of the existence of a fair at
Saint Ives[1] at this early period, where the King is stated
to have purchased robes for his brother Richard.

Upon the same Roll the King is found rewarding the
abbot and monks of Warden[2] for their losses and services
rendered near the town and at the castle of Bedford; which
probably relates to the disturbances a few years previous,
caused by Foulques de Breauteé, who seized and imprisoned the Judges in this castle.[3]   At the same page[4] of

[1] See page 1. The prescriptive right to take tolls in this fair is now in
course of litigation.

[2] See page 2.

[3] This occurred at the close of 1223. Braybrook, one of the judges, was
hurried into the strong castle of Bedford, and treated with great indignity;
the fortress was surrounded, and the manner of its being stormed points out
the way in which strong holds were then constructed. "In the first assault
was taken the barbican; in the second the outer ballia; at the third attack
the miners threw down the wall by the old tower, and, with great danger,
through a breach, made themselves masters of the inner ballia; at the
fourth assault the miners set fire to the tower, so that the smoke burst out,
the wall clove asunder, and the defenders yielded it up." *Matthew Paris.*

[4] See page 2.

this volume, is an entry of 1000*l.* paid to Hubert de Burgh, for the custody of Dover Castle, who is styled by Andrews the historian, the gallant defender of this fortress.[1] It is unnecessary here to state the circumstances under which Hubert de Burgh succeeded to the administration of the affairs of the realm upon the death of the Earl of Pembroke; this, with other incidents in history frequently referred to in the Pell Records, being matters of sufficient historical notoriety, are not noticed; but many names and rewards to persons who supported the King and his Chief Justiciary, aided by the influence of the Church, against the encroachments of the Barons, will be found extracted from these Rolls.

The object of the embassy sent to Lewis VIII., of France, successor to King Philip, demanding the restitution of Normandy, (Poitou and Guienne then being in danger,) having failed, preparations were made to reinforce Richard, Earl of Cornwall, the King's brother, in Gascony, both with men and money; and though King Henry subsequently sold these territories to the French King, the few extracts made from this Roll show the King's anxiety (at least at this period) to assist his brother in recovering the lost possessions, and retaining those threatened to be wrested from him.

The Editor regrets that the confined limits of this work would not allow him to furnish many interesting extracts

---

[1] Lyons, in his *History of Dover*, gives an interesting biographical account of this persecuted man, and of the various vicissitudes of his life. He states that the Bishop of Winchester was his implacable enemy; and, amongst other accusations, charged him with having taken a precious stone out of the King's treasury, possessing the extraordinary quality, that whoever had it with him would be victorious in the day of battle, and which he gave to Leoline, Prince of Wales, the King's enemy. *Lyons' History of Dover,* vol. ii. p. 148—158.

at this period, relating to Normandy, Gascony, Poitou, Guienne, and other provinces in France formerly subject to the King of England, as they probably would have supplied many deficiencies in Carte's[1] Catalogue of the Norman and Gascon Rolls, the earliest noticed by him being the 26th[2] Henry III. Some few extracts, however, relating to these provinces will be found on referring to the Index at the end of this volume; and further information on this subject may be gathered from the Rolls themselves.

It will be in order of time here to notice the portion of an early Roll of Accounts rendered into the Exchequer by the Jews, discovered amongst the Pell Records, and added in the Appendix,[3] from the heading of which a lithographic impression is annexed. Madox,[4] in his History of the Exchequer, makes frequent mention of the Jews and of their accounts rendered into the Exchequer, some as early as the reign of King Henry II.; and the late John Caley, Esq., in his learned treatise[5] "On the Origin or early Establishment of the Jews in England," states there were many repositories for the Jewish deeds established in England, but the greatest of these was in a

---

[1] A Catalogue of the Gascon, Norman, and French Rolls preserved in the archives of the Tower of London. London, 1743, two vols. folio, edited by Thomas Carte.

[2] Mr. Hardy, of the Tower, in the Introduction to his valuable edition of these Rolls, lately published, clearly proves that Carte was wrong in assigning the date of the 16th year of Henry III. to the Vascon Roll of the 26th Henry III. The Editor begs leave to refer the *learned in the abbreviated old Latin and Norman French* to this valuable collection of Mr. Hardy; and *the general reader of history* may consult his preface with advantage, wherein many previous errors of Carte are corrected.

[3] See Appendix, p. 506.

[4] See Madox's Hist. of Exchequer, pp. 14, 15, 77, 129, 150—177, 677, 721.

[5] See Archæologia, vol. viii., pp. 389—405.

particular part of the Exchequer at Westminster, called
Scaccarium Judæorum; and here all matters in which
the Jews had any concern were regulated by proper
officers appointed by the King, under the title of Justices
of the Jews.

The Roll now under consideration is not of such general
interest as some of those that have been lately discovered[1]
in the Exchequer, and of others which must have been inspected by the late John Caley,[2] Esq. It is only given as a
specimen of the earliest Roll of this nature yet discovered
in the Pell Office, and is curious inasmuch as it shows that
a great portion of the revenue derived from this class of
persons was paid by the Jewesses; this appears from
the payments made by Rachel, the daughter of David,
for an aid[3] to marry the King's sister; Margery, for a
chirograph, or star, to render an account;[4] and from many
other payments made by females.

Hume states that King Henry III. was noted for his
piety, devotion, and regular attendance on public worship,
and that the following saying of that monarch on the latter
subject is much celebrated by ancient writers; namely,
that when he was engaged in a dispute with Lewis IX.,

[1] By the unwearied and persevering exertions of C. P. Cooper, Esq.,
Secretary to the Record Commission, several of these early Rolls of Accounts
of the Jews, and also Jewish stars and chirographs, have been lately discovered amongst the heretofore unsorted Records of the Exchequer; which
it is hoped will be soon published to illustrate this obscure portion of our
history, and to show that this persecuted, but industrious and ingenious
class of the community, though then considered in a state of vassalage, were
yet main contributors to the necessities of the state.

[2] From a copy of Mr. Caley's work, before cited, with MS. notes, in the
possession of my brother, Charles Devon, Esq., I find frequent reference
made to a collection of Jewish documents preserved amongst the archives of
Westminster Abbey.

[3] See page 506.   [4] Ibidem.

of France, concerning the preference between sermons [1]
and masses, he maintained the superiority of the latter,
affirming that he would rather have one hour's conversation with a friend than hear twenty the most elaborate
discourses pronounced in his praise. This character
given of King Henry by the above, and by historians in
general, is fully corroborated in these Records: the
opinion he expressed in favour of mass and religious
ceremonies is also confirmed on referring to some of the
undermentioned payments.

The King presents a vest and a cup to the chaplains
of Saint Peter's,[2] Westminster; he grants 50 marks for
a pilgrimage to the Holy Land;[3] pays stipends to priests,
to say masses for the soul of Queen Eleanor,[4] his grandmother; makes oblations of cloths of gold and arras to
Christ Church, Bermondsey; also of musk and frankincense, together with a crystal vessel and cloths of arras
to the chapel of Saint Stephen's,[5] Westminster; presents
a ring, with an emerald, a gold clasp, and six baudekins,
to the church of Saint Paul's;[6] also mitres, to the Archbishop of Armagh,[7] and Bishop of Hereford;[8] gold and
other copes, a tunic and dalmatican, an albe, a gold
branch candlestick, chalices, and various other plate, &c.,
offered to divers chaplains and religious houses.[9] Incense
is offered in Saint Peter's Church, Westminster, on his brother Richard's return from the Holy Land:[10] 2000 poor
are fed for the salvation of his sister's soul, the Empress of

---

[1] The King himself preached a sermon in the Chapter House at Winchester, taking his text, "*Justice and peace have kissed each other.*" See
Baker's *Chronicle*, by Phillips, p. 83.

[2] See page 11.	[3] See page 12.	[4] Ibidem.
[5] Ibidem.	[6] See page 14.	[7] Ibidem.
[8] Ibidem.	[9] See page 18.	[10] See page 19.

Germany. Many oblations were made at the shrine of Saint Edward, and in Westminster Abbey, for religious purposes, such as lights to burn round the shrine,[1] and a great lamp in the body of the church; silver supplied to make a tabernacle,[2] to contain an ivory image, and to repair the sceptre[3] of the blessed Edward; and for rods and bars to bear the cross;[4] also a missal,[5] with a gradale and antiphone contained therein; an embroidered chesable, made by Mabilia,[6] of Saint Edmunds, with two Geneva cloths of silk, and another cloth from Milan, were offered on the return of Richard,[7] the King's brother; 126 rings were also offered at the feast of the Circumcision,[8] with very many other entries of a like nature, showing that this Monarch was exceeded only in pious superstition by the act of King Henry II., his grandfather, when he submitted to be scourged on doing penance at the tomb of Thomas à Becket, in Canterbury Cathedral.

INCIDENTS, EMINENT PERSONS, &c., NOTICED IN THIS REIGN.

An annual fee paid to Thomas, Earl of Flanders,[9] the King's uncle.

Payment to Humphrey de Bohun,[10] Earl of Essex and Hereford, for the custody of Dover Castle.

---

[1] See page 19.   [2] See page 21.   [3] Ibidem.
[4] Ibidem.   [5] See page : 2.   [6] See page 23.
[7] Ibidem.   [8] See page 24.   [9] See page 12.
[10] See page 13. Called the good Earl of Hereford, was Lord High Constable at the King's marriage, and godfather to Prince Henry. Though in great favour with the King, he sided with the barons, and was taken prisoner at the battle of Evesham, fighting against the King. For a fuller account of this Earl, see *Lyons' History of Dover Castle*, vol. ii. p. 209.

Payment to the cook[1] of Isabella, the King's sister, Empress of Germany.

Expenses of Edward,[2] the King's son, afterwards King Edward I.; and robes purchased for his household.

1010 marks paid to the men of Regula,[3] for damage sustained by them on building the castle there, and on surrendering their town to Richard, Earl of Cornwall, the King's brother.

Inquisitions taken of the chattels belonging to the Jews.[4]

Two hundred marks are paid to Bertram de Cryoll,[5] Constable of Dover Castle.

Payments to Bernard de Sabaudia, Constable of Windsor Castle, and for the garrison there; also, to Rylwin de Tywle, Bailiff of Windsor, to compensate the men of Windsor for damage sustained by them in making a foss[6] round the castle,

Ships provided to convey Warren de Munchens[7] and his attendants to Gascony, and to take the King's tents there.

Payment to Henry de Bracton,[8] the judge.

Stipend granted to the Hermit of Colemanneshegg.[9]

A daily stipend of 6d., granted to Master Henry de Abrinces,[10] the versifier.

---

[1] See page 15.   [2] See pages 15, 28.   [3] See page 17.   [4] Ibidem.
[5] See page 18. He was usually called the great Baron of Kent, was five times Constable of Dover Castle, and held the manor of Seaton, in Kent, by serjeanty; viz., to provide a man called a vautrer, to lead three greyhounds when the King should go into Gascony, so long as a pair of shoes of 4d. price should last. See *Lyons' History of Dover*, vol. ii. p. 208, and *Blount's Jocular Customs*, by Beckwith, p. 232.
[6] See page 20.   [7] See page 25.
[8] See page 33. This Henry de Bracton was the author of the treatise, "*De Legibus et Consuetudinibus Angliæ.*"
[9] See page 34.
[10] Ibidem. This is the first entry that has been found of the name

One thousand marks paid to the Pope,[1] due for his annual tax, in the fortieth year of this King's reign.

A messenger rewarded for bringing the first news of the safe delivery of the wife of William Chavenny.[2]

Simon de Montfort, Earl of Leicester, receives 400*l.* per annum for the dower of his wife Eleanor.[3]

A Roll[4] of the expenses for repairing and rebuilding part of the King's palace at Westminster, dated 43rd year of Henry III., is here introduced, which, amongst other particulars, gives an account of rebuilding his chamber, strengthening with iron the tunnel of the chimney, and

---

of the versifier or poet, from which probably the title of poet laureate of the present day takes its name. See note to the Editor's Introduction of the Issue Roll of Thomas de Brantingham, p. xxix. Andrews, in his History of Britain, p. 419, relates the following curious anecdote of this Henry the versifier. "In 1251, a bard, styled Master Henry the versifier, had 100*s.* allowed him as a fee of office. This Master Henry chanced to offend a humorous Cornish poet, named Michael Blaunpayne, or Merry Master Michael, by reflections on his country, which drew from the western rhymer a sharp satire, [in Latin,] in which Master Henry is thus described, [as translated by James Pettit Andrews:]

'The thigh of a sparrow, the feet of a goat,
Hare-lips, and boar's fangs, thee a monster denote;
Thou canst whine like a whelp, like a bull thou canst roar,
Thou art foul as a witch, and art as black as a Moor.
Thus peerless appearing, believe *me*, thy songster,
Thy grimly grimaces demonstrate a monster!'"

[1] See page 35.   [2] Ibidem.

[3] See page 40. This Eleanor was the King's sister, whom the said Earl married in 1238, and was publicly accused by the King of first corrupting his sister, and then marrying her to avoid scandal; they were forbidden to attend the churching of the Queen: on which accusation the Earl was much abashed, and left the kingdom, but was soon after received into favour.

[4] See from page 43 to page 74. This Roll may prove highly interesting to the architectural antiquary. I cannot omit expressing my thanks to Joseph Gwilt, Esq., F. S. A., a gentleman combining in an eminent degree the talents of the antiquary and architect, without whose able assistance I should have had great difficulty in translating many of the terms of art used in this Roll.

repairing the baths there, forming a drain from the
King's great kitchen to the Thames, and newly constructing another chamber over the Thames; with a description of the ornamental work, decorations, &c., done
to the same palace, including a payment to Master William,[1] the painter, for designing the picture of Jesse on
the mantelpiece of the chimney, and who is stated to have
cleaned and restored the painted walls of the King's
chamber. This Roll also furnishes a most minute account of the nature and quality of the stone and other
materials used, specifying from whence they were obtained; the names and class of workmen employed, the
rate of wages paid to each, with the time they were engaged upon the work, and a description is added of the
workmen's tools, hammers, planks, laths, tiles, nails, and
implements used.

A few extracts only are given from a household Roll[2]
of the forty-fourth year of the reign of King Henry III.,
being an account of the expenses during the year he went
to Paris to settle a treaty with the French King: for a
more detailed account of this Roll the reader is referred
to the note below.

EDWARD I.

In the Issue Roll of the first year of this monarch,
frequent mention is made of the death of his father,
King Henry III., who is stated, in a payment made to

[1] See page 64.   [2] See page 74.
[3] See note at page 77 of this volume, and page xvi of Introduction to Issue
Roll of Thomas de Brantingham, by the Editor.

his widow, Queen Eleanor, to have been buried on the day of Saint Edmund the king and martyr,[1] in the fifty-seventh year of his reign. Notice is also taken of the tomb erected for John of Windsor,[2] King Edward's infant son, born at Acre, in Palestine; on receiving the news of whose death the King is reported to have expressed but little sorrow, though deeply grieved by the loss of his father.[3]

At the commencement of this King's reign considerable repairs and decorations were made to Westminster Hall,[4] which, in all probability, were done in anticipation of the approaching coronation,[5] an event which had not taken place in this venerable building for many years preceding.

Immediately on this King's return to England, evidence of applying himself to correct the disorders arising from the loose administration of the laws during his father's reign, may be traced from the frequent payments to, and appointments of judges,[6] to proceed in their iters, the profits arising from which must have been considerable, as appears from the Receipt Rolls preserved in the Pell Office. The fines and heavy amercements arising in these iters were variously applied to

---

[1] See pages 78, 80.   [2] See page 78.

[3] Prince Edward had reached Sicily, on his return from the Holy Land, when he received intelligence of the death of his father, and he discovered a deep concern on the occasion. At the same time he learned the death of an infant son, John, whom his Princess, Eleanor of Castile, had borne him, at Acre, in Palestine; and appeared much less affected with that misfortune: the King of Sicily expressed a surprise at this difference of sentiment; but was told by Edward, that the death of a son was a loss which he might hope to repair; the death of a father was a loss irreparable. *Walsingham*, p. 44.

[4] See pages 78, 79, 82. See also Index, under Westminster.

[5] See page 84.   [6] See pages 80, 81, 87.

the King's necessities: one instance only, from many others, is here noticed, of an aid for the expenses of an expedition of Edward, the King's brother, to the Holy Land,[1] charged on the iter of the King's Justices, to Lincoln.

Although much of King Edward's time, at the early period of his reign, was occupied in redressing grievances at home, and in making preparations for the conquest of Wales, yet, on referring to several of the extracts here noticed, he appears to have found time for many charitable[2] and pious acts,[3] for improving his castle at Windsor,[4] the palace[5] and vineyard[6] at Westminster; for erecting the mews,[7] and forming his gardens[8] at Charing Cross, and for many private and public acts of piety, charity, and attention to his consort and children. .

INCIDENTS, EMINENT PERSONS, &c., NOTICED IN THIS REIGN.

Expenses of the household of Queen Eleanor,[9] mother of King Edward I., charged on the tallage of Adam Feteplace, a burgess of Oxford.

Messengers sent by the King to the Court of France.[10]

Letters sent to King Edward's sister, the Queen of Scotland.[11]

Payments to Nicholas Stapelton, William de Saham, Walter de Helyun, and Martin de Littelebury, the King's Justices,[12] during his absence from England.

[1] See page 96.   [2] See pages 83, 84.   [3] See page 82.
[4] See page 88.   [5] See page 89.   [6] See page 89.
[7] See page 90.   [8] See page 91.   [9] See page 77.
[10] See pages 78, 79.   [11] See page 79.   [12] See pages 80, 81, 87.

The archives of the Jews[1] at Winchester inspected, to ascertain if they had inrolled their debts.'

Sentence of excommunication pronounced by the Pope against Guido de Montfort,[2] published in England, Scotland, Ireland, and Wales.

Payments to John de Brittany,[3] on his return home.

The islands of Guernsey[4] and Jersey released to the King by Hugh de Turberville.

A loan granted by the knights templars,[5] at Paris, to King Edward I., whilst he was in France and in the Holy Land, of 28,189*l*. 8*s*. 4*d*., Tournois money.

A message is sent to Lewellin, the son of Griffin, Prince of Wales.[6]

Payments made to the knights templars, for their chaplains to perform divine service in the New Temple,[7] London, for the soul of King Henry III.

---

[1] See page 81.

[2] See page 83. This refers to the process of Pope Gregory X. against Guy de Montfort, son of Simon, Earl of Leicester, for having murdered, in the church of Viterbo, Henry, son of Richard, King of the Romans, and Earl of Cornwall. This was done at the solicitation of King Edward, cousin to the said Henry, who, during his stay at Rome, on his return from the Holy Land, obtained the condemnation of the murderers. See *Acta Regia*, vol. i. pp. 100, 101. See also an account of Guy de Montfort's death, in the *Excerpta Historica*, p. 267 ; a most delightful work, and ably edited: the general reader of history has cause to regret that it was not published in English. The Editor here begs to state that he has usually referred to translations, or works originally published in English, for the obvious reasons mentioned in his former publications; therefore, instead of quoting Rymer's Fœdera, he has preferred the Acta Regia, a Collection from that work, by Monsieur de Rapin Thoyras, published by Le Clerc, and translated by Stephen Whatley.

[3] See page 84.   [4] See page 85.

[5] See page 86. This loan was probably part of, or in addition to, the 70,000*l*. Tournois, advanced by Louis IX. for King Edward's crusade to the Holy Land, which he covenanted to repay at Paris, by instalments. For a curious account of this convention, vide *Excerpta Historica*, p. 266.

[6] See page 87.

[7] See page 88. One of King Henry's sons was buried in this church.

Peter de Skoteny[1] releases five knights' fees belonging to the half barony of Skoteny, from him and his heirs, to the King and his heirs, on condition that the said Peter might hold seventy-six oxgangs of land in Steynton, to be held of the King in capite, of the said half barony, by service of the twentieth part of a knight's fee.

Surrender, by Harvey de Cadurco, to the King, of a forge, &c., in the forest of Deane.[2]

Money borrowed at the Court of Rome,[3] repaid by the King.

Strict charge given for Oto de Grandison to be repaid 100*l.*, which he had delivered as a present from the King *to a certain foreign knight*,[4] on his departure.

Two thousand marks paid to Reymund de Nogerus,[5] the Pope's Nuncio, as a loan from the Prior of the hospital of Saint John of Jerusalem, for despatch of certain urgent business for the King.

A messenger sent from the King of England to the King of Norway.[6]

Stephen de Pencester[7] and Matthew Berille, constables of Dover Castle, appointed to the custody thereof.

Payments made on account of the King's sons, John

---

[1] See page 89. Sir Harris Nicholas, in his useful Synopsis of the Peerage of England, vol. ii. p. 581, states that this Peter de Scoteni was son and heir of Thomas, who died in 1277, and of whom nothing farther is known.

[2] See page 89. Both Sir Robert Atkyns and the Rev. Thomas Rudge, in their histories of Gloucestershire, are silent as to the early obtaining of iron in this forest; and Camden, in his *Britannia*, vol. i. p. 270, merely states that, subsequent to the reign of King Henry VI., rich veins of iron had been discovered; but the above entry indicates a much earlier working of this ore.

[3] See page 90.   [4] Ibidem.   [5] See page 91.   [6] Ibidem.

[7] See page 92. Stephen de Pencester was sheriff of Kent: he was a second time constable of this castle, and assisted the King in his expedition against Prince Llewellyn. He is stated to have been a learned man, and had all

and Henry,[1] whilst they resided at Windsor with Queen Eleanor.

Service performed in Saint Margaret's chapel, Westminster, for Margaret,[2] Queen of Scotland, the King's sister.

Payment to the Abbess and Nuns of Saint Antoine, near Paris, of a debt due from Eleanor, Countess of Leicester,[3] out of her dower on account of her husband William, late Earl Marshal.

Statues of King Henry III.[4] and Queen Eleanor,[5] formed in the burial-ground of the Abbot of Westminster.

the grants of lands and knights fees, with the services each knight owed to the castle, collected and made into a book, which was in being when Darell compiled his history. See *Lyons' History of Dover Castle*, vol. ii, p. 216.

[1] See page 93. The King's eldest and second sons, who died young during their father's lifetime.

[2] See page 96.   [3] See page 98.

[4] See page 99. Moule, in his elegant work on the Antiquities in Westminster Abbey, possibly refers to this statue or figure in the following description of his third plate of ancient oil paintings in this abbey; viz. PLATE III.

"PORTRAIT OF HENRY III.—This portrait, upon comparison, is found greatly to resemble *the features of the cumbent figure of the monarch upon his tomb*, in this church, which is the principal reason of its being assigned to Henry III., who commenced the re-building of the abbey in 1245."

Moule regrets that the figure on the fourth panel of the ancient enclosure, near the high altar, is entirely obliterated; but as he states the four canopies to this inclosure are similar in design to the sculptured sides of the monument of Eleanor, Queen of Edward I., it is not improbable that the vacant panel may have contained a drawing of that Queen from the statue above referred to.

[5] As Queen Eleanor died 29th November, 1290, anno 18 Edward I., and was buried in December following in Saint Edward's chapel, it may be objected that the statue here referred to could not be that of his Queen, but must have been intended for his mother Queen Eleanor. It should, however, be here stated that the Liberate and Receipt Rolls frequently contain entries of a date both prior and subsequent to that with which they are headed, indorsed, or known, as may be seen at pp. 99, 101, 103, 104, Roll 19 Edward I., which contains many entries of the twentieth and other years;

Payments for support of the chamber of Mary,[1] the King's daughter.

Several payments of black Tournois money to Florence, Earl, or Count, of Holland,[2] for the marriage of his eldest son.

Payments to William de Valencia,[3] the King's uncle, for the lands of Sibyll, the wife of Gerald Talbot, held in dower in the manor of Gainsborough; also for other lands assigned to the said William by King Henry III., saving the King's right in lands belonging to Robert de Vendenal.

Several payments to the King's Justices,[4] John de Metingham, Robert de Herteford, Elye de Bekyngham, William de Gyselham, and Robert de Thorp; also to Philip de Wilyheby, Chancellor of the Exchequer, John de Cobeham, William de Carleton, and Peter de Leycester, Barons of the Exchequer, and to William Juge,[5] attorney-general, for their respective services.

Payments to the Brethren and Sisters of Saint Catha-

---

the Roll of the seventeenth year might therefore contain entries of the eighteenth and nineteenth years; and as Queen Eleanor, the King's mother, was at this period a nun in the monastery of Ambresbury, and subsequently buried there, the above statue is most likely that referred to by Brayley in his Graphic and Historical Illustrator, where, at p. 232, describing Queen Eleanor's tomb in Westminster Abbey, he states, "The top is covered with a plate or table of gilt copper, on which lies *a statue of the deceased*, which also is of copper most richly gilt."

[1] See page 99.

[2] See page 99. He was one of the competitors for the crown of Scotland, descended from Ada, sister to King William.

[3] See page 100. William de Valencia, Earl of Pembroke, obtained a grant of a fair and other privileges, in Gainsborough, from King Edward I. *Magna Britannia*, vol. ii. p. 1435.

[4] See pages 100, 101.

[5] This name has generally been printed Inge, but is clearly written Juge on the Issue Rolls. *Vide Quo Warranto and Hundred Rolls, passim.*

rine,[1] near the Tower, on account of the enlargement of Tower[2] ditch.

Amongst the payments for articles supplied to the Exchequer, some are of a curious description, as for leathern forules to contain the Rolls of King[3] John, sacks for the Rolls of the fifteenths, and canvass bags for the money of the receipt.

William de Vescy appointed constable of Scarborough[4] Castle.

Release from the Abbot of Reading[5] of former grants to his predecessors, by letters patent of Kings John and Henry III.

Tomb of King Henry III.[6] repaired.

Letters to the Bishops respecting a tenth granted to the King as an aid for the Holy[7] Land.

Master Peter de Insula, Archdeacon of Exeter, pays the expenses of transcribing the Rolls of the ecclesias-

[1] Now the site of Saint Katharine's Docks. An interesting account of the Royal Hospital and Collegiate Church of Saint Katharine, compiled from Dr. Ducarel and other authentic sources, was published by J. B. Nichols, F. S. A., in 1824.

[2] See page 102. King Henry III. encompassed the Tower with a deep ditch; and King Edward I., soon after his accession to the throne, considerably improved the fortifications, by completing the works which his father had begun; and greatly enlarged the moat, or ditch, with which they were surrounded. Bayley's *History of the Tower*, pp. 16, 21.

[3] See page 103. Also *Mad. Hist. Exch.* pp. 725, 427, 742.

[4] See page 103. John de Vesci, on his return from a pilgrimage to the Holy Land, succeeded to the government of this castle, and Isabel de Beaumont, his second wife, kinswoman of Queen Eleanor, had the custody during her widowhood. William de Vesci, the brother and heir of John, succeeded Isabel de Beaumont. For a full account of this castle and the constables thereof, see *Hinderwell's History and Antiquities of Scarborough*, from p. 38 to p. 98.

[5] See page 104. The charters of this monastery are fully set out in the *Monasticon Anglicanum*, edited by Caley, Ellis, and Bandinel, title Reading.

[6] See page 105.

[7] *Ibidem.*

c

tical taxation[1] in the provinces of Canterbury and York; also expenses respecting a tenth granted in aid of the Holy Land.

The bulls of Pope Nicholas IV., granting a tenth[2] from the churches of England, Scotland, and Ireland, in aid of the Holy Land, transcribed and reduced into public form; upon which affair the King was attended at Ambresbury.

A portion only of a household Roll[3] of Edward, son of King Edward I., dated in the twenty-first year of his father's reign, has been extracted; the whole Roll is far too voluminous for insertion. This Roll is curious, inasmuch as it shows the daily expenditure of the Prince's household for one whole year, where he sojourned each day, states the names of the nobility and other persons who visited him, how long they stayed, and the time of their departure. Amongst the eminent guests that resorted to the Prince the following may be noticed: the Lord Bishop of Ely; Castellan de Bergles, his four knights, and the two sons of Lord R. de Typetot; Lord Hugh de Veer; the Earl of Gloucester, and his Lady the Countess, with a retinue of 200 knights, ladies, maids of honour, &c.; the Bishop of Durham; Lord John de

---

[1,2] See page 105. These two entries probably relate to the celebrated taxation of Pope Nicholas IV., begun in the year 1288, granting the tenths to Edward I. for six years, towards defraying the expense of an expedition to the Holy Land. A late discovery was made in the Court of Exchequer, Westminster, of a bag in which were fourteen long Rolls, containing an Ecclesiastical valor and taxation of the whole of Ireland, made by authority of Pope Nicholas IV.: upon these Rolls is an entry specifying that the same, together with other Rolls of the taxation of the goods of benefices of all Ireland, were received at the Exchequer, *Walter, Bishop of Exeter*, then being Treasurer, in the sixteenth year of King Edward I. *Cooper on the Public Records*, vol. i. p. 284.

[3] See from page 106 to page 112.

Berwick; Lord Peter de Sabaudia; Lord Edmund, the
King's brother, and his sons Thomas[1] and Henry, with a
great retinue; Edward, son of the King of Scotland;
Lady Agnes de Valencia; the Prior of Merton; Lord
and Lady de Vescy; the Earl of Lincoln and his four
knights; the wife of Walter de Bello Campo and her
retinue; the Abbess of Ambresbury, with her nuns,
attended by a great retinue; the Lord the King, with
many strangers to hunt in Ascheby Forest, who was also
attended by his steward and several of his household; the
Earl of Bar and Lord John de Brabant, with a numerous
suite; Thomas of Lancaster and Henry his brother; the
King's daughter,[2] attended by monks, and the whole
convent. The Prince is therein stated to have heard
mass at Salisbury, after which ceremony the Abbot,
Canons, and many of the choir dined with him. Another
household Roll, but without date, is also referred to; this,
in addition to similar information found in the before-
mentioned Roll, also furnishes the prices of provisions
supplied. Some few only, by way of example, are inserted,
showing at this date that a goose[3] was worth $4\frac{1}{2}d.$; a
capon, $2\frac{1}{2}d.$; one hundred eggs, $7d.$; a woodcock, $1\frac{1}{2}d.$;
a pound of tallow candles, $2\frac{1}{4}d.$; and a lamprey appears
to have obtained the enormous and disproportionate price
of $5s.$ $9\frac{3}{4}d.$

A payment of $20,000l.$, in part of $160,000$ livres of

[1] Probably the same that are subsequently called Thomas of Lancaster,
and Henry his brother.
[2] This was Mary, King Edward I[st's] sixth daughter by his wife Eleanor,
who at ten years of age was made a nun in the monastery of Ambresbury, at
the instance of Queen Eleanor, her grandmother; she lived, died, and was
buried there.
[3] See page 113.

black Tournois money, was made to John, Duke of Brabant,[1] due to him from the King for having furnished 2000 armed horsemen to fight against the King of France.

Payment to the Society of Merchants, called Friscobolders, for certain jewels made in France, and from thence obtained for the Pope.[2]

The assay[3] for Dublin delivered into the Tower, contained in a sealed purse preserved in a box.

Charter of Ralph Pippard[4] of his possessions in Ireland, delivered to the Chamberlains by the Treasurer at York.

Presents and payments made by the King and his Ambassadors to various Cardinals and their Deans in the court of Rome,[5] and to knights and servants belonging to the Pope's chamber; also a present from Edward, the King's son, of a gold cope to Peter Yspano, the Cardinal.

News of the safe delivery of Elizabeth, Countess of Holand,[6] brought to the King.

Letters taken to the King at Dumfermelyn,[7] and money, &c., sent to him in Scotland; an aid collected to marry his eldest daughter.

On the Issue Roll of Easter, 34 Edward I., is entered a memorandum stating that William de Tang, clerk and sacrist in the diocese of York, a notary public, *delivered into the Treasury a certain public instrument,*[8]

---

[1] See page 113.

[2] See page 114. Probably a present sent to Pope Boniface VIII. on his consenting to be an umpire of the differences between Philip, King of France, and Edward, King of England, not in the quality of Pope, but as a private person, under the name of Benedict Cajetan.

[3] See page 115.   [4] Ibidem.

[5] Ibidem.   [6] See page 116.   [7] See pages 116, 117.

[8] An interesting and important collection of Scotch instruments is now in course of publication, edited by that learned and indefatigable antiquary Sir Francis Palgrave. Should the instrument above referred to, still be in

containing thirty-five membranes signed by him, which
instrument is alleged to have been used as ratified in the
dispute that lately had arisen between the present King
of England and John, King of Scotland, and the nobility
and subjects of that kingdom, for the reconciliation of
the King of Scotland, and his nobility to the allegiance
and will of the King of England; also respecting
the homage and fealty to be done by the King of
Scotland and his nobility to the King of England; the
said instrument was delivered to William de Brichull and
William de Pershore, chamberlains of the King's Exchequer, and duplicates thereof into the King's Chancery
and Wardrobe.

EDWARD II.

The first remarkable entry noticed in this reign is the
delivery into the Exchequer of the King's[1] seal, by William
de Melton, Comptroller of the Wardrobe, which had been
used in England during his Majesty's absence; the delivery
is witnessed by Peter de Gavaston, Earl of Cornwall,
then designated the King's deputy in England, and is
stated to have been enclosed in a white leathern purse, or
bag, sealed with the Privy Seal of John de Langton,
Bishop of Chichester, Chancellor of England. The de-

existence and unpublished, the public will doubtless soon be put in possession
of it; for, in unremitting search to discover new materials for history, the
enthusiasm of Old Hearne seems to have revived in the person of Sir
Francis, to whom the compliment paid by Dibdin, to D'Israeli, of being the
modern "Indagator invictissimus of every thing that is curious and interesting in history and literature," is equally applicable.

[1] See page 118.

positing of this seal in the Exchequer appears to have
been attended with much publicity, being made in the
presence of the Chancellor, four Barons, and the Remembrancer of the Exchequer; it was entrusted to the care of
the Chamberlains of the same Court, to be kept in the
King's Treasury. The Roll of the 1st year of this King's
reign also notices the preparations made for his coronation;
and amongst other things directed to be obtained upon this
occasion, the following are to be found: cloth,[1] corn, beer,
large cattle, boars, sheep, pigs, poultry, fish, large fish,
small pike, lampreys, wood, coal, plates, dishes, saltcellars,
armour, beds, and apparel for the King's person; the
sceptre is also directed to be repaired, cloth purchased
at Abindon to cover the palace, and timber and planks are
stated to have been taken from Bustlesham[2] to the King's
palace at Westminster for the same purpose.

Many curious payments are also contained on this Roll
relative to the will[3] and burial of King Edward I., some

---

[1] See pages 120, 121.   [2] See page 132.
[3] See pages 122, 123. The only will of King Edward I. known to be in
existence is published in Rymer's Fœdera, new edit. vol. i. p. 195, and in
Nichols's Collection of Royal and Noble Wills. This will is dated at Acres,
in the 56th year of the reign of his father King Henry III. Nichols regrets
that no other will of this monarch has been discovered; but as the names of
the executors referred to in the above Issue Roll do not correspond with
those printed in Rymer or Nichols, it is clear that King Edward made a subsequent will or wills after he came to the Crown; this conjecture is confirmed
by Sir Francis Palgrave's recent work on the Ancient Kalendars and Inven-
tories of Records: who, at page cxlv of his Introduction to that work, gives the
following account of King Edward's wills. "Original will of Edward I., made
" before his accession to the Crown, he being described as ' Edward, the eld-
" est son of the Lord King Henry III.,' dated at Acres, the 56th year of his
" father's reign. This will is now lost, but a copy is entered in Register A. pre-
" served in the Chapter-house; and is therein stated to be deposited in the
" forcer, bound with iron, and marked with the sign of an index or hand.
" Furthermore a transcript of a will of Edward I. without date, and two
" original wills of the same sovereign, both indented and made under the

of which are not quite reconcileable with the accounts published of these transactions. Walter de Langeton, Bishop of Coventry and Lichfield, Henry de Blunteston, Luke de Wodeford, of the order of Preaching Friars, and Robert de Cotingham, are herein[1] described as executors to the will of King Edward I., and as such were paid 20,000 marks, for the expenses of the late King and his family, by command of the Treasurer. Payments were also made to, and by the said executors, upon various occasions, as for the expenses of the late King's children, Thomas, Edmund, and Eleanor; they distributed 100 marks to the poor for the salvation of the King's soul, and paid ten marks as a stipend to William de Horseden for remaining at Waltham[2] with the body of the deceased King; and remunerated the sumpter man for having provided torches and leather for the corpse, and furnishing horses for knights to ride in the late King's armour before his body, between the church of the Holy Trinity, London, and Westminster Abbey. They also appear to have paid some of the Queen's expenses; the apothecary's bill for Edward, Prince of Wales, the King's son, during his father's lifetime, together with other payments not here noticed: thus as some of the beforementioned payments were probably made in pursuance of directions contained in the will now under consider-

"great seal, and seal of his executors, who thus, according to the ancient "practice, signified their acceptance of the trust: all these instruments are "lost. The table of contents of the Register further notices another will of "Edward I., made at Ghent, in Flanders, in the 26th year of his reign, which "was also deposited in the beforementioned forcer. But this document has "shared the fate of the others, and can be no longer found, nor has any "copy been preserved; for, although it was evidently intended that the will "should have been entered in the Register, yet the pages to which the table "refers are left blank by the neglect or inattention of the transcriber."

[1] See pages 122, 123.　　　　　　　[2] Ibidem.

ation, it is not improbable, upon a more minute inspection of these Rolls, that further evidence of the contents of these wills may yet be found to supply the deficiency so much regretted by Sir Francis Palgrave.

The Issue Rolls of[1] about the period of the eighth year of this King's reign, are filled with payments for assembling the great army which marched against Scotland in the fruitless expedition previous to its defeat by Robert Bruce at Bannockburn; the entries of payments for the preparations made for this unfortunate and disastrous affair were too numerous to be extracted: the limits of this volume would only admit the few following notices relating to the affairs of Scotland, viz.:—

Payments to Lord William de Felton[2] for him to proceed to the Scotch war with five knights, forty soldiers, and those whose names were entered in a certain Roll delivered into the wardrobe.

One thousand pounds sent to Lord Eustace de Cotesbech,[3] at Berwick, Chamberlain of Scotland, for the expenses of the Scotch war; also one thousand marks paid to Humphrey de Bohun,[4] Earl of Hereford and Essex, for his last passage with the King to Scotland.

Many payments are made to persons proceeding to the Scotch war; to supply provisions for the King's passage to Scotland, and to men at arms in the marches there; to Lord Adomar de Valencia[5] for defence thereof, and to garrison

---

[1] See pages 120, 126, 127, 128.   [2] See page 119.
[3] See page 120.   [4] See page 129.
[5] See page 126. This was Lord Aymer de Valence, Earl of Pembroke, who formerly attended King Edward I. in the wars in Scotland. The commission appointing him to take the command of the army at this period is to be found in Rymer's Fœdera, vol. iii. p 491: it is dated at York, in August 1314; a portion of it is thus translated: To restrain the

the town of Berwick-upon-Tweed; also for mantles provided for the King's knights, and tunics for his valets going to the same war.

INCIDENTS, EMINENT PERSONS, &c., NOTICED IN THIS REIGN.

A curious description is given of the various kinds of cross-bows [1] and implements of war used at this period.

A palfrey purchased for the Countess of Cornwall, [2] also a chaplet and frontal of gold, and an alb with pearls, silk, tassels, &c., for the same countess.

Expenses and preparations made for the burial of Lady Eleanor, [3] the King's sister, at Beaulieu.

Queen Isabella pays one thousand pounds for the King to Lady Blanch, [4] of Brittany, out of her lands in Poitou, in aid to marry her daughter.

News brought from Ireland to the King from Lord Adomar de Valencia, [5] (Earl of Pembroke.)

Armour [6] provided for the King's use.

---

obstinate malice of our rebellious enemies the Scots, who not content with the flagrant acts of various kinds by them committed in our kingdom of Scotland, and on the borders of our kingdom of England, have now, to the dishonour, reproach, and damage of us and our good subjects, entered this very kingdom in a hostile manner, committing murders, depredations, burnings, sacrileges, and other evils without number, &c.

[1] See page 119.

[2] See pages 119, 120. This was the Earl of Gloucester's sister, the King's own niece, whom he married to his favourite Piers de Gavaston, created Earl of Cornwall, as a pretence to recall him from Ireland, where he had remained during his banishment.

[3] See page 124. King Edward I. had two daughters named Eleanor, the first by his wife Eleanor, who married Henry, Earl of Berry, in France; the second by his wife Margaret, who died in childbed.

[4] See page 125.   [5] See page 127.   [6] See page 128.

Price of wheat [1] and barley at this time; wheat 10*s*., and barley 6*s*. per quarter.

A crown of gold [2] made for the King.

Payments made, at the request of the Queen, to Master Albert Medici, for his journeys to Gascony concerning the affairs of the duchy of Aquitaine.[3]

Agreement between the King and Lord Robert de Umframville, Earl of Anegos,[4] respecting his castles of Hartbotle and Prudhou, held of the King in the Marches of Scotland, and for his retinue to garrison the said castles.

John de Morreue and Robert Barde,[5] two Scotch prisoners detained in the Tower of London.

Agreement between the King and Lord Henry de Bello Monte to defend the Castle of Norham [6] with eighty men at arms, &c.

Alms given to provide three days' entertainment for the Preaching Friars, holding their Chapter at Pampilloun, in Arragon;[7] viz. one day for the King, the second for the Queen, and the third for Prince Edward.

The Queen sends an embroidered cope to the Pope.[8] Lady Mary,[9] the King's sister, and Lady de Bourgh, go on a pilgrimage to Canterbury.

[1] See page 128.   [2] Ibidem.   [3] See page 129.

[4] See page 130. He was appointed a commissioner to treat with Robert Bruce and his accomplices for a truce; himself and his ancestors had held the castles of Hartbotel and Prudhou since the Conquest; he also had the valley of Rede, in which the castle of Harbotel was situate, held by service of defending it from wolves and thieves. See *Dugdale Bar.* vol. i. p. 504.

[5] See page 130.

[6] See page 131. John Balliol swore fealty to King Edward I. for the kingdom of Scotland in this castle, after judgment given in his favour at Berwick. For a full and interesting history of Norham Castle, see *Hutchinson's History of Durham*, vol. iii. p. 393.

[7] See page 132.   [8] See page 133.

[9] See page 134. A nun in the monastery of Amesbury. See note at page xxxiv of Introduction to the Issue Roll, 44 Edward III.

Allowance to Thomas, Earl of Norfolk,[1] for having continued Lord Edward de Balliol in his retinue, by the King's command.

Annuity granted to William Frauncels,[2] for services performed in the King's presence at Dunbar.

Rolls and Memoranda deposited in the King's Chapel, in the Upper Tower of London, of the reigns of Kings Henry II., Richard I., John, Henry III., and Edward I.[3]

The lesser volume of Domesday Book,[4] containing the counties of Essex, Norfolk, and Suffolk, repaired and bound.

A silver seal, old silver, and base money perforated, melted down for coining.

Payment of ten thousand pounds for the fleet and troops, sent to the duchy of Aquitaine,[5] and others made to Fulk Fitzwarren, for the same purpose: also to Robert Bendyn and John Sturmy, Admirals of the King's fleets, with several payments to the captains and other officers going in this expedition, and for supplying archers with arrows, &c., too numerous to be here noticed.

Bernard Trankalion, to repay the Constable of Bourdeaux[6] his expenditure in defending a confederacy against

[1] See page 134.   [2] Ibidem.   [3] See page 135.
[4] See page 135. Domesday Book was recently re-bound under the direction of the late John Caley, Esq.: the ancient covers are still preserved in the Chapter House, Westminster, consisting of two oak boards, covered with a rough leather, probably the original binding above referred to, though evidently since strengthened and embossed with the full-blown rose, worked on brass: the boards are eleven inches long and seven broad. The whole character of the binding exhibits a rude specimen of the art at this period, not possessing that finished workmanship of Charles Lewis, so enthusiastically described by Dibdin as adorning the rich volumes of purple and crimson morocco, gilt, which have passed through that learned author's hand.
[5] See pages 136, 137.   [6] See page 136.

the King of England's jurisdiction, by the French
King.

A description of armour[1] delivered into the Tower of
London, with the price affixed to each article. The Roll
of the 19th year of this King also contains a curious entry,
evidencing the existence of the art of engraving at this
early period; namely, a payment of 30s., to John de Cas-
tleacre, goldsmith of London, for engraving 300 dishes
and 300 saltcellars with a leopard, and for weighing the
same dishes and saltcellars, and engraving the weight on
the outside or back thereof. A payment is also added to
the engrosser of the Exchequer, for newly engrossing certain foreign accounts entered in the Red Book[2] of the
Exchequer.

EDWARD III.

The Issue Rolls of this period form nearly a regular
series, and furnish evidence of a much more connected
chain of events.

The first entry extracted in this reign is properly re-
ferable to the last, being a payment of two hundred
pounds to Thomas Berkeley and John Mautravers, for
the expenses of King Edward II., during his confinement
in Berkeley Castle.

Hume states that, whilst the King was in the custody
of Berkeley, he was treated with the gentleness due to his

---

[1] See page 138.
[2] For a full description of the contents of the Red Book of the Exchequer,
see *Cooper on the Public Records*, vol. ii. p. 309—325. See also *Madox's
History of the Exchequer*, vol. i. p. 624, and *Nicolson's English Historical
Library*, pp. 172, 173.

rank; but when the time of Mautravers and Gournay
came, every species of indignity was practised against
him, and that they eventually put the King to death in
the most cruel and barbarous manner possible to be con-
ceived. The murder is represented to have been committed by the order of Mortimer, in pursuance of the
equivocal sentence contained in the letter of Adam
Tarleton, Bishop of Hereford addressed to his keepers,
of, " Edwardum occidere nolite, timere bonum est;" and
it is stated that they availed themselves of Berkeley's absence, from indisposition, to perpetrate the act.   Several
payments appear upon the Issue Rolls both to Gournay
and Mautravers, particularly to the latter, who, subsequently to the murder, had a grant of 100*l.* yearly, as
Keeper of the Forests on this side Trent; and though
these payments furnish no conclusive evidence of guilt, yet,
if they are considered, as represented to be in the nature
of rewards for former services, a presumption arises not
favourable to the parties implicated.   Payments also will
be found for the removal[1] of the body of King Edward
II. from Berkeley Castle, to be interred in the Abbey
Church of Saint Peter, Gloucester.

The Rolls of the early period of this King's reign are
also occupied with entries relating to the coronation, and
marriage of the King with Philippa, daughter of the Earl
of Hainault : this marriage appears to have been celebrated
in the palace of the Archbishop of York.[2]   The match is
here described as popular and much spoken of;[3] and,
though previously contracted in haste by his mother,
Queen Isabella, on her return from France, with Morti-

---

[1] See pages 139, 140, 141.   [2] See page 140.   [3] Ibidem.

mer, to serve her own purposes, yet, in the result, was highly advantageous to the King. The frequent entries on these Rolls to furnish Queen Philippa with every thing requisite for her comfort and suitable to her estate, evince the King's attachment and attention to his consort, which he continued to manifest to the period of her death. Some few only of such payments could be extracted; amongst these will be found a curious description of a bed[1] provided for the Queen's lying-in, of green velvet, embroidered with gold, ornamented with sea sirens, and a shield with the arms of England and of Hainault; also a payment for a white robe,[2] worked with pearls, together with a velvet robe and carpets,[3] &c., obtained for her confinement at Windsor; her crown[4] is also stated to have been redeemed from pledge. Other payments on behalf of the Queen are continued on these Rolls throughout this reign, until we arrive at the fortieth year of the King, when we find a payment of 200 marks to Hawkin Liege,[5] from France, for the tomb of Queen Philippa;[6] and on the Roll of the 50th year, further payments appear for sculpture[7] and other expenses about the said Queen's tomb, in Westminster Abbey; certain ironwork was also obtained from Saint Paul's Church, and six angels, made of copper, were placed around the said tomb, and two alabaster images, erected upon a small marble tomb, for the infant son[8] and daughter of the Queen.

[1] See pages 144, 145.   [2] See page 145.   [3] See page 153.
[4] See page 171.   [5] See page 189.
[6] See Issue Roll of Thomas de Brantingham, 44 Edward III., p. 428, where the minister and brethren of Hounslow are paid 10 marks, of the King's alms, to offer prayers for the salvation of this Queen's soul.
[7] See pages 199, 200.
[8] See page 200. These must have been King Edward's sixth son, William, surnamed of Windsor, and his third daughter, Blanch, who both died young.

The payments connected with the affairs of Scotland commence in the sixth year of this King's reign, at which period he sent a knight to the King of Scotland,[1] to expedite certain business in the parliament of the said King, which must have been at the very period he was secretly lending his aid to Edward, the son of John Baliol, (having had an interview with him at Stamford,[2]) to recover the crown of Scotland against the then King David Bruce.

Shortly after King Edward's celebrated victory at Halydown Hill, we find him recognizing Edward de Baliol as King, and sending David de Wolloure[3] to prosecute certain business in that King's parliament, then held at Edinburgh. It is said by historians, that after King Edward had conquered Scotland, he considered Baliol as a mere dependant, and allowed him but five marks a day for his subsistence. This statement is in some measure confirmed by the Issue Roll of the 11th year of this King's reign, wherein an allowance[4] of 50s. daily is paid to that unfortunate monarch: the entry, however, immediately preceding,[5] shows that other payments were also made to him. Some few extracts are added, relating to the defeat of the Scots at the memorable battle of Durham,[6] where King David Bruce was defeated at the head of 60,000 men, and himself, and several of his supporters, made prisoners; amongst whose names we find a ransom paid for Duncan Magdowell and his son, Andrew Cambel,[7]

[1] See page 143.   [2] See page 146.   [3] See page 145.
[4] See page 146.   [5] Ibidem.
[6] This victory was attributable chiefly to the Archbishop of York, who not only assisted Henry Piercy, Ralph Nevil, and other great men of the North, to raise forces, but was actually in the battle, as appears from a letter of thanks to that prelate, from the Regent of England, dated in 1346, from the Tower.
[7] See page 152.

a Scotch knight, Sir William de Vaux, and other
men of note. Roger de Beauchamp[1] was sent to Berwick
to treat with the Scots, and bring David Bruys, King of
Scotland, to London ; but this duty, it would appear,
was eventually performed by Miles de Stapleton,[2] Sheriff
of York, who brought that King, after his defeat,
from Newcastle-upon-Tyne to London ; and it is a remarkable circumstance that we find both Kings of Scotland, at this period, receiving alms and assistance from
the King of England ; namely, 13s. 4d. daily paid to
David Bruys,[3] for the support of himself and his Chaplain ; and 40s. daily to Edward de Baliol. Some of the
payments made to the first-mentioned King are so
minute as even to particularize the price paid for his
jacket,[4] stockings, and riband for his hat, &c. The charges
for the medicines,[5] also supplied to this unfortunate King
during his captivity in the Tower,[6] may afford subject
of speculation to the medical profession,[7] as to the nature of his malady. He remained eleven years a prisoner in England, confined a portion of the time in
Odiham Castle,[8] and was at last ransomed for 10,000

---

[1] See page 156.   [2] See page 161.
[3] See page 157.   [4] See page 163.   [5] See page 166.
[6] Bayley, in his *History of the Tower*, p. 287, states, that the victory gained
over the Scots at Neville's Cross, near Durham, destined David Brus, their
King, together with the Earl of Fife, and above fifty other distinguished
chiefs, to confinement in that citadel. The King was taken by John de
Coupland, an esquire of Northumberland, whose name is gratefully recorded
in history, not only as the captor of the Scottish monarch, but for his valiant
deeds on that renowned day. See *Fœdera*, vol. iii. part 1. p. 102.

[7] The Editor must also refer to the learned profession for a translation of
some of the terms used in this bill, which he has partly printed in the
original Latin, not being sufficiently acquainted with the terms of art used
in prescriptions to render them into English.

[8] See page 166.

marks, on sufficient hostages[1] being given for his person.

The name of Edward the Black Prince is so intimately connected with the affairs of France, and associated with the circumstances attendant on his celebrated victories obtained at Cressy and Poitiers, that it was thought advisable to notice several of the entries relating both to the Prince himself and the results of his conquests in that kingdom.

The pension mentioned in Rymer to have been settled on Thomas Prior,[2] for conveying the news of the birth of Prince Edward to his father, is here noticed; as is also a further reward given to Catherine de Monte Acuto,[3] upon the same occasion, not noticed by Rymer. In the 15th year of this King's reign, allowance is made to the Prince of a sum of money, for the expenses of his household,[4] over and above the value of certain lands formerly assigned to him, which are asserted not to have been sufficient for this purpose.

Hume informs us that, after Edward had gained the battle of Poitiers, whilst he was laying siege to Calais, the flames of war were at the same time kindled in Britany; and that Charles de Bloys invaded that province, and invested Roche de Reim; but the Countess of Mountfort, reinforced by some English troops, under Sir Thomas Dagworth, attacked him during the night in his intrenchments, dispersed the army, and took Charles himself prisoner. The wife of Charles de Bloys, by whom he enjoyed his pretensions to Britany, assumed the government, and proved herself a rival to the Countess of Mountfort, both

[1] See page 169.
[2] See page 143.
[3] See page 160.
[4] See page 149.

d

in the field and cabinet. The King here acknowledges the eminent service of capturing Charles de Bloys, and rewards Sir Thomas Dagworth[1] with a payment of 4900*l*., in which enterprise Sir Thomas appears to have been assisted by John de Ipslyngrode,[2] who receives a reward of 1000*l*.

The next prisoner of importance mentioned is Lord Geoffrey de Charney, Governor of Saint Omer's, who corrupted Sir Emeric of Pavia, a Lombard, for 20,000 crowns, to deliver to him the castle and town of Calais.

The story[3] of King Edward sending for Sir Emeric, and discovering to him his intended treachery, is too well known for repetition, as are also the circumstances of the King privately proceeding to Calais, and fighting under the banner of Walter de Manny, when he totally defeated Lord Charney and frustrated his intentions. The honour of capturing Lord Charney fell to the lot of Sir John de Potenhale,[4] who, for this service, is here rewarded with a grant of 100 marks yearly.

We are compelled to pass over the names of Lord Dauboneye,[5] Sir Burseald, a French Knight, Count d'Assore, and other eminent persons made prisoners in the different provinces of France, previously to, and at the battle of Poitiers, in order to notice some of those brought captives to England, taken at this celebrated victory. Of these the most remarkable is John, King of France; for bringing the news of whose capture, with others of the French nobility, John le Cok,[6] of Cherbourg, was rewarded by

---

[1] See page 153.   [2] See page 154.

[3] See *Collins's History of Edward the Black Prince*, from page 29 to page 36. Several circumstances relating to this battle, mentioned by Collins, are fully confirmed by the Issue Rolls; Mr. James's late history of this Prince should also be consulted on this subject.

[4] See pages 156 to 158.   [5] See page 167.   [6] See page 165.

also entered on this Roll ; and many curious particulars relating to the mode of payment, the rate of exchange on
money paid, and the manner of conveying it from Calais
to the Tower of London, and from the Tower to the King's
private palace at Westminster, will be found on referring
to the entries contained in this Work, at pages 181, 182,
184, 189, 190.

Collins, in his *Life of Edward the Black Prince*, at p.
107, states that the Prince had some trouble in deciding
differences about the French prisoners: those whom he
designed to carry with him to England, and to whom the
Gascoigners laid claim, he bought of them ; but those
taken by the English he intended not to buy till they were
brought safe home. Among the prisoners bought of the
Gascoigners were Philip,[1] son of King John, the Earl of
Sancier,[2] and the Lord Craon,[3] whom he afterwards sold
to the King of England for 20,000*l.* It also appears from
our Records[4] that he purchased James de Bourbon Earl
of Ponthieu, of John de Greilley, Capital of Busche ; as
the King, by precept to his Treasurer and Chamberlains,
states that his son Edward had become bound to the
said John de Greilley in 25,000 old crowns, for James de
Bourbon and others, taken prisoner at Poitiers, and sold
to the said Prince. There were also heard before him the
several pretensions concerning the taking of the French

[1] See page 177, 190. He was the fourth son of John, King of France,
called Philip the Hardy, as Barnes states, from the circumstance of his
having given an English nobleman a box on the ear for serving King Edward III. before his father the King of France, at a feast ; the King of
England, forbidding the nobleman to revenge the affront, commended the
noble spirit of the young prince, by saying to him, " *Vous estes Philippe le
Hardi.*"
[2] See page 177.   [3] Ibidem.
[4] Rymer, tom. vi. p. 310.

Edward II.[1] to the master of the King's scholars, Cambridge, afterwards taken from him by Isabella, Queen of England.

Expense of providing a new seal for the see of Durham.[2]

Payments for support of Elizabeth,[3] daughter and heir of William, late Earl of Ulster.

Payment to Isabella de Lancaster,[4] a nun, at Ambresbury, for a book of romance purchased from her for the King's use.

Muniments in the King's Treasury relating to the duchy of Gascony,[5] delivered to Oliver de Ingham, Steward of Gascony.

An aid obtained to marry Eleanor,[6] the King's sister.

William Lewelyn, John de Breclote, and John de Cromhale[7] arrested by Henry Dymmok, and taken before the King's Council at York.

Expenses incurred about the funeral of John, late Earl of Cornwall,[8] the King's brother.

Provisions[9] supplied to Edinburgh and Striveling Castles, showing the price of wheat, malt, and peas at this period; also the price of lampreys.

Brother Aufricus, a monk of Saint Matthew, in Britany, arrives in England, to search for a gilt head of Saint Matthew.[10]

Alms distributed for carrying torches from Brentford

---

[1] See page 143.   [2] Ibidem.   [3] Ibidem.
[4] See page 144.   [5] See page 145.
[6] See page 147. See note page xli.
[7] See pages 147, 148.
[8] See page 148. Created Earl of Cornwall at twelve years of age, and died in Scotland unmarried.
[9] See pages 148, 149, 150,   [10] See page 153.

Payment to the Prior of Merton for oak obtained from his wood, near Reading, to form the round[1] table at Windsor.

Description of various instruments purchased to make an assay[2] of money.

Price of red herrings, sturgeon, stock fish, congers, and other[3] fish, paid to the Chamberlain of the town of Berwick-upon-Tweed.

Payments for divers pieces of armour obtained from the Merchants of Constance.[4]

The Earl of Dessemount,[5] from Ireland, in the King's custody for certain trespasses committed by him.

Certain thieves, in Sussex, to be arrested, who had robbed the Cardinal[6] of Rouen.

Payments to certain heralds, sent to France, Germany, Brabant, Flanders, and Scotland, to proclaim a tournament[7] to be held on the feast of Saint George.

[1] See page 164. This, it is presumed, is the celebrated round table, at which the Kings were accustomed to feast the twenty-five knights companions every Saint George's day. Charles II. made the last feast of this kind on the installation of the Duke of Buckingham, then Earl of Mulgrave. See *Ashmole's Berkshire*, vol. iii. p. 117.

[2] See page 164. [3] See page 165. [4] See page 166.
[5] See page 167. [6] See page 169.

[7] Ibidem. These heralds were sent to the different Knights of the Garter, at the early formation of this order, and to other Princes and nobility, to attend the splendid tournaments which were given on Saint George's day. The first Knights of the Garter were, the Sovereign, Edward III.; the Black Prince; Henry, Duke of Lancaster; Thomas, Earl of Warwick; Ralph, Earl of Stafford; William Montacute, Earl of Salisbury; Roger Mortimer, Earl of March; the Captal de Buche; John l'Isle; Bartholomew Burghwarsh; John Beauchamp; John de Mohun; Hugh Courtenay; Thomas Holland; John Grey; Richard Fitz Simon; Miles Stapleton; Thomas Walle; Hugh Wriothesley; Niel Loring; John Chandos; James de Audley; Otho Holland; Henry Eme; Zanchel D'Abericourt; and William Paynel. Many of these names will be found on referring to the Index at the end of this volume.

Payment to William Ser, a Gascon knight, of 1600 " guyenois," for expenses incurred by him in the retinue of John Chaundos, the King's deputy in France and Normandy, who was directed to receive the towns, &c., in the King's name, according to a treaty of[1] peace made at Calais between the King and John, King of France.

A description and value of horses[2] purchased for the King from the executors of the Bishop of Lincoln.

Edward the Black Prince[3] presents a lion and a leopard to the King.

A table, with images, made for the chapel at Windsor.[4]

Plate purchased by the King, and given to divers knights and others who came in the retinue of the Earl of Flanders;[5] furnishing a curious description of each piece of plate, with its value, form, and workmanship, to whom presented, &c.

Expenses of John, Duke of Lancaster, upon his going to Flanders respecting the nuptials between the Earl of Cambridge,[6] the King's son, and the Countess of Burgundy, daughter of the Earl of Flanders.

A Bible,[7] a Juvenal, and three books of romances, seized by the Sheriff of London from Henry de Tatton, and delivered to the King.

Payments to Lionel, Duke of Clarence, for the war in Ireland.[8]

The King stands godfather to the infant of Elizabeth, Countess of Athol.[9]

Thirty wild boars presented to the King of England by the King of France.

[1] See page 179.   [2] See page 180.   [3] See page 184.
[4] See page 187.   [5] See pages 185, 166.   [6] See page 187.
[7] Ibidem.   [8] See page 188.   [9] Ibidem.

de Wiclyf,[1] Clerk, is also sent in the retinue of the said Bishop upon the same embassy.

Payment to Elizabeth Chaundos, for her release to the King, of the Castle and Vicomtè of Saint Saviour's,[2] in Normandy.

Payments to Richard Dere and William Stapolyn for information by them given to the King's Council of the defective government of Ireland.[3]

Letter of Privy Seal sent to Oxford, directed to Master *John Wiclyf,*[4] Clerk, summoning him to appear before the King's Council in London.

An image of the Holy Mary, taken in a ship at sea, and sent to the King at his Manor of Eltham.[5]

Description and weight of plate purchased for the King of the executors of Sir Richard de Penbrugg.[6]

Reward for taking Sir John de Mistreworth,[7] a traitor, in Navarre, afterwards confined in the Tower of London, and the four quarters of his body sent to divers parts of England.

Knights of the Garter summoned to attend at Windsor on Saint George's[8] day.

Payment made by Geoffrey Chaucer to Philippa Chaucer,[9] his wife, a maid of honour to Philippa, Queen of England.

Payment to Joan, Princess of Wales, for the expenses of Richard, Prince[10] of Wales, afterwards King Richard the Second.

[1] See page 197.   [2] See page 199.   [3] Ibidem.
[4] See page 200. For an account of the charges made against Wiclyf for his heresies, see the *Annals of Oxford,* p. 493.
[5] See page 201.   [6] Ibidem.
[7] See pages 202, 203. He was drawn, hanged, and quartered at Tyburn for treason, having defrauded soldiers of their wages.
[8] See page 203.   [9] Ibidem.   [10] Ibidem.

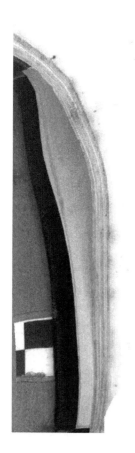

which the Lord the King rode from the city of London to Westminster at his coronation." That King Richard delighted in costly and high-bred horses is confirmed as well by this as by the frequent mention to be found of the spirited chargers he was accustomed to ride; and it is probable, from the great price here mentioned, that this charger may not have been inferior to the Monarch's celebrated horse Barbary, whose fondness for this animal is thus recorded by our immortal bard :—

> *K. Rich.* Rode he on Barbary? Tell me, gentle friend,
> How went he under him?
> *Groom.* So proudly, as if he distained the ground.
> *K. Rich.* So proud, that Bolingbroke was on his back!
> That jade hath eat bread from my royal hand;
> This hand hath made him proud with clapping him.
> Would he not stumble? Would he not fall down,
> (Since pride must have a fall,) and break the neck
> Of that proud man that did usurp his back?

On the Issue Roll of the 6th year of Richard II. are to be found preparations for his marriage with Anne, daughter to the Emperor Charles IV., to whom he had been previously affianced, which appear from payments made to the Duke of Hesse,[1] on his coming from the King of the Romans to England to treat with the King for the said marriage; and also from Michael de la Pole, the King's Chancellor, who had been sent to Milan and Rome, to the King of the Romans and Bohemia, upon the same subject,[2] Anne at this time being a prisoner, but was afterwards released from prison by King Richard. Certain knights and esquires were also sent to Calais to

---

[1] See page 223.   [2] See page 224.

assigned to a period of a later date than that here noticed.
From the following frequent references to cannon, cannoniers, guns, and powder, it would seem that the use of
this composition was not unfrequent even at this early
period ; viz.,

4th November, 1 *Rich. II.*—Payments were made to
John de Arundell for cannoniers [1] and engineers, remain-
ing with him as well in the town of Southampton as in
Corf Castle.

12th June, 1 *Rich. II.*—Amongst a curious list of
implements of war purchased, *two pipes of powder* [2] were
obtained by the celebrated Sir William Walworth and
John Philippot, for defending and fortifying the town of
Cherbourg in Normandy.

10th December, 3 Rich. II.—Payments by the Keeper
of Cherbourg Castle for ten [3] guns to throw stones, two of
which were of iron and eight of other metal, seven of the
said guns are described as casting large stones 24 inches in
circumference ; also for 200 lbs. of powder, 26 lbs. of saltpetre, and 24 lbs. of pure sulphur. In the same year Carisbrook Castle, [4] in the Isle of Wight, was supplied with
100 lbs. of saltpetre and 50 lbs. of pure sulphur. Payments were made in the 8th year of this King to Sir
Thomas Beauchamp, Captain of Carisbrook [5] Castle, for

---

[1] See page 206. Though gunpowder is stated to have been invented by
Schwartz, a German monk, at Cologne, in 1330, and great guns to have been
used by Edward III. at the battle of Cressy, in 1346; yet Aspin, Salmon, Tegg,
and other chronologists, state 1418 as the earliest use of them in England,
which is above thirty years subsequent to the date of the Issue Roll,1 Rich. II.

[2] See page 208.

[3] See page 213. This was upon Cherbourg being delivered to the English by the King of Navarre, who had extensive possessions in Normandy.

[4] See page 214. The French made a descent upon England at this
period, and committed great ravages in the Isle of Wight.

[5] See page 226.

five cannoniers, each having his cannon, and one cannonier with three cannons, and powder for the same cannons, to protect the Isle of Wight. In the same year Sir Simon de Burley,[1] Constable of Dover Castle, was also supplied with 12 guns, 2 iron patella, 120 stones for the guns, 100 lbs. of powder, and 4 stocks of wood to fortify and strengthen that castle. In the 9th year of this King, Porchester[2] Castle was supplied with cannon, espringolds, quarrells, and other artillery, from the Tower of London; 60 cannon and engines to throw large stones were supplied for fortifying the town of Calais. Many other entries are contained on the Rolls of this reign, showing the use of cannon and gunpowder at that period. Similar entries are frequent in the time of the succeeding monarch.

INCIDENTS, EMINENT PERSONS, &c., NOTICED IN THIS REIGN.

Redemption of the lands of the Duke of Britany,[3] Earl of Richmond, which were mortgaged to Lord John de Nevill, and redeemed for the maintenance of the said Earl and Joan, his wife, sister to the King.

[1] See page 227. While Sir Simon de Burley was constable of this castle, the French landed at Stanore, and burnt the town. Sir Simon was accused by the Archbishop of Canterbury of treachery; and, though the charge was not proved, the Duke of Gloucester ordered the knight to be beheaded. The Archbishop was in consequence adjudged guilty of treason, and directed to quit the kingdom and embark at Dover.

[2] See page 230.

[3] See page 205. He was styled John the Valiant, and was retained by Edward III. to serve the King in his wars in France: he married Joan, the daughter of Thomas de Holland, commonly called the Fair Maid of Kent; who afterwards married Edward the Black Prince. See *Dugdale's Baronage*, vol. i. p. 52, who cites "*Ex Autogr. penes Clerici Pell.*"

Sir Nicholas Dagworth[1] is sent to Ireland to inquire respecting the estate and government of that country, and to certify the King's Council thereof.

An assignment of 269*l*. 7*s*. 7*d*. was made to Ralph, Lord de Basset, of Drayton, for Reynerus Grymbald,[2] of Genoa, a prisoner, purchased of him for the King's use.

Edmund de Mortimer,[3] Earl of March, appointed by the King and his parliament to attend to the directions of the King's Council for governing the affairs and estate of the realm of England.

The Castle of Brest supplied with Burgundy wine, Robert Knolles[4] then being captain thereof: the wine was purchased by the Earl of Buckingham, Earl of Devon, John d'Arundel, Marshal of England, Michael de la Pole, Admiral of the North Fleet, Lord Fitzwalter, and other nobility in the King's service.

Charloto de Navarre,[5] a relation of the King of Navarre, detained in custody in the castle and town of Cherbourg, when the said castle, together with that of Morteyn, were delivered to the King by agreement with the King of Navarre, for a loan to him of 25,000 franks.

John Lamb, a Scotch Esquire, is rewarded for having killed Owynn de Gales,[6] the King's enemy, in France.

A curious description is inserted of the pearls formerly belonging to Alice Perrers,[7] the celebrated favourite of

---

[1] See page 205. [2] See page 206.
[3] See page 207. His son Roger was afterwards proclaimed heir apparent to the crown.
[4] See page 207. Sir Robert Knolles held this castle when the Earl of Buckingham, the King's uncle, went there with an army of 8000 men. Sir Robert had frequently fought under Edward the Black Prince, and subsequently suppressed the rebels under Wat Tyler.
[5] See page 208. [6] See page 209.
[7] See pages 209, 210. Usually written Alice Pierce.

King Edward III., amounting to the number of 21,868, which were seized by command of the King's Council, and delivered to the Clerk of the King's great wardrobe ; the value of each pearl is specified.

The Earl of Saint Paul,[1] the King's prisoner in France, to be delivered out of prison, and his ransom paid to Sir Thomas de Felton, the King's Steward in Gascony ; also payments to the said Earl for his brother, who remained as his hostage at Calais, in the retinue of the Earl of Salisbury.

Ceremonies to be observed upon the celebration of the anniversary[2] of King Edward III., King Richard's grandfather, in Westminster Abbey, for obsequies and burning lights round his tomb, &c.

John Katerine,[3] a Venetian dancing-master, dances and plays in the King's presence.

Payments made to Sir William Windsor,[4] for his expenses in the wars, and restitution made to him of certain lands which belonged to Alice Perrers, his wife, forfeited by judgment in parliament against the said Alice.

The King's engraver alters the great seal[5] and the seals of the King's Bench, Exchequer, and Common Pleas.

Thomas Johnson fights a duel with John Grey,[6] a

[1] See pages 210, 211, 212. This Earl was made prisoner in a skirmish near Lyques in 1375, and was presented to King Edward III. by the Lord of Gomuegines: he remained a long time prisoner in the Tower, but was at length removed to the "fayre castele of Wynsore," where he was allowed "to go and sport him a hawkyng between Wynsore and Westminster; he there met the future partner of his life." The Princess of Wales and her daughter the Lady Maud, "the fayrest ladye in all Englande," had then their residence in the castle ; and, as they sometimes met together " at daunsynge and carrollyng," there commenced that interchange of heart and feeling which soon produced their union. *Froissart.*

[2] See page 211.   [3] See page 212.   [4] See page 213.
[5] See page 214.   [6] See page 216.

traitor, at Calais, where other traitors were adjudged to
death.

Payment to the Clerk of the Works for repairing and
re-constructing the door broken by the common rebels
within the Tower of London.[1]

A crown, called the Spanish crown,[2] set with divers
precious stones, delivered to the keeper of the King's
jewels.

A duel fought upon the Marches of England and
Scotland between a certain Esquire of England and a
certain Esquire of Scotland.[3]

A loan of money advanced to the most Serene Prince,
Lord Wenceslaus,[4] King of the Romans and Bohemia,

---

[1] See page 217. Bayley, in his valuable *History of the Tower*, p. 32, refers to this outrage as follows :—" After the King had agreed to confer with
the rebels assembled under Wat Tyler at Mile-end, he went out of the
Tower to meet them ; before, however, the gates could be closed, a band of
the rebels rushed into the fortress and committed the most barbarous cruel-
ties. That worthy prelate, Simon Sudbury, Archbishop of Canterbury, the
Chancellor, and Sir Robert Hales, the Treasurer, whom they found in the
chapel, were dragged from their sacred refuge and led to instant execution ;
the villains then *broke open* and pillaged the royal apartments, and, entering
the chamber of the King's mother, treated her with the most wanton
brutality."

[2] See page 217.   [3] See page 218.

[4] See page 218. Wenceslaus was decreed unworthy of the imperial
crown for many reasons ; amongst others, for degrading the dignity of the
empire by suffering dogs to lie in the imperial bed-chamber. He drew on
himself the enmity of the church by endeavouring to reform it. He is dif-
ferently spoken of by different writers. Voltaire, Mezeray, and other authors,
paint him as a prodigy of cruelty and vice, and, amongst other atrocities,
accuse him of having roasted his cook alive for dressing his dinner amiss ;
his most intimate friend in Prague was the common executioner, and even
him he put to death at last, for not having taken him at his word when he
once bid him to cut off his head, and actually knelt down to receive the stroke.
He is also stated to have drowned a priest named John Nepomucene, (since
canonized,) because he would not reveal to him the confession of the Empress.
Chron. Belg.

for the more important and urgent affairs of the state of the Holy Church of Rome and the Roman empire.

A sergeant at arms sent from the parliament at Northampton to the priory of Durham, to arrest Sir Ralph de Ferrers,[1] and cause him to appear before the King and his parliament to answer certain charges.

Sir Hugh de Seagrave,[2] Treasurer of England, pays 1*l*. 5*s*. 4*d*. to provide a dinner for the nobility of the King's Council and knights of parliament attending at Westminster upon the affairs of the King and State.

Evidence furnished to John Cavendish, the King's Chief Justice, holding his session at Bury, in Suffolk, against the rebels aiding and abetting a certain monk[3] of that Abbey, who asserted he had the sanction for what he had done from the Court of Rome: this monk was afterwards summoned to appear ·before the King's Council in London, from Nottingham Castle, where he was confined prisoner.

Entries of large sums of money paid on account of the army sent to serve in the Crusades;[4] specifying the number and quality of the men engaged, and stating that the Venerable Father, Henry, Bishop of Norwich, was the Pope's nuncio and deputy in this Crusade against Antipope.

Payment to Sir Nicholas Brembre, mayor of London, for the safe conduct of John Northampton,[5] late mayor of

[1] See page 219.   [2] See page 221.   [3] See page 220.
[4] See pages 222, 223. It is well known that the Popes encouraged these Crusades, because, during the absence of kings and princes in Asia, they had more authority in their dominions, and because these princes commonly returning beggars, they were more submissive to the see of Rome than if they had been in a better condition. *Acta Regia*, vol. i. p. 29.
[5] See page 224. Stow states that John Northampton, Mayor of London, took strict order for suppression of usury, as had before been done by Sir Wil-

London, arrested in the city of London by order of the King's Council, and sent to Corf Castle.

William Craylyng, the King's messenger, sent to Gaunt, seized by the people of Lesclus,[1] in Flanders, and killed.

The King comes from Eltham to Westminster, there dines, and inspects his jewels.[2]

Payments to Arnald Brocas, Clerk of the Works, for constructing large warlike machines[3] in the Tower, ordered for certain urgent and secret affairs by the King and his Council; and also for making divers images and a tabernacle[4] placed over the head of an image made in the likeness of the King; also two images in the likeness of the King and Houell,[5] ordered at the King's pleasure to be put at the end of the great hall at Westminster; also for painting the images there, and repairing the King's bridge or landing-place at Westminster.

The Abbot of Waverley[6] directed to provide a horse for the King, to carry him towards Scotland.

The crowns[7] of King Edward III. and his Queen Philippa pledged to Anthony Bache, a certain merchant in France, for money advanced to pay the said King's troops in France: the said Anthony advances a further sum upon

liam Walworth, which was in part approved by the King. Stow adds that he was committed to perpetual imprisonment and his goods confiscated, but does not state why.

[1] See page 225. [2] See page 226. [3] See page 227.
[4] See page 228. [5] Ibidem. [6] See page 227.
[7] See pages 228, 229. Edward the Third's expensive wars with France obliged him to pledge his crown and jewels to the merchants of Flanders; soon after the accession of Richard II. they were placed in the hands of the Bishop of London and the Earl of Arundel, as security for the sum of 10,000l., which that monarch had borrowed of John Philipot and other merchants of London. *Rot. Pat.* 17 Edward III., p. 1. m. 8. *Rot. Pat.* 1 Richard II., p. 1. m. 25.

the same security to King Richard, to assist him in prosecuting his journey to Scotland.

Payment by Henry de Percy,[1] Keeper of the town of Berwick-upon-Tweed and the Marches there, to certain soldiers who had taken six traitors in the said Marches during the time he was custos there.

John Bottesham, goldsmith of London, provides the King[2] with a hunting-knife and horn, ornamented with gold, to be used in the woods.

Sir Hugh de Calverley[3] waits upon the King, by his command, attended by two knights, thirty-two esquires, and one hundred archers, to assist him against his enemies, and join the great army then assembled.

The Roll of the tenth year of King Richard II. is chiefly occupied with entries of payments for a large army raised at this period, to proceed to the different ports along the English coast to resist the King's enemies. The names of the commanders, with the number and quality of the men under their command, are specified, but are too numerous to be extracted: some few only, supplied from the Welsh counties, are noticed, which will be found at the pages referred to below.[4]

Payment to John Annesley and Isabella, his wife, one of the heirs of John Chandos, chevalier, who held the castle of Saint Saviour,[5] in the island of Constantyn, in

---

[1] See page 229.   [2] See page 231.

[3] See page 232. Pennant states that the last mention made of the celebrated warrior Sir Hugh de Calverley was in 1388. After the active part which, at the head of the "licentious companions," he took in the various fortunes of Peter the Cruel, he is said to have married a Queen Dowager of Arragon. His tomb is still kept in good repair at Bunbury in Cheshire. *Pennant.*

[4] See pages 231, 232.

[5] See page 233. Sir Richard Baker states that Katrington, here called

Normandy, of the gift and feoffment of King Edward III.
The said John prosecuted by duel in the King's presence,
in his palace at Westminster, one Thomas de Catherton,
for allowing the French to capture the said castle; upon
which duel fought in his presence, the King for a certain
time took the quarrel into his own hands, and granted an
annuity of 40l. to the said John and Isabella, and retained
the said John in his service.

Sergeants at arms were sent to the town of Kingston-
upon-Hull, to arrest Michael de la Pole,[1] Earl of Suffolk,
and take him before the King's Council; also to take Sir
Simon de Burlegh[2] and Sir William Elengham from London to Nottingham Castle and back again: also sent to Gloucester, to bring Nicholas Brembre,[3] the King's prisoner,
from Gloucester Castle, to appear before the parliament
and answer certain articles of treason charged against him
by the Duke of Gloucester and Earls of Derby, Warwick, Arundel, and Nottingham.—Sir Thomas Tryvet,
Sir John de Bello Campo, Sir Nicholas Dagworth,[4] and

Catherton, was a man of mighty stature, and Annesley a little man; yet
through the justness of his cause, after a long fight, Annesley prevailed,
and Catherton died the day after the combat. Fabian saith he was drawn
to Tyburn, and there hanged for his false accusation.

[1] See page 234. For the proceedings against him in parliament, *vide*
Rot. Parl. vol. iii. p. 232ᵃ.

[2] Judgment given against him reversed, and his estates restored to his
heirs.   *Rot. Parl.* vol. iii. pp. 358ᵇ, 464ᵇ. Proclamation thereon, &c.
Ibidem, 411ᵇ. Duke of Gloucester impeached for causing his judgment.
Ibidem, 376ᵇ. J. de Cobham impeached for passing judgment against him.
Ibidem, 381ᵇ. Sir Simon was once tutor and fellow in arms to the
Black Prince: to save him, it is said, the good Queen Anne was three hours
on her knees in vain to the hard-hearted Duke of Gloucester.

[3] Impeached of treason. *Rot. Parl.* vol. iii. p. 229ᵇ. Proclamation made
for revoking the judgment against him and others, &c. Ibidem, p. 411ᵇ.

[4] Sent on a commission into Ireland, but countermanded by the intrigues
of Alice Pierce. *Rot. Parl.* vol. i. p. 12ᵇ.

others, were also brought from Dover to London, charged with treason. The Duke of Ireland[1] also appears about this period to have been attainted, as the value of gold and other cloths belonging to him and the before-mentioned Nicholas Brembre are specified and accounted for to the King on the Issue Roll of the 11th year of this King's reign.

Sir Thomas Latymere summoned to appear before the King's Council with certain books and pamphlets in his custody, concerning *the error and perverse doctrine of the Catholic faith.*[2]

A commission is issued to inquire concerning the lands, lordships, &c., in the counties of Devon and Cornwall, belonging to the Duke of Ireland,[3] Robert Tresilian,[4] John Carey,[5] John Blake,[6] and others, forfeited by judgment in parliament : also 333*l.* 6*s.* 8*d.* paid to the King for the price of the Bishop of Chichester's[7] mitre, forfeited by reason of a judgment in parliament.

Payment to Henry Winchester, vicar of the King's

[1] See page 235. This was Robert de Veer, impeached of treason, &c., by the Lords appellants. *Rot. Parl.* vol. iii. p. 229ᵃ. Articles of his impeachment, Ibidem, 230ᵃ.

[2] See page 236. The Lollards were at this period much persecuted by the King at the request of his prelates. This sect, who had just lost two potent friends, the benevolent Anne and John of Gaunt, the latter of whom had passed over to Guienne, went so far as to deliver a remonstrance to parliament against ecclesiastical grievances ; but Sir Richard Story, who, with Sir Thomas Latimer, had carried it in, were obliged to abjure their errors, as is stated by Walsingham: the above entry probably relates to this abjuration.

[3] See page 236.

[4] Impeached of treason, &c., by the Lords appellants. *Rot Parl.* vol. iii. p. 229. Articles of his impeachment—found guilty thereon, and sentenced to be drawn and hanged—his heirs disinherited, lands, &c., confiscated—and hanged the same day at Tyburn. *Rot. Parl.* vol. iii. p. 237.

[5] See page 237. [6] Ibidem.

[7] See page 237. Impeached for his opinion upon the King's prerogatives ; pleads he was compelled to give the same as a Judge ; sentenced to death, but pardon of his life granted : banished to Ireland. *Rot. Parl.* vol. iii. pp. 233ᵃ, 238ᵇ, 239ᵇ, 240ᵇ, 241ᵃ.

free chapel, in his palace, Westminster, for furnishing a kalendar for the use of the King and Lords of the Council in the Star Chamber.[1]

The King's letters directed to the Chancellor and Proctors of the University of Oxford,[2] to quiet certain strifes and disputes between the scholars there.

The judgment of death and forfeiture of estates pronounced by parliament against Sir Robert Bealknap,[3] Chief Justice of the Common Pleas, is, upon petition of the prelates and nobility of the realm, remitted by the King, and an annuity of 40*l.* granted him for life, to issue out of his forfeited possessions. This Roll also contains a curious description of the horses and chattels belonging to Sir Robert.

Sir Philip de Courtenay,[4] the King's Deputy in Ireland, recompensed for the loss of his goods, &c., in Ireland, of which he was deprived by Robert de Veer, Duke of Ireland, from whom he escaped, together with his wife and children, with great difficulty.

Richard de Cicilia, a converted Jew, baptized by Robert, Bishop of London, in the King's presence, at his manor of Langley, and qualified as a Catholic to traffic with Christians out of England.[5]

Robert, Bishop of London, paid for providing a marble

---

[1] See page 237. Questions touching the King's prerogative referred to him. *Rot. Parl.*, vol. iii. p. 233*ᵃ*.

[2] See pages 237, 238.

[3] See page 240. Certain questions touching the King's prerogative referred to him,—impeached for his answers,— pleads he was compelled thereto,—sentenced to death, and forfeiture, &c.; but has pardon of his life :—banished to Ireland for life,—his banishment revoked, judgment against him reversed, and his estates restored. *Rot. Parl.* vol. iii. pp. 233*ᵃ*, 238*ᵇ*, 239*ᵃ*, 240*ᵇ*, 241*ᵃ*, 244*ᵃ*, 346*ᵇ*, 357*ᵇ*, 358*ᵇ*.

[4] See page 241.   [5] See page 242.

tomb, to be placed over the body of Edward,[1] brother of the King, buried in the church of the Friars Preachers of Children Langley.

Payments to the parish clerks and other clerks in the city of London, by the King's command, for their perform- ance, at Skinnerswell, of *the play of the Passion*[2] *of our Lord, and the Creation of the World.*

Letters of privy seal directed to the Archbishop of Armagh, the mayor, bailiffs, and commonalty of Dublin, Drogheda, and Cork; and to the Justices, Chancellor, and Treasurer of Ireland, concerning the state and governance of that country.[3]

Payment of 4*s.* 9*d.* to John Melton, a Clerk in the Receipt of the Exchequer, to provide a dinner for himself and his companion, and for arranging the Records of the Common Bench, taken from a place called Helle[4] to the King's Treasury.

[1] See page 244. This was Edward, the eldest son of Edward the Black Prince, born at Angolesme, who died at seven years of age.

[2] See page 244. This entry refers to the performance mentioned by Stowe in his *Survey of London*, p. 76, which seems, according to his authority, whatever it were, to have lasted three days. Stowe, however, does not give the name of the play; and in the above entry it is no doubt reversed, as that portion which related to the "Creation of the World" must have pre- ceded that of the "Passion of our Lord." This entry fixes the precise date in 1391, viz., after the feast of Saint Bartholomew, not given in any other Record. The sum paid was that which, more than two centuries afterwards, was annually given for the representation of a play before the King or Queen. Such particulars as are known upon this subject will be found in *Mr. J. Payne Collier's* "*History of Dramatic Poetry and the Stage*," vol. i. p. 18. This is unquestionably one of the earliest notices of the name and subject of any dramatic performance of the kind known; and there can be no doubt it was a miracle play, or series of scriptural representations. I find but one of an earlier name mentioned, called Saint Catharine, written, according to Matthew Paris, by Geoffrey, a Norman, abbot of Saint Albans, performed at Dunstable in 1110, in the canonicals of the monks, borrowed for the purpose.

[3] See page 245.

[4] Ibidem. The Records here mentioned to be brought from Helle are

The King grants to Leo, King of Armenia,[1] a pension of 1000*l.* a year, in reverence to God, and because the said King, by reason of his toleration in his own kingdom, had been expelled therefrom by the enemies of God and his own deluded subjects.

Peter Hiltoft, the King's engraver, engraves sixteen brass seals with crowns and letters round them, for sealing cloth in the county of Essex ; also a brass seal for the steward of the King's lordship of Haverford, in Wales.[2]

A gold ring, set with a diamond, sent as a present to the King of France,[3] by Sir Thomas Percy, who accompanied the embassy to treat for a peace between the said King and the King of England.

Payment to the Bishop of Salisbury of 20 marks for the price of a bed of green tarteryn, embroidered with ships and birds, which belonged to Sir Simon de Burley,[4] knight, forfeited by reason of a judgment against the said Sir Simon.

The mayor of the town of Northampton[5] expelled from his office by judgment in Chancery, and committed to Nottingham Castle : a writ directed to the men of the town to elect a new mayor from amongst themselves.

Remuneration to Roger Mortimer, Earl of March,[6] by reason of the destruction and invasion of his property in

now preserved in the Record Office, Chapter House, Westminster, in the custody of Sir Francis Palgrave. Helle and Paradise were two chambers under Westminster Hall.

[1] See pages 229, 245. Leo, King of Armenia, visited England in 1386. He endeavoured to unite the great European powers in a league against the infidels ; he succeeded not, but Richard gave him a handsome present in money and 1000*l.* per annum for life. *Walsingham.*

[2] See page 246.   [3] Ibidem.   [4] See page 250.

[5] See page 251.   [6] See page 252.

Ireland by the Irish, and custody of his lands granted, to enable him to resist the malice of his enemies there.

Presents of gold, worked cloth, plate, and jewellery, given to the knights and esquires who attended the Viscount de Meloun [1] on his embassy from France ; viz., amongst other things, is mentioned a large ruby set in a ring, worth 30*l.* ; a diamond set in a gold ring, worth 20*l.* ; and a great gold cup, worth 38*l.*, &c. : also payments for making two gold collars and a stud of gold, ornamented with pearls and precious stones, for the King's person ; and 46*l.* 10*s.* paid for two diamonds presented to the Bishop of London and the Earl of Arundel.

Payment to the Prior of Cork, in Ireland, for a marble coffin purchased to enclose the body of Thomas Russholk, [2] late Bishop of Chichester, who was buried in Ireland.

To Richard, Bishop of Chichester, for a piece of land with houses thereon, adjoining the burial-ground of the cathedral church of Chichester, [3] of the foundation of the progenitors of the Kings of England, whereon to erect a mansion for the vicars doing duty there.

Thomas Balymore, vicar of Llansthwell, [4] remunerated for the expense he was at during the time the King dwelt at his house on his passage to Ireland.

Curious description of tackle delivered to Thomas Lynne, master of the King's ship called the George ; [5] with an account of the price and weight of the cables, ropes, hawsers, &c., supplied to the same vessel.

Clement Atte Spice directed to seize into the King's hands the castle, lordships, and possessions of Thomas, Archbishop of Canterbury, [6] Thomas, Duke of Gloucester,

[1] See page 253.   [2] See page 254.   [3] Ibidem.
[4] See page 256.   [5] Ibidem.   [6] See page 264.

f

Richard, Earl of Arundell, and Thomas, Earl of Warwick, in the counties of Essex and Hertford, forfeited by virtue of a judgment against them in parliament.

A gold ring set with a ruby presented by the King to the Pope, taken by John Henritz, Prior of Launde, who was sent to the Court of Rome upon secret affairs.

Jewels purchased for the purpose of being presented as new year's gifts[1] from Queen Isabella; viz., a worked tablet with four sapphires and four rubies, price 26*l*., given to the Duke of Lancaster; a worked tablet of gold, with two sapphires, two rubies, and pearls, worth 25*l*., to the Earl Marshal; a tablet of gold worked with the image of Saint Catherine, with rubies, sapphires, and pearls, worth 28*l*., given to the Earl of Rutland; a diamond ring given to the Earl of Derby and Lady Beauchamp; with other presents.

A present sent from the King to Pope Urban[2] of a gold cup and a gold ring set with a ruby; also of a book of miracles of Edward, late King of England, whose body was buried at the town of Gloucester: with payment of expenses for taking the same presents from London to Florence.

David Panell, a felon, adjudged to death, for the murder of nine men[3] and one woman.

Exequies performed in the county of Essex for Robert, late Duke of Ireland.[4]

Richard, Bishop of Coventry and Litchfield, sent as the King's ambassador to Rome, respecting the canonization of King Edward II.,[5] buried at Gloucester.

John Mayheu[6] makes an offering of a small ship formed of silver to an image of the blessed Mary, in the town of

---

[1] See page 265.   [2] See page 259.   [3] See page 261.
[4] See page 262.   [5] See pages 248, 264.   [6] See page 267.

Aques, for his deliverance from danger during a storm at sea.

The bishops and nobility summoned to attend at Coventry to witness a duel to be fought there between the Dukes of Hereford [1] and Norfolk.

The King sends 1000 marks to the Duke of Hereford [2] at Calais, as a present.

The King pays 21*l*. 6*s*. 8*d*. for two bold falcons,[3] and 12*l*. for three lanerets, to be sent as a present to the King of Navarre; the price given for other descriptions of falcons purchased for presents is also stated.

The King allows Henry, the son and heir of Henry, Duke of Hereford,[4] 500*l*. yearly.

Allowance to Thomas, Duke of Surrey,[5] the King's Deputy in Ireland; also for conducting the son of Makmorgh and other persons of noble condition, sent as hostages from that country for the security of the peace there.

Payment of 2000*l*. to the Emperor of Constantinople,[6] to aid him in maintaining the war against the Saracens and others fighting against Christianity.

HENRY IV.

The Issue Rolls at the commencement of this reign, after noticing the solemnization of the new creation of

[1] See page 267. A long and interesting account of the parade and preparations for this duel, which never took place, will be found in *Brady's History of England*, vol. ii. p. 415.

[2] See page 268.   [3] Ibidem.

[4] See page 269. This and the previous grant to his father the duke, at page 268, immediately after his banishment, show that the King at this period entertained no resentment against his successor.

[5] See page 272.   [6] Ibidem.

knights made on Sunday next before the coronation of the King, by assembling the English, Scotch, and foreign heralds in the Tower,[1] and the meeting of the Lords and nobility in the Star Chamber to consult on the affairs of the Lord the King, (on which occasion rich cloths and cushions, worked with the arms, collar, and livery of King Henry IV., with tapestry and other cloths, were provided for the accommodation of the Council,[2]) proceed to trace some of those troubles which arose out of factions to which this King's reign was peculiarly subject, from his defective title to the crown, occasioned by a departure from the long familiarized hereditary succession of previous monarchs.

It is therefore proposed here to review some of the incidents which caused these insurrections, and to show their connexion with corresponding entries contained in the Issue Rolls of this period.

The first insurrection in this King's reign arose out of the daring conspiracy of the lords, contrived in the house of the Abbot of Westminster; namely, to invite the King to a joust or tournament at Oxford, and there to seize his person. This plot was providentially detected by the Duke of York, from the indenture of confederacy accidentally falling from the bosom of his son, the Duke of Aumerle, who visited his father previously to joining the conspirators at Windsor. The Issue Roll[3] of the first year of this King directs the lands and tenements of Thomas, Earl of Kent, John, Earl of Salisbury, Richard de Lomeley, and Thomas Blunt, knights, (who were conspirators in this plot,) to be seized into the King's hands, and inquiry to be made in various counties

---

[1] See page 274.   [2] Ibidem.   [3] See page 275.

respecting their goods and chattels. The names of some of the brave and loyal townsmen of Cirencester[1] are here noticed, and rewarded for arresting the Earls of Kent, Salisbury, and others who had lately rebelled against the King and his crown, and their expenses paid for taking the said rebels to Oxford, and ultimately bringing them to the King in London. The payment to John Cosin,[2] who probably was the gallant bailiff that headed his townsmen, is singularly worded, being for the " good service performed by the said John in manfully resisting, at Cirencester, Thomas, late Earl of Kent, and others who had traitorously risen against the King and his allegiance." Walsingham[3] and some other historians appear to have fallen into error in stating that the Earls of Kent and Salisbury,[4] together with Spenser, Lumley, and other traitors, were seized one day, and without further ceremony, according to the custom of the times, executed the next. The entry on the Issue Roll of Easter, 1 Henry IV., seems rather to contradict this assertion; namely, the mention of payments for fourteen days' attendance of the retinue of the *Earl of Rutland*[5] and the Lord Treasurer, sent to prosecute Thomas, late Earl of Kent, John, late Earl of Salisbury, Sir Ralph de Lomley, knight, and other rebels, who raised an insur-

---

[1] The transcriber has mistaken Cicester, in the original, for Chichester: it should be Cirencester. Rapin states, in his *Acta Regia*, vol. ii. p. 70, that some of the English historians will have it to be at Chichester, where four lords were attacked by the mayor; and others say it was Cirencester: the similarity of writing the place in ancient documents no doubt has occasioned this mistake.

[2] See pages 277, 278.   [3] Walsingham, p. 363.

[4] The Earl of Salisbury was a man of literature and genius. The celebrated Christiana of Pisa was fond of him, probably for listening to her productions, for she used to call him " Gracieux chevalier aimant dictiez, et luy meme gracieux dicteur." *Boivin's Mem. Liter.*

[5] See page 278.

rection at the feast of Epiphany against the King and his crown ; which rebels were taken at Cirencester by the men of the town.[1] The fate of the nobility and others implicated in this plot is lamented by Hume ;[2] who adds, that, when the quarters of these unhappy men were brought to London, no less than eighteen bishops and thirty-two mitred abbots joined the populace, and met them with the most indecent marks of joy and exultation. But the spectacle the most shocking to every one who retained any sentiment either of honour or humanity still remained. The *Earl of Rutland* appeared carrying on a pole the head of Lord Spencer, his brother-in-law, which he presented in triumph to Henry as a testimony of his loyalty. This infamous person, who was soon after Duke of York, by the death of his father, had been instrumental in the murder of his uncle the Duke of Gloucester; had then deserted Richard, by whom he was trusted ; had conspired against the life of Henry, to whom he had sworn allegiance; had betrayed his associates, whom he also seduced into this enterprise ; but, notwithstanding the baseness of his character, was appointed their prosecutor, presented with jewels, and received other marks of royal favour and distinction, as may be found on turning to the references of the Issue Rolls noted at the bottom of this page.[3]

Henry had scarcely quelled the conspiracy in England when fresh troubles broke out in Wales, encouraged by

---

[1] So pleased was Henry with the conduct of the women of Cirencester on this occasion, that he gave them by patent six bucks annually from his forest at Bredon, to the men only four ; and a pipe of wine to each sex. *Rymer's Fœdera.*

[2] See Hume, vol. iii. chap. 18.

[3] See pages 250, 265, 278.

Owen Glendour, an esquire of that principality, who, to revenge a wrong done to him by Lord Grey of Ruthen, excited the Welshmen to rebel, and endeavour to shake off the English yoke. To check this rebellion we find payments on the Issue Roll of the third year of this King were made to Henry Percy, son of the Earl of Northumberland, to continue the siege at Conway Castle, which he commenced immediately after the King's rebels had taken that fortress, and continued to besiege the same at his own costs, assisted only by the people of the country.[1] Messengers were also at this period despatched to the knights and esquires of the King's retinue to hasten to Wales with the King, to resist the malice of Owen Glendurdy[2] and other rebels there assembled. Several payments appear upon the Rolls of the same year to Prince Henry, the King's son, relating to this insurrection; a few only are noticed, amongst which will be found one to the Prince[3] for the wages of 100 men at arms, each to receive 12d. per day, and 400 archers, each at 6d. per day, who were sent with despatch to Hardelagh Castle, in North Wales, to remove the besiegers whom Owen Glendourdy and other rebels had sent to the castle aforesaid.[4] Remuneration was also made to the Bishop of Bangor for the losses occasioned to the possessions of the church of Bangor[5] by reason of the war there. Henry, Prince of Wales,[6] was the next year appointed the King's Deputy in Wales for one year, to see justice done on the rebels that should be found and taken there within the said year; and a list is furnished of the number of knights, esquires, and archers retained by him for this purpose. The entry

[1] See page 283. [2] See page 287. [3] See page 290.
[4] See page 290. [5] Ibidem. [6] See pages 293, 294.

immediately succeeding the above is a payment to messengers and couriers sent with writs to proclaim throughout
every county in England the death of *Henry Percy*,[1] together with other rebels, slain in the battle fought between
the King and the said rebels, on the part of the said
Henry Percy, near Shrewsbury; and the capture of
Thomas Percy, Earl of Worcester, in the said battle;
with directions to the keepers of all ports to prevent the
escape of the rebels.

. The rebellion in Wales was hardly quieted before fresh
disturbances broke out in Scotland, which, like the former,
terminated in the King's favour, as on the Issue Roll of
the seventh year will be found a reward given to Nicholas
Merbury for reporting to the King the acceptable news of
the success of the expedition at *Homeldon*,[2] near Wollure,

[1] See page 294. Shakspeare has chosen to make Hotspur fall by the
hand of Henry, Prince of Wales. Hollingshed says, "The king slew that
day with his own hand thirty-six of his enemies, and the troops of his party,
encouraged by his doings, fought valiantly, and slew the Lord Percy, called
Henry Hotspur." According to Speed, Percy was killed by an unknown hand.
The above proclamation was made in consequence of the reports that Hotspur was still alive. Stowe says, "Forasmuch as some people said that Sir
Harry Percy was alive, he was taken up again out of his grave and bound
upright between two mill-stones, that all might see that he was dead." *Chron.
of London*, 4to. p. 88.

[2] See page 302. Shakspeare represents Sir Walter Blount, and not Sir
Nicholas Merbury, as the person who brings the news of this battle to the
King.

"*K. Hen.* Here is a dear and true industrious friend,
Sir Walter Blunt, new lighted from his horse,
And he hath brought us smooth and welcome news.
The Earl of Douglas is discomfited;
Ten thousand bold Scots, two-and twenty knights,
Balk'd in their own blood, did Sir Walter see
On *Holmedon's* plains : of prisoners, Hotspur took
Mordake the Earl of Fife, and eldest son
To beaten Douglas," &c.

in Northumberland, under Henry, Earl of Northumberland,
against the King's Scotch enemies, to their destruction;
in which defeat four earls, many barons and bannerets,
with a great multitude of knights and esquires, as well
Scotch as French, are stated to have been taken and
drowned in the river Tweed.

The King at this period was compelled to keep a
watchful eye on France, which had shown a strong dispo-
sition to assist the Scotch in the late conflict with England, for which purpose we here find a payment to a spy[1]
for inquiring and searching into the intentions and purposes
of the French, and to certify and inform the Council
thereof. Preparations were also directed to be made for
the army to assemble and accompany the King to Calais,
and first to besiege that town. These hostile intentions,
however, were soon changed, as we find shortly afterwards
that Hugh Mortymer was sent to France to enter into a
contract of marriage[2] between the Lord the Prince and
the second daughter of the King of France; but as yet
the Editor has discovered no other proceedings relative to
this contract.

The King's second marriage with Joan, daughter of
Charles I., King of Navarre, widow of John de Montfort, surnamed Streamy, or the Conqueror, is frequently
noticed; and in the fourth year of the King's reign Lord
de Camoys is directed to conduct Queen Joan from Britany to England.[3] The expenses of the King's house-

Hotspur further refers to these prisoners in his well-known speech beginning,—

"My liege, I did deny no prisoners."

Many errors as to time, circumstance, and place, and attributing actions
to wrong persons, by Shakspeare, might be corrected by the Issue Rolls.
[1] See page 302. [2] See page 312. [3] See page 292.

hold at Winchester,[1] on the day of his marriage, are stated
to have been 333*l.* 6*s.* 8*d.*, and orders were issued for the
nobility and ladies to attend at the Queen's coronation, at
the celebration of which a singular circumstance is recorded, of Lord de Latymer releasing the right of his inheritance to the office of almoner, and receiving a remuneration for the almoner's dish placed before the Queen on
the day of her coronation.[2]

Frequent entries are also to be found on these Rolls
relating to the marriages and treaties for marriage of
the King's children. The following only could be noticed :—the Countess of Salisbury and a retinue are
appointed to attend the Lady Blanch,[3] the King's eldest
daughter, to Cologne, previous to the solemnization of her
marriage with Lewis Barbatus, Palatine of the Rhine
and Prince Elector ;—payment of 20,000 marks to the
King of the Romans on the day of the marriage :[4]—a
treaty for a marriage was also contemplated between
Lord Henry, Prince of Wales, and the daughter of Philippa, Queen of Denmark, references to which are given
in the pages noted below.[5]

The Editor has not discovered any entry on the Issue
Rolls to authenticate the remarkable story, taken from a
MS. in Christchurch College, Cambridge, to be found
in Peck's *Desiderata Curiosa*, and vouched by Clement
Maydestan : namely, that King Henry's corpse was
thrown into the Thames between Barking and Gravesend, " upon so frightful a rush of wind and waves
" pouring in, that eight barges, full of noblemen, who

[1] See page 296.   [2] See page 297
[3] See pages 283, 284, 285, 286, 292.
[4] See page 318.   [5] See pages 296, 311

"attended the funeral, were utterly dispersed, and in
" most extreme danger of being lost. Then we, who
" were entrusted with the royal body, being in the most
" imminent peril of our lives, by common consent threw
" it into the river, and straightway all was calm; but the
" coffin in which it had lain, and which was covered with
" gold cloth, we carried with great pomp to Canterbury,
" and interred it." The only notices of this King's
funeral, yet found, are those on the Issue Roll of the
1st year of King Henry V., of a payment to provide
90 banners,[1] ornamented with the arms of all the Kings
of Christendom, and other Nobles of different kingdoms
of the world, giving the price of each banner; also 50
geytons, painted with images, &c., placed around the
hearse ordered for the anniversary of the King's funeral,
within the Abbey of Christchurch, Canterbury; also
payments to the wax-chandler[2] for the hearse newly made
by Simon Prentot, placed in the said church on this
occasion, together with entire wax-lights and 120 torches
provided to burn around the hearse and in other places
within the church on the night and day of the anniversary
of the late King's funeral. A rather singular mark of
economy appears upon the same Roll, where the Treasurer
of England requests from the Archbishop and Prior of
Christchurch, Canterbury, a loan[3] of the very banners which
had been used at the burial of King Henry IV., and for
them to be placed on the hearse ordered for the anniversary
of the Lord Richard II., recently entombed in Westminster Abbey. The banners of Henry of Lancaster,
ornamented with the arms of all the Kings of Christendom, waving over the remains of his former rival, may be

[1] See page 325.   [2] See page 326.   [3] See page 327.

considered as carrying triumph beyond the grave, which
even the King himself had probably never contemplated.

The capture of James, son of Robert the Third, King of
Scotland, and his long detention as a prisoner both in this
and the subsequent reign, has excited so deep an interest
in the lovers of history, that it is to be regretted more
numerous extracts could not be admitted in this volume
to trace the progress of this unfortunate Monarch's captivity. Sufficient however are supplied to show that
though King Henry, contrary to every feeling of honour
and generosity, detained him a prisoner during the
existence of a truce, yet he fulfilled, with kindness and
liberality, the duties of a teacher, which he undertook
on hearing that the young Prince, when detained, was on
his way to the French Court for the advantages of education; the King sarcastically declaring that he understood
the French language sufficiently to instruct the Prince
himself. James appears to have been but nine years of age
when he embarked for France, under the care of the Earl
of Orkney; by stress of weather his ship was driven on the
English coast, near Flamborough Head. Hollinshed states
that the young Prince with his attendants were sent to confinement in the Tower; and, by the Issue Roll of the 8th
year of this King's reign, he appears to have been committed to the custody of Richard Spice,[1] Deputy Constable
there, to whom a payment is made for the said Prince, and
for John Toures, William Seton, John Gaffard, and Master
Dankirton, the chaplain, probably the companions spoken
of by Hollinshed. During the first years of his captivity
his freedom does not seem to have extended beyond the

[1] See page 305.

walls of the fortress to which he was consigned. In the
year 1407 he was removed from the Tower of London to
the castle of Nottingham, together with Griffin, son of
Owen Glendour,[1] who had been taken prisoner in the
battle of Usk; and on the Issue Rolls of the 10th year of
Henry IV. are payments to Lord Grey of Codnor, the
King's Chamberlain, and a powerful nobleman in Nottinghamshire, for the support of the said King of Scotland,
and of Griffin, the son of Owen Glendourdy.[2] Towards the
latter part of King Henry's reign the liberty of his royal
captive was less restrained; he was allowed his freedom within a prescribed district, and joined in the sports
of the field and in martial exercises. On the death of
Henry IV. King James was again placed under confinement in the Tower, with Murdoch, Earl of Fife, and
many of the Scotch nobility, as appears by the Issue
Rolls of the 1st and 3rd years of Henry V.[3] Sir John
Pelham had the custody and governance of the Scotch
King, and received an allowance of 700*l.* yearly for
support of his prisoner in food, clothing, and other
necessary things, as agreed upon between the said Sir
John and the King's Council.[4] James was afterwards
removed to Windsor Castle, and as soon as the new
King was peaceably settled on his throne the royal captive
seems to have been allowed his former freedom, till the
commencement of Henry's wars with France, when he
was again lodged in the Tower.[5] He was, however, still
bountifully supplied out of the royal treasure, and
frequently appeared at Court; and in the latter part of

[1] See *Pinkerton's History of Scotland,* vol. i. p. 81 and 82.
[2] See page 312. [3] See page 324. [4] See page 343.
[5] *Vide Bibl. Cotton. Vesp.* xiv. 105.

the King's reign accompanied him to France, upon which
occasion the Clerk of the King's Wardrobe is directed to
provide him with necessary apparel.[1] He was at the siege
of Melun in 1420; and, being subsequently appointed
with the Duke of Gloucester to invest the town of Dreux,
that place was surrendered to the Scottish King after an
arduous siege.   Death shortly afterwards terminated the
glorious career of King Henry V., an event which
occasioned King James's return to his ancient prison in
the Tower, and the renewal of negotiations which
speedily terminated in his release.   The Northern
Monarch was restored to his native country in 1423,
after a captivity of nearly eighteen years, upon delivering
several nobles of Scotland as hostages for payment of
40,000*l.* for his expenses during that period.   This
last mentioned circumstance is referred to in the Issue
Rolls of the 3rd, 5th, and 12th years of King Henry
VI., where it will be found that Sir Richard Nevile[2]
attended upon the Scotch King with knights, esquires,
&c., to the number of one hundred and sixty persons;
that Peter Cawode,[3] Esquire, conducted the hostages for
the said King from London to York, and there delivered
them to Sir Richard Nevile, after the King's oath[4] had
been received to perform those things he had promised;
and Richard, Earl of Salisbury, was paid for the expenses
of the said hostages, who appear to have amounted to the
number of fifteen.[5]

[1] See page 363.   [2] See page 293.   [3] See page 399.
[4] See page 388.   [5] See page 412.

INCIDENTS, EMINENT PERSONS, &c., NOTICED
IN THIS REIGN.

John Vaux appointed, by the Earl of Northumberland
and Westmoreland, Marshal of England, to hold a session
at Newcastle-upon-Tyne upon judgment of a duel to be
fought between the Earl of Salisbury[1] and Lord de
Morley.

John Mayheu, Master of a King's ship, presents the
King with a stone of adamant, ornamented and set in
gold.[2]

Knights and esquires arrive from France to prosecute
certain feats of arms against Sir John Cornewaill, knight,
and Janicas Darcass, Esquire, and are conducted to the
King's presence at York.[3]

Payment to the Countess of Huntingdon[4] for a black
bed with entire furniture, belonging to the chamber of the
late Earl of Huntingdon, forfeited to the King.

Ten pounds weight of silver used to make the great
seal and white privy seal, according to the form of a
certain pattern in the possession of John Edmunds,[5] the
goldsmith.

[1] See page 275. The brutal insolence of private pique overleaped every
decent restraint. The Lord Fitz-Walter, in the face of the house, challenged
Aumerle as a traitor, and Morley defied Salisbury for double treachery.—
Fabian.

[2] See page 277.　　　　　　　[3] See page 278.

[4] See page 279. The Earl of Huntingdon was the King's brother-in-law,
created Duke of Exeter by King Richard II. He was a steady adherent to the
late King, and was taken at Plesley in Essex, and after five days' imprisonment without trial, attended with circumstances of great cruelty, was beheaded, his head stuck on a pole, and placed on London Bridge; but at the
instance of his wife, the King's sister, it was afterwards removed and buried
with his body at Plesley.

[5] See page 279.

Payments to Sir John Stanley,[1] Lord Lieutenant of Ireland, for himself, 99 men at arms, and 300 archers in his retinue, to serve the King in his wars there.

The Merchants of Lynn capture Robert Logan,[2] a Scotch knight, and David Seton, clerk, Archdeacon of Rosse, at sea near the Marches : the prisoners were purchased from the merchants by the King, and John Elyngham was rewarded for bringing them from Lynn to London.

Sir Thomas Erpyngham purchases a sparrowhawk for the King, belonging to Thomas, late Earl of Kent,[3] for 16l.

Conditions upon which the custody of Roxborough[4] Castle is granted to Richard Lord Grey and Sir Stephen le Scrop, to complete the works there begun during the time of war, or during a truce.

A ship sent from Chester to Dublin to bring the King's son[5] from Ireland, together with the furniture of the chapel and ornaments thereof, which formerly belonged to the late King Richard.

The King's right of wreck to a vessel lost off the Isle of Scilly[6] to be ascertained.

Release to Manuel the devoted to God, Emperor of the Romans,[7] &c., for defence of the Roman empire against

---

[1] See pages 279, 292.

[2] See page 279. Sir Robert Logan commanded the Scotch fleet sent against the English; his first attack was designed against our fishermen, but before he came to action the greater part of his fleet was taken by certain English ships. *Sir John Hayward's Life of Henry IV.*, p. 308.

[3] See page 280.   [4] See pages 280, 281.

[5] See page 281.

[6] See page 281. The Scilly Islands are considered as part of Cornwall; the above with other franchises belonging to these islands are therefore now vested in the duchy of Cornwall. See *Troutbeck's Survey of the Scilly Islands.*

[7] See page 282. This Emperor was besieged in Constantinople by his

the enemies of the Christian faith, fighting against the cause of Christianity, of certain sums which he owed to the late King Richard II., in consideration of the great labour, charge, and expenses theretofore borne by the Emperor in the said cause, together with other Catholic Princes and faithful Christians.

Cloth of gold and other merchandise purchased of Richard Whityngton,[1] citizen and merchant of London, for the apparel and paraphernalia of Blanch, the King's eldest daughter, on her intended voyage to Cologne to solemnize her marriage with the son of the King of the Romans.

The King wounds Bertolf Vander Eme[2] in the neck in fencing with him, with the long sword, and in consideration thereof presents him with 10*l.*

The King is attended in his journey to Scotland[3] by twenty-two valets, tailors, tassel-makers, and carpenters, who took the King's pavilions and tents from London as well by land as by sea.

Payment of 12,000 marks yearly to Thomas,[4] the King's son, Deputy of Ireland, for men retained by him for the wars in that kingdom, and for the government of it.

---

nephew John and ten thousand Turks. Marshal Boucicault relieved the imperial city, and persuaded Manuel to resign the command, to sail with him to Europe, and endeavour to obtain assistance there.

[1] See page 283. This is the celebrated Whityngton, thrice Lord Mayor of London; his name is of very frequent occurrence on the Issue Rolls as a lender of money to the King. Some other references to his name will be found in the Index at the end of this volume.

[2] See page 284.

[3] See page 285.

[4] See page 287. A curious letter from this Prince, dated at Dublin Castle, is printed in Webb's translation of a French metrical history of Richard II., p. 249, giving an account of his entertainment in that castle, and of his difficulty in governing Ireland.

g

The Countess of Dunbarr[1] appeared before the King to prosecute certain affairs concerning her husband, herself, and their heirs, by particulars thereof delivered into the hanaper.

Eight collars purchased of Theodore, the goldsmith of London, and sent by the King's command to his sister, the Queen of Portugal,[2] for the King's infant nephew.

Payments to Henry, Earl of Northumberland,[3] and Henry Percy his son, keeper of the Scotch Marches, for the safe custody thereof, after the expiration of the truce entered into in the third year of this king.

A royal seat erected in Smithfield, where a duel was to be fought between the King's kinsman, Sir Richard Arundell, and a Lombard.[4]

Orders issued to arrest David Perot, Esquire,[5] of the county of Pembroke, to take him before the King and his Council, and to seize all arms in his possession.

Payments directed to be made to Thomas Sy, Esquire,[6] verger to the order of the Garter, in the same way as former vergers had been accustomed to be paid.

Ralph, Earl of Westmoreland, Marshal of England, paid for marshalling and appointing the lists in Smithfield, for a duel[7] to be fought between Yevan app Griffith Lloyt, appellant, and Perceval Soudan, knight, defendant, respecting certain articles of treason charged against the said Sir Perceval.

---

[1] See page 288.   [2] Ibidem.
[3] See pages 288, 290. The Earl of Northumberland also had a grant of the Isle of Man, with the privilege of carrying the sword called Lancaster on the King's left hand at coronations. This was the very sword which Henry wore when he landed at Ravenspur.
[4] See page 289.   [5] Ibidem.
[6] Ibidem.   [7] See page 291.

Two tablets purchased from Gamenshede and Albright, goldsmiths of London, delivered, by order of the Council, to John and Humphrey, the King's sons, to be by them presented to the Lady the Queen,[1] consort of the Lord the King; also a gold collar purchased for the King at his nuptials.

Divers silver vessels and jewels belonging to Edward de Mortimer[2] taken to the King's great Treasury at Westminster.

Edward, Duke of York,[3] appointed the King's Deputy in Aquitaine, with allowances for himself and retinue.

The King stands godfather to Henry, the son of John, Earl of Somerset,[4] and settles on him 1000 marks yearly.

An annuity granted to John Merbury[5] for his services to the King, and also because he had married Alice Old-castle, of the county of Hereford.

Payment for the safe custody of the two daughters of Lord le Despenser,[6] for certain causes in the hands of the Lord the King; also for conducting Lady le Despenser from London to Kenilworth Castle.

Parchment purchased for the enrolment of the Pell Records.[7]

The Earl of Douglas[8] committed to the custody of Roger Bradeshawe by the Lord the King, *from the time of the last battle fought near Shrewsbury* to the 21st August following, with expenses of his custody for twenty-seven days.

Proclamations made to arrest certain vagabonds[9]

[1] See pages 294, 295.
[2] See page 295.
[3] See page 297.
[4] See page 298.
[5] See page 299.
[6] See page 300.
[7] Ibidem.
[8] See page 301.
[9] See page 301. There was also a prohibition to prosecute those who said

spreading reports from town to town of the actual existence of King Richard II., and to keep them in safe custody until otherwise commanded by the King's Council ; also for the archbishops and bishops to pray for the good estate of the Lord the King and government of the realm.

Payment of 385*l.* 6*s.* 8*d.* for a gold collar,[1] worked with the motto " soveignez " and the letter S,[1] set with ten amulets, garnished with nine large pearls, twelve large diamonds, eight rubies, eight sapphires, together with a great clasp in shape of a triangle, with a large ruby set in the same, and garnished with four great pearls, delivered to the King at Winchester : another collar of gold set with precious stones was purchased for the King for 550*l.*

Payment to William Gascoigne,[2] Chief Justice of the King's Common Bench.

A scaffold directed by the King to be erected at Nottingham, for a duel to be fought between John Bulmer and Bertran Dusane.[3]

Chests and locks purchased for the preservation of the Pell Records[4] and memoranda of the Receipt of the Exchequer; also certain records inspected at Westmin-

innocently that King Richard was alive, dated July, 1402 ; but this order was not promulgated till several persons had been executed.

[1] See page 305. This was probably the collar of SS's formerly worn with the badge of the order of the Garter ; the amulets were frequently introduced in collars, and worn as charms against incantations. The precise form of the collar of the Garter was not fixed till the reign of Henry VIII., when it was ordered to weigh exactly thirty-two ounces—and to consist of two different links alternately combined. On the first of these is a red rose enamelled, which is surrounded by a blue enamelled garter, upon which appears the motto in letters of gold : the second link is the same in every respect, save that the rose in the centre is of white enamel. These links are united with lacs d'amour, or true-lovers knots, and from the middle of the collar is suspended the effigy of Saint George.

[2] See page 307.   [3] See page 309.   [4] See pages 309, 310.

ster for the profit and advantage of the King, with expenses attending the same; and a dinner provided for the Lord Treasurer, Barons, and Chamberlains of the Exchequer.

Knights of the Garter summoned[1] to appear at London on a certain day; Thomas, the King's son, then in Ireland, and Humphrey Stafford, also summoned to appear before the King in Chancery.

Doctor Nicholas Ryxton[2] and Sir John Colvyle sent to the Court of Rome upon the King's private affairs.

Proclamation of the truce agreed upon between the King's ambassadors and commissioners from the Earl of Burgundy.[3]

Sir Robert Umframvill[4] to communicate with the ambassador from the King of Scotland to prolong the truce lately entered into with that kingdom.

Proclamation made concerning the election of Pope Alexander;[5] also concerning the union of the church made and agreed upon at Pisa.

The Earl of Fyff[6] and other Scotchmen prisoners in Windsor Castle and Tower of London.

Expenses of making a new gate to the King's palace at Westminster, on the west side, towards the King's highway.[7]

[1] See page 310.
[2] See page 310. This Nicholas Ryxton, or sometimes called Riston, considering the strife between the then anti-popes, wrote the book *De Tollendo Schismate.*
[3] See page 311.
[4] See page 312. Sir Robert sailed with a fleet up the Forth as far as Blackness, took the grand galliot of Scotland, and carried back to the south fourteen tall ships, and so vast a booty of corn that he obtained the name of Sir Robert Mind-market.
[5] See page 313.   [6] See pages 314, 324.   [7] See page 317.

Richard Whityngton, citizen and merchant of London, advances money to pay for the charges and expenses of L'Ermyte de Foy Casyn [1] and other ambassadors from France.

The Lord Chancellor's barber [2] pays for fruit purchased by the keeper of the wardrobe.

HENRY V.

The progress of this King's glory and renown is to be traced rather through his military successes abroad than his domestic policy. The greater portion of his time being occupied in the conquest of France, left him but little leisure to attend to affairs at home. The Issue Rolls of this reign contain numerous payments to supply the King with men and arms, which enabled him to achieve his triumphs at Harfleur, Agincourt, Rouen, Meaux, and other places in Normandy and France; some circumstances connected with the accomplishment of which, together with the names of the prisoners mentioned throughout this reign in these Records, will first be noticed.

France having broken the treaty of Bretigny, pretending that it was null and void, and no peace since that period having been concluded between the two crowns, but truces only which did not in the least affect the rights of either party, was the foundation upon which Henry laid his pretensions to the crown of France, as the inheritance of his predecessors, from the time of his great-grandfather King Edward III.

To investigate his title to the crown of France we find

[1] See page 317.　　　　[2] Ibidem.

The remainder of the year was spent in unsuccessful negotiations, and war was declared at the parliament held at Leicester[1] in April 1414. Esquires were despatched to the Duke of Holland to provide shipping from Zealand for the King's voyage in person to France;[2] and on the 19th April, in the third year of the King's reign, a payment was made for a repast in the palace at Westminster, given to the Duke of Clarence and other Lords dining there, for advice to be had respecting the King's voyage to Harfleur.[3] Henry having embarked his army, which consisted of about 50,000 men, sailed on the 20th August, 1415, leaving his brother, the Duke of Bedford, Regent in England. He landed at Havre de Grace, and not many days after began the siege of Harfleur, soon after the commencement of which a commission was sent to the Constable of Dover Castle and Warden of the Cinque Ports, directing him to send all fishing vessels within those ports, supplied with men and tackle, to fish on the French coast for support of the King's army then at Harfleur.[4]

King Henry's arms having been crowned with success at Harfleur and Agincourt, provision is made on the Issue Roll for some of the prisoners of greater note. William Loveneye[5] is directed to provide for the charges and expenses of the household of the Dukes of Orleans and Bourbon, who were confined in Pomfret[6] and Somerton Castles, together with other earls, lords, and French knights, taken at the battle of Agincourt: provision is also made for the support of George de Clere[7] and three barons, his companions, with thirteen knights and seventeen

---

[1] See page 330.   [2] See page 340.   [3] Ibidem.
[4] See page 342.   [5] See page 344.   [6] See pages 352, 353.
[7] See pages 344, 345.

sence, yet it was found necessary to issue commissions, directed to knights and esquires, to assemble men at arms and archers to resist an insurrection in Scotland,[1] and to make war against that country, if necessary. Henry, during his war with France, seldom visited England, except for the purpose of obtaining subsidies or grants from his parliament; but a constant communication was kept up with him in Normandy, as is shown by some of the following entries on the Issue Rolls.

The Bishop of Saint David's,[2] the King's confessor, with his family, go to the King's presence in Normandy; the expenses of himself and clerks from Southampton to Cane are paid, and hokes, croches, and other ornaments, are provided for the King's chapel there.[3] Cloth is sent to the King for his army, and garters provided for the knights of the Garter at the feast of Saint George, to be celebrated in Normandy[4] in the fifth year of the King's reign. The King's specie and jewels were sent to him in Normandy[5] in the seventh year of his reign; and Walter Wodehall,[6] one of the organists of Saint Paul's Church, London, is appointed by the King's Council to proceed with five other organists to the King's presence in Normandy, and there to serve him in his chapel.

About this period it would appear the King's malady made him sensible his end was approaching; a malady which the surgeons at that period had not sufficient skill to cure. We find that Master Peter Henewer,[7] a physician, was sent by the Council to the King; but his com-

[1] See page 352.　　[2] See page 353.
[3] Ibidem.　　[4] See page 354.
[5] See page 361. Elmham states that the King was fond of church music, and frequently played on the organ.
[6] See page 361.　　[7] Ibidem.

year of the King, to solemnize the purification of the
Queen;[1] and Doctor Boyery was appointed her confessor,
and John Langton her chaplain. Divers ships and vessels
were retained at Southampton, Melcombe, and other ports
on the western coast, for the passage of the Lady the
Queen,[2] the Duke of Bedford, and her retinue, to France;[3]
and provision is made for her dower in the second year of
King Henry VI., prior to her marriage with Owen Tudor.

There are many entries on the Rolls of this reign referring to the persecutions against the Lollards and follow-
ers of the doctrines of Wicliff; some of those connected with
the proceedings against Sir John Oldcastle have been selected as the most interesting. Sir John was in great favour
with the King, who, it is said, personally remonstrated with
him to submit to the censure of the church, and abjure
the errors of Wicliff; upon his refusal to do so, his fate
is familiar to all, by his sufferings in Saint Giles's in the
Fields, where he was burnt as a heretic. Upon this
occasion a decree was drawn up by the Archbishop of
Canterbury, forbidding the scriptures to be translated
into English. The earliest notice of Sir John Oldcastle
on the Issue Rolls is to be found upon that of the first
year of this King's reign, where proclamation[4] is stated
to have been made that none of his Majesty's liege subjects should harbour Sir John, therein described as an
approved and convicted heretic, also offering a reward for
his apprehension. The King's proclamation seems to

---

[1] See pages 368, 370.
[2] See page 371. Lady Margaret Roos received 100 marks, Elizabeth Fitz
Hugh 20, and Katharine Chideok 40 marks, for accompanying the Queen in
this voyage; and Walden, the newly appointed confessor, received 10*l.* for
his journey to the King.
[3] See page 371.   [4] See pages 324, 330, 349.

INCIDENTS, EMINENT PERSONS, &c., NOTICED IN
THIS REIGN.

Preparations made for the King's coronation[1] at
Westminster Abbey, the palace, and Tower of London.

An image made in the likeness of the King's mother,
ornamented with the arms of England, directed to be
placed over her tomb in the King's college at Leicester,[2]
where she was buried.

Expenses paid for the custody of the wife of Owen
Glendourdi,[3] the wife of Edward Mortimer, and others,
their sons and daughters.

Offering by the King at the tomb of Saint Thomas,
Canterbury,[4] of a gold head-piece, ornamented with pearls
and precious stones.

Payment to William Gascoigne,[5] Chief Justice of the
King's Bench, of an annual allowance formerly made to
him by King Henry IV.

Payments to Joan, Countess of Hereford,[6] for releasing

[1] See page 321.
[2] Ibidem. The obscure account given of this tomb by Leland, in his
Itinerary, vol. i. p. 17, and copied by Throsby into his *History of Leicester*, in describing the collegiate church of Saint Mary's, is remarkable for the
little information possessed by these learned antiquaries on this point. Leland states, "There is a tumbe of marble in the body of the quire. They
"told me that a Countess of Derby lay buried in it, and they make her,
"I wot not how, wife to John of Gaunt or Henry the fourth. Indeade,
"Henry the fourth, wille he lived, was caulled Erle of Derby." A note is
added by Throsby, that, "according to Leland, Mary Bohun, Countess of
"Hereford, mother to Henry V., was buried withyn the quadrante of the
"area of the college." The above entry on the Issue Roll clearly explains
the doubt.
[3] See page 321.   [4] See page 322.   [5] Ibidem.
[6] See page 323. Probably the same circle described in the Parliament
Rolls, as garnished with 24 great and small rubies of divers sorts; 42
great and small emeralds of divers sorts; 7 sapphires of divers sorts, and
97 pearls, weighing 2lb. 3½oz.

assay[1] made in the presence of the Earl of Arundel and Barons of the Exchequer.

Information, furnished by John Kyngton, a monk[2] of Canterbury, respecting certain truces made between Lord Henry, late King of England, and other monarchs, &c.

Payments to Preachers in the Universities of Oxford and Cambridge to support the doctrine of the Catholic faith in the Universities[3] aforesaid.

Payment of 25,000 marks to the Executors named in the will[4] of Lord Henry, late King of England, for goods and chattels retained by the present King.

Expenses for building a ship[4] at Southampton, called the Holy Ghost.[5]

Payment to William Randolph, a citizen and goldsmith of London, of 976*l*. 0*s*. 10½*d*. for making twelve dishes of pure gold, four dozen chargers of silver, and eight dozen silver dishes for the King.[6]

The Prior of Mountgrace supplies certain books and other things, at the King's request, to the Abbey at Shene.[7]

---

[1] See page 333.   [2] See page 334.   [3] Ibidem.

[4] See page 335. Andrews states that Henry V. was the first English monarch who had ships of his own ; viz.

       " The Trewby, the Grace de Dieu, the Holy Ghost,
       " And many more which now be lost."

[5] See page 338.   [6] See page 340.

[7] Ibidem. This monastery was of royal foundation ; the charters are printed in *Dugdale's Monasticon Anglicanum*. p. 974, edit. 1655. The proem to these charters exhibits a curious instance of the pious feelings with which our ancestors were impressed previously to doing any public act, as it not only contains a short history of the sufferings of our Saviour, but shows the advantages of the Christian worship over that of the Jews under the Levitical law and Mosaic dispensation.

with this payment are specified, and the limitations contain much curious information relating to pedigree: a grant was also made to Thomas, Duke of Clarence, the King's brother, containing much information of a similar description.

Remuneration to John Horn,[1] a citizen and fishmonger of London, whose ship was arrested in the Prince's name, and afterwards plundered by the Welsh when taking provisions for the relief of Hardelagh Castle, then besieged by Lords de Talbot and Furnivale.

Payments to Gerard Spronge,[2] Esquire, for making divers cannon and carriages for the same, with other necessary things for their conveyance; also divers carriages for cannons, arblasters, and other things, as is fully contained in his account thereof.

Several payments appear on the Roll of the 4th year for shipping detained for the passage of the Earl of Hungary and other Lords of the retinue of the Emperor, proceeding with the King of England to the King of France upon certain especial and private affairs,[3] on which occasion tents ornamented with gold of arras, &c., were

[1] See page 338. Sir Harris Nicolas, in vol. ii. p. 139 of *Proceedings and Ordinances of the Privy Council*, gives at full length the petition of the said John Horne, to the King's Council, in Norman French, dated 13th December, 2 Hen. V., which in substance is nearly the same as the entry on the Issue Roll above referred to.

[2] See page 351. Amongst the acts of the Privy Council for this reign is also a petition from the above-mentioned Gerard Spronge, in the 2nd year of King Henry V., praying to be discharged on his account for the metal of a brass cannon called Messenger, weighing 4480 lbs., which was burst at the siege of Aberystwith; for a cannon called "Kynges doughtir," burst at the siege of Harlech; for a cannon which burst in proving it; for a cannon with two chambers; for two iron guns, and three other iron guns, with gunpowder, cross-bows, and arrows, delivered to various captains of castles and used at the aforesaid sieges.

[3] See pages 347, 348. This relates to the treaty of alliance between the

Conus Melver, goldsmith, paid for making a certain image of the Blessed Virgin Mary for Saint George's Chapel, in Windsor Castle.[1]

To James Styward,[2] calling himself the King of Scotland, payments for repair of his apparel.

Reward to Ralph, Earl of Westmoreland, for conducting William Douglas,[3] a Scotch prisoner, from the Marches of Scotland before the King's Council; payment to the Constable of the Tower for the above-named William Douglas, and for the following Scotch prisoners in his custody; viz. John Bloundelle,[4] John Daubeney, Reginald Homet, Master de Waranger, and John Blakemont.

The Remembrancer of the Exchequer directed to ascertain from Lady Scrop[5] what goods and jewels belonged to Lord Henry le Scrop, of Masham, which were forfeited to the King, and the expense of bringing the same from York to London.

The custody of Joan, Queen[6] of England, granted to Sir John Pelham, expenses thereof, and Peter Ofbace appointed her physician.

Lord Robert Ponynges, Hugh Halsham, and Thomas Hoo, knights, appointed to conduct the Duke of Bourbon,[7] the King's prisoner, to the King's presence in France, with the expenses of the men at arms, archers, and others of the retinue attending him.

Payments made by a recluse of the monastery of West-

---

[1] See pages 357, 358.
[2] See page 359.
[3] See page 361. A list of the jewels belonging to the above-named Lord will be found amongst the effects of King Henry V., enumerated in the *Rot. Parl.* vol. iv. pages 224ᵃ, 235ᵃ, 240ᵃ.
[4] See page 362.
[5] See page 358.
[6] See page 360.
[7] See page 363.

"Ewain Glendourdy,"[1] paid by direction of the Treasurer and Chamberlains.

Ralph de Gale and Colard Bloset, knights of France, the King's prisoners, committed to the custody of Thomas Barnaby, Constable of Caernarvon Castle.[2]

Sir John Colvyle to conduct Giles Lord de Camocy, Counsellor to the King of France, and other Ambassadors from the French King to the King of Scotland.[3]

Hearse and torches provided for the exequies of Thomas, Duke of Clarence,[4] the King's brother, entombed in Christ Church, Canterbury.

Payment to Sir William Meryng for conducting Arthur de Britany,[5] the King's prisoner, from Southampton to the King's presence at Milun in France.

Payment to John Robard, of London, scrivener, for writing twelve *books on hunting*[6] for the use of the Lord the King.

Dower assigned to Margaret, the widow of John Darcy,[7] chevalier, on taking her oath she would not marry again without the King's licence.

A zone of gold belonging to Queen Joan, pledged by her to Eleanor, the wife of Sir Almaric de Sancto Amando,[8] forfeited for non-payment of money borrowed.

Bartholomew Goldebeter, goldsmith of London, and other persons, appointed by the King's commission to order certain weights, rates, and scales, for regulating the weight of the noble, half noble, and ferling of gold, with other directions for weighing of gold at the Receipt of the Exchequer.[9]

[1] See page 332.   [2] See page 365.   [3] See page 366.
[4] Ibidem.   [5] See page 367.   [8] See page 368.
[7] See page 369.   [8] See page 370.
[9] See page 371. A curious document, relating to the above commission,

The Duke of Bedford's appointment as Protector or Guardian of the realm during the minority of the young King, and the Duke of Gloucester's investiture with the same dignity during the absence of his elder brother, explain the fact that most of the important events referred to by the Issue Rolls at this early period of the King's reign, are found connected with the names of those personages and the Council appointed by parliament to assist them in their administration; and consequently, that the King himself is seldom noticed.

The person and education of the infant Prince were committed to Henry Beaufort, Bishop of Winchester, his great uncle, and the earliest entries to be found on these Rolls alluding personally to the King, are an order to provide a house at Winchester[1] for the safe and secure custody of his chests of bows, arrows, stock, and stuff; and directions to purchase a quantity of plate and silver vessels for the King's use.[2]

The payments to the English and foreign heralds attending upon the young King show that he was installed a knight of the order of the Garter previously to the 6th year of his reign.[3]

On the Roll of the year following is a payment to Richard, Earl of Warwick and Albemarle, who, on the 1st June, in the sixth year of the King's reign, was, with the advice and assent of the Dukes of Bedford and Gloucester, and of all the Lords of the King's Great Council, appointed to be about the King's person, for the safe custody thereof; to exercise all pains and true diligence for his preservation; to instruct and inform him in manners

[1] See page 382.   [2] See page 385.   [3] See page 404.

expenses of her household, detailing many circumstances relating to her marriage.[1]

The Queen's coronation soon succeeded her nuptials, and the bishops, abbots, and nobility were thereupon summoned. We also find, upon this occasion, that five minstrels attended from the King of Sicily, two from the Duke of Milan, together with the ambassadors, esquires, and other attendants sent in the Queen's retinue by the King her father.[2]

It would occupy too much space were we to specify many other interesting payments connected with this Queen and her infant son Edward; the following, however, are entitled to notice, namely, that of 554*l*. 16*s*. 8*d*., made by the Queen, as well for an "embroidered cloth called crisome,[3] for the baptism of the Prince the King's son; and for 20 yards of russet cloth of gold, called tisshu, and 540 broun sable bakkes:" and to the prior and convent of Westminster for wax-lights, &c., burnt at the baptism of the said Prince Edward.

We are in like manner compelled, for the reason above stated, to pass over many other interesting payments made on behalf of the King during his sojourn at Kenilworth,[4] Coventry, and other places, previously to his seizure and confinement in the Tower of London, that the reader's attention may be directed to some of the more curious entries to be found in the Appendix to this volume.

So many conjectures and false assertions have been made relating to the imprisonment, death, and burial of

[1] See pages 449, 454.   [2] See pages 451, 452.
[3] See page 478.   [4] See pages 475, 476, 477, 478.

Henry; viz., for fourteen days,—4*l*. 5*s*.; together with many other payments on the same Roll for attendance on the King during his confinement in the Tower.

The historian of Croyland states, that after King Henry's death, his body was taken with " bylles and gleaves as he was thider brought " to Saint Paul's, where it lay for some days upon a bier, exposed to the view of the people; thence in a barge, solemnly prepared with torches, it was conveyed by water to Chertsey to be buried. But Hall, Grafton, and Hollinshed are not willing to allow that any decent respect was paid to the King's burial. They tell us that his corpse was conveyed to its resting-place at Chertsey " without priest or clearke, torch or taper, singing or saying;" though some of the following interesting memoranda, found on the Issue Rolls, evince the contrary to be the truth; and with these we must close the life of this unhappy monarch; viz. :—

To Hugh Brice.[1] In money paid to him, for such moneys expended for wax, linen, spices, and other ordinary expenses incurred for the burial of the said Henry of Windsor, *who died within the Tower of London ;* and for wages and rewards to divers men carrying *torches* from the Tower aforesaid to the cathedral church of Saint Paul's, and from thence to Chertsey, with the body,— 15*l*. 3*s*. 6½*d*.

To Master Richard Martyn.[2] In money paid to him at different times; namely, at one time 9*l*. 10*s*. 11*d*., for money by him expended for 28 yards of linen cloth of Holland, and for expenses incurred, as well within the Tower, as at the last departure of the said Henry; as also

[1] See page 495.   [2] See page 496.

Hall, who is copied by Grafton and Hollinshed, states
that "poore Kyng Henry the Sixte, a litle before deprived
of his realme and imperiall crowne, was now in the Tower
of London spoyled of his life, and all worldly felicitie, by
Richard, Duke of Gloucester (as the constant fame ranne);
which to thintent that King Edward his brother should
be clere out of all secret suspicion of sodain invasion
murdered the said Kyng with a dagger." But Hollinshed makes an important addition, and tells us nevertheless
that some writers, who he says were favourers of the
house of York, have recorded that after King Henry
understood the losses that had happened to his adherents,
the murder of his son, and the destruction of his friends,
he took it so to heart that he died. Stow follows the
statement of Fabian.

From these conflicting accounts it is impossible to
arrive at the truth. Probably much of the information
given by the before-named writers was obtained from
popular report, the last fountain to which the historian
should have recourse, as in every age men have shown
too strong a predilection for the marvellous and romantic.
The only legitimate test by which many events in English
history can be tried is the original record of them to be
found in the Issue Rolls and other authentic documents.
The investigation of these may appear uninviting and
laborious, but it often tends to important and satisfactory
results. Can any dispassionate reader of history, with
these resources before him, assert at the present day that
"no decent respect was paid to the burial of King Henry,"
and tell us that "his corpse was conveyed to Chertsey
without priest or clerk, torch or taper, singing or praying?" or that "the King was strykked with a dagger by

tenant in Ireland, with a yearly allowance to him for the
government thereof.

Former grants by Kings Edward III. and Richard II.
confirmed to the Dean and Canons of the King's free
chapel of Saint Stephen's,[1] Westminster, of certain
manors, advowsons, lands, and possessions therein mentioned, together with the nature of their tenure.

Plate purchased for the King's use; viz. a large silver
spice plate, with a gilt cover; three round saltcellars,
silver gilt, with covers; three candelabras, silver gilt, with
pykes, &c., specifying their weight and value.[2]

An account of the number of knights and men at arms
retained by Richard, Earl of Warwick;[3] Sir Geoffrey
Fitz Hugh, Lord Robert de Wylloughby, Lord Robert
Poynynges, and other commanders, to serve the King in
his wars beyond seas, under the Duke of Bedford, specifying the number of men each captain was to provide, &c.;
with an account of the expense of transporting the army
from Dover to Calais in passage-boats, called faircostes, &c.

Remuneration to Richard Hastynges, Constable of
Knaresburgh Castle, for conducting from the same
castle, to the Tower of London, William Constable[4] of
Scotland, James Lord Caldore, Robert, the son and heir
of Robert Mantalent, chevalier, Robert de Lisle, chevalier,
and William Abbernethy.

---

[1] See page 380. The late House of Commons. Stow says, the Dean
was usually of great confidence with the King, and often made a Bishop:
such was Sampson, Bishop of Litchfield and Coventry. The possessions
referred to in the above entry were conveyed, 3 Edward VI., to Sir Anthony
Aucher and Henry Polshed, Esquire. A curious rental of the possessions
of this chapel is preserved in the Auditor's Office of the land revenue.

[2] See page 385.   [3] See page 386, 387.   [4] See page 389.

Books to be produced before the King's Council to ascertain the amount of the temporalities of the see of Norwich.[1]

Payment to Robert Popyngay, executor of the will of Catharine Lardiner,[2] for a gold tabernacle, *with a piece of the holy garment placed in the middle thereof,* garnished with twenty-seven great pearls of the value therein described; which jewel is stated to have been pledged to raise men for the King's service in France, and afterwards restored to the Treasurer and Chamberlains of the Exchequer.

Payment to the Duke of Exeter for two gold cups, garnished with pearls and precious stones, purchased from the said Duke, to be presented to Prince Peter,[3] son of the King of Portugal, who had lately arrived in England.

Payment to Henry, Bishop of Winchester, late Chancellor, for his labour, costs, and charges, during the absence of the Dukes of Bedford and Gloucester, the King's uncles.[4]

Payment to Thomas Petit,[5] of Yorkshire, and others, for summoning divers of the nobility therein named to the parliament at Leicester.

A register written out of all the provinces of Bourdeaux and Gascony, also books of fealty and services due from

permanently appropriated to the use of the Council. *"The Lords sitting in the sterre chamber become a phrase."* See Palgrave's *Original Authority of the King's Council,* p. 38. The buildings containing the Star-Chamber and the old offices of the Exchequer have been lately taken down, and form part of the intended new houses of parliament.

[1] See page 393.   [2] See page 394.   [3] See pages 394, 395.

[4] See page 395. The Issue Rolls abound with payments to Cardinal Beaufort, Bishop of Winchester; his speech respecting money at his death is well known.

[5] See page 395.

been indicted for divers felonies, insurrections, murders, rebellions, errors, and heresies.[1]

Payments to John, Duke of Bedford, Regent of France, for his costs and expenses in coming from France at the request of the Council, for the tranquillity of England, at his own costs and charges; also for his return to France; and for Thomas, Duke of Exeter, and many other knights and esquires; giving an account of the shipping, men at arms, &c., retained on this occasion.[2]

Annuity granted to Paul Count de Valache,[3] who had arrived from Greece, in consideration that he was descended from noble blood, had been nearly destroyed and annihilated by the Turks and Saracens, the enemies of God, and had not wherewith to live except from the charity of good Christians.

Repayment of money borrowed to Richard Crosby, Prior of the cathedral church of Saint Mary, Coventry, and to other persons, for security of repayment whereof the late King, whilst he was Prince, pledged his great collar, called the Ikelton[4] collar, garnished with four

---

[1] See pages 398, 399. The writs for his apprehension describe him as "a certain son of iniquity," named William Wawe, convicted of many treasons and felonies, who had escaped from the Marshalsea prison and joined other felons, and robbed many churches and nunneries, offering a reward of 100*l.* to any one who should arrest him, and produce his body or head, alive or dead, before the Council; any person taking him should receive a free pardon for any crime except treason, that any city or borough taking him should have an exemption from payment of toll, and that no one should supply him with meat, or drink, or lodging, under severe penalty in such case provided. See *Acts of the Privy Council*, vol. iii. p. 257, 312.

[2] See pages 399, 400. [3] See pages 401, 402.

[4] See page 403. This is described among the jewels pledged by Henry VI. to Henry, Bishop of Winchester, Cardinal of England, "as a pusan of gold called Iklyngton Coler, garnisshed with iiii. rubes, iiii. greet saphers, xxxii. greet perles, and liii. other perles; the price cccl." *Vide Rot. Pat.* 17 Hen. VI. p. 2, m. 82.

described in a certain book remaining in the King's Remembrancer's Office of the Exchequer; which jewels were ordered to be sent to the Pope by the Bishop of London and John Lord le Scrop, Ambassadors to his Holiness.

Ten thousand masses to be said for the souls of departed knights of the Garter,[1] according to the ordinances of their foundation by King Edward III.

The Cardinal of Saint Eusebius receives the King's licence and authority to proceed to the King of Scotland, and confer with him upon certain great and weighty matters[2] concerning the King and realm of England; Henry Percy, Earl of Northumberland, is appointed to assist the Cardinal in his negotiations; and payments are made to the Earl of Salisbury, attending the Cardinal upon the same affairs.

The King of Scotland having failed in his agreement to pay the soldiers at Calais,[3] a new assignment for that purpose is made, charged on certain payments due from the Duke of Bourbon. Many payments are here entered on the Rolls for the fleet and army proceeding to France under the Cardinal of England, the King's uncle. Large sums of money were borrowed upon this occasion, and bonds given for repayment thereof, as well to the most holy Father the Pope as to the before-mentioned Cardinal.

Brother John Asshewell,[4] Prior of the Holy Trinity,

might merit recital, but a detailed account of these ornaments would require a space which neither the limits nor intention of this work will allow.

[1] See page 406.

[2] See pages 407, 408. These matters were touching the faith, honour, and usefulness of the universal Church, and the honour and welfare of the King's two realms.

[3] See page 408.

[4] See page 410. Margery Jourdemain, John Virley, Clerk, John Asshe-

France, specifying the number of earls, barons, knights,
archers, and armed men, serving under him.[1]

A penalty of 100*l.* obtained from Sir Thomas Wauton,
Sheriff of Bedfordshire and Buckinghamshire, *for permitting the election of Knights to Parliament*, and returning the same contrary to the statute.[2]

An assignment of money to Anne, Countess of Stafford,[3]
until it should be ascertained whether the castle and town
of Brenles, the lordships of Penkelly, Cantrecelly, and
Langoyt, and Alisaundres town, were parcel of the lordship
of Brecknock, in Wales.

Richard Gatone, Mayor of New Salisbury, seizes John
Keterige,[4] notoriously suspected, and afterwards convicted
of heresy, and thereby obtains a knowledge where to seize
John Longe and John Sharp, other traitors and heretics,
&c.

The Issue Roll of the 12th year of this King's reign
contains entries of repayments of immense sums of money
to Henry, Cardinal of England, Bishop of Winchester,

[1] See page 430. The privy council directed that he should be allowed
6000 marks yearly during the King's absence, and 5000 marks yearly
after his return, for his services as Lieutenant of England, especially for his
expenses in the apprehension and execution of the horrible and wicked
traitor to God and the King, who called himself Jak Sharp, and other heretics,
his accomplices.

[2] See page 416. In 1429, about the period above referred to, an important change was made as to the qualifications of voters for knights of
shires. These were now obliged to prove themselves worth 40*s.* per annum.
Before this time *every* freeholder might vote, and the vast concourse of
electors occasioned riots and murthers. *Twenty pounds* would, in modern
days, be barely an equivalent for our ancestors' 40*s.* The freeholders were
at the same time directed to choose two of the " fittest and most discreet
knights resident in their county ; or, if none such could be found, notable
esquires, gentlemen by birth, and qualified to be made knights, but no yeoman
or person of inferior rank." [*Henry, from the Statutes.*]

[3] See page 416.   [4] See pages 416, 417.

ford, in France, to Humphrey, Duke of Gloucester, and the Council, in England, was seized in the night-time by the King's enemies, whilst lying in bed, between Beauvais and Amiens, and taken into a wood, where he remained two nights and two days in despair of his life. The Gloucester herald at arms was also robbed and put to great and excessive charge about this period, when upon the King's affairs in France.[1]

Richard Grygge[2] proceeds, at imminent risk, in a boat, from Dover to Calais, to ascertain the safe arrival of the King at the latter place, and returns to inform the Duke of Gloucester and the Council thereof, at Canterbury.

Brother John Lowe appointed the King's Confessor, specifying the allowances to be made to him and his servants; which were to be regulated by the allowances made to the Confessors of former Kings, whose names are mentioned in this entry.[3]

The King's officers of the Receipt of the Exchequer appointed to remain at London and Westminster, in consequence of the courts of law being adjourned on *account of the plague.*[4]

A hearse and shields, painted with the arms of the Duke of Bedford,[5] furnished for his exequies and funeral, together with banners and other things provided, specifying the price of each article.

Guns, gunstones, gunpowder, arms, ammunitions, troops, and stores, sent to the town of Crotey,[6] giving a minute account of the payments for each.

Richard, Duke of York, retained by indenture in the

[1] See pages 417, 419.   [2] See page 418.   [3] Ibidem.
[4] See page 426.   [5] See pages 428, 437.   [6] See page 427.

Payment of dower to Sir Richard Wodevyle, for Jaquette, late wife of John, Duke of Bedford.[1]

Payments to Catharine de la Pole, Abbess of Berkyng, for the costs and expenses she had incurred for Edmund ap Meredith ap Tydier and Jasper ap Meredith ap Tydier, who had been committed to her custody.[2]

The greater portion of the Roll of Easter 17 Henry VI. (which is 70 feet in length) is occupied with the names of vessels retained to take the King's army to France,[3] specifying the names of the commanders, the number of knights, esquires, men at arms, and archers, serving under each captain, the names of the masters of the ships, and the number of mariners; with an account of the arms and provisions supplied for this expedition.

Expenses paid for the passage and repassage of the Lord Cardinal and others, Lords, Knights, and clerks, sent with him in an embassy to Calais, to treat for a peace; also for the passage and custody of the Duke of Orleans, going to the said town with Sir Richard Wodevyle in his retinue, upon certain affairs touching the King and his Council.[4]

Eleanor Cobham, Duchess of Gloucester, committed to the custody of Sir John Stiward and others, and afterwards to Ralph Lord de Sudeley, Constable of Kenilworth Castle, with twelve persons therein named, to be continually in attendance on her.[5]

---

[1] See page 436. [3] See pages 437, 438.
[2] Ibidem. [4] See pages 438, 439.

[5] See pages 440, 441, 448. The Duchess of Gloucester was charged with treason, for conspiring to take away the King's life by means of sorcery and enchantment, with the intent of advancing her husband to the throne; and Thomas Southwell, canon of Westminster, John Hume, a priest, Roger Bolingbroke, a priest, and Margery Jourdayn or Jourdemain, called *the Witch of Eye*, were apprehended and committed to prison as her accessaries,

Payments to doctors, notaries, and clerks, for their laborious employment respecting a superstitious sect of necromancers and persons charged with witchcraft and incantations.[1]

Sir Philip Boyle,[2] Knight, and a Baron of Arragon, performs feats of arms in the King's presence, at Smithfield, with John Asteley, the King's faithful and beloved subject.

Reward to Francis de Surienne, called l'Arrogonnoiz ;[3] an annuity granted to him for his services to the King, to maintain his estate of knighthood, and protect his wife and children from poverty.

Grant of 40*l*. to Owyn ap Tuder, by way of reward.

Payments to John Hampton, Esquire, for expenses incurred by him for labour bestowed upon the King's new college of the Blessed Mary, at Windsor.[4]

The Duke of Somerset retained as the King's Lieutenant and Captain General in Aquitaine, in which service he employed certain warlike instruments called "ribaultquines :"[5] also an account is given of the number of bows, arrows, lances headed with iron, long pavys with iron spikes, shovels, secnons, pekoys, leaden malets, and other necessaries, provided for his army; and a statement of wages paid to the officers and men serving under him.

Note.—The Roll of the 21st year of this King's reign

having, as was pretended, devised an image of wax to represent the King, whose person, through the medium of their witchcraft, was gradually to consume and die away, as the said image should melt before a slow fire. The learned Editor of the *Acts of the Privy Council* regrets that no notices relating to the imprisonment of the Duchess of Gloucester should occur on the Minutes of the Council: the Issue Rolls contain many curious entries concerning her.

[1] See page 440.   [2] See page 442.   [3] Ibidem.
[4] See page 443.   [5] See pages 444, 445, 446.

is nearly filled with payments for the army accompanying the Dukes of York and Somerset in this expedition, and contains a long list of the shipping, boats, and mariners employed.

The Archbishop of Canterbury, on hearing of the death of the Cardinal of Luxenburgh, Archbishop of Rouen,[1] sends his letters to the Pope, requesting that his Holiness would be pleased to abstain from promoting any person to the said archbishoprick until the King should write to him on the subject.

A jewel, called the George,[2] purchased from Sir William Estfield for 1333*l*. 6*s*. 8*d*.

Payments to the Prior of Kilmaynan,[3] attending the King's Council respecting a charge of treason made against him by the Earl of Ormond.

William Gedney sent by the King from Berkhamstead Castle to London, and from thence to the Bishop of Lincoln at Sleford, in Lincolnshire, to obtain a copy of the last will of King Henry V.[4]

Thomas Kerver,[5] a traitor, conducted from Berkshire to London, with a great posse, by Sir John Chalers, Knight, Sheriff of Oxford and Berks.

Payments to the Master of the hounds called " heireres," and 36 dogs called " rennynghoundys," and 9 greyhounds, charged on the profits of the counties of Bedford and Bucks.[6]

Lewis de Curtana presents the King with a consecrated rose from the Pope.[7]

---

[1] See page 447.   [2] See page 451.
[3] See pages 450, 451, 457, 461.   See also *Rot. Parl.* vol. iv. p. 198[b].
[4] See page 453.   [5] See page 454.
[6] See page 456.   [7] See page 457.

Payments to Philip Trehere, fishmonger, for instructing the Prior of Kilmaynan,[1] who lately appealed the Earl of Ormond of high treason, in certain points of arms, and for instructing and consulting with John Davy, who appealed John Cateur, armourer, of treason.

Recompense made to William Postell, gunner and maker of implements of war, who had served the King in his wars in France and Normandy for eighteen years, and had there lost his inheritance : also because certain cannon were taken from his house by direction of the King's Council in Normandy, during the siege of Harfleur,[2] and destroyed in the bombardment thereof.

John Hayne,[3] under arrest, and in the custody of the Constable of England, petitions the Council to be released, complaining that, during his confinement, he had lost great part of his inheritance, and that the King's enemies and rebels had seized and destroyed his castle, &c., at Porteseveston.

The President and fellows of Saint Margaret's and Saint Barnard's College, Cambridge,[4] relieved on account of their poverty.

Andrew Huls and John Solers sent, by direction of the King's Council, to communicate with Jack Cade,[5] calling

---

[1] See page 459.   [2] See page 461.
[3] See page 462.   [4] See page 464.
[5] See pages 466, 469, 470, 471, 476. Andrews's account of this insurrection in most particulars agrees with the above; some few variations will appear on a comparison; namely :—"Although Richard, Duke of York, was absent, having been sent to quell some disturbances in Ireland, yet, perhaps, it was not without his connivance that John Cade, a bold adventurer, (under the name of John Mortimer, and sometimes Sir John Amend-all,) at the head of a numerous rout of Kentish men, after having defeated and slain Sir Humphrey Stafford and his son, who had opposed him near Seven Oaks, dared to enter London in arms. There he beheaded the Lord Say and Seal, and Sir James Cromer, Sheriff of Kent, and, striking his staff on London

himself the Captain of Kent. The King directs Sir Thomas Tyrell and Richard Waller, Esquire, to go to Rochester and seize the goods belonging to John Mortimer, the traitor. Payments were also made to Alexander Eden, Sheriff of Kent, John Davy, and others of the same county, "for taking John Cade, an Irishman, calling himself John Mortimer, a great rebel, enemy, and traitor to the King, and for conducting him, together with Robert Spencer, a sworn brother to the said traitor, and William Parmenter, to the King's Council."

Payment to Richard, Duke of York, for his jewels stolen from the house of Philip Malpas, in the city of London, by Jack Cade, which jewels were afterwards delivered into the Receipt of the Exchequer. John, Cardinal Archbishop of York, proceeds to Rochester under the King's commission, to tranquillize the county, and recover plate, &c., stolen by Cade and his party.

Garter king at arms directed to conduct the Earl of Douglas, about to arrive in England from the Roman Court, to the King's presence, and to continue in attendance on him during his stay in England.[1]

John Kyrkeby, Philpot Morys, Thomas Bocher, and William Heyley, confined in Windsor Castle for treason;

stone, Cade exclaimed, 'Now I am master of London.' A general pardon dispersed the rabble, and Cade, endeavouring to escape, fell by the sword of Alexander Eyden, an esquire of Sussex, who, for that service, was knighted and made Governor of Rochester Castle," &c. The abovenamed Alexander Eden is called Iden by Rymer, in the *Fœdera*, vol. xi. p. 275, where may be found an account of Cade's capture by the said Sheriff of Kent.

[1] See pages 469, 472, 477, 480. This Earl Douglas was a most sanguinary monster. On his arrival from Rome he passed through England with a safe conduct. James, King of Scotland, received him with cautious kindness, invited him to his palace, and stabbed him with his dagger. Sir Patrick Gray (whose nephew he had most barbarously murdered) clove his skull with a battle axe, and armed men rushed in and covered him with wounds.

also a person called Lawless, a pirate, taken from Newcastle to the King's presence.[1]

Payment to John Hampton of expenses incurred for
plays and solaces performed before the Lord the King at
the feast of the Nativity of the Lord, in the 28th year of
his reign, and at the feast of Saint George, held at Windsor in the same year.[2]

Clarencieux King of Arms, and John Newport, Esquire,
sent to invest the Kings of Arragon and Poland with the
order of the Garter.[3]

A curious description is given of ordnance supplied by
Thomas Vaghan, the Master of the Ordnance, comprising,
amongst other things, serpentynes, colveryns, stones for
cannon balls, rybawdekyns with ten and four chambers
each, and gunners, carpenters, smiths, and match or lantern bearers to attend the same.[4]

Fetters purchased to secure Robert Ardern and John
Mattys in Kenilworth Castle, and to take them from
thence to the city of Hereford.[5]

A gilt garter, ornamented with pearls and flowers, presented to the King of Portugal.[6]

Robert Tomelynson charges John Atte Wode,[7] of Norfolk, with certain horrible treasons, conspiracies, and intentions against the King's person, the Queen, and the
Prince; which treasons the said Robert was ready to
prove, as might be demanded by the King's laws.

The more important entries in this volume having been
recapitulated with a view to draw particular attention to

[1] See pages 469, 470.   [2] See page 473.   [3] See page 474.
[4] Ibidem.   [5] See page 475.
[6] See page 480.   [7] See page 482.

k

them, it now remains only to notice a few others contained in the Appendix, which must be confined to King Edward IV., Richard, Duke of Gloucester, or to some few leading points in history : namely,

Payments are made for supplying wax for the hearse in the cathedral church of Saint Paul's, London, and for the exequies and performance of divine service for the salvation of the soul of the most noble and famous Prince of worthy memory the Duke of York, the King's father.[1]

A curious list of plate, arras, and other articles supplied to King Edward IV., among which is a payment for four pieces of arras, with a representation of the history of " Nabugodonoser," nine pieces of arras of the history of Alexander, six pieces with a representation of the Passion, one piece with the Judgment,[2] &c.

The King also about this period borrowed large sums of money ; among others appears a loan of 200_0l._ from Lewis de Gremaldys[3] and the merchants of Genoa.

The dresses, armour, and various other necessary articles supplied to the King, are equally curious, and not less minutely described than those before referred to. Cloth to make a " jaquette" for the King, with fustian, linen, lace, velvet, &c., to line and ornament the same, specifying the quantity and value of each article : trappings for horses, braices of mayle, brigganders, gauntlets, legharness, and other descriptions of armour, are also mentioned ; and medicines were provided against the plague. Many payments for suppressing the rebels in the county of Kent appear upon these Rolls, with the names of

---

[1] See pages 487, 488.   [2] See page 491.
[3] See page 492. For notices respecting this family see *Origines Genealogicæ*, p. 80, by Stacey Grimaldi, Esq.

the leaders and captains employed, with the number of
men under each commander, the quantity and quality
of arms and ammunition supplied :—the following entry
connected with this subject is singular ; viz.—Paid for
two casks of red wine, distributed to the citizens and inhabitants of the city of London after their conflict with the
King's rebels at Mile-End and elsewhere.[1]

The last extract noticed from this series of Rolls is a
payment to the master of the ship called the Little Jesus,
for the passage of a servant of Lord Hastyngs from
Dover to Calais, sent to Lord Dynham there, to convey to
him the first information of the demise of the most excellent and dread Prince, of happy memory, Edward IV.,
who is stated to have died on the 9th April.[2]

Many payments also appear upon the Issue Rolls about
this period to Richard, Duke of Gloucester, afterwards
King Richard III., amongst which the following are noticed :—

One thousand pounds paid by Richard, Earl of Warwick, for the expenses of Richard, Duke of Gloucester,
the King's brother.[3]

Payments to Richard, Duke of Gloucester,[4] for men at
arms and archers, under his command, specifying their
number and quality, and the daily pay to each; also for
the wages of fighting men under him in Scotland and
the marches thereof, and for repairing the walls of Carlisle : these payments show that he was at the head of an
army of 20,000 men, and was assisted in this campaign
by Alexander, Duke of Albany, brother to the King of
Scotland, relating to whom, and his preparations for the

[1] See page 495.
[2] See page 505.
[3] See page 490.
[4] See page 498.

k 2

war in Scotland, several entries will also be found in the Appendix.

Some few miscellaneous entries out of order of date have been introduced at the end of the Appendix, with a view to show that the interest of the Pell Records extends to a much later period than specified in the title page of this volume. Among these will be found

A payment in the 12th year of King Henry VII. to Sir Henry Willoughby and others for taking "Nicholas Joseph,[1] chief leader of the Cornish rebels;" Joseph and others were beheaded after their defeat at the battle of Blackheath. On the same Roll is to be found a payment to William Thomas, Esq., for capturing the brother of Lord Audely.

On the Roll of the 11th Elizabeth is a payment of 500*l*. to George, Earl of Shrewsbury, for the diet of Mary, Queen of Scots,[2] and 400*l*. paid to Valentine Brown, Esq., Treasurer of the town of Berwick, to remunerate divers soldiers attending upon the said unfortunate Queen. And in the 40th year of the reign of Elizabeth is noticed a payment of part of an annuity of 100*l*. to William Davidson,[3] Esquire, late one of the principal secretaries to the Lady the Queen, due to him for the quarter of the year ending at the feast of the Nativity of Saint John the Baptist, of that year; and it is worthy of remark that the secretary appears to have enjoyed this annual payment during the remainder of the Queen's reign and some time subsequent. Although it has been stated that Davidson[4] was imprisoned in order to

[1] See page 516.   [2] See page 517.   [3] Ibidem.
[4] See his circumstantial account of this transaction addressed to Walsingham, wherein he sufficiently justifies himself in the eyes of the world,

screen his mistress from the odium attached to the death
of the Queen of Scots, and was ruined by the exaction
of the fine of 10,000*l.*, imposed on him by the Court of
Star-Chamber, yet the remonstrances in his behalf by
Lord Burleigh, and the entreaties of the favourite Essex,
do not appear to have been entirely unavailing with his old
mistress the Queen ; or that his crime was considered so
great by her Majesty as to prevent the receipt of this pension, or yearly payment, long after his dismissal from
office.

The last payment but one in this volume is to Sir
Thomas Lucy,[1] knight, Sheriff of the county of Warwick, for the charges of fifty soldiers raised in that county,
and sent to Ireland in the 43rd year of Queen Elizabeth ;
and the work closes with payments made on settling the
accounts of Lady Margaret Hawkins and Thomas Drake,
Esquire, executors of John Hawkins and Sir Francis
Drake, the celebrated navigators.

The Editor cannot close this his third volume without
offering his sincere and unfeigned thanks to his friends
and the public for the patronage and encouragement he

in *Bayley's History of the Tower*, Appendix to vol. ii. first edition. Von
Raumer also, in his *Political History of England during the 16th, 17th, and
18th Centuries*, in reporting the conversation of the Queen, in an interview
with Chateauneuf, the French Ambassador, makes it appear that the fatal
catastrophe arose from Davidson inadvertently, contrary to the Queen's order,
showing the warrant she had signed to the Lords of the Council, who has-
tened to act on it, fearing that she might retract.

[1] See page 518. This must be the Sir Thomas Lucy ridiculed by Shakspeare under the name of Justice Shallow, in the Merry Wives of Windsor:

    Slen. They may give the dozen white luces in their coat.
    Shal. It is an old coat.

has received in his former publications. He has pursued
the plan originally adopted ; preserving as nearly as possible the original orthography of the Record in the spelling
of names of persons and places, and adhering to a literal
translation throughout the work. He is aware that in
some few instances difficulty may arise as to the imme-
diate identity of a person or place, from the varied spelling
of the same name on the original Record : this has been
in a great measure obviated by inserting a more modern
spelling in the Index, which, producing a double reading,
will generally remove all uncertainty.

This volume being also composed of extracts, and not
a selection of any particular series of events, may contain some discrepancies as to dates. In extenuation of this
circumstance (which must of necessity be incident to the
plan of giving extracts only) the reader is requested to
take into consideration the impossibility, from the variety
of subjects introduced, of tracing every entry to its
original date. It must be borne in mind that these extracts
are given to show the varied and interesting nature of the
Records; but it may with confidence be asserted, that
there would be little difficulty in tracing any given subject,
from its commencement to the close, in almost all cases
where the inquirer had time and inclination to prosecute
the search.

In many instances, particularly in the reigns of Edward III., Richard II., and Henry IV., one or two extracts
only have been taken from Rolls approaching one hundred
feet in length; each of which, if fully printed, would of
itself have formed a volume nearly the size of the present.
The Editor has also, for the reasons before stated, re-
stricted himself in his Introduction to attaching notes to

comparatively a few entries ; in some of these he fears he
has trespassed too much upon the reader's indulgence ;
though, while he offers his apology, he cannot refrain
from expressing his conviction that every entry extracted
is capable either of historical illustration, of elucidating
some points of history, or of rendering assistance to literary
inquiries.

In concluding this Introduction, the Editor has again
the pleasing task of expressing his acknowledgments to
Sir John Newport for his continued kindness, on all
occasions during the passing of this volume through the
press. He also entreats that Arthur Eden, Esq., the
Assistant Comptroller, and Ashburnham Bulley, Esq.,
Chief Clerk of the establishment, will accept his unfeigned
thanks for the facility they have afforded him while the
Work was in progress, evincing an equal anxiety with
the Comptroller-General that the public should be made
fully acquainted with the nature and contents of the important Records in their respective departments. The
Editor also begs to offer his sincere thanks to his brother,
Charles Devon, Esq., for the assistance he has received
from him throughout the Work.

FREDERICK DEVON.

April, 1837.

ERRATA.

ERRATA IN THE INDEX.

Fac-simile from a Drawing at the top of

17. Hen

nolte - nobke

ol.

Jsaac

Original at the Pell Office, in the Custody of The Right Hon.ble Sir Jo

Copied & Printed by J.Noble

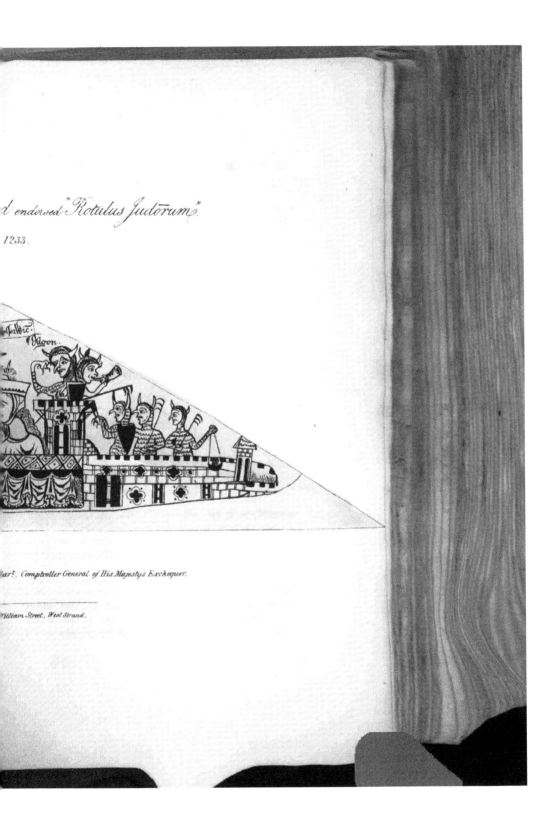

d endorsed "Rotulus Judēōrum".

1233.

ar.^t. Comptroller General of His Majesty's Exchequer.

illiam Street, West Strand.

EXTRACTS

FROM

THE PELL RECORDS.

HENRY III.

LIBERATE ROLL, 10 HENRY III.

HENRY, by the grace of God, King of England, Lord of Ireland, Duke of Normandy, Acquitaine, and Earl of Anjou. To his Treasurer and Chamberlains, greeting. Pay out of our Treasury to Walter de Kirkeham and Walter de Brackeley, clerks of our wardrobe, 200 marks, to purchase robes at the fairs of Saint Ives, for the use of Richard our brother. Witness ourself, at Westminster, the 30th day of April, in the 10th year of our reign, before the Justices.

Henry, by the grace of God, &c.—Pay out of our Treasury to Brother William, a Monk of Beaulieu, going on our embassy beyond sea, 2 marks for his expenses. Witness ourself, at Westminster, the 3d day of May, in the 10th year of our reign.

Henry, by the grace of God, &c.—Pay out of our Treasury to Simon Druel, our usher, half a mark, for taking twelve summonses from our Exchequer throughout England, and 6d. for wax to seal the same. Witness B. Bishop of Rochester, at Westminster, the 4th day of May, in the 10th year of our reign.

B

Henry, by the grace of God, &c.—Pay out of our Treasury
to the Abbot of Wardon 10 marks for this Easter Term, in the
10th year of our reign, in part payment of 20 marks which we
granted yearly to him and his monks of the same house, until we
should have provided them with 10 librates of land from the
escheats, or otherwise, as to us shall seem fit, in consideration of
the losses they have suffered near Bedford, and elsewhere, in the
siege which we made to the Castle of Bedford.   Witness ourself,
at Burewell, the 20th day of April, in the 10th year of our
reign.

Henry, by the grace of God, &c.—Pay out of our Treasury
to Brother Simon, a Canon of Begeham, 2 marks, to discharge the
expenses which he incurred when we sent him on our service to
the legate in France; also pay to the same Brother Simon, for
going as our ambassador beyond sea upon the embassy which we
sent him, 5 marks for his expenses, and 30s. for a palfrey purchased
for him, of our gift; also deliver to the same Brother Simon, for
the use of Engeram, who belonged to the household of William,
Earl of Salisbury, 30 marks, which we owed him at this Easter
Term, in the 10th year of our reign, for the 60 marks which
he yearly receives at our Exchequer; also pay to Adam de
Sancto Martino, and Ralph de Cambai, men of Anselm de
Winchester, 20s. of our gift.   Witness ourself, at Westminster,
the 5th day of May, in the same year.

Henry, by the grace of God, &c.—Pay out of our Treasury
to our faithful and beloved Hubert de Burgh, our Justice, 200l. in
part payment of 500l., which we owed him at this Easter Term,
in the 10th year of our reign, for the 1,000l. which he receives
yearly at our Exchequer for the custody of our castle of Dover;
also deliver from our Treasury to Thomas de Blundvill 25l.,
which we owed him at the same Term, as part of the 40l. which
he receives yearly at our Exchequer for the custody of our Tower
of London.   Witness ourself, at Westminster, the 4th day of
May, in the same year.

Henry, by the grace of God, &c.—Pay out of our Treasury to Richard de Hereford and Josceline de Oye 200*l.*, for the works of our castle at Dover. Witness ourself, at Westminster, the 6th day of May, in the 10th year of our reign.

Henry, by the grace of God, &c.—Pay out of our Treasury to our beloved in Christ, the Abbot of Saint Edmund, 10*l.*, which we owed him at Easter Term, in the 10th year of our reign, for the 20*l.* which he receives yearly at our Exchequer, by agreement made between us and the same Abbot, for the coinage and exchange, with the appurtenances at Saint Edmund's. Witness ourself, at Westminster, the 6th day of May, in the 10th year of our reign.

Henry, by the grace of God, &c.—Pay out of our Treasury to the Venerable Father in Christ, Richard, Bishop of Salisbury, 100*l.* for our 15ths which he lent us at Marlborough on Wednesday, on the morrow of the Epiphany of our Lord, in the 10th year of our reign, to pay our expenses. Witness ourself, at Westminster, the 8th day of May, in the same year of our reign, before our Justices, the Bishops of Bath and Salisbury.

Henry, by the grace of God, &c.—Pay out of our Treasury to the Venerable Father, Alexander, Bishop of Coventry, 100*s.*, which we owed him at Easter Term, in the 10th year of our reign, for the 10*l.* yearly which he receives at our Exchequer for Rugeley and Canok, in the same manner as William, formerly Bishop of Coventry, his predecessor, received the same. Witness ourself, at Westminster, the 7th day of May, in the 10th year of our reign, before the Justices.

Henry, by the grace of God, &c.—Pay out of our Treasury to Thurgis de Dover 50*s.*, which we owed him at Easter Term, in the 10th year of our reign, for the 100*s.* which he yearly receives at the Exchequer for his support in our service. Witness ourself, at Westminster, the 7th day of May, in the same year.

Henry, by the grace of God, &c.—Pay out of our Treasury to Norman, sent on our message to the Sheriffs of Essex, Hertford, Cambridge, Huntingdon, Norfolk, and Suffolk, 12*d.*

To Cornubiens, sent to the Sheriffs of Southampton, Dorset, Wiltshire, Devonshire, and Cornwall, 21*d.*

To John Blundus, sent to the Sheriffs of Berkshire, Oxfordshire, Worcestershire, Gloucestershire, and Herefordshire, 21*d.*

To Robert de Alemann, sent to the Sheriffs of Bedfordshire, Bucks, Northampton, Rutland, Lincoln, York, and Northumberland, 2*s.* 6*d.*

To Roger de Rupis, sent to the Sheriffs of Warwickshire, Leicestershire, Nottinghamshire, Derbyshire, Lancashire, and Westmoreland, 2*s.*

To John de Cantuar̃, going to the Sheriffs of Kent, 6*d.*

To Scogernell, going to the Mayor and Sheriffs of London, 6*d.*

To Robert de Turreny, going to Nottingham, 12*d.*

To William de Vendom, going to Southampton, 6*d.*

To William Cointerel, going to Windsor, 6*d.*

To Roger Passevaunt, going to Suffolk, 9*d.*

To William de Vendom, going to Windsor, Bedfordshire, and Norfolk, 18*d.*

To Cornubiens, going from Marlborough to London, 9*d.*

To John de Cantuar̃, going to Sandwich, 15*d.*

To William Cointerel, going from Marlborough to London, 6*d.*

To Geoffry de Ferendon, a messenger of the Justices, going to the Earls Warren and Essex, 12*d.*

To Robert Wastepain, going to Rodesthall, to the Earl of Salisbury, 4*d.*

To William Carectarius, going to Westminster, to the Earl Marshal, 6*d.*

To William Cointerel, going to Westminster, 6*d.*

To Cornubiens, going to Hertford, 6*d.*

To Robert le Herberun, going to Portsmouth, 9*d.*

To William Carectarius, going to the Sheriff of Southampton, 9d.

To Cornubiens, going to the Abbot of Bello, 6d.

To Scogernell, going to the Archbishop of Canterbury at Slindon and Dover, 15d.

To William Carectarius, going to the Sheriff of York, 2s.

To Scogernell, going to the Sheriff of Lincoln, 12d.

To Roger Passevaunt, going to the Abbots of Saint Alban's, Waltham, Saint Edmund, and the Official of the Lord Bishop of Norwich and Bishop of Ely, 15d.

To Cornubiens, going to the Bishops of Salisbury and Exeter, 18d.

To Robert Blundus, going to the Bishops of Worcester, Coventry, and Hereford, and to the Abbots of Malmsbury and Evesham, 27d.

To John Blundus, going to Lewes, to the Earl Warren, 6d.

To John de Cantuař, going to the Earls of Gloucester and Chester, 15d.

To Scogernell, going to the Earl of Ferrars, 15d.

To William de Verdom, going to the Earl of Chester, 9d.

To William Carectarius, going to the Earl of Ferrars, 12d.

To Roger de Rupis, going to the Sheriff of Worcester, 12d.

To Roger Passavant, going to the Sheriffs of Southampton and Devonshire, 15d.

To Robert de Herberun, going to the Sheriff of Norfolk and Suffolk, 6d.

To William de Verdom, going to the Sheriff of Cornwall and Devonshire, 2s.

To Scogernell, going to the Sheriffs of Southampton and Sussex, 15d.

To Carectarius, going to the Sheriffs of Northampton, Oxford, Lincoln, and Nottingham, 18d.

To Cornubiens, going to Leicester, to Stephen de Segrave; and to Nottingham, to William Gernun, 9d. Witness ourself, at Westminster, the 5th day of May, in the 10th year of our reign.

Henry, by the grace of God, &c.—Pay out of our Treasury
to our beloved and faithful R., Earl of Chester and Lincoln,
100*l.* in advance unto the feast of Saint John the Baptist, in the
10th year of our reign; also pay to Master Eustace, Archdeacon of
Lewes, 10*l.* of our gift, for his expenses; also pay to William, the
son of Warren, 55*l.* to make certain payments to 500 Welshmen
whom we have sent into Gascony to our Brother Richard; also
pay to Odo, the goldsmith, and his companions, keepers of the
works of our houses at Westminster, 40*l.* for the works done to
the same houses; also pay to William de Pratelle 10*l.*, which
we owed him at Easter, in the 10th year of our reign, for the
20*l.* yearly he receives at our Exchequer for the town of Aulton.
Witness ourself, at Westminster, the 8th day of May, in the
same year.

Henry, by the grace of God, &c.—Pay out of our Treasury
to Walter de Kirkeham and Walter de Brackeley, clerks of our
wardrobe, 216*l.* to purchase robes for our use and for our
Brother Richard, to be obtained from the fairs of Saint Ives.
Witness ourself, at Westminster, the 11th day of May, in the
10th year of our reign.

Henry, by the grace of God, &c.—Pay out of our Treasury
to Guido, clerk, brother of William, Earl Alvern, dwelling
in the schools at Oxford, 20 marks for his expenses, of our
gift. Witness ourself, at Westminster, the 15th day of May,
in the 10th year of our reign.

Henry, by the grace of God, &c.—Pay from our Treasury to
our beloved and faithful Richard Duket 10 marks, of our gift,
for his expenses. Witness ourself, at Westminster, the 16th day
of May, in the 10th year of our reign, before the Justices.

Henry, by the grace of God, &c.—Pay out of our Treasury
to Reynold de Bernevall and Brother Thomas, of the Temple,
22½ marks, for repairs, &c., of our great ship; also pay to the
6 masters of our great ship—to wit, to Stephen le Vel 1

mark, Germanus de la Rie 1 mark, John, the son of Sampson,
1 mark, Colmo de Warham 1 mark, Robert Gaillard 1 mark,
and Simon Westlegrei 1 mark. Witness ourself, at Westminster, the 17th day of May, in the 10th year of our reign. For
the mariners of the great ship.

Henry, by the grace of God, &c.—Pay out of our Treasury
to Thomas de Haia 16*l.* 10*s.* for the liveries of 11 of our soldiers
who remained, by our command, in our castle of Kenilworth,
whom we sent in our service into Gascony.

Henry, by the grace of God, &c.—Pay out of our Treasury
to John de Atya 25*l.*, which we owed him at Easter Term, in the
10th year of our reign, for the 50*l.* which he receives yearly
at the Exchequer, for the farm of Kingeston. Witness ourself,
at Westminster, the 8th day of May, in the 10th year of our
reign.

Henry, by the grace of God, &c.—Pay from our Treasury to
the Venerable Father, Joceline, Bishop of Bath, 25 marks, which
he delivered, by our command, to the Brethren of Chartreuse, for
our appointed alms, at this Easter Term, in the 10th year of our
reign. Witness ourself, at Westminster, the 4th day of May, in
the same year, before the Justices.

Henry, by the grace of God, &c.—Pay from our Treasury to
the Venerable Father, Joceline, Bishop of Bath and Wells,
19*l.* 15*s.*, which he paid at Bristol on the Vigils of Easter, in the
10th year of our reign, by our command, to 11 of our soldiers
living in our castle at Bristol, for their livery for 40 days, of
whom 8 take 12*d.* per day, and 3 take, per day, 7½*d.* Witness ourself, at Westminster, the 14th day of May, in the same
year.

Henry, by the grace of God, &c.—Pay from our Treasury to
our beloved Richard de Argentom 20*l.* for the works of our castle
at Hertford. Witness ourself, at Westminster, the 15th day of
May, in the 10th year of our reign.

Henry, by the grace of God, &c.—Pay from our Treasury to our beloved and faithful Henry de Cornhill, Chancellor of Saint Paul's, London, and to Godfrey de Craucumb, going in our service to Portsmouth, 20*l.* for their expenses, of our gift. Witness ourself, at Westminster, the 19th day of May, in the 10th year of our reign.

Henry, by the grace of God, &c.—Pay from our Treasury to Giles de Merk, whom we have sent into Gascony to our brother, 10 marks, of our gift. Witness ourself, at Westminster, the 19th day of May, in the 10th year of our reign.

Henry, by the grace of God, &c.—Pay out of our Treasury to Roger de Chester, for our well-beloved and faithful brother John, Constable of Chester, 15*l.* for this Easter Term, in the 10th year, of the 30*l.* which he receives from us yearly to maintain himself in our service. Witness ourself, at Westminster, the 15th day of May, in the 10th year of our reign.

Henry, by the grace of God, &c.—Pay from our Treasury to Engeram de Furnet 4 marks, of our gift, for his expenses; also pay to Philip de Cartret 3 marks, of our gift, and to William de Salmeles 3 marks, of our gift. Witness ourself, at Westminster, the 19th day of May, in the 10th year of our reign, before the Justices and the Bishops of Bath and Salisbury.

Henry, by the grace of God, &c.—Pay out of our Treasury to Reimund Gaillard, a man of Amaneus Columb, to the use of the said Amaneus and William Bernard, 200*l.*, which they lent to our brother Richard, the Earl of Poictou, for his support in our service in Gascony. Witness ourself, at Westminster, the 20th day of May, in the 10th year of our reign, before the Justices and Bishops of Bath and Salisbury.

Henry, by the grace of God, &c.—Pay from our Treasury to William de Casingham, at Easter Term, in the 10th year of our reign, 20*l.*, which he receives yearly, at the feast of Easter, for his maintenance in our service. Witness ourself, at Westminster,

the 20th day of May, in the same year, before the Justices and
the Bishops of Bath and Salisbury.

Henry, by the grace of God, &c.—Pay out of our Treasury
to Thomas de Haia 200*l.* for payment of our soldiers and cross-
bowmen; and to Richard de Hereford and Josceline de Oye 200*l.*
for the works of our castle at Dover; and 15*l.* 1*s.* 6*d.* for the same
works in the year preceding, for which the aforesaid Richard and
Josceline have rendered their account. Witness ourself, at Westminster, the 21st day of May, in the 10th year of our reign,
before the Justices.

Henry, by the grace of God, &c.—Pay from our Treasury to
Richard de Hereford and Jocelin de Oye, to the use of Master
Jordan, our carpenter, 30*s.*, in part payment of his livery. Witness ourself, at Westminster, the 21st day of May, in the 10th
year of our reign, before the Justices.

Henry, by the grace of God, &c.—Pay from our Treasury to
Bernard de Fonte, a man of Imbert de Fonte, for the use of
Peter Cucu, 300 marks, which the same Peter lent to Richard,
our brother, the Earl of Poictou, in Gascony, for his support in
our service. Witness ourself, at Westminster, the 19th day of
May, in the 10th year of our reign.

Henry, by the grace of God, &c.—Pay from our Treasury
to Randal le Barrer, for 11 pipes of white wine, 22*l.*, to wit, for
each cask 40*s.*; and for the carriage of the said pipes 8*s.* 6*d.*
Witness ourself, at Westminster, the 19th day of May, in the 10th
year of our reign.

Henry, by the grace of God, &c.—Pay from our Treasury
to our well-beloved and faithful Richard de Gray 200*l.*, for the
custody of our Islands of Guernsey, Jersey, and other Islands
there. Witness ourself, at Westminster, the 18th day of May, in
the 10th year of our reign.

Henry, by the grace of God, &c.—Pay from our Treasury to Brother Walter, Chaplain to the Queen Berengaria, and Martin, his servant, 1,000 marks, for the use of the said Queen, which we owed to her at the term of the Ascension of our Lord, in the 10th year of our reign. Witness ourself, at Westminster, the 24th day of May, in the same year.

Henry, by the grace of God, &c.—Pay from our Treasury to Robert de Auberville 10 marks, for the works at the Castle of Hastings. Witness ourself, at Westminster, the 23rd day of May, in the 10th year of our reign.

Henry, by the grace of God, &c.—Pay from our Treasury to Peter, the engineer of war-slings, going to our Castle at Corf, to make war-slings there, 4 marks, in part payment of his livery. Witness ourself, at Westminster.

Henry, by the grace of God, &c.—Pay from our Treasury to our 8 soldiers in our castle at Bristol, each of them receiving 12d. per day, and to our other 3 soldiers there, each of them receiving 7½d. per day, 19l. and 15s. for their livery for 40 days. Also pay to our 20 foot soldiers, of whom 10 have 3d. per day, and the other 10, 3½d. per day. Also for 21 liveries, and 1 mark for each of their liveries for 80 days—to wit, from the morrow of the close of Easter in the 10th year of our reign, unto Wednesday next before the feast of Saint Margaret, in the same year, counting each day. Witness ourself, at Westminster, the 25th day of May, in the same year, before the Justices and Bishops of Bath and Salisbury.

Henry, by the grace of God, &c.—Pay from our Treasury to Geoffrey le Moigne, going in our service to Gascony, 10 marks; and to William le Moigne, also going there on our service, 3 marks of our gift. Also pay to William, the son of William, the clerk of Master Philip de Haddam, 10 marks, at this Easter Term, in the 10th year of our reign, to the use of the same

Master Philip, for the annual tax of 20 marks which he receives
yearly at our Exchequer. Witness ourself, at Westminster, the
24th day of May, in the same year.

Henry, by the grace of God, &c.—Pay from our Treasury
to Walter de Kirkeham and Walter de Brakeley, clerks of our
wardrobe, 500*l*., to discharge our expenses. Witness ourself, at
Westminster, the 24th day of May, in the 10th year of our reign.

Henry, by the grace of God, &c.—Pay from our Treasury
to Godescall de Maghelins 210*l*., for going to Montgomery, for
works done at the same castle, and for liveries to our knights and
soldiers there; also deliver to the same Godescall 10*l*., as an
advance upon his rent of Michaelmas Term, in the 10th year of
our reign; also deliver to our beloved and faithful Warin, the son
of Joelis, 5 marks, of our gift, for his support in our service; also
deliver to Geoffrey de Sancto Dionisio 1 mark, of our gift, for his
expenses. Witness ourself, at Westminster, the 26th day of
May, in the 10th year of our reign, before the Justices and
Bishops of Bath and Salisbury.

Henry, by the grace of God, &c.—Deliver from our Treasury
to William de Castell 5 marks, to purchase a vest and a certain
cup for our Chaplain of Saint Stephen's, Westminster. Witness
ourself, at Westminster, the 25th day of May.

LIBERATE ROLL, 24 AND 25 HENRY III.

HENRY, by the grace of God, &c.—Pay out of our Treasury
to our beloved Brother John, our almoner, 4 marks for a certain
robe for his use, of our gift. Witness ourself, at Westminster,
the 24th day of September, in the 24th year of our reign.

Henry, by the grace of God, &c.—Pay out of our Treasury
to the Abbot of Westminster 1,000*l*., to be paid to the Prior of

the Hospital of Saint John of Jerusalem in France, for the use of the Earl of March. Witness ourself, at Westminster, 5th day of October, in the 24th year of our reign.

Henry, by the grace of God, &c.—Pay from our Treasury to Robert the Chaplain, ministring in the chapel of the Blessed Mary, in the Jewry, London, which was the synagogue, 60s. for the 22d year of our reign, and 60s. for the 23d year, which he receives yearly at our Exchequer, for his stipend. Witness ourself, at Westminster, the 13th day of August, in the 24th year of our reign.

Henry, by the grace of God, &c.—Pay from our Treasury without delay to Amaric de Sancto Amando 50 marks, of our gift, to make his pilgrimage to the Holy Land. Witness ourself, at Westminster, the 4th day of June, in the 24th year of our reign.

Henry, by the grace of God, &c.—Pay from our Treasury to our beloved clerk, Master Henry de Wintyn, 100 marks for the use of our beloved Uncle Thomas, Earl of Flanders and Hamoñ, for his annual fee, which he receives at our Exchequer. Witness ourself, at Westminster, the 4th day of October, in the 24th year of our reign.

Henry, by the grace of God, &c.—Pay out of our Treasury to Walter the Chaplain, for celebrating mass to the Blessed Mary in the chapel of Saint Peter, within the Keep of the Tower of London, 25s. for Michaelmas Term, in the 24th year of our reign.

Henry, by the grace of God, &c.—Pay out of our Treasury to Juon, a servant of our beloved Sister Isabella, Empress of Germany, 10l. for her expenses on returning home, of our gift. Witness ourself, at Westminster, the 16th day of October, in the 24th year of our reign.

Henry, by the grace of God, &c.—Pay out of our Treasury to the Prior of Lecton, for the use of the Monks of Font Eborald,

50s. for Michaelmas Term, which they ought to receive yearly, at our Exchequer, for the support of a chaplain to perform divine service for the soul of Queen Eleanor, our grandmother; and to Simon, the chaplain of Saint Stephen's, Westminster; and to William, the chaplain of Saint John's, Westminster, 50s.—to wit, to each of them 25s. for their stipends, from the feast of Saint Michael, in the 24th year, to the feast of Easter, in the 25th year of our reign.

Henry, by the grace of God, &c.—Pay out of our Treasury to Humphry de Bohun, Earl of Essex and Hereford, 200 marks for Michaelmas Term, in the 24th year of our reign, of the 400 marks which he receives yearly, at our Exchequer, for the custody of our castle at Dover. Witness ourself, at Westminster, the 14th day of October, in the 24th year of our reign.

Henry, by the grace of God, &c.—Pay from our Treasury to Edward, the son of Odo, our clerk, 6l. 14s. for four gold cloths purchased by our command for our use; also pay to the same 11s. 6d. for a certain cloth of arras purchased by our command, and offered in Christ's Church, Bermondsey; also pay to the same 4 marks 6s. for 44 half pennyweights of musk, (or frankincense,) and 1 bizant, purchased by our command, for our offerings, of which we gave 20 half pennyweights to the Blessed Edward, on the morrow of the translation of the Blessed Thomas the Martyr, in the 24th year of our reign, and 23 half pennyweights and 1 bizant on the day of Saint Peter ad Vincula there; also pay to the same 22s. for 24 half pennyweights of frankincense purchased by our command; also pay to the same 18s. 9d. for a certain cover made for a crystal vessel purchased by our command, and offered to the Blessed Edward on the same day; also pay to the same 12s. for a certain cloth of arras, purchased by our command, and put in our chapel of Saint Stephen's at Westminster; also pay to the same 50l. in discharge for our works done there by our command, from the day of Saint Botolph unto the day of Saint Oswald in the same year. Witness ourself, at Westminster, the 8th day of August, in the 24th year of our reign.

Henry, by the grace of God, &c.—Pay from our Treasury to our well-beloved clerk, Edward, the son of Odo, 12 marks for 4 baudekins, purchased by our order, and offered to the Blessed Edward at the feast of Saint Michael, in the 24th year of our reign ; also to the same 10 marks for a certain ring with an emerald, purchased by our command, and offered there in the same year; also to the same 37*s*. 6*d*. for a certain gold clasp, purchased by our command, and offered there; also to the same 1 mark for 5 pennyweights of frankincense, purchased by our command, and there offered ; also to the same 4 marks for a certain baudekin, purchased by our command, and given to Master Thomas, our chaplain, to make him a certain cope; also pay to the Messenger of the King of France, bringing a message from the same King, 10*l*., of our gift; also pay to the Friars Minors of Cambridge 10 marks, of our gift; also pay to the Cistercians and Friars Minors of London 2 marks; also pay to Brother John, our almoner, 10*l*., to be bestowed for our alms; also pay to Adam de Basinges 24 marks for 6 baudekins of gold, purchased by our command, and offered at Saint Paul's Church, London, at the feast of the dedication of the same; also to the same 22 marks for a certain embroidered chesable, and there offered at the same feast ; also to the same 7 marks for a certain mitre, purchased and given the Archbishop of Armagh; also to the same 7*l*. 0*s*. 2*d*. for a certain chesable of violet-coloured silk with a broad gold fringe, given to Saint Edward's; also to the same 25*s*. 7*d*. for a certain chesable with an entire vest for our chaplain of Kenington ; also pay to Master Joseph, the goldsmith, 14 marks for a certain mitre, purchased and given by our command to Peter de Aqua Blanca, [Bishop] elect of Hereford; also pay to Roger de Haverhull, our clerk, 60*s*. 20*d*. for a certain green banner with a gold cross and figures of gold on each side, purchased by our command, and offered to Saint Edward; also to the same 18*s*. 8*d*. for 14 half pennyweights of frankincense, offered at the church of Saint Paul's, London, at the feast of the benediction thereof; also pay to our beloved clerk, Edward, the son of Odo, 74*l*. 9*s*. 6*d*., in discharge of our works, done by our command, at Westminster, from

Sunday next after the feast of Saint Bartholomew the Apostle, in the 24th year of our reign, unto the feast of Saint Faith the Virgin, in the same year. Witness ourself, at Westminster, the 15th day of October, in the 24th year of our reign.

Henry, by the grace of God, &c.—Pay from our Treasury to Master Walter, keeper of our converted Jews, of London, 10 marks, for the term of Saint Benedict, at Easter, in the 24th year of our reign.

Henry, by the grace of God, &c.—Pay from our Treasury to Edward, the son of Odo, 8l. and 20d., to feed the poor in our great palace at Westminster; also to William de Haverhull 4l. and 40d., to feed 1,000 poor, for the soul .   .   .   .   .   . formerly our uncle. Witness ourself, at Westminster.

Henry, by the grace of God, &c.—Pay from our Treasury to Jordan, formerly cook to our dearly-beloved sister Isabella, Empress of Germany, 50s. yearly, for his support, so long as it shall please us.

Henry, by the grace of God, &c.—Pay from our Treasury to Adam de Benetley 70s. 6d., for a certain plain gilt cup purchased from him, and delivered to our clerk, by our command. Witness ourself, at Westminster, &c.

Henry, by the grace of God, &c.—Pay out of our Treasury to Master Walter de Dya and Hugh Giffard 20l. for the expenses of Edward, our son. Witness ourself, at Windsor, the 12th day of December, in the 25th year of our reign.

Henry, by the grace of God, &c.—Pay out of our Treasury to Wigan Briton, our servant, 10 marks, for a certain horse purchased for our use.

Henry, by the grace of God, &c.—Pay out of our Treasury to Adam de Basinges 4l. 19s. for a certain gold cope purchased by our command, and placed in our chapel at the feast of the Nativity of our Lord, in the 25th year of our reign; also to the same 24*l.* 1*s.* 6*d.* for a cope of red silk, given to the Bishop of Hereford, by our command, and for three chesables of red silk placed in our chapel, by our command, in the same year and day; also to the same 17*l.* 18*s.* 10*d.* for 2 diapered and 1 precious cloth of gold for a tunic and dalmatican entirely ornamented with gold fringe, purchased by our command, and placed in our chapel in the same year and day; also to the same 47*s.* 10*d.* for a chesable of silk cloth without gold, purchased by our command, and placed in our chapel in the same year and day; also to the same 24*l.* 13*s.* for two embroidered copes, purchased by our command, and placed in our chapel; also to the same 7*s.* 2*d.* for an Albe, embroidered with gold fringe, purchased by our command, and placed in our chapel; also to the same 17*l.* 1 mark for two embroidered chesables, purchased by our command, and placed in our chapel; also pay to our beloved clerk, Edward, the son of Odo, 13*l.* half a mark, for a certain cup of pure gold, purchased by our command, and given to Eleanor, our dearly-beloved Queen, at the feast of the Nativity of our Lord, in the same year; and pay to the same 16*s.* for the workmanship and gold of a certain branch candlestick, made by our command, and offered to the church of the Blessed Peter, Westminster, at the purification of Eleanor, our dearly-beloved Queen, in the same year; also to the same 18*s.* 6*d.* for the workmanship of 2 censers made for our chapel, and for pure gold, weighing 11½ dwts., to gild the same censers, by our command, in the same year and day; also pay to the same 5*s.* for pure gold, weighing 4 dwts., to gild a certain chalice for our chapel, by our command, and for the workmanship of the same, &c. Witness ourself at Windsor, the 12th day of January, in the 25th year of our reign.

Henry, by the grace of God, &c.—Pay from our Treasury to Segurus, our kinsman, whom we have recently knighted, 80 marks, of our gift. Witness ourself, at Windsor, the 15th January, anno 25°.

Henry, by the grace of God, &c.—Pay from our Treasury to our beloved and faithful John de Gatesden, 50*l.*, to discharge the expenses of our Queen. Witness ourself, at Marlborough, the 19th day of January, in the 25th year of our reign.

Henry, by the grace of God, &c.—Pay from our Treasury to our good men of Regula 25 marks, which remain unpaid of the 1010 marks which we owe them for the loss of their houses in building our castle of Regula, and for the loss of their houses and chattels on the entrance of our dearly beloved Brother Richard, Earl of Cornwall and Poitou, into the aforesaid town when it was surrendered to him. Witness ourself, at Windsor, the 11th day of January, in the 25th year of our reign.

Henry, by the grace of God, &c.—Pay from our Treasury to our beloved clerk Jeremy de Kaxton, 60 marks, for the expenses which he incurred in taking an inquisition of the chattels of the Jews, to be paid of our gift. Also, to our beloved clerk William Hardel, 60 marks, for taking a like inquisition, to be discharged of our gift. Witness ourself, at Westminster, the 8th day of January, in the 25th year of our reign.

Henry, by the grace of God, &c.—Pay from our Treasury to Edward, the son of Odo, 82*l.*, for a certain mitre made by our command, for the use of the Venerable Father Peter, Bishop of Hereford, of our gift; also pay to the same 43*l.* 6*s.* 8*d.*, for a certain garment with precious stones, made by our command, and placed in our chapel; also pay to the same 32 marks, for a certain textuary purchased by our command, and placed in the same chapel. Witness ourself, at Worcester, the 11th day of February, in the 25th year of our reign.

Henry, by the grace of God, &c.—Pay from our Treasury to our beloved and faithful John de Lexinton and Master Alexander le Seculer, for their expenses in performance of our business at the court of Rome, 100 marks of good money, new and perfect.

c

Also pay to our beloved and faithful Nicholas de Bolevill and Master John de Dya, for going to the court of Rome upon our affairs, 100 marks of good money, new and perfect, for their expenses. Witness ourself, at Worcester, the 12th day of February, in the 25th year of our reign.

Henry, by the grace of God, &c.—Pay from our Treasury to Roger, the usher of our Exchequer, 28s. 2d., for carrying 55 summonses to divers of our sheriffs, from the morrow of St. Hilary, in the 25th year of our reign, until Wednesday next before the feast of Saint Peter in Cathedraa, in the same year; also pay to the same 4s. 1d., for wax to seal the summonses, writs, &c.

LIBERATE ROLL, 26 HENRY III.

HENRY, by the grace of God, &c.—Pay out of our Treasury to Brother Hugh de Stocton, treasurer of the Templars, London, 5 marks, for half a mark and one pennyweight of incense purchased by our command, of which we took 40 half penny-weights for the church of the Blessed Peter, Westminster, on the coming into England of our beloved Brother Richard, Earl of Poitou and Cornwall, from the Holy Land, in the 26th year of our reign, &c. Witness ourself, at Westminster, the 24th day of April, in the 26th year of our reign.

Henry, by the grace of God, &c.—Pay out of our Treasury to our beloved and faithful Bertram de Cryoll, our constable of Dover, 200 marks, for Easter term last past, in the 26th year of our reign, &c. Witness ourself, at Portsmouth, the 7th day of May, in the 26th year of our reign.

Henry, by the grace of God, &c.—Pay out of our Treasury to Hugh Giffard and Master William Brun, 200l., for the support of Edward our Son, and his attendants residing with him in our castle of Windsor. Witness ourself, at Merewell, the 4th day of May, in the 26th year of our reign.

Henry, by the grace of God, &c.—Pay out of our Treasury to Gervase Purcell, 12 marks, to purchase a horse for his use, of our gift. Witness ourself at Westminster, the 12th day of April, in the 26th year of our reign.

Henry, by the grace of God, &c.—Pay out of our Treasury to Brother John, our almoner, 208*l*. 6*s*. 8*d*., to feed the poor, for the soul of the Empress, formerly our Sister, to wit, one-half at Oxford, and the other half at Ospringe, each of whom to have a penny for food; also pay to the same 8*l*. 6*s*. 8*d*., to feed 2000 poor persons, to wit, one-half at Ankerwick and the other half at Bromhal, for the soul of the same Empress. Witness ourself, at Winchester, the 30th day of April, in the 26th year of our reign.

Henry, by the grace of God, &c.—Pay out of our Treasury to the two chaplains ministering in the chapel of St. John at Westminster, 50*s*., &c. And to our said chaplains half a mark as a stipend for their clerk, and to provide a light in the chapel aforesaid. Also to three chaplains ministering in the chapel of Saint Stephen's at Westminster, 75*s*., for their stipends, &c. Witness ourself, at Windsor, the same year.

Henry, by the grace of God, &c.—Pay out of our Treasury every year to the Abbot and Monks of Westminster, 20*l*., which we have granted them, to be received at our Exchequer, to wit, 10*l*. at Easter, and 10*l*. at the feast of Saint Michael, to find 4 wax lights to be burnt about the shrine of Saint Edward at Westminster. Also pay yearly out of our Exchequer, at Michaelmas, to the Sacrist of Westminster, half a mark, for support of the great lamp which hangs in the body of the church of the Blessed Peter at Westminster. Witness ourself, at Westminster, the 20th day of April, in the 26th year of our reign.

Henry, by the grace of God, &c.—Pay out of our Treasury to our beloved and faithful Bernard de Sabaudia, 20 marks yearly, for the support of Ducelina his wife, who came to England at our especial request, which said 20 marks we grant of our will, to be paid her yearly at our Exchequer, so long as the said Ducelina shall remain in England, &c. In witness whereof we have caused these our letters to be made patent. Witness ourself, at Westminster, the 12th day of April, in the 26th year of our reign.

Henry, by the grace of God, &c.—Pay out of our Treasury to the wife of Reginald Hauberg, 5 marks yearly, for her support, so long as the said Reginald shall be with us beyond the seas in our service. Witness ourself, at Portsmouth, the 5th day of May, in the 26th year of our reign.

Henry, by the grace of God, &c.—Pay out of our Treasury every month, so long as we shall please, (after the month beginning the 4th day of May, in the 26th year of our reign,) to our beloved and faithful Bernard de Sabaudia, our constable of Windsor Castle, 25l. 15s. 8d., for the use of 4 knights in our aforesaid Castle, each of them taking 2s. per day; and for the use of 11 soldiers there, each of them taking 9d. per day; and for the use of 7 watchers there, each of them taking 2d. per day; and for the use of Burnell, the carpenter, and certain cross-bowmen, each of whom takes 6d. per day; also pay to the same Bernard for the use of the aforesaid 7 watchers 70s., to wit, to each of them 10s. for their stipends for one year, to wit, from the 4th day of May, in the 26th year of our reign.

Henry, by the grace of God, &c.—Pay out of our Treasury to Rylwin de Tywle, our Bailiff of Windsor, 7l. 5s., to be paid to our good men of Windsor, in recompense for the damage they sustained in taking down their houses for a foss, which we ordered to be made round our Castle of Windsor. Witness ourself, at Reading, the 26th April, in the 26th year of our reign.

Henry, by the grace of God, &c.—Pay out of our Treasury to Nicholas de Geneve, master of the tents, 20 marks, for a certain tent, which we purchased from him. Witness ourself, at Merewell, the 4th day of May, in the 26th year of our reign.

Henry, by the grace of God, &c.—Pay out of our Treasury to our beloved clerk Edward, the son of Odo of Westminster, 7s. 1d., for the weight of 7s. 1d. of silver, to enlarge a certain censer, made by our command for our chapel; and 10s. for the weight of 10 pennyweights of pure gold and quicksilver, to gild the same censer; also pay to the same 5s. for silver to make a certain small censer for our chapel, by our command; and 6½d. for the weight of 3 half pennyweights of pure gold to gild the said censer; also pay to the same 14d. for the weight of 14 pennyweights of silver to make a certain tabernacle to contain a certain image of ivory; also 22d. for the weight of 2 pennyweights of pure gold to gild the said tabernacle; also pay to the same 45d. for the weight of 4 pennyweights and a half of pure gold to repair the sceptre of the Blessed Edward, by our command; also pay to the same 9s. 9½d. for silver to make 9 small rods and three bars to bear the cross; and three shillings for the weight of three pennyweights of pure gold and quicksilver to gild the same, by our command; also pay to the same 18s. 3d. to make copes for ten monks of our chapel, and 6s. for the weight of 6 pennyweights of pure gold with quicksilver, to gild the same; also to the same 8s. 6d. for the weight of 8 pennyweights of pure gold and quicksilver to gild a certain chalice for our chapel; also pay to the same 30s. for the workmanship of all the things beforementioned, made by our command; also pay to the same 16 marks for 32 pieces of gold, each piece weighing 10 pennyweights, purchased by our command, eight of which pieces we offered at the tomb of the Blessed Edmund, at Saint Edmund's, at the feast of the same, in the 26th year of our reign; and four pieces of which we offered, on the day of the nativity of the Lord, in the church of the Blessed Peter at Westminster, in the same year; and 16 pieces there at the feast of the Blessed Edward, in the same year; and at the feast of the

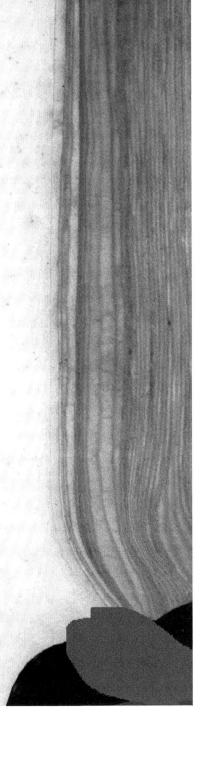

Epiphany, 4 pieces there, in the same year. Witness ourself, at Windsor, the 24th day of April, in the same year.

Henry, by the grace of God, &c.—Pay out of our Treasury to our beloved Clerk Edward, the son of Odo, 25 marks 5s., for gold weighing 33s. 10d. to make for us by our command clasps, with an alphabet; also pay to the same 40s., for 40 small emeralds purchased by our command for ornamenting the same clasps; also pay to the same 12 marks for the workmanship of the same clasps, for our use; also pay to the same 10 marks 10s., for gold weighing 14s. 4d. to make a certain zone which we gave to Eleanor, our beloved Queen; also 100s. for a certain clasp purchased for the use of Peter Chaceporc, which we gave on behalf of Eleanor our said Queen, and for a certain albe and stole ornamented with precious stones, offered in the church of Saint Peter's, Westminster, for the oblations of our said Queen Eleanor; also pay to the same 47s. 4½d. for bread, and for the custody of a certain Burster remaining at Westminster, by our command, from the day of Saint Tiburtius in the 25th year of our reign, until the vigil of Easter in the 26th year of our reign. Witness ourself, at Windsor, the 14th day of April, anno 26°.

Henry, by the grace of God, &c.—Pay from out of our Treasury to our beloved Clerk Edward, the son of Odo of Westminster, 38s. 3½d., for a certain entire vest purchased and sent to Radelay, by our command; also pay to the same 40s. for a certain missal, with a Gradale and Antiphone in the same volume, purchased and sent there by our command; also pay to the same 22s. 4d. for a certain silver chalice weighing 16s. 4d., purchased and sent there by our command. Witness ourself, at Windsor, the 24th day of April, in the 26th year of our reign.

Henry, by the grace of God, &c.—Pay out of our Treasury to Adam de Bakering 8s. 9d., for three yards of undressed cloth and 11 yards of white linen cloth purchased from him by our command for a certain altar cloth which the Earl of Flanders gave

us ; also pay to him 6s. 8d. for a certain cloth of silk and a fringe
purchased by our command to embroider a certain embroidered
chesable which Mabilia of Saint Edmund's made for us; and to
the same 5 marks for certain orfraies purchased by our command
for Saint Edward's cope, at the feast of the nativity of our Lord,
in the 26th year of our reign; also pay to the same 7 marks for
two cloths of gold purchased by our command and offered in the
church of the Blessed Peter, Westminster, at the feast of the
translation of the Blessed Edward, in the same year ; also pay to
the same 32s. for a certain cushion of silk cloth purchased by our
command and there offered, in the same year; also to the same
9 marks for two Geneva cloths of silk and for a Milan cloth purchased by our command, one of which we offered in the church
of Saint Paul, on the return of our well-beloved Brother Richard,
Earl of Poitou and Cornwall, and another in the church of Saint
Peter, Westminster, at the same return, in the same year, and the
other cloth was delivered into our wardrobe by our command;
also pay to the same 9 marks for three baudekins, purchased, by
our command, to offer in the church of the Blessed Peter, Westminster, by Edward, the son of Odo, our Clerk, at our departure,
after Easter, from Westminster, in the same year. Witness ourself, at Windsor, the 24th day of April, anno 26°.

Henry, by the grace of God, &c.—Pay from our Treasury to
Isabella, the wife of our beloved Clerk Robert of Canterbury, 5
marks, to purchase a robe for our use. Witness ourself, at Winchester, the 1st day of May, anno 26°.

Henry, by the grace of God, &c.—Pay from our Treasury to
Amaneus Bonelus, a Burgundian merchant, 182l., for 104 casks of
wine purchased for the stock of our castle at Dover—to wit, for each
cask 35s. Witness ourself, at Portsmouth, the 5th May, anno 26°.

Henry, by the grace of God, &c.—Pay to Richard Abel
12l. 5s. 3d. for 6 gold clasps, weighing 27s. 3d., purchased of him,
at Portsmouth, for our use, by the hands of P. Chacepore, keeper

of our wardrobe. Witness ourself, at Portsmouth, the 7th May, anno 26°.

Henry, by the grace of God, &c.—Pay from our Treasury to John Franc, the expenses for our Queen's gold, 38l. 9s. 8d., which we received from the chattels sold of John, formerly Earl of Lincoln, above the debt which the same Earl owed us, and which we will to be allowed to the executors of the will of the same Earl, for the gold which the aforesaid Earl owed us, on account of our Queen. Witness ourself, at Portsmouth, the 5th May, anno 26°.

. Henry, by the grace of God, &c.—Pay out of our Treasury to Robert, parson of the church of Saint Werburgh, keeper of our house of converted Jews, London, and to Lawrence de Frowic, 200 marks to purchase land for the same converts, of our gift. Witness ourself, at Portsmouth, the 5th day of May, in the 26th year of our reign.

. Henry, by the grace of God, &c.—Pay out of our Treasury to Margaret, who was the wife of Adam de Shoreditch, 46l. 16s. 11d., for a plain silver gilt cup and two clasps of the value of 10 marks, and 126 rings, purchased by weight for our use from the aforesaid Adam, by the hands of Peter Chaceporc, keeper of our wardrobe, at the feast of the Circumcision of our Lord, in the 26th year of our reign. Witness ourself, at Merewell, the 4th day of May, anno 26°.

Henry, by the grace of God, &c.—Pay out of our Treasury to Vilanus de Fossato, Ralph Page, and William Blund, our serjeants-at-arms, for the custody of our prisoners at our Tower of London, each of whom receives 12d. per day for his arrears, from the . . . day of March next after the close of Easter, in the 26th year of our reign, until the Tuesday in the finding of the Holy Cross, on the same day, counting each day; also pay to our 10 soldiers, dwelling in Windsor castle, each of whom also takes 12d. per day for their arrears during the same time. Witness ourself,

at Portsmouth, the 5th day of May, in the 26th year of our
reign.

Also after the departure of the Lord the King from England.

Henry, by the grace of God, &c.—Pay out of our Treasury to
Elye de Munteny, our servant, who received 12*d.* per day for
going as our messenger to Bristol, 40*s.*, in part payment of his
livery. Witness W. Archbishop of York, at Westminster, the 18th
day of May, anno 26°.

Henry, by the grace of God, &c.—Pay out of our Treasury to
Henry de Wengham, Clerk, 200*l.* to be expended in our service,
by the advice and command of our beloved and faithful William
Bardulph. Witness W. Archbishop of York, at Westminster,
the 20th day of May in the 26th year, by the same Archbishop,
with the advice of the Venerable Bishop of Carlisle and William
de Cantelupe.

Henry, by the grace of God, &c.—Pay out of our Treasury to
our beloved W. Hardel, 20 marks, to be taken to Portsmouth, to
freight two ships, to carry over our beloved and faithful Warren
de Munchens and his attendants; and to bring our great tent
after us into Gascony. Witness W. Archbishop of York, at
Westminster, the 24th day of May, anno 26°.

Henry, by the grace of God, &c.—Pay out of our Treasury to
John le Fol, W. Luvel, and Philip de Candoure, our huntsmen,
each of whom receives 25*d.* per day for themselves, their men,
horses, and dogs, for their liveries for 14 days 1*l.* 13*s.* 6*d.*,—to
wit, from Thursday next after the finding of the Holy Cross, unto
Wednesday next after the feast of Saint Dunstan, counting each
day. Witness W. Archbishop of York, at Westminster, the 22nd
day of May, anno 26°.

Henry, by the grace of God, &c.—Pay out of our Treasury to

William de Edmundestrop, 20s., for the expenses which he incurred in prosecuting our suit against Herbert, the son of P. Witness W. Archbishop of York, at Westminster, the 16th day of May, anno 26°.

Henry, by the grace of God, &c.—Pay out of our Treasury to John le Bon, a merchant of Rye, 13l. 15s. 8d., for the freightage of his ship, in which Nicholas de Bolevill was conveyed as our messenger. Witness W. Archbishop of York, at Westminster, the 16th day of May, anno 26°.

Henry, by the grace of God, &c.—Pay out of our Treasury to our beloved and faithful Bernard de Sabaudia, constable of Windsor Castle, 40s., for the livery of Geoffrey de Laundele our servant, dwelling in our Castle of Windsor, who receives daily 7½d. Witness W. Archbishop of York, at Westminster, 12th day of May, anno 26°.

Henry, by the grace of God, &c.—Pay out of our Treasury to our chaplain ministering in our chapel at our Tower of London, 25s. for Easter term, for payment of 50s., which he receives yearly for his services, &c.

Henry, &c.—Pay out of our Treasury to our beloved Brother Richard de Chilleham, 10 marks, as a loan. Witness W. Archbishop of York, at Westminster, the 26th day of May, anno 26°.

Henry, by the grace of God, &c.—Pay out of our Treasury to Adam de Haunstede, 15s. viz. which he paid to divers of our couriers for their expenses in going on our messages, as well to Scotland as to divers parts of England. Witness W. Archbishop of York, at Westminster, the 28th day of May, anno 26°.

Henry, by the grace of God, &c.—Pay out of our Treasury to Nicholas Spigenell and his companions, servants of our chapel, 11s. 3d., for 15 pounds of wax, to wit, 9d. for each pound; also to the same from our Treasury 32s. 6d. for 66 pounds of wax at 6d. per pound, which they used by our command for sealing our writs. Witness W. Archbishop of York, at Westminster, 31st day of May, in the 26th year of our reign.

Henry, &c.—Pay, &c. to Ralph Crast the waferer, 40s. of our gift, &c.

Henry, &c.—Pay, &c. to Robert le Sot, a messenger from our faithful and beloved W. Biset, 1 mark for his expenses, of our gift. Witness W. Archbishop of York, at Westminster, 2nd June, in the 26th year of our reign.

Henry, by the grace of God, &c.—Pay out of our Treasury yearly, to the Sacrist of Westminster for the time being, 50s., to purchase a cask of wine at the feast of Saint Botolph, which we granted him yearly of our gift for the performance of divine service. Witness W. Archbishop of York, at Winchester, 30th day of April, in the 26th year of our reign.

Henry, by the grace of God, &c.—Pay out of our Treasury to Aude de Buell, who was maid of honour to the Queen of Scotland, our sister, 5 marks, of our gift. Witness W. Archbishop of York, at Westminster, 1st June, anno 26°.

Henry, by the grace of God, &c.—Pay out of our Treasury to our beloved and faithful William de Haverhull, 208l. 6s. 8d., for the feeding at London, Windsor, and elsewhere which to our Council did seem fit, of 50,000 poor persons, each of whom had 1d. for food, for the soul of the Empress, formerly our sister. Witness ourself, at Winchester, the 30th day of April, anno 26°.

Henry, &c.—Pay, &c. to Philip de Caumdoner, who receives 21d. per day for the livery of himself, his men, horses, and dogs, 40s., &c. Witness W. Archbishop of York, at Ipswich, the 16th day of June, in the 26th year of our reign.

Henry, &c.—Pay, &c. to our beloved and faithful Henry de Tracy 100*l.*, to be taken to the Earl of Devon for the livery of his knights, soldiers, and sailors from Poitou, for the keeping of our peace. Witness W. Archbishop of York, at Norwich, the 23rd day of June, in the 26th year of our reign, by the same Archbishop before the whole Council.

Henry, &c.—Pay, &c. to Villanus de Fossato, Ralph Page, William Blund, our servants, for keeping of our prisoners in our Tower of London, &c.

Henry, by the grace of God, &c.—Pay, &c. to our beloved and faithful Bertram de Cryoll, 100 marks, to make four sailing vessels for our use, to be stationed at the cinque ports, where best it shall seem fit. Witness W. Archbishop of York, at Westminster, the 16th day of July, in the 26th year of our reign.

Henry, &c.—Pay, &c. to Joan, the wife of Ralph de Gorges, 4 marks, to purchase a robe and a cope. Witness ourself, at Portsmouth, 7th day of May, anno 26°.

Henry, &c.—Pay, &c. to Adam de Hainfield, 30*s.* 11*d.*, which he paid by our command to divers our couriers, for their expenses going as our messengers to divers parts of England. Witness W. Archbishop of York, at Westminster, the 15th day of July, anno 26°.

Henry, &c.—Pay, &c. to Walter de Kent and Jordan de Ainho, 46*l.* 4*s.* 5*d.*, to pay for the robes which were bought for the use of the household of Edward, our Son, against the feast of Pentecost, in the 26th year of our reign. Witness W. Archbishop of York, at Westminster, in the 26th year of our reign.

Henry, &c.—Pay, &c. to Giles de Erdington, for the use of Rose de Cokefield his mother, 8*l.* for the term of one year, which the aforesaid Rose hath in our manor of Kereseye, which belonged to Hubert de Ruylly, &c.

Henry, &c.—Pay, &c. to William Hardell, 113*l.* 8*s.*, for payment of the sailors in 109 ships remaining 7 days at Portsmouth, after our passage, of those ships which we commanded to be retained for our passage. Witness W. Archbishop of York, at Westminster, 22d day of July, anno 26°, by the Archbishop himself, before the whole Council.

Henry, &c.—Pay, &c. to Bernard de Sabaudia, Hugh Giffard, and William Brun, 200*l.*, for the works of our Castle at Windsor. Witness W. Archbishop of York, at Westminster, the 22d day of July, anno 26°.

Henry, &c.—Pay, &c. to Robert Brunman and Roger Fregge, or to either of them, for the use of our men of Yarmouth, 30*l.*, in part payment of 50*l.* which we owe them for herrings purchased to distribute in alms. Witness W. Archbishop of York, at Westminster, the 20th day of July, anno 26°.

Henry, &c.—Pay, &c. to William de Rummare, Knight, and to our beloved and faithful William de Cantilupe, 37*l.* 18*s.* 4*d.*, to pay the liveries of the knights and soldiers who resided in the fort in the Island of Lunday, from Saturday on the morrow of Saint Peter ad vincula unto Easter day, counting each day. Witness W. Archbishop of York, at Lambeth, the 26th day of July, anno 26°.

Henry, &c.—Pay, &c. to our beloved and faithful John de Grey, who came over to us into Gascony by our command, 30 marks, for his expenses. Witness, &c. as above.

Henry, &c.—Pay, &c. to Friaute, the wife of Griffin, son of Leuelin, 100*s.* for her support.

Henry, by the grace of God, &c.—Pay from our Treasury to Richard de Elandon, going as our messenger to Dover, 20*s.*, for his expenses. Witness W. Archbishop of York, at Windsor, the 5th day of August, anno 26°.

Henry, &c.—Pay, &c. to our beloved and faithful Thomas de Pavilly, 20 marks, to provide himself, and come to us into our service in Poitou. Witness, &c., the 8th day of August, anno 26°.

Henry, by the grace of God, &c.—Pay from our Treasury to our Sheriffs of London, 5000 marks and 100 marks, to be taken to Winchester, and from thence sent over to us in Poitou. Witness W. Archbishop of York, at Kennington, the 18th of August, anno 26°.

Henry, &c.—Pay, &c. to our Sheriffs of London, 500*l*., to be taken to Winchester, for payment of the liveries of the knights and soldiers who go with us to Poitou, and to freight the shipping and pay the wages of the sailors in the said ships who go over with us.

Henry, by the grace of God, &c.—Pay from our Treasury to our Exchequer at Michaelmas, in the 26th year of our reign, and to our faithful Hugh Giffard, 30 marks of our gift, to marry his daughter. Witness ourself, at Westminster, the 15th day of April, anno 26°.

Henry, &c.—Pay, &c. to Master Simon our carpenter, 100*l*. for the works done at our Castle of Windsor. Witness W. Archbishop of York, at Croydon, the 5th day of September, anno 26°.

Henry, by the grace of God, &c.—Pay out of our Treasury to our beloved and faithful Andrew Peverel 100*s*., for which he made a fine with us for his passage, and which he paid at our Exchequer because the same Andrew, by our command, sent, in lieu of himself, a certain knight for our service. Witness W. Archbishop of York, at Winchester, the 24th day of August, in the 26th year of our reign.

Henry, by the grace of God, &c.—Pay out of our Treasury to John de Schipford, bearer of these presents, 400*l*., to be taken to Portsmouth, and there to be delivered to William Hardell, our

Clerk, to expedite our business, with which we have instructed him. Witness W. Archbishop of York, at Winchester, the 26th day of August, in the 26th year of our reign.

Henry, by the grace of God, &c.—We command you, that you cause to be delivered to our Clerk, Edward of Westminster, money for the support of the works of Saint Edward's tomb at Westminster, and pay to the goldsmith for workmanship bestowed upon the same tomb, and for cutting marble for the same tomb, by our inspection, testimony, and advice; and to our beloved and faithful Robert Passelewe, when we shall have incurred the expense for the aforesaid works, we will command the same to be paid by our writ of liberate.

Henry, by the grace of God, &c.—We command that you cause to be paid to our beloved Clerk, Edward of Westminster, money to lead our chimney on the top of our hall at Westminster, and to paint the chapel of our beloved Queen there, and for sufficient support of our houses there, according to the view and testimony of good and lawful men; and when we shall have incurred such expenses, for this purpose, as may be necessary, we will cause our writ, for payment thereof, to be delivered to you. Witness ourself, at Merewell, the 2nd day of May, in the 26th year of our reign.

Issue Roll, Easter, 41 Henry III.

To the monks of Wrokeshall, 10 marks at Michaelmas Term, in the 41st year, for their appointed alms by letters patent.

To Henry, Brother of the illustrious King of Castile, 87 *l.* for the support of himself and retinue, to wit, for 87 days.

To Dentatius, a Florentine merchant, 67 *l.* for 30 casks of wine. ·

	£.	s.	d.
To Robert de Holeburn	3	0	5
To Thomas the Welshman	0	14	11½
To John the Welshman	0	1	7
To William Furmager .	0	12	0
To Walter the poulterer	0	16	6½
To Robert de Gannock .	0	11	1
To Robert Rufus . .	0	0	3
To William the Black .	0	4	6½
To Walter de Kyngeston	0	7	8½
To William Boby . .	1	13	2
To Geoffrey le Furmager	0	4	0
To Ely le Furmager .	0	2	2
To Wilkin le Furmager	0	0	6
To William of Bishopgate	0	1	0

For poultry obtained for the King's use by a writ.

Sum £51. 7s. 3d.

(With many others.)

To the hermit of Brehull, 50s. at Easter Term in the 41st year, for performing duty in the King's chapel of Brehull.

To Laurence Picher, a messenger of William de Chavenny, 40s., for the expenses which he incurred in coming for the fee of his lord.

To Margaret, Countess of Flaunders, 500 marks for the arrears of her annual fee of 500 marks.

To Domingo de Gawyak, a merchant, 62l. 2s. 6d., for 3550 lbs. of wax purchased for the King's use.

To Ralph le Spicer, of London, and Amphelisa his wife, 17 marks 5s. 8½d., for ale purchased from them for the King's use.

To John the chaplain, the King's almoner, 51l. 12s. 4d., for the exequies of Catherine the King's Daughter.

Henry de Castella 38l. in discharge of his expenses.

To Mansell, the King's tailor, 20 marks for making the King's tents.

To Simon de Wycomb, clerk to the Queen, 60l., in discharge of the expenses of the King's children.

To Henry de Ver, Earl of Oxford, 10 marks, at Easter Term in 41st year, for the third penny of the county, by writ patent.

To Alexander de Elmeden, 47s. 10½d. for the arrears of his wages in Gascony.

To Michael de Rednes, 50s., which he delivered to the Reeve of Saint Emelian, by the King's command.

To William of Gloucester, goldsmith, 10 marks, for a certain clasp, purchased from him to offer at the shrine of the Blessed Edmund of Pontiva.

To Guido de Leziniaco 150l., to wit, 100l. at Michaelmas Term, in the 40th year, for the manor of Derteford, and 50l. at the same Term of Saint Michael for his annual fee of 100l.

To Mariot, the wife of Robert de Ferars, 75l. 17s. 5½d., for palfreys, horses, harness, and other necessaries.

To William of Saint Ermin, 40 marks, at Easter Term in the 41st year, for his yearly fee of 40 marks.

To William de Trubbeville 5 marks, of the King's gift.

To Geoffrey de Leukenor 9 marks 8s., for his expenses in going to sell of the King's demesne woods.

To Ralph de Bakepuz 16l. 6s., for the arrears of his wages in Gascony.

To William de Trubbeville 5 marks, in discharge of his expenses during the time he was sick at London.

To Geoffrey de Bello Campo, 100 marks for the arrears of his fee, and for all debts which the King is bound to pay him.

To Ernald, the chaplain of the Saltu, 5 marks, for his support in the King's service, at Saltu, of the King's gift.

To Walter de Kyngeston, Ralph de la March, John de Oxford, Richard de Ambresbury and his companions, 33l. 7s. 4d., for divers kinds of poultry and fish, purchased from them for the King's use, whilst he was in Gascony.

To Master Simon de Welles, 5 marks and a half, for his expenses in coming to London and returning home.

To Henry de Bracton 25l. at Easter Term, in the 41st year, for his annuity of 40l.

To Mansell, the tailor, 100l. of the King's gift, to prepare himself against the King's going to Wales.

D

To Adam Bruning 25*., for 100 of sturgeon taken for the King's use.

To four chaplains, ministering in the chapel of Saint Stephen's, Westminster, 100*. for their stipends, from the feast of Easter unto the feast of Saint Michael, in the 41st year, by writ patent.

To two chaplains, ministering in the chapel of Saint John the Evangelist, half a mark for the stipend of a clerk, and to find lights during the same time, by writ patent.

To Richard, the hermit of Colemanneshegg, 30*. for his stipend during the same period.

To Edward of Westminster, 30*., for the support of a chaplain to perform divine service for Margaret the King's daughter, during same period, by writ patent.

To the Brethren of the Middle Temple, 4*l*., in part of 8*l*., appointed alms for the support of three chaplains to celebrate divine service at Easter Term in the 41st year, by writ patent.

To Roger, the usher of the Exchequer, 4*l*. 4*s*. for carrying divers summonses and writs to divers places in England, and for wax to seal the said summonses and writs.

For payments to the knights, chamberlain, clerks, and servants of the Exchequer, and for small issues thereof, as is contained in the great Roll of Writs, 38*l*. 7*s*. 11*d*.

To Buche, the slinger, who takes 12*d*. per day, 8*l*. 14*s*. for 114 days, to wit, from the morrow of Easter, on the 9th day of April, until Michaelmas day, including both days.

To Master Henry de Abrinces, the versifier, who receives 6*d*. per day, 4*l*. 7*s*., during the said period.

To Gervais, Usher to the Queen, who receives 2*d*. per day, 29*s*. for the same time.

To Henry le Tyeys, engineer to the King, of the war slings, who receives 4½*d*. per day, 3*l*. 2*s*. 3*d*.—to wit, from the morrow of Easter, the 18th day of April, in the 40th year, unto Michaelmas day in the same year, for 166 days, each day included.

To the same Henry, 3*l*. 11*s*. 7½*d*. for 180 and 11 days—to wit, from the morrow of Saint Michael, beginning the 41st year, unto

Easter day the 8th day of April in the same year, each day included.

To the Sacrist of Westminster, 20*l*. at Michaelmas Term, beginning in the 40th year, and at Easter Term in the same year, for the 20*l*. yearly which he receives, to find 4 wax torches around the tomb of the Blessed Edward, by writ patent.

To the same, 50*s*. for a cask of wine, purchased for performing divine service, at Easter term, in the 40th year, by writ patent.

To the same, half a mark, for the support of the great lamp, for the 40th year, by writ patent.

To the brethren of the guild at Westminster, appointed to ring the great bells at Westminster, 100*s*.—to wit, 50*s*. at Michaelmas term, in the 39th year, and 50 shillings at Easter, in the 40th year, for 100*s*. yearly, by writ patent.

To the keeper of the fabrick of the church at Westmintser, 3000 marks—to wit, 1500 marks at Michaelmas term, in the 39th year, and 1500 marks at Easter term, in the 40th year, for 3000 marks yearly, by writ patent.

To Ralph de Gorges, 20*l*.—to wit, 10*l*. at Easter term, in the 39th year, and 10*l*. at Michaelmas term next following, for his yearly fee of 20*l*.

To Brother John of Kent, a messenger from the Lord the Pope, 1000 marks for the use of the same Lord the Pope, which were owing to him, for the 40th year, for the annual tax of 1000 marks.

ISSUE ROLL, MICHAELMAS, 41 HENRY III.

To Rolland, clerk to the Queen of Cyprus, 10 marks, for his expenses in returning home, of the King's gift.

To a certain messenger bringing the first news of the safe delivery of the wife of William de Chavenny, 5 marks of the King's gift.

D 2

To Alexander, King of Scotland, 500 marks,

To Henry, brother of the King of Castile, 200 marks, } of the King's gift.

To the keepers of the works at Westminster, 200 marks, for the same works.

To the keeper of the wardrobe, 100 marks for the expenses of the Queen's household.

To Artaldus de Sancto Bomino, keeper of the King's wardrobe, 300 marks, for the expenses of the King's household.

To Richard, Earl of Cornwall, 57l. 10s. 8d., at Michaelmas erm, in the 40th year.

To the monks of Westminster 100s. for the support of a chaplain to perform divine service for the soul of Isabella, formerly Queen of England, by writ patent at Easter and Michaelmas terms in the 40th year.

To Simon de Montefort, Earl of Leicester, 200l. at Michaelmas term, in the 38th year, for part of the 400l. which he receives yearly for the dower of Eleanor, his wife, in Ireland.

To Peter Arnald Cordel, a messenger of Peter Reymund Cordel, 2 marks and a half.

To Domingo the good, and Arnaldus Reymond Dordayles, two marks and a half.

To Reginald de Perers, a messenger of Simon Grospermi, 40s.

To William de Monte Revelli, a valet of the Lord the King, 100s. of the King's gift.

To Henry de Malo Lacu, 5 marks, for the expenses which he incurred in going through divers counties of England, by command of the King.

To Master Albert, the chancellor of Mediolannen, 20 marks, for his expenses, of the King's gift.

To Nicholas de Stockbrugg, usher of the King's kitchen, 9l. 18s. 9d., for arrears of his wages in Gascony.

To Matthew de Subyr, 40s., for cloth purchased from him for the King's use.

To Thomas Esperun, 40*s.*, for the expenses he incurred in bringing the King's treasure to Suthwyk and to Portsmouth.

To Adam de la Ford, valet of Margaret, Queen of Scotland, 300*l.*, which the King of Scotland, his Lord, gave to him of the money which the same King owed, for the arrears of his marriage.

To the women of Kynton 100*s.* at Easter term, in the 40th year, for their 10*l.* yearly, by writ patent.

To two messengers of the Countess of Angolesme, and Isabella de Croun, the King's sister, 6 marks, for their expenses, of the King's gift.

To Michael de Weston, 74*s.*, for the arrears of his wages in Gascony.

To Vigerosus Yssue, 2 marks and a half, for his expenses, in part payment of the debts for which the King is bound to him.

To Sir Geoffrey de Cerys, Knight, to William de Chavigny, 10*l.* at Michaelmas term, in the 40th year, for his annual fee of 10*l.*

To Geoffrey de Lezingnan, 10 marks, for a certain palfrey purchased from him.

To Master Thomas, the King's surgeon, 50*s.*, for his expenses, of the King's gift

To Drogo de Barentino, 10*l.*, for palfreys, sumpter horses, and harness, for his two nephews whom the King, in Gascony, decorated with the belt of a Knight.

To Drogo de Barentino, going as the King's messenger beyond the seas, 30 marks for his expenses.

To Robert Russel, the Queen's servant, 20 marks, for the expenses of Catherine, the King's daughter.

To Raymond Guilli, a messenger from the good men of Joses, 20*s.*, for his expenses, of the King's gift.

To William Bonquer, 100*l* for his expenses going to the court of Rome.

To Master Peter de Lymeges, 40 marks, for his expenses, of the King's gift,

To Peter de Montefort, 25 marks, which he borrowed of Geoffrey Burlemunt, for his fee.

To Alan Burnell, 10 marks, for the loss of his horses in Gascony.

To the Monks of Westminster, 100*s.*, for the support of a chaplain to perform divine service for the soul of Richard, formerly Earl of Provence—to wit, at Easter and Michaelmas terms, in the 40th year, by writ patent.

To William de Monte Revell, 6*l.* 9*s.* 10*d.*, for the arrears of his wages in Gascony.

William of Gloucester, a goldsmith, 5 marks 14*d.*, for a gold clasp.

To Master William of Watford, 50 marks, for his expenses in going, as a messenger, to the King beyond seas.

To Artald de Sancto Romano, keeper of the King's wardrobe, 12 marks 6*s.* 8*d.* to do therewith what the King shall command him.

To Bernard de Castelnede, 4 marks, of the King's gift, for the losses and damages which he sustained by reason of the wars in Gascony.

To Henry de Castile, brother of the King of Castile, going to France, 40 marks, for the expenses of his attendants whilst he remained in England, taking per day 20*s.*, &c.

To Bertram de Bovell, valet to the King, and Bernard de Bovell, his brother, 10 marks, in part payment for the arrears of their wages.

To Master Nicholas de Plimpton, 100*s.* for the expenses of himself and his companions, for going on a message from the King to the Archbishop of Canterbury.

To Master Rustandus, 15 marks to be distributed to divers messengers coming to the King at Appelby.

To two chaplains ministering at the Tower of London, each of whom receives yearly 50*s.*—to wit, to each of them 25*s.* for their stipends—to wit, from the term of St. Michael in the 40th year, unto Easter in the 41st year.

To Pelerine of Luka, 80 marks, for 30 cloths of gold, purchased from him, for the use of the Queen, by Philip Lovell and W. de Bradeleg.

To Peter de Cuncys, 110s., for 20 frael of figs, purchased of him, for the King's use, by the hands of Roger the tailor.

ISSUE ROLL, EASTER, 42 HENRY III.

To John Maunsell, treasurer of York, 40 marks, which, by order of the King, he delivered to the Abbot of Tyron, and others, messengers from the King of Germany.

To William Braund, 67l. 4s. 9d., for 8 scarlet Lincoln cloths, taken from him, for the King's use, against his coming from Gascony.

To Eborard de Castrovyleyn, 107s. 8d., for the arrears of his stipend in Gascony, by writ, containing 7l. 7s. 8d. because the residue was to be paid in the wardrobe.

To Garsye Arnald, 36l., for 2000lbs. of wax, taken from him in London, for the King's use.

To Guido Boncunte, a merchant, 20 marks, of the King's gift, for the loss which he sustained, by reason of the loan he made to the Lord the King.

To William of Gloucester, goldsmith, 32l., for gold purchased of him for the King's use.

To Peter de Rivall, keeper of the King's wardrobe, 2000 marks, for the expenses of the King's household.

To Humfrey de Bohun, Earl of Hereford, 120l., for 50 casks of wine, taken from him in London, by Imbert Pugeys, for the King's use.

To William de Valencia, 100l. which he lent to the King, to be repaid by Robert, the son of Nicholas, for the manor of Dunham.

To the warders of the works of the chapel of Saint Martin le Grand, in London, 25 marks, to make 15 glass windows, and iron for the same, of the King's gift.

To Philip Lovell, 100 marks, which he delivered to Edward,

the King's Son, for the support of the garrison of the castle at Montgomery.

To Simon de Montefort, Earl of Leicester, 200*l.* at Easter Term, in the 42d year, for the 400*l.* which he receives yearly of the dower of Eleanor, his wife.

To William de Sancta Ermina, 20*l.*, which the King gave to him, of the chattels of William Isembard, Mayor of Wilton, who was hung.

To Martin de Amiens, 8*l.*, for a cloth of silk, purchased for the King's use.

To John, the notary, a messenger of the venerable father R. Cardinal of Saint Angeli, and to William de Miliant, messenger to a Lady of Calabria, 30 marks, for his expenses, of the King's gift.

To Finato, the King's proctor at the court of Rome, 30 marks —to wit, 20 marks at the term of the nativity of the Blessed John the Baptist, in the 41st year, and 10 marks at the term of the nativity of Saint John the Baptist, in the 42nd year, for 20 marks yearly.

To Peter de Rivallis, 100*l.* for the expenses of the King's household, delivered to Robert de la Bare, Robert le Marchant, and Nicholas de Winchelsea.

To John de Bosco, 90*l.* 13*s.* 6*d.*, for woollen cloth bought from him for the King's use.

To Hugh de la Penne, 150*l.*, in discharge of the expenses of the Queen's household.

To Richard Boxe, 76*s.* for 200lbs. of wax taken from him, and delivered to the sacrist of Westminster, by command of the King.

To Bernard Nicholas 5 marks for two cloths of gold.

To John Marescall, 11*l.* 2*d.*, for 4 horses, bought for the King's use, and delivered to four brethren of the order of Benedictines and Minors.

To the same, 69*s.* 7*d.* for the expenses of the same horses, and for harness, purchased for the use of the brethren aforesaid.

To the same John, 66*s.* 1*d.*, for harness, for the use of the brethren aforesaid.

To Nicholas de Handlou, 20*l.* at Easter term, in the 42nd year, for 40*l.* which he receives annually, for his support in the King's service.

To Roger de Whicester, 20 marks, at Michaelmas term, in the 41st year, for 40 marks which he receives yearly, so long as he shall continue in the office of justiciar.

To William of Gloucester, goldsmith, 20 marks, for working a certain precious cloth for the altar of the Blessed Edward.

To William of Gloucester, goldsmith, 60*s.* which he expended by command of the King, to repair a certain censer.

To Eustace Ruffus, merchant of Flanders, 12*l.* 16*s.* 8*d.*
To Hugh le Sweyn, 50*s.*
To Gerard de Middelburg, 4*l.* 7*s.* 6*d.*
To Gysekyn Cogeman, merchant of Germany, 43*s.* 9*d.*
To John de Luveke, 4*l.* 10*s.* 10*d.*
for oats, purchased of them for the King's use, by one writ.

To H. de Ver, Earl of Oxford, 10 marks, at Easter term, in the 42nd year, for 20 marks yearly, for the third penny of the county of Oxford, by writ patent.

To Peter de Montefort 25*l.*. at Michaelmas term, in the 40th year, for 50 marks yearly, which he receives for him and his heirs.

To Bartholomew le Spicer, 8*l.* 7*s.* 7*d.*, for nutmegs, figs, raisins, and cinnamon, purchased of him, for the King's use.

To Hugh de la Penne, clerk of the Queen's wardrobe, 1000 marks, for the arrear of divers expenses of the same Queen, to be accounted for at the Exchequer.

To Gerard de Bosco, a merchant of Bourdeaux, 70 marks, for 20 casks of wine, lately taken from him, for the Queen's use.

To Roger, an usher of the Exchequer, 43*s.*, for carrying summonses and writs to divers counties in England, and for wax to seal the said writs, as is contained in the great roll. In deliveries to the Knights, Chamberlains, Clerks, and servants of the Exchequer for other necessaries, as is contained in the great roll of writs, 39*l.* 17*s.* 6*d.*, from the day of the close of Easter, in the 42nd year, unto Saturday next after St. Peter ad vincula, in the same year.

To Master Henry, the versifier, who receives 6*d.* per day, 4*l.* 14*s.* 6*d.* for the said time.

To Richard, the chaplain, 25*s.*, for 50*s.* yearly, which he receives for the support of a chaplain, to perform divine service for the soul of Catherine, daughter of the Lord the King, during the same time, by writ patent.

ROLL OF EXPENSES FOR WORKS TO THE KING'S PALACE AT
WESTMINSTER.   ANNO 43 HENRY III.

Receipt touching the works to be done at the King's Court,
Westminster, viz. from the Feast of the Invention of the Holy
Cross, in the 43rd year of the reign of King Henry the IIIrd,
unto the feast of St. Michael following, 79*l.* 0*s.* 17*d.*; also
touching the aforesaid works after the Feast of St. Michael,
47*l.* 0*s.* 21½*d.*
                    Sum total of receipts, 126*l.* 3*s.* 2½*d.*

' Roll of Expenses incurred for the works of the Court of the
Lord the King at Westminster, from Monday after the Invention
of the Holy Cross, in the 43rd year of the reign of Henry, Son
of John, King of England, unto the nativity of our Lord next
following, viz. for taking down and rebuilding a chimney of the
chamber of the Lord the King, and binding and strengthening the
shaft of the said chimney outside with iron; and repairing the
laundry of the Court, and new making one great sewer or drain,
from the King's kitchen to the Thames; and one new cistern in
the King's Court; and newly constructing a certain outer common chamber in the King's Court adjoining the Thames; and
newly covering with lead the great chamber of the King's Stewards; and re-covering the King's kitchens with shingles, together
with the repair of the houses of the King's Court in divers places.

1st *Payment.*—The first payment for the aforesaid works of
the King's Court was made from the aforesaid Monday after
the Invention of the Holy Cross unto Sunday in the Vigil of
Saints Nerey and Acheley—to wit, for one week, including
the feast of Saint John Port Latin; which was made to
the plasterers and carpenters, viz.

Masons, Plasterers.—To Robert de Beverly, cutting away about
the King's chimney, for the same week, 3*s.*; and to John

Burglun for the same, 26*d.*; and to Henry de Wautham for the same, 26*d.*; and to William de Hampton for the same, 26*d.*

> Sum of the plasterers, 9*s.* 6*d.*

Free-stone.—And for five quarters of free-stone from Chalveden, bought of Ralph de Lamberhurst, for the chimney aforesaid, 7*s.* 6*d.*; and for one hundred weight of free-stone for the same, bought of Richard de Croiden, 6*s.*; and for three quarters of free-stone for the same, bought of Randulph de Wautham, 4*s.* 6*d.*

> Sum of the free-stone, 18*s.*

Grey-stone.—And for one ship load of grey-stone, for the use of the gutter aforesaid, bought of Richard le Corner, 6*s.*; and for one ship load of grey-stone, for the same, bought of Robert Fitz Alice, 5*s.*; and for one vessel load of grey-stone for the same, bought of Richard Fitz Jocelin, 4*s.*

> Sum of the grey-stone, 15*s.*

Lime.—And for felling and carrying old oak in the forest of Windsor unto the water side, wherewith to make lime for the works, 20*s.*; and for two new locks to the door of the Court and repairing two locks, 2*s.* 6*d.*

> Sum, 22*s.* 6*d.*
>
> Sum total of the first payment, 65*s.*

2nd Payment.—The second payment for the aforesaid works, was made from Monday in the feast of Saints Nerey and Acheley, in the 43rd year of King Henry, unto Sunday in the Vigil of Saint Augustine, for 15 days—to wit, the days containing the feast of the Ascension of our Lord, which was of the Lord the King; viz.

Masons.—To John Burglun, cutting away about the chimney for the aforesaid 15 days, with four of his companions, viz.

Reginald Sturmey, Henry de Wautham, William de Hampthon, Philip de Hildesle, 20s.—to wit, to each of them, 4s.

And to William de Badele, with two of his companions, cutting
about the laundry of the King's Court for the same 15 days,
viz. to Thomas de Kenefeg and Ralph de Oxford, 12s.—to
each of those three, 4s.

Sum of the plasterers' wages, 32s.

Carpenters.—To the carpenters, for the repair of the burnt roof
of the King's kitchen, viz. to William de Waudis with two
of his companions—to wit, John de Padinton, Henry de
Knythebrig, for the aforesaid 15 days, 12s.—to each of those
three, 4s.

Sum of the carpenters' wages, 12s.

Labourers.—And to labourers helping the plasterers and carpenters, viz. to Richard de Lichefeud, for 15 days, 2s. 3½d.;
and to Simon Russell, for the same time, 2s. 3½d.; and to
Roger de Chering, for the same time, 2s. 3½d.; and to Robert
de Oxford, for the same time, 2s. 3½d.

Sum of the workmen's wages, 9s. 2d.

Free-stone.—And for two hundred weight three quarters of free-
stone, for the use of the chimney and laundry, bought of Algar
de Brugge, 16s. 6d.; and for one quarter of free-stone, for the
same, bought of William de Brugge, 18d.; and for one hundred weight and a half of free-stone for the same, bought
of Ralph de Lamberhurst, 9s.; and for one hundred weight
one quarter of free-stone for the same, bought of Randulph de
Wautham, 7s. 6d.; and for one hundred weight of free-
stone, for the same, bought of Peter de Merscham, 6s.

Sum of the free-stone, 40s. 6d.

Sum total of the second payment, 4l. 13s. 8d.

3rd Payment.—The third payment was made from Monday in

the feast of St. Augustine, in the 43rd year of King Henry,
unto the Eve of Pentecost, for one week, without a holiday.

Masons.—To chisellers and bedders* about the King's chimney, viz. to Reginald Sturmey, John Burglun, Philip de
Hyldesle, Henry de Wautham, William de Hampthon,
John le Harper, Richard de Kermurth, Ralph de Waliden,
William de Bledelawe, 19*s.* 6*d.*—to each of the aforesaid
nine, 26*d.*; and to Robert de Beverly for the same week, 3*s.*;
and to William de Thame for two days, 12*d.*

The masons at the laundry, viz. to William de Bradele, Thomas
de Kenefeg, Ralph de Oxford, Robert Piks, for the same
week, 8*s.* 8*d.*, viz. to each of the aforesaid four, 26*d.*
            Sum of the plasterers' wages, 32*s.* 2*d.*

Smiths.—And to Master Henry de Lewes, for the iron work
which supported the mantel of the chimney of the King's
chamber, before it was taken down, for the aforesaid week,
4*s.*: and to William de Offinton, about the same, for the
same time, 18*d.*; and to Richard Smith about the same, for
the same week, 3*s.*
            Sum of the smiths' wages, 8*s.* 6*d.*

Carpenters.—And to four carpenters, about repairing of the
roof of the King's kitchen, for the same week, viz. to William
de Waud, John de Padinton, Nicholas de Eye, Henry de
Knythebrig, 8*s.* 8*d.*—to wit, to each of those four, 26*d.*
            Sum of the carpenters, 8*s.* 8*d.*

Labourers.—And to inferior workmen, viz. to Simon, the scaffold-
maker, for the same week, 18*d.*; and to William Millers,
15*d.*; and to John Porter 15*d.*; and to John Necks for four
days, 10*d.*; and to Martin, for the same time, 10*d.*; and to
five workmen, viz. to William de Priterwell, John Corant

* Men that bedded or laid the stones when chiselled or dressed.

Fulk, Reginald Fuhell, John Gynger, for two days carrying free-stone, cut from ashler,* unto the King's chamber, for the aforesaid chimney, 25d.—to wit, to each of those five, 5d.

And to three workmen who were with the smiths for the week aforesaid, 3s. 9d.—to each of them, 15d.; and to Adam de Auhlton for 4 days, 10d.; and to workmen with masons repairing the offices of the King's kitchen, viz. to Edmund the Brewer for the same week, 15d.; and to John Mityng, for the same time, 15d.; and to Ely le Breveter for the same time, 15d.

And to the workmen who dug the foundation for the great sewer or drain, viz. to Geoffry Wrenn, Durand de Eye, Hugh de Berking, Thomas de Eye, William de Feckam, 6s. 3d.—to each of the aforesaid five, 15d.

And to the labourers helping the masons about the laundry, viz. to Richard de Lichefeud, Simon Russell, Roger de Chering, for 15 days, 6s. 10½d.—to each of those three for the first week, 12½d. by reason of the feast intervening; and for the second week, 15d.

Sum of the labourers, 29s. 2½d.

Taskwork.—And to Robert English and his companions, to dress by taskwork for the laundry of the King's Court, 4s.; and for the carriage of free-stone cut from ashler, unto the King's chamber, for the use of the chimney, 21d.; and for the carriage of three ship-loads of grey-stone from the water to the hands of the workmen at the kitchen gutter, 21d.; and for laying down lead in the King's kitchen and repairing certain offices of the King's kitchen, for the rough stones 6s. 4d. Sum of the taskwork, 13s. 10d.

* Ashler is a term in masonry by which masons designate common free-stones as they come out of the quarry, of different lengths and thicknesses · 9 inches however is the ordinary thickness.

Free-stone.—And for two hundred weight three quarters of free-stone bought for the King's chamber, of Algar de Brige, 16*s.* 6*d.*; for two hundred weight three-quarters of free-stone, bought for the same, of Ralph de Lamberhurst, 16*s.* 6*d.* ; and for half a hundred weight of free-stone for the same bought of Richard de Croyden, 3*s.*; and for one hundred weight of free-stone for the laundry of the King's Court, bought of Randulph de Wautham, 6*s.*; and for half a hundred weight of free-stone for the same, bought of William de Bruge, 3*s.*; and for half a hundred of free-stone, for the same, bought of Peter de Mertsham, 3*s.*

Sum of the free-stone, 48s.

Lead, Ironwork.—And for four cart loads of lead bought at the fairs of Saint Botulf, by the hands of Richard Box of London, for the gutters of the King's great hall, and covering of the houses of the King's Court throughout, to be repaired, 8*l.* 8*s.* ; and for one hundred weight and a half of wrought iron bought at London, for the use of the chimney aforesaid, 25*s.*; and for three quarters of sea-coal to forge the iron for the aforesaid chimney, with the carriage and freight by water, 3*s.* 6*d.* ; and for 2000 iron nails, for the shingles bought at London of Henry de Bridge, 16*d.*

Sum, 9l. 17s. 10d.

Lime.—And for three hundred weight and a half of lime for the aforesaid chimney and laundry, bought of Agnes Calfonar of London, 17*s.* 6*d.*

Sand.—And to Richard de Celarer, for digging and carrying 36 cart-loads of sand, for the taskwork, 11*d.* ; and to Ralph de Bridge, for digging and carriage of as many cartloads of sand, for the taskwork, 11*d.*

Poles, Hurdles.—And to the relict of Richard de Eschep, for two dozen of hurdles and six bundles of poles, for making the scaffold for the chimney aforesaid; 5s. 3d.; and to Henry de Ponte, for six . . . and three . . 13d.; and to Richard le Cuver, for 3 buckets, 9d.

Sum, 26s. 5d.

Sum total of the third payment, 18l. 4s. 7½d.

4th Payment.—The fourth Payment was made from Thursday in the week of Pentecost, in the 43d year of King Henry, unto Sunday next before the Nativity of Saint John the Baptist, for fifteen days, and three days, including the Feast of Saint Barnabas the Apostle, by Tuesday, which was of the Lord the King, viz.

Masons.—To Richard de Eltham, a mason, for three days in the week of Pentecost, about the King's chimney, 2s. 3d.; and to William de Waudis, for the aforesaid three days, about the same, 3s.; and to Walter de Munden, for the same time, 13d.; and to Robert Piks, about the work of the chimney, for fifteen and three days, 5s. 1d.; and to Thomas de Kenefeg, about the same, for the same time, 5s. 1d.; and to Ralph de Waleden, for the same time, about the same, 5s. 1d.; and to Richard de Keruurth, for the same time, about the same, 5s. 1d.; and to Adam Fitz Warin, for four days, about the same, 17d.; and to John de Maldon, for the same time, 17d.; and to Gilbert Norman, for four days, about the same, 18d.; and to Walter de Waleden, for three days, about the same, 13d.; and to John Burglun, Philip de Hildesle, John le Harper, William de Hampton, Henry de Wautham, for fifteen days, about the same, 20s.—to wit, to each of those five, 4s.; and to Robert de Beverley, for one week, about the same, 2s. 6d.; and to Reginald Sturmy, for the same week, 22d.; and to Roger de Chichester, for one whole week, without a feast, 26d.

Bedders and Setters.—Viz. to William de Bledelawe, for fifteen days and three days, about the work of the chimney, 5s. 1d.;

E

and to Ralph de Oxford, for the week in which the feast happened and three days, 2*s.* 11*d.*; and to Henry de Biseber,
for the same time, 2*s.* 11*d.*; and to William de Bradele, for
the same time, 2*s.* 11*d.*; and to Bartholomew of Westminster, for one whole week, 26*d.*; and to William de Asscher,
for the same week, 26*d.*

Sum of the masons' wages, 76*s.* 9*d.*

Carpenters.—Viz. to William de Waudis, for fifteen days, about the
King's kitchen, and covering the gutter with boards, 4*s.*;
and to Henry de Knythebrige, for the same time, about
the same, 4*s.*; and to Odo, the carpenter, for three days,
about the same, 13*d.*; and to Roger Cornwus, for the same
time, 13*d.*

Sum of the carpenters, 10*s.* 2*d.*

Smiths.—And to Richard Smith, for the iron-work for the King's
chimney, for fifteen days and three days, 7*s.*; and to Richard
Smith, the younger, for one week, 22*d.*

Sum, 8*s.* 10*d.*

Taskwork.—Viz. to William de Thotull, upon taskwork, for
making the great kitchen sewer, 20*s.*; and to William de
Midhurst and his companions, for the carriage of free-stones,
cut for the King's chimney, 15*d.*; and to William de Cluse,
for making and mending the masons' hammers, for the time
preceding, 3*s.* 5½*d.*; and to William de Garden, for attending on the three feast days to receive the necessary materials
for the works aforesaid, 6*d.*

Sum, 25*s.* 2½*d.*

Labourers.—And to labourers helping the aforesaid masons
and carpenters, for the time aforesaid, viz. to Simon le Scaf-
folder, for three days, within the week of Pentecost, about the
scaffold for the King's chimney, 9*d.*; and to Walter Fitz
Elie, Martin William Millers, for one week and three days

helping at the chimney aforesaid, 5*s.*—to wit, to each of those three, 20*d.*; and to Roger de Chering, Geoffery Wrenn, Durand de Eye, Hugh de Berking, Thomas de Eye, and William de Feckam, who made the foundation of the great sewer aforesaid, for the time aforesaid, 17*s.* 6*d.*—to each of the aforesaid six, 2*s.* 11*d.*; and to Robert de Oxford, William Welbilove, Robert Chubbe, Stephen de Garden, John Malekin, Simon Russell, helping the masons and carpenters for the aforesaid fifteen days, 13*s.* 9*d.*—to wit, to each of those five, 2*s.* 3½*d.*; and to William de Coffle, John Mityng, William de Hendone, Robert de Eye, Walter de Brewer, John Cook, Richard de Hampslap, Hugh de Notyngham, John Havelove, William de Guldebury, John de Essex, Thomas de Thotull, for one week drawing the roller, to level the area of the garden near the cistern, 15*s.*—to wit, to each of those twelve, 15*d.*; and to William de Enefeud, Ely le Breveter, for two days, 5*d.*—to wit, to each of them, 2½*d.*, by the day; and to John Porter, for three days, 7½*d.*; and to Master Warin of London, with his three men, to clean the Queen's outer chambers, and those of the stewards in the King's Court, for four days, 4*s.* 5*d.*

Sum of the workmen's wages, 57s. 5½d.

Free-stone.—And for two hundred weight and a half of free-stone, for the chimney, cistern, and laundry, bought of Algar de Bruge, 15*s.*; and for one hundred weight and a half of free-stone, bought of Ralph de Lamberhurst, 9*s.*; and for one hundred weight and a half of free-stone, for the same, bought of William de Bruge, 9*s.*

Sum of the free-stone, 33s.

Grey-stone.—And for a vessel load of grey-stone, for the use of the great gutter, bought of Richard le Fort, 6*s.*; and for a ship-load of grey-stone, for the same, bought of Matthew de Ponte, 6*s.* 6*d.*

Sum of the grey-stone 12s. 6d.

Lime, Sand.—And to Agnes Calfonar, for 300 weight of lime
for the use of the sewer aforesaid and cistern, 15*s.*; and to
Ralph de Ponte, for twenty-five cart-loads of sand, carted
by task-work, 7⅝*d.*; to the same for seventy-three cart-loads
of sand, carried by taskwork, 19*d.*; and for mortar, lime, and
sand, bought of Master Hugh of Saint Alban, a monk, 3*s.*
                                        Sum, 20*s.* 2¼*d.*

Ironwork.—And to William de Cluse, for a certain ironwork for a
certain window in the King's kitchen, 26*d.*; and for three new
keys bought; for the amendment of certain locks in the King's
Court, 8*d.*; and to Henry of London Bridge, for 3000 nails
for laths, and 500 great nails for the use of the King's kitchen,
4*s.* 4*d.*; and for nineteen pounds of pitch and five pounds of
wax, bought for the use of the cistern of the King's Court,
14*s.* 1*d.*; and for half a hundred weight of charcoal, for mending the cistern, 7*d.*
                                        Sum, 21*s.* 9*d.*

Timber.—And for eighteen great pieces of oak, bought at Kyngeston, for the use of the outer chamber constructed in the King's
Court, 19*s.* 3¼*d.*; and for thirteen smaller pieces of oak for
the same, then bought there, 8*s.* 8¼*d.*; and for the carriage
of the aforesaid timber from Kyngeston to Westminster, 2*s.*
                              Sum of the timber, 30*s.*
    Sum total of the fourth Payment, 14*l.* 15*s.* 10¼*d.*

5th Payment.—The fifth payment was made from Monday on
the eve of the Nativity of Saint John the Baptist, in the 43rd
year of King Henry aforesaid, unto Sunday in the feast of
the Apostles Peter and Paul—to wit, for one week, containing the aforesaid feast of Saint John; which was for the carpenters.

Carpenters.—And to William de Waudis, Henry de Knythebruge,
    Odo Roger of Westminster, Simon de Northampton, Roger

Cornwus, carpenters, beginning to work about the construction of the outer chamber in the King's Court, for the same week, 13*s*.—to each of the aforesaid six, 26*d*.

Sum of the carpenters, 13*s*.

Plumbers.—And to William de Strande, for three weeks, about repairing the conduit of the laundry and cistern, 8*s*. 6*d*. ; and to John Govayr, for one day, 6*d*. ; and to John, his man, for three weeks, 4*s*. 3*d*. ; and to Simon le Plummer, for four days, 12*d*.

Sum, 14*s*. 3*d*.

Painters.—And to Richard Painter, for painting the wall on each side of the King's chimney, for nine days, 4*s*. 6*d*. ; and to John de Radinge, for eight days, about the same, 4*s*. ; and to Dendone, for fifteen days, about the same, 3*s*. 6*d*; and to a certain boy, preparing the colours for the aforesaid painters, for one week, 10*d*. ; and for divers colours bought for the same, 11*s*. 7*d*·

Sum, 24*s*. 5*d*.

Labourers.—And to five workmen helping the carpenters for the aforesaid week ; viz. to Walter Norris, William de Scyreburne, Stephen de Garden, John Porter, Durand de Eye, 5*s*. 2½*d*. —to wit, to each of them 12½*d*. ; and to eleven workmen for digging the foundation of the great sewer ; viz. to Roger de Chering, Geoffery Wrenn, Hugh de Berkyng, William de Feckam, Thomas de Eye, Philip de Turfeye, Adam de Diddewrth, Robert de Oxford, Hugh de Notyngham, John de Chelchuth, John de Essex, for the aforesaid week, 11*s*. 5½*d*.—to wit, to each of them, 12½*d*.

And to John Miting, Walter de Brewer, John Havelove, Thomas de Thotull, Roger de Knarebury, for four days about the same, and levelling the area of the garden with a roller, 4*s*. 2*d*.—to wit, to each of those five, 10*d*. ; and to William Fayrwife, Nicholas de York, Hugh le Paumer, Philip Fitz

William, Giles of Essex, for three days about the same,
3*s.* 1¼*d.*, to each of the aforesaid five, 7¼*d.*

　　　　　　Sum of the workmen, 23*s.* 11¼*d.*

Taskwork.—Viz., to William de Thotull, for the preparation of the
taskwork for the great gutter, which contained 16 perches and a
half, whereof he took for a perch of twenty feet, 3*s.* 4*d.*,—35*s.*

And to John Ginger and his companions for the carriage of free-
stone, the same for taskwork, 4*s.* 2*d.*; and to Ralph de Ponte,
for the carriage of half a hundred cart-loads of sand for the
taskwork, 18*d.*

　　　　　　Sum, 40*s.* 8*d.*

Grey-stone.—And for one ship-load of grey-stone for making
the gutter and quay under the aforesaid outer chamber,
bought of Ely de Meletone, 6*s.* 6*d.*; and for a ship-load of
grey-stone, for the same, bought of Henry Eldegrome, 5*s.*;
and to Alured de Strode for a ship-load of grey-stone for the
same, 6*s.*; and for a ship-load of grey-stone for the same,
bought of Robert Scyrlok, 6*s.*; and for a ship-load of grey-
stone for the same, bought of Richard Forti, 6*s.*

　　　　　　Sum of the grey-stone, 29*s.* 6*d.*

Chalk.—And for a ship-load of chalk for the same, bought of
Ely de Meletone, 2*s.* 4*d.*; and for a ship-load of chalk for the
same, bought of Hamond le Cogger, 2*s.* 7*d.*; and for a ship-
load of chalk for the same, bought of Thomas Long, 2*s.* 7*d.*;
and for two ship-loads of chalk, bought of Richard de Denyn-
tone, 4*s.* 4*d.*

　　　　　　Sum of white chalk, 11*s.* 10*d.*

Lime.—And for one hundred weight and three quarters of lime, for
the use of the gutter and quay aforesaid, bought of Richard
Calfonar, of London, 8*s.* 9*d.*; and for 300 weight of lime,
bought, for the same, of Agnes Calfonar, 15*s.*

　　　　　　Sum of the lime, 23*s.* 9*d.*

Ironwork.—And to Henry of London Bridge, for 8000 nails, for the laths, from him bought, 6*s.*; to the same, for 500 great nails, 20*d.*; also to the same, for 4000 and a half of nails, for the shingles, 3*s.* 9*d.*; and to Richard le Cuver, for the repair of the tools, 13*d.*

Sum, 12s. 6d.

Timber.—Viz. for forty-one pieces of oak, bought at Kingston, for the use of the outer chamber of the King's Court, 21*s.* 10*d.*; and for forty-nine small boards for the same, bought there, 13*d.*; and for three great posts of oak for the same, bought there, 7*s.* 6*d.*; and for the carriage of the aforesaid timber by water to Westminster, 2*s.*; and for 10,000 shingles, bought for the use of the aforesaid chamber, and for covering the King's kitchens, 70*s.*, price of the thousand, 7*s.*; and for the carriage of the aforesaid shingles by water from Kingston to Westminster, 6*s.* 1*d.*

Sum, 108s. 6d.

Sum total of the fifth payment, £15. 2*s.* 4½*d.*

6th Payment.—The sixth payment was made from Monday on the Morrow of the Apostles Peter and Paul, in the 43d year of King Henry aforesaid, unto Sunday on the Eve of the Translation of Saint Thomas the Martyr, for one whole week, viz. without a feast intervening.

Carpenters.—Viz. to five carpenters, working about the carpentry of the aforesaid outer chamber in the King's Court, to William de Waudis, Henry de Knythbrige, Roger of Westminster, Simon de Northampton, Roger Cornwus, for the aforesaid week, 10*s.* 10*d.*—to wit, to each of them, 26*d.*

Sum of the carpenters, 10s. 10d.

Labourers.—And to the labourers assisting the aforesaid carpenters, for the same time; viz. to Stephen de Garden, Roger de Chering, 25*d.*—to wit, to each of them 12½*d.*; and to five workmen drawing the roller to level the area of the gard-

about the cistern ; viz. to Geoffery Wrenn, Thomas de Eye,
John Malekyn, Adam de Diddeuurth, Robert de Sidwod, for
five days, 5*s.* 2½*d.*—to wit, to each of them 12½*d.*

Sum of the workmen, 7*s.* 3¼*d.*

Grey-stone.—And for a ship-load of grey-stone, for making the
aforesaid gutter and quay, bought of Matthew de Ponte,
6*s.* 6*d.* ; and for a ship-load of grey-stone for the same,
bought of Robert Scyrlok, 6*s.* ; and for a ship-load of grey-
stone for the same, bought of Philip de Ponte, 5*s.* 6*d.*

Sum of the grey-stone, 18*s.*

Lime.—And for one hundred weight one-quarter of lime, bought of
Richard Calfonar, of London, for the use of the aforesaid sewer
and quay under the aforesaid outer chamber, 6*s.* 3*d.* ; and for
twenty-nine pieces of oak, for the use of the same chamber,
bought at Kyngeston, 12*s.* 9*d.* ; and for the carriage of the
said timber by water to Westminster from Kyngeston, 2*s.*

Sum of the lime and timber, 21*s.*

Sum total of the sixth payment, 57*s.* 1½*d.*

7th Payment.—The seventh payment was made from Monday on
the feast of the Translation of Saint Thomas the Martyr, in
the 43d year of King Henry aforesaid, unto Sunday in the
feast of the Blessed Margaret the Virgin,—to wit, for fifteen
days, containing the aforesaid feast of St. Thomas, which was
of the Lord the King.

Masons.—To three masons cutting at the quay aforesaid for the
same fifteen days ; viz. to Richard de Colecester, Gervase
de Westminster, Henry Wytinge, 12*s.*,—to wit, to each of
them, 4*s.* ; and to Guydo de Brun, for the first week, 22*d.*

Sum of the plasterers, 13*s.* 10*d.*

Carpenters.—And to five carpenters, viz. to William de Waudis,
Henry de Knythebruge, Roger de Westminster, Simon de

Northampton, Roger Cornwus, working about the carpentry
of the aforesaid outer chamber, and putting the shingles
upon the King's kitchen, 20s.,—to wit, to each of the aforesaid five, 4s.

Sum of the carpenters, 20s.

Labourers.—And to five labourers assisting the aforesaid masons
and carpenters; viz. to Stephen de Garden, Roger de Chering, Geoffrey Wrenn, William de Gildesbury, Robert de
Sidwode, for the aforesaid fifteen days, 11s. 5½d.—to wit, to
each of them, 27½d.; and to five workmen, viz. to Nicholas
de St. Sepulchre, Thomas de Eye, Thomas Clerk, Walter de
Brewer, Walter Scales, working for two days, 25d.—to wit, to
each of them, 5d.; and to Gerard de Bisele, for repairing
the Queen's outer chamber, 12d.

And to seven workmen who unloaded a vessel of timber for the
use of the aforesaid common outer chamber, and carried the
same to the hands of the carpenters, 17½d.

Sum of the workmen, 16s.

Taskwork.—And to William de Thotull, on taskwork, for his
labour about the quay under the outer chamber, 10s.; and to
William de Bledelawe, with one workman, for one day's labour
about the cistern in the King's Court, 6½d.; and for the arrears
of two carpenters, for one day working in the King's kitchen,
6d.; and for the arrears of one workman, for three days about
the work of the chimney in the week of Pentecost, 7½d.;
and for cleaning of the Queen's outer chamber at one time
by two workmen, 5d.; and to William de Cluse, for the
making of the masons' hammers, 17d.; and to Richard de
Celarer, for carrying sand, for fifteen days, 3s. 8d.

Sum of taskwork, 17s. 2d.

Free-stone—And for four hundred weight and three quarters of
free-stone for the use of the quay aforesaid, bought of Ralph
de Lamher, 28s. 6d.

Sum, 28s. 6d.

Grey-stone.—And for a ship-load of grey-stone, for the use of the
gutter and quay aforesaid, bought of Philip de Ponte,
5*s.* 6*d.*; and for a ship-load of grey-stone for the same,
bought of Robert Scyrlok, 6*s.*

Lime.—And to Agnes Calfonar, of London, for one hundred
weight and one quarter of lime, bought for the use of the
aforesaid quay, 6*s.* 3*d.*; and to Richard Calfonar, of London,
for one quarter of lime, bought for the same, 15*d.*; and to
Ralph de Ponte, for carrying the sand for roughstone,
16*d.*; and for one lock bought for the use of the King's
Court, 6*d.*

Sum of the grey-stone, &c., 20s. 10d.

Timber.—And for twenty-nine pieces of oak, for the use of the aforesaid outer chamber, bought at Kingston, 8*s.* 11*d.*; and for 500
laths for the same, bought there, 3*s.*; and for the carriage
of the aforesaid timber by water from Kyngeston to Westminster, 2*s.*

Sum of the timber, 13s. 11d.

Sum total of the seventh payment, 6l. 10s. 3d.

8th Payment.—The eighth payment was made on Monday, in the
feast of Saint Margaret the Virgin, in the 43rd year of King
Henry aforesaid, unto Sunday next after the feast of Saint
Peter ad vincula, for the fifteen days containing the feast of
Saint Mary Magdalen by Tuesday, which was for the masons
and carpenters, and the feast of Saint James for Friday,
which was for the Lord the King, and the aforesaid feast of
Saint Peter by Friday in like manner, which was for the
masons and carpenters.

Masons.—Viz. to Richard de Colecester, for nine days cutting at
the quay aforesaid, 2*s.* 10*d.*; and to Guydo de Brun, for one
day about the same, 4*d.*; and to Richard de Eynesham, for
one day working in the King's Court to repair certain places,
22*d.*; and to Gervase de Westminster, for the aforesaid fifteen

days cutting at the aforesaid quay, 4s.; and to Henry.
Wyting, for the same time, about the same, 4s.

Sum of the plasterers, 13s.

Carpenters.—And to five carpenters, viz. to William de Waudis,
Henry de Knythbrige, Roger of Westminster, Simon de
Northampton, Roger Cornwus, working about the outer
chamber, and putting the shingles on the King's kitchens, 20s.
—to wit, to each of the aforesaid five, 4s.; and to Reginald de
Estwik, Thomas de Wyndesor, about the same for the same
time, 7s. 4d.—to wit, to each of them, 3s. 8d.; and to Richard
le Cuver, for one week about the same, 22d.; and to Gilbert
de Guldeford, about the same for 4 days, 14d.

Sum of the carpenters, 30s. 4d.

Labourers.—And to workmen helping the aforesaid masons and
carpenters for the aforesaid fifteen days, viz. to Stephen de
Garden, Roger de Chering, Robert de Sydwod, 5s 7½d.—
to wit, to each of the aforesaid three, 22½d.; and to William
de Guldeburg, for four days, 10d.; and to William de
Feckam, for one week, 12½d.

Sum of the labourers, 7s. 6d.

Taskwork.—Viz. to William de Thotull, for the preparation by
taskwork for labour at the quay with free-stone, 10s.; also to
the same William, upon taskwork, for the drain round the
laundry to be made in the King's Court, 7s. 6d.

And to two painters, for the arrears of one day's work on the
walls to be painted round the King's chimney, 12d.

And to William de Cluse, for making and mending the masons'
hammers, 6d.

And to Ralph de Ponte, with his carter, carrying the sand, for
five days, 20d.

Sum of taskwork, 20s. 8d.

Free-stone.—Viz. for one hundred weight of free-stone, for the use of the quay, aforesaid, bought of Richard de Croiden, 6*s.*; and for one hundred weight one quarter of free-stone for the same, bought of William de Bruge, 7*s.* 6*d.*; and for one quarter of free-stone for the same, bought of Randulph de Regat, 18*d.*; and for one quarter of free-stone for the same, bought of Ralph de Lamher, 18*d.*   Sum, 16*s.* 6*d.*

Lime.—And for one hundred weight of lime for the use of the aforesaid quay, bought of Richard Calfonar, 5*s.*; and for two hundred weight of lime for the same, bought of Agnes Calfonar, 10*s.*

                  Sum of the lime, 15*s.*

Boards.—And for 100 of great boards straightened, for mending and repairing the great gutter of the King's hall, 14*s.* 8*d.*

Ironwork.—And for 2000 nails for the laths, and half a hundred door nails, bought of Henry de Ponte, of London, 3*s.* 6*d.*

                  Sum, 18*s.* 2*d.*

Sum total of the eighth payment, 6*l.* 14*d.*

9th Payment.—The ninth payment was made from Monday next after the feast of Saint Peter ad vincula, in the 43rd year of King Henry aforesaid, unto Sunday in the feast of Saint Lawrence the Martyr, for one week without a feast.

Carpenters.—And to eight carpenters, viz. to William de Waudis, Henry de Knythbridge, Roger of Westminster, Simon de Northampton, Roger Cornwus, Reginald de Estwik, Gilbert de Guldeford, Richard le Cuver, working about the common outer chamber in the King's Court, and putting the shingles on the King's kitchens, for the aforesaid week, 17*s.* 4*d.*—to wit, to each of the aforesaid eight, 26*d.*; and to. Robert de Aldebury, for the same time, about the same, 18*d.*

          Sum of the carpenters, 18*s.* 10*d.*

Labourers.—And to three labourers, viz. Stephen de Garden, Hugh de Berking, Thomas de Eye, helping the carpenters for the same week, 3s. 9d.—to wit, to each of them, 15d.; and to three labourers, viz. to Robert de Oxford, John Porter, and John de Oxford, for three days moving the earth from the quay aforesaid, 22½d.—to wit, to each of those three, 7½d.; and to Gerard de Biseley, for repairing the outer chamber of the Lady the Queen at one time, 6d.

Sum of the workmen, 6s. 1½d.
Sum total of the ninth payment, 24s. 11½d.

10*th Payment.*—The tenth payment was made from Monday on the morrow of Saint Laurence the Martyr, in the 43rd year of King Henry aforesaid, unto Sunday in the feast of Saint Bartholomew the Apostle—to wit, for fifteen days, containing the feast of the Assumption of the Blessed Mary by Friday, which was for the carpenters.

Carpenters.—Viz. to nine carpenters, William de Waudis, Henry de Knythbrige, Roger de Westminster, Simon de North-ampton, Roger Cornwus, Reginald Estwyk, Gilbert de Guldeford, Richard le Cuver, Thomas de Wyndesor, working about the construction of the outer chamber, and putting the shingles on the King's kitchens, for the aforesaid fifteen days, 39s.—to wit, to each of them, 4s. 4d.; and to Robert de Aldebury, about the same, for the aforesaid time, 3s.

Sum of the carpenters, 42s.

Labourers.—And to two labourers helping the carpenters for the aforesaid fifteen days—to wit, to Stephen de Garden and Roger de Chering, 4s. 7d.—to wit, to each of them, 27½d.; and to Hugh de Berking, for one week and one day about preparing the foundation of the outer chamber of the King's Court, 17½d.; and to Thomas de Eye, for one week about the same, 15d.; and to Robert de Oxford, John Porter, and

John Oxford, about the same for three days, 22½d.—to wit, to each of those three, 7½d.

> Sum of the labourers, 9s. 2d.

Taskwork.—And to William de Thotull, for the preparation by taskwork for the sewer or drain about the laundry in the King's Court, 7s. 6d.; also to the same William for the carriage of sand for the use of the aforesaid sewer, 4s. 5½d.

> Sum, 11s. 11½d.

Lime.—And for one quarter of lime, for the use of the sewer about the laundry, bought of Agnes Calfonar, of London, 15d.

Timber.—And for 100 great boards for the aforesaid outer chamber, bought at Kyngston, 12s. 6d.; and for 200 laths of oak for the same, bought there, 16d.

Ironwork.—And for 200 and a half of iron nails for the planks, and 3000 nails for the shingles, and 2000 nails for the laths for the use of the aforesaid chamber and kitchen of the King, 8s. 6d.; and for two new locks bought for the Treasury door, 12d.; and for one tin lamp, for preserving a certain wax light in the chapel of Saint Stephen, by command of the Lord the King, 16d.

> Sum total of the tenth payment, 4l. 9s. 0½d.

11*th Payment.*—The eleventh payment was made from Monday on the morrow of the Blessed Apostle Bartholomew, in the 43rd year of the reign of Henry aforesaid, unto Sunday in the eve of Saint Giles—to wit, for one week, containing the feast of the Beheading of Saint John the Baptist by Friday, which was of the Lord the King.

Carpenters.—To nine carpenters, viz. to William de Waudis, Henry de Knythebrige, Roger de Westminster, Simon de

Northampton, Roger Cornwus, Reginald de Estwik, Gilbert de Gudeford, Richard le Cuver, Thomas de Wyndesor, for the aforesaid week, working about the aforesaid outer chamber, and putting the shingles on the King's kitchens, 16*s*. 6*d*.—to wit, to each of the aforesaid, 22*d*.; and to Robert de Aldebury, about the same, for the same week, 15*d*.

Sum of the carpenters, 17*s*. 9*d*.

Labourers.—And to two rlabourers, viz. to Stephen de Garden, Roger de Chering, helping the aforesaid carpenters for the aforesaid week, 25*d*.—to wit, to each of them 12½*d*.

Sum of the labourers, 25*d*.

Sum total of the eleventh payment, 19*s*. 10*d*.

12th Payment.—The twelfth payment was made from Monday, in the feast of Saint Giles, in the 43rd year of King Henry aforesaid, unto Sunday in the eve of the translation of Saint Edward the King for six weeks, containing the feast of the Nativity of the Blessed Mary to Monday, which was for the carpenters, and the feast of Saint Michael by Monday, in like manner, which was of the Lord the King's.

Bedders.—Viz. to Robert Busch, bedder, for five weeks, working about the sewer from the Queen's outer chamber unto the Thames, 10*s*. 2*d*.; and to Ralph de Oxford, for one whole week about the same, 26*d*.; and to Richard de Bureford, for four weeks about the same, 8*s*.; and to Geoffry de Pire, for two days about the same, 8½*d*.; and to Hugh de Merthon, for four weeks about the same, 7*s*. 8*d*.; and to Robert le Blund, for four days about the same, 17*d*.; and to Richard de Eynesham, for three weeks about the same, 6*s*. 6½*d*.; and to Roger de Essex, for fifteen days about the same, 3*s*. 8*d*.

Sum of the bedders, 40*s*. 4*d*.

Carpenters.—And to six carpenters, viz. to Simon de Northampton, William de Waudis, Henry de Knythebruge,

Roger Cornwus, Reginald de Estwik, Richard le Cuver, for
six weeks working about the aforesaid outer chamber, and
putting the shingles on the king's kitchens, 76s.—to wit, to
each of the aforesaid six, 12s. 8d.; and to Robert de Aldebury, for the same time, 8s. 9d.; and to Roger de Westminster and Thomas de Wyndesor, for five weeks, about the
same, 21s.—to wit, to each of them, 10s. 6d.; and to Gilbert de Guldeford, for three days, about the same, 13d.

Sum of the carpenters, 106s. 10d.

Painters.—And to Master William Painter, with his men, designing the picture of Jesse on the mantel of the king's
chimney, and for renovating and cleaning a painting on the
wall of the King's said chamber, 43s. 10d.; and for divers
colours bought for the same, 7s. 6d.

Plumbers.—And to three plumbers, for one week and three days,
about repairing the gutter of the King's hall, and stopping
up the holes above the steward's chamber, 6s. 3d.

Sum, 57s. 7d.

Labourers.—And to two labourers helping the carpenters for the
aforesaid time, viz. to Stephen de Garden, Roger de Chering, 14s. 2d.—to wit, to each of them, for the six weeks
aforesaid, 7s. 1d.; and to three workmen, viz. to Walter de
Neuport, Gerard de Biseley, William de Perham, for five
weeks helping the aforesaid bedders, 17s. 6d.—to wit, to
each of the aforesaid three, 5s. 10d.; and to Richard de
Lichefeud, for four weeks and two days about the same, 5s.;
and to Adam Miting, and to Simon Russell, for three weeks
about the same, 9s. 2d.—to wit, to each of them, 4s. 7d.;
and to John de Eynesham, for three weeks and two days
about the same, 3s. 10½d.; and to Fulk, for one week, with
a feast, 12½d.

Sum of the labourers, 50s. 9d.

Taskwork.—And for four perches of a certain brick wall, constructed to close up the way between the aforesaid outer chamber and the cloister of the King's chaplains, 3*s.* 6*d.*

Plumbers.—And to John Govayr and his companion, for laying and placing five fothers of lead in the gutter of the King's great hall, 25*s.*

And to three carpenters, for the arrears of one day's work, 12*d.*; and to Ralph le Verjur, for two days, 4½*d.*

Sand.—And to Richard Curteys, for 200 cart-loads and a half of sand for taskwork, 3*s.* 6*d.*; and for the hire of his cart for five days, 27*d.*; and to Richard de Celarer for 100 cart-loads of sand for taskwork, 2*s.*; to the same, for his cart with two horses at work for four days, 2*s.*; and to Walter de Chambers, for 100 cart-loads of sand for taskwork, 2*s.*; to the same for his cart for two days work, 8*d.* And to fifteen labourers, with two carmen daily, for fifteen days about cutting and turfing the grass of the Lord the King, 22*s.* 11*d.*

Sum, 65s. 2¼d.

Grey-stone.—The first week, for a ship-load of grey-stone, for the aforesaid gutter, bought of William Prudfot, 5*s.* 9*d.*; and for a ship load of grey-stone for the same, bought of Edmund Fitz Ralph, 5*s.* 9*d.*; and for a ship-load of grey-stone for the same, bought of Henry Muriweder, 5*s.* 9*d.*; and for a ship-load of grey-stone, for the same, bought of Robert de Hakeford, 5*s.* 9*d.*; and for a ship-load of grey-stone, for the same, bought of Richard Makevayr, 4*s.* 6*d.*

Sum, 27s. 6d.

Iron-work.—And to Henry de Ponte, for 7000 iron nails for the shingles for the covering of the King's aforesaid outer chamber,

F

and for putting the shingles on the kitchens, 10s. 6d.; to
the same, for 2000 nails for the laths for the same, 2s.

Sum, 12s. 6d.

Grey-stone.—Also, the second week, for a ship-load of grey-stone,
bought of William Prudfot, for the aforesaid gutter, 5s. 9d.;
and for a ship-load of grey-stone, bought of Edmund Fitz-
Ralph, 5s. 9d.; and for a ship-load of grey-stone for the
same, bought of Richard Fitz Jocelin, 4s. 6d.; and for two
ship-loads of white chalk for the same, bought of John
Eldegrom, 2s. 6d.

Sum, 18s. 6d.

Timber.—And for eighteen rafters and sixteen wedges of oak, for
the use of the aforesaid outer chamber, 8s. 6½d.; and for 200
rushes for strengthening the brick wall before the outer chamber
aforesaid, bought at Wytheflet, with the carriage by water to
Westminster, 2s.; and for litter to make the said wall, 6d.

Sum, 11s. 0¼d.

Ironwork.—And for 6000 tenails, for the use of the aforesaid
chamber and King's kitchens, 8s., price of the thousand,
16d.; and for 200 great nails for the planks, 3s. 2d.; and
for 4000 roof nails for the same, 6s. 8d.; and for 2000 nails
for the laths of oak, 2s.; and for 2000 nails for the laths of
deal, 22d.; and for 200 tenails, 6d.

Sum, 22s. 2d.

Also the fourth week, for 1000 laths of oak, bought of William de
Braye, 8s. 8d.; and for 4000 plain tiles and 100 and a half
of pantiles, for the covering of the houses of the King's
Court, 13s. 8d.

Also the fifth week, for 200 weight and a half of chalk for the
gutter of the outer chamber, bought at London, 12s. 6d.;

and for 2000 tenails and 2000 nails for the laths, bought of Henry of London Bridge, 4s. 8d.; and for 4000 forged nails for the pantiles, 7½d.; and for two new keys, bought with the reparation of certain locks of the King's Court, 20¼d.

Also the sixth week, for 500 tiles, bought of William de Smethefeud, 18d.; and to Henry of London Bridge, for 1500 nails for the shingles, 2s. 3d.

Sum, 45s. 7d.

Sum total of the twelfth payment, 22l. 18s.

13th Payment.—The thirteenth payment was made from Monday, in the feast of the translation of Saint Edward the king, in the 43rd year of the reign of King Henry aforesaid, unto Sunday next before the feast of the Apostles Simon and Jude (to wit), for fifteen days, containing the aforesaid feast of Saint Edward, which was for the carpenters; and the feast of St. Luke the Evangelist by Saturday, which was the Lord the King's.

Carpenters.—To three carpenters, viz., to Wiiliam de Waudis, Roger Cornwus, Henry de Knythebruge, about covering the King's kitchens, for the aforesaid fifteen days, 12s.; to wit, to each of the aforesaid three, 4s., and to Robert de Aldebury for the same time, 2s. 9d.

Sum of the carpenters, 14s. 9d.

Plumbers.—And to John le Plumber, working for two days, about mending the defects of the lead work beyond the steward's chamber, 8¼d.

Labourers.—And to two men helping the aforesaid carpenters and plumbers for the aforesaid time, viz., to Stephen de Garden, Roger de Chering, 4s. 2d.—to wit, to each of them 25d. for the fifteen days.

Sum, 4s. 10½d.

Ironwork.—And for 2000 great nails for the laths, and 1000

small nails for the same, bought of Henry of London
Bridge, 4s.; and for 6000 nails for the shingles for the use
of the King's kitchens, bought of the same person, 6s.

Sum, 10s.

Sum total of the thirteenth payment, 29s. 7½d.

14th Payment.—Payment the fourteenth was made from Monday,
on the eve of the Apostles Simon and Jude, in the 43rd year
of King Henry aforesaid, unto Sunday next after the feast
of Saint Martin, for three weeks, containing the aforesaid
feast of the aforesaid apostles, by Tuesday, which was for the
plasterers and carpenters; and the feast of All Saints by
Saturday, which was of the Lord the King; and the feast of
Saint Martin by Tuesday likewise, which was for the plasterers and carpenters.

Masons.—To masons working about the window in the house of
the Jews, viz., to John de Oxford, for three days, 6s. 2d.;
and to three masons, viz., to Richard de Chichester, John de
Eltham, Reginald Sturmy, for one week cutting at the same
window, 6s. 6d.—to wit, to each of those three, 26d.

Sum of the masons, 12s. 8d.

Carpenters.—And to three carpenters, viz., to William de Waudis,
Henry de Knythebridge, Roger Cornwus, for three weeks'
working about the shingles of the King's kitchens, 18s. 6d.,
to wit, to each of those three, 6s. 2d.; and to Robert de
Aldebury for the same time, 4s. 3d.; and to Gilbert Carpenter, John de Greneford, John de Padinton, for fifteen days,
about the same, 13s.—to wit, to each of those three, 4s. 4d.

Sum of the carpenters, 35s. 9d.

Smiths.—And to smiths, about making the ironwork which up-
held the shaft outside the kitchen of the King's chamber
against the force of the winds, viz., to Master Henry de

Lewes for the aforesaid three weeks, about making the aforesaid ironwork, 12*s*.; and to Simon the smith, for the same
time, 6*s*. 2*d*. ; and to William de Offinton, for the same time,
about the same, 4*s*. 3*d*.; and to Thorand, for the same time,
about the same, 4*s*. 9*d*.

Sum, 27*s*. 2*d*.

Labourers.—And to two labourers, viz., to Stephen de Garden
and Roger de Chering, helping the aforesaid masons and
carpenters, for the aforesaid three weeks, 6*s*. 3*d*.—to wit, to
each of them 3*s*. 1½*d*.; and to John Churant for four days,
10*d*.

Sum of the labourers, 7*s*. 1*d*.

Ironwork.—And for 2000 small nails for the laths, and 1000 large
nails for the same, 3*s*. 6*d*.; also for 4500 nails for the laths,
5*s*. ; and for 2000 great nails, and 300 and a half of nails
for the shingles, 9*s*. 0½*d*.; and for a certain new lock with a
key, for a certain door in the King's Court, 18*d*.

Sum, 19*s*. 0½*d*.

Sum total of the fourteenth payment, 101*s*. 8½*d*.

15*th Payment*.—The fifteenth payment was made from Monday
next after the feast of Saint Martin, in the 44th year of
King Henry aforesaid, unto Sunday in the feast of Saint
Andrew the Apostle, for fifteen days, containing the feast of
Saint Edward the King and Martyr, to Thursday, which was
of the Lord the King, and the feast of Saint Catherine the
Virgin, by Tuesday, which was for the masons and carpenters.

Masons.—Viz., to John de Oxford, working about the window
and benches in the house of the Jews, and for raising the
steps on the one part in the steward's chamber, for the aforesaid fifteen days, 4*s*.; and to Richard de Colecester, for one
week about the same, 2*s*.; and to Bartholomew de Westminster, for one week about the same, 2*s*.

Sum of the masons, 8*s*.

Carpenters.—And to six carpenters, viz., to William de Waudis, Roger Cornwus, Henry de Knithebruge, Gilbert Carpenter, John de Greneford, John de Padinton, for the aforesaid fifteen days, about repairing the King's kitchens and the seat of the Justices of the Bench, 24*s.*, to each of the aforesaid six, 4*s.*; and to Robert de Aldebury for the same time, 2*s.* 9*d.*

Sum of the carpenters, 26*s.* 9*d.*

Smiths.—And to Master Henry de Lewes, for making the iron-work for the chimney, for the aforesaid fifteen days, 8*s.*; and to Simon Smith, for the same time, 4*s.*; and to William de Offinton, for the same time, 2*s.* 9*d.*; and to Thorand, for the same time, 3*s.* 1*d.*; and to the aforesaid smiths for their diligence by night, for one month, about expediting the afore-said ironwork, 6*s.* 8*d.*

Sum of the smiths, 24*s.* 6*d.*

Labourers.—And to labourers helping the aforesaid masons and carpenters, for the aforesaid time, viz., to Stephen de Garden, for the same time, 25*d.*; and to Roger de Chering, for the same time, 25*d.*; and to three workmen, viz., to Walter de Saint Alban, William Millers, and John de Strande, helping and making a scaffold to fix the aforesaid ironwork, for one week, 3*s.* 1½*d.*—to wit, to each of them, 12½*d.*; and to two sawyers, viz., to William de Scyreburn, Walter Norris, for one week and four days, 3*s.* 9*d.*

Sum, 11*s.* 0½*d.*

Plumbers.—And to John Govair and William de Strande, for founding and laying eight fothers of lead above the steward's chamber, by taskwork, 40*s.*, taking for each fother 5*s.*; and to William de Cluse upon taskwork, for making the iron-work for the window of the Jews' house, with amend-ment of certain other things, 4*s.*; and for the cart of Master Odo for one day's work at the underwood, and carrying the lead, 6*d.*

Sum, 44*s.* 6*d.*

Sum total of the fifteenth payment, 114*s.* 9½*d.*

16th *Payment.*—The sixteenth payment was made from Monday
on the morrow of Saint Andrew the Apostle, in the 44th
year of the reign of the aforesaid King Henry, unto Sunday
on the morrow of Saint Lucy the Virgin, to wit, for fifteen
days, containing the feast of Saint Nicholas on Saturday, which
was of the Lord the King, and the feast of the Conception
of Saint Mary on Monday, which was for the carpenters.

Carpenters.—To six carpenters working about the seat of the
Justices of the Bench and putting the shingles on the King's
kitchens, viz., to William de Waudis, Roger de Westminster,
Roger Cornwus, Gilbert Carpenter, Henry de Knithbrige,
and to John de Padinton, for the aforesaid fifteen days, 24*s.*—
to wit, to each of those six, 4*s.* ; and to John de Greneford,
for one week, 22*d.* ; and to Robert de Aldebury, for fifteen
days, 2*s.* 9*d.*

Sum of the carpenters, 28*s.* 7*d.*

Masons.—And to John de Oxford, for the aforesaid fifteen days,
about raising the aforesaid steps, 4*s.* ; and to John le Plummer,
for one day, 4*d.*

Sum, 4*s.* 4*d.*

Smiths.—And to Master Henry de Lewes, for the first week, about
making the aforesaid ironwork, 4*s.*; and to Simon Smith,
26*d.* ; and to Thorand, 20*d.*; and to William de Offinton,
18*d.*, for the same week.

Sum of the smiths, 9*s.* 4*d.*

Labourers.—And to two labourers, viz., to Stephen de Garden
and Roger de Chering, helping the aforesaid carpenters for
the aforesaid fifteen days, 4*s.* 2*d.*—to wit, to each of them
25*d.*; and to two sawyers, viz., to Walter Norris and William de Scyreburn, for three days, 15*d.*, to each of them 7½*d.*

Sum of the labourers, 5*s.* 5*d.*

Plumbers.—And to John Govair and William de Strande, for

founding and laying eight fothers of lead above the steward's chamber by taskwork, taking for the fother, 5*s*.—40*s*.

Ironwork.—And to William de Cluse, for the preparation by task-work of the ironwork for the window of the Jews' house, 4*s.* 2*d*. To the same William, for making the ironwork to the seat of the Justices of the Bench, 14*d*.

Sum, 45*s.* 4*d*.

Carriage of the Sand and Clay.—And to Matthew de Eye with his cart, going for the sand and clay, to be placed under the lead beyond the steward's chamber, for three weeks, 6*s.*; and to Richard de Celarer for his cart with two horses, for fifteen days, 3*s.* 4*d*.

And to Walter de Chambers with his cart, going for the same, for one week and two days, 2*s.* 6*d*.

And to Master Odo for his cart, hired for one day, 6*d*.

Sum, 12*s.* 4*d*.

Lime.—And for one quarter of lime, bought at London, for ma-sonry work about the steps aforesaid, 15*d*.; and for four bundles of poles for the scaffold, 10*d*.; and for 100 of small wood, bought of William Jacob, for founding the lead, 4*s*.

Sum, 6*s.* 1*d*.

Sum of the whole sixteenth payment, 111*s.* 5*d*.

17th Payment.—The seventeenth payment was made from Sun-day on the morrow of Saint Lucy the Virgin, in the 44th year of King Henry, unto Sunday in the feast of St. Thomas the Apostle,—to wit, for one week without the feast.

Carpenters.—To seven carpenters, viz., to William de Waudis. Roger de Westminster, Roger Cornwus, Gilbert Carpenter, Henry de Knythbruge, John de Greneford, John de Padinton, for the aforesaid week, about repairing the King's bridge, and putting up the seat of the Justices of the Bench, 15*s*. 2*d*.; to each of the aforesaid six, 26*d*.; and to Robert de Aldebury for the same week, 18*d*.

> Sum of the carpenters, 16*s*. 8*d*.

Masons.—And to John de Oxford, for the aforesaid week, about raising the aforesaid steps, and the filleting beyond the ends of the lead, covering near the walls, and repairing the plaster, 26*d*.; and to William de Bledelawe, for the arrears of one day's work, about setting a window in the house of the Jews, 4½*d*.

> Sum of the masons, 2*s*. 6½*d*.

Plumbers.—And to John Govayr and William de Strande, for twelve fothers and a half of lead by taskwork, founded and laid beyond the great chamber of the King's stewards. 62*s*. 6*d*.

> Sum, 62*s*. 6*d*.

Labourers.—And to two labourers, viz., to Stephen de Garden and Roger de Chering, helping the carpenters and masons for the aforesaid week, 2*s*. 6*d*.—to wit, to each of them 15*d*.; and to two sawyers, viz., to Walter Norris and William de Scyreburn, for the same week, 30*d*., to each of them 15*d*.; and to a certain labourer for the arrears of two days' works with the masons in the house of the Jews, 5*d*.; and to Roger de Chering, for three days, between the feast of St. Thomas the Apostle, and the day of the nativity of our Lord, about repairing the laundry of the King's Court, 7½*d*.

> Sum of the workmen, 6*s*. 0½*d*.

Ironwork.—And for 2000 of tenails, bought of Henry de Ponte, for the use of the houses of the King's Court, 2*s*. 6*d*.; and for 4000 nails and 200 board sawnails, and 200 nails for the planks for the same, 8*s*.

And for 300 weight of iron, bought at London, with the carriage
and passage by water of the ironwork, for the use of the
King's chimney, 50*s.*—price of the hundred weight, 16*s.* 6*d.*;
and for 10 quarters of sea coals, for forging the aforesaid
ironwork, 10*s.*

Sum, 70*s.* 6*d.*

Sum total of the seventeenth payment, £7. 18*s.* 3*d.*

Sum total of all the expenses about the petty works of the
King's Court, Westminster, in wages to the workmen, and for
all purchases made, from Monday next after the Invention
of Holy Cross, in the 43rd year of the reign of Henry, son of
King John, King of England, until the day of the nativity
next following, £126 17*s.* 8½*d.*

Thereof the Lord the King owes 14*s.* 6*d.*, which as yet remain to
be paid, for ironwork for the King's chimney.

HOUSEHOLD ROLL FOR THE ENTIRE 44TH YEAR OF THE
REIGN OF KING HENRY III.

Tuesday, on the feast of the Apostles Simon and Jude, at
Westminster.—The dispensary, 1*l.* 14*s.* 2*d.*; the buttery, 3*s.* 4*d.*;
the kitchen, 12*l.* 15*s.* 5½*d.*; the scullery, 13*s.* 7*d.*; the salsary,
2*s.* 1*d.*; the hall, 5*d.*; venison, 4*d.*; the chamber, 9*d.*; the
chamber billets, 6*s.* 8*d.*; the stable, 17*s.* 8½*d.*; the grooms,
1*l.* 1*s.* 10*d.*; the horses, 1*l.* 17*s.* 0*d.*

Sum, 21*l.* 13*s.* 4*d.*

The store of wax, 46 pounds; whereof for the chapel 18 pounds.

For the Queen's horses, &c.—The stable, 11*s.* 11½*d.*; the grooms,
7*s.* 8*d.*; the horses, 7*s.* 9*d.*

Sum, 1*l.* 7*s.* 4½*d.*

For the entertainment of 150 religious persons.—The dispensary, 6*s.* 3*d.*; the buttery, 2*s.* 10½*d.*; the kitchen, 10*s.* 10*d.*
Sum, 19*s.* 11½*d.*

Wednesday following, &c. [The route and daily expenditure of the King and his attendants are then given, until their arrival at Paris and return to Westminster.]

Wednesday following, at Paris.—The dispensary, 1*l.* 9*s.* 9*d.*; the buttery, 2*l.* 8*s.* 5*d.*; the kitchen, 5*l.* 0*s.* 6*d.*; the scullery, 1*l.* 5*s.* 5*d.*; the salsary, 2*s.*; the hall, 2*s.* 8*d.*; the hall billets, 4*s.*— the chamber, 1*l.* 0*s.* 6*d.*; the chamber billets, 14*s.*; the stable, 1*l.* 5*s.* 10½*d.*; the grooms, 1*l.* 19*s.* 6*d.*; the horses, 3*l.* 19*s.* 9*d.*
Sum, 19*l.* 6*s.* 4½*d.*

The stock of wax, 42 pounds, whereof in the chapel and for alms, 8 pounds and a half.

For the Queen's horses, &c.—The stable, 17*s.* 9½*d.*; the grooms, 10*s.* 1*d.*; the horses, 16*s.* 3*d.*
Sum, 2*l.* 4*s.* 3*d.*

For entertainment of 150 religious persons.—The dispensary, 6*s.* 3*d.*; the buttery, 3*s.* 3½*d.*; the kitchen, 5*s.* 3*d.*
Sum, 14*s.* 9½*d.*

Thursday following, at the same place.—The dispensary, 3*l.* 6*s.* 5*d.*; the buttery, 4*l.* 16*s.* 9*d.*; the kitchen, 15*l.* 14*s.* 10*d.*; the scullery, 1*l.* 12*s.* 4*d.*; the salsary, 11*s.* 1*d.*; venison, 2*d.*; the hall, 1*s.* 2*d.*; the hall billets, 4*s.*; the chamber, 6*s.* 6*d.*; the chamber billets, 16*s.*; the stable, 1*l.* 3*s.* 5*d.*; the grooms, 1*l.* 9*s.* 6*d.*; the horses, 3*l.* 15*s.* 9*d.*
Sum, 33*l.* 17*s.* 11*d.*

Stock of wax, 62 pounds, whereof for the chapel and in alms, 10 pounds.

For the Queen's horses, &c.—The stable, 16*s.* 5½*d.*; the grooms, 10*s.* 1*d.*; the horses, 16*s.* 3½*d.*

Sum, 2l. 2s. 10d.

For the entertainment of 150 friars.—The dispensary, 6*s.* 3*d.*; the buttery, 3*s.* 3½*d.*; the kitchen, 10*s.* 9*d.*

Sum, 1l. 0s. 2½d.

Friday following, at the same place.—The dispensary, 2*l.* 19*s.* 0½*d.*; the buttery, 3*l.* 12*s.* 11½*d.*; the kitchen, 18*l.* 6*s.*; the scullery, 1*l.* 7*s.* 8*d.*; the salsary, 2*s.*; the hall billets, 4*s.*; the chambers, 4*s.* 2*d.*; the chamber billets, 19*s.* 1*d.*; the stable, 1*l.* 3*s.* 5*d.*; the grooms, 1*l.* 9*s.* 4½*d.*; the horses, 3*l.* 18*s.* 6*d.*

Sum, 34l. 7s. 0d.

The stock of wax, 61 pounds, whereof for the chapel 9½ pounds.

For the Queen's horses, &c.—The stable, 1*l.* 4*s.* 6*d.*; the grooms, 9*s.* 11*d.*; the horses, 16*s.* 9*d.*

Sum, 2l. 11s. 2d.

For the entertainment of 150 religious persons.—The dispensary, 6*s.* 3*d.*; the buttery, 3*s.* 3½*d.*; the kitchen, 5*s.* 5*d.*

Sum, 14s. 9½d.

Saturday following, at the same place.—The dispensary, 2*l.* 13*s.* 11½*d.*; the buttery, 2*l.* 18*s.* 1*d.*; the kitchen, 19*l.* 8*s.* 3*d.*; the scullery, 1*l.* 7*s.* 9*d.*; the salsary, 1*s.* 8½*d.*; the hall, 8*d.*; the hall billets, 4*s.*; the chamber, 1*s.* 7*d.*; the chamber billets, 1*l.* 0*s.* 7*d.*; the stable, 1*l.* 3*s.* 5*d.*; the grooms, 1*l.* 10*s.* 0*d.*; the horses, 4*l.* 1*s.* 4½*d.*

Sum, 34l. 11s. 4½d.

Stock of wax, 69 pounds, whereof for the chapel 11 pounds.

For the Queen's horses, &c.—The stable, 16*s.* 5½*d.*; the grooms, 9*s.* 11*d.*; the horses, 16*s.* 9*d.*

Sum, 2l. 3s. 3½d.

For the entertainment of 150 religious men.—The dispensary, 6*s.* 3*d.*; the buttery, 3*s.* 3½*d.*; the kitchen, 5*s.* 5*d.*

Sum, 14*s.* 10½*d.*

Sum, 205*l.* 7*s.* 11½*d.*, approved.*

---

1 EDWARD I.

ISSUE ROLL OF EASTER TERM, IN THE FIRST YEAR OF THE REIGN OF KING EDWARD, SON OF KING HENRY III.

To Luke of Lucca, a merchant, whom the King sent to the fairs at Leny to execute certain special business for the King there, 50*l.*; delivered to him to pay certain merchants there in the name of the King.

To Luke of Lucca, 1000*l.*, in part payment of the King's own debts, for which the King was bound to him before the death of the Lord King Henry, paid by him for the aforesaid King.

To Eleanor, mother of the King of England, 10 marks, for the 10 marks which the Lord King Henry gave to the same Eleanor for the expenses of her household, out of the tallage of Adam Feteplace, then a burgess of the King at Oxford, delivered to her by John de Wathele her clerk.

* This Roll forms a diary of the King's expenses whilst in France and England, which are added up every day and week; it also gives authentically his route and stay at each place, the time of his embarkation, &c. commencing on Tuesday, the 28th day of October, at Westminster, from whence the King proceeded to Feversham, Whitsand, and Dover, where he embarked on the 13th November. The King's route may be then traced from Boulogne to Paris, where he remained five weeks; thence to St. Omers, where he continued two months; and then on his route home, where he arrived at the end of the month of April. An account of the expenses of each department in the household is given, amounting in the whole to 7500*l.* for one year.—Vide Issue Roll, 44 Edw. III. Pell Records, p. xvi., of the Introduction.

To Eleanor, Queen of England, mother of the King, who received daily from the day of Saint Edmund the King and Martyr, on which day the body of Henry, King of England, of renowned memory, was buried, unto the feast of Saint Hilary next following, 10 marks for her expenses, provided by the King's Council, 366*l.* 1 mark ; paid to John de Wathele, Gilbert de Chalfunt, and R. Burnel.

To the prior and brethren of Chartreuse, 25 marks, at Easter term last past, of those 50 marks yearly which they receive at the King's Exchequer in pure and perpetual alms, by a charter of King Henry our great grandfather.

To Master Robert de Beverley, 6*l.* 16*s.* 4½*d.*, for the stipends of divers workmen employed about the tomb of John de Windsor, the King's son, for sixteen weeks ; paid to the same.

To the same Master Robert, 1*l.* 6*s.* 1*d.* for the stipends of divers workmen for repairing the King's great hall at Westminster, for the time aforesaid, paid to the same.

To Henry de Cadurcis, 50*l.*, as a loan until the King's return to England ; but if the King shall cause that sum to be remitted on his return for the loss which the same Henry had sustained on account of the removal of a certain forge by the King in the forest of Saint Briavell, then the same Henry shall be therefrom discharged, &c.

To Gervaise the usher, 24*s.*, for 2*d.* daily which he receives at the Exchequer, from the day of the burial of the Lord King Henry unto Easter next following,—to wit, for 74 days ; paid to him.

To Master Ralph de Merlawe, sent as the King's messenger beyond seas to expedite the business of the same King in the Court of the King of France, 30 marks paid to him for his expenses.

To Master William de la Cornere, sent as the King's messenger beyond seas, to expedite the business of the same King in the Court of the King of France, 40 marks for his expenses; paid to William his chaplain.

To Master John Clarel, sent as the King's messenger beyond seas to expedite the business of the same Lord the King in the Court of the King of France, 40 marks for his expenses; paid to John de Stokewell his clerk.

To Thomas Scot, a messenger, 5s., for his expenses in going, by the King's command, with certain letters from the King to the King and Queen of Scotland.

To Thomas de Saint Sepulchre, engineer of the King's war-slings in the Tower of London, who received $7\frac{1}{2}d$. per day for his wages and arrears of his wages, from the day of the burial of Lord Henry, the King's father, unto the feast of the Purification of the Blessed Mary next following, and from the same feast each day $7\frac{1}{2}d$. for his wages unto the feast of Pentecost next following, 5l. 18s. $1\frac{1}{2}d$.

To Stephen, the King's painter, 40s., in part payment of his wages for whitewashing and decorating the King's great hall at Westminster.

To Master Robert de Beverley, the King's plasterer, 40s., to purchase colouring for decorating and whitewashing the King's great hall at Westminster.

To Stephen, the King's painter, 2 marks, for his stipend for whitewashing the King's great hall at Westminster; paid to the same.

To Thomas de Pampelworth, clerk of Geoffrey de Picheford, constable of Windsor Castle, and keeper of the King's boys in the same castle, 60l., for the expenses of the boys aforesaid.

To Robert Le Naper, who receives 2*d.* daily, 1*l.* 11*s.* 6*d.*, for 189 days—to wit, from the morrow of the burial of the Lord King Henry III. in the 57th year of his reign, unto the day of Pentecost, in the first year of the reign of King Edward I., counting each day.

To Walter, the King's painter, 77*s.*, for the arrears of his wages for eleven weeks—to wit, from the day after the Epiphany of our Lord, in the 51st year of the reign of the Lord King Henry, until the Lord's day after the Annunciation of the blessed Mary in the same year.

To Master Ralph de Beverley, keeper of the works at the Tower of London, 20*l.*, to provide necessaries for the works of the Tower aforesaid, by view of Alan le Hurer and Master Thomas of Saint Sepulchre, overseer of the works aforesaid.

To Robert de Cerne, who receives 3*d.* per day, 2*l.* 7*s.* 3*d.*, for 189 days—to wit, from the morrow of the burial of the Lord King Henry III., from the 57th year of the reign of the same King, to the day of Pentecost next following, in the first year of the reign of King Edward, counting each day.

To Master Robert de Beverley, the King's plasterer, 3*l.* 8*s.*, for his support from the feast of Saint Hilary in the 1st year of the reign of King Edward, unto the feast of Pentecost next following—to wit, for 136 days, including each day, in lieu of 6*d.* daily which he was accustomed to receive by grant of Lord King Henry made to him for the life of the said Master Robert.

To Nicholas de Stapelton, one of the King's justices assigned to hold pleas before the King, 20 marks this time, in discharge of his expenses for the time that he remained in the King's service in the office aforesaid, and also for the time which he remained in the King's service until the King's return to England.

To Luke de Lucca, a merchant of Lucca, 1000 marks, to be

paid to Philip Bemanuchu, a citizen of Genoa, which the King commanded to be paid to the same Philip by his letters patent for payment of the debt which the King owed to him.

To William de Saham, one of the King's justices assigned to hold pleas before the King, 10 marks, in part payment of the expences of himself and his clerks attending with him in the pleas aforesaid.

To Walter de Helyun, one of the King's justices appointed to hold the pleas of the Lord the King, 10 marks, as an advance from the King until his return into England.

To Adam of Winchester, whom the King lately sent to Bristol, Exeter, Hereford, Worcester, Warwick, and Gloucester, to inspect the archives of the Jews in the towns aforesaid, and to inrol the debts contained in the same, 5 marks, for his expences about discharging the business aforesaid.

To Eleanor, the King's mother, 200*l.* in part of her support by loan from the King.

To Catherine, who was the wife of William de Saint Germain, formerly servant of the Lord King Henry of renowned memory, father of King Edward, 1 mark, for the arrears of 3*d.* daily, which the same Catherine receives at the King's Exchequer, by charter of the said King's father.

To William, warden of the Tower of London, 1 mark, for the arrears of his stipend, which he receives for his support in the service of the Lord King Henry, father of the present King Edward.

To Mary, who was the wife of Walter Achard, 10*s.*, for the arrears of 50*s.* which the aforesaid King Henry, at the time of his death, owed to the aforesaid Walter for the time that he was in the service of King Henry II.

To Joan de Hamul, formerly the wife of Roger de Assewell, deceased, 100s.; which were in arrear to him for 12l. 15s. 3¼d., for which the Lord King Henry, father of the King, owed to the said Roger, formerly her husband, for the arrears of wages of the same Roger during the time he remained in the service of the King's father.

To Roger le Herberur, formerly servant of the Lord King Henry, the King's father, 10s., for the arrears of 2¼d. daily, which he receives at the King's Exchequer.

To Master Robert de Beverley, 6l. 11s. 5¼d., to finish the painting and whitewashing of the King's great hall at Westminster, and for a stipend to the workmen executing the works aforesaid.

To the brethren of the hospital of Saint Giles, London, 30s., in part payment of 60s. yearly, which they receive at the King's Exchequer by charter of the Lord King Henry, great grandfather of the present King and royal progenitor of the Kings of England, for the support of a chaplain to perform divine service in the chapel of the hospital aforesaid.

To the King's two chaplains, for performing divine service in the chapel of the blessed Stephen at Westminster, for the soul of the King's father; to one of the King's chaplains, for performing divine service for the soul of the aforesaid King, in the church of the blessed Mary at Westminster; and to two chaplains of the King, for performing divine service for the soul of the King's father aforesaid, in the hermitage of the Charing, for their stipends, from the feast of the Nativity of the Lord last past unto the feast of Saint Michael next following, in like manner as they have been accustomed to receive the like stipends in the time of the aforesaid King Henry III.; delivered to them by a writ.

Sum, 10l. 2s. 6d.

To brother Reginald and Richard his companion, the King's

chaplains, for performing divine service in the chapel of the Tower of London, each of whom receives yearly 50*s.* for his stipend of 100*s.* for the arrears of their stipends, from the feast of Saint Michael last past unto the feast of Easter next following, and for their stipends from the same feast of Easter unto the feast of Saint Michael next following; paid to them the sum of 100*s.*

To Lawrence, the son and heir of Roger, formerly usher of the King's Exchequer, 12*s.*, for taking twenty-four of the King's summonses to divers counties in England, from the morrow of the close of Easter in the 1st year of the King's reign, unto Saturday next before the feast of Saint Peter ad vincula in the same year.

To Robert le Naper, formerly a servant of the Lord King Henry, half a mark, for his arrears of 2*d.* daily, which the same Robert receives at the King's Exchequer by letters patent of the same Lord King Henry.

Sum total of the whole issues of this Roll, from the morrow of the close of Easter unto Saturday next following after the feast of the blessed Peter ad vincula, 4086*l.* 0*s.* 4½*d.*

ISSUES IN THE MIDDLE TIME.

To Thomas de Mymmes 35 marks, for his expenses in going as the King's messenger to Lincoln, York, Durham, and Carlisle, and from thence to Scotland, Ireland, and Wales, to publish the sentence, pronounced by the Lord the Pope, in those parts, against Guido de Montefort.

To John de Rowell, clerk, imprisoned at Newgate for certain trespasses, 1 mark, for his support—to wit, from those 54 marks found in the custody of the same John on the day he was taken for the trespasses aforesaid.

1 EDWARD I.

ISSUES OF MICHAELMAS TERM, IN THE FIRST YEAR OF THE
REIGN OF KING EDWARD, SON OF KING HENRY.

To Master Robert de Beverley, the King's mason, 50*l*., therewith to erect a stage for the feast of the King's Coronation, thereon to be held.

To John Tartarin, formerly servant of Lord King Henry, father of the present King, decrepit with age, for the arrears of 2*d* and 1½*d*. daily, which the same John hath been accustomed to receive, by grant of the King's Father aforesaid, by his letters patent.

To Juliana de Estri, formerly laundress to Eleanor, Queen of England, the King's mother, 4 marks, in advance from the King for her support until the King's return to England.

To William de Karrois, valet to our beloved and faithful John of Brittany, returning home, 40*s*., for the arrears of his fee which the aforesaid John his Lord had been accustomed to receive at the exchequer of the Lord King Henry, father of the present Lord the King.

To Maurice de Croun, kinsman to the King, 120 marks, as a loan from the King until the King's return into England, on condition that he then restore the same money to the King.

To Walter Paulin and William the engineer, and to the King's soldiers whom the King sent to Bergevenny, to remain in the fort of the castle there, 4*l*. 7*s*. 6*d*. for their wages advanced—to wit,

from Sunday next after the feast of All Saints, in the first year of
our reign, unto the day of St. Hilary next following, including
each day.

To John Pykard and his three companions, foot cross-bowmen,
sent with the aforesaid King's soldiers to the place aforesaid, and
there to remain in the fort of the castle aforesaid, 70*s*., in advance
upon their wages for the time aforesaid.

To Master Conard, maker of cross-bows, 1*l*. 0*s*. 8½*d*., for repairing with horn six cross-bows delivered to him by the Constable
of Windsor Castle, and again returned to the aforesaid Constable
by the said Conard, by the King's command, to be kept in the
castle of the King at Windsor.

To Ralph de Wodeburg, 10*l*., in part payment of the debts
which the King owed him for horses and other things lately received from him, for the King's use whilst beyond seas.

To John Hardele, 17 marks, for a certain palfrey purchased
by him for the King's use, from Theobald de London.

To Hugh de Turberville, 30*l*., for 145*l*. which the King owed
to the aforesaid Hugh for a certain sum of 360*l*., for the release of
his term in the islands of Guernsey and Jersey, which he held of
the King at farm.

To Juliana, who was the wife of Hugh Bradeleye, deceased,
60*s*., for which the said Juliana released to the King 6*l*. 18*s*. 8*d*.,
which were in arrear to him for 100*s*., which the aforesaid Hugh in
his lifetime was accustomed to receive yearly at the exchequer, by
letters of the Lord King Henry, father of the present Lord the
King.

To Master Henry de Woburne, the deaf man, 7*l*. 12*s*. 1*d*., for which he released to the King 2½*d.*, that he was accustomed to receive daily at the Exchequer, and for all arrears thereof.

To Roger de Oylly, 28 marks, for which he released the 42 marks that the King owed to the same Roger for corn and hay, purchased for the King's use at his church of Misterton; paid to John de la Wade.

Payments made to Isabella, the widow of Alan, the smith; to Eugina, the widow of Henry de la Bere; and to Alice, the widow of Henry de Roinges, for which they respectively released to the King certain sums of money due to their late husbands.

ALSO OF ISSUES AFTER THE FEAST OF SAINT HILARY.

To Brother Stephen de Fuleburn, 20 marks, in part payment of 20*l.*, which the same Brother Stephen lent, by the King's desire, to Thomas de Boulton for the use of Gilbert the King's chaplain, paid to the same Gilbert of the King's gift, for building at the new hospital which the same Gilbert had began to build, &c.

To Matilda, the wife of Master Walter de Saundon, the King's cook, 6 marks,—to wit, 1 mark at Easter term last past, and 5 marks at Michaelmas term next following, which were in arrear to her for the 10 marks yearly which the King granted to the same Matilda, for her support until his return to England.

To Brother Henry, under treasurer of the house of the knights templars of Paris, procurator to Brother John de Turno, treasurer of the same house, 2000 marks, in part payment of 28,189*l.* 8*s.* 4*d.* Tournay money, for which the King was bound to the same treasurer, on account of a loan made to him whilst he was in the Holy Land, and also in France.

To William de Plumton, sent as the King's messenger to Lewellin, the son of Griffin, Prince of Wales, 40s., for his expenses.

To John Hardele, 8 marks, for the expenses and keep of five of
the King's palfreys, and for the wages of five grooms to look after
the same palfreys, from the day of the Nativity of the Lord last
past unto the day of the Purification of the Blessed Mary next
following; also to the same John, 10 marks, for a certain palfrey
purchased for the King's use.

To William de Staunford, usher of the chapel of Eleanor,
Queen of England, the King's mother, who receives 3½d. daily at
the Exchequer, by letters patent of Lord King Henry, by the
hands of the Sheriff of Essex, of the appointed alms, 10l., for
which the same William released to the King the aforesaid 3½d.
daily, together with the arrears thereof.

To Martin de Littelebury, the King's justice assigned to hold
pleas before the King, 20l., for an advance upon his fee which
others had before been accustomed to receive by reason of the
office aforesaid; paid to Master William Dayrel.

To Hugh de Kendale, 10 marks, for his expenses in going to
the King beyond the seas, by the King's command.

To Robert Burnel, Archdeacon of York, 50 marks, for the 50
marks delivered to the King's beloved and faithful John de
Burgh, in part payment of the money which the King owed to
the same John, according to the form of an agreement made between the King and the aforesaid John; paid to Master Robert
de Langley.

4 EDWARD I.

WRITS FOR PAYMENTS AT EASTER TERM IN THE FOURTH YEAR
OF THE REIGN OF KING EDWARD, SON OF KING HENRY.

Edward, by the grace of God, King of England, Lord of Ireland, and Duke of Acquitain, to his Treasurer and Chamberlains,
greeting,—Pay out of our Treasury to our beloved in Christ, the
Prior and Brethren, the Carthusians, 25 marks, at Easter term,
in the fourth year of our reign, for the 50 marks yearly, which
they receive at our Exchequer. Witness ourself, at Kenington,
the 22nd day of April, in the year aforesaid.

Edward, by the grace of God, &c.—Pay from our Treasury
to our beloved and faithful Geoffrey de Pycheford, Constable of
our Castle at Windsor, and custos of our manor of Kenington,
200l., to expedite our works by view of the surveyors of the same
works there. Witness ourself at Westminster, the third day of
November, in the third year of our reign, by Hugh the son of
Oto, sent by the Lord the King.

Edward, by the grace of God, &c.—Pay out of our Treasury,
from the day of the death of the Lord King Henry, our father,
of renowned memory, for each year, to our beloved the Master and
Brethren of the Knights Templars in England, 8l., which our said
father granted them by his charter to be received yearly at our
Exchequer, for the support of three chaplains, daily for ever, to perform divine service in the New Temple, London, one of whom is to
perform service for our aforesaid father, the other for all Christian
people, and the third for the faithful deceased, as was accustomed
to be done in the time of our aforesaid father. Witness ourself

at Westminster, the 14th day of November, in the third year of
our reign.

Edward, by the grace of God, &c.—Pay from our Treasury
to Peter de Skoteny 40 marks, for the release which he made
to us of the five knights' fees which he held of us in capite,
belonging to a moiety of the barony of Skoteny, and which he
for ever quit claimed from him and his heirs to us and our heirs, so
nevertheless that the same Peter might hold seventy-six ox-gangs
of land with the appurtenances, in Steynton, which are extended, at
64s., and which belong to the half barony aforesaid, of us in capite,
by the service of the twentieth part of a knight's fee. Witness the
King, at Westminster, the 4th day of May, in the fourth year
of our reign.

Edward, by the grace of God, &c.—Pay from our Treasury to
Peter Lof, 100s., due at Easter term last past, for the 100s. which
he receives yearly at our Exchequer until of our more abundant
grace we shall have provided him with an ecclesiastical benefice
without cure, or otherwise provide for him. · Witness ourself, at
Westminster, the 8th day of May, in the fourth year of our
reign.

Edward, by the grace of God, &c.—Pay out of our Treasury
to Richard Wolward, keeper of our houses and court at Westminster, 1 mark, there to dress our vines, as heretofore, in the preceding years, hath been accustomed to be done. Witness ourself,
at Westminster, the 4th day of May, in the fourth year of our
reign.

Edward, by the grace of God, &c.—Pay out of our Treasury
to our beloved and faithful Hervey de Cadurco, 500 marks, for
the release and quit claim which the same Hervey made of a
forge which he had in our forest of Dene, and which he quietly
surrendered into our hands from himself and his heirs for ever;
and cause to be received from him the letters patent by which

the forge aforesaid was granted to him, &c., provided that any
money which the same Hervey may have borrowed at our Exchequer on account of the forge aforesaid be allowed. Witness
ourself at Westminster, the 4th day of May, in the fourth year
of our reign.

Edward, by the grace of God, &c.—Pay out of our Treasury
to Scantinus de Scala, a citizen and merchant of Florence, or to
his messenger bearing these present letters, 2000 marks sterling,
which we formerly borrowed at the court of Rome, and you shall
be allowed the same in your account. Dated at Bayonne, the 18th
day of November, in the second year of our reign.

Edward, by the grace of God, &c.—Pay from our Treasury to
Bones, a Florentine merchant, 1000l., which we lately borrowed
in the Court of Rome. Dated at Acquitaine, the 13th day of
November, in the first year of our reign.

Edward, by the grace of God, &c.—Pay out of our Treasury
to our beloved and faithful Oto de Grandison, 100l., which of our
gift he delivered to a certain foreign knight at his departure; and
this by no means omit, as you respect us and our honour. Dated
at Odiham, under our privy seal, the 30th day of August, in the
second year of our reign.

Edward, by the grace of God, &c.—Pay out of our Treasury
to Matthew de Charrun, 140l. 8s. 7½d. for expenses incurred about
our mews at the Charing, and other our works there, and whereof
a view was made before you, by which it appears that the same
Matthew had expended in the same works 140l. 8s. 7½d., of which
said money the said Matthew as yet hath received nothing, as he
saith. Witness ourself at Brehull, the 28th day of July, in the
third year of our reign.

Edward, by the grace of God, &c.—Pay from our Treasury to
Paul le Arblaster and William le Arblaster, our servants, 20

marks, to wit, to each of them 10 marks, in part payment of their wages and debts, and for them to purchase harness therewith; and this in no wise omit. Witness ourself at Upravene, the 16th day of December, in the fourth year of our reign.

ISSUE ROLL OF MICHAELMAS TERM, IN THE FOURTH YEAR OF THE REIGN OF KING EDWARD, SON OF KING HENRY, BEGINNING THE FIFTH.

To Brother Joseph, Prior of the hospital of Saint John of Jerusalem, in England and Brethren of the same house, 2000 marks, paid to Master Reymund de Nogerus, chaplain and nuncio of the Lord the Pope; and to Brother John de Derelington for the 2000 marks which the same Prior and Brethren received as a loan from the same, for the dispatch of certain urgent business for the King.

To Eleanor, the King's mother, Queen of England, 580*l.*, at Easter term, in the fourth year of the King's reign, which the King granted her in aid of her dower, until after an extent of her lands should be made, so that the King might calculate her dower; paid to John de Wathel, clerk, and Luke of Lucca.

To Master Robert de Beverley, keeper of the King's works, 97*l.* 17*s.* 7½*d.*—to wit, for lead, timber, planks, nails, and divers other necessary things purchased by him, to make the King's mews at Charing, and likewise to make the King's kitchen-garden; paid to the same and to William de Staunford his clerk.

To Roger Brun, 100 marks, for his expenses which he incurred in going as the King's messenger to the Lord the King of Norway, by command of the King.

To Master Thomas Beck, keeper of the King's wardrobe, 3000*l.*, for the expenses of the King's household; paid in dis-

charge thereof to Master William de Luda and Thomas de Goneys, clerk of the King's wardrobe.

To the Abbess of Fontevrault, 184*l.* 5*s.*, which were in arrear
to her during the time of Lord King Henry, father of the
present Lord the King, for her annual fee of 82*l.* 10*s.* 4*d.*, which
she receives at the King's Exchequer; paid to the same and John
de Wydyhull, clerk.

To the same Abbess, 138*l.* and 1 mark, which were in arrear to
the same Abbess during the time of the aforesaid King, for the
aforesaid annual fee that the aforesaid Abbess received at the
Exchequer aforesaid; paid to the same and to John de Wydyhull,
clerk.

To Reymund de Alemaunt, of Bourdeaux, 46*l.* 13*s.*, for twenty
casks of wine purchased from him for the King's use, by the
hands of Gregory de Rokesle and Matthew Columbarius, the
King's butlers.

To Peter Gwyll, de Monte Albano, 162*l.* 6*s.* 8*d.*, for 73
casks of wine, purchased from him for the King's use, by the
hands of Gregory de Rokesle and Matthew de Columbarius, the
King's butlers.

To Stephen de Pencester, Constable of the King's castle of
Dover, 14*l.* and half a mark, for Michaelmas Term, in the fourth
year of King Edward, beginning the fifth, 28*l.* 13*s.* 4*d.*, which the
King granted him yearly, to be received for his support so long
as he should have the custody of the castle aforesaid; also to
the chaplain, servants, watcher, and engineer, dwelling in the
aforesaid castle, and for their robes.

To Isabel, who was the wife of William de Hastentot, 15*l.* 10*s.*,
at Michaelmas Term, in the fourth year of the reign of King
Edward, beginning the fifth, which the Prior of Barnewell is

bound to pay yearly at the King's Exchequer for the farm of the manor of Chesterton, and which the Lord King Henry, father of the present King, lately granted to the said William de Hastentot, to hold to him and his heirs by the hands of the aforesaid Prior, until he should provide him with twenty librates of land, and which the said King's father, after the death of the aforesaid William, formerly her husband, granted to the aforesaid Isabella, to hold and receive to the same Isabella for support of herself and their children, until the lawful age of the heir of the aforesaid William, formerly her husband, as is fully contained as well in the letters patent of the aforesaid now King, as in the letters patent of King Henry aforesaid.

To Robert de Veer, Earl of Oxford, 20 marks, at Easter term, in the fourth year of the reign of King Edward, and Michaelmas term next following, for his annual fee of 20 marks which he receives at the King's Exchequer during his life; paid to Robert Carbonel, his knight.

To R., Bishop of Bath and Wells, the King's Chancellor, 14l. 13s. 4d., for countersigning two charters to the use of the Abbot of Dernhall, one to wit, for the land of Conewardel, and the other for the land which belonged to Roger de Clyfford, in Weverham ; paid to Henry de Lenn, his clerk.

To Roger de Clyfford, junior, Justice of the King's forest on this side Trent, 50l., at Michaelmas term, in the 56th year of the late King's reign, for his annual fee of 100l., which the King granted him, to be received at his Exchequer so long as he should be in the office aforesaid ; paid to Thomas de Goneys and William de Herlawe, clerks.

To Adam de Bradenham, chaplain, 77l. 8s., paid by his own hands to divers creditors of John and Henry, the King's late children, at Windsor, deceased, during the time the said King's children lately lived at Windsor with the King's most dear mother,

Eleanor, Queen of England; paid to Augustin de Plessetis, the Queen's valet.

To William de Chester, 30 marks, as well for the discharge of 4*d.* daily, which he was accustomed to receive of the appointed alms, by the hands of the Sheriff of Surrey, and from the town of Bedford, as for the release of all arrears thereof; paid to Robert de Chester, clerk.

To the Abbot and convent of Messenden, 50 marks, for the release of 50*s.* yearly, which they have been accustomed to receive by the hands of the Sheriff of Buckinghamshire for the time being, for the support of a certain chaplain, to perform divine service in the abbey aforesaid, for the soul of Hugh de Saunford; paid to Master William de Luda, clerk.

To Ralph de Wodeburgh, 110*l.*, who by his deed surrendered and quit claimed to the Lord the King, and his heirs, or assigns, for himself and his heirs, for ever, 10*l.* yearly, which he had of the gift of a certain William de Huntrecumb, and which he was accustomed yearly to receive by the hands of the Abbot of Stratford, for those 20*l.* which the said Abbot was accustomed to render at the King's Exchequer.

To Nicholas Corbet, who married Margery, the daughter and a heir of Hugh de Bolebek, deceased, who held of the King in capite, 60*l.*, for the vesture of sixty acres of wood in Langeley Park, which descended in purpartie to the same Nicholas and Margery, which same belonged to the inheritance of Richard de Munfychet, deceased; which same vesture, the aforesaid Nicholas and Margery granted to the Lord the King, for the sum above said; paid to William de Hamelton, clerk of the chancery.

To Roger de Lancaster, who married the daughter and a heir of Hugh de Bolebeck, deceased, who held of the King in capite, 60*l.*, for the vesture of sixty acres of wood in Langeley Park;

which descended in purpartie to the same Roger and daughter of the said Hugh, which belonged to the inheritance of Richard de Munfychet, deceased; which same vesture the aforesaid Roger and daughter granted to the Lord the King for the money aforesaid; paid to the aforesaid William de Hamelton.

To Peter de Roffiah, a merchant of Gascony, 28 marks, for seven casks of wine purchased of him when the King was last at Lindhurst, to be expended in the King's household.

To Alexander le Ryche and Thomas le Ryche, merchants of Andeuro, 80*l.*, which Matthew Berille, formerly constable of the King's castle of Dover, received from them as a loan, and which the said Matthew expended in provisions for the castle aforesaid, as appears by inspection of the King's letters patent granted to the aforesaid Matthew; paid to the same by J. de Wydehull, clerk.

To Eleanor, Queen of England, the King's mother, 532*l.* 18*s.* 3½*d.*, at Michaelmas term, in the fourth year of the reign of King Edward, beginning the fifth, for her yearly fee of 1065*l.* 16*s.* 7*d.*, for the residue of the dower which the Lord King Henry, father of the present King, lately assigned to her by his charter for certain lands and tenements; which said residue in such lands and tenements for certain causes she had not received; paid to John de Wathel, her clerk.

To John de Northampton and his companions, skinners, of London, 30*l.*, for part payment of the relief of Hugh de Mortimer which remained to be paid for the residue of 63*l.*, which were assigned to them for the same relief before the death of the Lord King Henry, father of the present King, as the King is informed by the Record of the Barons of the King's Exchequer, in part payment of the debt for which the same King's father was bound for skins purchased from them for the use of the aforesaid King Henry.

To Walter de Helyun, lately sent to divers places in the realm to expedite the King's business, receiving 20*l.* for payment of his expenses concerning the business aforesaid, in two tallies, made to John de Baunton.

To Geoffrey le Squeller, 10*l.*, as well for the release of those 100*s.*, for two robes which he hath yearly been accustomed to receive, as for the release of all arrears thereof.

To Walter de Tuthull, a chaplain, performing divine service in the chapel of Saint Margaret of Westminster, for Margaret, the King's sister, Queen of Scotland, who receives 60*s.* yearly for his stipend so long as he shall perform divine service in the church aforesaid, 30*s.*, to wit, for Easter term, in the fourth year of the reign of King Edward.

To Edmund, the King's brother, 300*l.*, part of those 1700 marks which are in arrear to him for 2600 marks which the Lord King Henry, father of the King, lately granted to the same Edmund in aid of his going to the Holy Land, to be received from the issues of the iters of the Justices in their last iter for the county of Lincoln, and of which the same Edmund received from the issues of the iter aforesaid, 600*l.*, as the King was informed by the Treasurer and Barons of the Exchequer; paid to the Earl of Cornwall, by assignment to the same earl.

---

15 EDWARD I.

WRITS FOR PAYMENTS, 15 EDWARD I.

Edward, by the grace of God, King of England, Lord of Ireland, and Duke of Acquitaine, to his Treasurer and Chamberlains, greeting,—Pay from our Treasury to our beloved mother, the Lady Eleanor, Queen of England, 409*l.* 19*s.* sterling, which our beloved clerk, Master William de Lud, keeper of our wardrobe, received for the expenses of our household, by the hands of the merchants of Lucca, for money assigned to our same mother out of the customs of Bourdeaux. Witness ourself, at Blanke-ford, the 1st day of June, in the 15th year of our reign. By bill of the wardrobe.

Edward, &c.—Pay, &c., to our beloved clerk, Master Odo, of Westminster, 20 marks, for the expenses which he incurred in coming to us from London to Oloroun, in Biern, upon our affairs, and from thence returning to London. Witness, &c., at Oloroun, in Biern, the 5th August, anno 15°.

Edward, &c.—Pay, &c., to Robert Poterel, $7\frac{1}{2}d$. daily, from the morrow of the Holy Trinity last past, until our return to England, which we granted to be received at our Exchequer for his wages during the time aforesaid. Witness, Edward, Earl of Cornwall, our kinsman, at Westminster, the 24th day of October, in the 15th year of our reign.

Edward, &c.—Pay, &c., to our beloved in Christ the Abbot of Colchester, 100 marks, for the release and quit claim which the same abbot made for himself, his convent, and successors, to us and our heirs of the advowson of the church of Ledred, and of all right and claim which he had, or could have, in the same; to-gether with a certain annual pension to his house belonging, pay-able from the same church, which the same Abbot had been ac-customed to receive; and take from the same Abbot his deed of release and quit claim for the advowson and pension aforesaid, sealed with the seal of his chapter. Witness, &c., at West-minster, 29th April, anno 14°.

Edward, &c.—Pay, &c., to our beloved clerk, Richard de Rowell, 20l., which we granted him in support of his expenses which he had incurred, as well in taking inquisitions in the counties of Cumberland and Westmoreland, by our command, as for the per-formance of divers other our affairs, from the morrow of the close of Easter last past, until the end of the Translation of the

H

Blessed Thomas the martyr, next following. Witness ourself, at
Westminster, the 1st day of July, anno 13°.

Edward, &c.—Pay, &c., to the Abbess and Nuns of Saint Antoine, near Paris, 63*l*. 1*s*. 8*d*., for 220*l*. 16*s*. (Parisian money),
which Eleanor, formerly Countess of Leicester, bequeathed to the
same by her will for a debt which she owed them, and for which
we were bound to the same Countess in lieu of the inheritance
of the Earl Marshal for assignment of her dower in Ireland
and West Wales, on account of William, late Earl Marshal, her
first husband, as appears by former letters patent of discharge
from the executors of the aforesaid Countess, made to us and
our heirs, and to all others whomsoever concerning the said
money, given under the seal of the same executors and our seal
of office, so that the heir of the aforesaid Earl Marshal, who remained charged at the Exchequer for payment thereof, should be
discharged, &c.   Witness ourself, at Paris, 17th July, anno 14°.

Edward, &c.—Pay, &c., to our beloved in Christ the Master
and Brethren of the hospital of the Blessed Mary of the Teutonics,
in Jerusalem, 40 marks, for those 40 marks yearly which Lord
King Henry, our father, by his charter, granted them to be received at his Exchequer until there should be competent provision
made for the same Master and Brethren, by our aforesaid father,
or his heirs, out of certain lands in England of that value.
Witness, &c., at Westminster, 28 April, anno 14°.

---

17 EDWARD I.

LIBERATE ROLL, 17 EDWARD I.

To John Bacon and Richard de Cancea, attorneys, executors
of Eleanor, of good memory, formerly Queen of England, the
King's consort, 407*l*. 10*s*. 4½*d*., for the appraisement of the goods
and stock valued at the manor of the said Queen, and purchased
for the King's use at divers prices.

To the same, 609*l.* 14*s.* 7½*d.*, for so much money received for the farms and issues of the manors which belonged to the aforesaid Queen, from the time of her death unto Tuesday next after the feast of the Purification, in the 20th year: paid to the said John and Richard at divers times, and according to divers particulars.

To Hugh de Kendale, for erecting a certain house in the burial-ground of the Abbot of Westminster, in which the statues of King Henry and Eleanor, Queen of England, late consort of the present King, were being made, 116*s.* 4½*d.*

---

19 EDWARD I.

WRITS FOR PAYMENTS, 19 EDWARD I.

Edward, by the grace of God, King of England, Lord of Ireland, and Duke of Acquitaine, to his Treasurer and Chamberlains, greeting,—Pay from our Treasury to our dearly beloved daughter Mary, 100*l.*, for Michaelmas Term, in the 19th year of our reign, of those 200*l.* which we granted her yearly, to be received at our Exchequer, for support of her chamber. Witness ourself, at Bristol, the 3rd day of October, in the 19th year of our reign. By writ of privy seal.

Edward, &c.—Pay, &c., to Ela, Countess of Warwick, 25*l.*, of those 50*l.* which we granted her for life, to be received yearly at our Exchequer, for the manor of Dimmok, which she surrendered to us. Witness, &c., at Bristol, 1 October, anno 19°.

Edward, &c.—Pay, &c., to Florence, Earl of Holland, 1000*l.* sterling, for the 4000*l.* of black Turnois money, in part payment of a certain sum of money which we owed to the same Earl for the marriage of his eldest son, which he granted to us. Witness ourself, at Northampton, 16 May, anno 19.°

Edward, &c.—Pay, &c., to our beloved in Christ the Abbess of
Fontevrault, 41*l*. 5*s*. 2*d*., at Michaelmas Term, of the 82*l*. 10*s*. 4*d*.
which she receives at our Exchequer of our appointed alms.
Witness ourself, at Bergevenny, 22 October, anno 19°.

Edward, &c.—Pay, &c., to our beloved and faithful uncle,
William de Valencia, 7*l*. 19*s*. 1¼*d*., at Michaelmas, of the 15*l*.
18*s*. 0¾*d*., which we granted him yearly; to be received at our
Exchequer, for the land which Sibyll, who was the wife of
Gerard Talebot, holds in dower, in the manor of Geynesborough,
which belonged to the aforesaid Gerard, and which after the death
of the same Sibyll will remain to the aforesaid William and
his heirs, in satisfaction of fifty librates of land, assigned to the
aforesaid William in the aforesaid manor of Geynesborough, by
the Lord King Henry, our father, in part satisfaction of a yearly
fee of 50*l*., granted to the same William and his heirs, by our
aforesaid father, until satisfaction should be made to them for the
fifty librates of land aforesaid, by our said father, or by his heirs.
Witness, &c., at Bergevenny, 26 October, anno 19°.

Payment made to the same William deValencia, of 55*l*.16*s*. 3¾*d*.
for the 111*l*. 12*s*. 7½*d*., which he ought to receive at the Exchequer for the value of so much land which the Lord King
Henry, our father, for himself and his heirs, granted to the same
William and his heirs, &c., saving to us our demand and challenge
in the lands which belonged to Robert de Vendenal, held by the
said William. Tested as above.

Edward, &c.,—Pay, &c., to our beloved and faithful John de
Metingham, Robert de Herteford, Elye de Bekyngham, William
de Gyselham, and Master Robert de Thorp, our justices of the
Bench, 115 marks,—to wit, to the aforesaid John 30 marks, and
to the aforesaid Robert de Herteford 25 marks, and to each of the
aforesaid Elye,William, and MasterRobert 20 marks atMichaelmas
Term, in the 19th year of our reign, for their annual fees, which
we granted them to be received for the offices aforesaid. Witness.

ourself at Westminster, the 28th day of November, in the 20th year of our reign.

Edward, &c.—Pay, &c., to the Master of the house of Saint Lazar, of Burton, procurator of the lepers of Saint Lazar, of Jerusalem, in England, 40 marks, for the use of the lepers aforesaid for Michaelmas Term, in the 19th year of our reign, for those 40 marks which the Lord King Henry, our father, by his charter, (which we have seen,) granted to the lepers aforesaid yearly to be received at his Exchequer at the term aforesaid, of his appointed alms. Witness, &c., at Hereford, the 3rd day of November, anno 19°.

Edward, &c.—Pay, &c., to our beloved and faithful John le Butiller, 30s., for the 18th and 19th years of our reign,—to wit, 15s. for each year, which we granted him yearly to be received, &c., in recompense for three quarters of wheat which were extended yearly at 15s., and which the Master and Brethren of God's house of Postesmouth received each year from the manor of Wymering, which, together with the corn aforesaid, was extended at 40l. yearly, and which we granted to the same John according to that extent in part satisfaction of sixty librates of land, which we granted to be assigned to him for the manor of Ryngwode, which he surrendered and quit-claimed to us, &c. Witness ourself, at Westminster, the 1st December, anno 20°.

Edward, &c.—Pay, &c., to our beloved and faithful Philip de Wilyheby, Chancellor of our Exchequer, John de Cobeham, William de Carleton, and Peter de Leycester, our barons of the same Exchequer, 160 marks,—to wit, to each of them 40 marks at the terms of Easter and of Saint Michael, in the 19th year of our reign, for their annual fees, which we granted them to be received for their offices aforesaid. Witness, &c., at Westminster, the 2nd December, anno 20°.

Edward, &c.—Pay, &c., to William Juge, 80l., in aid of the expenses which he incurred in prosecuting and defending our affairs, from the feast of the Holy Trinity, in the 15th year of our reign, from which time we retained the same William in our service, unto the feast of the Holy Trinity in the 19th year,—to wit, for four whole years, viz. for each year, 20*l.* Witness, &c., at Berewick-upon-Tweed, 12th August, anno 19°.

Edward, &c.—Pay, &c., to our beloved servant Hugh de Louthre, 20*l.*, for Easter and Michaelmas Terms, in the 19th year of our reign,—to wit, for each term 10*l.*, which we granted him in aid of his expenses which he incurred in prosecuting and defending our affairs. Witness, &c., at Stebenheath, 11th December, anno 20°.

Edward, &c.—Pay, &c., to our beloved in Christ the Master, Brethren, and Sisters of the hospital of Saint Catherine, near our Tower of London, 11 marks and 2*d.* for the 18th and 19th years of our reign,—to wit, for each year 5 marks, 6*s.* 9*d.*, which we have granted them to be received yearly, in recompense of the damage they sustained by the enlargement of the ditch which we caused to be made around the Tower aforesaid. Witness, &c. at Westminster, the 30th November, anno 20°.

Edward, &c.—Pay, &c., to the venerable Father John, Bishop of Winchester, 1000 marks, which he lent us in the 19th year of our reign, and receive from him his letters patent acknowledging the receipt thereof, together with our letters patent which he hath thereon. Witness, &c., at Westminster, 2nd December, anno 20°.

Edward, &c.—Pay, &c., to Lawrence de Lodelaw 1000 marks, which 1000 marks at our request he paid to Richard Guydicois and his companions, our merchants of the society of Ricardoz, of Luca, in part payment of a certain debt which we owe to the same merchants, and for which the same merchants have our letters patent, and upon making this payment receive from the

same merchants our letters aforesaid. Witness ourself at Stebenheath, 11 December, anno 20°.

Edward, &c.—Pay, &c., to the Abbot of Vale Royal, 200*l.*, for
the works of their monastery, and for other things which we owe
them. Witness, &c., at Saint Albans, 14th July, anno 18°.

Edward, &c.—Pay, &c., to the usher of the Exchequer, 9*s.*, for
taking eighteen summonses to divers of our counties in England,
&c.; and 39*s.* for taking forty-seven writs for his daily allowance at
divers places in England; also pay to the same usher, 8*s.* 7*d.*, for
wax to seal the same summonses and writs, &c.; also pay to the
knights, chamberlains, clerks, and servants of the Exchequer, and
for other small necessary issues during seventy-eight days, &c.,—
to wit, to the two chamberlains, each receiving 8*d.* per day, 104*s.*;
to three scribes, each receiving 5*d.* per day; to the usher of the
Exchequer, 5*d.* per day; to the four tellers, each 3*d.* per day;
to the watchmen and for a light, 1½*d.* per day; and for thirty
dozen of parchments, purchased for the Rolls of the receipt, and
for certain Rolls of the great Exchequer, and other necessaries,
30*s.*; for matts purchased for the house of the barons of the receipt, and for the chapel near the house of receipt, and rushes
for the same, 13*s.*; for a certain leather forul, purchased to contain
the Rolls of King John; for a certain canvas sack to contain the
Rolls of the 15ths.; for a certain coffer, with two locks and keys
to contain the Remembrancer's Rolls, 14*s.* 6*d.*; for one new chest,
purchased to contain divers particulars of divers accountants, 4*s.*6*d.*;
and for twenty-six dozen of canvas bags, purchased to contain
the money of the receipt, 52*s.*; for porterage, of money carried
from the Receipt to the Treasury, and back from the Treasury
to the Receipt, 3*s.* 6*d.*; for one skin of leather to file the tallies,
and a box purchased to contain the King's letters; to the precen-
tor of Westminster, for ink for half a year, 3*s.* 4*d.*

Edward, &c.—Pay, &c., to our beloved and faithful William de
Vescy, constable of our castle of Scarborough, 25*l.* for the term of

Saint Michael, in the 18th year of our reign, of the 50*l.* which we granted him yearly to be received by our commission, so long as he should have the custody of that castle. Witness ourself, at Kingisclipston, 29th October, anno 18°.

Edward, &c.—Pay, &c., to our beloved in Christ the Abbot of Reading, 100*l.*, as well for the release and quit claim which the same Abbot made for himself and his convent to us and our heirs, of the 10 marks yearly which he and his predecessors have been accustomed to receive at our Exchequer by grant of Lord Henry, of renowned memory, formerly King of England, our father, for the mark of gold yearly which John, formerly King of England, our grandfather, granted them by his charter, to be received at the same Exchequer in pure and perpetual alms, as for the release and quit claim of all arrears thereof; and before this payment shall be so made receive from him the charter of our aforesaid grandfather, and also the charter of our aforesaid father, which thereof he hath, and also the letters patent of release and quit claim from the same Abbot, as well for the aforesaid 10 marks yearly for the aforesaid mark of gold yearly, as for all arrears thereof. Witness, &c., at Westminster, the 6th day of February, anno 20°.

Edward, &c.—Pay, &c., to our beloved Florence, Earl of Holland, 2500*l.* sterling for 10,000*l.* of black Turnois money, in part payment of a certain sum of money for which we are bound to him for the marriage of John his eldest son, for the use of Elizabeth our daughter, taking from the same earl his letters patent of discharge upon receipt of the money aforesaid. Witness ourself, at Devises, the 26th September, anno 19°.

Edward, &c.—Pay, &c., to our beloved clerk, Walter de Langueton, keeper of our wardrobe, 10,000*l.*, for the expenses of our household. Witness, &c., at Coldstream, 1st August, anno 19°. Also pay to the same 10,000*l.*, for the same purpose. Witness, &c., at Westminster, 11th January, anno 20°.

20 EDWARD I.

MEMORANDA ROLL OF THE PELL, MICHAELMAS, 19 BEGINNING
20 EDWARD I.

To William Sprot and John de Ware, for providing latten metal for the tomb of King Henry, to repair the metal upon the same by the hands of Hugh de Kendale, 20*l.*; paid to the aforesaid Hugh.

To three of the King's messengers, bearing letters under the seal of the Bishop of Winchester, concerning the taxation of a tenth granted to the Lord the King in aid of the Holy Land, directed to the vicar of the Archbishop of York, the Bishops of Carlisle, Saint David's, and other bishops in England and Wales, and to all the bishops in the kingdom of Scotland, concerning the affairs of the tenth aforesaid, &c., 40*s.*

To Master Peter de Insula, Archdeacon of Exeter, for the stipends and salaries of certain scribes for transcribing the Rolls of the ecclesiastical taxation in the provinces of Canterbury and York, which Master Gifford delivered to Master William de March, Treasurer of the Exchequer, and for parchment purchased for the same; and also for the expenses of the same Master Peter coming from Exeter by command of the aforesaid Treasurer upon the business of the tenth granted in aid of the Holy Land, and for the expenses of Master Peter de Avebyr, being with him upon the same business, 103*s.* 4*d.*

To Master John Bush, a notary public of London, for transcribing and reducing into a public form the bulls of Lord Pope Nicholas the Fourth, which he granted to the present King for a tenth from the churches of England, Scotland, and Ireland in aid of the Holy Land, in compensation for his labour and

for certain expenses which he incurred in going to the King
at Ambresbury upon the same business, 100s.

To Master John of Gloucester, clerk, assigned to inspect, keep,
and examine the money arriving at Dover from beyond seas and in
the parts adjoining, for his expenses, 100s.

---

21 EDWARD I.

HOUSEHOLD ROLL of LORD EDWARD THE KING'S SON, beginning the 21st year of the reign of King Edward his
Father, during which time William de Bliburgh was keeper
of his wardrobe.

Wax, 32½ lb. Wine for the chapel, stock, 25 4 lb. gallons, &c. — Thursday at the feast of the blessed King Edmund, the 20th day of November at Stanewell.—The dispensary, 24s.10d.; the buttery,12s.8d.; the kitchen, 58s. 6½d.; the scullery, 10s. 7½d.; the salsary, 5s. 2d.; the hall, 5s. 1d.; the chamber, 20d.; the stable, 19s. 4½d.; for wages, 5s. 6d.; for alms, 12d. — Sum, 7l. 4s. 5½d.

Wax, 29 lb. Wine for stock, 24 gallons, &c. — Friday following at Hylindon.—The dispensary, 20s. 7d.; the buttery, 14s. 3d.; the kitchen, 39s. 10½d.; the scullery, 7s. 8d.; the salsary, 2s. 6½d.; the hall, 7s. 8d.; the chamber, 7s. 5d.; the stable, 19s. 7d.; wages, 5s. 6d.; alms, 3s. — Sum, 6l. 8s. 1d.

Saturday following at Rick-
mansworth.—The dispensary,
22*s.* 3*d.*; the buttery, 9*s.* 9½*d.*;
the kitchen, 43*s.* 8½*d.*; the
scullery, 7*s.* 11½*d.*; the sal- Sum,
sary, 5*s.* 3*d.*; the hall, 4*s.* 9*d.*; 6*l.* 4*s.* 0*d.*
the chamber, 3*s.* 6*d.*; the
stable, 20*s.* 3⅓*d.*; wages,
5*s.* 6*d.*; alms, 12*d.*

Sum of the three days, 19*l.* 16*s.* 6½*d.*

Note.—This Roll then proceeds to give the daily expenditure of the prince's household, adding up the amount of
each day; the total is carried out to the right-hand margin of
the Roll, and the daily totals are again added up at the end
of each week, which in the whole amount to 3896*l.* 7*s.* 6½*d.*,
being for a period of one year. The name of the place where
the prince sojourned each day is also stated, and on the
dorse of the Roll, which consists of ten membranes, is contained the names of the nobility and other persons who dined
with the prince, stating when they arrived and departed.

The following dates are taken from the first of those membranes, upon the dorse of which is entered the names of those
persons who dined with the prince, and the marginal number
is a reference to the dorse of the same membrane; which entry beginning with the words *" Isto die Martis,* &c., renders
it impossible to ascertain the exact day of the month.

Saturday, the 4th day of January, at Langley.

m. 2 dors. On this Tuesday there dined with the Lord the Prince the
Lord Bishop of Ely.

On this Thursday came to dine the Lady Countess of
Gloucester, with her knights, ladies, clerks, and certain
esquires, receiving nothing except from the Marshal, and
they went away on the Saturday after dinner.

Wednesday, February, at the feast of the Purification.

m. 3 dors.   On this Saturday there came Castellan de Bergles, with him four knights and two sons of Lord R. de Typetot, and on the day following after breakfast departed.

On this Tuesday came Lord Hugh de Veer and Lord Stephen Fitzwalter, and Lords P. and I. de Matteburgh, and departed on Wednesday.

On this Thursday came John de Brabant and two sons of Lord Edmund from the tournament at Dunstaple, with a great retinue; and Lord John de Brabant, on Sunday after breakfast, departed towards Canterbury, and part remained in our retinue.

On this Sunday John de Brabant returned from Canterbury.

On this Tuesday after breakfast departed John de Brabant, and the two sons of Lord Edmund.

On Tuesday came Lord Earl of Gloucester and the Lady the Countess to dinner, with a retinue of 200 knights, ladies, maids of honour, and esquires, and they received nothing except from the Marshal, and departed on Thursday following; the Lady the Countess, before her departure, with her maids of honour and esquires, breakfasted.

On this Saturday there dined with the Lord the Prince, the Lord Bishop of Durham and a certain bishop and brother minor, who belonged to the retinue of the Bishop of Durham, and Lord John de Berwick. The Bishop departed after dinner, and Lord John de Berwick stayed all night.

Sunday 22nd March.—Feast of Palm Sunday.

m. 4 dors.   On this Wednesday came Lord Peter de Sabaudia.

On this Tuesday there was at dinner with the Lord the Prince and the Ladies, Lord Edmund the King's brother.

Wednesday following the 26th day of April at Mortlake.

m. 5 dors.   On this Thursday there were at dinner with the Lord the Prince and the Ladies, the Lord Bishop of Durham and Thomas and Henry, sons of Lord Edmund, and John de Brabant.

On this feast of Pentecost there were with the Lord the Prince, Edward, son of the King of Scotland, Lady Agnes de Valencia, the Prior of Merton, Master I. de Lacy, the two brothers of . . . de Leyburn, knights, and Lady de Vescy, who returned seven days ago, and many others, strangers, with her.

On this Monday came Castellan de Bergles, and with him three knights, and stayed all night, having hay and corn for their horses, and continued there ; on the same day Lady de Valencia, and Lady de Vescy, and the son of the King of Scotland, departed after breakfast.

On this Tuesday departed before breakfast Lady de Valencia and Castellan, and Lord de Vescy after dinner.

On this Wednesday there dined with the Lord the Prince, the Earl of Lincoln, and with him four knights.

On this Thursday there dined with the Lord the Prince, John de Bar, Roger le Mohaut, Roger de Leyburn, Castellan de Bergles, and with him three knights, the wife of Walter de Bello Campo, with one knight and five ladies, and many esquires, strangers, who came upon the marriage of Eleanor, daughter of John de Mereworth.

On this Sunday, at the feast of the Trinity, there was at dinner with the Lord, the Lord Bishop of Durham, the

Archbishop Gibelee, who came in his retinue, and is a brother minor.

Memorandum, that the sum of this Wednesday was charged for the expenses of Brother Roger, who was sick at Bernes,—to wit, for his expenses on Monday and Tuesday preceding, 27s. 10½d.

Thursday following the last day of May.

m. 6 dors.   Memorandum, that the sum of this Friday was charged for the expenses of Brother Roger, sick at Bernes,—to wit, for his expenses on the Wednesday and Thursday preceding, 34s. 7d.

On this Wednesday came the Lady Maria, Abbess of Ambrisbury, with her, five nuns and a great retinue, and two sons of Lord Edmund with their household, and departed on Sunday after dinner.

On Wednesday came to dine, John de Brabant, and with him were thirty horses and twenty-four grooms at wages, the two sons of Lord Edmund,—to wit, Thomas and Henry, with thirty horses and twenty-one grooms, and remained at our expense in all things, and also for hay, oats, and wages of the grooms.   They remained Thursday, Friday, Saturday, Sunday, and continued to remain on Monday, and were charged for those days.   John de Brabant and Thomas and Henry, sons of Lord Edward, breakfasted at Kyngeston, going to . . . . . at Fulham, and were at great charge, &c.

On this Tuesday the Lord the Prince held his Commons in the great hall of the Lord Archbishop.

Wednesday following, the 5th day of July, at Chillam.

m. 7 dors.   On this Monday there dined with the Lord the Prince, Lord William de Langley and Lord John de Berwick.

Sunday, 16th August, at Winchester.

m. 8 dors.   On this Tuesday there were in the Society of the Lord
the Prince, John de Brabant, the two sons of Edmund, also
there came the Lord the King, and very many strangers
to hunt in the forest of Ascheby by command of the Lord
the King, and tarried with the Lord the Prince the Wednesday and Thursday following.

On the two days of Monday and Tuesday, and on Wednesday, there were with the Lord the Prince, the steward of
the Lord the King, the hunters, Welshmen, and very many
others of the King's household at all charges.

On this Wednesday the Lord the King dined with the
Lord the Prince.

On this Thursday there were with the Lord the Prince,
Thomas of Lancaster and Henry his brother. Thomas
departed on the morrow, and Henry remained with the
Prince on account of illness.

On this Tuesday the Lord the Prince rode to Salisbury
and heard high mass, and there were with him at dinner
the abbot, canons, and many others of the choir, also very
many of that county.

On this Wednesday there dined with the Lord the Prince,
the King's daughter, a monk and some other monks.

On this Thursday there were at dinner with the Lord the
Prince, before her departure, the Lady the King's daughter, some monks with the whole convent of monks and their
household.

On this Tuesday the Lord the Prince, with his household,
dined at Weston with Lord John de Weston.

Wednesday next after the 27th day of September, at Melksham.

m. 9 dors. On this Saturday there were present in the retinue of the Lord the Prince, the Earl of Bar and John de Brabant, with a great suite, and many knights of the King's household.

Note.—On Membrane 10, at the end of the Roll, which closes on Thursday after the 15th day of November, is the following summary or total added of the whole expenditure; viz.—

Sum of wine for the stock from the beginning unto the end of this Roll, 3891 gallons 1 pitcher, which make 74 casks 6 gallons 1 pitcher, reckoning 52½ gallons for 1 cask, from which are subtracted 13½ casks and 4 gallons of wine for wine expended by the gallon before Easter in the present year, &c.

Sum of wax of the whole Roll, 10,149 lbs.

Sum total of this Roll, 3611*l.* 6*s.* 9*d.*; approved.

And this is the sum total of the Roll for necessary expenses, messengers, gifts, oblations, and for divers particulars allowed upon this account, as appears at the end of the same Roll, 285*l.* 0*s.* 9½*d.*

Sum total of both Rolls, 3896*l.* 7*s.* 6½*d.*

The same William de Bliburgh hath received at divers times, whereof he answers in the 21st year, 3966*l.* 16*s.* 1*d.*

And so the same William remained in arrear at the end of this account, 70*l.* 8*s.* 6½*d.*, which is charged upon him, and whereof he answered in the 22nd year in the month of May, and so is here therefrom discharged.

Note.—There is also another Household Roll of a somewhat similar nature to the last, but without date, though evi-

dently about the same period; the names of the guests are also
entered on this Roll, and the price of the provisions purchased
is added, some few of which are extracted below; viz.

2 Geese	9d.	7 Fieldfares	2d.
8 Cocks	16d.	100 Herrings	10¼d.
2 Capons	5d.	50 Whelkes	12d.
2 Pullets	2d.	4 Mullets	1s. 5d.
3 Woodcocks	4½d.	Roach and Dace	6d.
100 Eggs	7d.	6 Stockfish	10½d.
1 Falcon	14d.	1 Lamprey	5s. 9¾d.
2 Rabbits	10d.	1 Stick of Eels	3d.
1 Pheasant	12d.	Half a basket of Cod-	18d.
1 Woodcock	1½d.	lings and Haddock,	
12 Snipes	4½d.	1 Basket of Place	2s. 6d.
4 lb. of Tallow Candles,	9d.	1 Piece of Sturgeon	12d.
		50 Eggs	3d.

ISSUE ROLL, EASTER, 22 EDWARD I.

To Gilbert de Gaunt, 1232*l*., for the manors of Folkyngham,
Edenham, Hekynton, and Barton-upon-Humber, which the King
purchased from him; paid to him by the hands of divers persons, as appears on the dorse of the writs of liberate thereof made.

LIBERATE ROLL, EASTER, 23 EDWARD I.

To John, Duke of Brabant, 20,000*l*. sterling, in part payment
of 160,000*l*. of black Turnois money, which the King owed
him for the services which the same Duke was bound to perform
for the Lord the King, with 2000 armed horsemen, against the
King of France, as between the same King and the aforesaid
Duke fully it was agreed.

I

To Walram, Lord de Mountjoye de Faukemont, 75*l.*, for 300*l.* of black Turnois money, the value of which the King granted he might receive at his Exchequer—to wit, one-half at the term of Saint Michael, and the other half at Easter last past, for his annual fee, &c.

To Ruffin de la Ferarde, 80*l.*, for a bay war horse, which the Lord the King purchased from him in the month of November last, for his own use.

ISSUE ROLL, EASTER, 30 EDWARD I.

23rd May.—Five hundred pounds, paid to Betin de Friscobold and his companions, merchants, of the society of Friscobolders, of Florence, for certain jewels made in France by the same merchants, for the use of the High Pontiff; delivered by the hands of the said Betin and Cracie his clerk, to the said Betin and his companions, at London, for the 1000*l.* which Master Nicholas de Ocham brought there on Monday, in seven days of Pentecost; paid to him on the eleventh day of June, in the present year; and the remaining 500*l.* they then delivered to Master Amantus de la Bret, as appears, &c.

Half a mark paid to John de Malling, a fishermen, for a sturgeon for the King's use, taken in the river Ouse, near the city of York; by command of P. de Willoughby, deputy to the present Treasurer. W. de Persore paid the same, on the 30th day of July.

MEMORANDA ROLL OF THE PELL, MICHAELMAS, 30 EDWARD I.

Memorandum that the Treasurer delivered to the Chamberlains, on the 18th day of October, in the present year, the assay made for the Exchange of Dublin, in Ireland, into the Tower of London, on Wednesday at the feast of St. Peter ad vincula, in the

30th year; which same assay remains in the custody of the Chamberlains, in a certain box, contained in a certain sealed purse within the said box.

Memorandum that the Chamberlains received by delivery of the Treasurer, at York, on Thursday, the 28th day of November, in the present year, a charter of Ralph Pippard, which he made to the Lord the King, of all the manors, castles, towns, lands, and tenements, together with knights' fees, advowsons of churches and religious houses in Ireland, which the same Ralph held on the day of making the charter aforesaid.

Master John de Droknesford, keeper of the King's wardrobe, on the 24th day of November, paid 10s. to John de Lumpuce, for binding two books of the fees of England, newly written out, by command of Peter de Willoughby, deputy to the Treasurer.

MEMORANDA ROLL OF THE PELLS, MICHAELMAS, 31 EDWARD I.

The Bishop of Coventry and Lichfield, Treasurer.—Payments made by Master John de Droknesford, keeper of the King's wardrobe, anno 31 Edward I.

15th October.—Paid to William de Aston, clerk to the Bishop of Coventry and Lichfield, so much as the same William had paid for the King at the Court of Rome, to divers Cardinals in the said Court, for fees which the King owed, and for the King's other necessary payments—to wit, to Master Gillinus de Pergamo, of St. Nicholas, in prison; to Tully, dean to the Cardinal, for his fee for the whole 31st year of King Edward, 50 marks; to brother Gentilus, by the title of Saint Martin in the mountains, priest to the Cardinal, 25 marks; to Master Luke de Flysco, of Saint

Mary, in Via Lata, dean to the Cardinal, for the said whole year, 50 marks; to divers knights and servants of the chamber of the Lord the Pope, of the gift of the Ambassadors from the King of England, 11*l.* 1 mark; to divers couriers sent from the Court to the King, 4 marks; and for divers expenses incurred about Master Bartholomew, from Florence, who was taken ill on his journey to Rome, 43*s.* 4*d.*; and for a gold cope, purchased and presented to Master Peter Yspano, the Cardinal, on behalf of Lord Edward, son of the King of England, 86*l.* 1 mark. And be it remembered that the said Lord John de Droknesford hath fully delivered all the said particulars by delivery of William de Eston, together with three letters of discharge from the said three Cardinals, for their fees aforesaid.

18th October.—10 marks paid to Master Thomas de Querl, for jewels and other things provided for the passage of the Lady the Queen beyond the seas; by command of the Treasurers, John de Droknesford and John de Sandale.

22nd November.—50 marks paid to Huward de Seyru, valet to Elizabeth, Countess of Holand and Hereford, by the hands of Brach Gerard, of the King's gift, for the news which he brought to the King of the delivery of the aforesaid Countess.

January.—To Master John de Droknesford, keeper of the King's wardrobe, upon his writ of liberate, containing 2000 marks, which is dated at the town of Saint John of Perth, the 15th day of July, in the 31st year of King Edward; paid 7*s.* to John de Langeton, clerk to the Treasurer, for so much money which he delivered to Robert le Porter, for carrying the Treasurer's letters from the town of Leen to Dumfermelyn to the King; and to David, the courier, for taking letters from the same Treasurer, from Coldham, to the Archbishop of Canterbury, in Kent, upon the King's affairs—to wit, to the aforesaid Robert, 5*s.*, and to the said David, 2*s.*, on the 15th day of January.

[Several entries on this roll for collecting and taking money into Scotland for the King's use, also for collecting an aid to marry the King's eldest daughter.]

EASTER, 34 EDWARD I.

Memorandum—that on this present Tuesday, next after the octaves of the Holy Trinity—to wit, on the 7th day of June, Andrew, formerly William de Tang, clerk sacrist in the diocese of York, a public notary, by authority of the Apostolic See, delivered into the Treasury a certain public instrument, containing thirty-five membranes, signed by him, which public instrument was used as ratified in the dispute lately arising between the present King of England and John, King of Scotland, and the nobility and subjects of his kingdom, for the reconciliation of the said King of Scotland and the nobility of that kingdom to the faith and will of the said King of England; and respecting the homage and fealty done by the same King of Scotland and his nobility to the King of England; which said instrument was made in testimony of the acts done in these premises. And on the same day the instrument aforesaid was delivered to William de Brichull and William de Pershore, Chamberlains of the King's Exchequer, &c. And on the same day a like instrument was delivered into the King's Chancery, and another like instrument into the wardrobe of the Lord the King, &c.

1 EDWARD II.

Memorandum, that on the 15th day of March there came to
the Exchequer William de Melton, comptroller of the King's
wardrobe, and brought the King's seal which had been used in
England during the time the King was abroad this present year,
under which seal the King's writs, that were issued from the
King's Chancery in England, were sealed during the above period,
by testimony of Peter de Gavaston, Earl of Cornwall, then the
King's deputy in England, and the same seal was contained in a
certain purse of white leather, sealed with the privy seal of John de
Langeton, Bishop of Chichester, Chancellor of England, and was
delivered on the same day at the Exchequer, in the presence of
John de Sandale, Chancellor of the same Exchequer, William
de Carleton, Roger de Hegham, Master Richard de Abingdon,
and Master John de Everdon, barons; and Walter de Norwick,
Remembrancer of the same Exchequer. And immediately the
said seal, in the said purse, so sealed, was delivered to the Chamberlains of the Exchequer, to be kept in the King's Treasury—
to wit, to Henry de Loutergarshale, chamberlain, John Devery,
clerk to the Treasurer at the Receipt of the Exchequer, and
John de Bukingham, clerk of Lord William de Pershore, chamberlain, &c., in the presence of the said John de Sandale, the
Barons, and Remembrancer.

To John de Benstede, keeper of the King's wardrobe, upon his
writ of liberate, containing 20,000 marks, dated at Nottingham,
the 1st October, in the first year.—Paid 4l. to Thomas de
Couplonde, Nicholas Lovel, Robert Lovel, and Ernon de
Merk, the King's falconers, to each of them 20s.—On the 6th of
October, 10 marks paid to John de Eggleshale, a valet of the
King's household, to provide for his office in the hall of North-

ampton Castle, against the coming of the king there.—On the 18th day of October, 14*l.* 0*s.* 3*d.* paid to divers persons, as follows—to wit, to Albinus, the cross-bowman, of London, for two cross-bows of three feet, 16*s.*; for two cross-bows of two feet, 10*s.*; for nine cross-bows of one foot each, 31*s.* 6*d.*—To Master Richard of Bayonne, cross-bow maker, for four cross-bows of two feet, 20*s.*, and for three cross-bows of one foot each, 10*s.* 6*d.*; and to the said Albinus, for thirty balders for the said cross-bows, 33*s.*; for cord, nuts, and other necessary apparatus for the said cross-bows, 19*s.* 1*d.*—To William Courad, for 5100 darts for the said bows, 115*s.* 2*d.*; and to the said Albinus, for flaskets and cord to pack and cover the said bows, 18*s.*; and to the said William Courad, for a case to put the said darts in, 8*s.*—Expenses for carrying the said bows from London to Striveling Castle, to fortify the same castle.

Paid, on the 24th day of October, 500*l.*, to Lord Peter de Gaveston, Earl of Cornwall, by the hands of Robert de Wellesworth, clerk of the said Earl, for so much money which the same Lord the Earl lent in the wardrobe for the Lord the King.

Paid, on the last day of October, 10*l.*, to John de Rippele and Nicholas de Lughteburgh, clerks, for their expenses in going to divers parts of England to make preparation for the Scotch war, &c.

Paid, on the 4th of November, 52*l.*, to Richard de la Bayr, for two war horses, purchased from him for the King's use, the one a bay and the other white spotted.—20*l.* paid to Adam de Billing, for a roan coloured palfrey, purchased from him, and given by the King to the Countess of Cornwall.

Paid 173*l.* and half a mark to Lord William de Felton and five knights, his companions, and forty servants, for an advance of wages, on their going into Scotland, there to remain in the war, whose names are entered in a certain roll delivered into the King's wardrobe by command of the Treasurer.

Paid, on the 15th of November, 1000*l.* to Sir William de Felton, knight, and John de Wrockwardyn, clerk, to be taken to Berewick upon Tweed, and there delivered to Lord Eustace de Cotesbech, Chamberlain of Scotland, to pay for the King's expenses there in the war, &c.

[Here follows a long list of payments to persons proceeding to the Scotch wars, with their expenses for provisions, &c.]

Paid, on the 25th of November, 20*l.* to John Lamb, a mariner, to provide a certain ship appointed for the passage of the Lord the King, by command of the Treasurer.

[This part of the Roll contains a full account of the King's preparation for the Scottish war, and of payments made for his passage to Scotland.]

Paid, on the 2nd of December, 20*l.* to John de Lincs, of London, and Richard de Campes, of the same place, by their own hands, to provide and purchase by view of William de Berton, clerk, and William Corrad, for the King's use, the under-written things :—wine, honey, vinegar, cross-bows with strings of hemp for the cross-bows, darts, and divers other things, as appears by a commission which the same John and Richard have under the seal of the Exchequer, which is dated at Westminster, the 25th day of November, in the now first year ; by command of the Treasurer.

Paid, on the 13th of December, 30*l.* to Peter de Sparham, by the hands of Godin, his boy, for divers tassels of gold, a chaplet and frontal of gold, and for an alb with pearls and silk, and divers other mercery of this sort, purchased from the same Peter by the King's command, and given by him to the Countess of Cornwall and to other ladies and maids of honour then with him; by command of the Treasurer.

Paid, on the 30th of December, 200*l.* to Richard Poterel son of Richard Poterel, citizen and draper of London, by his own hands, to provide cloth for the King's coronation.——

6th January, 100*l.* paid to Adam Wade, Thomas de Wrotham, John le Huthereve, Roger le Palmer, and John de Romeneye, corn chandlers, of London, chosen by the mayor and sheriffs of London to provide corn for the coronation, &c.——On the same day, 40*l.* paid to Nicholas Picot and Nigell Drury, Sheriffs of London, to provide beer for the said coronation.——9th January, 100*l.* paid to Ralph Ratespray and Nicholas Doreman, merchants, of London, to provide large cattle and boars for the coronation.—— On the same day, 50*l.* paid to John Fairhod, Thomas de Hales, Thomas Wastel, Roger le White, and John de Talworth, wood [and coal] merchants, to provide wood and coal for the said coronation.——On the 11th of January, 200*l.* paid to Thomas Brun, poulterer, of London, chosen by the mayor and sheriffs of London to provide poultry for the coronation of the Lord the King. ——On the same day, 80*l.* paid to Henry de Say, the King's butler.——On the 12th day of January, 100*l.* paid to Adam de Foleham, of London, to provide fish for the coronation.——Same day, 20*l.* paid to John le Discher, of London, for him and his companions, to provide plates, dishes, and saltsellers, for the coronation.——50*l.* paid to Walter de Haken, fishmonger, of London, for him and his companions, to provide large fish for the coronation; also 20*l.* paid to Henry de Redenhale, to provide small pike for the coronation; also 40 marks paid to Hugh de Bungey, for making armour, beds, and apparel for the Lord the King on the day of his coronation; also 10 marks paid to Gilbert de Taunton, for a saddle made for the King, by command of the same King; also, on the same day, 33*l.*, for three pair of silver helmets, purchased and delivered to Master Thomas de Butterwick, clerk to the said keeper, by the hands of the Treasurer, to be sent to the Court of Rome, by command of the Treasurer; also 10 marks paid to George de Percy, for a palfrey and a saddle given to the same George by the King.——100 marks paid to Edward de Lovekyn, on the 15th January, to provide sheep, pigs, large cattle, and things of this kind, against the coronation of the Lord the King.——On the 17th January, 100*s.* paid to Ralph de Stok, for certain clerks sent to divers places to provide cloth to cover the hall at the King's coronation. ——On the 23rd January, 15*l*. 10*s*. paid to Master Ralph de Stoke, by the hands of John Brame, a Brabant merchant, for cloth purchased from him for the King's body.——On the 26th January, 40 marks paid to Hugh de Bungeye, for making armour and apparel for the King's body for the day of his coronation : on the same day, 200*l*. paid to Thomas Brun, chosen by the mayor and sheriffs of London to provide poultry for the king's coronation.——On the 29th day of January, 10 marks paid to Henry de Redenhale, to obtain from Gloucester lampreys for the King ; by command of the Treasurer.——On the 29th day of January, 20*l*. paid to Roger de Frowyk, by his own hands, for repairing a sceptre, and for other works against the coronation ; by command of the Treasurer, &c.

Paid, on the 5th February, 272*l*. 10*s*. 4*d*. to Master Richard de Lutheburgh, clerk, by his own hands, for so much money as the same Master Richard lent to the Lord the King at Boulogne, against the festivity of the nuptials of the same Lord the King there, as appears by a letter patent of the said keeper, acknowledging the receipt of the same money, dated at Boulògne, the 26th January, in the present year, remaining in the possession of the Chamberlain.

CHARGE OF THE EXECUTORS OF LORD EDWARD, LATE KING OF ENGLAND.

To Walter de Langeton, Bishop of Coventry and Lichfield, Henry de Blunteston, brother Luke de Wodeford, of the order of Preaching Friars, and Robert de Cotingham, Executors of the will of Lord Edward the King, deceased,—200*l*., paid to the aforesaid brother Luke and Robert, by their own hands, on the 4th day of October, upon the writ of the said Executors of liberate, containing 20,000 marks, which is dated at Nottingham, the first day of October, in the first year, for payment of the expenses

of the said Lord the King, deceased, and his family; by command
of the Treasurer.——To the same Executors, on the 9th day of
October, 53*l*. 6*s*. 8*d*. paid to Master John de Claxton, by his
own hands, for the expenses of the Lords Thomas and Edmond, the
King's sons, deceased, and Eleanor, daughter of the said King;
by command of the Treasurer.——To the same, on the 3rd day
of November, 100 marks paid to the aforesaid brother Luke
and Robert, by their own hands, to distribute to the poor for the
soul of the King; by the Treasurer's command.——To the same,
on the 15th day of November, 10 marks, paid to William de
Horseden, by his own hands, for his stipend and labour whilst
remaining at Waltham with the body of the deceased King; by
command of the Treasurer.——On the 27th day of November,
40*s*. paid to William Attefenne, the sumpter-man, for the great
labour he sustained in providing torches and leather for the
body of the deceased King.——On the 14th day of December,
100*l*. paid to Master Andrew Lumbard, by the hands of Andrew Boncristien, for horses purchased from him for knights
to ride in the King's armor before his body, between the church of
the Holy Trinity, of London, and Westminster, for two days.——
On the 28th day of December, 100*l*. paid to the Lady the Queen,
by the hands of John de Tunford, for her expenses from the day of
the death of the Lord the King unto the day of his burial; by
command of the Treasurer.

On the 14th day of March, in the middle time after the feast
of Saint Hilary, at the close of the Exchequer, 50 marks paid
to the same, by the hands of John de Sellyngg, apothecary, of
London, for various drugs purchased from the same John in divers
years, for the use of the Lord the King, whilst he was Prince of
Wales.——On the 16th day of March, 10 marks paid to Master
William de Hodocote, the King's cook, by his own hands, for the
debt which was owing him out of the wardrobe of the Lord the
King whilst he was Prince of Wales; by command of the
Treasurer.

To Robert de Thorp, keeper of the King's mines in the county of Devon, and to the Abbot of Tavistock, controller of the said mines, upon his writ of liberate, containing 200*l.*, which is dated at Westminster, the 11th December, in the 1st year of the reign of King Edward; paid 20*l.* to the said Robert on the 18th day of November, by his own hands, for working the mines aforesaid, by command of the Treasurer.

To Master James de Levesham, the King's smith, in the Tower of London, to whom the Lord the King granted daily 8*d.*, for his wages, so long as he should remain in the office aforesaid, 5 marks, &c.

ISSUE ROLL, MICHAELMAS, 4 EDWARD II.

21st October.—Twenty marks paid to John de Chaucomb, by his own hands, of the King's gift, for the news which he brought to the same Lord the King, respecting the Lady Eleanor le Despenser; by the King's command.

28th August.—Twenty marks paid to Sir Robert de Haustede, junior, knight, by his own hands, for the expenses and preparations made for the burial of the body of the Lady Eleanor, the King's sister, at Beaulieu, by command of the Treasurer; also on the 20th of November, 100*l.* paid to Henry de Ludgareshale, for the same purpose.

12th November.—In two tallies made—to wit, one to Robert de Thorp, for the issues of the King's mines in the county of Devon, containing 200*l.*; and the other to John de Sandale, for the farm of the manor of Eshford, containing 40*l.*, by command of the Treasurer.

20th November.—Eighty-seven pounds ten shillings paid to Lady Isabella, Queen of England, by the hands of Lord

William de Bougdone, her Treasurer, in part payment of 1000*l.* sterling, due to the same Lady the Queen, for so much money paid by the same Lady the Queen for the Lord the King to the Lady Blanch, of Brittany, out of the issues of her lands in Pontieu, of the King's gift, in aid of marrying a certain daughter of hers; by command of the Lord the King by privy seal.

ISSUE ROLL, EASTER, 8 EDWARD II.

5th May.—Paid to Lord William, Bishop of Exeter, 100*l.*, by a tally made to him, for the custody of the land which belonged to Thomas de Cogan, to have the same for his expenses in going with certain other nobility of the King's council to France, upon certain business of the Lord the King, touching the duchy of Acquitaine, and there prosecuting the same.

On the same day 50 marks were paid to Sir Maurice de Berkeley, knight, by the hands of the Abbot of Croyland and Nicholas de Cambridge, in part payment of 1000*l.*, which he receives of the Lord the King for the custody of the town of Berwick upon Tweed—to wit, from the feast of Pentecost last past, for one year following, fully to be completed, as appears by a certain indenture made between the same Lord the King and the aforesaid Maurice, one part whereof remains in the wardrobe; for which said 50 marks, the letters of acquittance of the aforesaid Maurice, testifying the receipt of the money from the aforesaid Abbot and Nicholas, remain in the custody of the chamberlain.

7th May.—Paid to Lord Adomar de Valencia, Earl of Pembroke, 50*l.*, by the hands of Master Walter Alisaundre, his chaplain, for his expenses in going to the Court of the Lord the King of France, in the retinue of the Lord Bishop of Exeter and others of the King's council, upon the King's affairs in those parts, touching the duchy of Acquitaine.

Monday, 19th May.—Paid to Sir Bartholomew de Badlesmere, knight, 266*l.* 13*s.* 4*d.*, by the hands of the merchants of the society of Bardolph, of Florence, for payment of that which he receives from the Lord the King, for himself and his men at arms, with him in the Marches of Scotland, living in the retinue of Lord Adomar de Valencia, Earl of Pembroke, and of other noblemen there, on behalf of the Lord the King.

5th June.—Paid to Sir Robert de Montealto 60*l.*, by the hands of Master William de Melton, for that which he received of the Lord the King, whilst he remained in the retinue of certain other English nobility in the Marches of Scotland.

9th June.—Paid 9*l.* 10*s.* to Master Robert de Welle, receiver of the King's provisions at Carlisle, by his own hands, for the wages of divers men at arms, hoblers, archers, and other persons, going with him from London to Carlisle, and there remaining in his retinue, &c.

Paid to Master Stephen le Blound, Chamberlain of Scotland, 78*s.* 9*d.* by his own hands, for the wages of divers men at arms, hoblers, archers, and others, going with him from London to Berwick, and there appointed to remain in the garrison of the said town.

14th June.—Paid 20*s.* to Thomas Springet, William Kempe, and Edmond de Grenewiz, mariners, the money received by their own hands of the King's gift, for their labour in taking a whale, lately caught near London Bridge.

3rd July.—Paid 280*l.* to Lord Adomar de Valencia, Earl of Pembroke, by the hands of William de Lavenham, his receiver, receiving the money in the presence of Sir William de Cleidone, his knight, in part payment of the 2000 marks which the aforesaid Adomar receives from the Lord the King by agreement made with him—to wit, for the allowance which he receives for the defence of the Scotch Marches, for himself and his men at arms remaining here with him, as appears, &c.

13*th July.*—Paid to Master Alexander le Convers 1200*l.*, received by his own hands, for the wages of divers mariners sailing together to the islands of Scotland and Ireland, from Bristol and elsewhere, &c.

Paid to Walter Waldeshef, butler to the Lord the King, 1000 marks, by the hands of the mayor and citizens of London, as an allowance for his office, &c.

30*th July.*—Paid to Stephen le Convers 20*s.*, by his own hands, for his expenses in taking the letters of Master Alexander le Convers from Bristol to the Lords the Archbishop and Treasurer, and returning with letters from them directed to the said Master Alexander, concerning the sailing of the fleet upon the affairs of the Lord the King there.

1*st August.*—Paid to Adam, the messenger of Lord Adomar de Valencia, 40*s.*, by his own hands, for certain news which he brought to the King from the said Lord Adomar from Ireland ; also on the 8th of August 26*s.* 8*d.* to Thomas de Dummere, valet of Sir Edward Darel, Knight of Yorkshire and Constable of Werk Castle, of the King's gift, for the good news which he brought to the King from those parts.

16*th August.*—Paid to William le Clerk, of London, 8 marks, for that which was owing to him in the wardrobe, for eight pots of brass and one great brass pot, purchased of him for the King's use, and delivered to John de Somers, the King's scullion, by letters close of the aforesaid keeper, directed to the Lord Treasurer thereof, &c.——12*l.* paid to John Hereward, for that which is due to him for vessels purchased from him for the King's kitchen—to wit, one *black robyn*, price 20 marks, and for platters and such like, &c.

18*th August.*—Paid 16*l.* 4*s.* to Master John le Hauberger, for certain small armour for the King's use, and for repairing the King's armour ; a particular whereof is contained in a certain schedule, sealed with the seal of the said John, and remaining amongst the bills of the wardrobe, &c.

[This Roll contains numerous payments for the preparations of the King and his army in Scotland.]

ISSUE ROLL, MICHAELMAS, 9 EDWARD II.

18*th October.*—Paid 132*l.* to Sir Alexander de Claveryngg, knight, by the hands of the Bishop of Norwich and the Sheriffs of Shropshire and Staffordshire, for 120 quarters of wheat, price the quarter, 10*s.*; and 240 quarters of barley, price the quarter, 6*s.*, purchased from the same, &c.

26*th November.*—Paid 20 marks to Roger Frowyk, goldsmith, of London, by his own hands, in advance for making a crown of gold for the Lord the King, by command of the said Lord the King, by privy seal thereon; directed to the Lord Treasurer, &c. [There is yet owing to the same Roger, for making the said crown, 23*l.* 6*s.* 8*d.*, and other payments for the same are entered on this Roll.]

24*th November.*—Paid 8*l.* to Richard Golde, Master of the King's ship called the Peter of Westminster; to Richard Atte Wose, master of the King's ship called the Bernard of Westminster; to John Mut, master of the King's ship called the Marioun of Westminster; and to Richard Councedeu, master of the King's ship called the Mary of Westminster, each of them receiving 40*s.* by their own hands, for the equipment of the ships aforesaid.——10*l.*, paid to John de Taillour, of Rochester, master of the King's ship called the Catherine of Westminster, for the wages of himself and his men for the equipment of the same ship. [The names of other ships are also mentioned.]

5th December.—35*s*. paid to Brother John, of Wrotham, Prior of the order of the Preaching Friars, of London, by their own hands, of the King's Almoner, for seventy brethren of the aforesaid convent, as the same Brother John acknowledged before the Treasurer—to wit, to each of the same brethren, 6*d*., for performing divine service at the anniversary of the Lady the Queen, mother of the present Lord the King, by command of the same Lord the King, &c.

8th December.—266*l*. 13*s*. 4*d*. paid to Lord Humphrey de Bohun, Earl of Hereford and Essex, by the hands of Master Geoffrey de Clare, his clerk, in part payment of 1000 marks due to the aforesaid Lord the Earl, for the allowance which he ought to have received for his last passage with the Lord the King to Scotland, as fully appears by certain letters of privy seal of the Lord the King, thereupon directed to the Treasurer, upon which the same sum is indorsed, remaining amongst other writs of mandamus.

9th December.—20*s*. paid to William Ward, valet of the King's chamber, as an advance on the wages assigned him by the Lord the King, to keep certain private chambers for the King in the palace of the said Lord the King at Westminster.

16th December.—24*l*. 19*s*. 7½*d*. paid to Master Albert Medici, clerk, in part payment of 61*l*. 12*s*. 11½*d*., due to the aforesaid Albert, for his expenses in going from London to Gascony, there remaining and returning, and again going back, upon the affairs of the Lord the King, touching the duchy of Acquitaine, as appears by a certain bill delivered into the wardrobe, upon which the sum is indorsed; and now there is satisfaction made to the aforesaid Master Albert for the whole debt aforesaid, at the request of the Lady the Queen, consort of the Lord the King, &c.

K

17th January.—200 marks paid to Lord Robert de Umframville, Earl of Anegos, by the hands of William de Overtone,
his chaplain and attorney, in part payment of 700 marks which he
receives of the Lord the King, by agreement made between them,
for his two castles—to wit, Hartbotle and Prudhou, which he
holds on behalf of the King in the Marches of Scotland, with
forty men at arms and eighty hoblers, in the castle of Prudhou,
and also with twenty men at arms and forty hoblers, retained in
his retinue, to harass the enemy, &c.; to be paid for as is fully contained in the transcript of the agreement remaining amongst the
writs of mandamus, by the King's mandate of privy seal thereupon, directed to the Treasurer, &c.

12th February.—Half a mark paid to Simon de Miravalle, a
fishmonger of London, for a certain fish called a " sturgoun,"
caught at Woolwich by the men of the said Simon, and afterwards,
on the 23rd day of March, presented in a certain barrel, salted to
Master William de Northwell, clerk of the King's kitchen, for
the King's use.

To David Atte Hope, the King's smith at Westminster, and
Bernard de Lescar, maker of the King's spears and lances, 4*d.*
a day each whilst they were employed; 16*s.* 4*d.* to the aforesaid
David and Master Bernard, for a certain great millstone by them
purchased and provided to properly point the heads of the King's
spears and for other similar works, &c.; also 60*s.* paid to John de
Norton, surveyor of the King's works within the King's palace
at Westminster, &c.; to purchase iron, steel, and sea coal to
make divers heads for the King's lances, &c.

8th March.—10 marks paid to Philip de la Beche, valet of the
King's household, for himself and his companions, for their expenses in remaining at the Tower of London for the custody of
John de Morreue and Robert Barde, Scotch prisoners, imprisoned
in the Tower aforesaid by command of the Lord the King, under
privy seal directed to the Treasurer.

10*l.* paid to Lord John de Crumwelle, knight and steward of the King's household, by his own hands, for his expenses, sent by the same Lord the King and his council to la Pole to appease and settle a quarrel and strife which had arisen between the Lords Griffin de la Pole and John de Charletone, &c.

19*th March.*—266*l.* 13*s.* 4*d.* paid to Lord Henry de Bello Monte, knight, by the hands of Gerrard de Chartres, his valet and attorney, made before the Treasurer in part payment of those 1000 marks which he was to receive from the Lord the King for remaining at the castle of Norham, for the defence of those parts, with 80 men at arms, by agreement made with him, as is contained in a certain indenture made between him and the Lord the King, one part of which remains in the wardrobe, &c.

27*th March.*—20*l.* paid to Master Adam de Brugges, farrier to the Lady the Queen, consort of the Lord the King, and to William de Watford, keeper of the palfreys of the same Lady the Queen, by the hands of John de Salisbury, for a bay horse purchased by them of John Fleg, a horsedealer of London, and delivered to them to carry the litter of the said Lady the Queen.

6*th November.*—10*l.* paid to Master Martin Fisshacre, at the request of Lord Hugh le Despenser, senior, for restoring one of his horses for the King's service at Stryvelyn, in the 7th year, &c.

8*th November.*—100 marks paid to Lord Thomas de Brothertone, brother of the Lord the King, in part payment of 124*l.*16*s.* 8*d.* due in the wardrobe for the expenses of Edward de Balliol in the 5th and 6th years, as appears by a certain bill, &c.

17*th November.*—20*l.* 7*s.* 10*d.* paid to Gilbert de Wygeton, clerk, at the desire of the Lady Queen Margaret, for monies by him at divers times paid for the King, as appears by a certain bill of the wardrobe remaining in the Treasury.

To Nicholas de Tykhull, late clerk of the works at the King's palace at Westminster, in advance, &c.—to wit, for the carriage of timber and planks from the wood of Bustlesham to Westminster, for the King's palace against the coronation of the same Lord the King, together with the wages of the carters and divers men as well for the carriage aforesaid as for carrying of divers cloths purchased at Abindon to cover the said palace, as is contained in a certain indenture made between the aforesaid Nicholas and Thomas Danvers, late Sheriff of Oxford and Berks, &c.,— 14*l.* 4*s.* 2*d.*

Issue Roll, Easter, 10 Edward II.

12th April.—49*s.* 10*d.* paid to Guido de Villars, an esquire to the Lady the Queen, the King's consort, by his own hands, at the request of the said Lady the Queen, for so much money due to him, &c.

13th April.—20 marks paid to Roger de Gretford, the King's bailiff at the manor of la Nayte, to complete certain works there began for the Lord the King by his command.

15th April.—20*l.* paid to Brother Richard de Brumfield, of the convent of Preaching Friars, of London, of the King's alms, for three days' entertainment of the Brethren of the said order, who met together to hold their general chapter at Pampilloun, in the kingdom of Arragon, at the feast of Pentecost last past,— to wit, one day for the Lord the King himself, the second day for the Lady the Queen his consort, and the third for the Lord Edward their son, by command of the Lord the King, under his privy seal, thereupon directed to the Treasurer and Chamberlains.

26th April.—220*l.* paid to Lord Robert de Mortimer of Wygemore, by the hands of Lord Walter, bishop of Exeter, in part payment of 2000*l.* which he received from the Lord the King for the wages of certain men at arms in the retinue of the same Lord Roger going to Ireland in the King's service, &c.

6th May.—8*l.* 0*s.* 4*d.* paid to Walter de Spaldingg, the King's goldsmith, by his own hands, for making a silver image, weighing 10 marks, for the use of the Lord the King, which said image the King so commanded to be made, &c.

17th May.—50 marks paid to Rose, the wife of John de Bureford, a citizen and merchant of London, by her own hands in part payment of 100 marks due to the same Rose for an embroidered cope for the choir, lately purchased from her to make a present to the Lord High Pontiff from the Lady the Queen, consort of the Lord the King, and sent by the King's messengers going to the court of the said Lord High Pontiff.

18th May.—13*l.* 9*s.* 1½*d.* paid to Simon de Swanelound, merchant, by his own hands, in satisfaction of 115*l.* 3*s.* 4*d.* due to the same Simon for cloth purchased from him, and by him delivered to the Lord the King into his wardrobe, to make mantles for the King's knights and tunicks for his valets, going with him to Scotland; by command of the said Lord the King, under his privy seal, directed to the Treasurer, remaining amongst other writs of mandamus of Michaelmas term last past.

4*l.* paid to Hugh de Bungeye, by his own hands in advance for making a bed for the Lord the King, &c., and 20*l.* paid to Master Ralph de Stokes, clerk of the King's great wardrobe, by the hands of Master Richard de Monte Pessulano, his clerk, to purchase a carpet and bauker for the King's use, and also for making the bed of the same Lord the King.

21st May.—20 marks paid to Master Henry de Shirokes, clerk of the King's wardrobe, by his own hands, for the expenses of the

Lady Mary, the King's sister, and Lady de Bourgh, going on a pilgrimage to Canterbury, &c.

22nd April.—10*l.* paid to Lord Thomas, Earl of Norfolk, by the hands of Sir Giles de Trumpetone, his knight, as an advance upon that which is due to the same Earl for the allowance which was directed to be made him from the Lord the King for the continuance of Lord Edward de Balliol in his retinue, by the King's command, under the privy seal thereupon directed to the Treasurer and Chamberlains, &c.

To William Herle, one of the King's sergeants, 10*l.*, paid to him on the 25th day of May, by the hands of the executors of the will of Guy de Bello Campo, late Earl of Warwick, for this present Easter Term, for the 20*l.* yearly which the King granted him in aid of his expenses in prosecuting and defending the affairs of the said Lord the King, by writ of liberate dated at Windsor, the 28th April, in the 10th year, &c.

To William Fraunceis, to whom the King, by his letters patent, granted 50 marks yearly, to be received out of the farm of the city of York, on account of the kind service he lately performed for the King in his presence at Dunbar—to wit, at the feast of Saint Michael, 25 marks, &c.

To William de Everdone, one of the Remembrancers of the Exchequer, to whom the King, by his letters patent, granted 30*l.* yearly to be received at the Exchequer, &c., until he should provide him with a competent ecclesiastical benefice for the good services he had performed, as well for Lord Edward, formerly King of England, as for the present Lord the King, &c.

ISSUE ROLL, MICHAELMAS, 14 EDWARD II.

To the Ushers of the Receipt, for string purchased by them for divers rolls and memoranda of the time of Kings Henry the Second, Richard, John, Henry the Third, and Edward, the son of King Henry, put in the King's chapel in the Upper Tower of London; received the money, the 4th day of April, by the hands of Hugh de Braye,—12s.

To Hervey de Staunton, Chancellor of the Exchequer, 20 marks, paid to him on the 6th day of March, by the hands of Thomas de Todydone, his clerk, for his fee at this present Michaelmas Term. By writ, &c.

To William the bookbinder, of London, for binding and newly repairing *the book of Domesday*, in which is contained the counties of Essex, Norfolk, and Suffolk, and for his stipend, costs, and labour; received the money the 5th day of December, by his own hands,—3s. 4d.

ISSUE ROLL, MICHAELMAS, 15 EDWARD II.

To William de Haustede, keeper of the Exchange of London, for old money particularised and found in the Treasury at the Tower, delivered to the custody of the office of Treasurer and Chamberlains for melting and coining the same, together with a silver seal broken, and eight small pieces of silver, and also one piece of melted silver arising from false money perforated at the receipt, a memorandum whereof is fully noted in the memo-randa of the greater Exchequer, amongst the records of this term,—17l. 14s. 6d.

Issue Roll, Easter, 17 Edward II.

To Bernard Trankalion, to whom the King of his especial grace granted 500*l.* of small Turnoise money of his gift, in aid of his expenses incurred in defending the confederacy moved against him and his subjects by the King of France and his subjects concerning the King's jurisdiction, and which the same King commanded should be paid to his constable of Bourdeaux for the time being, for that which the aforesaid King's constable at Bourdeaux had directed to be expended in the King's said affairs since the quindene of the present feast of the Nativity of Saint John the Baptist, and that the said 500*l.* should be paid to the said Bernard at the said quindene, excepting 5 marks of the same sum, which the King commanded to be paid to the Procurator of the aforesaid Bernard for prosecuting the business aforesaid, &c.

To Nicholas de Hugate, clerk, whom the Lord the King appointed receiver of his monies to be expended for his affairs in the duchy of Acquitane, upon his writ of liberate containing 10,000*l.*, to be paid to him for the expenses of a certain fleet of ships and men, as well horse as foot, going in the service of the said King to the aforesaid duchy, which writ was dated at Westminster, the 1st of May, anno 17°, &c.—133*l.* 6*s.* 8*d.* was paid to him on the 28th May, by the hands of Fulk Fitzwarren Banaret, which the Lord the King commanded the same Fulk to pay, &c., to wit, 66*l.* 13*s.* 4*d.* to prepare himself to go in the King's service to the duchy of Gascony, and 66*l.* 13*s.* 4*d.* for his wages, which he received of the King in the service aforesaid, which said money the same Fulk bound himself to forfeit the same to the King if for any cause it should happen he should not go over to the same parts, which bond, &c. —To the same, on the 28th May, 66*s.* 8*d.*, paid by the hands of John Devery appointed to prepare and expedite certain ships in the counties of Southampton, Somerset, Dorset, Devon, and Cornwall, for the King's services in Gascony, as to the same John by the said Lord the King fully it was enjoined, which said John received daily 2s. for his wages so long as he was attending to this business. By writ of great seal, &c., dated at Westminster, 27th May, anno 17°, &c.

On the 20th June, 59s. 7d. paid to divers fletchers of London for 100 smooth arrows purchased for the King's use, and delivered to the aforesaid Nicholas to be given to divers archers sent to Gascony.—On the 10th August, 10l. paid to Master Robert Bendyn, captain and admiral of the King's fleet of all the ships proceeding from the mouth of the river Thames westward, in the King's service, by the hands of Thomas de Hornynton, his valet, for the expenses of the same Robert, going in the King's service abovesaid, by writ of the great seal, dated at Hanle, 8th August, anno 18.—On the 16th August, 10l., paid to Master John Sturmy, captain and admiral of the King's fleet, of all ships about to proceed in the King's service from the mouth of the river Thames northwards, going upon the service aforesaid, &c. [The payments made on account of this expedition are too numerous to be extracted, the names of many of the captains and officers proceeding therein are mentioned, together with an account of the arms furnished them, &c.]

ISSUE ROLL, EASTER, 18 EDWARD II.

To Richard de Worcester, keeper of the mine of the Lord the King at Burlond, in the county of Devon, 50l., paid to the same on the 15th day of June by his own hands, for the works there done in the mine aforesaid. By writ of great seal for that purpose, directed to the Treasurer and Chamberlains, dated at Westminster, the 15th day of June, in the 18th year, &c.

To the Abbot and Convent of Westminster, to whom King Henry, formerly King of England, grandfather of the present

King, by his charter granted and confirmed for himself and his heirs, for the honour of God and of Saint Edward the King, especial patron of the present King, by the hands of the said King's grandfather, or by his Queen, or their heirs, whether they be in or out of the kingdom, that there should be rendered by the hands of the Treasurer of the said grandfather or of the present Lord the King, or who for the time shall be Treasurer, 24 halfpenny weights of frankincense, yearly for ever, in the name of chevage, upon the high altar in the church of Westminster—to wit, 12 half pennyweights at the feast of the burial of the aforesaid Saint, and 12 halfpenny weights at the feast of the Translation of the same Saint, as in the charter aforesaid fully is contained; the price of each halfpenny weight of frankincense, 20d., as appears by the account of John de Drokenesford, late keeper of the King's wardrobe, rendered at the Exchequer for the 27th, 28th, and 29th years—10l.

ISSUE ROLL, MICHAELMAS, 19 EDWARD II.

Memorandum that on the 7th day of February, Nicholas le Clerk, armourer of London, came here, and brought one part of a certain indenture made between him and John de Weston, Constable of the Tower of London, testifying that the same Nicholas had delivered to the same Constable 100 coats of mail, 100 covered helmets, and 100 pair of iron gauntlets, the price of each coat of mail, 7s., of each helmet, 3s. 4d., and each pair of gauntlets aforesaid, 1s. 8d.; and so the whole price of the armor aforesaid is 60l., of which sum he received 30l., in part payment for the aforesaid armor, which said armor the King commanded to be provided for fortifying the Tower aforesaid.

1 EDWARD III.

ISSUE ROLL, EASTER, 1 EDWARD III.

To Thomas de Berkle and John Mautravers, upon their writ of liberate containing 200*l.*, paid to them for the expenses of Lord Edward, late King of England, father of the present King, which writ is dated at Alderwyk, the 5th day of this month of July, and remains here. In money paid to the same by the hands of Richard de Harsfeld, valet of the aforesaid Thomas, in part payment of the said writ—66*l.* 13*s.* 4*d.*

ISSUE ROLL, MICHAELMAS, 1 EDWARD III.

4th February.—To Robert de Wodehouse, keeper of the King's wardrobe, for the price of 174 florins from Florence, price each florin as purchased 39½*d.*, paid to the same keeper by the hands of John de Houton his clerk, for one pound and one mark of gold to make oblations on the day of the coronation for the Lord the King:—and in like manner was delivered 104 florins and a mark of 70*s.*, by the King's command under the privy seal, which was used before he received the government of this kingdom, which is here amongst the writs and mandates of this first year,—28*l.* 12*s.* 6*d.*

ISSUE ROLL, MICHAELMAS, 2 EDWARD III.

23rd October.—To Hugh de Glanvill, clerk, assigned to him by the Treasurer and Barons of the Exchequer for the expenses

incurred upon removal of the body of Lord Edward, late King
of England, father of the present King, from Berkeley to the
abbey of Saint Peter Gloucester. In money paid to the same
by his own hands for the expenses aforesaid, by mandate of privy
seal, which is dated at Nottingham the 10th day of October last
past;—answered for here &c.,—5*l.*

18*th December.*—To Nicholas de Hugate, clerk, appointed by
the King to superintend the preparation of the apartments in the
palace of the Archbishop of York, to celebrate the solemnization
of the King's marriage. In money, paid to the same by his own
hands, for the preparations thereof, by writ of privy seal,—40*l.*

4*th March.*—To Roger, Bishop of Coventry and Litchfield,
lately sent upon a message for the Lord the King to Hainault,
to contract a marriage between the Lord the King and the
daughter of the Earl of Hainault, from the 8th day of October
last past, on which day he set out for Nottingham, the Lord the
King at that time being there, and proceeded in his journey to
the parts aforesaid, until the 23rd day of January next following,
on which day he returned to the King at York, in the retinue of
the daughter of Earl Hainault aforesaid, including each day for
108 days, receiving 3*l.* 6*s.* 8*d.* daily for his expenses,—360*l.*; and
also for his passage and re-passage in going and returning, as
above, 20*l.* And for the expenses of John de Hoby, his clerk,
sent by the same Bishop from Hainault to the Lord the King,
with letters of credence to hasten this much spoken of marriage;
and also concerning divers other affairs of the Lord the King, from
the 29th day of October last past, on which day he proceeded on
his journey from the parts aforesaid to the same King, unto the
8th day of December next following, on which day he returned
from the King to the parts aforesaid, taking each day 18*d.* for his
expenses,—2*l.* 17*s.* 0*d.*; and also for his passage and re-passage in
going and returning as above, 13*s.* 4*d.*, receiving the money in one
tally, made on the same day to Roger, Bishop of Coventry and

Litchfield, charged upon the tenths, granted by the Clergy to the King, &c.—383*l*. 10*s*. 4*d*.

ISSUE ROLL, EASTER, 3 EDWARD III.

To Robert de Sutlyngton, for himself and three chaplains performing divine service daily in Saint Edward's chapel, within the King's castle of Windsor, and for two clerks assisting the said chaplains in the chapel aforesaid, by his writ of liberate containing 26*l*. 13*s*. 4*d*., for their wages and stipends from the feast of Saint Michael last past unto the same feast next following, &c.,—13*l*. 6*s*. 8*d*.

ISSUE ROLL, EASTER, 4 EDWARD III.

8th May.—To Master Thomas de Garton, keeper of the King's wardrobe, in money, paid to him by the hands of John Brokaz, for the purchase of the three undermentioned chargers,—to wit, one called Pomers, of a grey colour, with a black head, price 120*l*.; another called Labryt, dappled with grey spots, price 70*l*.; and the third, called a Bayard, of a bright brown bay, with the two hind feet white, price 50*l*. :—by writ of privy seal, dated at Woodstock, &c.,—240*l*.

ISSUE ROLL, MICHAELMAS, 4 EDWARD III.

26th February.—To Hugh de Glanvill, clerk, lately assigned to him by the Treasurer and Barons of the Exchequer, for the expenses incurred upon the removal of the body of Lord Edward, late King of England, father of the present King, from Berkeley to the Abbey of Saint Peter Gloucester; in one tally, made this day to Thomas de Rodberg, sheriff of Gloucester, upon the men of the town of Bristol, containing 28l. 6s. 8d., for the remainder of his account, and paid to the aforesaid sheriff, for so much money paid by the same Thomas to the aforesaid Hugh for the expenses aforesaid, as appears by the letters patent of the same Hugh acknowledging the receipt of the same money, which remains discharged in the Hanaper of this term, By writ of privy seal, dated at Nottingham, the 10th day of October, in the first year of the present King, and remaining amongst the mandates of Michaelmas term, in the second year of the present King,— 28l. 6s. 8d.

Issue Roll, Easter, 6 Edward III.

2nd June.—To a certain goldsmith of London, in money, paid to him by his own hands, for making a certain great seal for the Chancery of the Lord the King,—5l.

3rd June.—To Master William la Zousche, clerk of the King's great wardrobe, in money, paid to him by the hands of John le Charer, for making a certain chariot for the use and behoof of Lady Eleanor, the King's sister, by writ of liberate containing 1000l. Paid to him for furniture for the said Eleanor, amongst the mandates of Michaelmas term last past,—20l.

14th July.—To William de Boveye, one of the clerks of the Exchequer, for extracting from Domesday Book the names of the towns noticed in the same book under the title of "Terræ Regis," to be had for evidence in assessing the tallage newly to be assessed by the Council. In money, paid to him by his own hands for his labour by the Treasurer and Chamberlains,—3s. 4d.

Issue Roll, Michaelmas, 6 Edward III.

2nd October.—To Simon de Bury, master of the King's

scholars at Cambridge, to whom the Lord the King, in recompense for the books of the laws and canons which Lord Edward, late King of England, father of the present King, gave him, and which afterwards, by command of the Lady Isabella, Queen of England, were taken away from the aforesaid Simon, granted him 10*l.* of his gift. In money paid to him by his own hands in discharge thereof, by writ of privy seal, &c.,—10*l.*

20*th October.*—To Hugh le Seler, of York, for making a new seal for the regulation of the see of Durham, now vacant by the death of Lewis, of good memory, late Bishop of the see aforesaid (and now in the hands of the King), weighing 1*l.* 17*s.* 8*d.* for which the same Hugh received 30*s.* on the 8th of October last past, and now on this day the remaining 7*s.* 8*d.* for the weight aforesaid, and 20*s.* for the workmanship of the same seal, also for the loss in fusing the said, 1*l.* 17*s.* 7*d.* By writ of great seal amongst the mandates of this term,—1*l.* 9*s.* 7*d.*

25*th November.*—To Sir William de Shaishull, knight, sent to the King of Scotland to expedite the business of the Lord the King of England, in the parliament of the said King of Scotland, in money, paid for his expenses,—13*l.* 6*s.* 8*d.*

18*th February.*—To the Countess of Ulster, in money, paid to her by the hands of John de Hamburg, for the 100 marks which the King lately granted to the same Countess to be received yearly at his Exchequer, for the support of Elizabeth, daughter and heir of William, late Earl of Ulster, deceased, from the time of his death so long as the same Elizabeth should remain in the custody of the aforesaid Countess her mother,—33*l.* 6*s.* 8*d.*

ISSUE ROLL, EASTER, 9 EDWARD III.

26*th May.*—To Thomas Prior, valet of the Lord the King, to whom the Lord the King (for the welcome and desirable news

he brought to the same King concerning Edward his eldest
son) granted him, by his letters patent, 40 marks, to be received
yearly at his Exchequer during the life of the same Thomas, or
until the same Lord the King should provide him with forty marks
of land or rent, to hold during his life, &c.,—13*l.* 6*s.* 8*d.*

30*th May.*—To Catherine de Monte Acuto, in money, paid to
her by the hands of William de Northwode, in part payment of
200 marks which the Lord the King commanded to be paid her
for the 500 marks which the said Lord the King granted her for
the welcome news she brought him of the birth of his son, &c.

5*th June.*—To John, Earl of Cornwall, in money, paid to him
in discharge of 500*l.* which the Lord the King commanded to be
paid him of his gift, in aid of his expenses in going to Scotland,
—500*l.*

To Isabella de Lancaster, a nun of Aumbresbury, in money,
paid to her by the hands of John de Gynewell, for payment of
100 marks 'which the Lord the King commanded to be paid her
for a book of romance purchased from her for the King's use,
which remains in the chamber of the Lord the King,—66*l.* 13*s.*4*d.*

9*th June.*—To Bartholomew de Burghassch, in money, paid to
him by the hands of the Bishop of Lincoln, as an advance upon
that which the King might owe him upon his account as receiver
of Pontieu, for his fee during the time the said Bartholomew was
steward there, &c., 80*l.*

To Master William la Zousche, late clerk of the King's great
wardrobe, in money paid to John de Colonia, the King's armourer,
by the hands of Theodoric his brother, in part payment of 203*l.*
due to him in the wardrobe aforesaid, for divers costs and charges
by him incurred, about making a bed of green velvet embroidered
with gold,—10*l.* 28*th June.*—A further payment made to the said
William of 486*l.* 5*s.* 5½*d.*, which is owing to him in the wardrobe

aforesaid, for divers costs and charges by him incurred, about making the said bed of green velvet embroidered in gold with sea sirens, bearing a shield with the arms of England and Hainault, and for making a white robe worked with pearls, and a robe of velvet cloth embroidered with gold of divers workmanship, made by him against the confinement of the Lady Philippa, Queen of England, and for divers furniture made by him for the King's use, as appears by five bills sealed with the seal of the said clerk, in which the money below noted is entered, &c.,— 91*l.* 15*s.* 7*d.*

29th July.—To David de Wolloure, clerk, lately sent to Scotland to prosecute certain business for the Lord the King at the parliament of Edward de Balliol, King of Scotland, then called at Edinburgh. In money paid to him in discharge of 24*s.*, which the Lord the King commanded to be paid him for eight days,—to wit, for each day, 3*s.*, for his expenses in going to the parts aforesaid, &c.,—24*s.*

12th August.—To Nicholas de Acton, one of the Chamberlains of the Exchequer, sent by the Council with two clerks from York to London to order a certain great seal for the rule of the realm of England to be newly made; also there to deliver to Oliver de Ingham, steward of Gascony, certain muniments in the King's Treasury touching the said duchy; for going, tarrying, and returning eighteen days, including the first and last day; and in money allowed for the expenses of his clerks, men, and horses, by a particular of the same expenses which remains in the hanaper of this term. By writ of the great seal amongst the mandates of this term,—5*l.* 12*s.* 8½*d.*

18th August.—32*l.* paid to John Denton for the safe custody of the Earl of Murrief, the King's enemy, taken in the war, and detained in the King's prison at Bamburgh ; also another payment on the 23rd of August for taking the same Earl from York to Nottingham castle.

L

[This Roll contains payments for making divers tunicks for the Knights and Esquires proceeding to the Scottish war, and other preparations for the same purpose.]

ISSUE ROLL, EASTER, 11 EDWARD III.

17th May.—To Edward, King of Scotland, kinsman of the Lord the King, in money, paid to him in discharge of 100 marks, which the Lord the King commanded to be paid him for his expenses in coming to the Lord the King at Stamford to his council.   By writ of privy seal, &c.,—66*l.* 13*s.* 4*d.*

15th July.—To Edward, King of Scotland, in money paid to him by the hands of William de la Pole, mercer, of Hull, for the 50*s.* daily which the Lord the King granted him for the support of himself and family, &c.,—66*l.* 13*s.* 4*d.*

ISSUE ROLL, MICHAELMAS, 11 EDWARD III.

4th November.—To Matthew de Crauthorn, keeper of the mine in Devonshire, in one tally, made this day to the Abbot of Torre, collector of the fifteenths and tenths granted from the laity to the King in the county of Devon, containing 60*l.* of the same fifteenths and tenths, paid to the same Abbot by the hands of Ralph Spek, in allowance for so much money which the said Abbot paid to the aforesaid Matthew for the works in the mine aforesaid, &c.,—60*l.*

23rd November.—To John Bray, usher of the receipt, in money, paid to him by his own hands,—to wit, 8*l.* 17*s.* 6*d.*, for 187 gallons of honey, price the gallon, 10*d.*; and for 78 gallons of honey, 2*l.* 18*s.* 6*d.*, price the gallon, 9*d.*, purchased for the use of the Lord the King, by order of his Council; also for two empty casks purchased by him to put the said honey in, 10*s.*; which said casks, with the honey, the same John delivered to Thomas de Rokeby, sheriff of York, by indenture, &c., for the use of the Lord the King, taken to Strivelyn, and there lately delivered for the supply of the castle of that town. By writ for providing victuals as above, —12*l.* 6*s.*

To William de Northwell, clerk of the great wardrobe of the Lord the King, by the hands of Nicholas de Wyght, tailor to the same Lord the King, in payment of 29*l.* 6*s.* 9*d.*, due to him in the wardrobe aforesaid, as well for divers costs and expenses by him incurred for making the robes and divers other garments for the person of the said King, between the 1st of April in the ninth and 29th of September in the tenth year, as for his wages, he being from the Court during the same time,—17*l.* 2*s.* 9*d.* [There are other payments to the King's tailors entered on this Roll.]

7th December.—To Thomas de Blaston, one of the Barons of the Exchequer, in discharge of 20 marks which the King granted him for his expenses in going lately by the King's command to divers places, religious persons, and others, to obtain from them an aid to marry Eleanor, the King's sister, &c.,—13*l.* 6*s.* 8*d.*

12th December.—To Philippa, Queen of England, in money, allowed to Master Paul de Monte Flor, clerk, for a loan made to the Queen by the same Master Paul for divers robes which the same Master Paul bought and provided beyond the seas for the use of Philippa, Queen of England, the King's most dear consort, and for Edward, Earl of Chester, as appears by the letters of the said Queen testifying the receipt thereof, &c.,—1333*l.* 6*s.* 8*d.*

24th January.—To Henry Dymmok, one of the Ushers of the Exchequer, lately sent by the King's patent writ, which is amongst the mandates of this term, to seek for, arrest and take a certain William Lewelyn, and to bring him before the King's Council at York ;—for his going, tarrying, and returning at divers times, from the last day of July last past unto the last day of September next following. In money allowed to the same for his expenses, and for others going with him upon the business aforesaid &c.,—6*l.* 12*s.* 0*d.* [Also another payment to the same Henry for arresting John de Breclote and John de Cromhale.]

12th February.—To Bartholomew de Barde and his companions, merchants, of the society of Bardolph, of Florence, in money paid to them in discharge of 100*l.* which they paid by command of the Lord the King to William de Cusaunce, clerk, for expenses incurred about the funeral of John, late Earl of Cornwall, brother of the said Lord the King, as appears by letters patent of the said William, testifying the receipt of the said money, &c.,—100*l.*

Issue Roll, Easter, 14 Edward III.

4th May.—To Thomas de Rokeby, keeper of Edinburgh and Strivelyn castles, by the hands of Robert Baious and others, merchants, of Barton-upon Humber, by a tally delivered this day to the same merchants by the hands of the same Robert, containing 380*l.* 13*s.* 6*d.*, from the biennial tenths granted to the King in the fourteenth year, arising in the see of York,—to wit, for 674 quarters of wheat and malt, price the quarter, 9*s.*; and for 309 quarters 2 bushels of peas, price the quarter 5*s.*, delivered to Thomas Gretheved and John de Laton, his deputies, in the castles aforesaid, for the munition thereof, as appears by counterparts of certain indentures, &c., and by an indenture made between the Duke of Cornwall and the same merchants for the price of the same provisions remaining in the possession of the parties aforesaid, &c.,—80*l.* 13*s.* 6*d.*

ISSUE ROLL, EASTER, 15 EDWARD III.

21st May.—To William de Cusaunce, keeper of the King's wardrobe, by a tally delivered this day to Walter Dastyn, sheriff of Gloucester, containing 12*l.* 5*s.* 8*d.*, for the issues of his baili-wick, in allowance for so much money paid by the same keeper to the aforesaid sheriff, for the price of forty-four lampreys purchased by the same keeper, and provided for the use of the King's household by letter of the same keeper cancelled in the hanaper, of this term, &c.,—12*l.* 5*s.* 8*d.*

ISSUE ROLL, MICHAELMAS, 15 EDWARD III.

28th October.—To William de Munden, clerk of the Duke of Cornwall, for money by him paid for writing divers letters and other memoranda sealed with the seal of the said Duke, touching divers royal affairs, &c.,—13*s.* 6*d.*

8th November.—To Robert de Chaster, a courier, sent with let-ters to the Duke of Cornwall at Dover, in money paid to the same for his expenses,—8*d.*

20th November.—To Edward, Duke of Cornwall, in part pay-ment of 1000*l.* which the King lately granted him in aid of the expenses of his household, because the land which the Lord the King heretofore assigned to the same Duke was not sufficient for the expenses of his household aforesaid, and for other charges incumbent to be supported and maintained by him in the same household. By writ of privy seal, &c.,—106*l.* 13*s.* 3*d.*

Issue Roll, Michaelmas, 16 Edward III.

10th *November.*—To Robert de Tonge, by the hands of the Bishop of Durham, by a tally raised this day, containing 246l. 11s. 4½d., for many debts due to the same Bishop, in discharge of so much money which was lately owing to the aforesaid Bishop, —to wit, for 896 quarters of corn, price each quarter, with the advantage, 4s. 3d., and 556 quarters 3 bushels of oats, price the quarter, 2s., purchased from the aforesaid Bishop for the King's use, by his Council, and delivered to John de Thynden, deputy of Robert de Tonge, late receiver of the King's provisions at New-castle-upon-Tyne, by the attorney of the said Bishop,—viz. John de Asheby, as appears by the accounts of the said John de Thynden for the receipt of the same provisions,—246l. 11s. 4½d.

21st *November.*—To John de Chaundeler, of Bread-street, London, for wax purchased of him to provide wax-lights to be burnt around the body of Lord Edward, formerly King of England, grandfather of the present Lord the King, buried in the monastery of Westminster,—3l. 19s. 10d.

To Sir Robert Pawyng, knight, in part payment of 25 marks payable to him at Michaelmas term last past, for those 50 marks yearly which the King granted him for the good service performed to the King, and that he might the better be able to maintain the estate and military order which he had received from the King.

Issue Roll, Easter, 17 Edward III.

3rd *May.*—To William de Edyndon, keeper of the King's wardrobe, for the price of eight pieces of silver in plate, weighing 68l. 15s. 7d., received from John Moneroun, keeper of the King's mines in Cornwall, and delivered into the King's wardrobe, to make silver vessels for the King's household. By writ, &c.,—68*l.* 15*s.* 7*d.*

14*th July.*—To John Moneroun, keeper of the King's mine in Devonshire, in money, paid to him by his own hands in discharge of 80*l.*, paid by him for working three shafts in the same mine to the King's use. By writ of privy seal amongst the mandates of this term,—80*l.*

ISSUE ROLL, EASTER, 18 EDWARD III.

31*st July.*—To Robert Chapman, one of the workmen in the King's mine, in the county of Devon, coming to London to inform the Council of a certain new mine [discovered] in Cornwall. In money paid to him of the King's gift, to return to the same parts,—6*s.*

9*th September.*—To Edward le Balliol, King of Scotland, in money paid to him by the hands of Sir Robert Gower, knight, as an advance upon that which was in arrear of a certain allowance which the Lord the King of England lately granted to the same King of Scotland for the expenses of his household—to wit, 40*s.* per day in the time of peace and 60*s.* per day in the time of war; by writ current of the great seal remaining amongst the mandates of Easter Term of the 15th year, and by another writ of Privy Seal amongst the mandates of this term,—680*l.*

ISSUE ROLL, MICHAELMAS, 21 EDWARD III.

14*th November.*—To Thomas de Lucy, Sheriff of Cumberland, by a tally raised this day in his own name of the issues of his bailiwick, containing 306*l.* 19*s.* 2½*d.*, paid to the same Thomas in part payment of 700*l.*, which the Lord the King lately granted in recompense for the ransom of Duncan Magdowell and his son, whom the same Thomas took in the war in the Marches of Scotland, as appears by the King's letters patent of the Great Seal, which the same Thomas hath in his possession indorsed with the underwritten sum, &c.,—306*l.* 19*s.* 2½*d.*

21st November.—To Peter de Sancto Marcello, a valet from the Roman court, in money paid to him for that which was in arrear of a certain annual allowance of 40*l.*, which the Lord the King by his letters patent lately granted to the same Peter for the news which he brought to the said King of the consecration of the present Pope. By writ, &c.,—20*l.*

17th February.—In money paid for making the seal for Lyonell, keeper of England, son of the Lord the King, by writ of the same keeper amongst the mandates of this term,—1*l.* 13*s.* 2*d.*

3rd March.—To Thomas de Musters, Thomas de Ulvyngton and John Eryon, in discharge of 50 marks which the Lord the King commanded to be paid them in recompense for the ransom of Andrew Cambel, a Scotch knight, lately taken by them in the war at Durham, and brought by them at the King's command to the Tower of London, and there delivered to John Darcy, constable of the same Tower. By writ, &c.,—33*l.* 6*s.* 8*d.*

Issue Roll, Easter, 22 Edward III.

4th July.—To Sir Robert de Herle, knight, in discharge of 100*l.* which the Lord the King commanded to be paid him of his gift, because the same Robert delivered to the King, William de Vaux, a knight of Scotland, whom he lately took in the wars at the battle of Durham,—100*l.*

Issue Roll, Easter, 23 Edward III:

8th May.—To Sir Thomas de Gourney and Sir Peter de

Audele, knights, who went in the King's service to the town of Saint John the Evangelist and there remained in the King's service. In money paid to them in part payment of 80*l.*, which the Lord the King commanded to be paid to the same Thomas and Peter in aid of their preparations, &c.,—53*l.* 6*s.* 8*d.* [This Roll contains several similar entries of payments made to knights and other persons then in the King's service.]

25*th May.*—To Sir Thomas de Dagworth, knight, in part payment of 4900*l.* which the Lord the King granted him for the good services he had performed for the same Lord the King, and especially for capturing Charles de Bloys, the King's prisoner, calling himself the duke of Britany, &c.,—100*l.*

18*th June.*—To Brother Aufricus, a monk of Saint Matthew in Britany, who came to England to search for a certain gilt head of Saint Matthew. By writ of this term,—3*l.* 6*s.* 8*d.*

ISSUE ROLL, MICHAELMAS, 23 EDWARD III.

In money paid to fifty poor persons of the King's alms for carrying torches from Brentford to London with the body of William, the King's son,—50*s.*

ISSUE ROLL, EASTER, 24 EDWARD III.

14*th April.*—To Master Bernard de Casselon, nuncio from the Lord the Pope, coming as a messenger to the Lord the King, for the price of a cup with a silver ewer, given him of the King's gift, &c.,—7*l.* 13*s.* 4*d.*

19*th April.*—To Philippa, Queen of England, in money paid to her for twelve carpets purchased and provided for her last con-

finement at Windsor. By writ of Easter Term in the twenty-
second year,—60*l.*

4th May.—To Roger le Mortimer, a banneret, in money, paid
to him for his wages in the war and for his men at arms, and
archers going with him in the King's service beyond seas,—
321*l.* 13*s.* 4*d.*

2nd June.—To John de Grymstede, a goldsmith of London, in
part payment of 4*l.*, paid to him for engraving a certain seal
for the Lord the King for Ireland, by order of the Council,—2*l.*

4th June.—To Gerard de Tournaye, the King's armourer, in
money paid to him in part payment of 72*l.* due to him in the
King's wardrobe for plated armour, helmets, gauntlets, and
corsets of plate and divers other armour made for the King's
use, &c.,—17*l.* 13*s.* 4*d.*

To William de Wynterton, clerk of the Chancery, in money
paid to him for writing two charters of the foundation of the
King's chapel at Westminster,—6*s.* 8*d.*

1st July.—To John de Ipslyngrode, in money paid to him in
part payment of 1000*l.* which the Lord the King commanded to
be paid him of his gift for the efficient services which the same
John lately most meritoriously performed in capturing Charles
de Bloys, the King's enemy, in Britany, as appears by the King's
letters patent, which the same John thereupon hath in his possession indorsed with the underwritten sum. By writ of Privy Seal,
—100*l.*

15th July.—To William Mugge, chaplain of the King's chapel
at Windsor, in money paid to Thomas Cheiner, of London, in
discharge of 140*l.* lately due to him for a vest of velvet embroidered with divers work, purchased by him for the chaplain
aforesaid, &c.,—80*l.*

15th July.—To Sir John Ward, knight, lately taken in the war in France, in money paid to him of the King's gift in aid of his ransom. By writ of privy seal,—14*l.* 6*s.* 8*d.*

To William de Retford, keeper of the King's wardrobe, in money paid to him for money received of the Earl of Fife of Scotland, in part payment for the ransom of the same keeper, &c., —333*l.* 6*s.* 8*d.*

13th September.—In money paid as well for the wages of divers mariners retained in divers ports of England, as well from the north as the south, for the passage of the Lord the King by sea, and to arrest and take the Spanish enemy's fleet assembled to destroy the coasters upon the English coast, as for the wages of the clerks and divers other ministers sent to pay the wages aforesaid, and to retain shipping, in the month of August last past, as appears by the particulars of the payments thereon made remaining in the hanaper of this term,—1106*l.* 0*s.* 4*d.*

ISSUE ROLL, MICHAELMAS, 24 EDWARD III.

20th October.—To Thomas de Haukeston, constable of Tykhill Castle, in money paid to him in discharge of 96*l.* 14*s.*, due upon an account made with him for the custody and support of the Duke of Britany and his attendants, residing within the castle aforesaid, &c.,—96*l.* 14*s.*

4th December.—Money remaining in a bag for the making and regulating the assay elsewhere, therewith, by order of the Treasurer and barons, 46*s.* 6*d.*

7th December.—To John Cok, late clerk of the King's great wardrobe, by the hands of John Silvery, of Valenciens. In money paid to him in discharge of 1700 florins de Scuto, paid to the same John for making a certain bed for the use of the Lady Philippa, Queen of England. By writ, &c.,—84*l.* 6*s.* 8*d.*

4th February.—To Sir John de Potenhale, knight, for going upon the King's affairs to Calais to conduct Geoffrey de Charny a prisoner to London. In money paid to him of the King's gift for his expenses by writ of privy seal,—20*l.*

Issue Roll, Easter, 26 Edward III.

4th May.—To Sir Roger de Beauchamp, knight, sent to Berwick to treat with the Scots, and to bring David Bruys, king of Scotland to London. In money paid to him for his expenses, &c., —26*l.* 13*s.* 4*d.*

15th May.—To Martin Pardy, of Pystoy, in money paid to him for a certain stone called a "dyamand," purchased from him for the said Lord the King, &c.,—20*l.*

18th May.—To Sir Thomas de Kyngeston, knight, lately taken in the battle near Calais in the retinue of John de Bello Campo. In money paid to him of the King's gift in aid of his ransom, &c., —100*l.*

To Martin Pardy of Pystoy, in money paid to him for a certain crown purchased from him for the King, &c.,—100*l.*

26th May.—To Martin Pardy of Pystoy, in money paid to him for a gold ewer garnished with divers precious stones. By writ, &c. —133*l.* 6*s.* 8*d.*

5th June.—To Elizabeth de Vaux, in discharge of 10 marks which she lent to the Lord the King at the receipt of the Exchequer on the 14th day of November last past, paid to her on restoring a certain tally for the loan, as appears in the Roll of receipts of that day,—6*l.* 13*s.* 4*d.*

1st August.—To Sir John de Molyns, knight, in money paid to him by his own hands in part payment of 550*l.*, which the Lord the King directed to be paid him for the manor of Henly, purchased of him for the King's use. By writ, &c.,—50*l.*

To David de Bruys, King of Scotland, receiving daily 13*s.* 4*d.* for his support, in money paid to him as an advance in discharge of his same allowance,—to wit, from the 7th day of July last past unto the 5th day of August next following, for 30 days, both days included. By writ of Privy Seal amongst the mandates of Michaelmas Term last past,—20*l.*

14th August.—To Edward de Balliol, King of Scotland, in money paid to him by a tally raised this day in the names of the collectors of the King's customs and subsidies in the port of London, in discharge of 140*l.*, payable to him for a certain allowance of 40*s.* which the Lord the King lately granted to the same King of Scotland for the expenses of his household,—to wit, from the 12th day of May last past unto the 21st day of July next following for 70 days, both days included. By writ of privy seal amongst the mandates of this term,—60*l.*

21st August.—To Richard de Gretham, chaplain to David de Bruys, King of Scotland, in money paid to him of the King's alms in aid of his expenses,—1*l.* 6*s.* 8*d.*

ISSUE ROLL, MICHAELMAS, 26 EDWARD III.

11th October.—To John de Ellerton, the King's serjeant at arms, sent upon the King's affairs to bring Ralph de Camoys, knight, to London. In money paid to him for his wages by order of the Council,—1*l.*

12th October.—To Robert de Swylyngton, lately taken in the war at Calais by the French enemies. In money paid to him of the King's gift in aid of his ransom. Made by writ of privy seal, &c.,—33*l.* 6*s.* 8*d.*

5th November.—To Sir John de Potenhale, knight, to whom the Lord the King by his letters patent lately granted 100 marks, yearly to be received at the Exchequer out of the farm of the priory of Saint Faith's, at Horsham, for the good services by him performed for the said Lord the King, and especially for taking Geoffrey de Charny, a French knight, whom he lately captured in the battle at Calais, in money paid to him by a tally raised this day in the name of the Alien Priory of Saint Faith's of Horsham, containing 33*l.* 6*s.* 8*d.*; paid to the same John in discharge of 50 marks, payable to him for his said allowance, &c.,—33*l.* 6*s.* 8*d.*

9th November.—To Sir Thomas de Gourney, knight, for his journey to Gascony, in the retinue of Isabella, the King's daughter, in money paid to him for the wages of himself and of other men at arms going in her retinue to the same parts, &c.,—30*l.*

3rd December.—To William de Cusaunce, late keeper of the King's wardrobe, in money paid to him in part payment of 307. 9*s.* 3½*d*, due upon an account made with him before Richard de Feriby, Master John de Rodeswell, and John de Kyngeston, late auditors of the King's chamber, for the goods which belonged to the Earl of Cornwall, an account of which were sent to the Exchequer with the King's writ of "Mittimus," &c., —81*l.* 14*s.* 2*d.*

12th December.—To Eleanor, the Empress, in money paid to her in part payment of 500 marks, which the King of his gift had commanded to be paid in aid of her expenses whilst she remained in England by order of the King's Council. By writ of privy seal amongst the mandates of this term,—150*l.*

22nd May.—To Ralph, Earl of Stafford, by a tally raised this day from the fifteenths granted to the clergy in the twenty-fifth year, containing 1000*l.*, granted to the said Earl of the King's gift for lately capturing Burseald, a French knight, in the war in Gascony. By writ of privy seal amongst the mandates of this term,—1000*l.*

8th June.—To John Clermount, a French knight, lately prosecuting before the Lord the King against John Charnell, clerk, claiming him as his prisoner, whom he had delivered to him by consideration of the Lord the King and the Court, and who was afterwards granted to the same Lord the King. In money paid to the same John de Clermount, of the King's gift, for the price of 4000 Florence nobles, and for the price of one palfry purchased for his use, &c.,—1008*l.* 13*s.* 4*d.* Also for the price of four cups with a gilt ewer enamelled, with two great cups, delivered to the knights and valets coming in his retinue, of the King's gift, &c.; and in money paid to a certain minstrel of the said John Clermount of the King's gift, 100*s.*,—66*l.* 8*s.* 9*d.*

15th June.—To Richard de Grymesby, the King's goldsmith, in money paid to him for the weight of a certain image of Saint Thomas the Martyr, which the Lord the King gave to John, Archbishop of York, for an oblation made at Canterbury. By writ, &c.,—40*l.*

16th July.—To William Clerk, a courier of the King's wardrobe, going on a pilgrimage to Jerusalem and Mount Sinai. In money paid to him of the King's alms in aid of his expenses,—1*l.* 6*s.* 8*d.*

27th October.—To Alice de Latimer, a recluse anchorite, in money paid to her of the King's alms in aid of her support,—20s.

14th November.—To Edward de Balliol, King of Scotland, in money delivered to him in advance by the hands of Thomas Bride, his valet, in discharge of 40s. daily which the Lord the King by his letters patent lately granted to the same King of Scotland, in aid of the expenses of his household, until otherwise he should provide for his estate—to wit, from the 22nd day of July last past until the 3rd day of September next following, for forty-three days, each day included, by writ of privy seal amongst the mandates of Easter term last past,—86l.

16th November.—To divers messengers and couriers sent to divers parts of England with writs of the seal of Saint George, directed to all knights of the order of Saint George, to come to Windsor, in money delivered to them for their wages,—1l. 6s. 8d.

To Thomas Priour, valet of Philippa, Queen of England, to whom the Lord the King, by his letters patent, lately granted 40 marks, yearly to be received at the Exchequer, as well for the good service rendered by him to the same Lord the King as for the pleasant news which the same Thomas brought to the Lord the King of the birth of Edward, Prince of Wales, &c.,—13l. 6s. 8d.

To John, a canon of Saint Catherine's, the King's picture painter, in money delivered to him for painting a picture which the same John was commanded to paint by the Lord the King, with images for the chapel in Windsor Castle, &c.—13l. 6s. 8d.

To Sir John Avenal, knight, in part payment of 1000l., which the Lord the King commanded to be paid him of his gift, because the same John rendered into the King's hands Roland Daneys, whom he lately took in the war in Britany, as appears by letters patent of the great seal, which the same John thereof hath in his possession, endorsed with the underwritten sum, &c.—13*l.* 6*s.* 8*d.*

ISSUE ROLL, MICHAELMAS, 27 EDWARD III.

21st December.—To John de Saint Philibert, in money by him received of John Maleweyr and his companions, merchants, in part payment of 700 marks which the Lord the King commanded to be paid him for the manor of Caieswell, with the appurtenances, in the parish of Bray, in the county of Berks, and for other goods and chattels purchased from him to the King's use, &c. —350*l.*

ISSUE ROLL, MICHAELMAS, 28 EDWARD III.

9th October.—To Richard de Grymesby, a goldsmith in the Tower of London, in money paid to him for certain images made in honour of Saint Thomas the Martyr, and delivered to the venerable father John, Archbishop of York, of the King's gift, for his oblation at Canterbury, &c.—7*l.* 8*s.* 5*d.*

12th March.—To Henry de Vaus, a messenger sent on secret business of the Lord the King to Britany, in money paid to him of the King's gift, for his expenses. By writ of privy seal, &c.—5*l.*

ISSUE ROLL, MICHAELMAS, 29 EDWARD III.

18th March.—To Miles de Stapleton, sheriff of York, for taking David de Bruys, King of Scotland, from the town of Newcastle-upon-Tyne to London, 200 marks, paid for the expenses of the said King. By writ of privy seal of this term—13*l.* 6*s.* 8*d.*

M

18th April.—To Robert de Thorp, late one of the Justices appointed to hear and determine divers trespasses committed in the University of Oxford. In money paid to him of the King's gift, for his expenses in going, tarrying, and returning in the same journey,—6*l.* 13*s.* 4*d.*

9th May.—To a certain groom of Charles de Bloys, coming with lampreys to the Lord the King, sent by the same Charles. In money paid to him of the King's gift,—2*l.*

23rd May.—To divers messengers and couriers sent to divers parts of England with writs of great seal directed to divers sheriffs, to make proclamation at the University of Oxford. In money paid to them for their wages,—1*l.* 15*s.* 8*d.*

13th June.—To Robert Halmark, of London, in money paid to him for making scales for the King's use at the receipt of the Exchequer,—2*l.*

2nd July.—To John de Mountford, in money paid to John de Grenewych, a goldsmith of London, for making a certain seal for the use of the said John,—13*s.* 4*d.*

3rd July.—To the Venerable Father, the Bishop of Mendieu, coming upon an embassy to the Lord the King on behalf of the Emperor of the Romans. In money paid to him of the King's gift for the value of a certain ring purchased of John Adam, an apothecary of London, 50*l.*; and for the value of a certain scarlet cloth purchased of John de Bures, 21*l.* By writ, &c.—71*l.*

To Richard Hake, in money paid to him in discharge of 40 marks, which the Lord the King owed to the same Richard, because the same Richard surrendered to the Lord the King the manor of Caieswell, in the county of Berks, which he held for the term of his life by demise of John de St. Philibert, which said manor remains to the Lord the King after the death of the same John and Margaret his wife, by a fine thereof levied in the Court of the Lord the King between the said Lord the King and the said John and Margaret. By writ, &c.—26*l.* 13*s.* 4*d.*

9th July.—To Bartholomew de Burgharssh the father, in money paid to him in discharge of 44*l.*, paid to him in the 28th and 29th years, for the twenty-two years which he received the same for the support of the heir of Hugh le Despenser, in his custody,—44*l.*

ISSUE ROLL, EASTER, 30 EDWARD III.

8th June.—To John de Castello, who quitted the Jewish errors, and is newly converted to the Christian faith, in money paid to him of the King's gift in aid of his support. By writ of privy seal, &c.—2*l.*

11th July.—To William Trussell, constable of Odyham Castle, in money, paid to him for divers necessary things purchased for the person of David de Bruys, King of Scotland,—to wit, one tunick, one jacket, 2*l.* 5*s.*; two pair of stockings, 5*s.*; three pair of socks, 22*d.*; cloth for a robe, 1*l.* 5*s.*, for the lining thereof, 10*s.*; one riband for a hat, 13*s.* 4*d.*; and for two pair of linen cloths, 6*s.* By writ, &c.—5*l.* 6*s.* 2*d.*

2nd August.—To William de Morton, a goldsmith of London, in money paid to him for making a certain seal for the King's use,—3*l.*

20th August.—In money paid by William of Wykham, for the keep of the King's eight dogs at Windsor, for nine weeks, taking for each dog three farthings per day: and for the wages of a boy to keep the said dogs during the same time, 2*d.* per day, —2*l.* 11*s.*

ISSUE ROLL, MICHAELMAS, 30 EDWARD III.

6th October.—To Henry de Southworth, in money paid to him in discharge of 20 marks which the Lord the King commanded to be paid him of his alms in aid of his support, because the same Henry had lost the sight of both eyes from the shooting of a certain arrow which casually struck him in the left eye in the King's service beyond sea, in Gascony, in the retinue of Ralph Earl of Stafford. By writ of great seal,—13*l.* 6*s.* 8*d.*

5th December.—To Master Pascal, the physician, in money paid to him of the King's gift for the cure performed by him upon Elizabeth, Countess of Ulster. By writ of privy seal,—13*l.* 6*s.* 8*d.*

18th December.—To the Prior of Merton, in money paid to him by the hands of Geoffrey de Chaddesley, one of the canons of the same place, in full satisfaction of the money due to the same Prior for fifty-two oaks taken from the wood of the same Prior, near Reading, for the round table at Windsor, which said oaks were carried to Westminster for the King's workmen there. By writ of privy seal, &c.—26*l.* 13*s.* 4*d.*

2nd March.—To William de Rothewell, keeper of the King's chamber within the Tower of London, in money paid to him for divers instruments purchased of Eustace de Glaston, late clerk of Richard de Grimesby, to make an assay of the money,—to wit, one table with a column and a [gibcrake,] bordered with small pieces of divers colours inlaid ; one pair of small scales for the subtle assay, one pair of small pincers, one little case with the small weights, viz., one pennyweight of twenty-four grains, one half pennyweight of twelve grains, three drachms of silver, and two pair of weights each containing six grains, and six pair of weights for silver each for one grain, half a pannel of parchment, containing half a grain ; another piece of paper containing eight grains, one table of oak, one standing balance and gibcrake of box-wood, one pair of great and one pair of long pincers; also a bellows with a brass pipe, to blow the assay, one pair of iron shovels, one pair of tables of box-wood, to place a pair of scales on, one pair of weights, one case to put the large scales in, and one pair of pincers,—3*l.* 6*s.* 8*d.*

ISSUE ROLL, MICHAELMAS, 31 EDWARD III.

14th October.—To Sir Thomas de Swynnerton, knight, lately taken in the war in Scotland. In money paid to him of the King's gift for his ransom, &c.—100*l.*

To John'le Cok of Cherburgh, in money paid to him in discharge of 25 marks which the Lord the King commanded to be paid him of his gift for the pleasing intelligence which the said John brought to the Lord the King of the capture of John King of France and others of the French nobility at Poytiers. By writ, &c.—16*l.*13*s.*4*d.*

21st October.—To Philipp of Navarre, a knight, in money paid to him of the King's gift, for his homage done to the same Lord the King. By writ of privy seal amongst the mandates of this term,—666*l.* 13*s.* 4*d.*

24th October.—To Master John de Bolton, late chamberlain of the town of Berwick-upon-Tweed, for the price of five lasts of (9000) red herrings, price 50 marks, and two lasts of white herrings, price 12*l.*, with 5 marks for the freightage and carriage thereof: and for the price of two barrels of sturgeon, price 6*l.*; 1300 stock fish, price 21*l.* 5*s.*; eighty-nine congers, price 13*s.* 9*d.*; and 320 mulwels, price 20 marks; paid to the said John for his office by Robert Monk, purveyor of the King's household, as appears by an indenture made between the said John and Robert, remaining in the hanaper of this term,—102*l.* 14*s.*

18th November.—To Thomas Atte Feryie, serjeant at arms of the Lord the King, dwelling at the Castle of Odiham, to keep David de Bruys, King of Scotland, there as the King's prisoner. In money paid to him in advance upon his wages,—8*l.* 10*s.*

25th November.—To Richard d'Armes, in money, paid to Henry Spicer and Cosine, his brother, merchants, of Constance, in money paid to them in part payment of 404*l.*, paid for 123 pair of plates, 123 pair of helmets and caps of iron, 89 pair of plated gauntlets, 89 pair of vanbraces, and as many back pieces, 155 targets and as many lances, purchased from them by the Lord the King. By writ of privy seal, &c.—200*l.*

In expenses for the Chancellor, Treasurer, Earl of Arundel, Guido de Bryenne, Walter de Manny, and others of the council of the Lord the King tarrying at Westminster for two days at the time when the news came of the capture of John, King of France, —4*l.* 3*s.* 4*d.*

9th December.—To Robert de Langeton, the King's serjeant at arms, lately taken in the war, near Calais, by the French enemy. In money paid to him of the King's gift in aid of his ransom. By writ of privy seal amongst the mandates of this term,—40*l.*

15th March.—In money paid to John Adam, an apothecary, of London, for 2 lb., [de fyn madyan,] price 4*s.*; 3¼lb. of sperm-aceti, price 8*s.* 3*d.*; 2½lb. of white powder, price 5*s.*; 6¼lb. [de zucre caffatyn,] price 13*s.*; [et pro uno electuario condayl] 2lb., price 18*s.*, purchased for the medicine of David de Bruys, King of Scotland, remaining in prison within the Tower of London, —2*l.* 12*s.* 9*d.*

17th March.—To John de Haddon, the King's serjeant at arms, sent to Odyham, to bring David de Bruys from thence to London. In money paid to him for his wages,—1*l.*

ISSUE ROLL, EASTER, 32 EDWARD III.

17th May.—To the Earl of Dessemount, from Ireland, remaining at London in the King's custody, for certain trespasses committed by him against the said King. In money paid to him by the hands of John, the son of John, his valet, for his expenses. By writ of privy seal,—20*l.*

7th June.—To John Morice, son of Thomas, Earl of Dessemount, remaining in England for certain affairs concerning the Lord the King. In money paid to him by the hands of John, the son of John, his valet, for his expenses. By writ of privy seal, —13*l.* 6*s.* 8*d.*

7th July.—To Sir Gilbert le Despenser, knight, in part payment of 600*l.* due for the advowson of the churches of Walkefield and Dewsbury, in the diocese of York, purchased from him to the King's use, and appropriated to the Chapel of Saint Stephen, the protomartyr, within the palace of Westminster. By writ of this term,—500*l.*

ISSUE ROLL, MICHAELMAS, 32 EDWARD III.

4th October.—To Robert de Ufford, Earl of Suffolk, in money paid to him in part payment of 3000 florins, (de scuto vetero,) price of each florin, 45¼*d.*, which the King commanded to be paid him for his share of the ransom of the Earl d'Aussore, taken in the war, at the battle of Poytiers. By writ, &c.—562*l.* 10*s.*

5th October.—To Sir John de Wynkefield, Knight, in money paid to him, in part payment of 2500 marks, paid to him for Lord Dauboneye, his prisoner, taken by him at the battle of Poytiers,

and purchased of him for the King's use. By writ of privy seal,
&c.—333*l.* 6*s.* 8*d.*

6*th October.*—In money paid for wine and perry purchased at
Westminster for the King's Council by William de Dyghton,
clerk,—2*s.*

To Walter Norman for his seventeen companions, lately remaining in the King's barge, as well by day as by night, upon the
Thames, near the Sauvoye, for the safe custody of John, King of
France, each of them receiving per day 3*d.* for their wages. In
money paid to them in discharge of their wages,—to wit, from the
2nd day of September last past, unto the 15th day of September
then next following, for fourteen days, counting each day. By
writ of privy seal amongst the mandates of Easter term last past,
—2*l.* 19*s.* 6*d.*

14*th November.*—To John Greyley, captain de Buche, Stephen
Dax, Menant de Casaux, Arnald Tuyll de Puch, Levand Ray-
mon, Drostauh, Arnaud de Puy, Peter de Casaux, and others.
In money, paid to them in discharge of 2356*l.* 15*s.* 5*d.*, for the
value of 12,500 florins, [de scuto vetero,] the price of each florin
3*s.* 9½*d.*, paid to them at Michaelmas term last past for those
25,000 florins, [de scuto vetero,] for which the Lord Prince of
Wales by his letters patent, obligatory was bound to the aforesaid
John, Stephen, Menant, Arnald, Levand, Drostauh, and Peter, for
the purchase of James de Bourbon, Earl of Pontieu, late their
prisoner, for the King's use, as appears by the letters obligatory
of the same Prince, indorsed with the underwritten sum and the
letters of acquittance thereof, remaining in the hanaper of this
term,—2356*l.* 15*s.* 5*d.*

1*st December.*—To Master John de Welwyk, a clerk, sent on the
23rd of January, in the twenty-eighth year, to Gascony, to certify
to the Council of the Lord the King, concerning the bounds and

limits of the duchy of Acquitaine. In money paid to him, as well for his expenses as for his passage and re-passage, and all other charges incurred by him in the same voyage. By writ of privy seal, —25*l.* 14*s.* 8*d.*

To the same Master John, on the 5th day of November, in the twenty-sixth year, sent to Scotland, to receive the hostages for the person of David de Bruys, King of Scotland. In money paid to him for his expenses, &c.—10*l.*

17*th January.*—To Miles de Stapelton, in money paid to him by the hands of William de Helmesley, for his wages in going as the King's messenger to Normandy. By writ of privy seal, &c.,—50*l.*

24*th January.*—To John Mayn, the King's serjeant at arms, and John Bone, lately sent to Sussex, to arrest certain thieves who had robbed Cardinal of Rouen of certain goods and chattels. In money paid to them for their expenses,—to wit, to John Mayn 3*l.* 10*s.*, and to John Bone 1*l.* By writ of great seal, &c. —4*l.* 10*s.*

9*th March.*—To William Volaunt, John Haveregge, Rolinet de Lancaster, Roger de Corby, and Cayser, king of the heralds, sent to France, Germany, Brabant, Flanders, and Scotland, to proclaim the tournament to be held on the feast of Saint George. In money paid to them for their expenses, viz., Volaunt, 10*l.*, Haveregge, 10*l.*, Cayser, 6*l.*, and Corby, 6*l.* By writ, &c.—32*l.*

13*th March.*—To a certain Esquire of Cardinal Perigord, for bringing to the Lord the King a certain charger as a present from the said Cardinal. In money paid to him of the King's gift, with 20*s.* given to a certain groom riding upon the same charger, &c.—13*l.* 6*s.* 8*d.*

[This Roll also contains the names of several persons taken prisoners at the battle of Poitiers, with an account of their ransom; amongst the rest, of Arnold Doudenham, Marshal of France, &c.]

Issue Roll, Easter, 33 Edward III.

3rd May.—To John, Duke of Britany, in money, paid to him of the King's gift, for his armour and equipment at the last tournament at Smythfield, held on the 4th day of March last past, and for the expenses of himself and his household incurred by reason of the said tournament. By writ of privy seal, &c.— 13*l.* 8*s.* 11*d.*

23rd May.—To the President and Monks of the Blessed Mary of Grace, near the Tower of London, in discharge of 66*s.*, which the Lord the King commanded to be paid them,—to wit, for a certain legend of the Saints, purchased for the use and benefit of the Abbot aforesaid, 30*s.*; and for the delivery of a portfolio to the same Abbot, pledged to John Cory, 24*s.*; also for the illuminating of a gradual, 12*s.* By writ of great seal, &c.—3*l.* 6*s.* 0*d.*

6th July.—To John Curraunt, in money paid to him in discharge of 58*l.* which the Lord the King ordered to be paid him for jewels purchased of him for the marriage of the Earl of Richmond, and the Lady Blanche, daughter of the Duke of Lancaster,—to wit, for one ring with a ruby, 20*l.*, and for a belt garnished with rubies, emeralds, and pearls, 18*l.*; and for a trypod with a cup of silver gilt, 20*l.* By writ of privy seal, &c.—58*l.*

15th July.—To Thomas de Chynham, clerk of the chapel of Philippa, Queen of England, in money paid to him of the King's gift, for his fee for performance of three marriages in the same chapel, viz., Margaret, the King's daughter, the daughter of the Earl of Ulster, and John, Earl of Richmond. By writ of privy seal, &c.—10*l.*

19th July.—To Philippa, Queen of England, in money paid

to her by the hands of the Earl of Arundel, in part payment of
300*l.* which the Lord the King granted to the same Queen, to re-
deem a certain crown of hers which had been pledged for so much
money. By writ, &c.,—100*l.*

20th July.—To William de Rothwell, keeper of the King's
wardrobe within the Tower of London. In money paid to him for
the purchase of 4000 bowstaves for the King's use,—40*l.*

25th July.—To Roger de Mortimer, Earl of March, in money
paid to him in discharge of 4000 marks which the Lord the King
commanded to be paid him for the marriage of Edmond his son
and heir. By writ of privy seal, &c.—333*l.* 6*s.* 8*d.*

12th September.—To the Abbot of the blessed Mary de Grace,
near the Tower of London. In money paid to him for a certain
Bible purchased by the same Abbot for the use of his house aforesaid. By writ of great seal, &c.—6*l.* 13*s.* 4*d.*

To William Volaunt, king of the heralds and minstrels, being
at Smythfield at the last tournament there, in money paid to them
of the King's gift, &c.,—40*l.*

ISSUE ROLL, MICHAELMAS, 33 EDWARD III.

10th November.—To James de Loreygne, of Scotland, remaining upon the faith and peace of the Lord the King, in money
paid to him in discharge of 10 marks, which the Lord the King
commanded to be paid him. By writ of privy seal,—6*l.* 13*s.* 4*d.*

22nd November.—To William de Rodom, in money paid to
him in discharge of 80*l.* which the Lord the King commanded
to be paid him of his gift, as a reward for his good services to
the same Lord the King, for taking William de Tours, valet, in
the Scotch wars, in the Marches of Scotland, &c.,—80*l.*

10th December.—To Simon Bochel, in money paid to him in discharge of 216*l.* 13*s.* 4*d.* which the Lord the King commanded to be paid him for 2000 pearls purchased for the marriage of Margaret, the King's daughter, and the daughter of Lionel, Earl of Ulster. By writ of privy seal amongst the mandates of this term,—216*l.* 13*s.* 4*d.*

4th February.—To John Galeys, in money paid to him in discharge of 10*l.* which the Lord the King commanded to be paid him in recompense for the loss which the said John sustained for the accommodation of his houses at the Mile-hend during the time the body of Isabella, late Queen of England, the King's mother, remained there with the King and his household. By writ of great seal, &c.—10*l.*

22nd February.—To John, Duke of Britany, in money, paid to him in discharge of 26*l.* 15*s.* 5*d.* which the Lord the King commanded to be paid him of his gift, for the expenses of himself and household and others remaining in his retinue, for eight days, whilst the same Duke remained in London during the time of the tournament at Smithfield. By writ, &c.—26*l.* 15*s.* 5*d.*

ISSUE ROLL, MICHAELMAS, 34 EDWARD III.

11th October.—To Robert Dys, lately taken in France and wounded in both hands, to whom the Lord the King granted 10 marks yearly, to be received at the Exchequer in aid of his support. By letters patent, &c.—3*l.* 6*s.* 8*d.*

26th October.—To John de Chichester, a goldsmith of London, in money paid to him in discharge of 139*l.* 7*s.* 4*d.* which the Lord the King commanded to be paid him for divers jewels purchased from him for the marriage of the Earl of Richmond, the King's son, and Blanch, daughter of the Duke of Lancaster. By writ of privy seal, &c.—139*l.* 7*s.* 4*d.*

2nd March.—To Benedict Zakarie, in money paid to him in discharge of 30*l.* which the Lord the King commanded to be paid him for two silver buckles purchased of him, and delivered to Isabella, the King's daughter, to be presented to the Countess of Richmond. By writ of privy seal,—30*l.*

10th March.—To John de Wadesword, for conducting Lord Dauboney, a prisoner of the Lord the King, to the castle of Tykhull, in money paid to him for his expenses,—2*l.* 13*s.* 4*d.*

To John de Thorp, a clerk, lately sent beyond sea to the Lord the King upon secret business, in money paid to him in discharge of 10 marks which the Lord the King commanded to be paid him for the 20 marks which the King granted him in recompense of the damage and loss which he sustained at the town of Winchelsea during the time the French enemy hostilely entered into the said town and plundered and burnt the same. By writ, &c.—6*l.* 13*s.* 4*d.*

For the loss of gold money broken up, paid to Bartholomew Chaunges into the Exchange,—4*s.* 11*d.*

ISSUE ROLL, EASTER, 35 EDWARD III.

7th April.—To Thomas de Brynchesbye, valet, to whom the Lord the King, by his letters patent, lately granted 100*s.* yearly, to be received at the Exchequer, for the gratifying intelligence which the same Thomas brought to the Lord the King of the capture of Charles de Bloys; also of the defeat of the Scotch at the battle of Durham. In money delivered to him in discharge of the 50*s.* payable to him for this his allowance,—to wit, at Easter term last past. By his writ current of great seal amongst the mandates of Easter term in the 23rd year.—50*s.*

16th April.—To John de Neubury, clerk of the great wardrobe of the Lord the King, by the hands of Melisius de Shepensteth, in discharge of 132*l.* 3*s.* due to him in the great wardrobe aforesaid, for a beautiful work with skins of ermine, as appears by a bill of the said clerk,—132*l.* 3*s.*

14th May.—To the Lord of Capene, in money paid to him in discharge of 800 florins de scuto vetero, price each florin 45½*d.*, with 17½*d.* sterling, paid to him in part payment of 3000 florins de scuto vetero, for payment of which Lord Edward, the Prince of Wales, by his letters, bound himself to the same Lord for the Count de Vendosme, his late prisoner, purchased from him by the said Prince to the use of the Lord the King, which [letters] the same Lord hath in his possession, indorsed with the sum underwritten, &c.,—100*l.*

14th May.—To Arnald Reymund,Viscount de Anoita, in money delivered to him by the hands of Gerald de Meuta, in discharge of 840 florins de scuto vetero, price the florin 45½*d.*, delivered to him in discharge of 4499 florins de scuto vetero due to the same Viscount for those 15,000 florins de scuto vetero for which Lord Edward, Prince of Wales, bound himself by his letters to the same Arnald for the Count of Joigny, his late prisoner, purchased from him by the said Prince for the use of the Lord the King, as appears by the letters obligatory of the said Prince which the same Arnald hath in his possession, cancelled in the hanaper of this term,—158*l.* 7*s.* 6*d.*

15th May.—To William de Lambhuyth, one of the canons of the chapel of Saint Stephen, Westminster, in money paid to him in discharge of 100*s.* which the Lord the King commanded to be paid him for the sealing of certain bulls in the Court of Rome, concerning the said chapel. By writ of privy seal amongst the mandates of this term,—5*l.*

To Henry de Snayth, keeper of the King's private wardrobe

within the Tower of London, by the hands of John de Cornewaill, engineer, in discharge of 21*l*. 18*s*. 10*d*. due to him for divers things purchased of him to the King's use, viz., for 11,600 darts, 16 balisters, and 5 guns. By writ of privy seal amongst the mandates of this term,—21*l*. 18*s*. 10*d*.

19*th June*.—To John de Chychester, a goldsmith of London, in money paid to him for making two silver seals for the privy seal of the Lord the King. By writ of privy seal amongst the mandates of this term,—7*l*. 18*s*. 8*d*.

2*nd July*.—To the Sacrist of Westminster, in money paid to him for renewing the wax around the body of Lord Edward, late King of England, grandfather of the present Lord the King. By writ of the great seal amongst the mandates of this term,—2*l*. 10*s*.

3*rd July*.—To John, Duke of Britany, in money paid to him in discharge of 20*l*. which the Lord the King commanded to be paid him of his gift in recompense of so much money lent by him, and paid to divers minstrels at his marriage. By writ, &c.—20*l*.

To Sir Thomas de Uvedale, knight, sent as a messenger from the Lord the King to France concerning the affairs of the Earl of Mountfort. In money paid to him for his wages,—60*l*.

10*th July*.—To the Executors of the will of Henry, late Duke of Lancaster, in money paid to them in part payment of 1602 marks 6*s*. 8*d*., paid to them for certain jewels purchased from them to the King's use, &c.—400*l*.

19*th July*.—To Walter de Manny, a banneret, in money paid to him by the hands of Richard de la Vache, in discharge of 500 marks paid to him for certain lands called Ryssyndon, in the island of Shepey, purchased from the same Walter for the King's use. By writ, &c.—333*l*. 6*s*. 8*d*.

Issue Roll, Michaelmas, 35 Edward III.

18th November.—To the Lord the King in his chamber, by his own hands, at Westminster, in money paid to him in discharge of 2800 marks paid to him for jewels purchased by the Lord the King to be delivered of the King's gift to John, King of France, and other nobility in his retinue. By writ of privy seal, &c.—525*l.* 17*s.* 4*d.*

To the same Lord the King, in money paid to him into his chamber aforesaid, for three rings purchased by the same Lord the, King, delivered as a present to the said King of France at Calais, viz., two rings, one with a ruby and one with a diamond, price 250 marks; and one ring with a great diamond, price 65*l.* By writ of privy seal,—231*l.* 13*s.* 4*d.*

———

Issue Roll, Easter, 36 Edward III.

9th May.—To John de Elmrugg and Thomas Elyot mayor of Corf, in money delivered to them for the repairs of the houses within Corf Castle. By writ, &c.—20*l.*

13th May.—To Havekin Petit, a valet of Lord d' Engayn, for bringing to the Lord the King from the same Lord a certain charger. In money paid to him in discharge of 10 marks, which the Lord the King commanded to be paid him of his gift. By writ, &c.—6*l.* 13*s.* 4*d.*

To a certain clerk of Master Thomas de Nevill, a canon of York, for bringing to the Lord the King a certain vest which belonged to the Blessed Peter the Apostle. In money paid to him by the hands of William of Wykham in discharge of 100*s.* which the Lord the King commanded to be paid him of his gift. By writ, &c.—5*l.*

3rd June.—To John de Chichester, a goldsmith, of London, in money, paid to him in discharge of 1*l.* 12*s.* 6*d.*, as well for making a chain for the privy seal of the Lord the King, as for the weight of silver by him found for enlarging the said chain. By writ of privy seal, &c.

13th June.—To Elizabeth de Vaux, one of the maids of honour of Philippa, Queen of England, to whom the Lord the King granted 40 marks yearly, &c. for the good services bestowed by her upon the same Queen, &c. In money, paid to her by the hands of Ralph de Bukeston her husband, in discharge of 20 marks, &c., —13*l.* 6*s.* 8*d.*

21st June.—To William Strokelady, in money paid to him by his own hands, in part payment of 44*l.* 15*s.* 9*d.* due to him in the King's wardrobe for divers provisions purchased from him and expended in the King's household, &c.,—22*l.* 7*s.*

4th July.—To the Executors of the will of Richard Wolveston, in money paid to them by the hands of Nicholas de Westerdale, in discharge of 33*l.* which the Lord the King commanded to be paid them for a great missal and an antiphone purchased from them for the free chapel of Saint Stephen's, Westminster, &c., —33*l.*

25th July.—To Edward, Prince of Wales, in money, paid to him by the hands of Peter de Lacy, in part payment of 20,000*l.* due to him for certain prisoners taken in the war by the same Prince at the battle of Peyters, and purchased by the Lord the King from the same Prince, viz., for Philip, son of the King of France, the Earl de Sanser, and Lord de Croon, as appears by the King's letters patent which the same Prince thereof hath in his custody, indorsed with the sum under-written, &c.,— 3333*l.* 6*s.* 8*d.*

Issue Roll, Easter, 37 Edward III.

6th May.—To Beatrice, the widow of Thomas de Berewose, executrix of the will of the same Thomas, &c., in discharge of 200 marks which the Lord the King commanded to be paid her for a certain crown purchased from her for the King's use, —133*l.* 6*s.* 8*d.*

17th May.—To Edward de Balliol, King of Scotland, in money paid to him by the hands of William de Aldeburgh, knight, in discharge of 1000 marks which the Lord the King commanded to be paid him because the same Edward by his charter had given and granted to the Lord the King and his heirs the castle and town of Helicuria, in Vymeo, under the dominion of Pontieu, &c.,—666*l.* 13*s.* 4*d.*

22nd June.—To the Abbot, Prior, and Convent of Westminster, in money, paid to them by the hands of the same Prior, in part payment of 100 marks which the Lord the King commanded to be paid them of his gift in recompense of the expenses and charges by them incurred about the removal of a certain water mill, situate near the King's palace of Westminster, and for erecting a certain other mill; also for timber, stones, and other things, purchased for the same mill and for the carriage and grinding of their corn, and malt, &c.,—20*l.*

Issue Roll, Michaelmas, 37 Edward III.

18th October.—To Robert Burgeys, a courier, sent with a commission to John de Kyrketon, to come to parliament. In money, paid to him for his wages,—3*s.* 4*d.*

29th October.—To Matthew de Torkesey, clerk of the King's navy, by the hands of Roger de Sutton, for the purchase of twenty-eight quintals two stone of white flax, 109 quintals three stone and

fourteen lbs. of bastard flax, and one quintal of black flax, purchased for the King's use of Robert Budde and his companions,
men of the town of Bridport, &c.,—66*l*. 13*s*. 4*d*.

15*th November*.—To Lionel, Earl of Ulster, by the hands of
Robert de Hadham, by a tally levied this day in the names of
Walter Atte More and William de Keynes, for the value of the
marriage of Margaret, the sister and heir of John Blount, containing 240*l*., paid to the same Earl in allowance for the value of
the same marriage, which said marriage, together with the custody
of all the lands and tenements with the appurtenances in Mor-
thesthorn, in the county of Dorset, which belonged to the aforesaid John, being in the hands of the King after the death of
the aforesaid John by reason of the minority of the aforesaid
Margaret, with all things belonging to that custody, were granted
to him on the 7th November, in the 34th year.   By writ of great
seal, &c.,—240*l*.

1*st December*.—To Master Robert de Wykford, clerk, in money
paid to his own hands for the manor of Werpesdon with the appurtenances, in the county of Surrey, purchased of the same
Robert by William of Wickham, clerk, for the King's use,
—533*l*. 6*s*. 8*d*.

3*rd December*.—To William Ser, a Gascon knight, in money,
paid to him by his own hands, in part payment of 1600 "guyenois"
owing to the same William, as well for the good services by him
bestowed upon the Lord the King, as for the costs and expenses by
him incurred in the affairs of the Lord the King in the retinue of
John Chaundos, the King's deputy in France and Normandy to
receive the towns, castles, and lands in those parts, belonging to
the Lord the King by treaty of peace made at Calais between the
same Lord the King and John, King of France, as appears by the
King's letters patent of privy seal which the said William thereof
hath in his custody, indorsed with the underwritten sum, &c.,
—133*l*. 6*s*. 8*d*.

17th February.—To William de Manton, keeper of the King's wardrobe, by the hands of Thomas Spigurnell, keeper of the King's great horses, in discharge of 119*l.* 6*s.* 8*d.* paid to the same Thomas for the purchase of divers horses from the Executors of the will of John, late Bishop of Lincoln, viz., one free sorrel courser, price 20 marks; one courser, spotted with white, price 20 marks; one courser, of à roan colour, from Pappeworth, price 20 marks; one roan coloured courser from Tolney, price 20 marks; one brown bay courser, price 25 marks; one roan courser from Cranbourn, price 10*l.* 13*s.* 4*d.*; one brown bay courser, price 11*l.* [With several other horses, describing their colour and from whence obtained.]

28th February.—To Pelegrin de Caux, brother of Bernard de Troye, in money paid to him in discharge of 10 marks which the Lord the King commanded to be paid him of his gift, in part satisfaction of a reward which the Lord the King was bound to pay to the same Bernard for the capture of John, King of France, at the battle of Peyters, 6*l.* 13*s.* 4*d.*

1st March.—To Charles, Lord de Memorancy, of France, in money paid to him by the hands of Peter Vanne, his attorney, in part payment of 20*l.* which the Lord the King commanded to be paid him of his gift, in recompense of so much of the sum which Joan, late Queen of Scotland, owed the same Charles, as appears by the letters of attorney of the same Charles remaining in the hanaper of this term.

3rd March.—To Matilda Rous, prosecuting at the King's Council the claim of Dionisius de Morbek, who asserted whilst he lived that he took John, king of France, in the war, at the battle of Poytiers. In money, paid to her of the King's gift in aid of her expenses, &c.,—3*l.* 6*s.* 8*d.* [There are other payments on these Rolls relating to this affair.]

2nd April.—For the ransom of the King of France, 29,981*l.* 8*s.*, for those 400,000 florins de scuto, of which two are worth one noble of gold, English money, received at the town of Calais by the hands of Henry Pycard and his companions, in part payment of 600,000 of like florins due to the Lord the King of England, for the first payment of the said ransom, according to the form of a treaty made between the same Kings; also 123*l.* arising from the increase on payments of divers sums for the ransom aforesaid, as appears by the Memoranda Roll of the Exchequer of the 39th year, amongst the Records of Trinity term, paid and delivered at divers times to divers persons, and as is also contained in the Memoranda of the Pell of the 36th and 37th years,—to wit, for a greater value over than for which they were received from the King of France, viz., for a certain sum arising from such increase upon payment of the aforesaid sums, the receipt whereof was charged on the 8th day of March, in the 35th year, as is contained within the said sum of 123*l.*; also 16*l.* 13*s.* 4*d.* arising from the advantage of the coinage on each pound of gold coined for the ransom aforesaid, which the King thereon had and received upon each pound received from the King of France, 20*d.*, and for the payments thereof made to divers persons, as is premised, and for which there was allowed them only at the said coinage, 18*d.*; and so there arose to the King's use 2*d.* upon every pound by the Record aforesaid.

For the same ransom, by the hands of Ralph Maillard and Nicholas Brake, 17,066*l.* 13*s.* 4*d.*, for the value of 98,200 florins de scuto, of which two are worth one noble, viz., in money of nobles, 7388*l.* 13*s.* 4*d.*; and for 653*l.* of gold weighing in money called franks 9678*l.* 0*s.* 1*d.*; and for 1150 marks the remainder of this payment which was received, as appears by the Roll of Receipt, on the 30th day of January and 24th February last past, &c.—Sum, 47,197*l.* 3*s.* 11*d.*

ISSUE ROLL, EASTER, 38 EDWARD III.

2nd April.—To the Lord the King, in his chamber at Westminster, on the aforesaid second day of April, in this 38th year, by his own hands, there being personally in the presence of the same Lord the King the Venerable Father Simon, Bishop of Ely, Chancellor of England, William of Wickham, keeper of the privy seal, and Gauterus de Barde, master of the King's money. In divers sums of money in gold received for the ransom of the King of France, which said gold was placed in the Treasury within the Tower of London,—to wit, in 2062*l.* 19*s.* 8½*d.*, in weight of divers gold money being the first payment made for the said ransom, at Calais, and received by Henry Pycard and his companions; which said sum by weight is worth by computation 30,104*l.* 8*s.*, the pound weight being computed at 14*l.* 18*s.* 5*d.*, the advantage in weight amounting to 9½*d.* for each pound weighed which was not deducted, for the reason noted in the particulars remaining in the hanaper of this term. And for 17,066*l.* 13*s.* 4*d.* received for the same ransom by the hands of Nicholas Brake and Ralph Maillard,—to wit, in gold nobles, 7388*l.* 13*s.* 3*d.*; and for 653 pounds weight of gold in franks—19,678*l.* 0*s.* 1*d.*, as appears by the said particulars of the declaration of this said sum remaining in the hanaper aforesaid; which said sums the said Lord the King acknowledged to have been delivered to him as aforesaid on the said second day of April; so that the same King is willing that any other persons shall be charged therefore, but by virtue of the same delivery to him, the Treasurer, Chamberlains, and other persons whomsoever are therefrom exonerated and discharged, it being in the King's possession. By writ of privy seal, —47,171*l.* 1*s.* 4*d.*

8th April.—In money paid by Richard de Normanton, for carriage of the gold for the ransom of the King of France from the Tower of London to the private palace at Westminster, together with 23*d.* paid to James Chaundeller, of the parish of Saint Mildred, London, for a certain chest purchased from him for the Treasury within the Tower aforesaid ; also for other costs and charges incurred by him for the same gold, by view and direction of the Chamberlair,—11s. 4d.

18th April.—To Sir Nicholas Dammory, knight, sent to Canterbury and Dover for the safe conduct of the body of John, late King of France. In money, paid to him for his expenses, by writ of privy seal, &c.,—6l. 13s. 4d.

19th April.—In money, paid for an oblation of the Lord the King at the church of Saint Paul, London, on the day of the exequies of John, late King of France,—6s. 8d.

9th May.—To Henry de Ruston and the good men of the town of Scarborough, in money paid to them by the hands of the same Henry for the amendment and repairs of the key of the aforesaid town. By writ, &c.,—100l.

Issue Roll, Michaelmas, 38 Edward III.

6th December.—To divers Lords and others coming to England in the retinue of the Lord King of Scotland to ratify a treaty of peace between the Lord the King of England. and the said King of Scotland, viz., to the Earl of Douglas, for the price of a gilt cup weighing in gross by money 100s. 9d., and worth 10l. 18d.; to Robert de Eskyn, a Scotch knight, for the price of a silver cup weighing in gross by money, 4l. 19s. 3d., and worth 9l. 18s. 6d. ; to Master Walter, clerk of the privy seal of the King of Scotland, for the price of a gilt cup weighing 102s. 5d., value 10l. 4s. 10d.; to a certain clerk to the steward of the King of Scotland's household, for the price of a gilt cup weighing 4l. 18s. 9d., and worth 9l. 17s. 6d.; to two knights of the same King's household for the price of two gilt cups weighing 110s. 9d. and worth 11l. 18d.; to the son of the Queen of Scotland for the price of a gilt cup weighing 75*s*. 4*d*., and worth 6*l*. 5*s*. 4*d*.; to a certain notary for the price of a silver cup weighing 66*s*. 1*d*., and worth 4*l*. 16*s*. 1*d*.; to a certain esquire called Heryng, for the price of a silver cup weighing 71*s*. 8*d*., and worth 4*l*. 15*s*. 8*d*.; to two other esquires for the price of two silver cups weighing 7*l*. 3*s*. 4*d*., and worth 9*l*. 11*s*. 4*d*. By writ of privy seal amongst the mandates of this term,—76*l*. 12*s*. 3*d*.

8th December.—To Gilbert Prince, a painter, of London, in money paid to him in discharge of 24*l*. due to him in the King's wardrobe for banners and divers other things purchased from him for the exequies of Joan, late Queen of Scotland, as appears by the bill of William de Manton, late keeper of the wardrobe aforesaid, &c.,—24*l*.

1st February.—To William de Mulsho, clerk of the King's works at Windsor, in money paid to him by the hands of John de Asshehurst, for the purchase of 100 chaldron of coals for the King's use. By writ, &c.,—31*l*. 13*s*. 4*d*.

24th February.—In money paid by Richard de Normanton, for expenses incurred at the Tower for divers Lumbarders and others remaining there for one day to weigh the gold for the ransom of the King of France, 1*l*. 10*s*. 2*d*.

ISSUE ROLL, EASTER, 39 EDWARD III.

17th May.—To Peter de Ekeston and Robert Herbrak, coming from Gascony with a lion and a leopard the gift of Edward, Prince of Wales. In money paid to them of the King's gift, &c.,—5*l*.

19th June.—To William Spalding, the King's sergeant at arms, sent to conduct the Duke of Orleans to Bolognia, in money paid to him for his wages,—2*l*. 13*s*. 4*d*.

21st June.—To John, a canon of Saint Catherine's, painter to the Lord the King, in money paid to him for making a table whereon the same John was directed by the Lord the King to paint images for the chapel within Windsor Castle. By writ of privy seal,—13*l.* 6*s.* 8*d.*

31st June.—In money paid to Thomas Hessey, a goldsmith of London, for divers cups and other silver plate purchased from him for the King's use, and delivered of the King's gift by the hands of Helmyng, Leget at Dover, to divers knights and others coming there in the retinue of the earl of Flanders—viz. to Lewes de Nemours, one tripod with a cup and ewer, and one salt-seller silver gilt and enamelled, weighing by the goldsmiths' weight 38 marks, 5*s.* 2¼*d.*, price 200 marks;—to the constable of Flanders an ewer, gilt and enamelled, weighing by the same weight 42*s.*, price 6*l.* 11*s.* 9*d.*, together with a certain cup delivered to the same constable from the plate in the charge of William Sleford; —to the *Lord de Pouke and Simon Topet, chaplain, a cup silver gilt, with fretwork enamelled in the bottom with two wodewosez, and one ewer silver gilt, delivered to the same Lord de Pouke, and one dish of silver gilt, delivered to the aforesaid Simon, weighing together by the same weight 14 marks, 8*s.* 6*d.*, and worth 26*l.* 6*s.* 11½*d.*;—to Sir Roger Boteleyn, a silver cup, gilt, embossed with azure, weighing by the same weight 5 marks, 8*s.* 11*d.*, and worth 9*l.* 16*s.* 3¼*d.*;—to Sir John Bouer, a silver cup, gilt and enamelled with roses, weighing by the same weight 4 marks, 10*s.* 10*d.*, and worth 8*l.* 6*s.* 4*d.*;—to Sir Peter de Montagu, a cup in form of a chalice, gilt and enamelled on the top, with a white eagle, weighing 5 marks, 3*s.* 4*d.*, worth 9*l.* 2*s.*;—to Sir John Doyle, a silver cup, gilt and enamelled at the bottom with a griffin, weighing 5 marks, 3*s.* 4*d.*, worth 9*l.* 2*s.*;—to Sir John Hauley, a silver cup gilt, standing upon three lions, worth

* The word prefixed to the names in the original is "Dominus," which does not here in all instances denote a title of nobility, but only of courtesy; as applied to the clergy, it is equivalent to magister, or master, and to laymen, knight, esquire, lords of manors, &c.

8*l.* ; and also to the same Sir John a silver cup, gilt and
enamelled on the top with a star, worth 6*l.* 7*s.* 10*d.*;—to Sir
Frederick de Hasbrok, a silver cup, gilt and enamelled with a
rose, worth 9*l.* 7*s.* 0½*d.* ;—to Sir Robert Hauteyn, a silver cup,
gilt and enamelled with three rows of rubies on the top, worth
6*l.* 4*s.* 3½*d.* ;—to John Kaiamit, a silver cup gilt, with a white
eagle standing upon three angels, worth 9*l.* 11*s.* 11*d.* half a
farthing ;—to William de Hasfield, a silver cup gilt ;—to
William de la Camere the same ;—to Stephen de Lemport, a
silver cup, gilt and enamelled ;—to Clays Bovyn, a silver cup,
gilt and enamelled ;—to Stathyn de Vanes, a silver cup gilt and
enamelled ;—to John Van Mwute, the value of a silver cup, viz.
3*l.* 2*s.* 2*d.*;—to Lamkin Vaghenare, to Master John le Mareschall,
to Giles Babbe, to Tydeman Bergh, to Frank, the messenger from
Flanders, to Lord Godfrey de Delf, to each a silver cup, gilt,
with the weight and value added ;—to Thomas Spygurnell, a cup,
standing upon three lions, and the value of a silver cup ;—to
Sir Gerard de Nassenham, a cup in form of a chalice, standing
upon three lions ;—to Sir John de Bouer, a like cup ;—to Sir
Peter de Dylf, a like cup ;—to Sir Busigald, a silver cup, gilt, with
a white pelican on the top ;—to Sir Warner de Woshyn, a cup in
shape of a chalice, standing upon three angels ;—to the King's
messenger from Denmark, a silver dish, gilt ;—to Thomas Atte
Hyll, a messenger from the King of Scotland, a silver cup, gilt,
standing upon three lions, with a green top; together with many
other cups of different descriptions, such as godels, ciphos, &c.

14*th July.*—To William Courteray, embroiderer of London,
in money paid to him by his own hands, in discharge of 350*l.*
which the Lord the King commanded to be paid him for a vest
purchased from the same William for the said Lord the King,
By writ, &c.,—250*l.*

28*th August.*—To Thomas de Dryffeld, in money paid to him
by the hands of John de Neuton, in discharge of 100 marks which
the Lord the King commanded to be paid him for the wages of

himself and his men, lately remaining in France by the King's direction to receive possession of the castles of Roche super You Inay in Berry, and Peyton, according to a treaty made between the Lord the King and his council and the Dukes of Orleans, d'Angeon, and de Berry, and others of the household of the King of France. By writ of privy seal,—666*l.* 13*s.* 4*d.*

ISSUE ROLL, MICHAELMAS, 39 EDWARD III.

22nd November.—To John, Duke of Lancaster, in money paid to him by the hands of William de Bukbrugg, for his expenses in going to Flanders respecting the nuptials between the Earl of Cambridge, the King's son, and the Countess of Burgundy, daughter of the earl of Flanders. By writ, &c.,—400*l.*

10th December.—To Walter de Berney and John Deynes, late Sheriffs of London, in money paid to them for the price of divers books, viz. one bible, one portiforium, one Juvinal, three books of romances, of little value, for which the same Sheriffs were charged at the Exchequer, in their account for the value of the goods and chattels which belonged to Henry de Tatton, which said books were taken into the King's hands because it was certified to the King that the said books related to the solemnity of the feasts, and were of great value. By writ of the great seal of this term,—3*l.* 1*s.* 6*d.*

To John de Lyndesey, in money paid to him by his own hands, in part payment of 50*l.* which the Lord the King commanded to be paid him for a certain table with figures purchased from him for the King for the chapel of Saint George, in Windsor Castle. By writ of privy seal amongst the mandates of this term,—20*l.*

Payment of 100 marks yearly to John Paladyn, the King's physician.

ISSUE ROLL, MICHAELMAS, 40 EDWARD III.

23rd October.—To William de Lyndeseye, a carver of wooden images in London, in money paid to him in discharge of 10 marks, which the Lord the King commanded to be paid him of his gift as a reward in addition to a former sum paid him, for making a certain table with images of wood for the chapel of the Lord the Ki g, in the new works within the castle of Windsor purchased from him, also in recompense of the cost by him incurred for the carriage of the same table from London to the castle aforesaid, &c.,—6*l.* 13*s.* 4*d.*

29th October.—To Lionel, Duke of Clarence, in money paid to him by the hands of Robert de Assheton, John Joce, and John de Hylton, for the wages of himself, his men at arms, and archers retained by him in the war in Ireland in the service of the Lord the King. By writ of privy seal,—1333*l.* 6*s.* 8*d.*

6th November.—To divers minstrels at Windsor, present at the marriage of Isabella, the King's daughter, the Lady de Courcy, in money paid to them of the King's gift. By writ, &c.,—100*l.*

To Elizabeth, Countess of Athol, in money paid to her by the Lord the King at Windsor, of the said King's gift, at the time the same Lord the King held the infant of the same Countess there at the holy font. By writ of privy seal,—100*l.*

15th November.—To John de Padbury, in money paid him by the hands of his wife in part payment of 24*l.* 15*s.* 4*d.*, due to him upon his account made at the Exchequer for the receipt of his wages and expenses in going on a certain voyage in the King's service to Gascony, in the retinue of Thomas de Aldeshels, to the Prince of Wales, in the 31st year; also for the costs and expenses by the same John incurred for taking 10,000 lbs. of gold to the same Prince. By writ of privy seal,—10*l.*

6th December.—To Robert de Holm, chaplain, in money paid to him for the expenses of Edward Palmer, for the youngest son of the Lord the King, in the custody of the same Robert to be instructed in the science of grammar. By writ of privy seal, &c., —4l.

14th January.—To John de Brampton, clerk, in money paid to his own hands for binding a certain book called the Book of Memoranda of the Receipt of the Exchequer,—3s.

14th January.—To John de Teuso and John de Boys, hunts-men to the King of France, for presenting to the Lord the King of England thirty wild boars as a present from the said King of France. In money paid to him of the King's gift, viz. to the afore-said John de Teuso, 10l., and to the aforesaid John de Boys, 5 marks. By writ of privy seal,—13l. 6s. 8d.

To William Courteray, of London, embroiderer, in money paid to him for orfries and other things by him purchased for a velvet vest for the King, therewith embroidered with pelicans, images, and tabernacles of gold, and for workmanship by him done in repairing the same vest, &c.,—20l.

20th January.—To Hawkin Liege, from France, in money paid to him in discharge of 200 marks, which the Lord the King commanded to be paid him for making the tomb of Philippa, Queen of England, the King's consort. By writ of privy seal, &c.,—133l. 6s. 8d.

23rd January.—To John le Meaugre, called Burcigald, mar-shal of France, in money lately received by assignment made to him for the ransom of the King of France for the price of 2000 royal florins, reckoning 7 for three nobles, due to the same John at the terms of the Nativity of Saint John the Baptist in the 38th year, and the Nativity of our Lord in the 39th year, for those 2000 florins de scuto yearly, which the Lord the King, by his letters patent under the great seal, lately granted to the same John, as well for the homage done by him to the same Lord the King as for the grateful services by him bestowed and hereafter to be conferred upon the same King, as appears by letters patent, &c.,—285*l.* 14*s.* 2*d.*

To William de Dormantz, chancellor of Normandy. In money by him lately received by assignment made to him by letters patent under the great seal of the King's Chancery, for the ransom of the King of France for the value of 400 royal florins, price of each florin 2*s.* 10½*d.*, of which royal florins seven were reckoned for three nobles, due to the said William at the term of Saint John the Baptist in the 39th year, &c.; also for those 200 florins de scuto yearly which the Lord the King lately granted to the same William, &c., as well for his homage, &c., as for good services, &c., —47*l.* 12*s.* 6*d.*

24*th January.*—To John, son of the King of France, the Duke de Berri and d'Auvergne, in money paid to them by their own hands as an advance, to be restored at the feast of the Nativity of Saint John the Baptist last past, as appears by letters obligatory from the same John remaining in the custody of the Treasurer and Chamberlains of the Exchequer. By writ of privy seal,—666*l.* 13*s.* 4*d.*

Issue Roll, Easter, 41 Edward III.

1*st February.*—To Peregrine, a valet of the Duke of Berry, coming to the Lord the King and Philippa, Queen of England, with the pleasing news of the birth of the son of the Duchess of Berry, in money paid to him, &c., of the gift of Philippa, Queen of England, &c.,—26*l.* 13*s.* 4*d.*

5*th May.*—To Simon Royer, by the hands of Sir Frank de

Hale, knight, in money paid to the hands of the said Frank by Perceval Royer and William Chaumberleyn, in discharge of 1100 marks which the Lord the King commanded to be paid to the same Simon for a certain crown purchased from him for the King's use. By writ, &c.,—266*l*. 13*s*. 4*d*.

15*th May*.—To Fulk Van Brombury, a messenger from Lord de Pruys, for presenting to the Lord the King divers falcons from the same Lord. In money paid to him of the King's gift, for the price of 100 Florence crowns, &c.,—16*l*. 13*s*. 4*d*.

1*st June*.—To Ingelram, Falconar, coming to the Lord the King with letters from the Duchess of Lancaster with news of the birth of a son of the same Duchess, in money paid to him of the King's gift. By writ, &c.,—5*l*.

5*th July*.—To Franskinus Forsset, valet of the Lord the Prince of Acquitaine, for bringing to the Lord the King a certain charger from Henry the Bastard of Spain, taken at the battle of Nazery, in Spain, in the conflict between the same bastard with Peter, King of Spain, in money paid to him of the King's gift, for the value of 100 Florence crowns. By writ, &c.,—16*l*. 13*s*. 4*d*.

ISSUE ROLL, MICHAELMAS, 43 EDWARD III.

25*th October*.—To Stephen Rummelowe, constable of the King's castle of Nottingham. In money paid to his own hands, 68*s*. 9*d*., due upon an account made with him at the Exchequer, as well for the receipt of, as for the costs and expenses of making a baptismal font, with a cover for the same, within the King's chapel there, and for other works done in the same castle as is contained in the 41st roll of accounts. By writ, &c.,— 3*l*. 8*s*. 9*d*.

15*th November*.—To John de Sleford, clerk of the King's

private wardrobe, by the hands of Godfrey Sadler, in money paid to the same Godfrey by Helming, Legate, for sixty targets purchased from the same Godfrey for the King's use, &c.,—3*l.* 6*s.* 8*d.*

3rd February.—To Edward, Prince of Wales and Acquitaine, by the hands of Peter de Lacey, his receiver, for the value of certain Florence nobles paid to him for his wages in the war, and as a reward to his men at arms and archers going in the service of the Lord the King to Gascony,—to wit, for the ransom of the King of France, &c.,—6200*l.*

19th February.—To Henry de Sneyth, clerk of the King's great wardrobe, by the hands of John Blaton, embroiderer. In money paid to Philippa, Queen of England,—to wit, by the hands of Simon de Worstede, 60*l.*, and by the hands of Richard de Ravenesere, 194*l.*, in discharge of 313*l.* due to the same Queen, for satin with silk and gold cloth from Cyprus by him purchased for a bed from the same John Blaton for the King's use,—254*l.*

5th March.—To Thomas Hervy, receiver of the Duke of Clarence, in money paid to him for the expenses of the said Duke and his men, going to Milan concerning a marriage between the same Duke and the daughter of Galiache, Lord of Milan,—to wit, by his own hands 8500 marks, and by the hands of Philip de Popham 1000 marks, &c.,—6333*l.* 6*s.* 8*d.*

ISSUE ROLL, EASTER, 45 EDWARD III.

6th May.—To John Innocent, one of the Clerks of the receipt, in money paid to him as a gift for his labour and diligence in writing the indentures [made] between the venerable Father Thomas, Bishop of Exeter, late Treasurer of England, and Sir Richard le Scrop, knight, now Treasurer, concerning dive s jewels, silver vessels, and other things relating to the office of

Treasurer, by order of the Treasurer and Barons of the Exchequer,—20*s.*

23*rd May.*—Allowance of 2*s.* a day for the support of John de Nevell, a knight of France, whilst he was a prisoner in the Tower, viz., from the 1st of March to the 24th of May, being 85 days,——8*l.* 10*s.*

24*th May.*—To William de Newby, a valet, sent with two letters from the Lord Treasurer, directed to Alexander de Cokeburn, of Scotland, and Alan de Strother, to certify to the Lords Chancellor and Treasurer the names of those persons who made a certain payment of 4000 marks for the ransom of the King of Scotland, and for taking letters of acquittance and safe conduct to the said persons at the term of the Nativity and Saint John the Baptist. In money paid to him for his expenses,—13*s.* 4*d.*

6*th June.*—To Peter Maceon, of Nottingham, by a tally raised this day, containing 50 marks, which the Lord the King commanded to be paid him in discharge of 300 marks which the same Lord the King owed to the same Peter for a table of alabaster made by him, and placed upon the high altar within the free chapel of Saint George, at Windsor. By writ of privy seal, &c.,—33*l.* 6*s.* 8*d.**

ISSUE ROLL, EASTER, 46 EDWARD III.

15*th April.*—To Alice de Perrers, in money paid to her own hands in discharge of 397*l.* which the Lord the King commanded to be paid her,—to wit, 197*l.,* for jewels and divers other things purchased from the said Alice for the use of the said Lord the

* *Note.*—The Issue Roll for the 44th year of King Edward III. has already been printed at length. Vide Issue Roll of Thomas de Brantingham, translated by Frederick Devon, 1835.

o

King against the feast of the Nativity of our Lord in the 44th
year; also 200*l.* for divers other jewels and things purchased
from the same Alice, for the use of the same Lord the King,
against the feast of the Nativity of our Lord last past.   By writ
of privy seal amongst the mandates of this term,—397*l.*

ISSUE ROLL, MICHAELMAS, 47 EDWARD III.

6th October.—To divers messengers and couriers, sent to all
parts of England, on this 6th day of October, with writs of great
seal directed to all Archbishops and Bishops of England, also to
the Abbots, Priors, Earls, Barons, and other Lords, and to all
Sheriffs of England for ordering the parliament to assemble at
Westminster in fifteen days of Saint Michael last past, prorogued
and adjourned unto the morrow of All Souls then next happening, by reason that the Lord the King had returned to England
from the voyage made by him at sea.   In money paid to them
for their wages, as appears by the particulars entered in a certain
great paper book remaining in the receipt of the Exchequer,
—8*l.* 6*s.* 8*d.*

12th October.—[To divers messengers sent with writs of the
great seal to summon the under-mentioned persons to the above-
named parliament], viz., writs directed to the Earl of March; Sir
Hugh Burnell, knight; John de Monte Acuto; Sir William
Botreux, knight; Sir Luke de Ponynges, knight; Sir John de
Wylughby, knight; Sir Robert de Holand, knight; the Earl
of Suffolk; to Prince John, King of Castile and Leon; to
Humphry, Earl of Hereford; William, Earl of Salisbury; Thomas,
Earl of Warwick; Hugh, Earl of Stafford; Edward, Lord le De-
spenser (and to very many others).

18th October.—To Rudekin Van Bamberlowe, Esquire, from
Germany.   In money paid to him by the hands of John Philipot,
in discharge of 340*l.* which the Lord the King commanded to be

paid him of his gift for Matthew Saberwyk, a prisoner of the said Rudekin, purchased from him by the Lord the King for his use, &c.,—100*l*.

10*th November.*—To John Knouseley, sent on the 30th day of October last past with a writ under the great seal, directed to Lord Basset, to conduct himself well in the quarrel which had arisen between him and the Earl of Warwick. By writ, &c.,—3*s*. 4*d*.

21*st February.*—To John Crull, a valet sent to the North on this day with a commission under the great seal directed to Henry le Scrop, Ralph de Hastyngs, knight, and to Roger de Fulthorp, to hear, determine, and settle a certain dispute and strife which had arisen between Henry Lord de Percy and William Douglas, of Scotland, respecting the custody of the marches of the kingdom of England near Scotland; also with letters of privy seal directed to the Bishop of Durham, Lord de Percy, and Henry le Scrop, concerning the same business. In money paid to him for his wages, —1*l*. 10*s*.

31*st March.*—To Catherine Swynford, in money paid to her in discharge of 20 marks which the Lord the King commanded to be paid her of his gift, for announcing to the same Lord the King the news of the birth of a daughter of the Queen of Spain, consort of John, King of Castile and Leon, and Duke of Lancaster. By writ, &c.,—13*l*. 6*s*. 8*d*.

16*th April.*—To Ralph Swyft, a courier sent this day with writs under the great seal directed to the Sheriffs of London, Lincoln, and York, to arrest mariners and detain them as the King's prisoners, so long as it shall please him, on account of the rebellion and disobedience of the same mariners, they having refused and denied obedience to the King's service and mandates. In money paid to him for his wages,—8*s*. 4*d*.

22*nd December.*—To the venerable Father Simon, Bishop of

London, sent as a messenger from the Lord the King to Bruges, in
Flanders, to treat with certain French deputies for a peace to be had
between the Lord the King and his adversary of France. In money
paid to him by the hands of John Rysyng, a monk, and John
Charnel, for his expenses. By writ of privy seal amongst the mandates of this term,—133*l.* 6*s.* 8*d.* [Also payments to Sir Richard
Stafford, Sir Ralph Ferrers, and others sent with the said Bishop,
are entered on this Roll.]

10*th January.*—To a certain valet, coming with writs directed
to the Lord the King from the Duchess de Bares, the King's
kinswoman, announcing to the same Lord the King the news of
the birth of a child of the same Duchess. In money paid to him
in discharge of 10 marks which the Lord the King commanded
to be paid him of his gift, &c.,—6*l.* 13*s.* 4*d.*

To John de Nevell, a prisoner of the Lord the King in the
Tower of London, in money paid for divers cloths purchased and
delivered to the same John of the gift of the said Lord the King,
for his clothing, against the feast of the Nativity of our Lord last
past,—to wit, for eleven yards of black cloth, price the yard 4*s.* 6*d.*,
—2*l.* 9*s.* 6*d.*; and for making up of the same, 6*s.* 8*d.*; also for
the fur of one gown, one surtout, and a coat, 11*l.* 3*s.* 10*d.*; as
appears by the particulars remaining in the hanaper of this term,
—14*l.*

5*th February.*—To John de Sleford, clerk of the King's great
wardrobe, in money paid to the same John for the purchase of
cloth of gold for the exequies of the Earl of Hereford and the
Countess of Arundell, &c.,—48*l.*

ISSUE ROLL, EASTER, 48 EDWARD III.

18*th May.*—To Edward, Prince of Wales, for two payments
to him by the hands of Sir Alan de Stokes, knight, made in the

presence of the same Prince,—to wit, at one time 1000 marks, and at another time 3000 marks, in discharge of 4000 marks which the Lord the King commanded to be paid him in aid of maintaining his estate, &c.,—2666*l.* 13*s.* 4*d.*

2*nd June.*—To Sir William de Windsor, knight, late the King's deputy in Ireland, in money paid to him by the hands of Alice Perrers in discharge of 1615*l.* 3*s.* 11*d.*, which the Lord the King commanded to be paid him for the costs and expenses of the men of the same William who had lately arrived in Ireland before the coming of the said William into the said land, for the time which his said men remained in the King's service in Ireland before the arrival of the said William as aforesaid. By writ of privy seal, &c., —569*l.*

31*st July.*—To the venerable Father John, Bishop of Bangor, sent as a messenger from the Lord the King to the town of Bruges, in Flanders, to treat with the Bishop of Pampelone and other ambassadors of the Lord the Pope there, upon certain articles touching the Lord the King and his realm of England. In money paid to him by the hands of Walter de Somerton, brother of the order of the Preaching Friars, for his wages. By writ, &c.,—133*l.* 6*s.* 8*d.*

To Master John de Wiclif, clerk, sent in the retinue of the said Bishop to the same town of Bruges to treat with the same ambassadors concerning the said articles, in money paid to him by his own hands for his wages. By writ of privy seal, &c.— 60*l.* [Further payments are entered on this Roll to other persons sent on the same embassy.]

9*th September.*—To Reginald Baker, of the town of Westminster, in money paid to his own hands of the King's alms, for the support of Jakeman, an idiot, in the retinue of the late Queen of England, by direction of the Treasurer and Chamberlains of the Exchequer,—1*l.* 6*s.* 8*d.*

22nd September.—To Henry de Wakefield, keeper of the King's wardrobe, by the hands of William Strete, the King's butler. In money paid to John Oetanebroke, for one cask of vinegar purchased from the said John, to be expended in the King's household,—2*l.* 13*s.* 4*d.*

23rd September.—To Thomas Shardelowe, the King's attorney in the Bench. In money paid to him by his own hands, of the King's gift, for the labour and diligence exercised by him in recovering 20 marks to the King's use, for the value of a hoy [craere] which belonged to Thomas de Langeton, condemned for felony and hung, then being in the hands of John Robyn of Grenehyth. By order of the Treasurer and Chamberlains,—1*l.*

23rd September.—To William Beaufey, one of the tellers of the Receipt, sent to the town of Berwick-upon-Tweed for 4000 marks for the ransom of the King of Scotland, to be received there, due at the term of the Nativity of Saint John the Baptist last past. In money paid to him for his wages in going, tarrying, and returning, viz. from the 7th day of June last past unto the tenth day of July next following, for thirty-four days, each day included, receiving 5*s.* per day during the time aforesaid, 8*l.* 10*s.*; also for the wages and expenses of two valets going and returning in the retinue of the same William upon the same business, each of them taking per day 1*s.*—3*l.* 8*s.*; for the hire of three horses from the town of Newcastle-upon-Tyne to Berwick, and for their expenses for ten days, 1*l.* 2*s.* 8*d.*; also for the wages of a valet sent to Edeneburgh, in Scotland, with a safe conduct, directed to Walter Bygar, chamberlain to the King of Scotland, to repair to the said town of Berwick with the money aforesaid, 6*s.* 8*d.* By writ, &c.,—13*l.* 8*s.* 4*d.*

ISSUE ROLL, MICHAELMAS, 48 EDWARD III.

10th December.—To Elizabeth Chaundos, in money paid to her in discharge of 120*l.* which the Lord the King commanded to be paid her of his gift, by reason that the same Elizabeth released and quitted claim to the same Lord the King all right and claim which she had in the castle and vicomté of Saint Saviour's, in Normandy. By writ of privy seal,—120*l.*

ISSUE ROLL, EASTER, 50 EDWARD III.

22nd April.—To John Knouseley, a messenger, sent with a writ of great seal directed to the Earl of Arundell to come to the parliament, in money paid to him for his wages,—5*s.*

30th May.—To Richard Dere and William Stapolyn, from Ireland, in money paid to them by their own hands, viz., to each of them 100*s.*, in discharge of 10*l.* which the Lord the King commanded to be paid them of his gift for their trouble in lately coming from Ireland and residing at London, to inform the King's Council of the defective government of the land aforesaid. By writ of privy seal,—10*l.*

31st May.—To John Orchard, a stonemason, of London, in money paid to him by his own hands for making divers images, in the likeness of angels, for the tomb of Philippa, late Queen of England, within the abbey of Saint Peter, Westminster. By writ, &c., —5*l.*

28th June.—To Stephen de Haddele, valet of the King's household, in money paid to him by the hands of John Orchard, stonemason, 100*s.*, &c., in discharge of 18*l.* 2*s.* which the Lord the King commanded to be paid him for divers costs and expenses incurred about the tomb of Philippa, late Queen of England, within the abbey of the blessed Peter at Westminster ; for the portage and carriage of a certain iron work from the church of St. Paul's, London, unto the same abbey, 10*s.*; for making eight bars and two plates of iron, together with a battlement around the said iron work, 62*s.*; also for painting the same iron work with a red colour, 30*s.*; for six angels of copper placed around the said tomb, and 12*l.* for two images of alabaster placed upon a small marble tomb for an infant son and daughter of the Queen, 20*s*. By writ of privy seal, &c.,—18*l*. 2*s*.

4th July.—To John Skilfull, of Swanesey, in money paid to his own hands, 12*l*. 6*s*. 8*d*., which the Lord the King commanded to be paid him for sixty-two fish called pikes, [luces,] purchased of him for the King's use to re-stock the pond called Babworth Pond; also for the carriage of the same fish from Swanesey to the pond aforesaid. By writ, &c.,—12*l*. 6*s*. 8*d*.

18th July.—In money paid by the hands of John Buck for a certain coffer purchased to contain the rolls and memoranda of the accusations against William de Windsor,—8*l*.

23rd September.—To Alan de Barley, a messenger, sent with a letter of privy seal, on the 22nd September last past, to Oxford, directed to Master John Wiclyf, clerk, to repair to London to the King's Council. In money paid to him for his wages,—5*s*. [This Roll also contains entries of payments to messengers sent to divers nobility therein named, requesting them to attend the funeral of Edward Prince of Wales.]

ISSUE ROLL, MICHAELMAS, 50 EDWARD III.

20th November.—To John Vendour, of Newark, coming by command of the Council from Lincoln to bring Sir William de Cantelupe, knight, to the Tower of London, upon suspicion had against him for the death of Nicholas de Cantilupe, his brother, slain ; and there safely and securely to keep him in the King's prison until otherwise respecting the same William it should be ordered by the said King and his Council. In money paid, &c., in discharge of 100*s*. which the Lord the King commanded to be paid him for the wages and expenses of himself and his men going with him in his retinue for the safe custody of the aforesaid William. By writ, &c.,—5*l*.

16th January.—To Nicholas de Twyford, a goldsmith of London, in money paid to his own hands, for engraving and making a seal ordered by the King for the Lordships of Glomorgan and Morgannok, lately belonging to Edward Lord le Despenser, deceased, being in the King's hands by reason of the minority of the son and heir of the aforesaid Edward. By writ, &c., —2*l.* 10*s.*

24th January.—To William de Wylughes, keeper of the old fabric of the cathedral church of [St.] Paul, London, in money paid to him in discharge of 40*l.* which the King commanded to be paid him for an iron tomb lately placed over the tomb of the Venerable Father Michael, late Bishop of London, without the West porch of the same church, purchased of the same Henry for the King's use for the tomb of Philippa, late Queen of England, within the abbey of the Abbot of Saint Peter, Westminster, &c.,—40*l.*

5th February.—In money paid by the hands of Robert Sybthorp, one of the Chamberlains of the Exchequer, for the carriage and safely conducting an image of the Holy Mary, lately taken by John de Ryngeborne in a certain ship upon the sea, from Westminster to the King's manor of Eltham, delivered to the Lord the King by direction of the Treasurer and Chamberlains of the Exchequer,—6*s.* 8*d.*

27th February.—To William de Mulsho, keeper of the King's wardrobe, by the hands of Thomas Brayles, for the value of divers silver vessels purchased from the executors of the will of Sir Richard de Penbrugg, knight, weighed in the presence of the Lord de Nevill, steward, John Ispre, Comptroller of the King's household, Richard de Beverley, the King's cofferer, and Helmyng Leget, —to wit, for the price of eight silver chargers, weighing by the goldsmiths' weight 23*l.* 0*s.* 10*d.*; seven dozen of silver dishes, weighing by the same weight 103*l.* 6*s.* 1*d.*; four dozen and six silver saltcellars, weighing by the same weight 17*l.* 10*s.* 9½*d.*;

four small silver saltcellars, by the same weight 3*l*. 0*s*. 5½*d*.; four
silver pots, weighing by the same weight 13*l*. 15*s*. 9*d*.; six silver
cups, with a cover made in the shape of a goblet, weighing by the
same weight 9*l*. 1*s*. 5*d*.; twenty-four plain silver cups, weighing
by the same weight 23*l*. 2*s*. 11½*d*.; two silver plates for spices,
weighing by the same weight 3*l*. 15*s*. 8½*d*.; four silver basins,
weighing by the same weight 13*l*. 4*s*. 7*d*.; two silver ewers, weighing
by the same weight 3*l*. 17*s*. 6*d*.; and one round basin, with a silver
water-jug, by the same weight, 7*l*. 6*s*. 10*d*., &c.,—233*l*. 6*s*. 8*d*.

27th March.—To Adam de Hertyngdon, clerk of the works of
the Lord the King at Windsor. In money paid to him by the
hands of William de Lokyngton for making a new bell for the
King's clock within the castle aforesaid, &c.,—50*l*.

ISSUE ROLL, EASTER, 51 EDWARD III.

9th April.—To Sir William de Faryngton, knight, in money
paid to his own hands for the costs and expenses he incurred for
carrying the four quarters of the body of Sir John de Mistreworth,
knight, a traitor to the King, to divers parts of England. By writ
of privy seal, &c.,—20*l*.

11th April.—To Lopinus de Saint Juliane, an esquire from
Gascony, in money paid to his own hands in discharge of 500
marks, which the Lord the King commanded to be paid him of
his gift, in recompense for the costs and expenses incurred by him
for taking Sir John de Mistreworth, knight, in Navarre, a traitor
to the King, and for the safe passage and conduct of the said
John from Navarre to England. By writ, &c.,—333*l*. 6*s*. 8*d*.

13th April.—To divers messengers and couriers sent on the
12th day of April last past to divers parts of England with letters
of the King's signet, directed to the Earl of Stafford, Lord de

Basset, Lord de Nevill, Sir Hugh de Wrottesley, Sir John Sulley, and Sir Nigel Loryng, knights of the garter, to repair to Windsor at the feast of Saint George next coming, &c.,—2*l.* 9*s.* 8*d.*

5th May.—To Walter Chipenham, under-constable within the Tower of London, in money allowed for so much money by him paid for the expenses of Sir John de Mistreworth, knight, and one of his esquires, traitors against the King, confined in the King's prison within the Tower aforesaid, in the custody of the said Walter, for eight days, &c.,—13*s.* 4*d.* [There are other payments on this Roll respecting these traitors; one on the 15th May, of 1*l.* 6*s.* 8*d.*, for bringing them from Bristol to London.]

ISSUE ROLL, MICHAELMAS, 51 EDWARD III.

27th November.—To Philippa Chaucer, one of the maids of honour of the chamber of Philippa, late Queen of England, to whom the Lord the King granted 10 marks yearly, to be received at the Exchequer during her life, or until otherwise he should provide for her estate. In money delivered to her by the hands of Geoffrey Chaucer, in discharge of the 5 marks payable to her for this her allowance,—to wit, at Michaelmas term last past. By writ of liberate amongst the mandates of this term,—3*l.* 6*s.* 8*d.*

20th December.—To Joan, Princess of Wales, in money paid to her by the hands of William de Fulborne, in discharge of 200*l.* which the Lord the King commanded to be paid her for the support and expenses of Richard, Prince of Wales, being in her retinue,—200*l.* [Further payments are entered on this Roll for the said Prince, wherein he is styled Duke of Cornwall and Earl of Chester.]

11th March.—To John Compton, one of the King's archers of his crown. In money paid to him for the expenses of himself, and other archers in his retinue, coming from Gloucester to London to conduct and deliver up Thomas Pardoner and Reginald Clerc, forgers of the seal of the Lord the Pope then taken in those parts, in the office of the King's Marshalship; also for hire of horses for the same Thomas and Reginald, and for divers other costs incurred for their safe conduct, as appears, &c.,—6*l*.

21st March.—To John Eliot, a messenger, sent with letters of privy seal, directed to the Archbishop of Canterbury, the Bishops of Chichester, Rochester, Durham, the Earl of Arundell, and Lord de Percy, to repair to London to the King's Council on Thursday then next after the feast of Easter. In money paid to him for his wages,—10*s*. [Like letters were sent to the Bishop of Salisbury, the Earl of Salisbury, and Roger de Beauchamp; to the Earls of Warwick, Stafford, and Lord de Basset; to the Earls of March, Suffolk, and Lord Fitzwauter; to the Bishop of Lincoln, and many others of the nobility.]

23rd March—To William Danvers, late esquire of the King's chamber, by a tally raised this day, containing 10*l*., in part payment of 43*l*. 18*s*. due to him in the King's wardrobe, as well for his wages in the war as for robes, re-stocking his horses, and his passage back, as appears by the bill of William Farlee, late keeper of the wardrobe. By writ, &c.,—10*l*.

RICHARD II.

20th October.—To John Lord de Nevill, by assignment made this day, containing 2000 marks, for which John Duke of Britany, Earl of Richmond, was bound to the same John de Nevill, for the lands of the Earl of Richmond mortgaged to the said Lord de Nevill by the said Duke, which said 2000 marks the Lord the King, with the consent of his Council, for restitution to be made of the said lands to the said Earl, and for the maintenance of his estate, also for the support of himself, and Joan, his wife, sister of the same Lord the King, had granted to be paid to the aforesaid Lord de Nevill in discharge of the Earl aforesaid. By writ of privy seal of this term,—1333*l.* 6*s.* 8*d.*

30th October.—To Henry de Burton, sent by direction of the Council to Devonshire, to make search for gold in those parts for the King's advantage. In money paid to him for his wages in going to the parts aforesaid upon the said business. By writ, &c., —3*l.* 6*s.* 8*d.*

30th October.—To Sir Nicholas Dagworth, knight, sent upon the King's affairs to Ireland, to inquire concerning the estate and government of the same land, and also of the estate, conduct, and condition of the men at arms, archers, and others dwelling there at the King's charge for the protection of the land aforesaid, and to certify to the King's Council respecting the articles aforesaid. In money paid to him for his wages, &c. By writ, &c.,— 182*l.* 10*s.*

4th November.—To John de Arundell, in money paid to him by assignment made this day in discharge of 234*l*. 19*s*. 4*d*. due upon an account made with him at the Exchequer of account for the wages of himself, his knights, esquires, archers, cross-bowmen, cannoneers, and engineers with him, and remaining as well in the town of Southampton as in the King's castle at Corf, for the safe custody thereof, at different times. By writ, &c.,—234*l*. 19*s*. 4*d*. [This Roll also contains an account of payments made for the repairs, &c., of Corf Castle.]

25th January.—To Sir Richard le Scrop, knight, steward of the King's household, sent to the Northern parts to attend on the day appointed there to be held for the Marches between the Lord the King and his adversary the King of Scotland. In money paid to him for his wages, &c.,—66*l*. 13*s*. 4*d*.

5th April.—To Sir Alured de Veer, knight, by two tallies raised this day, containing 100*l*., paid to the same Alured in discharge of 200*l*. which the Lord the King commanded to be paid him of his gift for a charger which the same Lord the King had of the gift of the said Alured, and upon which charger the same Lord the King rode from the city of London to Westminster at his coronation. By writ of privy seal amongst the mandates of this term,—100*l*.

ISSUE ROLL, EASTER, 1 RICHARD II.

4th June.—To Ralph, Lord de Basset, of Drayton, by two tallies levied this day in his own name, containing 269*l*. 7*s*. 7*d*., paid to the same Ralph by the hands of John Leyr, his clerk, in discharge of the same sum which he restored to the Lord the King at the receipt of his Exchequer, in seven tallies lately assigned to the said Ralph for Reynerus Grymbald, of Genoa, a prisoner of the same Ralph, bought of him for the King's use,—to wit, on the

5th day of November, in the 51st year of the reign of King Edward III., &c.,—269*l.* 7*s.* 7*d.*

5th August.—To Edmund de Mortimer, Earl of March, appointed by the Lord the King, with the assent of the prelates, nobility, and commonalty of the realm of England, in all respects to attend to the directions of the King's Council for regulating the war and governing the affairs of the estate of this realm of England, by a tally levied this day upon the subsidies in the port of Saint Botolph, containing 200*l.*, paid to the same Earl by the hands of Walter Compton, clerk, for that which was due to him for wages received by him during the time he was attendant upon the Council aforesaid. By general writ, &c.,—200*l.*

27th September.—To Gilbert Prince, of London, painter. In money paid to him by the hands of John Bacon, in discharge of 44*l.* due to the same Gilbert in the great wardrobe of the Lord King Edward III., grandfather of the present King, for ornamenting a pair of curtains for a certain great bed of the said Lord King Edward; also for four small banners for the minstrels' trumpets, ornamented with the arms of the said King Edward, as appears by the bill of John Sleford, clerk of the said wardrobe, &c.,—44*l.*

28th May.—To Robert Knolles, captain of Brest castle, in Britany, by the hands of Quassant Marey, a merchant of the city of Bayonne. In money received by the same Quassant from William and John, receivers, for the price of 2356 franks, due to him for 132 pipes of wine from Burgundy, purchased of the same Quassant by the Earl of Buckingham, Earl of Devon, John d'Arundell, Marshal of England, Lord de Latymer, John de Cobbeham, of Kent, Michael de la Pole, admiral of the King's North fleet, Lord Fitzwauter, and Ralph de Ferrers, late in the King's service at sea, for supply of the said castle of Brest, &c.,—376*l.* 4*s.*

12th June.—To John Lincoln, in money received by him from William Walworth and John Philippot, received to purchase and provide 300 quarters of wheat, 200 quarters of beans, 60 casks of wine, one cask of oil, 100 chaldron of sea coals, 10,000lb. of iron, one barrel of brass, two horse-mills, 1000 planks for wainscoting, 20,000 nails, two carts, six horses, with harness for the same, two pipes of powder, 40 war slings, 10,000 quarells, 200 bows, 700 quivers of arrows, and 200 lances, for defending and fortifying the castle and town of Cherburgh, in Normandy, as appears by bill, &c.,—666*l.* 13*s.* 4*d.*

To Charloto de Navarre, a relative of the King of Navarre, in money by him received from the said William and John, received in full satisfaction for wages, in the war, of forty men at arms and forty cross-bowmen of Navarre, as a special guard for the person of the same Charloto, remaining in safe custody in the castle and town of Cherburgh from the 27th day of June last past, on which day the said castle was delivered into the hands of the Lord the King by a certain agreement made between the Lord the King and the said King of Navarre, unto the first day of November then next following. By bill of privy seal, &c.,—300*l.*

To the same Charloto, the son of Lord Lewis of Navarre, Pascaceus de Ilardye, and Master Garceo de Garro, proctors. In money by them received in full satisfaction of 25,000 franks which the Lord the King granted as a loan to the same King of Navarre upon the aforesaid treaty, and by agreement made between the same Lord the King and the aforesaid King of Navarre for the giving up of the castles of Cherburgh and Morteyn, as appears by the letters of acquittance of the same proctors for the receipt of the sum underwritten. By bill, &c.,—2312*l.* 10*s.*

ISSUE ROLL, MICHAELMAS, 2 RICHARD II.

4th December.—To John Lamb, an esquire from Scotland, because he lately killed Owynn de Gales, a rebel and enemy of the
King in France, on his passage to England to explain certain
affairs to the Lord the King and his Council. In money paid
to his own hands, in discharge of 20*l.*, which the Lord the King
commanded to be paid him. By writ of privy seal, &c.,—20*l.*

25th February.—To John Orewell, the King's serjeant at arms,
sent by command of the Council to Gloucester for a certain clerk,
who lately brought bulls from Acquitaine to England, and who
for anti-popery was imprisoned in Gloucester Castle, to take him
from the same prison to Windsor Castle. In money paid to his
own hands for the expenses of himself and his clerk, and for
hire of their horses in coming from the castle of Gloucester to
Windsor aforesaid, &c.,—3*l.* 6*s.* 8*d.*

ISSUE ROLL, EASTER, 2 RICHARD II.

21st May.—To Alan de Stokes, clerk of the King's great
wardrobe, for the value of divers pearls, part of the jewelry of
Alice Perrers, appraised at divers prices, lately received by Simon
de Burgh, Esquire, William Blakemore, the King's serjeant at
arms, and other persons, appointed by command of the Council to
seize certain goods of the same Alice in the King's name,—to wit,
for the value of 600 pearls, the price of each 20*d.*,—50*l.*; 1700
pearls, the price of each 10*d.*,—70*l.* 16*s.* 8*d.*; 5940 pearls, the
price of each 5*d.*,—123*l.* 15*s.*; 1800 pearls, the price of each 4*d.*,
—30*l.*; 2000 pearls, the price of each 4*d.*,—50 marks; 1380 pearls,
the price of each 6*d.*,—34*l.*10*s.*; 500 pearls, the price of each 2*d.*,
—4*l.* 3*s.* 4*d.*; 3948 pearls, the price of each 3*d.*,—49*l.* 7*s.*; 000

P

pearls, the price of each 1½d.,—25l.; and 30 ounces of pearls, worth in the gross 50l.; delivered to the same clerk by the hands of the Treasurer and Chamberlains of the Exchequer, &c.,—469l. 18s. 8d.

24th May.—To Geoffrey Chaucer, to whom the present Lord the King, on the 18th day of April, in the first year of his reign, by his letters patent, granted 20 marks yearly, to be received at the Exchequer at the feasts of Saint Michael and Easter by equal portions, for the good services performed and hereafter to be performed by him to the same Lord the King, and in recompense of a pitcher of wine charged by the Lord King Edward, grandfather of the present King, upon the port of the city of London, by the hands of the butler of the same King Edward and his heirs, also lately granted by letters patent to be received daily during the life of the said Geoffrey. In money paid to him by assignment made this day in discharge of 12l. 4s., paid to him for this his allowance, —to wit, as well rateably from the aforesaid 18th day of April unto the feast of Saint Michael next following, as for the term of Easter last past. By writ, &c.,—12l. 13s.

6th June.—To Sir Robert Rous, knight, sent by direction of the Council in the retinue of the Earl of Saint Paul, a French prisoner to the King, to the town of Calais, to deliver the same Earl out of the King's prison. In money paid to the same Robert for his own wages, and for the costs and expenses of the aforesaid Earl, &c.,—66l. 13s. 4d.

20th June.—To Richard Stoke, a courier, sent to Somerset and Dorset with a letter of privy seal directed to John Burghersh and John Radyngton, knights, to come for the county of Somerset aforesaid, to the King's last parliament held at Westminster, upon certain affairs concerning the King. In money paid to him for his expenses,—6s. 8d.

8th July.—To Reginald de Hatton, clerk in the office of the

King's great wardrobe, paid to his own hands and to John de
Hermesthorp, for divers purchases, costs, and expenses incurred
on the 21st day of June last past, for celebration of the anniversary
of the Lord King Edward III., grandfather of the present King,
in the church of the blessed Peter of Westminster, viz.: to the
sacrist and other officers of the same church for ringing the bells
and performance of divers other obsequies on the same day, 13*s.*4*d.*;
to the keeper of the reliques for the safe custody thereof and of
the tomb, and for wax lights burnt upon the same tomb, 6*s.* 8*d.*;
to the same sacrist for wax purchased to be constantly burning
in two wax lights about the tomb of the same King Edward the
grandfather, 14*l.* 5*s.* 6*d.*; to the brethren of the four orders
within the city of London, for celebrating divine worship in the
said church on the day of the same anniversary, a gift of 4
marks; to Roger Elys, for four wax lights, each of 8 lbs. weight,
ordered to be burnt on the vigil and day aforesaid, 18*s.* 8*d.*; and
in distributions to the poor, for the soul of the said grandfather,
9*l.*; to forty poor persons bearing torches, 13*s.* 4*d.*; and for the
placing of four candelabras, and the portage and carriage thereof,
and for wax, from London to Westminster; also for other small
expenses incurred on the vigil and day of the anniversary aforesaid, 15*s.* 10*d.* By writ of privy seal, &c.,—29*l.* 6*s.* 8*d.*

16*th July.*—To the Lord the King, in his chamber, for the
price of two drinking-cups and two silver ewers, gilt, purchased
of Nicholas Twyford, a goldsmith of London, and delivered
to the said Lord the King in his chamber aforesaid, for the marriage of Sir Philipp de Courtenay, knight, and Anne de Wake, his
wife. By writ of privy seal, &c.,—22*l.* 17*s.* 4*d.*

2*nd August.*—To the Earl of Saint Paul, a prisoner to the
King, brought from France, for going to the town of Calais to
make a certain payment there for his ransom. In money paid to
him in advance, to be restored by the same Earl to William Eremyn, treasurer of the town of Calais, before the departure of the
same Earl from the town aforesaid,—50*l.*

16th August.—To Sir Thomas de Felton, knight, late the King's steward in Gascony, by assignment made to him this day in the name of the Earl of Saint Paul, of France, a prisoner to the King, for the price of 30,000 franks, the ransom of the same Earl,—to wit, in part payment of 5765*l.* 7*s.* 9*d.*, &c., for which the Lord King Edward, grandfather of the present King, was bound to the same Thomas by his letters obligatory under the great seal; by account made with him at the Exchequer, &c., and for the receipt of the wages and fees of the same Thomas and his men going with him, in the service of the same Lord the King in Gascony, as appears by the said letters obligatory under the great seal, remaining in the possession of the same Thomas, indorsed with the underwritten sum, &c.,—5000*l.*

7th September.—To John de Notyngham, clerk of the receipt, sent to Buckingham to search for certain money under ground, or treasure hid in the earth in those parts. In money paid to him by his own hands, as well for the hire of horses as for costs by him incurred for the wages of miners and other labourers making the search aforesaid,—2*l.*

ISSUE ROLL, MICHAELMAS, 3 RICHARD II.

12th March.—To John Katerine, of Venice, a dancing-master. In money paid to his own hands in discharge of 10 marks which the Lord the King ordered to be paid him of his gift, because he played and danced in the presence of the King.— By writ, &c.,—6*l.* 13*s.* 4*d.*

10th December.—To John Walssh, receiver of the King's provisions at Cherburgh. In money paid to him by John d'Arundell, Marshal of England, late keeper of the castle and town of Cherburgh, at the time he was discharged from the custody aforesaid, for the under-mentioned things remaining there for the King's use for the defence and provision of the castle and town aforesaid,:

viz. : for ten guns to throw stones, two of which are of iron and eight of other metal, seven of the said ten guns casting large stones twenty-four inches in circumference, and the three remaining casting large stones fifteen inches in circumference ; 200 lbs. of powder, 26 lbs. of saltpetre, and 24 lbs. of pure sulphur, which said guns, powder, saltpetre, and pure sulphur, were paid for at the Exchequer in the account of the 17th day of June, in the eighth year, &c.

ISSUE ROLL, EASTER, 3 RICHARD II.

1st August.—To John Brauderer, of Southampton, the King's serjeant at arms, sent to Cornwall to arrest John Treverthian, and John, his son, William Carnello, Prior of Bodmyn, and others, for certain misprisions by them committed against the King's peace. In money paid to him, &c.,—2*l.*

· *12th September.*—To the Lord the King, by the hands of John Rose, valet of the King's chamber, as well for *the price of a Bible written in the Gaelic language, as for two volumes, contained in two leather cases, one book containing the Romance of the Rose, the other book containing the Romances of Percevall and Gawayn,* delivered to John Bacon, as appears by the counterpart of a certain indenture made between the aforesaid John Bacou and John Rose, and by writ of privy seal, directed to the said John Bacon, concerning the delivery of the said books and Bible, remaining in the Hanaper aforesaid. By general writ of privy seal above alleged,—28*l.*

29th May.—To Sir William Windsor, knight; in money paid to him by the hands of Nicholas Rouney, in discharge of 200*l.*, which the Lord the King commanded to be paid him of his gift, in aid of the charges by him incurred for 100 men at arms retained by him at his own costs to serve the Lord the King in his wars, and for his absence for half a year ; also on account of restitution made to the same William of certain lands which belonged to Alice Perrers, wife to the said William, forfeited to the Lord the King by reason of a judgment pronounced against the said Alice in his parliament held at Westminster in the first year. By writ, &c.,—200*l.*

17*th August.*—To John Sampson, the King's receiver in the Isle of Wight, in money paid to him by the hands of Richard Ryngeborne, Esquire, and Sir Thomas Beachamp, knight, for purchasing and providing 100 lbs. of saltpetre and 50 lbs. of pure sulphur, to supply the King's castle at Carisbrook, in the aforesaid island,—6*l* 10*s.*

ISSUE ROLL, MICHAELMAS, 4 RICHARD II.

28*th November.*—To Geoffrey Chaucer, in money paid to his own hands in discharge of 14*l.* due upon an account made with him at the Exchequer of account, for receipt of his wages and expenses in going upon the King's message to Lombardy, in the 1st year of the reign of King Richard II. By writ of privy seal, &c.,—14*l.*

31*st January.*—To William Geyton, the King's engraver in the Tower of London. In money paid to his own hands in discharge of 50*s.* which the Lord the King commanded to be paid him for alterations by him made, as well on the great seal used in the Chancery as upon the King's seals used in the King's Bench, Exchequer, and Common Bench, at the commencement of this King's reign. By writ of privy seal, &c.,—2*l.* 10*s.*

To the Prior of the Hospital of Saint John of Jerusalem, in England, by indenture and by writ of the great seal in these words: Richard, by the grace of God King of England and France, and Lord of Ireland, to the venerable Father in Christ Thomas, by the same grace Bishop of Exeter, our late Treasurer, greeting: Whereas we have committed to our beloved brother in Christ Robert Hales, Prior of the Hospital of Saint John of Jerusalem in England, the office of Treasurer of our Exchequer, to hold with all things belonging to that office so long as it shall please us, as in our letters patent thereof made fully is contained : We command you that you deliver to the same Prior the rolls, keys, and all other things touching that office which are in your custody, to be kept in the form aforesaid. Witness ourself at Westminster, the 1st day of February, in the fourth year of our reign. [*Note.* Letters patent, appointing different officers under the Crown, are sometimes fully set out on these Rolls.]

6th February.—To John Wetherhird, a messenger sent, during the time of holding the parliament at Northampton, from the town of Northampton to London, by command of the Council, to seek out a certain clerk of Ralph de Ferrers, for certain causes in custody under arrest in the city of London, and to bring the same clerk to the parliament aforesaid, there to answer concerning certain articles. In money, &c.,—10s.

6th March.—To Geoffrey Chaucer, an esquire of the King. In money paid to his own hands, by assignment made to him this day, in discharge of 22l., which the Lord the King commanded to be paid him of his gift in recompense of his wages, and the charges by him incurred in going as well in the time of King Edward, grandfather of the present King, as a messenger of the same grandfather, to Mounstrell and Paris, in France, on account of a treaty of peace pending between the aforesaid grandfather and his adversary of France; as in the time of the present Lord the King, to make a communication respecting a marriage to be had between the same Lord the King and the daughter of his said enemy of France. By writ of privy seal, &c.,—22l.

ISSUE ROLL, MICHAELMAS, 4 RICHARD II.

11th March.—To Thomas Johnson, in money paid to him, by
assignment made this day, in discharge of 20 marks which the
Lord the King commanded to be paid him for his expenses in
fighting a duel with John Grey, a traitor against the King, at
the town of Calais, and for succeeding in the capture of five
other traitors adjudged to death at the town aforesaid. By writ
of privy seal amongst the mandates of this term,—13*l.* 6*s.* 8*d.*

6th April.—To William de Patryngton, keeper of the King's
wardrobe, in money paid to him by the hands of John Carper,
the King's cofferer, distributed to the poor on the day they were
fed of the King's alms,—133*l.* 6*s.* 8*d.*

ISSUE ROLL, EASTER, 4 RICHARD II.

10th May.—To John, Duke of Lancaster, sent on the King's
behalf to the North to attend on the day of the Marches appointed
to be held there between the Lord the King and the people of
Scotland, viz., on the morrow of the Trinity next happening. In
money paid to him by the hands of John Norfolk, his clerk, viz.,
in money at the receipt of the Exchequer, 1000*l.*, and by assignment made to him this day for his wages,—1333*l.* 6*s.* 8*d.*

30th July.—To Sir Thomas Percy, knight, and Hugh Calveley.
captain of the castle of Brest, in Britany, by three tallies levied
this day, containing 500 marks, paid to the same Thomas and
Hugh, by the hands of the aforesaid Thomas, for the safe custody
of the castle aforesaid. By writ, &c.,—333*l.* 6*s.* 8*d.*

20th September.—To Arnald Brocas, clerk of the works of the
Lord the King within the palace of Westminster and Tower of

London, Windsor Castle, and divers others of the King's castles and manors. In money paid to him by the hands of William Hanneye, comptroller of the works aforesaid, for repairing and constructing the door broken by the common rebels within the Tower of London,—3*l.* 6*s.* 8*d.*

20th September.—To Richard Hauberger, of the Tower of London. In money paid to him by his own hands for the purchase and making of a certain bridle and an (aventail) for the King, —2*l.*

23rd September.—To the Lord the King, in his chamber, by the hands of Baldwin de Radyngton, keeper of the King's jewels in the same chamber, for the price of a crown called the Spanish crown, set with divers precious stones, delivered to the said Baldwin, by John Bacon, into the King's chamber aforesaid, as appears by the counterpart of a certain indenture made between the aforesaid John and Baldwin. By writ of privy seal, &c.—1719*l.*13*s.*4*d.*

ISSUE ROLL, MICHAELMAS, 5 RICHARD II.

10th October.—To Sir John Harleston, knight, 1583*l.* 6*s.* 8*d.*, for his share of the ransom of William de Bordes, a knight of France, taken in the war in Normandy by a soldier in the retinue of the said John,—1583*l.* 6*s.* 8*d.*

9th December.—To William de Patryngton, keeper of the King's wardrobe, in money paid to him by the hands of John Carper, the King's cofferer, for the wages of the knights and esquires sent to Calais, there to await the arrival of the Lady the Queen of England. By writ of privy seal, &c.,—536*l.* 18*s.* 9*d.*

To divers messengers and couriers sent to divers parts of England and Wales with writs of the King's great seal, directed to the King's escheators, to seize into the King's hands the lands of the

late Earl and Countess of March, by reason of the death of the
same Earl and Countess, which they held of the Lord the King
in capite.   In money paid to them, &c.,—5l.

To Pezenuslaus, Duke de Techmensis, Couranus de Kreyg, master
of the court, and Peter de Wauteberg, master chamberlain of
the most Serene Prince and Lord, Lord Wenceslaus, King of the
Romans and Bohemia.   In money paid to them by the hands of
Hervey Berzebo on account of a valid, lawful, and actual loan for
the use of the said King of the Romans, for the important
and more urgent affairs of the state of the Holy Church of Rome,
the Roman empire and kingdom aforesaid, to be restored, as appears by letters obligatory made by them to the said Lord the
King, remaining in a certain box in the King's Treasury, &c.,—
1114l. 3s. 10d.

To Sir William Faryndon, knight, sent to the North, by command of the King's Council, to make preparations for a duel to
be fought upon the Marches between England and Scotland between a certain esquire of England and a certain esquire of Scotland.   In money paid to him by his own hands, in discharge of
20l. which the Lord the King commanded to be paid him for his
expenses.   By writ, &c.,—20l.

16th December.—To William de Monte Acuto, Earl of Salisbury, late captain of the town of Calais, in money paid to him
by the hands of Nicholas Wychyngham, in discharge of 100 marks
which the Lord the King commanded to be paid him in recompense and satisfaction of the costs incurred by the same Earl for
the support and custody of the brother of the Earl of Saint
Paul during the time the said brother of the Earl of Saint
Paul remained as an hostage at Calais, in the retinue of the said
Earl of Salisbury, for the aforesaid Earl of Saint Paul, then
a prisoner.   By writ, &c.,—66l. 13s. 4d.

17th December.—To Sir Simon de Burley, knight, for the

charges of his embassy in two voyages to treat for the marriage between our Lord the King and the sister of the King of the Romans and Bohemia. By writ, &c.,—10*l.* 9*s.* 4*d.*

21st December.—To divers knights, esquires, and other officers of the court of the King of the Romans and Bohemia, coming in the retinue of the Lady Anne, Queen of England, sister of the said King of the Romans, from Bohemia to the town of Calais, and returning from the said town of Calais, by direction of the Lord the King and his Council, to their homes. In money paid to them for the price of 1052½ franks, each frank valued at 3*s.* 2*d.* sterling; together with 5*d.* sterling for those 1800 franks paid by John de Monte Acuto, steward, and Simon de Burley, under-chamberlain of the King's household, received at the said town of Calais from Edward Halstede and Ralph Bathill, attorneys of Nicholas Brembre, a citizen of London, viz., in discharge of 250 marks which the Lord the King commanded to be paid of his gift to the same knights, esquires, and officers, as a reward for the purposes aforesaid. By writ, &c.,—166*l.* 13*s.* 4*d.*

25th February.—To Nicholas Adam, the King's serjeant at arms, lately sent by command of the Lord the King from the town of Northampton, during the time the last parliament was there held, to the priory of Durham, to place Sir Ralph de Ferers, knight, under arrest at the said priory, and to cause him to appear before the Lord the King and others of the nobility at the said parliament, to answer to certain articles charged against him in the parliament aforesaid. In money paid to his own hands for the wages and expenses of the said Ralph, and for the hire of horses; also for the expenses of others his valets coming in the retinue of the same Nicholas for the safe conduct of the same Ralph, for the reason aforesaid, &c.,—6*l.* 13*s.* 4*d.*

24th March.—To John Asheby, an esquire coming from the castle of Cherburgh, in Normandy, upon a message to the Lord the King, to certify and declare to the same Lord the King and his Council the condition of the soldiers in the garrison of the castle aforesaid, and want of provisions within the aforesaid castle. In money paid to him for the wages and expenses of his coming over, and for hire of a boat, with twenty-four mariners in the same, for his repassing upon the King's message to the castle aforesaid, &c.,—5*l.*

To divers messengers and couriers sent to all parts of England with writs of the King's great seal, directed to all sheriffs, to make proclamation throughout England of the statutes enacted at the King's parliament held at Westminster on the morrow of All Souls, in the 5th year of the present King. In money paid, &c., —6*l.* 15*s.*

In money paid to Hugh Seagrave, Treasurer of England, for so much money by him expended for the expenses of certain nobility of the King's Council, and other knights, appointed by the counties to attend the parliament then held at Westminster, for one day's dinner at the King's charge, to expedite certain special business touching the state of the Lord the King, &c.,— 1*l.* 5*s.* 4*d.*

ISSUE ROLL, EASTER, 5 RICHARD II.

21*st April.*—To Richard Stoke, a courier sent to Gloucester and the Marches of Wales with divers writs directed to William de Wyndesore, John Lovell, and others, knights, to come to London to the King's parliament, there to be holden on the morrow of the Exaltation of the Holy Cross, in the 5th year. In money paid to him for his wages,—6*s.* 8*d.*

16*th May.*—To William Droit, John Droit, and John Langor, masters of three ships from Dunkyrk, in Flanders. In money paid to them by the hands of the same John Langor, by assignment made to them this day, in discharge of 13*l.* 10*s.*, which the

Lord the King commanded to be paid them according to an agreement made between the Council of the Lord the King and the said William, John, and John, for the freightage and shipping of five chargers, palfreys, and of other horses, for conducting the retinue of Anne, Queen of England,—to wit, for each horse 5s., from the town of Calais to Dover, on the coming of the said Queen into England. By writ of privy seal,—13l. 10s.

4th August.—To John Ellerton, the King's serjeant at arms, sent in the month of December, in the third year, to Norfolk and Suffolk, to seize into the King's hands Mirabilla, daughter and heir of John Aspall, who held of the King in capite, and to bring the said Mirabilla to London before the King's Council, to dispose of the custody of her as should be ordered by the Council for the King's advantage, being occupied in the said business twelve days: also sent at another time by command of the Council in the third year to the town of Bury, in the county of Suffolk, to John Cavendissh, the King's Chief Justice, there holding a session, to inform him of certain evidence against the rebels aiding and abetting a certain monk of the abbey of the same town; the Abbot of the same abbey having asserted that he had sanction for what he had done from the Court of Rome; employed in the said business for eight days: also sent a third time to arrest Sir Robert Howard, knight, and to bring him before the King's Council to answer certain articles put to him by the said Council; employed in the same business for ten days. In money paid to his own hands for his wages, taking per day 2s. 6d. during the time aforesaid,—3l. 15s. 0d.

4th August.—To John Palyng, of London, goldsmith, in money paid to his own hands in discharge of 100 marks which the Lord the King commanded to be paid him for a worked fillet, with one large ruby, two sapphires; and for three rings of pearls, each ring of four pearls, and one great diamond placed in the middle of each, purchased from the same John, by the King's command, for the use of Anne, Queen of England, by Richard de Abber-

bury, chamberlain of the same Queen. By letter of privy seal,
—66*l.* 13*s.* 4*d.*

ISSUE ROLL, MICHAELMAS, 6 RICHARD II.

26th November.—To Sir Hugh de Seagrave, knight, Treasurer
of England, lately appointed by a commission of the Lord King
Edward, grandfather of the present King, one of the Justices to
hear and determine certain articles touching the Stannaries in the
counties of Devon and Cornwall. In money paid in discharge
of 40 marks, for his charges, &c., which the Lord the King
granted by advice of his Council, &c.,—26*l.* 13*s.* 4*d.*

In money paid to the boy Bishop, appointed in honour of
Saint Nicholas, the Bishop, at the feast thereof held in the King's
chapel, Westminster, of the King's gift, by direction of the Treasurer and Chamberlains,—1*l.*

23rd February.—To John Morewell, the King's serjeant at
arms, sent by command of the Council from London to Nottingham Castle to a certain monk of the convent and abbey of
Bury, for certain reasons in custody in the said castle, to desire
him to come to London, and appear before the said Council. In
money paid to him for his wages, and hire of horses for the said
Prior's riding to London, and for the expenses of the same Prior
for the cause aforesaid,—2*l.* 17*s.*

ISSUE ROLL, EASTER, 6 RICHARD II.

9th May.—To the Venerable Father Henry, Bishop of Norwich, deputy and especial Nuncio of our most Holy Father, Pope
Urban, in the crusade against the anti-pope, and the schismatics
adhering to and favouring them. In money paid to him by the
hands of John Philippot, citizen of London, from the fifteenths

granted to the Lord the King, in the sixth year, for wages in the war, and as a reward for 2500 men at arms and 2500 archers going in his retinue to Flanders and France, to serve as well in the crusade aforesaid, as for the Lord the King in his war in the parts aforesaid, for one whole year. By two writs of privy seal amongst the mandates of Michaelmas term last past,—6266*l.* 13*s.* 4*d.* [This Roll contains other entries of payments for the army appointed for the purposes above mentioned.]

20th May.—To Florymund, Lord de le Sparre, in money paid to him by assignment made this day upon the subsidies of wool in divers ports of England, for the price of 10,000 franks, to be paid as a loan during the King's pleasure. By writ, &c.,—1666*l.* 13*s.* 4*d.*

6th June.—To William Dounebrigg, one of the auditors of the Exchequer, appointed by command of the Council to audit and revise the accounts of divers receivers and ministers of the King in Cornwall and Devonshire, because they were not accustomed to render account at the King's Great Exchequer. In money paid to him, &c., for his wages and expenses, viz., from the 21st day of February last past, on which day he departed from London to Lostwithyell for the purpose aforesaid, unto the 10th day of March next following, for eighteen days, taking each day 6*s.* 8*d.* for his wages, &c.,—6*l.*

13th July.—To the Lord the King, in his chamber, in money paid to William Walsham, the King's almoner, by assignment made to him this day, in discharge of 40*l.* which the same William paid as a loan to the Lord the King, in his chamber aforesaid, for the expenses lately incurred by the said Lord the King for the Duke of Hesse; and for others, messengers, coming from the King of the Romans to England to treat for a marriage between our said Lord the King and the sister of the King of the Romans and Bohemia aforesaid. By writ of privy seal, &c.,—40*l.*

ISSUE ROLL, MICHAELMAS, 7 RICHARD II.

9th January.—To Sir Michael de la Pole, Chancellor of England, lately sent from England to Milan, and from thence to the court of Rome, to the King of the Romans and Bohemia, as the King's messenger, to enter into a treaty for a marriage to be had between the said Lord the King and Anne, Queen of England, taken prisoner in those parts under the safe conduct of the same King of the Romans, upon her return from the parts aforesaid. In money paid to him, by assignment made this day, in discharge of 933*l.* 6*s.* 8*d.* which the Lord the King commanded to be paid him in recompense of so much money which the said Michael paid for the release of the said Queen from the prison aforesaid, and because the same Lord the King, with the advice of his Council, promised to satisfy him for the loss which he had incurred on account of the embassy aforesaid. By writ, &c.,— 933*l.* 6*s.* 8*d.*

5th March.—To divers messengers and couriers sent to all parts of England with writs under the King's great seal, directed to the Prelates, the Duke of Lancaster, Earls, Barons, and other nobility of the realm, to come to Salisbury to the King's parliament, there to be held on Wednesday after the feast of Saint George, in the seventh year. In money paid to them for their wages, as appears by the particulars remaining in the Hanaper of this term,— 8*l.* 6*s.* 8*d.*

30th March.—To Sir Nicholas Brembre, Mayor of London, in money paid to him by his own hands for so much money by him paid for the safe conduct of John Northampton, late Mayor of London, for certain causes detained under an arrest within the city of London, and by advice of the King's Council sent to Corf Castle, there to be safely kept at the King's will; also for the costs and expenses of certain valets, and for the hire of horses for the safe custody of the said John riding from the said city to the aforesaid castle, &c.,—22*l.*

ISSUE ROLL, EASTER, 7 RICHARD II.

2nd May.—To Nicholas Auncell, a messenger sent from the town of New Salisbury with a writ of the King's great seal, directed to the Constable of Dover Castle, to summon the Barons of the cinque ports to the King's parliament to be held at the town of Salisbury aforesaid. In money paid to him for his wages,—10s.

26th May.—To John, King of Castille and Leon, Duke of Lancaster. In money paid to him by the hands of Sir Hugh Seagrave, knight, Treasurer of England, in advance upon a certain fee of 100 marks which the same Duke receives yearly from the "avoueries" in North Wales, by the hands of the Chamberlain there,—100l.

15th June.—To Natalicia, who was the wife of William Craylyng, which said William was lately sent to the town of Gaunt as a messenger from the King, and was taken in the said message by persons of Lesclus, in Flanders, and killed on account of the message aforesaid. In money to the same Natalicia, paid to her own hands of the King's alms, in aid of discharging the debts of the said William, &c.,—13l. 4s.

22nd June.—To Sir John de Burley, knight. In money paid to his own hands, by assignment made this day, in discharge of 500 marks, which the Lord the King commanded to be paid him of his gift, in aid of his ransom, having been lately taken a prisoner in Germany at the time when the said John was last sent as the King's messenger to the King of the Romans and Bohemia. By writ, &c.,—200l.

13th August.—In money paid to a clerk of the King's Chancery, for writing a copy of a certain papal bull, to obtain the opinion of some discreet men upon certain articles contained in the said bull,—1s.

Q

To Alan Stokes clerk, of the King's great wardrobe. In money paid to him by the hands of Pincheron, of London, jeweller, for making divers buttons for the person of the Lord the King. By writ, &c.,—20*l.*

ISSUE ROLL, MICHAELMAS, 8 RICHARD II.

11th November.—To Sir Thomas de Beauchamp, knight, late captain of Caresbrok Castle, in the Isle of Wight. In money paid to him by assignment made this day for wages in the war of his men at arms, cross-bowmen, archers, and others lately residing with him, for the protection and safe custody of the same castle in the island aforesaid. By writ, &c.,—45*l.* 15*s.*

To the same Sir Thomas. In money paid to him, viz., by the aforesaid assignment, 4*l.* 5*s.*; and in money paid to his own hands for so much money by him disbursed, viz., to five cannoniers, each having his cannon; and to one cannonier with three cannons, for the hire of the same cannoniers and cannons, and for powder purchased for the same cannons late in the King's service in the retinue of the said Sir Thomas for the protection of the island aforesaid against the King's enemies, who in certain galleys at sea lately made an attempt to invade the island aforesaid. By writ of privy seal, &c.,—26*l.* 5*s.*

12th November.—To Merric de la Ville Nove. In money paid to his own hands in discharge of 24*l.* 3*s.* 4*d.* which the Lord the King commanded to be paid him for so much money which the said Merric paid to divers men for armor and other necessary preparations for the duel waged between him and John Walshe, &c., —24*l.* 3*s.* 4*d.*

14th November.—For expenses incurred at Westminster by the King's command, upon the secret arrival there of the said Lord the King from his manor of Eltham, to dine and to inspect his jewels, and upon other his private affairs,—2*l.* 5*s.*

24th December.—To Arnald Brocas, clerk of the King's works within the palace of Westminster and Tower of London, and at divers other of the King's castles and manors. In money paid to him by the hands of John Hermesthorp, one of the chamberlains of the receipt, for ordering, making, and amending of divers large warlike machines, made in the Tower by order of the King and his Council, intended for certain urgent and secret affairs by the said King and his Council. By writ of privy seal,—9*l.* 5*s.* 7*d.* [Other payments of a similar nature are entered on this Roll.]

11th February.—To Arnald Brocas, clerk of the King's works in the palace of Westminster and Tower of London. In money twice paid to him by the hands of Walter de Walton, for making divers images ordered at the King's pleasure for the great hall at Westminster. By writ, &c.,—6*l.*

ISSUE ROLL, EASTER, 8 RICHARD II.

1st May.—To Sir Simon de Burley, knight, Constable of Dover Castle, for the price of 12 guns, 2 iron "patella," 120 stones for the guns, 100 lbs. of powder, and 4 stocks of wood, purchased of William, the founder, of London, and delivered to the said Simon by the hands of William Hanney, clerk, for fortifying and strengthening of Dover Castle,—97*l.* 10*s.*

26th June—To John Eliot, a messenger sent with a writ of the King's great seal, directed to the Abbot of Waverley, to send a horse to London to carry the King towards Scotland. In money paid to him for his wages, 3*s.* 4*d.* [Also a writ sent to the Abbot of Tame for the like purpose, and to take knights, and other persons, accompanying the King to Scotland.]

27th June.—To Anthony Bache, merchant. In money paid to him by the hands of Guido de Sinoche, in part payment of 11,720*l.* 2*s.*, for which the Lord King Edward, grandfather of the present King, was bound to the same Anthony, by his letters obligatory, for several sums of money borrowed of him for the wages of divers men at arms and archers in the late King's service, in parts beyond seas, also for the delivery of certain crowns of the said Lord King Edward, the grandfather, and Philippa, late Queen of England, pledged in France, as appears by the said letters obligatory remaining in the possession of the said Anthony, indorsed with the underwritten sum, which said assignment is now made with the advice of the King's Council, because that the said Anthony hath now lent to the King's use 2000*l.*, in his great necessity, to assist him in his journey to Scotland, the said King going in his own person,—666*l.* 13*s.* 4*d.*

ISSUE ROLL, MICHAELMAS, 9 RICHARD II.

14th November.—To a certain Esquire of France, who lately arrived in the retinue of Guichard Marzei, a knight of France, passing through England upon a message to the King of Scotland with the King's licence, paid for the price of a piece of worsted striped with black and white, purchased of John Organ, a citizen and merchant of London, delivered to the same Esquire of the King's gift,— 1*l.* 13*s.* 4*d.*

30th November.—To Arnald Brocas, clerk of the works of the Lord the King within the palace of Westminster and Tower of London, and of divers others the King's castles and manors. In money paid to him by the hands of Walter Walton, for making a tabernacle over the head of an image, made in the likeness of the King, placed at the end of the great hall, Westminster. By general writ of privy seal, &c.,—2*l.*

15th December.—To Arnald Brocas, clerk of the King's works within the palace of Westminster, Tower of London, and divers other the King's castles and manors. In money paid to him by the hands of Walter Walton, for making two images, in likeness of the King and "Houell," the same placed at the end of the

King's great hall within the palace of Westminster. By general writ of privy seal,—2*l.*

12th February.—To the King of Arminia. In money paid to his own hands in discharge of 1000*l.* which the Lord the King commanded to be paid him in gold nobles, upon his departure from England. By writ, &c.,—1000*l.*

29th March.—To Simon de Burgh, Treasurer of the town of Calais, and receiver of the King's provisions there. In money paid to him, viz. by the hands of William Wodeward, for making of sixty cannon, 10*l.*, and by the hands of Roger Cromp, 5*l.*, for the forming of stones to be thrown by engines for fortifying and defending of the town of Calais,—15*l.*

3rd April.—To John Butt, a messenger sent to the west with letters of the King's signet, directed to Matthew Gourney, Guido de Bryen, John Sully, and other knights of the garter in those parts, to delay the feast of Saint George so ordered for certain reasons by the said Lord the King. In money paid to him for his wages,—1*l.*

7th April.—To Henry de Percy, (the son,) late keeper of the town of Berwick-upon-Tweed, and the marches thereof. In money paid to him by assignment made this day in discharge of 30*l.* which the Lord the King, with the advice of his Council, commanded to be paid him of his gift in the name of a reward, because the said Henry had paid a fine and agreed with certain soldiers in the Marches of Berwick for their ransom, by reason they had taken six traitors in the said marches at the time when the said Henry was custos there,—to wit, for each of the said traitors, 100*s.*, who by judgement of the laws of the said marches, on account of their treason aforesaid, by command of the said Henry, were condemned to death. By writ of privy seal,—30*l.*

22nd March.—To Sir John Golofre, knight of the King's chamber, to whom the Lord the King, by letters patent, granted the manor of Tybest with the appurtenances, in the county of Cornwall, in lieu of forty pounds yearly; to have and to hold the manor afore-said with the appurtenances, and all issues and profits thereof arising, from the day of the death of the mother of the Lord the King, during his life; which said manor, with the appurtenances and profits thereof arising, were in the hands of the executors of the said King's mother, by virtue of the King's letters patent, granted by the said Lord the King to his same mother in her lifetime, and confirmed to the said executors after her death, to have and to hold to the said executors for one whole year after the decease of his said mother, in the same manner as all lordships, lands, and rents were assigned to his aforesaid mother in dower. In money paid to the said John, by assignment made this day, in discharge of 40*l.* which the Lord the King commanded to be paid him in recompense of so much money that was in arrear to the said John, as should be of the value of the said manor with the appur-tenances, for the year aforesaid, by reason of the grant made by the said Lord the King to his aforesaid mother, and confirmation to her executors of the manor as aforesaid. By writ of privy seal amongst the mandates of this term,—40*l.*

ISSUE ROLL, EASTER, 9 RICHARD II.

15*th May.*—In money paid to Richard Stanlak, clerk of Sir Robert Bardolf, knight, for the carriage of cannon, espringolds, quatrells, and other artillery from the Tower of London to Porchester Castle, for the munition and defence of the castle aforesaid, &c.,—16*s.*

To Arnold Brocas, clerk of the works of the Lord the King within the palace of Westminster, Tower of London, and divers other of the King's castles and manors. In money paid to him for painting the images in the great hall at Westminster, and for repairing a bridge at Westminster, &c.,—5*l.*

29*th May.*—To John Moubray, a priest in the county of Lincoln, who lately appeared before the King's Council, and offered, by certain evidence, to search for and take within the said county and elsewhere, divers traitors coiners of the King's money. In money paid to his own hands, by advice of the said Council, for his expenses in travelling and pains taken in the business aforesaid. By writ of privy seal, &c.,—10*l.*

26*th June.*—To Roger Longe, the King's sergeant at arms, sent by direction of the King's Council from the town of Reading to Somersetshire and Dorsetshire, to seize into the King's hands, in the name of wardship, other daughters and heirs of Sir John Mautravers, knight, deceased. In money, paid to him for his wages and expenses in going, &c.,—1*l.* 6*s.* 8*d.*

5*th July.*—To the Lord the King, in his chamber, by the hands of John Bottesham, of London, goldsmith, for a knife to be used in the woods, and a horn ornamented with gold, weighing sixteen ounces less one drachm of gold, made by him for the Lord the King for his hunting horn, in the summer season this ninth year, together with the making thereof and tassels of green silk for the same,—25*l.* 17*s.* 4*d.*

ISSUE ROLL, MICHAELMAS, 10 RICHARD II.

16*th October.*—To Rees ap Tuder, William ap Tuder, and six of his companions, Esquires, Captains of one hundred and twenty archers of the county of Carnarvon; Eignon ap Gryffyth ap Ħ and two of his companions, esquires, captains of forty archers from the county of Merioneth; Eignon ap Ithell ap Gurgeny and one of his companions, an esquire, captain of forty archers from the county aforesaid; Ithell ap Blethin ap Ithell, Howell ap Tuder ap Ithell, William ap Merith ap Griffitz, David Vaghan ap David Lloit Ithel, Moil ap David Ithell, each a captain of twenty Welsh archers, and Howell ap Joreward, and three of his com-

panions, governors and captains of sixty archers, who lately came
from the marches of Wales to the Lord the King, by his command at the feast of Saint Michael last past, and with the said
archers and their retinue, ordered to resist the malice of the King's
enemies and join a great army, to be assembled at divers ports
along the English coast, which said men had not tarried or inhabited within the limits of sixty miles of the city of London, as
stated upon their oath taken before the Lord Treasurer and
Chamberlains. In money paid to them by their own hands, at
different times, for their wages in the war, and for their men aforesaid, for a certain period within the space of one month after the
feast aforesaid, during which time they were coming towards
London and there remained in the parts adjacent, and returned by
virtue of the King's command aforesaid. By general writ, &c.,—
125*l.* 7*s.* [*Note.* This Roll contains many similar entries of payments made to the captains and leaders of the English army at
this time assembled.]

20th October.—To Sir Hugh de Calveley, knight, who lately
came to the Lord the King, by his command, at the feast of Saint
Michael last past, with two knights, thirty-two esquires, and one
hundred archers in his retinue, to resist the malice of the King's
enemies, ordered to join a great army to be assembled at divers
ports upon the coast, which said men had not tarried or inhabited
within the limits of sixty miles from the city of London, by the
oath of their attorney Hugh, taken before the Lord the Treasurer
and Chamberlains. In money paid to them by assignment made
this day, for the wages of themselves and their men, for a certain
period within the space of one month after the feast aforesaid,
during which time they were coming to London, and in the parts
adjoining remained, and returned by virtue of the King's command
aforesaid, &c.,—120*l.* 8*s.*

ISSUE ROLL, EASTER, 10 RICHARD II.

17th June.—To William, Duke de Gelre [of Gueldres.]   In money paid to him by the hands of James de Mountford and Colard de la Zenendre, for a certain annual fee granted him by the Lord the King, to be received at the Exchequer during his life on account of the homage, fealty, and good services performed and to be performed by the said Duke to the said Lord the King, &c., —500*l.*

18th June.—To Alan Stokes, clerk of the great wardrobe of the Lord the King.   In money paid to him by the hands of Reginald Hatton, his clerk, for providing a sword ornamented with silver, gilt, purchased for the King's person.   By writ of liberate, &c.,— 13*l.* 6*s.* 8*d.*

22nd July.—To John Annesley and Isabella, his wife, one of the heirs of John Chandos, chevalier, deceased, who held of the Lord the King in fee the castle of Saint Saviour, with the appurtenances, in the island of Constantyn in Normandy, of the gift and feoffment of Lord Edward, grandfather of the present King, which said John prosecuted a certain quarrel by duel before the now Lord the King in his palace at Westminster against Thomas de Catherton, on account of the capture of the aforesaid castle by the French; and afterwards, when the aforesaid John and Thomas contended together in the presence of the Lord the King in the same duel, the Lord the King, for a certain time, took the said quarrel into his own hands; and to the said John and Isabella, on the 26th day of May in the ninth year, granted, by his letters patent, 40*l.*, yearly to be received at the Exchequer during their lives and the longer liver of them, as well in recompense of a full reward which the said John, by reason of the plaint aforesaid, and the aforesaid John and Isabella, by any other pretence, could demand the castle aforesaid from the aforesaid King, as also because that the aforesaid John was retained to attend the said Lord the King both in peace and war.   In money paid to them, &c.,—20*l.*

27th November.—To John Warburton, an esquire of Earl of Arundell. In money paid to him by assignment made this day, in part payment of 135*l.* 14*s.* 5½*d.*, due upon account made with him at the Exchequer of accounts, as well for his receipts as for costs incurred by him for amending the causeway walls and fortification of the King's town of la Rye, also for making a drawbridge and two turrets there, a well, and a kitchen within the tower of the aforesaid town, and also for the wages of the said John, four archers, one cannonier, and one engineer, lately residing in the fortification of the aforesaid town. By writ, &c.,— 66*l.* 13*s.* 4*d.*

9th December.—To Sir Hugh le Despenser, knight, lately taken in the war, in the King's service, in Flanders, by the King's French enemies. In money paid to him, &c., in part payment of 200*l.* which the Lord the King commanded to be paid him of his gift in aid of his ransom. By writ, &c.,—98*l.* 6*s.* 8*d.*

20th December.—To Thomas Sayvill and John Elyngeham, the King's sergeant at arms, appointed by the King's commission to go to the town of Kyngston upon Hull, to arrest Michael de la Pole, Earl of Suffolk, for certain causes, and bring him before the Lord the King and his Council. In money paid to him, &c.,— 6*l.* 13*s.* 4*d.* [Also payments for taking Sir Simon de Burley and Sir William Elingeham from London to Nottingham Castle, and for bringing them back again.]

28th January.—To John Orewell, Richard Hembrigg, and Thomas Atte Mille, the King's sergeants at arms, sent to Gloucester to bring Nicholas Brembre, a prisoner in the King's castle of Gloucester, from the said castle to London, to appear before and answer in the King's parliament upon certain articles of treason charged against him by the Duke of Gloucester, Earls of Derby, Warwick, Arundel, and Nottingham. In money paid to them, viz., to each of them 5 marks for their wages, costs, and expenses incurred by them in going, tarrying, and returning, and for the hire of men and horses for the purpose aforesaid, &c.,— 10*l.* [Similar payments were made on the 22nd of February and the 11th of March, for bringing Sir Thomas Tryvet, Sir John de Bello Campo, Sir Nicholas Dagworth, and others, from Dover to London, also charged with treason.]

13*th February.*—To William Dounebrigg, late one of the auditors of the King's Exchequer. In money paid to him by assignment made this day, for the costs and expenses incurred by him, in the 10th year of the present King, in going from the city of Exeter, by direction of the Lord Treasurer, to Lostwytiell in Cornwall, to audit the accounts of divers of the King's ministers in the counties of Devon and Cornwall, which they were accustomed to render before the auditors of Lord Edward, late Prince of Wales, viz. for fifteen days, during which time he was employed and occupied in the business aforesaid, receiving each day 6*s.* 8*d.* By writ, &c.,—5*l.*

2*nd March.*—To Thomas Moubray, Earl of Nottingham, marshal of England, viz. for the price of three cloths of gold, one piece of velvet, and one piece of linen cloth of Reyns, of the goods of the Duke of Ireland, forfeited to the King, and delivered to the aforesaid Earl by the Treasurer and Chamberlains of the Exchequer, as a loan to be restored at the King's pleasure,— 44*l.* 13*s.* 4*d.*

14*th March.*—To Richard, Earl of Arundell, admiral of England. In money paid to him,—to wit, by the hands of Robert Pubblewe, his clerk, in money counted at twice,—6466*l.* 13*s.* 4*d.*; and by the hands of the aforesaid Robert, for the price of ten cloths of gold which belonged to Nicholas Brembre, forfeited to the King, 40*l.*; also by the hands of Thomas Kardyngton, clerk of Edward, Earl of Devon, in money, 200*l.* for his wages in the war, and as a reward for the men at arms, archers, and others going

with him in the King's service in a certain voyage upon the sea.
By writ, &c.,—6706*l.* 13*s.* 4*d.*

ISSUE ROLL, EASTER, 11 RICHARD II.

2nd May.—To Edward Doo, the King's sergeant at arms, sent
with a writ of the King's great seal, directed to Sir Thomas Latymere, knight, to come to London and appear before the King's
Council with certain books and pamphlets in his custody *concerning the error and perverse doctrine of the Catholic faith as is said.*
In money paid to him for his wages,—13*s.* 4*d.*

14th May.—To Sir John Kentwode, knight, and William Hor-
bury, clerk, appointed by the King's commission to inquire in the
counties of Devon and Cornwall concerning all the lands, lordships,
rents, and of the goods and chattels which belonged to the Duke
of Ireland, Robert Tresilian, John Cary, John Blake, and other
persons, forfeited by virtue of a judgment pronounced against their
persons in the King's last parliament held at Westminster. In
money paid to them, &c.,—50*l.* 10*s.* 6*d.* [Robert Tresilian,
Chief Justice, and John Cary, Chief Baron, were condemned to
die, as appears by following entries on this Roll.]

11thSeptember.—To William de Pakyngton, keeper of the King's
wardrobe, by the hands of William Mancester, for the price of a
chariot, which lately belonged to Sir John Salesbury, knight, forfeited to the Lord the King and delivered to the said William
for the King's use,—2*l.*

To John Slegh, the King's butler, keeper of the King's castle
of Tyntagell, in Cornwall, for the price of vestments of rich silk,
of a red and blue colour, consisting of a chesable, two albs, two
scarfs, two maniples, two frontlets,—to wit, one with the images of
the Blessed Mary and Saint John and one a covering for the body,
one pulpit cloth, and two curtains, valued at 10 marks; which said

vestments the Lord the King commanded to be delivered to the same John in the said castle for the use of a certain chantry, for ever to be held within the said castle, &c.,—3*l.* 6*s.* 8*d.*

ISSUE ROLL, MICHAELMAS, 12 RICHARD II.

9th December.—To the Lord the King, in his chamber. In money paid into the same chamber : viz. for the price of a mitre which belonged to the Bishop of Chichester, forfeited to the said Lord the King by reason of a judgment pronounced against the said Bishop in the King's last parliament held at Westminster, for having performed certain secret affairs at the will of the King in the chamber aforesaid,—333*l.* 6*s.* 8*d.*

17th December.—To Henry Wynchester, one of the vicars of the King's free chapel in the palace at Westminster. In money paid to him by the hands of John Melton, clerk, in discharge of 7*s.* due for a certain kalendar, purchased of him for the King's use, viz. to be kept for the use of the Lords of the Council in the star chamber. By order of the Treasurer and Chamberlains,—7*s.*

30th January.—To John Merland, an esquire of Sir Peter de Courtenay, knight, lately captured in the war in the King's service upon the sea, by the King's French enemies, then in the retinue of Sir Hugh le Despenser, knight. In money paid to him by assignment made this day, in discharge of 400 franks which the Lord the King commanded to be paid him of his gift, at the request of the Earl of Nottingham, in aid of payment for his ransom. By writ, &c.,—66*l.* 13*s.* 4*d.*

13th March.—To John Elyngeham, the King's sergeant at arms, sent with all haste to the town of Oxford with letters of the King's privy seal, directed to the Chancellor and Proctors of the

University of Oxford, to quiet certain strife and disputes which
had arisen between the scholars there. In money paid him for
his wages, expenses, and hire of horses, for the sake of hastening the message aforesaid,—1*l.* 6*s.* 8*d.*

Issue Roll, Easter, 12 Richard II.

3rd May.—To Master John Ondebey, Robert Cotum, clerks,
and William Houghlot, one of the tellers of the receipt of the Exchequer, sent from London to Langeley with the King's best
crown, by command of the said Lord the King and the Lords of
his Council, there to be delivered into the King's wardrobe. In
money paid to their own hands, for their expenses and for the
hire of horses and archers for the safe conduct and carriage of
the crown aforesaid. By order of the Treasurer and Chamberlains,—2*l.*

17th May.—To Matthew de Gournay, a banneret. In money
paid to him by assignment made this day, by the hands of Thomas
Hankyn, in discharge of 37*l.* 6*s.* 10*d.*, due to him upon an account
made at the Exchequer of Accounts, having been lately retained
in the King's service in the war, to dwell in the town of Calais for
the safe custody of the same town, with certain men at arms and
archers of his retinue,—to wit, for the wages of the said Matthew,
his men at arms, and archers aforesaid, for one quarter of a
year, and as a reward to the said men at arms during the time
aforesaid; also for the re-passage of the same Matthew and his
retinue, &c.,—7*l.* 6*s.* 10*d.*

6th July.—To Robert Markeley, the King's sergeant at arms,
sent to Essex to inquire concerning a certain gold mine reported
to have been found in those parts. In money paid to him at twice,
for his expenses in going, tarrying, and returning on the business
aforesaid,—4*l.*

14th July.—To John Elyngeham and Robert Markeley, the King's sergeants at arms, sent to Worcester with a certain commission, under the King's great seal, to arrest certain persons in the forest of Dene, as is said, for blaspheming the King's person, and to cause them to appear before the King's Council. In money, &c.,—2*l.* 13*s.* 4*d.*

15th July.—To Henry de Percy, son and heir of the Earl of Northumberland. In money paid to him by assignment made this day, in part payment of 1000*l.* which the Lord the King, with the advice of his Council, commanded to be paid to the same Henry of his gift in aid of his ransom having been lately taken in the Scotch war, &c.,—500*l.*

23rd August.—To Sir Richard Stury, a knight of the King's chamber, going to Calais in the retinue of Roger Walden, treasurer of the aforesaid town, to supervise a payment to be made by the same Roger to the soldiers of the same town, vacated by reason of a truce made between the Lord the King and his adversary of France, by order of the King's Council, &c.,—20*l.*

ISSUE ROLL, MICHAELMAS, 13 RICHARD II.

7th October.—To Geoffrey Chaucer, clerk of the works of the Lord the King within the palace of Westminster, Tower of London, and divers others the King's castles and manors. In money paid to him by assignment made this day,—to wit, by the hands of John Hermesthorp, clerk of the works near the Tower. By writ of liberate amongst the mandates of Easter term last past,—66*l.* 13*s.* 4*d.* [*Note.*—This Roll contains several other payments to Geoffrey Chaucer, as clerk of the King's works.]

20th October.—To Thomas, Duke of Gloucester, Henry, Earl of Derby, Richard, Earl of Arundell, Thomas, Earl of Warwick, and Thomas, Earl Marshall and of Nottingham, by assignment made to them this day, containing 1995*l.* 1*s.* 8*d.*, which the Lord the King commanded to be paid to the same Duke and Earls, with the consent of his Council, in discharge and full satisfaction of 20,000*l.* granted by the same Lord the King to the aforesaid Duke and Earls, in the last parliament held at Westminster. By writ of privy seal amongst the mandates of this term,— 1995*l.* 1*s.* 8*d.*

5th November.—To Sir Robert Bealknap, knight, who, by force of a judgment pronounced against him in the King's last parliament assembled at Westminster, was condemned to death; and all and singular the manors, lands, and tenements, goods and chattels whatsoever, which belonged to the aforesaid Robert, were seized into the King's hands, as forfeited to the King, for the reason aforesaid: whereupon the said Lord the King being moved with mercy and piety, and wishing and being desirous to make a competent provision for the support of the same Robert, towards whom he was moved with pity, did remit and pardon the execution of the judgment aforesaid, at the request of very many of the pre-lates, great men of the estate, and other nobility of this realm, lately attending the said parliament; and of his especial grace, with the assent of his Council, on the 13th day of July, in the 12th year of his reign, granted to the same Robert 40*l.* yearly, to be re-ceived during his life out of the issues and revenues of the manor, lands, and tenements aforesaid, to be paid by the hands of the farmers thereof for the time being, &c., according to an ordinance of the parliament aforesaid. In money paid to him by the hands of Juliana, his wife, viz., by assignment made to the same Juli-ana this day, 20*l.*, and in money counted, 20*l.*, &c.—40*l.* [A list of the horses, with a description of them, belonging to the said Robert, is entered on this Roll.]

6th November.—To John Morewell, the King's sergeant at arms, sent to Norwich to arrest John Sutton, and to bring the same John before the King's Council. In money paid to him for his wages and expenses, and for the hire of horses for the sake of expediting the journey aforesaid,—4*l.* 6*s.* 8*d.*

6*th November.*—In money paid for the expenses of the Lords the Chancellor, Treasurer, Keeper of the King's privy seal, and other Lords of the Council, for their dinners at Westminster, attending there for three whole days to forward certain business concerning the state of the King and kingdom. By command of the Treasurers and Barons,—9*l.* 14*s.* 11*d.*

13*th November.*—To David Blod, sent to Norwich in the retinue of John Morewell, the King's sergeant at arms, to arrest John Sutton, late servant of Thomas de Chippenham. In money paid to him for his expenses in going and returning upon the business aforesaid,—1*l.* 6*s.* 8*d.*

17*th November.*—To Sir Philip de Courtenay, knight, late the King's deputy in Ireland, deprived of all his goods and chattels which he had there, as well silver vessels, beds, and furniture for the chapel, chambers, hall, and kitchen, as of his horses, arms, and weapons, and of all other his goods whatsoever, by the officers of Robert Veer, then Duke of Ireland, by force of the King's letters at that time there sent. And the same Philip, a long time before the end of his term, by an indenture made between the said Lord the King and himself, was on no account to be removed from the said office contrary to the form of the indenture aforesaid; being also himself in danger of arrest and imprisonment, from which himself, his wife, and children, with great difficulty and danger escaped and came into England with great trouble. In money paid to him by assignment made this day in part payment of 1000 marks which the Lord the King, with the advice of his Council, and by treaty and agreement made between the said Council in the King's name and the said Philip, commanded to be paid him, &c., as well in recompense of all his goods, chattels, and other things, as above said, despoiled and lost, as for the damage by him

R

sustained by reason of his removal before the end of the term limited in the aforesaid indenture, contrary to the form of the said indenture; also for all other losses which he had suffered or sustained by whatsoever means or causes aforesaid. By writ of privy seal, &c., of Easter, in the 11th year, and by letters of acquittance from the same Philip of all the causes and circumstances aforesaid made to the Lord the King, remaining in the hanaper of this Michaelmas term, of the 12th year.—66*l.* 13*s.* 4*d.* [This Roll contains further entries relating to this matter.]

14th December.—To Richard de Cicilia, a converted Jew, lately baptized by the Venerable Father Robert, Bishop of London, at the manor of Langeley, in the presence of the Lord the King, on account of which the said Lord the King granted to the said Richard a certain annuity of 10*l.,* to be received at the Exchequer for term of his life in aid of his support. In money paid to him by assignment made this day in discharge of 50 marks which the said Lord the King commanded to be paid him as a reward, because that, as yet, the aforesaid Richard had received nothing of the annuity aforesaid, and also to qualify him as a Catholic to traffic with certain Christians out of England. By writ, &c.,— 33*l.* 6*s.* 8*d.*

25th January.—To Adam de Thorp, a goldsmith, of London. In money paid to his own hands for engraving a certain brass seal with the arms of the Lord the King; ordered by the King's Council for the office of Chancellor in the King's lordship within the county of Pembroke,—1*l.* 13*s.* 4*d.*

7th February.—To Douglas. a herald from Scotland, for the price of 15 nobles, each noble reckoned at 8*s.,* which the Lord the King commanded to be delivered to him of his gift. By writ, &c., 4*l.*

10th February.—To Edward, Earl of Devon. In money delivered to him by agreement made this day for payment of 86*l.* 18*s.* 7*d.* owing upon an account made with him at the Exchequer of accounts, for receipts, wages, and rewards to himself, his men at arms and archers with him in a certain voyage in the King's service, in the first year of his reign, made beyond the sea, in the retinue of the Earl of Buckingham. By writ, &c.,— 43*l.* 8*s.* 7*d.*

·ISSUE ROLL, EASTER, 13 RICHARD II.

11*th May.*—To John, Duke of Lancaster. In money paid to him by assignment made this day in discharge of 150*l.* which the Lord the King commanded to be paid him in discharge of the arrears of a certain annuity of 100 marks which he was accustomed to receive from the issues of the county of Chester, by the hands of the King's Chamberlain of Chester for the time being, out of certain profits called "avoueries," belonging to the castle and lordship of Halton of the aforesaid Duke, in the county aforesaid. By writ of privy seal, &c.,—150*l.*

25*th May.*—To David de Lyndesay, a Scotch knight. In money paid to him, viz., in money counted 100*l.*, and for the price of a cup and a silver ewer with gilt covers, purchased of Richard Brok, goldsmith, of London, 6*l.* 16*s.* 8*d.*, which the Lord the King commanded to be paid him of his gift, by writ of privy seal, &c.,—106*l.* 16*s.* 8*d.* [With many other payments and presents made to Scotch knights, entered upon this Roll.]

17*th June.*—To divers messengers and couriers sent to divers parts of England with writs of the King's great seal directed to all Sheriffs of England, to forbid the taking of any money in wedges, mass, or plate, out of the kingdom of England. In money paid to them, &c., as appears by their particulars remaining in the hanaper of this term,—5*l.* 6*s.* 8*d.*

19*th July.*—To William Pakyngton, keeper of the King's

R 2

wardrobe. In money paid to him by assignment made this day, viz., by the hands of Stephen Ingram, clerk, 100 marks, upon the arrival of the Countess of Saint Paul into England, &c.—[making, together with other payments,—116*l.* 13*s.* 4*d.*]

ISSUE ROLL, MICHAELMAS, 14 RICHARD II.

23rd February.—To Henry de Percy, son of the Earl of Northumberland, lately captured in the war by the King's Scotch enemies. In money paid to him by John Hermesthorp, one of the Chamberlains of the Exchequer, with the assent of the King's Council, and on the petition and request of the knights of the counties and commonalty of the realm of England, at the King's parliament held at Westminster in the 13th year, &c., when it was ordered that 3000*l.* be paid to the said Henry of the King's gift, in aid of payment of his ransom, &c.,—1000*l.*

ISSUE ROLL, EASTER, 14 RICHARD II.

27th April.—To the Venerable Father Robert, Bishop of London, by a tally raised this day containing 100 marks, paid to the same Bishop in discharge of the same sum which the King commanded to be paid him for the costs and expenses incurred by him for providing a certain marble tomb to be made, and now lately ordered to be placed over the body of Edward, brother to the said now Lord the King, buried within the church of the friars preachers, of Children Langeley. By writ of privy seal, &c.,— 66*l.* 13*s.* 4*d.*

11th July.—To the clerks of the parish churches, and to divers other clerks in the city of London. In money paid to them in discharge of 10*l.* which the Lord the King commanded to be paid them of his gift, on account of the play *of the Passion of our Lord and the Creation of the World*, by them performed at Skynnerwell, after the feast of Saint Bartholomew last past. By writ of privy seal amongst the mandates of this term,—10*l.*

12th August.—To Henry le Scrop, son of Sir Stephen le Scrop, knight. In money paid to him in discharge of 20*l.* which the Lord the King commanded to be paid him of his gift in aid of his expenses in lately coming from Barbarie. By writ, &c.,—20*l.*

To John Elyngeham, the King's sergeant at arms, sent by direction of the King's Council to Ireland, with letters of privy seal directed to the Archbishop of Armagh, Primate of Ireland, the mayor, bailiffs, and commonalty of Dublin, Drogeda, and Coork ; also to the Justices, Chancellor, and Treasurer of Ireland, upon certain affairs touching the estate and governance of the land aforesaid. In money paid to his own hands for his expenses,— 6*l.* 13*s.* 4*d.*

ISSUE ROLL, MICHAELMAS, 15 RICHARD II.

7th December.—In money paid to John Melton, one of the clerks of the receipt of the Exchequer, for the costs and charges incurred for himself and his companions for a dinner at Westminster, attending there one whole day to arrange divers records of the King's Common bench, together with the porterage thereof from a certain place called Helle, to the King's Treasury. By order of the Treasurer and Chamberlains,—4*s.* 9*d.*

12th December.—To Leo, King of Arminia, to whom the present Lord the King, on the third day of February, in the 9th year of his reign, by his letters patent, granted 1000*l.* yearly, to be received at the Exchequer at the terms of Saint Michael and Easter,

by equal portions, in reverence to God, and because the aforesaid
King, by reason of his toleration in his own kingdom, was expelled therefrom by the enemies of God and his own deluded
subjects; the same to be allowed until he should, by God's assistance, recover his kingdom aforesaid.   In money delivered to him
by the hands of Francis de Meyre, his chamberlain, as an advance
upon this his allowance.   By writ of liberate amongst the mandates of this term,—333*l.* 6*s.* 8*d.*

4th March—To Peter de Hiltoft, the King's engraver, residing
within the Tower of London.   In money paid to him, viz., to his
own hands, for the workmanship and engraving of sixteen brass
seals, with crowns and letters engraved round them, for the sealing of cloth sold, deposited in the county of Essex; and for the
engraving of a brass seal with two impressions of the King's arms,
for the office of steward or receiver of the King's lordship of Haverford, in Wales, which by the death of John Clannowe hath now
come into the King's hands.   By writ, &c.,—5*l.*

5th March.—To Sir Thomas Percy, knight, under-chamberlain to the King, sent to France, together with the Duke of Acquitaine and Lancaster, and others, in the King's embassy, to treat for
a peace between the Lord the King and his adversary of France,
viz., for the price of a gold ring, set with a diamond, delivered to
the said Thomas, to present to the King of France, on behalf of the
Lord the King, of the gift of the said Lord the King.   By writ of
privy seal amongst the mandates of this term,—26*l.* 13*s.* 4*d.*

ISSUE ROLL, EASTER, 15 RICHARD II.

4th May.—To Sir John Golafre, knight, keeper of the castle
and town of Chierburgh, in Normandy.   In money paid to him,
viz., by the hands of Andrew Neuport, the King's sergeant at arms,

for the safe custody of the castle and town aforesaid. By writ of privy seal, &c.,—500*l.*

To Thomas, Duke of Gloucester, the King's deputy in Ireland. In money paid to him by the hands of Edmund Brokesburn, his esquire, at divers times, for the wages of himself, his men at arms, and archers going with him in the King's service to Ireland afore-said, for the safe custody of the land aforesaid. By writ of privy seal, &c.,—6333*l.* 6*s.* 8*d.*

19*th June.*—To the Venerable Father Richard, Bishop of Coventry and Litchfield. In money paid to him by assignment, made this day, for his wages and expenses, on being sent as the King's ambassador to Scotland, to oppose an attempt made against the form of the truce lastly affirmed. By writ, &c.,—60*l.* [Also a payment of 26*l.* 13*s.* 4*d.* to Sir Ralph Percy, sent with the said Bishop in the same embassy.]

6*th July.*—To Alexander Dothelee, clerk. In money received by him, at Nottingham, for the costs and expenses incurred for the purchase and providing of a bell ordered for the King's chapel within the manor of Eltham. By writ of privy seal, &c. —16*s.* 8*d.*

To two minstrels from the King of Aragon. In money received by them at Nottingham in discharge of 1*l.* 6*s.* 8*d.* which the Lord the King commanded to be paid them of his gift. By writ, &c.,—1*l.* 6*s.* 8*d.*

15*th July.*—To the Venerable Father Robert, Bishop of London. In money paid to him by assignment made this day in his own name, in discharge of 100*l.* which the Lord the King commanded to be paid him for so much money by the same Venerable Father paid to divers persons by the King's command, viz., to Master William Storteford 40 marks, as a reward to the same Master William for prosecuting the affair in the Roman Court respecting the canonization of Edward, great grandfather of the said now Lord the King, whose body was buried at Westminster; also for the procuring iron-work to be placed around the tomb of Edward, brother of our said Lord the King, at Childerlangley, 40 marks; to a certain esquire of the Duke of Gelre [Gueldres] 18 marks; and to certain proctors, notaries, scribes, and messengers, employed in the business aforesaid concerning the canonization, 52 marks. By writ, &c.,—100*l.*

10*th September.*—To Alexander Domynyk, clerk. In money received by him from the Venerable Father J., Bishop of Salisbury, Treasurer of England, for the costs and labour by him incurred in the sessions held at Nottingham, Windsor, and elsewhere, to inquire concerning divers articles objected against the citizens and commonalty of the city of London. By writ, &c.,—3*l.* 6*s.* 8*d.* [Like payments were made to Robert Cherlton, chief justice, and to others employed upon the same business.]

20*th September.*—To John Orewell, the King's sergeant at arms, sent by the King's command for the safe conduct of Hanard Cambernard, an esquire of the King of France, and to John Caleu, captain of Liske, viz., from England to France. In money by him received, &c.,—6*l.* 13*s.* 4*d.*

To Andrew Hagge and Blanche, his wife, kinswoman of the King; to whom the present Lord the King, on the 5th day of February last past, by his letters patent, granted 40*l.* yearly, to be received during their lives, or the longer liver of them, by reason of the marriage aforesaid. In money received, &c.,—10*l.*

To Sir Thomas Dalston, knight. In money by him received from the venerable Father John, Bishop of Salisbury, Treasurer of England, in discharge of 40*l.* which the Lord the King commanded to be paid him in aid of discharging his ransom, having been lately taken in the war by the King's enemies. By writ, &c., —40*l.*

To Robert Crull, the King's Treasurer in Ireland. In money received by him from John Elyngeham, the King's sergeant at arms, at Dublin, in the said land of Ireland, to retain armed men according to the discretion of the Justices, the Chancellor, and others of the King's Council there, for the safety and defence of the land aforesaid. By writ of privy seal, &c.,—1333*l.* 6*s.* 8*d.*

ISSUE ROLL, MICHAELMAS, 16 RICHARD II.

15th October.—To the venerable Father the Bishop of Man. In money by him received from the venerable Father John, Bishop of Salisbury, and Treasurer of England, in discharge of 100 marks which the Lord the King commanded to be paid him for the charges and labour incurred and undergone by him in prosecuting certain affairs for the Lord the King in the islands, by command of the said Lord the King. By writ, &c.,—66*l.* 13*s.* 4*d.*

30th October.—To Stephen Percy, clerk, sent from London to Queensborough Castle, there to ask for the King's great crown, and bring it from thence to Westminster, to be delivered to the Lord the King, for celebrating the solemnization of the translation of Saint Edward the King and Confessor, in the church of the blessed Peter, Westminster, on the 13th day of October last past. In money paid to his own hands for his wages and expenses, and for the expenses of certain archers riding in his retinue for the safe custody and conduct of the same crown; also for the hire of horses to hasten and expedite the business aforesaid,—2*l.* 4*s.* 11½*d.*

14th December.—To divers messengers and couriers, sent to all the counties of England with writs of the great seal, directed to the Sheriffs of the counties aforesaid, to prohibit the receipt of nobles into the currency of England, made from the coinage of the Duke of Burgundy, on account of the less value thereof in comparison with the English nobles. In money paid to them for their wages and expenses,—4*l.* 13*s.* 4*d.*

9th January.—To William Piers, a converted Jew, to whom the present Lord the King, by his letters patent, granted 2*d.* daily, to be received during his life at the Exchequer, &c., because the same William was converted to the Christian faith, and lately baptized into our law. In money paid to him, viz. to his own hands, in discharge of 1*l.* 10*s.* 4*d.*, &c. for 182 days, &c. By writ, &c.,—1*l.* 10*s.* 4*d.*

To the Lord the King in his chamber. In money paid into the said chamber, viz. by the hands of Lord John de Beaumond, 100 marks, by the hands of Guido Mone, for bringing the bones of Sir John Pauley, knight, to England, 10*l.* 16*s.* 8*d.*; by the hands of the aforesaid Guido and Thomas, his clerk, 402*l.* 10*s.*; by the hands of John Maudeleyn, 20*l.*, in part payment of 2000*l.* paid to the said Lord the King for Easter Term last past, for the 4000*l.* reserved and appointed to be received yearly at the Exchequer at Michaelmas and Easter Terms, by equal portions, for an allowance to his chamber aforesaid,—500*l.*

7th March.—To the venerable Father John, Bishop of Salisbury. In money paid to him in discharge of 20 marks which the Lord the King commanded to be paid him of his gift, for the price of a bed of green Tarteryn, embroidered with ships and birds, consisting of a covering, a tester, and a half coverlet with three curtains, valued at the same sum, which bed belonged to Sir Simon de Burley, knight, deceased, forfeited to the King by reason of a judgment pronounced against the said Simon. By writ, &c.,—13*l.* 6*s.* 8*d.*

1st April.—To John Draxe, the King's sergeant at arms, appointed by a commission under the King's great seal to arrest John Gaynesburgh, and to bring the said John to London before the King's Council. In money paid to his own hands for his wages and expenses,—6*s.* 8*d.*

To John Hereford, the King's sergeant at arms, sent from London to the lordship of Irchynfeld, near the forest of Dene, in the county of Gloucester, to arrest a certain chaplain for opening a mine by command of the Lord de Talbot, and to bring him to London before the King's Council to answer for certain treasure found hid in the said land. In money paid for his wages and expenses, &c.,—2*l.* 13*s.* 4*d.*

ISSUE ROLL, EASTER, 16 RICHARD II.

21st May.—To Nicholas Auncell, a messenger sent to the town of Northampton with a writ of great seal, directed to the honest men of the same town, to elect from amongst themselves, and appoint a mayor in the said town, because the former mayor there had been expelled and put out of his office aforesaid, by judgment given against him in Chancery. In money paid to the same Nicholas for his wages,—10*s.*

To John Draxe, the King's sergeant at arms, sent from London to the King's castle at Nottingham, to safely and securely conduct the mayor of the town of Northampton to the said castle of Nottingham, for certain reasons expelled from his office of mayoralty, and to retain him in custody in the said castle during the pleasure of the Lord the King and his Council. In money paid to him for his wages and the hire of horses, &c.,—5*l.*

9th June.—To Robert Bysshopesten. In money paid to him, viz. by assignment made this day, 10*l.* and in money counted and in hand paid 5 marks, in discharge of 20 marks which the Lord the King commanded to be paid him as well in recompense of the cost and labour which he lately incurred and sustained by riding in the retinue of two esquires from France, by command of Walter, Bishop of Durham, and William Beauchamp, knight, then conservators of the truce made between our Lord the King and his adversary of France, to cause the said truce to be proclaimed in the towns of Gand and Bruges, as also in consideration of the loss which the said Robert sustained during the time he was detained a prisoner in the town of Gand upon the charge of certain persons, who affirmed against the said Robert that the letters upon which the said truce had been proclaimed were forged and not true. By writ of privy seal, &c.,—13*l.* 6*s.* 8*d.*

7th July.—To Roger de Mortimer, Earl of March. In money paid to him by the hands of Walter Brugge, clerk, by assignment made this day in his own name in discharge of 1000 marks which the Lord the King, with the assent of his Council, commanded to be paid to the said Earl from his Treasury, in consideration and on account of the attack and invasion made by the King's Irish enemies upon the Lordships and possessions of the same Earl in Ireland, by which they had been entirely devastated and destroyed, and by reason thereof, the same Lord the King granted to the aforesaid Earl the custody of his lands and lordships aforesaid, to the end that he might more powerfully resist the malice of the enemies aforesaid. By writ of privy seal, &c.,—666*l.* 13*s.* 4*d.*

12th September.—To Thomas, Earl Marshal and of Nottingham, the King's kinsman. In money paid to him in discharge of 200*l.*, which the Lord the King commanded to be paid to the same Earl to celebrate a marriage between the son of the same Earl and the daughter of the Earl of Huntyngdon, also a kinsman of the Lord the King aforesaid. By writ of privy seal,—200*l.*

To Alan Stokes, late clerk of the great wardrobe of the Lord the King, by the hands of Gilbert Prince, a painter, of London. In money paid to the same Gilbert by the hands 'of Thomas, his clerk, for the performance of divers works of his art, and delivered to the said Alan for the King's use. By writ, &c.,—650*l.* 13*s.* 7½*d.*

ISSUE ROLL, MICHAELMAS, 17 RICHARD II.

6th October.—To Nicholas Auncell, a messenger, sent with a letter of the King's privy seal, directed to Sir Thomas Swynbourne, knight, to appear before the King's Council concerning certain matters to be objected against the same Sir Thomas by the said Council. In money paid to him for his expenses, &c., —8*s.* 4*d.*

13th October.—To the Viscount de Meloun, of France, now lately arrived on behalf of the King of France upon an embassy to the Lord the King. In money paid to the same Viscount for the knights and esquires coming in his retinue, for the price of the underwritten articles of the King's gift; viz. twenty pieces of baudekin of a blue and white colour, price 2*l.* 6*s.* 8*d.*; two pieces of cloth of gold, blue, price the piece 20*l.*; six pieces of cloth of gold, of a black colour, price 5*l.*6*s.*8*d.*; one cloak of velvet, worked with gold of Cyprus, price 42*l.*; one large ruby set in a ring, price 30*l.*; six silver cups, gilt, price 21*l.*; a diamond set in a gold ring, price 20*l.*; and one great gold cup, price 38*l.* By writ of privy seal, &c., —249*l.* 13*s.* 4*d.*

3rd December.—To Drugo Barantyn and Hans Doubler, goldsmiths, of London. In money paid to them for making two collars, and one stud of gold ornamented with pearls and precious stones, for the Lord the King's person,—66*l.* 13*s.* 4*d.* [This Roll also contains many payments for plate and jewels given as presents; amongst others, on the 15th January, 461*l.* 10*s.* paid for two diamonds, one given to the Bishop of London and the other to the Earl of Arundel.]

6th December.—To Robert Selby, clerk, treasurer of the town of Calais, in money paid to him in discharge of 50*l.* which the Lord the King commanded to be paid him of his gift, to the end that he should pay for the finances of John Lancaster, chevalier, who has been for a long time and as yet is detained a prisoner in the kingdom of France, as the said Lord the King is informed. By writ, &c.,—50*l.*

To Alice Windsor, in money paid to her in discharge of 200*l.* which the Lord the King commanded to be paid her from his Treasury, in payment and full satisfaction of 1000 marks, which the said Lord the King was indebted to the said Alice on account of a loan received by the hands of Sir Simon de Burley, knight, deceased, as appears by letters of acquittance of the said Alice, remaining &c.,—200*l.*

To Brother John Grey, Prior of Cork, in Ireland. In money paid to him in discharge of 40 marks, which the Lord the King commanded to be paid to the said Prior of his gift, viz. for a marble coffin purchased to inclose the body of Thomas Russholk, late Bishop of Chichester, who was buried in Ireland, 20 marks; also as a remuneration and reward given to the servants of the said Bishop for the time they remained in the service of the said Bishop, 20 marks. By writ, &c.,—26*l.* 13*s.* 4*d.*

Issue Roll, Easter, 17 Richard II.

6th May.—To the venerable Father Richard, Bishop of Chichester. In money paid to him by the hands of Robert Bussh, his clerk; viz. by assignment made this day, 36*l.* 13*s.* 4*d.*, and in money counted 20 marks, in discharge of 50*l.* which the Lord the King, of his especial grace, commanded to be paid to the same venerable Father for a piece of land, with certain houses thereupon built, adjoining to the burial ground of the cathedral church of Chichester, of the foundation of the progenitors of the said Lord the King, purchased by the said Lord the King from Robert Blundell, right heir to the said piece of ground, to erect thereon a mansion for the vicars serving God in the said church, to hold to the said vicars and their successors for ever of the grant of the aforesaid Lord the King, to the honour of God and of Saint Richard, enshrined and exalted. By writ, &c.,—50*l.*

21*st May.*—To the Queen of Sweden and Denmark. In money paid to her by the hands of Ludwyk de Camera, in discharge of 40 marks which the Lord the King commanded to be paid to the said Queen, of his gift, for the price of a gold cup purchased of Barantyn, the goldsmith, of London, &c.,—26*l.* 13*s.* 4*d.*

30*th May.*—To Richard, Earl of Arundell and Surrey. In money paid to him by the hands of Sir William Heron, knight, in discharge of 40 marks which the Lord the King commanded to be paid him of his gift, to be delivered to Anne, Queen of England, in discharge to the said Earl from the said Queen for the like sum demanded from the aforesaid Earl by the aforesaid Queen for a certain other sum of 40 marks, paid by the said Earl into the King's Chancery, for the marriage of Philippa, consort of the said Earl, late wife of John de Hastinges, Earl of Pembroke, deceased. By writ, &c.,—26*l.* 13*s.* 4*d.*

3*rd June.*—In money paid for boatage and carriage of the statue made in likeness of Anne, late Queen of England,—to wit, from London to Shene. By direction of the Treasurer and Chamberlains,—3*s.*

17*th June.*—To John Michell, the King's sergeant at arms. In money paid to him for the carriage of 1500 lbs. of wax obtained by the same John at Hadle, in the county of Suffolk, and from thence brought to London and delivered to Roger Chaundeler, of London, provided for the hearse at the funeral of Anne, late Queen of England,—13*s.* 4*d.*

10*th July.*—To divers messengers and couriers sent with letters of privy seal, directed to the Archbishops, Bishops, Abbots, Priors, and Deans and Chapters of the cathedral churches, in each county of England, to pray for the soul of Anne, late Queen of England, deceased. In money paid, &c.,—7*l*. 6*s*. 8*d*.

19*th July.*—In money paid to Lamkyn Lokyer, for the repair of a pair of scales at the receipt, to weigh certain sums of silver, which said scales heretofore have been used in the said receipt. By direction of the Treasurer,—1*s*. 8*d*.

25*th August.*—To Thomas Balymore, vicar of Llansthwell. In money received by him from the Lord the Treasurer, in discharge of 40*s*., which the Lord the King commanded to be paid him of his gift, on account of the great charge to which the same vicar was lately subject, at the time when the Lord the King dwelt in the house of the said Vicar on his passage to Ireland. By writ, &c.,—2*l*.

5*th September.*—To John Carp̄, keeper of the great wardrobe of the Lord the King, by the hands of Thomas Lynne, master of the King's ship called the George, for the price of divers things and tackle belonging to the same ship, purchased and provided by Richard Rowe, mariner of the town of Greenwich, and delivered in Flanders to the same Thomas by the said Richard for the tackle and steerage of the ship aforesaid; viz. five cables, weighing 5941 lbs.; two "upties," weighing 802 lbs.; two "scotes," weighing 348 lbs.; two "lollers," weighing 120 lbs.; three warping ropes, weighing 584 lbs.; one hawser for "bayropes," weighing 300 lbs.; one winding rope, weighing 488 lbs.; as appears by the counterpart of a certain indenture made between them of the delivery of the things aforesaid, &c.,—44*l*. 1*s*. 8½*d*.

ISSUE ROLL, MICHAELMAS, 18 RICHARD II.

3*rd November.*—To Robert Markeley, the King's sergeant at arms, sent in the retinue of Sir Robert Whyteney, knight, and John Melton, clerk, beyond seas to give up the castle of Cher-

burgh to Carloto de Beaumond, of Navarre. In money paid to
him for his wages,—7*l.* 6*s.* 8*d.*

7*th December.*—To John Henriz, Prior of Launde, sent upon
the secret affairs of the Lord the King to the Roman cóurt. In
money paid to his own hands for the price of a gold ring set
with a ruby, delivered to the said Prior, to be presented to our
most holy Father the Pope, of the King's gift. By writ, &c.,—
20*l.*

10*th December.*—To the sacrist of the church of the blessed
Peter of Westminster. In money paid to him in discharge of 100
marks which the Lord the King commanded to be paid him according to the discretion of the venerable Father John, Bishop of
Salisbury, Treasurer of England, as a reward for and in the names
of the monks of the same church, for the pains which the said
monks had undergone and sustained in performing the exequies
of Anne, late Queen of England, in the same church before the
feast of the Assumption of the Blessed Mary last past, and in
recompense and full satisfaction of certain oblations which might
have been required from the Abbot and monks of that place, by
the Lord the King, for the same exequies, and for the hearse in the
same church constructed for the honour of the said Queen; also
as a reward to the ministers for ringing the bells and for other
exequies performed by the said ministers at the solemnization of
the exequies aforesaid. By writ, &c.,—66*l.* 13*s.* 4*d.*

22*nd March.*—To John Carp, keeper of the King's wardrobe,
by the hands of Master John Middelton, the King's physician. In
money paid, to wit, by assignment made this day, viz. by the
hands of John Waddesworth, apothecary of London, 10*l.* 8*s.*, and
by the hands of John Salman, apothecary of the same place,
4*l.* 13*s.* 4*d.*, as well for providing spices and electuary for the
King's body, as for bottles, electrines, phials, and other necessary
things belonging to his profession, purchased by the same Master
John of the said John Salman for the use of the Lord the King

s

aforesaid, as appears by two bills indented of the same articles remaining in the hanaper of this term,—15*l.* 1*s.* 4*d*

28th January.—In money paid for two large wooden chests,
bound with iron, for carrying 1600*l.* of gold and silver put into
them to be safely and securely taken to Ireland. By direction of
the Treasurer and Chamberlains,—2*l.*

3rd April.—To Master Henry Yevely and Stephen Lote,
citizens and stone masons, of London. In money paid to their own
hands for the 200*l.* by them to be received of the King's gift,
for making and constructing a tomb of pure marble, together
with the whole workmanship belonging to the marble, according
to the form of a certain indenture between the same Lord the
King and the said Master Henry and Stephen,—viz. to be
made for the said Lord the King and Anne, late Queen of
England, whose body is buried in the Church of Saint Peter,
Westminster. By writ, &c.,—66*l.* 13*s.* 4*d.* [The total amount of
issues contained on the Roll for this term is 121,029*l.* 15*s.* 6*d.*,
amongst which are many payments on the King's preparing to go
to Ireland.]

3rd April.—To Richard Clifford, clerk of the great wardrobe of
the Lord the King, by the hands of Gilbert Prince, the King's
painter. In money received by him of John Innocent, by the hands
of Thomas his clerk. By writ, &c.,—20*l.*

ISSUE ROLL, EASTER, 18 RICHARD II.

20th April.—To Sir William Arundel, knight, Constable of the
King's castle of Rochester. In money paid to him by assignment
made this day, by the hands of Elie Reyner, esquire, for repairing
a defect of the new tower near the bridge in the castle aforesaid.
By writ, &c.,—26*l.* 13*s.* 4*d.*

24th April.—To Peter Merk and James Monald. In money paid to them by the hands of the same Peter, in discharge of 6*l.* 19*s.* which the Lord the King commanded to be paid them for so much money by them paid for costs incurred about the carriage and portage of a gold cup and a gold ring set with a ruby; also *a Book of the Miracles of Edward, late King of England, whose body was buried at the town of Gloucester,*—to wit, from London to the city of Florence, to make a present of the same to our most holy Father Pope Urban, on behalf of the Lord the King. By writ, &c.,—6*l.* 19*s.*

To William, Lord de Roos. In money paid to him by the hands of Guido Mone, receiver of the King's chamber, in discharge of 200*l.* which the Lord the King commanded to be paid to the said William of his gift, on account of the marriage solemnized between the said William and Margaret d'Arundell, kinswoman to the said Lord the King. By writ, &c.,—200*l.*

30th April.—To John Godmanston, clerk of the works of the King's great hall within the palace of Westminster. In money paid to his own hands for the works in the hall aforesaid, —133*l.* 6*s.* 8*d.*

21st May.—To Robert Thorley, the King's receiver in the counties of Devon and Cornwall. In money paid to him by assignment made this day, in discharge of 40*l.* which the Lord the King commanded to be paid him in the name of a special reward of his gift, for the costs and expenses incurred by him in his office for the seven years last past, and as a recompense and acknowledgment; directed to be paid by the said Lord the King for the exertion and great diligence the same receiver had exercised towards the merchants, and because he had received an increase upon the coinage of the tin in those parts within the time aforesaid, amounting to the sum of 2500*l.*, being more than had been accustomed to be received in previous years from the coinage aforesaid. By writ of privy seal amongst the mandates of this term. By writ, &c.,—40*l.*

s 2

8th June.—To John Carp, keeper of the King's wardrobe. In money paid to him by the hands of John Spenser, his clerk, for payment of the seamen's wages for the King's passage, on coming with his army from Ireland to England. By general writ, &c.—1000*l.*

21st June.—To John Elyngeham, the King's sergeant at arms, sent to Leeds with the King's second crown, there to be delivered to the Lord the King. In money paid to his own hands for his wages, and for the hire of men and archers to ride with him, for the safe conduct of the crown aforesaid,—1*l.* 6*s.* 8*d.*

2nd July.—To John Elyngeham, the King's sergeant at arms, sent to the city of Salisbury with a writ of the King's great seal, directed to the mayor and commonalty of the city aforesaid, to appear at Westminster before the King's Council, upon certain matters to be objected against the said mayor and commonalty on behalf of the said Council. In money paid to him for his wages and expenses,—2*l.*

15th July.—To the Venerable Father, Robert, Archbishop of Dublin, sent as the King's Ambassador to France, there to treat concerning the King's marriage. In money paid to his own hands for his wages. By general writ, &c.—140*l.*

[*Note.*—This part of the Roll contains entries of payments to the Bishop of Saint David's; Edward, Earl of Rutland; Thomas, Earl Marshal and of Nottingham; John, Lord de Beaumont; Sir William le Scrop, and others employed in the treaty for the marriage of the King with Isabella, daughter of Charles VI., King of France, afterwards married to Charles, son and heir of the Duke of Orleans.]

15th July.—To John Drax, the King's sergeant at arms, appointed by commission under the King's great seal to make inquiry concerning all the lands and tenements which belonged to

John Crestelton, in the county of Warwick, seized into the King's hands because the aforesaid John was a bastard, and died without heir issuing of his body. In money paid to him for his wages, &c.,—2*l.*13*s.* 4*d.*

19*th July.*—To Thomas Beverle, an esquire of Scotland. In money paid to him in discharge of 45*l.* which the Lord the King commanded to be paid him of his gift, in preparing for the said Thomas horses, armour, and other necessary things for his body, and other costs by him incurred for the duel to be fought between him and Walter Strathern, in an appeal determined at the town of Berwick. By writ, &c.,—45*l.*

19*th July.*—To John Preston. In money paid to his own hands, in discharge of 2*l.* 6*s.* 8*d.* which the Lord the King commanded to be paid him of his gift, on account of the cost and labour by him incurred in a prosecution against David Panell, a felon, adjudged to death for the murder of nine men and one woman, killed by the said David, as the said Lord the King was informed. By writ, &c.,—2*l.* 6*s.* 8*d.*

29*th July.*—In money paid to John Burgh, clerk, for the hire of horses and men for the safe conduct of the King's second crown from London to Eltham, on the vigil of the Assumption of the Blessed Mary last past. By direction of the Treasurer and Chamberlains,—6*s.* 8*d.*

To Richard Clifford, clerk of the King's great wardrobe. In money paid to him for the pledge of a certain book of Master Henry Bowet, pledged to the said Richard. By writ, &c.,— 5*l.* 6*s.* 8*d.*

29*th July.*—To Robert Fox, appellant for the Lord the King, in a cause against a certain Yon de Wyron. In money paid to him in discharge of 40*l.* which the Lord the King commanded to be paid him for the costs and preparation made for the same

Robert, on account of a duel fought between them at the town of
Calais.   By writ, &c.,—40*l.*

ISSUE ROLL, MICHAELMAS, 19 RICHARD II.

16th October.—To William Thirnyng, one of the Justices of
the Common Bench, receiving yearly 40 marks for his fee in the
office aforesaid.   In money paid to him by the hands of William
Vaux, in discharge of 20 marks paid to him for this his fee.   By
writ, &c.,—13*l.* 6*s.* 8*d.*

14th December.—To Sir Thomas Percy, knight, steward of the
King's household.   In money paid to him by the hands of Nicholas Roscelin, of the Exchequer, in discharge of 58*l.* 5*s.* 1½*d.*
which the Lord the King commanded to be paid him for performance of the last exequies of Robert, late Duke of Ireland, in
the county of Essex, beyond other sums by the same Thomas before received for the purpose aforesaid.   By writ aforesaid, &c.,—
58*l.* 5*s.* 1½*d.*

To Master Peter, sacrist of the church of the Blessed Peter,
Westminster.   In money paid him by the hands of John Haxey,
in discharge of 20*l.* which the Lord the King commanded to be
paid him, as well for painting the covering of the tomb of Anne,
late Queen of England, buried within the said church, as for the
removal of a tomb near the tomb of the said Queen; also for
painting the same tomb so removed, and for painting an image to
correspond with another of the King placed opposite in the choir
of the aforesaid church.   By writ, &c.,—20*l.*

To Thomas Credy, the King's sergeant at arms.   In money
paid to his own hands, for the expenses and costs by him
incurred for the carriage of 800 marks from Devonshire to London, recovered from William Cary, of the county of Devon, for the

King's use, being for the goods of John Cary, brother of the said William, forfeited to the said Lord the King, by reason of a judgment pronounced against the said John in the King's parliament held at Westminster in the eleventh year,—2*l.* 13*s.* 4*d.*

19th February.—To Thomas, Earl Marshal and of Nottingham, captain of the town of Calais. In money paid to him by the hands of Roger Jouderell, in discharge of 200 marks which the Lord the King commanded to be paid him for appointing the lists, and for other charges incurred for a duel fought within the lists between Robert Fox, appellant, and Yon de Wyron, defendant, at the town of Calais, aforesaid. By writ of privy seal, &c.,—133*l.* 6*s.* 8*d.*

1st March.—In money paid at divers times to divers masons, carpenters, and other labourers at the works of the King's great hall within his palace at Westminster; also to certain artificers, for forming of two images of copper, in likeness of the King and the Queen, paid for their drink, by command of the Treasurer, of the King's gift,—2*l.* 13*s.* 4*d.*

To Robert Maceon, vicar of the church of Kyngslangeley. In money paid to his own hands, 8*l.* 17*s.* 6*d.*, which the Lord the King commanded to be paid him for a missal and a chalice partially gilt, and delivered to the same church of the King's gift and alms. By writ, &c.,—8*l.* 17*s.* 6*d.*

ISSUE ROLL, EASTER, 20 RICHARD II.

30th May.—To Richard Clifford, clerk of the King's great wardrobe. In money paid to him, viz., by assignment made by the hands of Roger Rouland, for making the Queen's chariot, 400*l.*; and by the hands of William Dynestan, citizen and clothier of London, 200*l.*, for his office, &c.,—600*l.*

28th June.—To the Venerable Father Richard, Bishop of Coventry and Litchfield, sent as the King's Ambassador to the Court of Rome, respecting the canonization of Edward II., late King of England, whose body was buried in the church of the Blessed Peter, Gloucester. In money paid to him by assignment this day for his wages. By writ, &c.,—133*l.* 6*s.* 8*d.*

14th July.—To Master Henry Yeveley and Stephen Lote, citizens and stonemasons, of London. In money paid to them by assignment made this day, for the 250*l.* to be received of the Lord the King, for a tomb of pure marble made and constructed by them, together with the whole workmanship of the marble, according to the form of a certain indenture between the said Lord the King and the said Henry and Stephen, viz., made for the said Lord the King, and for Anne, late Queen of England, whose body is buried in the church of the Blessed Peter, Westminster. By writ, &c.,—100*l.*

ISSUE ROLL, MICHAELMAS, 21 RICHARD II.

16th October.—To Clement Atte Spice, appointed, together with others, to seize into the King's hands all castles and lordships, lands, tenements, reversions, fees, advowsons, franchises, liberties, and all other possessions which belonged to Thomas, Archbishop of Canterbury ; Thomas, Duke of Gloucester ; Richard, Earl of Arundell ; Thomas, Earl of Warwick, in the counties of Essex and Hertford, within the liberties and without ; and to make inquiries concerning the goods and chattels which belonged to the same Archbishop, Thomas, Richard, and Thomas, in the counties aforesaid. In money paid to them by assignment made this day, as well for their wages, as for the carriage of the goods of the said Duke from the counties aforesaid to London, there to be delivered for the King's use,—6*l.* 13*s.* 4*d.*   [*Note.*—It appears by entries upon this Roll that the possessions and goods of the abovementioned persons were forfeited to the Lord the King by virtue of a judgment pronounced against them in the then present parliament, held at Westminster; and that Thomas Wodyfeld was sent to arrest their horses, &c., in Middlesex, Surrey, and Sussex; also inquiry was directed to be made concerning the possessions of some of the aforesaid persons in Cornwall and Devonshire.]

22nd October.—To John Paylyng, a merchant, of London. In money paid to him by assignment made this day, in discharge of 116l. 6s. 8d., which the Lord the King commanded to be paid him for certain jewels purchased of him for the new gifts of Isabella, Queen of England, at the feast of the Nativity of our Lord last past, viz., to the aforesaid John, for a worked tablet with four sapphires and four rubies, price 26l., given to the Duke of Lancaster;—to the same John for a worked tablet of gold, with two sapphires, two rubies and pearls, value 25l., given to the Earl Marshal;—to the same for a tablet of gold, worked with the image of Saint Catherine with rubies, sapphires, and pearls, value 28l., given to the Earl Rutland; to the same John for a gold stud set with three sapphires and three rubies, price 15l. 13s. 4d., given to the Duchess of Lancaster; to the same John for two diamond rings, price 12l., given to the Earl of Derby and Lady Beauchamp; to the same John for a diamond ring worth 5l., given to the Lady de Ponynges; and to the same John for two rings of sapphires, worth 4l. 13s. 4d., given to the companion of the Queen's confessor and to Herteman Hauberk. By general writ of privy seal for new gifts to the same Queen amongst the mandates of Michaelmas term, anno 20, along with divers other names,— 76l. 6s. 8d.

7th November.—To Roger Elys, of London, chandler, deceased. In money paid to the executors of the same Roger by assignment made this day, in discharge of 41l. 8s. 10d. due to the same Roger, upon an account made with him at the Exchequer of Accounts, for receipts, purchases, charges, and expenses incurred by the said Roger by direction of the Treasurer of England, as well for the burial of the body of Anne, late Queen of England, as for providing four hearses upon the days of celebrating the solemnity of the exequies of the said Queen, viz. at Wandsworth; the priory of Saint Mary de Overe; St. Paul's; and the Blessed Peter, at Westminster; together with the carriage and re-carriage of the aforesaid hearses, and wax lights for the same, from London to the places aforesaid, and from thence to London, at different times in the month of June, in the 17th year, and in the months of July and August, in the 18th year. By writ of privy seal amongst the mandates of this term, in the 19th year,—41*l.* 8*s.* 10*d.*

30th January.—To John Carp̄, keeper of the King's wardrobe. In money paid to him by assignment made this day by the hands of Thomas More, the King's cofferer, for certain provision made for the expenses of the King's household, against his going into Ireland; by his writ of liberate as above,—600*l.*

21st February.—To Richard Maudelyn, clerk. In money paid to his own hands, for the reparation and amendment of the defects of the houses and other buildings within the Castle of Dublin, in Ireland, against the arrival of the Lord the King in the land aforesaid. By writ, &c.,—100*l.*

ISSUE ROLL, EASTER, 21 RICHARD II.

22nd April.—To Thomas Crauley, Archbishop of Dublin, lately sent upon the King's embassy to the Court at Rome, to our most Holy Father, Pope Urban, for the safe estate and prosperity of the most holy English church. In money paid to him by the hands of Henry Mory, his clerk, for his wages,—66*l.* 13*s.* 4*d.*

22nd May.—To Thomas, Duke of Surrey. In money paid to him by assignment made this day, in part payment of 100 marks which the Lord the King commanded to be paid him for certain charges of the Lord de Cobeham and his servants, being in the custody of the said Duke, by appointment of the said Lord the King, viz., from the first day that the said Duke had the same custody unto the holding of the King's parliament at Shrewsbury. By writ, &c.,—20*l*.

24*th July.*—To divers heralds and minstrels attending at the feast of Saint George last past, held at Windsor, in the presence of the Lord the King. In money by them received of William Waxcombe, clerk there, in discharge of 25 marks which the Lord the King commanded to be paid them of his gift, on account of the solemnization of the feast aforesaid. By writ, &c.,—16*l*. 13*s*. 4*d*.

31*st July.*—To John Mayheu, master of the King's ship, called "la Trinité de la Tour." In money paid to his own hands, in discharge of 100*s*. which the Lord the King commanded to be paid him, viz., for the charges and expenses incurred by him for the carriage and portage of a small ship made of silver, which the same John, in a certain voyage first made in his said ship to Burgundy, in quest of wine there for the King's use, made a vow, during a storm and danger of the sea in the said voyage, to take as an offering to the image erected in the town of Aques to the honour of the most Holy Mother Mary, for the prosperity and safety of his ship aforesaid; also for the hire of a boat by water from Sandwich to Gravesend, together with a stipend to four mariners navigating the same boat, and for the carriage of certain masts and tackle belonging to the same ship,—5*l*.

31*st August.*—To divers messengers and couriers sent to all and singular the counties of England with writs of privy seal, directed to the Archbishop of Canterbury and certain other Bishops within the realm of England; and to divers Barons, Knights, and Esquires of the King's retinue, to assemble themselves in person, with all haste, at the city of Coventry, in the presence of the Lord the King, there to witness a duel to be fought between the Dukes of Hereford and Norfolk in the city aforesaid. Also with writs under the great seal directed to the Escheators in divers counties of England, to make certain executions in their office for the King's advantage. In money paid to them for their costs and wages,—6*l.* 10*s.*

Issue Roll, Michaelmas, 22 Richard II.

18th October.—To Henry, a messenger, sent with two letters of privy seal directed to Sir William Sturmy, knight, and Lawrence Dru, to come to the King's Council with all possible haste, respecting certain affairs of the kingdom. In money paid to his own hands for his wages and expenses,—10*s.*

28th October.—To Henry, a messenger, sent with a writ of great seal directed to the Earl of Gloucester, requesting him not to cross the seas. In money paid to him for his expenses,—16*s.* 8*d.*

7th December.—To John Colton, Archbishop of Armagh, Primate of Ireland, sent to the Roman Court upon certain secret affairs of the King. In money paid to him for his wages for going and returning on the message aforesaid,—266*l.* 13*s.* 4*d.*

To Hugh Curteys, esquire. In money paid to his own hands, as well for his costs and expenses, as for the expenses of Robert Markeley, the King's sergeant at arms, sent to Calais with 1000 marks, there to be delivered to the Duke of Hereford of the King's gift, as well for his passage by sea ; and also for the hire of horses on the road, to expedite the message aforesaid,—1*l.* 6*s.* 8*d.*

11th February.—To Sir Baldwin Bereford, knight, the King's master falconer. In money paid to him by the hands of Oliver Manou, in discharge of 77*l.* 13*s.* 4*d.* which the Lord the King commanded to be paid to the same Baldwin, for certain falcons purchased by the said Baldwin for the King's use, viz., for two bold falcons, price 21*l.* 6*s.* 8*d* ; for three lanerets, price 12*l.*, purchased of Haukin Hamme, and given to the King of Navarre, as a present from the King; for two falcons, price 12*l.*; for one falcon and one laneret, price 8*l.*, purchased of Haukin Ferers; for two falcons, price 10*l.*, purchased of Haukin Germyng, and given by the said Lord the King to the Earl of Salisbury; for two falcons, price 9*l.* 6*s.* 8*d.*, purchased of Peter Helmond; and for two lanerets, price 100*s.*, purchased of Hayne de Brugge, for the use of our Lord the King aforesaid. By writ of privy seal, &c.,—77*l.* 13*s.* 4*d.*

5th March.—To Henry, son and heir of Henry, Duke of Hereford. In money paid to him by the hands of Peter Melbourn, an esquire, for part of those 500*l.* yearly which the present Lord the King granted to the said Henry, to be received at the Exchequer at a certain term, so long as it should please the Lord the King.—10*l.*

26th March.—To John Eneor, an esquire, sent to Leicester for the safe conduct of 1000*l.*, there to be delivered for certain reasons to the Executors of the will of John, late Duke of Lancaster. In money paid to his own hands for his costs and expenses, and for a horse to carry the sum aforesaid,—1*l.*

27th March.—To the Abbot of Saint Albans. In money paid to him by the hands of Master Robert Botheby, in discharge of 100 marks which he lent to the Lord the King at the Exchequer, viz., on the 22nd August, in the 20th year, as appears in the Rolls of the Receipt of that day; and as appears by the letters obligatory of the great seal of the said Lord the King, &c.,—66*l.* 13*s.* 4*d.*

ISSUE ROLL, EASTER, 22 RICHARD II.

14th April.—To John Chamberlain, clerk of the King's navy. In money paid to his own hands, as well for the repairs of decayed ships and for necessary alterations in the same, as for the new constructing of certain others on account of the voyage of the said Lord the King with his army to Ireland,—100*l.*

To Nicholas Broker and Godfrey Prest, citizens and copper-smiths of London. In money paid to their own hands, for gilding two images, resemblances of the King and Queen, made with copper and latten, and crowned, with their right hands joined, and the left hands of the said statues holding a sceptre, with a rod and a cross between the said statues, also a table for the taber-nacle, with the whole apparatus; with other images and things made, of their mystery or art, as in a certain indenture between the Lord the King and the said Nicholas and Godfrey more fully is contained,—100*l.*

26*th April.*—To Adam Attewoode, keeper of the King's beds. In money paid by his own hands, in discharge of 112*s.* 6*d.* which the Lord the King commanded to be paid him; viz., for the wages of two servants attending and remaining with him in the Tower of London as well for the safe custody of the beds of the said King, as of Isabella, Queen of England, then being there when the said Queen was brought from France to England; viz., for the wages of each of the two said servants, receiving 3*d.* per day from the 1st day of August last past, unto the feast of the Puri-fication of the Blessed Mary next following, including a period of 185 days,—4*l.* 12*s.* 6*d.*; and for the costs of the aforesaid Adam during the same time, riding to London to explain the state, and to make declaration of his office in this behalf to William, Earl of Wiltshire, Treasurer of England,—20*s.* By writ, &c.,—5*l.* 12*s.* 6*d.*

2*nd May.*—To Sir Peter de Craon, knight, Lord de la Fert Bernard, to whom the present Lord the King, on the 15th of Oc-tober last past, for 4000 crowns of the price or value of 500*l.* English money, received at the Exchequer by his letters patent, on account of the homage and vassalage of the same Peter, had become a liege man, and for having done liege homage to the said Lord the King. In money paid to him by the hands of John Seintemors, as an advance upon this his allowance,—150*l*.

3rd May.—To John Scalby. In money paid to his own hands, in discharge of 100*s.* which the Lord the King commanded to be paid him of his gift, as a reward for the information given by him to the King's Council, by virtue of which information the said Lord the King recovered, against certain persons in the city of London, certain silver vessels of the value of 100 marks and upwards, which belonged to Thomas, late Earl of Warwick, by forfeiture of the same Earl, belonging to the same Lord the King; which said vessels for a long time were concealed and eloigned, contrary to the form of the proclamation thereof made, in prejudice to the King, until the time that the said John inquired after, and gave information of the vessels aforesaid. By writ, &c.,—100*s.*

To William le Scroop, Earl of Wiltshire, Treasurer of England. In money paid to his own hands, in discharge of 1074*l.* 14*s.* 5*d.*, due upon account made with him at the Exchequer of Account, for charges and expenses by him incurred, as well for the safe conduct of Thomas, late Earl of Warwick, to the Isle of Man, and for the support of the same late Earl there, after judgment given against the said late Earl in the King's parliament held at Westminster in the 21st year, as also for the costs and expenses incurred by the said Earl of Wiltshire for the support of divers Irish hostages in his custody after the King's coming from Ireland, unto the first day of April, in the 22nd year. By writ of privy seal, &c.—1074*l.* 14*s.* 5*d.*

To the Abbot and Convent of the church of the Blessed Peter, Westminster, by the hands of Sir Richard le Scroop, knight. In money paid to the same Richard by the hands of Nigell Hornyngton, clerk, for the value of a certain stock of wine purchased from the same Richard for the use of the said Abbot and Convent, within the manors of Oteford and Cowehouse, in the county of Middlesex,—88*l.* 13*s.* 4*d.*

3rd May.—To Nicholas Skelton, the King's sergeant at arms, sent to Ireland in the conduct of the son of Makmorgh and certain other persons of the more noble condition of the King's Irish enemies, sent as hostages into the kingdom of England for security of peace in the same land. In money paid to the same Nicholas for his wages and expenses, and for the charges of the said persons, and for the hire of horses to conduct them from London to the land aforesaid,—4*l.*

13th May.—To Thomas, Duke of Surrey, deputy of the Lord the King in Ireland, for three years next following, fully to be completed, receiving 11,500 marks yearly for himself and his men for governing the land aforesaid. In money paid to him by the hands of Richard Gascoigne, esquire,—to wit, for the wages of the same Duke and his men remaining in the King's service for the safe custody of the land aforesaid. By his writ current, &c.,—116*l.* 13*s.* 4*d.*

To the Emperor of Constantinople. In money paid to him by the hands of Reginald Grille, a merchant of Janua, by assignment made to him this day, charged upon the customs in the port of Southampton, in discharge of 2000*l.* which the Lord the King commanded to be paid to the same Emperor in aid and relief to maintain the war of the said Emperor in resisting the malice of the Saracens and others warring and fighting against the faith which they are effecting and hastening, (as is said) to the destruction of Christianity in those and the neighbouring parts. By writ of privy seal amongst the mandates of this term,—2000*l.*

30th June.—To Thomas Lamport, citizen and goldsmith of London. In money paid to him by assignment made this day, in discharge of 8*l.* 13*s.* 4*d.* which the Lord the King commanded to be paid for silver provided by him to make a certain ship ordered of the King's alms, and for gilding the same against the feast of the Nativity of our Lord last past ; also for like silver by him provided to repair six shields of silver engraved with divers arms upon two candelabras, which belonged to John, late Duke of Lancaster, and given by the said Lord the King to the Abbot and Convent of Westminster, there ever to remain,—8l. 13s. 4d.

HENRY IV.

―――

ISSUE ROLL, MICHAELMAS, 1 HENRY IV.

22nd November.—To Henry Grene, King of the heralds, from
Scotland, to the English heralds, and others from foreign parts,
present at the Tower of London on Sunday next before the
coronation of our Lord the King Henry IV., to solemnize the
new creation of divers knights there made by the said Lord
the King. In money paid to them by the hands of the said
Henry, in discharge of 20 marks, which the Lord the King
commanded to be paid to the same heralds of his gift. By writ,
&c.—13*l.* 6*s.* 8*d.*

To John Ederyk, usher of the receipt of the Exchequer. In
money paid to him by the hands of Henry Somere, in discharge
of 7*l.* 18*s.* 10*d.* which the Lord the King commanded to be paid
him for five rich cloths and twelve cushions worked with the arms
and collar, of the livery of the Lord King Henry IV.; also for
tapestry work, and a dozen of green cloths purchased and provided
by the same John by command of the Council, the said rich
cloths and cushions provided for the advantage and accommodation of the Lords and nobility appointed to consult together on
behalf of our said Lord the King in the Star Chamber, within the
King's palace at Westminster. By writ, &c.,—7*l.* 18*s.* 10*d.*

1st December.—To Thomas Tuttebury, clerk, keeper of the
King's wardrobe. In money paid to him by the hands of John
Crouche, citizen and vintner, of London, for nine casks and one
pipe of sweet Spanish wine, two butts of Romeney, and one butt

of Malvesyn, purchased from the said John for the use of the household. By writ, &c.,—94*l.* 10*s.*

26*th January.*—To John Lokyngton, clerk, appointed by commission, under the great seal, to seize into the King's hands all the lands and tenements which belonged to Thomas, Earl of Kent, John, Earl of Salisbury, Richard de Lomeley, and Thomas Blount, knights; also to inquire concerning the goods and chattels of the same, in whosesoever hands they might be, in the counties of Surrey, Southampton, Berks, Wilts, Dorset, Devon, and Cornwall. In money paid, &c.,—6*l.* 13*s.* 4*d.*

4*th February.*—To Reginald Spicer, Roger Carnill, John Colman, Richard Small, and others, of the town of Chichester. In money paid to them in hand, in discharge of 12*l.* 7*s.* 9*d.* which the Lord the King commanded to be paid for certain costs and expenses incurred by them, as well for arresting the Earls of Kent and Salisbury, and other rebels, who lately rebelled against the Lord the King and his crown, as for charges by them incurred for the safe conduct of certain rebels so taken by them to the town of Oxford, and afterwards for like expenses which they were put to, for the safe conduct of their goods to London, and there delivered to the Lord the King. By writ, &c.,—12*l.* 7*s.* 9*d.*

17*th February.*—To Thomas Tuttebury, clerk, keeper of the King's wardrobe. In money paid to him by the hands of William Pampleon, esquire, for expenses incurred for the carriage of the body of Richard, late King of England, from the town of Pomfrait to London. By writ, &c.,—66*l.* 13*s.* 4*d.*

21*st February.*—To John Vaux, appointed, by the Earl of Northumberland and Westmoreland, Constable and Marshal of England, a Commissioner, and Deputy, to hold a session at the town of Newcastle-upon-Tyne for judgment of a duel there to be fought between the Earl of Salisbury and Lord de Morley. In money paid to him in discharge of 100*s.* which the Lord the King

T 2

commanded to be paid him for the costs and expenses by him incurred in the journey aforesaid.   By writ, &c.,—5*l.*

20th March.—To William Loveday, clerk of the King's great
wardrobe, sent by the King's command upon the said King's secret
affairs to the castle and town of Pountfreyt.   In money paid to
his own hands for the costs and expenses of himself and his men
riding with him, and for their return on account of the King's
service aforesaid,—3*l.* 6*s.* 8*d.*

To a certain valet of Sir Thomas Swynford, knight, coming
from Pountfreyt Castle to London, to certify the King's Council
concerning certain matters for the King's advantage.   In money
paid him for his wages and expenses, and for the hire of a horse
for the sake of expediting his journey aforesaid,—1*l.* 6*s.* 8*d.*

To a certain other valet, sent from London, by direction of the
King's Council, to Pountfreyt Castle, for the protection and safe
custody of the body of Richard the Second, late King of England.
In money paid to his own hands for his wages and expenses,—
6*s.* 8*d.*

To Robert Eslakby, the King's almoner, in money received by
him from Henry Somere, clerk, to be distributed amongst certain
religious persons [priests], to celebrate one thousand masses for
the salvation of the soul of Richard the Second, late King of
England, deceased, whose body is buried at Langeley, by the command of our Lord the King aforesaid,—16*l.* 13*s.* 4*d.*

7th April.—To Stephen Ingram, clerk, appointed to pay
the expenses and costs of Isabella, late Queen of England,
made by the hands of Richard Clifford, clerk, junior, keeper of
the wardrobe of the same Isabella, the late Queen.   In money
paid to John Norman, wheeler, of London, by the hands of Henry
Somere, for money due to the same John for the repairs and
amendment of divers chariots, " whyrlys," and wheels, and for

divers other things purchased from the same John, by the said Richard Clifford, for the use of Isabella, the aforesaid late Queen, as appears by the Bills, &c.,—7*l.* [*Note.* There are many payments on this Roll relating to the late King Richard the Second and Queen Isabella his wife.]

———•———

ISSUE ROLL, EASTER, 1 HENRY IV.

3rd May.—To Henry Roberts, sergeant, dwelling near Guildhall, in the city of London; William Oliver, grocer, of Boklersbury; Giles Allartisson, and Thomas Joly. In money paid to them by the hands of the aforesaid Henry, in discharge of 16*l.* 8*s.* 2*d.*, which the Lord the King commanded to be paid them,—to wit, to the aforesaid Henry 8*l.* 8*s.* for 24 "quarell gunnes," at 7*s.* each; to the aforesaid William 6*l.* 17*s.* 8*d.*,—to wit, for 300 pounds of saltpetre, price 4*d.* per lb., and for 100½ lbs. of pure sulphur, at 4½*d.* per lb.; to Giles Allartisson 20*s.*, for 40 lbs. of wadding; and to Thomas Joly 2*s.* 6*d.*, for 10 lbs. of emery at 3*d.* per lb., purchased from them for the King's use.—16*l.* 8*s.* 2*d.*

5th June.—To John Mayheu, one of the masters of the King's ships. In money paid to him by the hands of Henry Somere, clerk, in discharge of 40*l.* which the Lord the King commanded to be paid him of his gift as a reward for a stone of adamant ornamented and set in gold, presented by the said John to the aforesaid Lord the King. By writ of privy seal,—40*l.*

To Thomas Tuttebury, clerk, keeper of the King's wardrobe, in money paid to him by the hands of John Wardale and William Pamplyon, for the costs and charges incurred for the carriage of the body of Richard, late King of England, from Pountfreyt Castle to London. By writ of liberate to the said keeper as above,—13*l.* 6*s.* 8*d.*

26th June.—To John Cosin, of Chichester, to whom the present Lord the King, on the 27th of January last past, by his letters patent, granted 100 marks, yearly to be received at the Exchequer during his life, &c., for the good service performed by the said John in manfully resisting, at Chichester, Thomas, late Earl of Kent, and others who had traitorously risen against the said King and his allegiance. In money paid to him by assignment made this day in discharge of 11*l.* 9*s.* 2*d.*, for this his allowance; viz. ratably from the aforesaid 27th day of January until the last day of March then next following, for 73 days, including each day. By writ of liberate, &c.,—11*l.* 9*s.* 2*d.*

6*th July.*—To John Orewell, the King's sergeant at arms, sent to York for the conduct of certain knights and esquires who had come from France to England to prosecute certain feats of arms against Sir John Cornewaill, knight, and Janicus Darcass, esquire, to be performed in the presence of our Lord the King at York. In money paid to the same John by his own hands for his wages, —5*l.*

13*th July.*—To John Burgh, clerk of the Receipt, lately appointed by the Lord Treasurer to go in his retinue to make certain payments to divers persons, which were ordered to be made by our Lord the King to those in the retinue of the Earl of Rutland and the said Lord Treasurer, sent to prosecute Thomas, late Earl of Kent, John, late Earl of Salisbury, Sir Ralph de Lomley, knight, and other rebels who raised an insurrection at the feast of the Epiphany of our Lord last past against our Lord the King and his crown, which said rebels were taken at Chichester by the men of the same town. In money paid to his own hands, as well for his expenses in going and returning in the retinue of the said Earl and Treasurer for fourteen days, as also for the wages of a valet accompanying him, and for the hire of three horses for the journey aforesaid. By direction of the Treasurer and Chamberlains,—6*l.* 13*s.* 4*d.*

To Elizabeth, Countess of Huntingdon. In money paid to her

by the hands of Henry Somere, for payment of 10*l.* which the Lord the King commanded to be paid to the said Countess of his gift, for the price of a black bed with entire furniture, and for other furniture for the chamber, which belonged to John, late Earl of Huntingdon, adjudged to be forfeited by the said Earl to the Lord the King. By writ, &c.,—10*l.*

14*th August.*—To John Edmunds, a citizen and goldsmith of London. In money paid to him by assignment made this day for the value or price of 10 lbs. weight of silver, used in a great seal for the Chancery and for a white seal for the office of privy seal, made by the said John for the King's use, according to the form of a certain pattern remaining in possession of the same John, delivered to him by our Lord the King aforesaid,—13*l.* 10*s.*

ISSUE ROLL, MICHAELMAS, 2 HENRY IV.

26*th October.*—To Sir John Stanley, knight, the King's deputy in Ireland, for the three years next following. In money paid to him by assignment made this day, by the hands of John Aldeleine, for the wages of himself, ninety-nine men at arms, and three hundred archers, retained or to be retained in the retinue of the said John, to serve the said Lord the King in his wars in the said land of Ireland during the term aforesaid. By writ, &c.,—1000*l.* [There are several other payments to this Lord Lieutenant during the time of his appointment in Ireland.]

22*nd November.*—To John Brandon and his companions, merchants, of the town of Lenn. In money paid to them, by assignment made this day, in discharge of 500 marks which the Lord the King commanded to be paid to the same John and his companions, on account of Robert Logan, a Scotch knight, and David Seton, clerk, archdeacon of Rosse in Scotland, prisoners to the same merchants, captured by them at sea in the war near the marches of Scotland, and purchased by the same Lord the King from the

said merchants to his own use for the sum aforesaid. By writ, &c.,
—333*l.* 6*s.* 8*d.*

11*th December.*—To John Perant, the King's sergeant at arms,
sent, on the 26th day of November last past, to the county of
Kent to arrest Thomas Yoxflet, clerk, and to bring him safely
and securely before the King's council. In money paid to him
for his wages and expenses, and for the hire of horses on the road
to expedite his message aforesaid,—1*l.* 13*s.* 4*d.*

To the Sacrist of the church of Saint Peter's, Westminster. In
money paid to him in discharge of 50*s.* for the last year, ending
at the feast of Easter, to renew the wax lights burning round the
body of Lord Edward, of renowned memory, son of Henry, formerly King of England, our progenitor, buried in the said church,
as heretofore hath been accustomed to be done. By writ, &c.,—
2*l.* 10*s.*

To John Brampton, a spy, sent, by command of the King's
council, to France, to watch for and obtain news in those parts
concerning the estate and condition of the King's enemies there.
In money paid to him, &c., for his wages and expenses,—2*l.*

14*th December.*—To Sir Thomas Erpyngham, knight, the
King's chamberlain. In money paid to him by the hands of
Henry Somere, clerk, in discharge of 16*l.* which the Lord the
King commanded to be paid to the said Thomas for the price
of a sparrowhawk, which belonged to Thomas, late Earl of Kent,
to have of his gift. By writ, &c.,—16*l.*

5*th February.*—To Richard Lord de Gray and Sir Stephen le
Scrop, knights, keepers of the King's castle of Rokesburgh, upon
the marches of Scotland, for the three years next following, beginning the 4th day of September last past; receiving for the same
custody, according to the tenor of an indenture made between the
Lord the King and them, viz. during the time of the war, after the

rate of 4000 marks yearly, until the works there newly begun, and a ditch near to and before the said works, should be repaired and finished; and on completion of the said works during the said time of war, after the rate of 3000 marks per annum, and during the time of a truce 2000 marks per annum, for the custody aforesaid. In money paid to them by the hands of Hugh Curteys, by assignment made to him this day, for the custody of the castle aforesaid. By writ of privy seal, &c.,—376*l.* 9*s.* 7*d.*

5*th March.*—To Henry Dryhurst, of West Chester. In money paid to him by assignment made this day, as well in discharge of 84 marks which the Lord the King commanded to be paid him for eight pipes of red wine, purchased of him and expended in the King's household at Chester, price of each pipe 10½ marks, as for the payment of 20 marks which the Lord the King commanded to be paid him for the freightage of a ship from Chester to Dublin; also for sailing to the same place and back again to conduct the Lord the Prince, the King's son, from Ireland to England, together with the furniture of a chapel and ornaments of the same, which formerly belonged to the late King Richard the Second, deceased. By writ of privy seal, &c.—69*l.* 6*s.* 8*d.*

26*th March.*—To Robert Markeley, the King's sergeant at arms, lately appointed, together with James Chidley, John Herlee, and others, by the King's commission, to inquire concerning 1800 marks which belonged to John Cary, now appertaining to the King by reason of forfeiture made by the same John; also to inquire respecting a certain barge belonging to Patrick Galue, of Ireland, going to Genoa laden with copper, tin, cloth of Linn, and innumerable other things, wools, and merchandize, about the 20th year of King Richard the Second; which vessel, from the tempestuous and boisterous state of the sea, was cast ashore at the Isle of Silly, and there was taken into the hands of John Colshull and others in those parts, to the defrauding of the King, as is said. In money, paid to the said Robert by the hands of Roger Haldanby, clerk, for his wages,—4*l.* 13*s.* 4*d.*

To Manuel Paleologue, the devoted to God, Emperor of the Romans et semper Augustus. In money paid to him by the hands of Brother Peter Holt, Prior of the hospital of Saint John of Jerusalem, in Ireland, in discharge of 3000 marks of gold, which the Lord the King commanded, of his especial grace, to be paid to the same Emperor from his Treasury, to have of his gift, in recompense of such sum due during the time of the late King Richard the Second, after the conquest to be collected and levied from the clergy and people of his realm of England, for the defence of the Roman empire against the invasion of the enemies of the Christian faith fighting against the tenets of Christianity; received by Reginald Grill, merchant of Genoa, to be paid to the said Emperor within a certain term now past, as plainly appears by letters obligatory of the said Reginald, by which he was bound to the said Lord King Richard and his heirs, and in default of such payment within the term limited the same had then come to the hands of the said Lord the King; nevertheless the present Lord the King, regarding and considering the great labour, charge, and expenses heretofore borne by the said Emperor in furthering the said affairs under his direction, together with other Catholic Princes and faithful Christians, granted to the aforesaid Emperor the said sum for the reasons above specified, as appears by the letters of acquittance of the aforesaid Emperor, acknowledging the receipt of the sum aforesaid, remaining in the hanaper of this term. By writ, &c.,—2000*l.*

ISSUE ROLL, EASTER, 3 HENRY IV.

15th April.—To John Strete and others, men of the town of Dover. In money paid to them, by assignment made this day, by the hands of the aforesaid John, in discharge of 92*l.* 6*s.* 8*d.*, which the Lord the King, with the assent of his Council, commanded to be paid to the same persons, as well to provide a passage for Isabella, late Queen of England, to Calais, as for the return of the lords, ladies, and other persons who accompanied the said Lady the

Queen to England; which said sum, for the passage and return aforesaid, amounts to 79*l.*, as the Earl testified before the Council of the said Lord the King, for which he lately accounted to the men of the town aforesaid; also by reason that Lord de Grey, admiral of the North fleet, in like manner had testified before the said Council that 20 marks were due to the said men for two passage boats, one a farecoaster, and the other a boat hired for the passage of the Emperor of Constantinople to Calais. By writ of privy seal amongst the mandates of Michaelmas term last past,—92*l.* 6*s.* 8*d.*

19*th April.*—To Master John Chaundeler, clerk, appointed, by the Lord the King and his Council, Treasurer to Blanch, the King's eldest daughter. In money paid to him by assignment made this day, by the hands of Richard Clifford, clerk, junior, for ten cloths of gold and other merchandize purchased of Richard Whityngton, citizen and merchant of London, 215*l.* 13*s.* 4*d.*; and by the hands of William Cromer, citizen and clothier of the said city, 380*l.*, for the apparel and paraphernalia of the said Blanch in her next voyage to Cologne, for the solemnization of a marriage between the son of the King of the Romans and the said Blanch. By writ, &c.,—595*l.* 13*s.* 7*d.*

19*th April.*—To Henry Percy, son of the Earl of Northumberland. In money paid to him by assignment made this day by the hands of Thomas Karnica, his clerk, in discharge of 200*l.* which the Lord the King, with the assent of his Council, commanded to be paid him as a reward for the costs and expenses incurred by the said Henry, having it in command by the King's late letters to continue the siege round Conway Castle, which the said Henry had began there immediately after the King's rebels lately took the said castle, which said Henry continued the said siege for four weeks, at his own costs, without the assistance of any one except the people of the country. By writ of privy seal,—200*l.*

21*st April.*—To Sir Peter Holt, knight. In money paid to him received of John Norbury, late Treasurer of England, for the costs and expenses of Emanuel, Emperor of Constantinople, whilst he was at Calais before his arrival in England, at the time when our Lord the King was with his army in Scotland,—400*l*.

8*th May*.—To Thomas Barbour, of Walkerne, for having brought a certain traitor into the presence of the Lord the King and ;his Council. In money paid to his own hands for the pains and expenses incurred by him in this behalf, of the King's gift. By writ, &c.,—5*l*.

8*th May*.—To Bertolf Vander Eme, who fenced with the present Lord the King with the long sword, and was hurt in the neck by the said Lord the King. In money paid to his own hands, of the King's gift. By writ, &c.,—10*l*.

To Henry Soweleby, Chamberlain to the venerable Father Henry, Bishop of Bath and Wells, Treasurer of England, appointed by the said Treasurer to provide clothes, linen, and other necessaries for Roger Stanlak, the King's idiot, in the custody of the said Treasurer. In money paid to him to provide such necessaries for the use of the said idiot, &c.,—13*s*. 4*d*.

11*th May*.—To Robert Longe and Thomas Messingham, servants of William Terry and Thomas Tuttebury, sent from the North into the King's presence to announce to him the news of the capture of a certain ship, sent to Scotland to victual those parts. In money paid to him by his own hands for his labour and expenses,—13*s*. 4*d*.

To Elizabeth, Countess of Salisbury, appointed by the Lord the King and his Council to pass over in the retinue of the Lady Blanch, eldest daughter of the Lord the King, to Cologne, for the solemnization of her marriage. In money paid to her by the hands of John Grene, her esquire, for her wages in the affair aforesaid,—100*l*.

[*Note.* This Roll contains payments made to John, Earl of Somerset, Richard, Bishop of Winchester, Thomas Chaucers, and several other distinguished persons, including a long list of servants, who accompanied the Lady Blanch on her departure to be married.]

11*th May.*—To a certain woman, prosecuting certain affairs for the King, concerning which, as is asserted, great profit and advantage would arise to the Lord the King. In money paid to her own hands for her expenses,—1*s.* 8*d.*

To Stephen Vyne, embroiderer, whom Lord Richard the Second, after the conquest, late King of England, on account of the good report made to our most dear uncle the said late King, by the Duke de Berry and d'Auverne, of the skill of the said Stephen in the art of embroidery, he was appointed chief embroiderer to the said late King and his most dear consort, the late Queen of England; and for this reason there was granted to the same Stephen, 6*d.* daily, to be received yearly at the Exchequer during his life, or until otherwise he should be provided for in his estate, &c. In money paid to him by the hands of his wife, in part payment, &c.,—2*l.*

12*th June.*—To John Drayton, sergeant of the King's pavilions and tents. In money paid to him, by assignment made this day, in part payment of 40*l.* 3*s.*, due upon an account made with him at the Exchequer of Accounts, for the receipts and wages of twenty-two valets, tailors, tassel-makers, and carpenters, going with the King's pavilions and tents from London, in the King's journey to Scotland, as well by land as by sea, between 17th of July in the second year and the feast of Saint Michael then next following. By writ, &c.,—33*l.* 6*s.* 8*d.*

21*st June.*—To Master John Chaundeler, clerk, appointed by the Lord the King and his Council to attend as Treasurer to the Lady Blanch, the King's eldest daughter. In money paid to his own hands, receiving the money from Henry Somere, at Orewell, in part payment of 20,000 marks, to be paid to the King of the Romans according to covenants for payment thereof made be-ween our said Lord the King and the King of the Romans, and affirmed by divers lords and nobility of the kingdom, by their writing obligatory, payable on the day of the solemnization of the marriage between the son of the said King of the Romans and the said Lady Blanch, this being the first term for payment. By writ, &c.,—5333*l.* 6*s.* 8*d.* [There are other payments entered on this Roll relating to the above marriage, one on the 26th Septem-ber of 14*l.* 11*s.* 8*d.* paid to the said Henry Somere, for taking 9500 marks to Ipswich to be delivered to the said John Chaundler, Treasurer to Lady Blanch.]

27th June.—To divers of the King's messengers, sent to each county of the kingdom of England with the King's commissions, directed to certain persons, for due punishment to be inflicted on those who, to excite the people to an insurrection against the King and his peace, publicly proclaimed and affirmed that Richard the late King was still living. In money paid to them for their wages and expenses in going on the message aforesaid,—6*l.* 13*s.* 4*d.*

3rd July.—To divers of the King's messengers, sent to each county of the kingdom with the King's letters, directed to the sheriffs of the same counties, commanding that they should cause proclamation to be made within their bailiwicks of a general par-don, graciously granted by the Lord the King to his liege subjects, and to declare that it was not the intention of the King to punish any of his liege subjects for slanderous reports made before the time of this proclamation concerning the existence of Richard, the late King, except the principal actors and favourers of this oblo-quy, any of whom, as is contained by the tenor of the said letters, should at that time receive condign punishment. In money paid to them for their wages in going on the message aforesaid,—5*l.*

15th July.—To William Loveney, clerk of the King's great

wardrobe. In money paid to him by the hands of Thomas Gloucester, the painter, in discharge of 36*l.* 2*s.*, which he lent to the
Lord the King, &c.,—36*l.* 2*s.*

15*th July.*—To divers messengers, sent with letters of the King's
privy seal, directed to the knights, esquires, and other persons of
the King's retinue, to hasten to Wales, there to proceed with the
Lord the King, to resist the malice of Owen Glendurdy and other
rebels there against the King. In money paid for their expenses,
7*l.* 3*s.* 4*d.*

21*st July.*—To Nicholas Usk, Treasurer of the town of Calais.
In money paid to him, with the assent of the Council, by assignment made this day, by the hands of John Norbury, esquire,
captain of the castle of Guynes, for having made a new tower
within the dungeon of the castle aforesaid called the "Cupe," by
survey and control of the King's comptroller of the town of Calais.
By writ, &c.,—666*l.* 13*s.* 4*d.*

To Thomas, the King's son, the King's deputy in Ireland for
the three following years, receiving for himself and all and singular the men retained for the war and government of the said land,
12,000 marks yearly. In money paid to him by the hands of Sir
Stephen le Scrop, knight, and Walter de Thebaud receiving the
money from the Treasurer, for himself and his men, retained to
go with him, to serve the Lord the King in his wars, and for the
safe custody and government of the land aforesaid, according to
the force and effect of a certain indenture made between the said
Lord the King and himself. By general writ of privy seal of
Easter term, in the second year,—1200*l.*

26*th September.*—To divers messengers, sent with commissions
and writs under the great seal, directed to the Archbishops,
Bishops, Abbots, Priors, Dukes, Earls, Barons, and divers others,
knights of the counties, to prorogue parliament unto the morrow
of Saint Michael next coming. In money paid to them, &c.,—
6*l.* 8*s.* 4*d.*

3rd October.—To Christian, Countess of Dunbarr. In money paid to her by the hands of Columbe, her son, in discharge of 40*l.* 19*s.* 3½*d.* which the Lord the King commanded to be paid to the said Countess of his gift, for her charges and expenses in coming from the North into the presence of the Lord the King, by his command, to prosecute certain affairs concerning her husband, herself, and their heirs, as appears by the particulars exhibited by the said Countess remaining in the hanaper of this term. By writ, &c.,—40*l.* 19*s.* 3½*d.*

26th October.—To the Lord the King in his chamber. In money delivered into his chamber by the hands of John Elvet, receiver of the same chamber, by assignment made this day in discharge of 250*l.* which the Lord the King commanded to be paid into the same chamber, for eight collars purchased of Theodore, the goldsmith, of London, and sent, by the King's command, to his sister, the Queen of Portugal, for the King's infant nephew. By writ of privy seal,—250*l.*

28th October.—To the Venerable Father John, Bishop of Rochester, appointed by the King's commission, together with William Heron, Lord de Say, to inquire and proceed against an attempt made to seize land in Picardy and Normandy, after the last treaty made between the kingdoms of England and France. In money paid to them for their expenses, &c.,—66*l.* 13*s.* 4*d.*

11th November.—To Henry, Earl of Northumberland, and Henry Percy, his son, keepers of the East and West Marches, near Scotland. In money paid to them by the hands of Thomas Carnika, clerk, for the safe custody of the marches aforesaid after the completion of the truce ending at this present feast of Saint Martin,—500*l.*

12th November.—To Richard Cressy, one of the ushers of the

King's hall, of the household, directed to order, at the King's expense, a royal seat to be made within the place at Smithfield, where a tournament was appointed between the king's kinsman, Sir Richard Arundell, knight, and a certain Lombard. In money paid to him by the hands of Thomas Lath, in discharge of 14*l*. 12*s*. 3*d*. which the Lord the King commanded to be paid him for constructing and erecting the seat aforesaid. By writ, &c., —14*l*. 12*s*. 3*d*.

17th November.—To John Michell, the King's sergeant at arms, appointed by the King's Commission, together with Thomas Carreu, chevalier, sent to arrest and take before the Lord the King and his Council, when he should be captured, David Perot, esquire, of the county of Pembroke, to answer for certain contempts done by himself and others, which were objected against him by the said Council on the part of the King ; also to seize all goods and chattels of the said David wheresoever they should be found, and all arms in his possession, and place them in safe and secure custody, until otherwise should be directed by the King. In money paid to him for his wages,—3*l*. 16*s*. 8*d*.

9th December.—To Thomas Sy, esquire, to whom the present Lord the King, on the 9th day of December, in the first year of his reign, granted, by letters patent, the office of verger to the knights of the order of the garter, within the castle of Windsor ; for term of his life receiving 12*d*. per day, out of the revenues and issues of the castle aforesaid, by the hands of the Constable, or his deputy there, for the time being, in the same manner as was received by Walter Whitehors, in the aforesaid office, and to have and occupy the said office in the same manner as the aforesaid Walter occupied the same. In money paid to his own hands, by assignment made this day, in discharge of his said wages ; viz., from the aforesaid 9th day of December, in the first year, unto the 1st day of December, in the third year ; for 721 days, not including the first or last day, &c. By divers writs, &c., —36*l*. 1*s*.

U

12th December.—To Henry Percy, son of the Earl of North-umberland, keeper of the King's town of Berwick-upon-Tweed, and the East Marches of Scotland. In money paid to him by assignment made this day, by the hands of Thomas Carnika, 44*l.*; and in counted money, by the hands of the aforesaid Thomas, 2000*l.*; for the wages of himself, his men at arms, and archers, with him, for fortifying and safe custody of the town and East Marches aforesaid, in the time of war between the kingdoms of England and Scotland. By writ, &c.,—2044*l.*

14th December.—To Henry, Prince of Wales. In money paid to him by the hands of Sir Richard Aston, knight, in discharge of 420*l.* which the Lord the King commanded to be paid to the said Prince, for the wages of 100 men at arms, each receiving 12*d.* per day; and 400 archers at 6*d.* per day each, for one month, which said men at arms and archers were sent with despatch to Hardelagh Castle, in North Wales, to remove the besiegers whom Owen Glendourdy and other rebels against the King had sent to the Castle aforesaid. By writ, &c.,—420*l.* [This Roll contains many payments to Henry, Prince of Wales, after-wards King Henry V., relating to this insurrection, too long and numerous to be here inserted.]

18th January.—To Thomas, Bishop of Bangor. In money paid to his own hands, in discharge of 100 marks, which the Lord the King, of his especial grace, ordered to be paid him as a reward, because a great part of the possessions of the Church of Bangor, as the King is informed, were destroyed by reason of the war in North Wales; also in consideration of the great ex-pense incurred by him in attending the King's Council after his coronation unto the present time. By writ, &c.,—66*l.* 13*s.* 4*d.*

3rd February.—To the Venerable Father Walter, Bishop of Durham. In money paid to him by assignment made this day, by the hands of William Lokton, in part payment of 72*l.* 1*s.* 3*d.*, due upon an account made with him at the Exchequer of account, for receipt of his wages and expenses in going in the King's service to Calais, to restore Isabella, Queen of England, to her father, the King of France, in the second year of the present King's reign. By writ of privy seal, &c.,—72*l.* 1*s.* 3*d.* [A payment of 73*l.* 6*s.* 8*d.* was also made to John, Bishop of Hereford, on the 14th November, employed on the same business.]

To William Loveny, clerk of the King's great wardrobe. In money paid to him by assignment made this day, by the hands of Thomas Prince, the King's painter, for his office. By his writ current,—10*l.*

14*th March.*—To Ralph, Earl of Westmoreland, Marshal of England. In money paid to him by the hands of John Darell, in discharge of 5 marks, which the Lord the King commanded to be paid him for the marshalling and appointing in order the lists at Smithfield, for a duel to be determined between Yevan app Griffith Lloyt, appellant, and Perceval Soudan, knight, defendant; respecting certain articles of treason charged by the said appellant against the said defendant. By writ, &c.,—3*l.* 6*s.* 8*d.*

14*th March.*—To Thomas More, clerk, keeper of the King's wardrobe. In money paid to him by the hands of Robert Watterton, master of the King's horses, for the purchase of horses at the fair last held at Staunford, for the use of the King's household,—133*l.* 6*s.* 8*d.*

To John Aldelyme, senior, to whom the present Lord the King of his especial grace, by his letters patent, granted 40*l.* yearly, to be received at the Exchequer during his life, &c., in recompense, because the said John restored into the Chancery of the present King, to be cancelled, the letters patent of the late King, Lord Richard the Second, after the conquest, made to him of the offices of Escheator, clerk of the market, and keeper of the weights and measures in Ireland, with the weighage and other profits belonging to the said office, to hold during his life. In money paid to him, &c.,—20*l.*

To the Earl of Somerset, appointed, by the King and his Council, to conduct the Lady Blanch, the King's eldest daughter, to Cologne, there to solemnize her marriage. In money paid to him, by the hands of John Burton, his clerk, for his wages in going to the parts aforesaid for the purpose aforesaid,—66l. 13s. 4d.

ISSUE ROLL, EASTER, 4 HENRY IV.

28th May.—To Richard Gaynesburgh, to whom the present Lord the King, by his letters patent, granted 10l. yearly, to be received during his life at the Exchequer, &c., as well for the good services by him bestowed upon the Lord the King for the last fifteen years, as also in consideration that he is visited with the infirmity of leprosy. In money paid to him by the hands of John Langerigge. By writ, &c.,—10l.

1st June.—To Sir John Stanley, knight. In money paid to him by assignment made this day, by the hands of John Aldelyme, in discharge of 1500l., &c., for the restitution of three tallies lately assigned to the said Sir John Stanley, for the custody of Ireland; viz., by two tallies, &c.,—1500l.

25th June.—To Thomas, Lord de Camoys, directed to safely conduct the Lady Queen Joan from Britany to England. In money paid to him by assignment made this day for his wages,—100l.

To Joan, Countess of Hereford. In money paid to her by assignment made this day, in discharge of 200 marks which the Lord the King commanded to be paid her, with the assent of his Council, for the maintenance of Richard, son and heir of the Earl of Oxford, a minor, and their servants attending, by direction of the King, in the retinue of the said Countess for two years previous to the date of these presents; viz., to the 22nd June, in the fourth year, over and above 100l. per annum, lately granted to the said Richard by the Lord the King in aid of the support of the

said Richard, until he should attain his full age. By writ, &c.,—
133*l.* 6*s.* 8*d.*

17th July.—To Simon Gaunstede, clerk, in money paid him
by assignment made this day, by the hands of John Mapilton, in
discharge of 20*l.* which the Lord the King, with the assent of his
Council, commanded to be paid him, for the great labour he un-
derwent in writing the Originalia in Chancery, in the second and
third years of this King's reign ; viz., for each year, 10*l.*, in the
same way as heretofore hath been accustomed to be received. By
writ, &c.,—20*l.*

To Sir Thomas Talbot, knight, keeper of the King's castle of
Moungomery, in Wales. In money paid to him by assignment
made this day, for the wages of himself, his men at arms, and
archers dwelling with him, for the protection and safe custody of
the castle aforesaid,—100*l.* [Also a payment to the said Sir
Thomas Talbot, on the 7th December, of 38*l.* 6*s.* 8*d.*, for the defence of Richard's castle against the Welsh rebels.]

To Richard Kays, the King's sergeant at arms, appointed by
letters of commission, under the great seal of the Lord the King,
to arrest a certain John Rogers, then in the county of Dorset, and
to bring him before the Treasurer and Barons of the King's Exchequer, to answer to certain articles propounded to him by the
said Treasurer and Barons, concerning the benefit of the King and
this kingdom. In money paid, &c., for his wages and expenses
in going upon the business aforesaid,—1*l.*

To Henry, Prince of Wales, eldest son of the King, ordered by
the Lord the King, with the assent of his Council, to be the
King's deputy in his country of Wales for one whole year, beginning the first day of April last past, receiving for the said year
8108*l.* 2*s.*, to see justice done to the rebels who should happen to
be found and taken there within the year aforesaid. In money
paid to him by the hands of John Wynter, his receiver, for the
wages of four barons and bannerets, 20 knights, 476 esquires, and

2500 archers, retained by him for the safe custody of the country aforesaid, and trial of the rebels aforesaid. By writ, &c.,— 666*l.* 13*s.* 4*d.*

To divers messengers and couriers sent to all and singular the counties of England, as well with writs for proclamation to be made within the said counties, of the death of Henry Percy, together with other rebels, slain in the battle fought between the King and the said rebels on the part of the said Henry Percy, near Shrewsbury; and of the capture of Thomas Percy, Earl of Worcester, in the said battle; as also with other writs directed to each keeper of all passage boats whatsoever, in all the ports of England, to prohibit the passage of all persons whomsoever, until otherwise thereon they should receive command from the Lord the King and his Council. In money paid to them by the hands of John Skelton, clerk, for their wages and expenses,—5*l.* 10*s.*

20th July.—To Thomas Tuttebury, clerk, late keeper of the King's wardrobe. In money paid to him by assignment made this day, viz., by the hands of William Pamplion,—9*l.* 2*s.*; by the hands of Thomas Fulham, for tin vessels purchased from the same Thomas,—98*l.* 6*s.* 3*d.*; by the hands of Robert Dyne, for fish purchased of him,—253*l.* 9*s.*; by the hands of Thomas Lathe, William Noke, and Alexander Tresorer,—14*l.* 6*s.* 1*d.*; and by the hands of Walter Whitby, clerk,—7*l.* 14*s.* 5*d.*, due to the said persons, &c.,—382*l.* 17*s.* 9*d.*

To Everard Gamenshede and Albright, the goldsmiths, of the city of London. In money paid to them by assignment made this day, in discharge of 79*l.* which the Lord the King commanded to be paid them for two tablets purchased from them, and delivered at the will and direction of the said Lord the King to his sons John and Humphrey, by the advice of his Council, to be presented, by the said John and Humphrey, to the Lady the Queen consort of the said Lord the King, on his coming to Winchester. By writ of privy seal, 79*l.*

4th September.—To the Lord the King, in his chamber. In money paid into the said chamber, by assignment made this day, by the hands of John Whitewll, jeweller, in discharge of 500 marks which the Lord the King commanded to be paid to the said John, for a gold collar purchased from him at the time of the nuptials of the said Lord the King and the Queen, for the use of the said Lord the King. By writ, &c.,—333*l.* 6*s.* 8*d.*

ISSUE ROLL, MICHAELMAS, 4 HENRY IV.

19th October.—In money paid to divers porters, for the portage of divers silver vessels and jewels which belonged to Edward de Mortimer, from the river Thames to the King's great Treasury at Westminster, for their labour,—8*d.*

7th December.—To Gawyn de Dunbarr, son of the Earl of March, of Scotland, to whom the present Lord the King, on the 10th day of March last past, with the advice of his Council, by his letters patent, granted 40*l.* yearly, &c., because the said Gawyn was retained to continue personally in attendance upon the Lord the King during his life, until otherwise for his estate it should be ordered. In money paid to his own hands; viz., ratably from the aforesaid 10th day of March until the last day of the same month, for twenty-one days, the last day and not the first included. By writ, &c.,—2*l.* 6*s.* 8*d.*

7th December.—To Sir Thomas Beaufort, knight, keeper of Lodelowe Castle. In money paid to him by the hands of Matthew Penketh, &c., for the wages of himself, his men at arms, and others dwelling with him in the garrison of Lodelowe Castle, in Wales, to resist the invasion of the rebels there,—88*l.* 18*s.* 9*d.*

9th December.—To the Venerable Father, Bishop of Bangor, (together with other persons,) sent upon the King's embassy to the kingdoms of Sweden, Denmark, and Norway, to treat for a marriage to be had between Henry, Prince of Wales, and the daughter of the Queen of the kingdoms aforesaid; and between the eldest son of the said Queen and Philippa, the King's daughter. In money paid to his own hands, receiving the money from the mayor, bailiffs, and honest men of the town of Lenn, for their wages, passage, and re-passage by sea, in going upon the aforesaid embassy,—20*l*. [*Note.*—There are other payments entered on this Roll relating to these intended marriages.]

3rd February.—To William Loveney, clerk of the King's great wardrobe. In money paid to him at different times; viz., by the hands of Thomas Kent, painter, receiving the money from William Wexcomb, clerk, for painting a certain chariot ordered for the Lady Philippa, daughter of the Lord the King, 5*l*.; and in money received by the hands of John Gadyer, goldsmith, from the aforesaid William, for making certain pommels for the chariot aforesaid, 10*l*., by virtue of his office,—15*l*.

19th February.—To Thomas More, clerk, keeper of the King's wardrobe. In money received by him from the Bishop of Winchester, at Winchester, for the expenses of the King's household on the day of the solemnization of the marriage there between the Lord the King and Joan the Queen,—333*l*. 6*s*. 8*d*.

22nd February.—In money paid for Roger, an idiot of the Lord the King, in the custody of the Lord Treasurer, at the charge of the said Lord; viz., for shoes, socks, shirts, and other necessaries, to be provided for him so long as the same Roger should happen to remain at the charge of the said Lord the King. By direction of the said Treasurer and Chamberlains,—13*s*. 4*d*.

To several messengers and couriers sent to divers counties of England, with letters of privy seal directed to divers lords and ladies, and others, knights, to come to the coronation of the Lady Joan, Queen of England. In money paid to them for their wages and expenses,—1*l*. 10*s*.

To Edward, Duke of York, appointed the King's deputy in the territory and dominion of Acquitaine, for the term of three years next following, fully to be completed, receiving for himself, the earl, knights, esquires, and such a sufficient number of archers as should appear to him necessary to be retained for the safe custody of the territory and dominion aforesaid, 25,000 marks for each year, during the term aforesaid, according to a truce remaining between the kingdoms of England and France. In money paid to him by the hands of Robert Eggerley, for the wages of himself and his men aforesaid, dwelling with him, for the government and safe custody of those parts. By writ, &c.,—300*l.*

1st March.—To John, Lord de Latymer, for having released his right of inheritance to the office of almoner, belonging to him and his heirs, on the day of the coronation of the Lord the King or Queen of England, for the time being. In money paid to his own hands, receiving the money from Ralph, Lord de Nevill, in discharge of 40 marks which the Lord the King, with the assent of his Council, commanded to be paid him for release of the almoner's dish for Queen Joan, placed before the said Queen on the day of her coronation ; which said dish the said Lord de Latymer claims of right to belong to him, as his ancestors heretofore, in like cases, have been accustomed to have the said dish. By writ, &c., —26*l.* 13*s.* 4*d.*

26th March.—To John Domegode, lapidary, of London. In money paid to his own hands, for making and engraving a metal seal, ordered by advice of the King's Council for the subsidies of 3*s.* per ton, and 12*d.* for the lb. in the port of Plimouth, in the county of Cornwall. By direction of the Treasurer and Chamberlains,—3*s.* 4*d.*

ISSUE ROLL, MICHAELMAS, 5 HENRY IV.

9th November.—To Richard Vaux, sent by direction of the King's Council with the seal of the Earl of Northumberland, to be delivered to the said Earl. In money paid to his own hands, for his wages and expenses in going and returning for the cause aforesaid. By order of the Treasurer and Chamberlains,— 1*l.* 6*s.* 8*d.*

30*th November.*—To Henry, the son of John, Earl of Somers, the King's godchild, whom the said Henry the Lord the King held at the sacred font, to which said Henry the present Lord the King gave 1000 marks, to have and receive the same to him and the heirs male of his body begotten, yearly to be paid at the Exchequer at Easter and Michaelmas terms, by equal portions, until the same Henry, his godson, should be provided with 1000 marks of land or yearly rent, to be held to him and his heirs male aforesaid for ever, &c. In money paid, &c.,—200*l.*

10*th December.*—To John, Earl of Somers, captain of the castle and town of Calais. In money paid to him by the hands of Henry Merstan, clerk, in money counted,—88*l.* 9*s.*; and for the price of three silver gilt cups, one ewer, and a salt cellar, which belonged to Sir Thomas Percy, knight, forfeited to the King,—43*l.* 18*s.* 4*d.*; for the wages of 50 men at arms and 100 archers, ordered by the Lord the King and his Council to go in his retinue to the town of Calais, there to remain for forty days in the fortification of the castle and town aforesaid, above a certain number of soldiers for the retinue of the captain, from ancient time kept there, for the safe custody of the town and castle aforesaid,—132*l.* 7*s.* 4*d.*

21*st December.*—To William Loveney, clerk of the great wardrobe of the Lord the King. In money paid to him by the hands of Thomas Basham and Walter Gauteron, for divers bonds which belonged to Sir Henry Percy, knight, forfeited to the King for his office. By writ, &c.,—300*l.*

To Thomas Langeley, keeper of the King's privy seal. In money paid to his own hands, for the price of divers vessels of silver, gilt, which belonged to Thomas Percy, late Earl of Worcester, forfeited to the King, and sold to the said keeper, as an advance upon his accustomed fee in his office,—8*l.* 9*s.* 5*d.*

31st January.—To Henry, Prince of Wales. In money paid to the same Prince by the hands of Thomas Saundres and John Stevenes, of Bristol, by assignment made this day, &c., to purchase and provide 66 pipes of honey, 12 casks of wine, 4 casks of sour wine, 50 casks of wheat flour, and 80 quarters of salt, provided by the said Thomas and John, with the assent of the King's Council, in the port aforesaid, to be carried by the said Lord the Prince in divers ships by sea, for victualling and providing the King's castles of Karnarvon, Hardelagh, Lampadern, and Cardygan.

27th February.—To John Merbury, to whom the present Lord the King, on the 18th March, in the third year of his reign, of his especial grace granted 10 marks yearly, to be received at the Exchequer, &c., for the good and grateful service by him bestowed and to be bestowed upon the same Lord the King; and also because that he married Alice Oldecastle, of the county of Hereford. In money paid to him by the hands of the Bishop of Saint David's, &c.,—10*l.*

ISSUE ROLL, MICHAELMAS, 6 HENRY IV.

2nd December.—To Sir Richard de Aston, knight, of the county of Chester. In money paid to him by assignment made this day, in discharge of 256*l.* which the present Lord the King of his especial grace, and for the good and grateful service bestowed and thereafter to be bestowed by the same Richard upon the said Lord the King, directed to be paid to the said Richard of his gift, in part payment of 333*l.* 6*s.* 8*d.* which the Lord the King granted him, in aid of payment of 1000 marks, for his ransom, for which the said Richard was bound, &c.,—256*l.*

13th December.—To William, Lord de Roos, of Hamelak. In money paid to him by assignment made this day, in discharge of 100*l.* which the Lord the King commanded to be paid him as a reward, to be had of his gift, in consideration of the good and laudable services performed by the same William to the said Lord the King in the office of Treasurer of England ; as also for the great pains, costs, and expenses which the same William lately incurred and sustained in going to the North, by command of the said Lord the King, to receive at Berwick certain bonds made by certain Scotch prisoners to Henry Percy, deceased, and bringing the same from thence to the Lord the King at Pountefrayt Castle, &c. By writ, &c.,—100*l.*

To John Grove, valet, ordered and deputed by the Lord the King to safely and securely keep, at the costs of the said Lord the King, the two daughters of Lord le Despenser, being for certain causes in the hands of the said Lord the King. In money paid to him, &c., for the expenses of the daughters of Lord le Despenser aforesaid,—1*l.*

3rd February.—To Joan, Queen of England, in money paid to her, by assignment made this day, by the hands of William Denys, clerk, her receiver, as an advance upon a certain annuity of 10,000 marks, yearly received at the Exchequer,— 147*l.* 18*s.* 8*d.*

2nd March.—To Elming Leget, esquire, in money paid to his own hands for the expenses and safe conduct of the Lady le Despenser from London to the King's Castle of Killyngworth, there to be safely and securely kept,—10*l.*

In money paid to Nicholas Neubold, one of the Clerks in the Receipt of the King's Exchequer, for parchment purchased by him therewith to make rolls for the enrolment of the Pells of the same Receipt. By writ, &c.,—5*s.* 1½*d.*

1st May.—To Roger Bradeshawe, in money paid to him, by assignment made this day upon the Sheriff of Stafford, in discharge of 30*l.* which the Lord the King, with the assent of his Council, commanded to be paid to the said Roger, in recompense as well for the charges of the Earl of Douglas, lately committed to the custody of the said Roger by the said Lord the King, from the time of the last battle, fought near the town of Shrewsbury, unto the 21st day of August then next following for twenty-seven days, as for the charges of the said Roger and other men of the said Roger hired for the safe custody of the said Earl during the time aforesaid.   By writ, &c.,—30*l.*

18th July.—To divers messengers, sent to all and singular the counties of England with writs under the great seal, directed to the Sheriffs of the counties aforesaid, commanding them to make proclamation within the said counties for the arrest of certain vagabonds spreading reports from town to town, and safely and securely to keep the said vagabonds so arrested until otherwise it should be commanded in this behalf by the King and his Council; also with commissions and writs under the same great seal, directed to the Archbishops and Bishops to pray for the good estate of the said Lord the King and government of the whole realm of England.   In money, &c., paid for their wages and expenses, &c.,— 5*l.* 8*s.* 4*d.*

3rd November.—To Nicholas Merbury, to whom the present Lord the King granted 40*l.*, yearly to be received at the Exchequer during the term of his life, at Michaelmas, &c., as well for the good services by him performed and thereafter to be performed for the said Lord the King, as also because the same Nicholas was the first person who reported for a certainty to the said Lord the King the good, agreeable, and acceptable news of the success of the expedition lately made at Homeldon, near Wollore, in Northumberland, by Henry, late Earl of Northumberland, and other his liege subjects in that county against the King's Scotch enemies to their destruction, in which said expedition four earls, many barons and bannerets, with a great multitude of knights and esquires, as well Scotch as French, were taken, and also a great multitude slain and drowned in the river Tweed. By writ, &c.,—10*l*.

3rd December.—To Gilbert Talbot, chevalier, son of Richard Talbot, chevalier, in money paid to him, by assignment made this day, in part payment of 200*l*. which the Lord the King, of his especial grace, commanded to be paid him as of his gift, &c., in recompense because the same Gilbert, on account of his minority, was in custody of the Lord the King, &c., and had only for his support 100 marks, &c., by reason whereof he was much indebted, &c.; also in recompense because the said Gilbert ought to have had more for his support, during the previous four and a half years in consideration of the great expense he sustained in the service of the said Lord the King and his most dear son the Lord the Prince. By writ, &c.,—120*l*.

27th February.—To a certain messenger, sent to France to inquire and search into the intentions and purposes of the French enemy, and with all possible dispatch he was able to certify and inform the Lord the King, or his Council, of the intentions and purposes of the enemies aforesaid. In money paid to him, by assignment made this day, in discharge of 10 marks which the Lord the King commanded to be paid him for his wages and expenses in going and returning upon the message aforesaid. By writ, &c.,—6*l*. 13*s*. 4*d*.

26th March.—To Henry Messenger, a messenger sent with a writ directed to Lord de Bellomonte, to appear before the Lord the King in his Chancery at a certain day named in the said writ. In money paid to him for his expenses in going and returning with the message aforesaid,—13*s*. 4*d*.

To John Curson, esquire, ordered by the Lord the King and his Council, with the advice of his parliament held at Coventry, to make payments to certain lords, men at arms and archers retained by him to go to the lordship and castle of Cotyff, in Wales, for the rescue thereof. In money paid to him, by assignment made this day, by the hands of Sir Thomas Erpyngham, knight, for the rescue of the said lordship and castle. By writ, &c.,—20*l*. [*Note.* There are several other payments entered on this Roll for the same purpose.]

ISSUE ROLL, EASTER, 7 HENRY IV.

20th April.—To Sir John Skelton, knight, in money paid to his own hands as an advance upon a certain annual allowance of 100 marks, granted to him for term of life on account of taking Mordak Stiward, a Scotch prisoner, and delivering him into the King's hands,—66*l.* 13*s.* 4*d.*

. . . *May.*—To Simon Blakebourn, the King's sergeant at arms, appointed by the King's commission to proceed to the North and arrest Richard Rowdoun, and bring him safely and securely before the King's Council. In money paid to him for his wages and expenses,—1*l.* 6*s.* 8*d.*

7th June.—To Richard Lord de Grey. In money paid to him, by the hands of Thomas Burgh, his attorney, in discharge of 92*l.* which the Lord the King commanded to be paid to the said Lord de Grey, of his gift, in recompense of 92*l.* which the said Richard received from the manors of Brymesgrove and Kyngesnorton with the appurtenances, which belonged to Edward Mortymer, chevalier, reserved to the same Lord the King for one whole year, from the feast of Easter in the fifth, to Easter in the sixth year, &c., according to an order made in the last parliament of the said Lord the King, held at Coventry. By writ, &c.,—92*l.*

28th July.—To Richard Clifford, junior clerk of the wardrobe to the Lady Philippa, the King's daughter, Queen of Sweden, Denmark, and Norway. In money paid to him, by assignment made this day, by the hands of Richard Whityngton, citizen and mercer of London, for pearls and cloth of gold purchased from him at the solemnization of the marriage between the said Philippa and the King of the Romans in those parts. By writ, &c.,—248*l.* 10*s.* 6*d.*

ISSUE ROLL, MICHAELMAS, 8 HENRY IV.

24th October.—To divers messengers and couriers, sent with letters and writs under the great seal, directed to all Sheriffs of the counties of England, to make proclamation within the said counties for the Lord the King, for rescue to be made of the town of Calais and marches thereof. In money paid to them for their expenses, &c.,—4*l.*

To divers messengers, sent with letters of privy seal, directed to the lords, knights, and esquires of the King's retinue, to prepare themselves with the greatest possible speed, in the best way they could, to proceed in the King's army to the town of Calais to resist the malice of the enemies of his adversary the King of France, which he purposed to do by besieging the said town of Calais and other castles, of the marches adhering thereto. In money paid, &c., for their wages and expenses,—3*l.* 16*s.* 8*d.*

29th October.—To William Loveney, ordered and appointed, by the Lord the King and his Council, Treasurer of the household of the Lady Philippa, Queen of Sweden, Denmark, and Norway. In money received by him from Thomas Lord de Furnyvall, Treasurer of England, by the hands of Henry le Scrop, 122*l.*; by the hands of Richard, Clerk to the Lord Treasurer, 515 marks; by the hands of divers brewers for the price of thirty casks of beer, purchased from them, 48*l.*; and by his own hands, for the price of divers silver and gilt vessels, 316*l.* 9*s.* 11*d.*, for the expenses of the household of the said Queen in her journey to the parts aforesaid to solemnize the marriage between the King of the Romans and the said Philippa, celebrated in those parts, —829*l.* 16*s.* 7*d.*

3*rd November.*—To Christopher Tildesley, a citizen and goldsmith of London. In money paid to him, by assignment made this day, in discharge of 385*l.* 6*s.* 8*d.*, which the Lord the King commanded to be paid him for a collar of gold, worked with this motto "soveignez" and the letter S, and ten amulets garnished with nine large pearls, twelve large diamonds, eight rubies, eight sapphires, together with a great clasp in shape of a triangle, with a great ruby set in the same and garnished with four great pearls, which said collar, with the whole garnishing aforesaid, was delivered to the said Lord the King, at Winchester, for the said sum, then proved to be of a reasonable price and merchandise by those who, at that time, had a good knowledge of the value of the said collar. By writ, &c.,—385*l.* 6*s.* 8*d.*

10*th December.*—To Richard Spice, deputy constable of the Tower of London. In money paid to him, by assignment made this day, in discharge of 59*l.* 13*s.* 4*d.*, which the Lord the King, with the assent of his Council, commanded to be paid him for the expenses of the son of the King of Scotland, John Toures, William Seton, John Gaffard, and Master Dankirton, chaplain, being under the custody and governance of the said Richard within the Tower aforesaid, from the 6th July last past, &c. By writ, &c.,— 54*l.* 6*s.* 5*d.*

ISSUE ROLL, EASTER, 8 HENRY IV.

1*st June.*—To Richard Lord de Grey, of Codenore, chamberlain to the Lord the King. In money paid to him by the hands of Thomas Burgh, his clerk, as well for the expenditure of the King of Scotland, for whom 6*s.* 8*d.* per day was assigned to him by advice of the King's Council, as for the expenses of Griffin, the son

x

of Owen Glendour and Owen ap͠p Griffith ap͠p Richard, to whom also, by advice of the Council, were assigned 3*s.* 4*d.* per day, who were committed to the custody of the same Lord; viz. on the 12th day of the present month of June. By writ, &c.,—40*l.* [*Note.* There are several other payments for the above purposes entered on this Roll.]

15th July.—To a certain spy, coming from France with news communicated by him to our Lord the King concerning the intentions and purposes of the French. In money paid to him by the hands of the Treasurer of England, in aid of his costs and expenses in coming to our said Lord the King for the cause aforesaid,—3*s.* 4*d.*

Issue Roll, Michaelmas, 9 Henry IV.

16th November.—To Sir John Tiptot, knight, keeper of the King's wardrobe. In money paid to him by the hands of William Kynelmerssh, clerk, receiving the money from James Byllyngford, for the marriage of the heir of Henry Scogan, 20*l.*; and of John Lord de Haryngton, for the marriage of the heir of Fulk Fitz Waryn, 700 marks; and by the hands of Arnald Buada, for the expenses of the Queen's household, upon her going from Haveryng to Gloucester, 100 marks; and by the hands of Robert Tunstall, cofferer, for the expenses of the household of the same Queen removing from Gloucester to Malmesbury, 10 marks. By writ, &c.,—560*l.*

To Henry, Prince of Wales. In money received by him, by the hands of John Straunge, his Treasurer of war, for the wages of the aforesaid Treasurer at Gloucester, with 120 men at arms, each receiving 12*d.* per day, and 360 archers, each receiving 6*d.* per day, for one quarter of a year, then remaining at the abbey of Stratfleure, and keeping and defending the same from the malice of those rebels, who had not submitted themselves to the obedience of the Lord the King, and to ride after and give battle to the rebels, as well in South as in North Wales. By writ, &c.,—666*l*. 13*s*. 4*d*.

To Humphrey, the King's son. In money paid to him, by assignment made this day, out of those 6000*l*. granted to the King in the 8th year, by the commonalty of his kingdom, to be disposed of at his pleasure, in discharge of 200 marks which the Lord the King, of his especial grace, directed to be paid to the same Humphrey, his son, in aid of the payment of 5000 marks, which by writ he was bound to pay for the reversion of the lands and tenements which belonged to Matthew Gourney, chevalier, deceased. By writ, &c.,—1333*l*. 6*s*. 8*d*.

16*th January*.—To Simon Flete, esquire, keeper of the private wardrobe of the Lord the King within the Tower of London. In money paid to his own hands, for making a new large cannon,—13*l*. 6*s*. 8*d*.

20*th January*.—To Drugo Barantyn, a citizen of London. In money paid to him, by assignment made this day, out of those 6000*l*. granted to the King in the 8th year by the commonalty of the realm, to be disposed of at his pleasure, in discharge of 550*l*. which the Lord the King commanded to be paid for a collar of gold, garnished with precious stones, purchased from the said Drugo, and by him delivered into the King's chamber for the King's use. By writ, &c.,—550*l*.

1*st February*.—To William Gascoigne, Chief Justice of the King's common bench, receiving yearly 40*l*. for his fee in the office aforesaid. In money paid to him, by the hands of Robert Mauleverer, his esquire, in discharge of 20*l*. paid to him for this his fee,—20*l*.

17*th March*.—To Simon Flete, esquire, keeper of the private wardrobe within the Tower of London. In money paid to his own hands for newly making and constructing a certain great cannon newly invented by the Lord the King himself. By his writ current, &c.,—25*l.* 6*s.* 8*d.*

20th March.—To the Lord the King in his chamber. In money paid into the said chamber, viz. by the hands of Richard Lord de Grey, receiving the money from John Hende by letter of the King's signet,—100*l.*; and by the hands of the same John Hende for two gold flaskets, pledged to the same John for 400*l.*; and by the hands of the same John for certain cloths of gold, pledged to the said John,—65*l.* 10*s.* 7*d.*; which said flaskets and gold cloths were delivered to our Lord the King, at Mortlake, by the Lord Bishop of Bath and Wells, Treasurer of England, in the month of June last past,—565*l.* 10*s.* 7*d.*

ISSUE ROLL, EASTER, 9 HENRY IV.

25th April.—To William Loveney, late clerk of the great wardrobe of the Lord the King. In money paid to him, by the hands of John Hende, citizen and clothier of London, for woollen cloth purchased from him for garters provided against the feast of Saint George last past. By writ current,—103*l.*

To Sir John Cheyney, knight, the King's ambassador at the Court of Rome, to prosecute certain secret affairs for the King there. In money paid to him, by the hands of Philip de Albertis, for his wages whilst there upon the King's affairs aforesaid. By writ, &c.,—100*l.*

23rd May.—To the Lady Philippa, Queen of Sweden and Denmark. In money paid to her, by assignment made this day, in discharge of 20*l.* which was lent to the Lord the King at the receipt of the Exchequer, by restitution of a tally lately assigned to the same Queen; viz. on the 18th day of May last past, as appears in the Roll of Receipts, &c.,—20*l.*

11th June.—To Nicholas Blakeburn, late the King's admiral in the north. In money paid to him, by assignment made this day, in discharge of 166*l.* 13*s.* 4*d.* which the Lord the King, with the assent of his Council, commanded to be paid him in satisfaction of certain money due, as well for his protecting the sea as for conducting the Queen of Denmark to those parts. By writ, &c.,—166*l.* 13*s.* 4*d.*

7th July.—To Richard Cressy, esquire, sergeant of the hall of the King's household. In money paid to him in part payment of 107*s.*, which the Lord the King commanded to be delivered to him, therewith to pay the carpenters and workmen employed in making a certain scaffold at Nottingham, by command of the Lord the King, against the day of the duel appointed to be fought there between John Bulmer, appellant, and Bertran Dusane, defendant. By writ, &c.,—4*l.*

11th July.—To William Loveney, clerk of the great wardrobe of the Lord the King. In money paid to him, by the hands of Roger Wise, for the carriage of certain beds of the said Lord the King to the North, against the coming of the ambassadors from the French King to the presence of the Lord the King then being there. By writ, &c.,—6*l.* 13*s.* 4*d.*

In money paid to Henry Botolf for divers chests, locks, and other necessary things purchased by him for the preservation of the Pell Records and Memoranda of the Receipt of the Exchequer, then in the house of the Treasurer of England, and for other small expenses incurred by direction of the Treasurer and Chamberlains of the Exchequer,—16*s.* 10*d.*

ISSUE ROLL, MICHAELMAS, 10 HENRY IV.

4th December.—To Sir John Pelham, knight. In money paid to him, by assignment made this day, in his own name, for the

support of the Earl of March and his brother in the custody of
the said John,—163*l.* 6*s.* 8*d.*

In money paid for the expenses of the Lord Treasurer, Barons,
Chamberlains, and other officers, as well of the Exchequer as of
the receipt thereof, for their dinner, being engaged at Westminster
for one whole day to expedite certain business, especially concerning the estate of the Lord the King and his realm; also to inspect certain records there for the profit and advantage of the
said Lord the King, by direction of the Treasurer, Barons, and
Chamberlains aforesaid,—2*l.* 17*s.* 5½*d.*

To John Thomas, John Asshewell, and Robert Wygton, messengers, sent with letters of the King's signet, writs under the
great seal, and letters of privy seal, directed as well to the
knights of the garter, to be at London on a certain day named in
the same letters, as to Thomas, the King's son, then in Ireland,
and to Humphrey Stafford, junior, to appear before the Lord the
King in his Chancery in eight days of Saint Hilary next happening, to answer to certain articles and matters objected against the
said Humphrey on behalf of the said Lord the King. In money
paid for his expenses, &c.,—2*l.* 16*s.* 8*d.*

To Master Nicholas Ryxton, Doctor of Laws, sent as a messenger from the Lord the King to the Court of Rome, upon private affairs intimately concerning the estate of the Lord the King,
and for the benefit of the realm. In money paid to him for his
wages in going, tarrying, and returning upon the message aforesaid. By writ, &c.,—100*l.* [Sir John Colvyle, knight, also received 100*l.*, sent with the said Nicholas Ryxton upon the same
business.]

1st March.—To John Nevill, son of the Earl of Westmoreland,
keeper of Rokesburgh Castle. In money paid to him, by assignment made this day to Robert Rolleston, for the wages of his men
at arms and archers dwelling with him for the protection and safe
custody of the castle aforesaid. By writ, &c.,—200*l.*

ISSUE ROLL, EASTER, 10 HENRY IV.

26th April.—To Richard Clifford, clerk, master of the King's wardrobe. In money paid to his own hands, 40*l.*; by the hands of Hugh Nettylham, 40*l.*; and by the hands of John Leversegge, 24*l.* 10*s.*, for the purchase of gold Tartrin cloth, from Cyprus, and other stuffs, to make garters therewith against the feast of Saint George, in this tenth year. By writ current, &c.,—104*l.* 10*s.* [Other payments are entered on this Roll for the purchase of other stuffs for the liveries of the knights of the garter at the said feast of Saint George.]

17th May.—To Thomas Wodyngfeld, the King's sergeant at arms, appointed, by commission under the King's great seal, to proceed from the mouth of the Thames to the North, publicly to proclaim the truce last agreed upon between the Ambassadors of the said Lord the King and the Commissioners of the Earl of Burgundy, in those towns, ports, and other places, which to him should appear most necessary. In money paid to him for his wages in going and returning upon the business aforesaid,—3*l.* 6*s.* 8*d.* [Similar payments to Richard Kays, for proceeding westward from the mouth of the Thames, to make the like proclamation.]

To Sir William Bourchier, knight. In money paid to him by assignment made this day, in discharge of 159*l.* 13*s.* 4*d.*, due to him upon an account rendered before the Treasurer and Barons of the Exchequer, by virtue of the King's letters of privy seal, lately directed to the Barons, on account of a voyage made by the said William, at the King's command, to Denmark and Norway, to treat with Isabella, Queen of Denmark, for a marriage to be had between the Lord Henry, Prince of Wales, and the daughter of Philippa, Queen of Denmark. By writ of privy seal,—3*l.*

23rd May.—To Richard, Lord de Grey, the King's chamberlain. In money paid to him by the hands of Richard Maydeston,

for the support of the King of Scotland, Griffin, the son of Owen
Glendourdy, and other prisoners, in his custody. By writ, & c
—78*l*. 13*s*. 4*d*. [Also other payments appear on this Roll upon
the same account.]

To Hugh Mortymer, esquire, lately twice sent, by the King's
command, to France, to enter into a contract of marriage between
the Lord the Prince and the second daughter of his adversary, the
King of France. In money received by him from Richard Maydeston, in discharge of 150*l*. which the said Lord the King, with
the assent of his Council, commanded to be paid him as a reward,
on account of the great costs and expenses which he had incurred
and sustained, to support the King's honour in this journey, beyond the sums of money by him lately received at the receipt of
the Exchequer for his wages upon the business aforesaid. By
writ, &c.,—150*l*.

To Simon Flete, esquire, clerk of the King's private wardrobe
within the Tower of London. In money paid to him by the
hands of Richard Merlawe, &c., for the purchase of iron and sea
coal, therewith to make cannon for the King's use,—210*l*. 8*s*. 8*d*.

16*th July*.—To John Derby, one of the King's miners of his
silver mine, in the county of Devon, which expecting to find there,
the farm thereof, by the advice, and upon the responsibility of the
Lord the Treasurer, and Barons of the Exchequer, and of other
Lords of the King's Council, was leased to the said John. In
money paid to him by the hands of Robert Welton, as a loan to
be restored,—13*s*. 4*d*.

To Sir Robert Umframvill, knight, appointed by commission of
the Lord the King to treat and communicate with the Ambassador from the King of Scotland upon the Marches there, as well
for prolonging of the truces lately entered into between the Ambassador of the said Lord the King and the Ambassador of the
said King of Scotland, as for redressing an attack lately made

upon the Marches aforesaid, contrary to the tenor of the aforesaid
truces.   In money received by him from the hands of William
Massy, &c., for his wages in the embassy aforesaid,—20*l.* [Sir
John Mitteford and Sir Richard Tempest received similar payments upon the like business.]

ISSUE ROLL, MICHAELMAS, 11 HENRY IV.

10th October.—To divers messengers, sent to all and singular
the counties and ports of England, with writs under the great
seal directed to the Sheriffs of the counties aforesaid, to make proclamation in the said counties concerning the election of our Pope
Alexander; also concerning the union of the Church made and
agreed upon at the city of Pisa; also with writs of great seal
directed to the collectors of the ports aforesaid, for them to demand writs under the great seal directed to such collectors from
all merchants shipping wool in the ports aforesaid, &c.   In
money paid to their own hands for their wages and expenses in
going and returning upon the messages aforesaid,—5*l.* 10*s.*

To Hugh Helwys, clerk, a notary public.   In money paid to
his own hands, by consideration of the Treasurer and the Chamberlains, for making and writing out an instrument made between
our Lord the King and three owners and other good merchants
belonging to three Venetian gallies, which arrived at the port
of London in the tenth year, and there remained for a long time,
having incurred the full forfeiture of their goods and merchandize
contained in the said gallies, for not having paid custom, and
for that reason were adjudged forfeited to the Lord the King;
which said owners and merchants paid a fine of 2000 marks to
our Lord the King, to have the said gallies and merchandize restored to them, notwithstanding the forfeiture aforesaid.   And
moreover the said owners and merchants, for the safe conduct
of their gallies aforesaid, granted a remise, release, and quit claim
to the same Lord the King, from them and their heirs, as is fully
contained in the said instrument, &c.,—13*s.* 4*d.*

To Henry, Prince of Wales. In money paid to him by the hands of John Straunge, his clerk, for the wages of 300 men at arms and 600 archers, cannoniers, and other artificers, for the war, who lately besieged the castle of Hardelagh, in North Wales,—44*l.* [Other payments are entered on this Roll relating to the siege of this castle.]

To divers messengers sent with commissions and writs under the great seal directed as well to the Archbishops, Bishops, Abbots, Priors, Dukes, Earls, and Barons, as to Sheriffs, Mayors, and Bailiffs of counties, cities, and boroughs, to elect Knights for the counties, cities, and boroughs aforesaid, to appear at the King's parliament ordered to be held at Bristol. In money paid to them by their own hands, for their wages and expenses in going and returning upon the message aforesaid,—6*l.* 15*s.*

13*th November.*—To Sir John Stanley, knight, Constable of Windsor Castle. In money paid to him by assignment made this day, by the hands of John Horsey, for the expenses and costs of the Earl of Fyff and other Scotchmen under his custody, in the castle aforesaid,—38*l.* 6*s.* 8*d.*

ISSUE ROLL, EASTER, 11 HENRY IV.

27*th May.*—To Alice, Countess of Kent. In money paid to her by the hands of Richard Hastynges, in discharge of 5 marks which the Lord the King, with the assent of his Council, commanded to be paid her for the costs and expenses incurred by her for conducting the son and heir of the Earl of Somerset from Makesey to Lamhith, there to produce the said heir to the King's presence. By writ of privy seal, &c.,—3*l.* 6*s.* 8*d.*

17*th July.*—To Sir Thomas Beaufort, knight, the King's Admiral at sea. In money paid to him, viz., by the hands of Sir John Kixley, knight, 10*l.*; by the hands of John Mortimer, 10*l.*; by

the hands of Stephen, his clerk, at different times, 1217*l.* 13*s.* 4*d.*;
and by the hands of William Horneby, his clerk, 766*l.* 13*s.* 4*d.*;
for the wages of himself, his men at arms, and archers; and for
the wages of the masters, constables, and mariners, of divers
ships, boats, and barges, appointed for the protection of the sea
aforesaid.   By writ, &c.,—2400*l.* 13*s.* 4*d.*

[*Note.*—This part of the Roll contains entries of re-payments of
divers sums of money borrowed from (inter alios) the Abbot of
Woubourne, 166*l.* 13*s.* 4*d.* ; the Abbot of Gloucester, 66*l.* 13*s.* 4*d.*;
the Abbot of Tewkesbury, 26*l.* 13*s.* 4*d.* ; the Prior of Lanthony,
20*l.* ; the Prior of Worcester, 20*l.* ; the Abbot of Evesham,
26*l.* 13*s.* 4*d.*; the Abbot of Bury St. Edmonds, 100*l.* ; the Abbot
of Leicester, 40*l* ; the Abbot of Croiland, 33*l.* 6*s.* 8*d.* ; the Abbot
of Pershore, 20*l.*; the Abbot of Saint Albans, 66*l.* 13*s.* 4*d.* ; the
Abbot of Waltham, 33*l.* 6*s.* 8*d.* ; Joan, Countess of Hereford,
333*l.* 6*s.* 8*d.* ; the Bishop of Lincoln, 66*l.* 13*s.* 4*d.*; the Earl of
Arundell, 129*l.*; the Earl of Warwick, 50*l.*; with very many
others, from whom various sums of money are specified to have
been borrowed.]

31*st July.*—To Robert Thorley, esquire, Treasurer of the town
of Calais.   In money paid to him by the hands of John Gerard,
esquire, captain of the new tower at the port of Calais, for the
wages of himself, his men at arms, and archers, dwelling with
him, for the defence and safe custody of the tower aforesaid,—
338*l.* 5*s.*

ISSUE ROLL, MICHAELMAS, 12 HENRY IV.

9*th December.*—To divers messengers, sent twice, as well with
writs of the great seal directed to each Sheriff of England, to make
proclamation within his county, that every person who was able to
expend 40*l.* per annum beyond reprises, should by himself appear before the Council of the Lord the King, previous to the feast
of the Purification of the Blessed Mary, to receive the order of

knighthood, or to treat and agree with the said Council to pay a fine wherefore he refused to accept the order aforesaid; and also with writs under the great seal of the said Lord the King, and letters from the Treasurer of England, directed to each of the customers and keepers of all ports in England, to make search in the said ports, that not any money, coined or in mass, should be taken out or exported from the said ports, in the name of any English or foreign merchant, or other person whomsoever, without especial warrant thereupon to be obtained, and directed to the said keepers or customers; and also with letters of privy seal directed to the Archbishops, Bishops, Abbots, Priors, Dukes, Earls, and Barons, to be at Westminster on the morrow of Saint Valentine, there to assemble of the King's Council, and deliberate for the best advantage and benefit of the Lord the King and the whole kingdom. In money paid to their own hands for their wages and expenses,— 8l. 10s.

23rd March.—To Richard Cressy, sergeant and usher of the King's hall. In money paid to his own hands in discharge of 10l. 11s. 3d. which the Lord the King commanded to be paid him for so much money by him paid and applied for erecting a complete scaffold ordered for the King himself, and other persons attendant upon him during the time of the last tournament in Smithfield, there performed in the presence of the said King. By writ, &c.,—8l. 11s. 4d.

ISSUE ROLL, EASTER, 12 HENRY IV.

26th April.—To Richard Clyfford, clerk of the King's great wardrobe. In money paid him by assignment made this day, by the hands of Hugh Nettelham, his clerk, for making garters for Saint George's day last past, celebrated at Windsor. By writ, &c.,—44l.

12th May.—To Robert Rolleston, clerk of the King's works

within the palace of Westminster and Tower of London. In money paid to him by assignment made this day, for the purchase of timber, stone, and other stuff, and for the wages of carpenters, stone masons, and other workmen, for making a new gate to the King's palace at Westminster, on the west side, towards the King's highway. By writ current, &c.,—33*l.* 6*s.* 8*d.* [Subsequent payments on the 15th May, of 198*l.*, and on the 28th May, of 137*l.* 14*s.* 4*d.*, were made for the like purpose.]

23rd July.—To Sir Thomas Bromflet, knight, keeper of the King's wardrobe. In money paid to him by the hands of Thomas Rokes, his clerk, at divers times receiving the money from the fines of knights, in part payment of 1600*l.*, ordered and appointed by the Council of the said Lord the King, for one year's expenses of his household. By writ, &c.,—888*l.* 6*s.* 8*d.* [Many similar payments appear upon these Rolls.]

22nd August.—To Hugh, Lord de Burnell. In money paid him by assignment made this day, by the hands of Richard Whityngton, citizen and merchant, of London, in discharge of 100 marks which the Lord the King, with the assent of his Council, commanded to be paid him for the charges and expenses directed by him to be expended upon l'Ermyte de Foy Casyn and other Ambassadors, from France, lately sent to our Lord the King to treat upon certain affairs, viz., for the conduct of the said Ambassadors from the town of Dover to Gloucester to the King's presence there. By writ, &c.,—66*l.* 13*s.* 4*d.*

25th September.—To John Shepherd, one of the creditors of Richard Kyngeston, late keeper of the King's wardrobe. In money paid to him by the hands of Roger Broun, barber to the Lord Chancellor, in discharge of 100*s.* 6*d.* due for fruit purchased of him during the time the said Richard was late keeper of the said wardrobe, &c.,—5*l.* 0*s.* 6*d.*

23rd February.—To Lewis, Count Palatine of the Rhine, High Seneschal of the holy Roman empire and Duke of Bavaria. In money received by him from Sir John Pelham, Knight, Treasurer of England, by the hands of Frederick de Mitra, esquire, in discharge of 1000 marks which the Lord the King, with the assent of his Council, commanded to be paid to the said Duke, in part payment of 5000 marks, for payment of which the said King was bound to the same Duke by his writing obligatory, for the marriage of the Lady Blanch, eldest daughter of our said Lord the King, lately married to the same Duke, as appears by the letters of acquittance of the said Frederick, &c. By writ, &c.,—666*l.* 13*s.* 4*d.*

3rd November.—To William Byngley, the King's minstrel. In money paid to his own hands, from the Treasurer of England, upon the King's verbal command, to purchase apparel for his person,—2*l.* 6*s.* 8*d.*

15th November.—To Nicholas Frost, bowyer, Stephen Sedar, fletcher, Ralph, the stringer, and divers others of the said mysteries. In money paid to them, viz., to the aforesaid Nicholas and others of his mystery, for 500 bows,—31*l.* 5*s.*; to the aforesaid Stephen and others of his mystery, for 1700 sheaves of arrows,—148*l.* 15*s.*; and to the aforesaid Ralph and others of his mystery, for forty gross of bow strings,—12*l.*; purchased from them, and sent by the King's command to Acquitaine, for the use of the Duke of Clarence and others in his retinue, to resist the King's enemies in those parts. Also for divers vessels, barrels, and boxes, to contain the said bows, arrows, and bow strings; also for the safe carriage thereof, and for the porterage, carriage, lighterage, freightage, and small charges incurred in the business aforesaid,—32*l.* By writ, &c.,—224*l.*

23rd November.—To Thomas Bromflet, keeper of the King's wardrobe. In money paid to him by assignment made this day by the hands of Thomas Chaucers, the King's chief butler, for wine purchased of John Dorde, for the expenditure of divers foreigners, in divers embassies and messages lately sent to the King's presence, viz., as well for the Ambassadors of the Duke of Burgundy, as for John Carnyan and other Ambassadors coming to the King at Coldherber, on behalf of the said Duke, and for the Ambassadors from the Dukes of Berry, Orleans, and Bourbon, the Counts Armynak, and Lord de la Bret; and also for the Ambassadors from the Duke of Britany, lately residing at the Friars Preachers, London. By writ, &c.,—191*l.* 6*s.* 4*d.*

25th January.—To John Michel and John Drax, the King's sergeants at arms, sent by command of the Lord Treasurer to arrest a certain John Milner, a mariner of Greenwich. In money paid to him for his costs and expenses, as well for his boatage from London to Greenwich twice, and attendance to arrest the aforesaid John, as for the hire of horses for the said John to ride from London to Mortelak, and for going there twice, and once in the night time, fully to inform the Lord the King of the whole truth of certain facts in these premises, by direction of the Treasurer and Chamberlains of the Exchequer. . . .

22nd February.—To John Petit, to whom the present Lord the King, by his letters patent, granted 100*s.,* yearly to be received at the Exchequer during his life, for the good services performed, and to be performed by him, for the said Lord the King, &c.,—5*l.* 16*s.* 8*d.*

1st March.—To Robert Rolleston, clerk of the King's works. In money paid to him by the hands of Henry Somers, for repairing the inclosure and lodge of the park at Kenyngton,— 15*l.* 13*s.* 7*d.*

17th March.—To Richard Whityngton, citizen and merchant, of London. In money paid to him by assignment made this day, in discharge of 1000*l.* which he lent to the Lord the King at the receipt of the Exchequer, viz., on the second day of March last past, as appears in the Receipt Roll of that day,—1000*l.*

HENRY V.

———

ISSUE ROLL, EASTER, 1 HENRY V.ISSUE ROLL, EASTER, 1 HENRY V.

4th May.—To Robert Rolleston, clerk, appointed and ordered by our Lord the King to erect a new scaffolding for his coronation within the Abbey of Saint Peter, Westminster; also to make and construct anew certain other works, as well within the palace of Westminster, as within the Tower of London, prepared for the coronation of our said Lord the King. In money paid, &c. By writ, &c.,—26*l.* 13*s.* 4*d.*

20th May.—To William Godezer, a citizen and coppersmith, of London. In money paid to his own hands, in advance for newly devising and making an image in likeness of the mother of the present Lord the King, ornamented with divers arms of the Kings of England, and placed over the tomb of the said King's mother, within the King's college at Leicester, where the mother of the aforesaid Lord the King is buried and entombed,—43*l.*

27th June.—To John Weele, esquire. In money paid to his own hands, for the expenses of the wife of Owen Glendourdi, the wife of Edmund Mortimer, and others, their sons and daughters, in his custody in the city of London at the King's charge, by his command. By writ of privy seal,—30*l.*

4th July.—To the Lord the King in his chamber. In money paid into the said chamber by the hands of Master Richard Courtenay, receiver thereof, receiving the money from Lord Thomas, Earl of Arundell, Treasurer of England, in discharge of

Y

160*l.* which the Lord the King commanded to be paid to the said Richard for a gold head piece in shape of a man's head, ornamented with pearls and precious stones, offered by the said Lord the King, in person, at the tomb of Saint Thomas, at Canterbury.   By writ, &c.,—160*l.*

To John Berns, a goldsmith and citizen, of London. In money paid to his own hands, as well for engraving two pair of duplicate seals ordered for the principality of North and South Wales, as for the value in troy weight of 6 marks of silver, used to make the same, and for the manual labour thereof, 4*l.* ; in discharge of 10*l.* paid him for the engraving and workmanship aforesaid.   By writ, &c.,—10*l.*

7th July.—To William Gascogne, late Chief Justice of the Bench of Lord Henry, father of the present King, receiving yearly 40*l.* for his fee in the office aforesaid. In money paid to him by the hands of William Bekwyk, &c.; also to the same William, to whom the said Lord Henry, late King of England, father of the present King, by his letters patent, granted 120*l.*, yearly to be received at the Exchequer at Michaelmas and Easter terms, by equal portions, as an increase above his ancient appointed fee in the said office, that he might be able more decently to support his estate and expenses, which by reason of his office was requisite, so long as he should happen to continue in that office. In money paid to him by the hands of Robert Mauleverer, &c., —79*l.* 3*s.* 0¼*d.*

[*Note.*—The payments of the salaries and allowances to all the Judges and law officers of this period appear upon this Roll; the above payment only is selected on account of its being made to the judge who committed the King to prison when he was Prince of Wales.]

13th July.—To Richard Whityngton, citizen and merchant, of London, mayor of the staple of the town of Calais. In money paid to his own hands, for costs and divers other expenses incurred by him and his servants, in bringing Robert Ekford from York, before the Treasurer and Barons of the Exchequer, to answer upon certain causes and matters objected against him on behalf of the Lord the King, for the King's advantage. By order of the Treasurer and Barons of the Exchequer,—1*l.* 7*s.* 10*d.*

17*th July.*—To John Sewale, a messenger, sent to Thomas, Archbishop of Canterbury, with a letter from Thomas, Earl of Arundell and Surrey, Treasurer of England, directed to him, to borrow a certain sum of money for the King's use. In money paid to his own hands, &c.,—10*s.* [There are several similar letters, addressed to the Bishops and other persons, to borrow money for the King's use.]

24*th July.*—To Joan, Countess of Hereford. In money paid to her by the hands of Nicholas Neubold, in part payment of a greater sum which the Countess ought to receive from our Lord the King for her right and share of interest in a certain clasp which formerly belonged to Lewis de Clyfford, sold by the said Countess to the said Lord the King. By writ of privy seal, &c., —400*l.*

To John Oldecastell, Chevalier Richard Colfox, Walter Gayton, Thomas Berebowe, and John Andrew, executors of the will of Lewis Clyfford, chevalier, deceased. In money paid to them, in part payment of 1200 marks, due to the same executors for a clasp of gold, set with precious stones, which belonged to the aforesaid Lewis, and sold to our said Lord the King. By writ, &c.,—133*l.* 6*s.* 8*d.*

To John, the King's brother, keeper of the town of Berwick and the East Marches of Scotland. In money paid to him by assignment made this day, by the hands of John Squyr, esquire, for the wages of himself, his men at arms, and archers, dwelling with him, for the safe custody of the town and East Marches

aforesaid, from the 20th March last past.   By writ, &c.,—
1335*l*. 10*s*. 8*d*.

Issue Roll, Michaelmas, 1 Henry V.

10*th October*.—To divers messengers, sent to each county of
England, as well with writs under the great seal, to make proclamation on behalf of the King that none of his liege subjects
should harbour John Oldecastell, an approved and convicted
heretic, under penalty of forfeiting all things for doing contrary
thereto which could be forfeited to the Lord the King; and also
with other writs to cause proclamation to be made on behalf of
our Lord the King in all cities, boroughs, and counties of England,
that no one should take the goods, chattels, or victuals of any
person, without prompt payment for the same being made, as between the buyers and sellers, in such cases should be agreed upon,
(the said Lord the King and his consort only excepted).   In
money paid to them for their expenses in going, tarrying, and
returning upon the messages aforesaid.   By general writ, &c.,—
5*l*. 1*s*. 8*d*.

To Richard Threll, esquire.   In money paid to his own hands,
for the expenses of the King of Scotland, the Earl of "Fyth,"
and other prisoners within the Tower of London, being there at
the King's costs, immediately after the discharge of Robert Morley, chevalier, late keeper of the Tower aforesaid, as appears by
the parcels of the said Richard, delivered to Lord Thomas, Earl
of Arundell and Surrey, Treasurer of England, and to the Chamberlains of the Receipt of the Exchequer, remaining in the hanaper of this term,—3*l*. 17*s*.

To Joan, Queen of England.   In money paid to her by the
hands of Parnelle Broket and Nicholas Alderwych, in part payment of a greater sum due to the said Queen upon a certain pri-

vate agreement made between the said Queen and the present Lord the King; and especially concerning the marriage of the Earl of March, purchased and obtained from the said Lady the Queen by the said now Lord the King whilst he was Prince of Wales. By writ of privy seal, &c.,—100*l.*

17th October.—To John Damport, a messenger sent to the town of Calais with a certain commission of the Lord the King to proclaim a truce lately concluded between the Ambassadors as well of our King of England and France, as of the French King, at Lellyngham, to continue,—to wit, from the first day of October last past, unto the rising of the sun on the first day of June, then next following. In money paid to his own hands, for his expenses in going, tarrying, and returning upon the message aforesaid. By writ, &c.,—1*l.* 13*s.* 4*d.*

8th November.—To the Prior and Convent of Christ Church, Canterbury. In money paid to them in discharge of 10*l.* which the Lord the King commanded to be paid, of his gift, for divers banners borrowed of them, to put on the hearse, ordered to be placed within the church of the Blessed Peter, Westminster, for the exequies of Lord Richard, late King of England, by direction of the Lord the King, now lately entombed there. By writ of privy seal, &c.,—10*l.*

15th November.—To Thomas Kent and Thomas Wryght, citizens and painters of London. In money paid them in discharge of . . . which the Lord the King commanded to be paid them, as was agreed upon in gross between Thomas, Earl of Arundell, Treasurer of England, and the said Thomas and Thomas,—to wit, for making 90 banners, with entire stuff for the same, ornamented with the arms of all the kings of Christendom and other nobles of different kingdoms of the world, the price of each banner, one with the other, 16*s.* 8*d.*; and 50 "gytons," with divers arms, price of each, one with the other, 3*s.*; and . . . . . . of valances, painted with images, price of each valance, one with the other . . . placed upon and around the hearse ordered for the anniversary of Lord Henry, father of the present King, within the abbey of Christ Church, Canterbury, at the feast of the Holy Trinity last past. By writ of privy seal,—36*l.* 15*s.* 4*d.* [Further payments for the above anniversary are entered on the Roll of Easter term of this year.]

To Simon Prentot, wax chandler, of London. In money paid to his own hands, in discharge of 200*l.* which the Lord the King commanded to be paid him, as was agreed upon in the gross between the said Treasurer and Simon, viz., for a hearse to be newly made by the said Simon, and placed on the vigil of the Holy Trinity last past, in Christ Church, Canterbury, together with entire wax lights and all other preparations necessary for the said hearse ; and also for making of 120 torches to burn around the hearse, and in other places within the church aforesaid, on the night and day of the anniversary of Lord Henry, late King of England, father of the present Lord the King, buried within the church aforesaid. By writ, &c.,—100*l.*

1*st December.*—To John Rygall, a messenger of Lord Thomas, Earl of Arundell, Treasurer of England. In money paid to his own hands, at divers times, for expenses incurred by him for the carriage of iron, bow staves, and " bromstons," as well from the Tower of London, as from divers other places within the city of London, unto the house of the said earl, called Pountenayshyn, there to be safely and securely kept for the King's use. By direction of the Treasurer and Chamberlains,—5*s.* 5*d.*

To John Wyddemer, joiner, of London. In money paid to his own hands, as well for the wages and expenses of himself and his men, riding with him to Langley, to provide a bier, and other stuffs there ordered for the carriage of the body of Richard, late King of England, from thence to the abbey of the Blessed Peter, Westminster, there to be newly buried ; in part payment of 4*l.* By writ of privy seal amongst the mandates of this term,—2*l.*

[Other payments are entered on this Roll, relating to the removal and burial of the said late King Richard II.]

To Giles Thorneton, servant of the chandry of the King's household. In money paid to his own hands at different times, viz., at one time, 24*l.* 4*s.* 6*d.*; at another time, 18*l.*; at another time, 1*l.* 6*s.* 8*d.*; as well for furnishing 120 torches, newly provided, to burn by the way, around the body of Richard, late King of England, brought from Langley to Westminster, as for the carriage of the said torches to Langley aforesaid and to Saint Albans, —43*l.* 11*s.* 2*d.* [Another payment, of 22*l.*, to the brethren of Langley, is entered on this Roll on the 22nd February, upon the removal of King Richard's body from Langley to Westminster Abbey.]

To William Twyford, valet to Lord Thomas, Earl of Arundell, Treasurer of England, sent with a letter from the said Treasurer, directed to the Archbishop of Canterbury, to borrow from the said Archbishop and Prior of Christ Church, Canterbury, the banners which were provided for the anniversary of the Lord Henry, father of the present Lord the King, held at Canterbury, to be placed upon the hearse ordered at Westminster for the anniversary of the Lord Richard, late King of England, there recently entombed. In money paid to his own hands for his expenses in going, tarrying, and returning,—1*l.* 6*s.* 8*d.*

To William del Chaumbre, valet of the said Earl. In money paid to his own hands, for expenses and other charges incurred for the burial and exequies of the wife of Edward Mortimer and her daughters, buried within Saint Swithin's Church, London. By writ of privy seal amongst the mandates of this term, —1*l.*

4*th December.*—To Ralph Alienore, and John Weddesbury, valets, and John Lincoln, groom, appointed by the Lord the King to keep the parliament chamber and the chamber of the King's

Great Council. In money paid to them by the hands of the aforesaid John Weddesbury, in part payment of 100s. which the Lord
the King commanded to be paid them, viz., to each of the said Ralph
and John Weddesbury, 40s, and to the aforesaid John Lincoln, 20s.,
to have of the King's gift, for the great pains by them taken in keeping the chambers aforesaid, as well in the time of Lord Henry,
father of the present Lord the King, in his last parliament held at
Westminster, as in the parliament of the present Lord the King,
now lately held at Westminster, in like manner as hath been accustomed to be allowed from ancient time to such persons. By
writ, &c.,—4l.

To Thomas Barbour and John Broun, valets of the Earl of
Arundell. In money paid to their own hands for their expenses
and wages, and the expenses of divers other persons with them at
Westminster, as well for softening and melting the wax, now
lately ordered for the hearse at the anniversary of Lord Richard,
late King of England, kept within Westminster Abbey, as for
taking the remnant of the same wax therefrom, and safely and
securely keeping it for the King's use; which said wax was afterwards delivered to the clerk of the spicery of the Lord the King,
for the use of his household. By order of the Treasurer and
Barons of the Exchequer,—1l. 6s. 8d.

11th December.—To John Wade, chaplain of the Lord the
King. In money paid to his own hands, in discharge of 100
marks which the Lord the King commanded to be paid him, to
be distributed by direction of the said King, for the soul of Richard, late King of England, on the way by which the bones of the
said King were ordered to be carried from Langley to the abbey
of the Blessed Peter, Westminster, there to be newly interred.
By writ of privy seal, &c.,—13l. 6s. 8d.

To Oliver Martin, a Portuguese merchant. In money paid to
his own hands, in part payment of 384l. which the Lord the King
ordered to be paid him for 96 pipes of Algarve wine, price of

each pipe, 4*l.*; purchased of him for the King's use for his stock. By writ, &c.,—201*l.* 10*s.* 2*d.*

27th January.—To the Venerable Father Henry, Bishop of Winchester, Chancellor of England. In money paid to him by the hands of Nicholas Calton and John Forest, in discharge of 826*l.* 13*s.* 4*d.* which the Lord the King commanded to be paid to the said Venerable Father, in recompense of so much money by him lent to the said Lord the King whilst he was Prince of Wales. By writ, &c.,—826*l.* 13*s.* 4*d.*

To the Abbot and Convent of Saint Peter, Westminster. In money paid to him by the hands of Richard Haroughden, a monk of the abbey aforesaid, for new works done to the body of the church of Saint Peter, within the abbey aforesaid. By writ, &c.,—66*l.* 13*s.* 4*d.*

To Joan, Queen of England. In money paid to the said Queen, by the hands of Robert Okebourn, in part payment of a certain greater sum agreed upon between our said now Lord the King whilst he was Prince, and the said Queen, for the marriage of Edward, Earl of March. By writ, &c.,—100*l.*

To Robert Sapurton, the King's sergeant at arms, appointed by a commission of the Lord the King to detain certain ships, together with sufficient mariners, as well for embarking the French Ambassador, Lord le Bret, the Bishop, and others in his retinue; as also Lord le Scrop, Hugh Mortimer, Master Henry Ware, Ambassadors of our Lord the King, going with the said Ambassadors to Paris, there to confer upon certain articles of great weight intimately concerning the estate of the Lord the King. In money paid to his own hands for the wages of the masters of the ships and mariners retained by him for the voyage aforesaid,—66*l.* 13*s.* 4*d.*.

[Payments to the keepers of the beds, cloths, and great clock, within the palace of Westminster are frequently entered on the Rolls.]

To Charles of Navarre, to whom Lord Henry, late King of England, by his letters patent, granted 250 marks to be received yearly for the good services performed and to be performed by him to the same late King Henry, which said letters patent the present Lord the King confirmed on the 29th day of June last past. In money paid to him by the hands of Charles de Beaumond, his son, in part payment of the greater sum payable to him for this his allowance; viz. rateably from the aforesaid 29th of June to the last day of September then next following. By writ, &c.,— 40l.

16th February.—To Henry Botolff. In money paid to his own hands for four pair of fetters, two pair of manacles, and six pair of "cleralls," with locks for the same, purchased by the said Henry for the King's use, and sent to Thomas Erpyngham, steward of the King's household, for certain traitors lately taken at Eltham and elsewhere to be imprisoned. By direction of the Treasurer and Chamberlains of the Exchequer,— 16s. 8d.

To divers messengers, sent with writs under the great seal, directed to each Sheriff of England, to make proclamation in every city and borough within his county of the prorogation of parliament to the last day of April next happening, and then to be held at Leicester; also with writs under the same seal directed to the same sheriffs, to make proclamation within their same counties to seize Sir John Oldecastell, knight. In money paid for their expenses in going and returning, &c. By writ, &c.—7l. 1s. 8d.

In money paid to certain constables of Smithfield, for having kept a careful watch in the night time to take Sir John Oldecastell, knight, and also chiefly, for having found and seized certain books of the Lollards, in a certain house of a parchment maker, the same having been taken to our Lord the King; paid of the gift of the said Lord the King to the persons aforesaid. By writ of privy seal, &c.,—1*l.*

To John Maihewe and others, his companions, jurors, impanelled upon an inquest held for the King at Westminster, upon certain traitors and rebels against the King's person, then lately taken. In money paid by the hands of the said John in discharge of 6*l.* which the Lord the King ordered to be paid them of his gift. By writ, &c.,—6*l.*

To William Hokhust, servant of Thomas, Earl of Arundell, Treasurer of England. In money paid to him for expenses incurred within the Tower of London, upon ordering a certain breakfast for the said Treasurer, and Henry le Scrop, Lord de Roos, and the mayor of London, appointed by the King's commission with others there, to try certain traitors who lately rebelled against the person of the Lord the King, then within the Tower aforesaid, and further to do what justice in that behalf should require. By writ, &c.,—2*l.* 16*s.* 8*d.*

To John Sewalle, a messenger, sent in all possible speed with a letter of privy seal, directed to Sir Hugh Luterell, knight, upon certain matters contained therein touching the escape of John Oldecastell. In money paid, &c.,—1*l.*

To John Welde, clerk, in the office of privy seal, and to five others, his companions, directed by the Lords of the King's Council to write copies of divers truces concluded in the time of the progenitors of the said Lord the King, in order that the ambassadors of the said Lord the King, directed to go in an embassy from the said King to Paris in France, might have a more perfect inspection of the same truces. In money paid to them, viz. to each, 6*s.* 8*d.*, as an especial reward for writing the copies aforesaid. By direction of the Lords of the King's Council aforesaid, &c.,—2*l.*

19*th February.*—To John Barton, a valet of Sir Robert Morley, knight, and others his companions, for watching and searching about a house in Smythfield which belonged to William the parchment maker, in which said house John Oldecastell now lately dwelt. In money paid to their own hands in discharge of 20s., which the Lord the King commanded to be paid them as a special reward for the reason aforesaid. By direction of the Treasurer and Chamberlains,—1l.

To a certain Welshman, coming to London, and there continuing for a certain time to give information respecting the conduct and designs of "Ewain Glendourdy." In money paid to his own hands for his expenses, and as an especial reward for the cause aforesaid. By direction of the Treasurer and Chamberlains of the Exchequer,—1l.

20th February.—To John Wyddemer, joiner, of London. In money paid to his own hands in discharge of 4l., which the Lord the King commanded to be paid him for making and providing a "horsbere," a coffin [cista], and other necessary things for the carriage of the body of Richard, late King of England, from Langley to Westminster, there to be newly buried. By writ of privy seal,&c.,—2l.

To John Stevenes, of Bristoll, ordered by the Lord the King to inspect the making a great cannon at the town of Bristoll, there made for the King's use., &c. In money paid to his own hands, as well for iron, coal, and timber, purchased by him, as for divers other costs and expenses by him incurred on account of the cannon aforesaid. By writ, &c.,—107l. 10s. 8d.

To John Wyddemer, joiner. In money paid to him for a certain chest purchased of him, ordered to stand within the Receipt of the King's Exchequer, as well to contain certain truces concluded between the Kings of England and divers other Kings at different times on either side, as for memoranda and other evidences to be put in the said chest for their safe custody, for the King's advantage, and benefit of his realm. By direction of the Treasurer and Chamberlains of the Exchequer,—13s. 4d.

22nd February.—In money paid for so much money in gold delivered from the pix, within the Tower, for an assay made in the presence of the Earl of Arundell, Treasurer of England, and the Barons of the Exchequer, which said assay, after it had been melted in the fire, remained within the bag at the Exchequer.

To William Warde and John Thorlethorp, jointly appointed by a late commission of our Lord the King, under the great seal, to hear and determine all matters of account whatsoever, of all receivers, bailiffs, reeves, and other officers whomsoever, belonging and appertaining to, and within the duchy of Cornwall. In money paid to their own hands in discharge of 60*s.* which the said Lord the King commanded to be paid them for their wages; each of them receiving 5*s.* per day,—3*l.*

To Thomas Burton, the King's spy. In money paid to his own hands in discharge of 100*s.*, which the Lord the King ordered to be paid to the said Thomas of his gift, and as an especial reward for the great pains and diligence exercised by him, for his attentive watchfulness to the operations of the Lollards, now lately rebellious, also because he fully certified their intentions to our said Lord the King for his advantage. By writ, &c.—5*l.* [This Roll contains payments for writs of general pardon to all Lollards, excepting those only specially named in such writs, together with many other particulars relating to the Lollards.]

ISSUE ROLL, EASTER, 2 HENRY V.

16th April.—To Sir William Neuport, knight, constable of Beaumarey's Castle. In money paid to him, by the hands of Thomas Barneby, for the wages of himself, his men at arms, and archers dwelling with him for the protection and safe custody of the castle aforesaid. By writ, &c.,—40*l.*

16th July.—To Sir Walter Hungerford, knight, sent as the

King's ambassador to the King of Hungary the Emperor, upon
certain especial matters intimately affecting our said Lord the
King. In money paid to his own hands for his passage and re-
passage by sea, in going and returning upon the embassy aforesaid.
By writ, &c.,—5*l.* [Master Simon Sydenham, Doctor in Laws,
Sir Hertank Van Clux, and John Waterton, Esquire, were sent
upon the same embassy.]

To Master John Kyngton, a monk. In money paid to him in
discharge of 5 marks, which the Lord the King commanded to be
paid him, of his especial grace, to have of his gift for expenses
incurred by him in coming from Canterbury into the King's presence, at Westminster, by his command, to give information upon
certain causes and matters, required by our said Lord the King
and his counsel touching certain truces made between Lord Henry,
late King of England, and Prusia, &c. By writ, &c.,—3*l.* 6*s.* 8*d.*

19*th July.*—To the P.ior and Convent of the order of
Preachers, in the University of Oxford, to whom the present
Lord the King, on the 28th of November, by his letters patent,
in the 1st year of his reign, granted 50 marks yearly, &c., to be
received so long as the King should please to support the doctrine
of the Catholic faith in the university aforesaid. In money paid
to them, by the hands of brother John Lambe, in discharge of 25
marks, paid of the King's alms, &c.,—16*l.* 13*s.* 4*d.* [A payment is also made to the same order in the University of Cambridge there to support the same doctrine of the Catholic faith.]

To Thomas, Duke of Clarence. In money paid to him, by the
hands of William Glym, clerk,—150*l.*, and by the hands of Sir
William Bowes, knight—100*l.* ; in advance upon a certain yearly
allowance of 500*l.* granted to the same Duke and Margaret his
wife, &c.,—250*l.*

To John Leventhorp, one of the executors named in the will of
Lord Henry, late King of England, father of the present Lord the

King, together with the venerable fathers Henry, Archbishop of York, and Thomas, Bishop of Durham, John Pelham, and Robert Waterton. In money paid to their own hands in part payment of 25,000 marks, granted and assigned to the aforesaid executors by the King for goods and chattels of the said King's father, now retained in the King's possession. By writ current of the great seal,—4000*l.*

To John Lord de Furnivall, the King's deputy in Ireland. In money paid him for the wages of himself, his men at arms, and archers remaining with him for the protection and safe custody of the land aforesaid,—100*l.*

To William Soper, of the town of Southampton. In money paid to his own hands at divers times; viz. at one time, 60*l.*, at another time, 28*l.* 4*s.* 2*d.*, at another 108*l.*, at a fourth time 300*l.*, for building the King's great ship called the "Holigost," which was lately built at Southampton,—496*l.* 4*s.* 2*d.* [There are several payments on the Rolls for building this and other ships.]

ISSUE ROLL, MICHAELMAS, 2 HENRY V.

27th October.—To Richard Beauchamp, Earl of Warwick, sent as the King's ambassador to the general council held at Constance before our Lord the Pope, the Emperor, and others there assembled for the salvation of Christian souls; also for certain other causes concerning our said Lord the King with respect to the said Emperor. In money paid to him, by the hands of John Shirley, his esquire, for his wages in going and returning upon the embassy aforesaid. By writ, &c.,—333*l.* 6*s.* 8*d.* [*Note.* This Roll also contains payments to other persons accompanying the said Earl of Warwick upon the same embassy; viz. to Henry Lord Fitz Hugh,—200*l.*; Sir Walter Hungerford,—100*l.*; Master John Honyngham, Doctor in Laws,—100*l.*; and Sir Ralph Rocheford, —100*l.*]

30th October.—To Richard Beston, clerk. In money paid to his own hands, at twice, for the expenses of Copin de Viesville, ambassador from the Duke of Burgundy, then in the city of London at the King's charges,—40*l.*

To William Hokhirst, clerk to Lord Thomas, Earl of Arundell and Surrey, Treasurer of England. In money paid to his own hands for the expenses of the Chancellor, Treasurer, Lords of the Council, Justices, and other officers of the King's Court, dining one day at Westminster at the King's cost, there attending in the Exchequer Chamber of the Lord the King for the election of sheriffs and escheators for each county of England; also to certify and deliver to the Lord the King the names of those persons so elected according to custom, for his advice to be taken thereon. By direction of the Treasurer and Chamberlains, &c.,—7*l.* 11*s.* 10*d.*

To Nicholas Merbury, esquire. In money paid to his own hands for forming 10,000 stones for guns for the King's use, and for the carriage thereof to London,—66*l.* 13*s.* 4*d.*

3rd November.—To Thomas Beauforth, Earl of Dorset, sent as the King's ambassador to Paris, in France, to treat and confer with the King of France upon certain business, and secret affairs affecting our said Lord the King, and especially concerning the benefit of his kingdom. In money paid to him, by the hands of John Burton, his servant, for his wages, passage, and re-passage at sea in going and returning upon the embassy aforesaid,—166*l.* 13*s.* 4*d.* [Further payments appear upon the Roll of Easter Term, anno 2°, for the same embassy; viz. to Thomas, Bishop of Durham, and Richard, Bishop of Norwich, each 166*l.* 13*s.* 4*d.*; to Richard Lord Grey of Codnore,—100*l.*; to Sir William Bouchier, Sir John Philipp, and Master Philip Morgan, Clerk, Doctor in Laws,—50*l.* each; to Master Richard Holme, a licentiate in laws, William Porter, esquire, &c.]

3rd December.—To Elizabeth Whittewell, to whom Lord

Richard the Second, late King of England, of his especial grace, and with the assent of his Council, in consideration of the good services which the said Elizabeth bestowed upon his consort the late Queen of England, by his letters patent granted her 10*l.* yearly for life to be received, &c., which said letters the present King hath confirmed. In money, &c. By writ, &c.,—3*l.* 6*s.* 8*d.*

5th December.—To Richard of York, son of Edward, late Duke of York, to whom Lord Richard, late King of England, by his letters patent, gave and granted 350 marks, yearly to be received during the term of his life, at the Exchequer, at the usual terms, by equal portions, above the 100*l.* which he receives yearly for term of his life, from the aforesaid King, out of the issues of the county of York, by the hands of the Sheriff there for the time being, by virtue of a grant thereof made to him after the death of his most dear aunt, the late Duchess of York, until the said late King should provide the said Richard, his young relative, with the sum of 500 marks in lands, rents, or in marriage for his competent estate, &c., which said letters the present King confirmed on the 13th day of June, in the first year of his reign. In money paid, &c. By writ, &c.,—284*l.* 19*s.* 1*d.*

To Stephen Patryngton, the King's Confessor, to whom the said Lord the King, by his letters patent, granted for the support of himself, his companion and servants dwelling in the King's household, and for four horses and a hack, 3*s.* per day, amounting to, &c.; also for four grooms to look after the said horses, each receiving 1½*d.* per day, amounting to, &c.; and also for small necessary expenses 116*s.* yearly, amounting in all to 69*l.* 10*s.* 6*d.* yearly. In money paid, &c. By writ, &c.,—34*l.* 15*s.* 3*d.*

4th February.—To Edward, Duke of York, son and heir of Edward, late Duke of York, to which said Edward, then Earl of Cambridge, and to the heirs male of his body issuing, the Lord King Edward, great grandfather of the present Lord the King, by his letters patent, granted 1000 marks to be received yearly at the

z

Exchequer of the said great grandfather, &c., to have and to hold until the said Earl and his heirs male should have manors, lands, &c. (besides the manors of Foderyngey and Ansty, and other manors with the appurtenances, which were granted to the Earl the father and to the said Edward the son in the time of Kings Richard, and Henry father of the present Lord the King, &c.) in lieu of the 1000 marks aforesaid, as appears, &c., in part payment thereof, &c., but deducting 94*l.* 8*s.* 9½*d.* paid to Henry Lord le Scrop and Joan, his wife, late wife of Edward, late Duke of York, father of the said Edward, being a third part belonging to the said Henry and Joan for the dower of the said Joan, &c., which letters patent the present Lord the King hath ratified and confirmed. In money paid, &c. By writ, &c.,—66*l.* 13*s.* 4*d.*

To William Soper, of the town of Southampton. In money paid to him, by the hands of Robert Broun, carver, for the purchase of timber, and making a swan and an antelope for the King's new great ship, called the "Holigost," lately built at Southampton, paid at twice; viz. at one time, 40*s.*, and at another time 4 marks —4*l.* 13*s.* 4*d.*

20th February.—To John Horn, a citizen and fishmonger of London, to whom the present Lord the King, of his especial grace, commanded 100 marks to be paid, because, during the time that the said Lord the King was Prince, certain ships of the said John, laden with provisions, were at that period arrested in the Prince's name for victualling the Lords de Talbot and Furnivale and their men lying siege to the castle of Hardelagh; and after the arrival of the said John with the ships at the siege aforesaid, he there delivered part of the said provisions for relief of the aforesaid lords and men, and afterwards the Welsh rebels lying in ambush took as well the said John as his ships and money so received for the sale of the said provisions, as also the residue of the victuals aforesaid remaining unsold, and imprisoned the said John until he paid a fine of 20 marks to the said rebels for his ransom. In money paid to his own hands, receiving the money in several bonds of divers English merchants, in discharge of 100 marks aforesaid, which the said Lord the King commanded to be paid him for the reasons aforesaid. By writ, &c.,—66*l.* 13*s.* 4*d.*

20th February.—To William Soper, of the town of Southampton. In money paid to him, by the hands of William Stone, for painting the King's great ship lately built at Southampton; viz. with swans and antelopes and divers arms, also with the royal motto called "une sanz pluis" in divers parts of the said ship, —7*l.* 6*s.* 8*d.*

26th February.—To Richard Dewe, one of the Ushers of the Exchequer. In money paid to him for so much money paid for divers expenses incurred for the carriage of 21 sarplars of wool, lately forfeited at Newcastle; viz. from the King's palace at Westminster into the hall thereof, and from thence to a certain house of the staple near Westminster. By order of the Treasurer and Barons of the Exchequer,—13*s.* 4*d.*

26th February.—To Roger Castell, esquire. In money paid to his own hands, for the carriage of 250 " waynscotes and regale," therewith to make doors, windows, and other works, to a chamber in the water under Kyllynworth Castle, —6*l.* 13*s.* 4*d.*

27th February.—To John Wilcotes, esquire, receiver general of the duchy of Cornwall. In money paid to his own hands, receiving the money in his own name, in discharge of 100*l.* which the Lord the King commanded to be paid to the said John, to be received of his gift, as a special reward for the great costs and expenses incurred by him for the safe conduct of the King's money, received by him from the duchy aforesaid, taken to Westminster, and there delivered into the receipt of the said King. By order of the Treasurer and Chamberlains of the Exchequer,— 100*l.*

To William Randolf, a citizen and goldsmith, of London. In

money paid to his own hands, at different times, as well for
making twelve new dishes of pure gold, as for four dozen chargers
of silver, and eight dozen silver dishes for the King's use,—
976*l.* 0*s.* 10½*d.*

To Richard Cliderowe and Reginald Curteys, esquires, ordered
by the Lord the King to go to Seland and Holand, to treat, as
well with the Duke of Holand, as with other persons of those
parts, to provide ships for the King's present voyage in person,
to accompany him abroad. In money paid to them by the hands of
Thomas Burton, citizen and grocer, of London, &c., therewith to
pay divers masters and mariners of the ships aforesaid, &c.,—
2000*l.*

ISSUE ROLL, EASTER, 3 HENRY V.

11*th April.*—To the Prior and Convent of Mountegrace. In
money paid to them by the hands of the said Prior, in discharge
of 100*l.* which the present Lord the King commanded to be paid
to the said Prior and Convent, to have of his gift, in part payment
of a greater sum granted by the King to them for certain books
and other things ordered by them for their abbey of Shene, now
lately ordered to be provided there by the said Lord the King.
By writ, &c.,—100*l.*

19*th April.*—To William Hokhyrst. In money paid to his
own hands, for costs and expenses incurred by him for a certain repast made within the palace of Westminster to the Duke
of Clarence and other lords dining there, for their advice to be
had respecting the King's present voyage to Herfleu and Normandy. By writ, &c.,—23*l.* 12*s.* 1½*d.*

18*th May.*—To Sir William Bourghchier, knight, lately sent in
the King's embassy to Paris, in France, in the retinue of the
Bishops of Durham and Norwich, and Earl of Dorset, to confer

and treat with the French King upon certain secret articles and matters concerning our said Lord the King, and especially touching the benefit of his kingdom. In money paid to his own hands, &c., for his costs and expenses, &c., from the 10th of December, in the second year, unto the 13th March then next following, for his passage, &c. By writ, &c.,—50*l.*

To John Copelston, junior, and divers other persons coming from the county of Devon to London with a certain sum of 573*l.* 6*s.* 8*d.*, borrowed from the Dean and Chapter of the cathedral church of Exeter; the Mayor of the town of Exeter; the Abbot of Tavystok; the Prior of Lanceton; the Abbot of Bukfast; Robert Gary Prior of Plymton; Alexander Chambernoun Mayor of the town of Plymouth; John Bonell, and John Copelston. In money paid to the aforesaid John Copelston, junior, and his companions, for the safe conduct of certain of the King's jewels, valued at 800*l.*, delivered to the aforesaid persons as security for the said sums borrowed of them under conditions contained in certain indentures made between our Lord the King and the said John and his companions, &c. By writ, &c.,—10*l.*

ISSUE ROLL, MICHAELMAS, 3 HENRY V.

4th October.—To Richard Norton, a messenger, sent with the greatest speed with a certain commission of the Lord the King, under his great seal, directed to the Constable of Dover Castle and Warden of the Cinque Ports, or his deputy there, relating to certain pressing and urgent affairs chiefly concerning certain matters for the honour of the kingdom of England and the advantage and benefit thereof; strictly enjoining and commanding the said constable and warden that, on seeing the aforesaid commission, they personally go to the Cinque Ports aforesaid, and other places adjoining the said ports, where fishermen commonly reside and dwell, and strongly enjoin and command all and singular the fishermen of the ports and places aforesaid, according to their numbers, to be chosen on behalf of the King, without delay to proceed to the town of Harfleu with their boats and other vessels, and with their nets, tackle, and other things, necessary to fish upon the Norman coast, near the town aforesaid, for support of the King's army there. In money paid to their own hands, &c. By writ, &c.,—1*l.*

15*th October.*—To divers messengers, sent with great speed to all and singular the counties of England, as well with commissions as writs under the great seal of the Lord the King, directed to the Archbishops, Bishops, Abbots, Priors, Earls, Barons, and Sheriffs of the counties aforesaid, for the prorogation of parliament unto the morrow of All Souls next happening, then to be holden at Westminster, before Lord John, Duke of Bedford, Keeper of England, in the absence of our Lord the King beyond seas. In money paid to them, &c. By writ, &c.,—6*l.* 5*s.*

To Nicholas Mandit, the King's sergeant at arms, appointed by a commission under the King's great seal, to arrest John Foxholes, Thomas Blase, and others named in the said commission, lately residing with Lord Henry le Scrop, of Masham, a traitor against the King, and safely and securely to bring them to London, there to answer before the Council of the Lord the King, upon certain matters objected against them on behalf of the said King's Council during his absence. In money paid to him, &c. By writ, &c.,—2*l.* 13*s.* 4*d.*

To Master Robert Benham, sent to the town of Calais with divers medicines, ordered as well for the health of the King's person, as for others of his army who went with him. In money paid to him, &c.,—10*l.*

28*th October.*—To Thomas, Duke of Clarence, the present King's brother, to whom the Lord the King, on the 14th July, in the first year of his reign, by letters patent, granted 2000 marks yearly, to him and the heirs male of his body, to be received, &c. And Lord Henry, late King of England, father of our said now Lord the King, of his certain knowledge, by his letters patent, granted to the said Thomas, and Margaret his wife, the custody of all castles, lordships, parks, manors, lands, &c., which belonged to John, late Earl of Somerset, deceased, which were held of the said Lord the King, the father, in capite, on the day he died, and which, by the death of the said Earl, by reason of the minority of Henry, son and heir of the said Earl, came to the hands of the said King the father; and by a certain inquisition taken before William Nutborne, late escheator to the said King's father, in the county of Middlesex, on the 28th day of June, anno 11, Henry IV., and returned into chancery, &c., it was found that the aforesaid late Earl died on Palm Sunday, then last past, possessed of 500*l.*, yearly to be received at the Exchequer, to hold to him and the heirs male of his body, by letters patent of the said King's father, &c., which letters patent to the said Thomas and Margaret the present Lord the King confirmed. In money paid to the said Duke, by assignment made this day, &c. By writ, &c.,—666*l.* 13*s.* 4*d.*

30th October.—To a certain Bishop and Knight, who lately arrived from the King of Denmark, upon a message to our Lord the King from their King aforesaid. In money paid to their own hands, for the price of two silver gilt cups and two ewers, which belonged to Henry, Lord le Scrop, forfeited to the King, and delivered to the said Bishop and Knight of the King's gift, upon their departure home. By writ, &c.

14th December.—To Sir John Pelham, knight, to whom the present Lord the King, on the 22nd February last past, committed the custody and governance of James, King of Scotland, during the pleasure of the said King; and in consideration thereof there was granted yearly, by letters patent, &c., to the said John, 700*l.*, yearly for support of the said King in food, clothing, and other necessary things, incumbent for him, so long as the said John should have the custody and governance of the said King, at certain places

.which between the King's Council and the aforesaid John should be agreed upon. In money paid to him by assignment made this day, in discharge of 421*l.* 2*s.* 11½*d.*, paid for this his allowance, as well rateably from the aforesaid 22nd February last past, unto the last day of March next following, for 37 days, the last but not the first day included, as for the terms of the Nativity, Saint John the Baptist, and Saint Michael, last past. By writ, &c.,—421*l.* 2*s.* 11½*d.*

20th December.—To William Loveneye, esquire, ordered and appointed by the Lord the King to provide for the charges and expenses of the household of the Dukes of Orleans and Bourbon, and of other Earls and Lords, the King's French prisoners, continuing for a time at Windsor. In money paid to his own hands, in advance for the costs and expenses of the Dukes, Earls, and Lords aforesaid,—26*l.* 13*s.* 4*d.* [There are further payments entered on this Roll, made on account of the abovenamed and other prisoners taken at the battle of Agincourt.]

23rd December.—To Sir William Bourchier, knight, ordered and appointed by the Lord the King for the support of George de Clere and three Barons, his companions, and thirteen knights, the King's prisoners, lately taken at Herfleu, then in his custody within the Tower of London, at the King's costs. In money paid to him in advance, by the hands of Sir Roger Aston, knight, by agreement made with him at 1*l.* 6*s.* 8*d.* per day, for the expenses of the same prisoners,—14*l.* 13*s.* 4*d.*

10th January.—To the Lord the King, in his chamber. In money paid to his said chamber, by the hands of Sir John Rothenale, knight, paying the money from the fifteenths and tenths, in discharge of 1000 marks which the said Lord the King commanded to be paid into his chamber, in order to make a payment to Sir John Greye, knight, in part satisfaction of a larger sum granted by the King to the said Sir John Greye, for the ransom of the Count de Ewe, lately taken at Agincourt, and sold to the

Lord the King by the said Sir John. By writ of privy seal,
&c.,—666*l.* 13*s.* 4*d.*

29*th February.*—To the Agincourt herald, sent with letters of
privy seal from the Lord the King, directed to the Emperor, the
Duke of Bavaria, and other Dukes, Earls, and Lords, in foreign
parts, to announce to the said Lords certain matters and affairs
intimately concerning our said Lord the King. In money paid to
his own hands, for his expenses, &c. By writ, &c.,—16*l.* 13*s.* 4*d.*
[Also a payment of 23*l.* 6*s.* 8*d.* to Gloucester herald, sent to the
Kings of Castile, Leon, Portugal, and Navarre, upon the like
important affairs.]

To Thomas Barnaby, Treasurer of the town of Harfleu. In
money paid to his own hands, out of the money arising from the
second fifteenths and tenths granted by the laity to the King in
the second year of his reign, for the wages and rewards of the
captains, bannerets, knights, and men at arms; also for the wages
of the gunners, archers, masons, carpenters, and labourers, constantly remaining there for the safe custody of the town aforesaid,
reparation of the walls, and making rebuildings there. By writ of
privy seal, &c.,—4892*l.* 2*s.*

18*th March.*—To Sir William Bourchier, knight, Constable of
the King's Tower of London. In money paid to him by the
hands of Sir Roger Aston, knight, his deputy, as well for the expenses of the King of Scotland, as for seventeen of the King's
prisoners, lately taken at Harfleu, in France, and committed to
the custody of the said constable, viz., the aforesaid seventeen
prisoners, from the 18th of December last past, and the aforesaid King of Scotland from the 28th of January, then next
following; receiving for the aforesaid King of Scotland, 13*s.* 4*d.*,
and for the aforesaid seventeen prisoners, 1*l.* 6*s.* 8*d.* per day, by
agreement made with him for the King's advantage, so long as
he should have the custody of the prisoners aforesaid,—
106*l.* 13*s.* 4*d.*

30th April.—To Edward Courteney, son of the Earl of Devon,
retained for a quarter of a year to attend our Lord the King, and
serve him at sea, for the protection thereof, and defence of the
realm of England. In money paid to him by the hands of
Robert Carey, esquire, out of the money arising from the second
fifteenths and tenths, for the wages of the said Edward, his five
knights, 343 men at arms, and 700 archers, retained for forty
days by the said Edward, to serve the King at sea for the purpose
aforesaid, during the said period. By writ, &c.,—1416*l.* [Pay-
ments were also made to John, Earl of Huntingdon, John, Lord
Clifford, and others employed upon the same service.]

27th May.—To several messengers sent with divers writs, under
the King's great seal, directed to each Sheriff of England, to make
proclamation in divers places within their counties, at which to
them it should seem most fit, for proroguing the truce lately concluded between the Lord the King and the powers of Flanders;
and also that all knights, esquires, and valets of the King's retinue,
should appear at Westminster on a certain day specified in the
same writs, with their best preparations, to go with our Lord the
King upon his next voyage to sea, to be made by him in person.
In money paid them for their costs, &c.,—4*l.* 6*s.* 8*d.*

5th June.—To Simon Flete, esquire, keeper of the King's private wardrobe within the Tower of London. In money paid him
by the hands of William Wodeward, founder, for the purchase
and providing of cannon and gunpowder and other stuffs for the
King's voyage at sea, &c.,—40*l.*

[This Roll also contains several payments for guns, gunpowder,
and other preparations for the King's voyage at this period; and
also payments for the Emperor Sigismund and Duke of Holand,
with their retinue, at Westminster, and for the Emperor's household,
removing from Westminster to Leeds, whilst visiting England.]

27th June.—To Henry Bromley, one of the King's sergeants at arms, ordered by the King's Council to detain shipping for the passage of the noble Earl of Hungarie and other lords of the retinue of the Emperor, sufficient to accompany the said Emperor to France, proceeding there upon divers private affairs to be declared to the King of France, on behalf of the said Emperor. In money paid to his own hands, for his costs and expenses in going, tarrying, and returning, &c.,—1*l.*

23rd July.—To divers messengers sent to each county of England with writs under the great seal of the Lord the King, directed to each Sheriff in the counties aforesaid, to make proclamation that all knights, esquires, valets, and other persons of the King's retinue, should repair to Dover before the 18th August next happening, to accompany the Lord the King with their best equipment to Calais, upon certain causes, especially concerning the said Lord the King and the whole commonalty of his kingdom. In money paid, &c.,—4*l.* 16*s.* 8*d.*

29th July.—To our Lord the King, in his chamber. In money paid into the same chamber by the hands of John Broune and John Burnham, for costs incurred for the carriage of tents, ornamented with gold and cloth of arras, with hangings and sides of arras, and other their appurtenances whatsoever, for our said Lord the King and the Emperor to dwell in at Calais, during the time of their stay there,—20*l.*

To Richard, Earl of Warwick, sent as the King's Ambassador to the Duke of Burgundy, to treat with him upon certain secret affairs concerning our Lord the King and good of his whole realm. In money paid to him by the hands of John Botissham, rector of Hanslape, his receiver, &c., for his wages and passage by sea in the embassy aforesaid. By writ, &c.,—40*l.* [John Waterton and John Burghop were also sent in this embassy.]

29th July.—To Master Raymund Banneret, clerk, from the city of Burgundy, coming, on behalf of the authorities of the same city, to the King's presence, to make a declaration to the said Lord the King concerning the state and government of the said city and the country adjacent. In money paid to his own hands by the King's oral command, to have of his gift, for the labour, costs, and expenses incurred and sustained by him in coming to the King's presence upon the business aforesaid,—16*l.* 13*s.* 4*d.*

10*th August.*—To Sir John Rothenale, knight, keeper of the King's wardrobe. In money paid to him, arising from the fifteenths and tenths, viz., by the hands of John Feriby, receiving the money from a certain attorney of the Lord de Talbot, dwelling in Grayes Inn, at the house of the Treasurer of England, for the expenses of the household of the Emperor whilst at Eltham. By writ, &c.,—200*l.*

In money paid for a pair of large "trussying cofers," bound with iron, purchased by command of the Lord Treasurer, to take in them 4000*l.* from London to Calais to the King's presence, to make divers payments there for the benefit of the King and his kingdom. By general writ, &c.,—8*s.*

3*rd September.*—To John Burgh, clerk to the Treasurer of England. In money paid to his own hands, as well for his wages, being sent by the Treasurer's command, and advice of the King's Council, from London to Sandwich, with a certain sum of money, there to be delivered to certain masters and sailors retained by the Lord the King, as well for the embarkation of himself and retinue to Calais, as for embarking and safe conduct of the Emperor to " Durdraught," and for going, tarrying, and returning in eighteen days, on the business aforesaid, receiving 10*s.* per day; also for the hire of horses and divers archers, to ride with him for the safe conduct of the aforesaid money, in the said journey,—11*l.* 5*s.* 4*d.*

ISSUE ROLL, MICHAELMAS, 4 HENRY V.

14*th December.*—To Thomas Henlemsted, of Southwerk, " dyker." In money paid to his own hands in advance upon covenants, contained in a certain indenture made between our Lord the King and the aforesaid Thomas, to pay him 800*l*., under certain conditions expressed in the same and agreed upon for the removal, clearing, and taking away a mound, and for making a foss without the walls of the King's town of Herfleu.   By writ, &c.,—200*l*.

18*th January.*—To John Damport and Thomas de la Howe, messengers, sent to divers counties of England, with writs under the King's great seal, directed to the Sheriffs of the counties afore-said, to cause proclamation to be made to arrest and take the body of Sir John Oldecastell, knight, wheresoever he might be found, and safely bring him to the King's presence, under certain rewards contained in the said writs.   In money paid to them, &c.,—2*l*.

14*th March.*—To Robert Berd Clerk, surveyor for the building a certain great ship for the King called the Gracedieu, newly built at Southampton.   In money paid to him, by assignment made the 20th of February last past, in advance for building the ship afore-said,—500*l*.

ISSUE ROLL, EASTER, 5 HENRY V.

21*st April.*—To Thomas, Duke of Clarence, the present King's brother, to whom the said now Lord the King and Lord Henry, late King of England, his father, by their divers letters patent, granted 1846*l*. 13*s*. 4*d*. yearly to be received at the Exchequer, &c.   In money paid in part of the said allowance, &c.,—178*l*. 1*s*.

To John, Duke of Bedford, the present King's brother, to whom the said Lord the King, of his especial grace, and in recompense of the lands, tenements, and possessions of the inheritance of Percy, which the said Duke lately held, and which he restored to Henry de Percy for 3000 marks yearly to be received by him and his heirs male; viz. 1000 marks thereof at the King's Exchequer, and 2000 marks at the receipt of the duchy of Cornwall, &c., until the said Duke should be recompensed with other lands, lordships, or possessions, to the true yearly value of the said 3000 marks, &c. In money paid in part payment, &c.,—334*l.* 6*s.* 8*d.*

To Humphrey, Duke of Gloucester, brother of the present King, to whom the said King, by his letters patent, granted yearly, to him and the heirs male of his body issuing, &c., 500 marks, to be received at the Exchequer, &c. In money paid in part payment, &c.—166*l.* 13*s.* 4*d.*

To William Houswyf, of the county of Leicester, to the men of the town of Nottingham, William Garton, of Lutrerworth in the county of Leicester, John Burton, parson of the church of Norton, in the same county of Leicester, Sir Thomas Dymmok, knight, and others of the county of Lincoln, John Darell [and many others.] In money paid to them, by divers assignments made this day, in discharge of 503*l.* 13*s.* 4*d.* which they had lent to the King at the Exchequer, &c.,—503*l.* 13*s.* 4*d.*

29*th April*.—In money paid to divers labourers for carrying three coffers with the muniments of Henry le Scrop, late Lord of Masham, forfeited to the King, from the Receipt of the Exchequer to the King's Treasury within the abbey of Westminster, there to be safely kept, by agreement made with them in gross for their labour,—2*s.*

12*th May*.—To our Lord the King in his chamber. In money paid into his said chamber out of the money arising from the finances of the Earl of Vendom, by the hands of Lord de la Barde, for certain lands and tenements purchased of him in Acquitaine for our Lord the King, for the expenses of his chamber aforesaid,—1000*l.*

25th May.—To two knights from "Ducheland," residing with the Emperor at Constaunce. In money paid to them, by the hands of Sir John Tiptot, knight, by the King's verbal command, to hold of his gift,—90*l.*

30th June.—To Henry Botolff, a messenger, sent from London to Southampton with a letter from the mayor of the city of London, directed to William Kynwolmerssh, then being there, directing him to certify concerning the state of certain ships in the river Thames for their safe conduct to the port of Southampton, for fear of the enemy who had assembled in numbers at sea. In money paid to his own hands for his costs and expenses, and hire of horses, sent with the greatest speed upon the message aforesaid,—10*s.*

15th July.—To Gerard Spronge, esquire. In money paid to his own hands, received from Robert Whitegreve at Southampton, in part payment of 470*l.* 7*s.* 5*d.*, due to him upon an account rendered at the Exchequer of Accounts, as well for divers sums of money by him received in the King's chamber as at the Receipt of the Exchequer, and elsewhere, for making of divers cannon and carriages for the same, with other necessary things for their conveyance, as for divers carriages for cannons, arblasters, and other things, as is fully contained in his account aforesaid. By writ, &c.,—76*l.* 14*s.*

To our Lord the King in his chamber. In money paid into his chamber by the hands of John Broune, received from Robert Whitegreve, at the time of the King's passage to France, for the expenses of his chamber aforesaid,—2666*l.* 13*s.* 4*d.*

To Sir John Rothenale, knight, the King's Treasurer at War. In money paid to him, viz., by the hands of John Turburbury, 93*l.* 15*s.* for the wages of sixteen miners, and by the hands of

Peter Lowart, esquire, 20*l.* for the wages of himself and his men, retained by the King for his voyage aforesaid. By writ, &c.,— 112*l.* 15*s.*

To Sir Nicholas Montgomery, knight. In money paid to his own hands, received from the aforesaid Robert Whitegreve, in advance for the safe conduct of the Duke of Bourbon, the King's prisoner, from Portchester to Somerton Castle, there to be securely kept,—10*l.* 13*s.* 4*d.*

To Sir John Rothenale, knight, the King's Treasurer at War. In money paid to him, by the hands of Conus, a goldsmith, for the wages of divers miners from Lieges, retained by our Lord the King for his voyage aforesaid. By writ, &c.,—20*l.*

ISSUE ROLL, MICHAELMAS, 5 HENRY V.

21st October.—To different messengers, sent to divers counties of England with commissions of the Lord the King, directed to the knights and esquires of the counties aforesaid, to prepare and assemble together divers men at arms and archers to resist the evil of the insurrection in Scotland, and to make war with them if it should be necessary, also to muster together, as often as required, for the cause aforesaid, &c. In money paid for their costs and expenses, &c.,—2*l.* 13*s.* 4*d.*

To William Wykeham, one of the sergeants of the Sheriff of Southampton, to which said Sheriff it was strictly commanded, by divers writs from the King, that he should take Richard Wyche and William Broune, chaplains, if they could be found within his bailwick, and safely conduct them to the King's Council at Westminster, to make disclosures to them concerning certain sums of money that belonged to Sir John Oldecastell, knight, forfeited to the King. In money paid to the said William

Wykeham for his costs and expenses, incurred as well in searching for and obtaining knowledge of their persons, as for capturing
and safely bringing them to Westminster. By writ, &c.,—1*l.* 10*s.*

4th November.—To John Darell, esquire. In money paid to
him, by assignment made this day, as an especial reward for his
labour, costs, and expenses incurred whilst he was the King's
escheator in the county of Kent, sometimes riding with twenty
and sometimes thirty horsemen, for fear of the soldiers and
others malefactors adhering to, and obstinately favouring John
Oldecastell, as well to seize the lands, tenements, goods, and
chattels of the said John Oldecastell as to deliver such goods and
chattels, &c., according to the King's command, &c., —6*l.* 13*s.* 4*d.*

10th November.—To the venerable Father in Christ the Bishop
of Saint David's, the King's Confessor. In money paid to him,
by assignment made this day, for the hire of divers ships, boats,
and passage boats, for the passage of himself and family by sea to
Normandy, to the King's presence there,—34*l.* 18*s.*

15th November.—To John Rothenhale, keeper of the King's
wardrobe. In money paid to him, by assignment made this day,
by the hands of John Hotoft, esquire, for wine purchased by
Thomas Chaucere, the King's chief butler, and sent to Pountfret
for the use of the Dukes of Orleans and Bourbon, and others the
King's French prisoners there. By writ, &c.,—20*l.* 14*s.*

23rd November.—To Sir John Rothenhale, knight, keeper of
the King's wardrobe. In money paid to him, by the hands of
John Chaddesden, for the purchase of divers "hokes and croches"
to ornament the King's chapel at Cane in Normandy. By writ,
&c.,—1*l.* 6*s.* 8*d.*

1st February.—To Robert Leversegge, clerk, for making, by
the King's advice, divers purchases and provisions for the wardrobe, &c. In money paid to him, by the hands of Thomas

2 A

Stanes, viz., at one time, 100*l.*, a second time, 40*l.*, and a third time by bond, 81*l.* 3*s.* 4*d.*, for the purchase of cloth for the King's army in Normandy; by the hands of John Cavendyssh, citizen and embroiderer of London,—10*l.*, to purchase garters for the livery of the knights of the garter at the feast of Saint George then next happening, to be celebrated in Normandy,—231*l.* 3*s.* 4*d.*

3rd March.—To Sir John Rothenale, knight, the King's Treasurer at War. In money paid to him, viz. by the hands of Thomas, Duke of Exeter, receiving the money; viz. from Geoffrey Coket and Robert Whitegreve,—1886*l.* 1*s.* 9*d.*; of Richard Knyghtley,—900*l.*; and of Thomas Stokdale,—955*l.* 9*s.*; for the wages of the said Duke, 5 bannerets, 18 knights, 236 men at arms and 780 archers: by the hands of Thomas, Duke of Clarence, receiving the money from the Tellers of the Exchequer,—878*l.* 4*s.*; for the wages of one Earl, one baron, five knights, 53 men at arms and 180 archers: by the hands of Edward Holand, Earl of Mortayne,—658*l.* 8*s.* 9*d.*; for the wages of one knight, 39 men at arms, and 120 archers: by the hands of Henry Lord Fitz Hugh,—1110*l.* 10*s.* 6*d.*; for the wages of one baron, two knights, 77 men at arms, and 240 archers: and by the hands of Sir Gilbert Umfravile, knight,—824*l.* 18*s.* 8*d.*; for the wages of two knights, 58 men at arms, and 180 archers, retained by our Lord the King to serve him in France for one whole year in his war there; viz. for one quarter of a year. By divers writs, &c.,—7103*l.* 9*s.*

9th March.—To Robert Rodyngton, esquire. In money paid to his own hands, receiving the money from Richard Coventre, in advance for making a certain tower at Portsmouth for protection of the King's ships and defence of the said town and country adjoining, there newly built at the King's charges. By writ, &c., —50*l.* [There are several other payments for the erection of this tower.]

ISSUE ROLL, EASTER, 6 HENRY V.

9th May.—To divers masters and mariners in four barges and four balingers, retained by the Lord the King in the fleet commanded by Richard Lord Scrop, of Bolton, to serve the King at sea with his retinue, for a quarter of a year, for the protection thereof. In money paid to him by the hands of Richard Ulverston, clerk, in discharge of the wages of the said masters, and for wages and rewards to the mariners aforesaid, &c.,—474*l.* 10*s.*

To William Yalton, William Richeman, and William Tenderle, masters of three of the King's "Karaks;" also to 3 constables, 3 carpenters, 12 masters, 896 mariners, and 65 boys and pages in the said 3 karaks, 2 great ships, 4 barges, and 6 balingers, appointed by the King's Council to serve him in the fleet commanded by Sir John Arundell, knight, deputy to Thomas Duke of Exeter, retained by the said Lord the King for the protection of the South part of the sea for half a year. In money paid, &c.,—794*l.* 13*s.* 1*d.*

To Richard Rawe, Master of the King's balinger called the Swan. In money paid to him for embarking Stephen Haxton, sent to the Lord the King with letters from the keeper of England and other lords, directed to our Lord the King in Normandy, concerning a certain agreement made with him by Nicholas Banaster on behalf of the King for conveying persons to Normandy, &c.,—3*l.* 6*s.* 8*d.* [This Roll contains very many payments for preparations made to supply the fleet and troops, sent to Normandy at this period, with arms, provisions, money, &c.]

1st June.—To Master Peter Altobasse, physician. In money paid to him, by the hands of Richard Baldelwelle, his servant, in discharge of 40*s.* paid to him for divers medicines purchased and provided, with the advice of the King's Council, and applied

2 A 2

for the cure of Lord de Touteville, the King's prisoner, for a long time detained with sickness in the castle of Moresende. By writ, &c.,—2*l.*

1st July.—To Sir John Rothenale, knight, the King's Treasurer at War. In money paid to him by the hands of John Hexham, in advance for payments made by him for the wages and rewards to masters and mariners of the port of the town of Bristol, for embarking the Prior of Kylmaynan, 200 horsemen, and 300 foot, from Waterford in Ireland, to go to the King's presence in France, there retained to serve him in the war. By writ, &c.,—91*l.* 17*s.*

16th July.—To the venerable father in Christ, the Bishop of Bangor, sent by the King's Council from London to Southampton to consecrate a certain King's ship, there newly built, called the Gracedieu. In money paid to him by the hands of Nicholas Banaster, for his costs and expenses in going and returning for the purpose aforesaid. By direction of the Treasurer and Chamberlains of the Exchequer,—5*l.*

26th September.—To divers brethren of four orders. In money paid to them by the King's especial command, of his alms, to celebrate certain masses for the souls of Lord de Grey, of Codnore, and Sir John Blount, knight, who died in Normandy,—17*l.* 10*s.*

27th September.—To Panton Ebron, master of the ship called the Hilde of Whitby, and William Walton, master of the balinger called the Michell, of Southampton. In money paid to their own hands, received from Nicholas Banaster; viz. to the aforesaid Panton,—10*l.*, and to the aforesaid William,—100*s.*, for the safe conduct of the King's confessor, and clerks of the King's chapel from Southampton to Cane, in Normandy, to the King's presence there, according to a certain covenant made with them by the said Nicholas for the King's advantage,—15*l.*

ISSUE ROLL, MICHAELMAS, 6 HENRY V.

3rd October.—To John Straunge, clerk of the King's works. In money paid to him, viz. by the hands of Robert Broune, carver, for carving divers swans in the King's chamber at Shene,—52*s.*; by the hands of Sir Roger Aston, knight, for cleansing the King's ditch round the Tower of London,—10*l.*; and by the hands of John Henry, of Penterych, Richard Hunt, of Notfield, and Henry Saxby, of Cotenhore, for 9½ fothers 401 quarters 14 lbs. of lead, purchased from them for the King's works at Shene,—55*l.* 0*s.* 8*d.* In advance, &c.,—67*l.* 12*s.* 8*d.*

22nd October.—To divers brethren of different orders. In money paid to them, by the King's command, for 2000 masses for the souls of Edward, Earl of Morteyn, and Gilbert Lord de Talbot, who died in Normandy, to be devoutly celebrated by the same brethren,—16*l.* 13*s.* 4*d.*

11th November.—To our Lord the King in his chamber. In money paid to the same chamber, by the hands of Conus Melver, goldsmith, for the value of 20 lbs. 3½ oz. of silver in mass, purchased for repairing an image of the blessed Mary for the King's chapel of Saint George, in Windsor Castle, price the lb. 30*s.*,—30*l.* 8*s.* 4*d.*

28th November.—To Henry Southwell and his companions, clerks in the King's Remembrancer's Office, in the Exchequer. In money paid to them, by assignment made this day, for writing a certain book of divers ordinances to be observed in the King's Exchequer aforesaid, sent by the King's command to Cane. By direction of the Treasurer and Barons of the Exchequer aforesaid, —40*s.*

23rd February.—To Simon Flete, keeper of the King's private wardrobe within the Tower of London. In money paid to him, by the hands of John Mathewe, for making two cannons with three chambers in each, and two cannons with two chambers in each,—5*l.* 10*s.* 5*d.*

To our Lord the King in his chamber. In money paid to the same chamber, to the hands of divers goldsmiths of London, for 24 collars of gold purchased from them and sent to the said Lord the King at Roan, &c.,—79*l.* 12*s.* 6*d.*

To Margaret Merssh. In money paid to her in discharge of 35*s.*, for eighteen pair of fetters and eight pair of manacles, made by her and delivered by the King's command to the constable of the Tower of London. By writ, &c.,—1*l.* 15*s.*

11*th March.*—To our Lord the King in his chamber. In money paid to the same chamber, by the hands of Conus Melver, goldsmith, for making a certain image of the blessed Virgin Mary for Saint George's Chapel, within the King's castle of Windsor,—30*l.*

Issue Roll, Easter, 7 Henry V.

1*st May.*—To our Lord the King in his chamber. In money paid into the same chamber, by the hands of John Romayne, for making a certain round basin for the chamber aforesaid,—20*l.*

13*th May.*—To James Styward, calling himself the King of Scotland. In money paid to him, by the hands of John Leo, his servant, in advance for repairing divers apparel belonging to his person. By writ of privy seal,—20*l.* [The abovenamed Styward is called both John and James on this Roll.]

20*th May.*—To Sir Thomas Burton, knight. In money paid to his own hands in advance for the support and expenses of Arthur de Bretayne Earl of Richmond, the Earl of Vewe, and Sir John Meugre, knight, the marshal of France, otherwise called Sir

Burcegant of France, the King's prisoners, in the custody of the said Sir Thomas at Fodryngey, at the King's charges,—20*l.*

19th June.—To Sir Walter Pole, knight, sent as the King's ambassador to the King of Poleyne and Lords of Prucia, to treat concerning certain discords pending between them, and to confer with and obtain a good peace between them according to the instructions given him by the King and the Council. In money paid, &c. By writ, &c.,—66*l.* 13*s.* 4*d.*

5th July.—To Roger Keston, master of the grammar school at Cornhill, London. In money paid to his own hands "pro tabula doctrina," and for the exhibition of Walter Heuse, then in the King's custody by reason of his minority; viz., from Michaelmas, anno 6, to 18th July following, &c.,—4*l.* 11*s.* 4½*d.*

24th July.—To Ralph, Earl of Westmoreland. In money paid to him, by the hands of Thomas Stokdale, as an especial reward, given him by the advice of the King's Council, for the costs and expenses incurred by him for the safe conduct of William Douglas, a Scotch prisoner, from the West Marches of Scotland to Westminster, and there delivered, to await the order of the King's Council,—20*l.*

24th July.—To Thomas, Duke of Exeter. In money paid to him, by the hands of Philip Caxton, his attorney, in advance as well for 1000*l.* yearly, paid at the King's Exchequer, as for the support of the Earl of Oxford, in the King's custody by reason of his minority,—158*l.* 12*s.* 3½*d.*

20th August.—To Lady Margery le Scrop, to whom Lord Geoffrey le Scrop, (brother and heir of Henry, late Lord le Scrop, who forfeited certain gold and silver vessels and other goods and jewels which belonged to the said Henry, then in the custody of the said Geoffrey,) pledged the same for 103 marks, to be faithfully paid on a certain day agreed upon between them. In money paid to her, by assignment made th day, by the hands of Thomas

Broket in part payment of 103 marks, paid to the said Lady
Margery in discharge of the jewels aforesaid taken in the King's
hands by reason of the forfeiture of the said Henry, and delivered
to the custody of the Treasurer and Chamberlains,—66*l.* 13*s.* 4*d.*

To Richard Pepyr, one of the esquires of the Lady Bergeveney,
and Hans, a messenger of the said Lady. In money paid to them,
&c., by the Treasurer of England, as an especial reward to them
for their costs and expenses in coming from Haryngton, in
the county of Worcester, to London to give information to the
King's Council respecting certain goods which belonged to brother
John Randolf, of the order of Friars Minors, being for certain
reasons seized and taken into the King's hands, &c.,—2*l.* 6*s.* 8*d.*

25*th August.*—To Sir Roger Aston, knight, deputy to Sir
William Boucher, knight, constable of the Tower of London.
In money paid to his own hands in advance for the expenses of
John Bloundelle, John Daubeney, Reginald Homet, Master de
Waranger, John Blakemont, and William Douglas, the King's
Scotch prisoners, for each of them 4*s.* per week, being within the
Tower aforesaid, in the custody of the said Roger, at the King's
charge,—20*l.*

26*th August.*—To Thomas Stokdale and Richard Knyghtley,
clerks, sent from London to Normandy, by command of the
Treasurer of England, with 33,333*l.* 6*s.* 8*d.*, to be delivered to
John Rothenale, the King's Treasurer at War, by the hands of
John Feryby, cofferer, by command of the said Lord the King at
Roan. In money paid to them, &c., to each of them 5*s.* per day,
in going, tarrying, and returning, viz. from the 9th of February,
in the sixth year, the day on which they began their journey
from the city of London, to the 8th of June in the seventh year,
on which day they returned to the city aforesaid, being 120 days,
each day included, &c.,—60*l.*

26*th August.*—To Nicholas Banaster. In money paid to his
own hands as well for the carriage of salt, "ermonyak and vert-

gres," with a horse, and also divers of the King's specie and jewels at different times, with seven carts from the city of London to the port of Southampton, as for the freightage of divers furniture for the Earl of Vewe, Arthur de Bretayn, Sir Thomas Burton, knight, and others sailing in their retinue from the port of Southampton to Herfleu, going to the King's presence there,—12*l.* 8*s.*

ISSUE ROLL, MICHAELMAS, 7 HENRY V.

27th October.—To Thomas Broket, Remembrancer on the Treasurer's side of the Exchequer, appointed by the Treasurer of England to communicate with Lady le Scrop and ascertain for a certainty what goods and jewels belonged to Henry le Scrop, Lord of Masham, which were forfeited to the King. In money paid to his own hands, for the costs and expenses by him incurred for the carriage and safe conduct of the goods and jewels aforesaid from the city of York to the city of London, together with his own expenses, &c.,—8*l.*

28th October.—To Walter Wodehall, one of the organists of the cathedral church of Saint Paul's, London, appointed by the King's Council to proceed, in company with five other organists, abroad to the King's presence, there to serve the King in his chapel. In money paid to his own hands for the costs and expenses of his passage by sea, in going to the parts aforesaid for the reason aforesaid. By writ, &c.,—5*l.*

To Master Peter Henewer, physician, appointed by the Lord the King and his Council to go to the said Lord the King in Normandy. In money paid to him, &c., for the costs and expenses of his passage by sea, &c.,—10*l.*

22nd November.—To William Thorley, chaplain, William Dyolet, Richard Laudewarnake, Thomas Wodeford, and Gerard Hesyll, clerks and singers ordered by the King's Council to proceed to the King's presence in his duchy of Normandy, there to serve him in his chapel. In money paid to their own hands for the costs and expenses of their passage by sea in going to the parts aforesaid for the reason aforesaid. By writ, &c., —25*l.*

To Richard Whytyngton, citizen and alderman of London. In money paid to him, by the hands of Richard Knyghtley, in discharge of 2000 marks which he lent to the Lord the King at the Receipt of his Exchequer, on the 12th of June, in the fifth year, as appears by the Roll of Receipts, &c.,—333*l.* 6*s.* 8*d.* [*Note.* It also appears by these Rolls that Richard Whytyngton, thrice Lord Mayor of London, advanced other large sums of money to the King.]

27th November.—To Sir John Pelham, knight, appointed, by the King's Council, for the governance and safe custody of Joan, Queen of England. In money paid to him by the hands of Richard le Verer, her esquire, in advance for the support and safe custody of the Queen aforesaid,—166*l.* 13*s.* 4*d.* [Master Peter de Ofbace was appointed the said Queen's physician.]

ISSUE ROLL, EASTER, 8 HENRY V.

6th May.—To John Sewalle and William Bolton, messengers. In money paid to them, viz. to the aforesaid John for his expenses, sent, by command of the Treasurer, from Southampton to Windsor with a letter, directed to Roger Noble, keeper of the vests of the King's chapel of Windsor, to take certain books, vestments, and other ornaments of the King's chapel from Windsor to Roan, —6*s.* 8*d.* [with other payments, amounting to]—1*l.*

24th May.—To Robert Rolleston, clerk of the King's great wardrobe. In money paid to him as an advance for purchasing and providing divers necessary apparel for James, King of Scotland, to proceed, by the King's command, to his presence in France, there to serve him in his war,—86*l.*

25*th June.*—To Robert Lord Ponynges, Hugh Halsham, and Thomas Hoo, knights, ordered and appointed by the King's Council for the safe and secure conduct of the Duke of Bourbon, the King's prisoner, from the seaport, where he should be received on board to sail to France to the King's presence. In money paid to them, viz. to the aforesaid Lord de Ponynges for his wages at 4*s.* per day, to nineteen men at arms each 12*d.*, and forty archers, to each 6*d.* per day,—32*s.*; to the aforesaid Hugh at 2*s.* per day, nine men at arms and twenty archers for their wages as above,—14*l.* 14*s.* [with other payments to the said Thomas, 19 men at arms, and 40 archers, &c.,]—73*l.* 10*s.*

12*th July.*—To James, King of Scotland. In money paid to him, by the hands of divers persons, as well for armour and other preparations for his person in the war, as for horses, tents, banners, and divers other things provided and purchased for him and other men attending him by order of the King's Council, upon his departure to foreign parts to go to the King's presence. By writ, &c., —42*l.* 6*s.* 8*d.*

ISSUE ROLL, MICHAELMAS, 8 HENRY V.

2*nd October.*—To our Lord the King in his chamber. In money paid in the said chamber, viz. by the hands of William Meuston, for the price of harps, purchased by him for the King and Queen,—8*l.* 13*s.* 4*d.*; also paid by the hands of a certain recluse within the monastery of Westminster,—4*l.*; and by the hands of the Bishop of Rochester 2000 marks for the expenses of the chamber aforesaid,—1346*l.*

29*th October.*—To Thomas Wodevill, esquire. In money paid to him, by assignment made this day, by the hands of Richard Knyghtley, in advance for the custody and support of the

Lords de Stutvile and Gancourt, the King's prisoners, being in his custody at the King's charge,—100*l.*

21st January.—To divers brethren of different orders in England. In money paid to them, by the King's especial order, for them devoutly to celebrate 1000 masses for the soul of Hugh de Stafford, Lord de Bouchier, one of the knights of the order of the garter, who died abroad,—6*l.* 13*s.* 4*d.*

To Sir John Rothenale, knight, late keeper of the King's wardrobe. In money paid to him,—to wit, by the hands of Hans Bemer, keeper of a nest of falcons called Melons,—40*s.*; by the hands of William Countrevour, the King's falconer, for the wages of the falconer and keep of the falcons,—11*l.* 18*s.* 11*d.*, charged upon the expenses of the King's household. By writ, &c.,—13*l.* 18*s.* 11*d.*

30th January.—To John Aclan, one of the King's valets of the Crown. In money paid to his own hands in discharge of 20*l.* which the Lord the King commanded to be paid him for certain bows, arrows, and bow-strings, ordered by the King's especial command, to be sent to the most powerful Prince the King of France, father [in-law] of the said King of England. By writ, &c.,—20*l.*

To Nicholas Auncell, John Sewalle, and Henry Botolf, messengers, sent to divers counties of England with writs under the King's privy seal, directed to divers Bishops, Abbots, Priors, and other prelates, also to divers temporal lords and other persons, to be in attendance at Westminster on the third Sunday in Easter, there to solemnize the coronation of Catherine, Queen of England. In money paid to them, &c.,—1*l.* 13*s.* 4*d.*

8th February.—To Ralph, Earl of Westmoreland, to whom the Lord the King commanded that he should direct, in his town of Berwick-upon-Tweed, Mordoc Styward, son of the Duke of Al-

bany, to be interchanged by him for Henry, Earl of Northumberland, promising to the same Earl of Westmoreland that he would
pay the costs by him incurred, as well for the delivery of the said
Mordoc, as for the reception of the said Earl to the amount of 200*l.*,
for which delivery and reception of the said Earl of Northumberland and Mordok, the said Earl of Westmoreland incurred divers
expenses to the amount of the said 200*l.* and more, as it appeared
to the King; and further after the coming of the said Earl of Northumberland to the castle of Raby, the aforesaid Lord the King, by
his letters patent, likewise commanded the said Earl of Westmoreland to incur expenses for the said Earl of Northumberland's
appearing in the King's presence, by virtue of which command
the aforesaid Earl of Westmoreland commanded to be paid to the
officers of the said Earl of Northumberland 100 marks for their expenses in going to the King's presence as aforesaid. In money
paid, &c.,—30*l.* 3*s.* 4½*d.*

8th February.—To Nicholas Skericorn, John Skericorn, William Bayldon, Richard Gibson, John Hancok, John Croxton,
Richard Ireland, David Gibson, and Richard Hansman. In
money paid to them, &c., in discharge of 10*l.* which the Lord the
King commanded to be paid them for their labour, costs, and expenses in conducting, by the King's command, brother John Ran-
dolff, of the order of Friars Minors, of Shrovesbury, viz. from the
castle of Gailard, within the King's duchy of Normandy, to the
King's city of London, and there delivering him to the constable
of the Tower of London, by order of the King's Council. By
writ, &c.,—10*l.*

27th February.—To Thomas Barnaby, constable of the King's
castle of Caernarvan. In money paid to him, &c., in discharge
of 12*l.* 13*s.* 4*d.*, due to him upon his account, &c. for costs and
expenses incurred by him about the safe custody and support of
Ralph de Gale and Colard Bloset, knights of France, the King's
prisoners, lately committed to his custody by the King, and for
conducting the said prisoners, by virtue of divers letters directed

to him, from the castle aforesaid to the city of London, and there delivering them to Humphrey, Duke of Gloucester, keeper of England. By writ, &c.,—12*l.* 13*s.* 4*d.*

To Robert Darcy, esquire, one of the executors of Joan de Bohun, late Countess of Hereford. In money paid to him, by assignment made this day, &c.,—advanced for the purchase of the live and dead stock from him and other executors of the said Countess, purchased for the King's use,—442*l.* 17*s.* 5*d.*

11*th March.*—To Sir John Colvyle, knight, sent by the King's especial command to conduct Giles Lord de Camocy, counsellor of the King of France, and three other ambassadors of the French King, sent on behalf of the said King to Scotland, there to confer concerning certain affairs of England, France, and Scotland, viz. for going from the city of London to the parts aforesaid. In money paid, &c.,—26*l.* 13*s.* 4*d.*

Issue Roll, Easter, 9 Henry V.

1*st April.*—To James, King of Scotland. In money paid to his own hands, by the King's oral command, in discharge of 52*s.* 1*d.* which the said Lord the King commanded to be paid to the said James, to have of his gift, for private expenses incurred by him at Leicester, on the day of the Lord's Supper last past,—2*l.* 12*s.* 1*d.*

24*th April.*—To Simon Prentot, a wax chandler, of London. In money paid to him, in part payment of 85*l.*, which the Lord the King commanded to be paid, &c., viz., to make a new hearse, and place it within Christ Church, Canterbury, together with the entire wax lights and the whole preparation belonging to the said hearse ; also to make 100 torches to burn round the said hearse and other places in the said Church, during the day and night of the exequies of Thomas, Duke of Clarence, the King's brother, entombed within the church aforesaid, &c.,—40*l.*

9th May.—To Sir William Meryng, knight. In money paid to his own hands, in discharge of 10*l.* 12*s.* 7*d.*, due to him, &c., for costs and expenses incurred by him about Arthur de Britany, the King's prisoner, during the time he was in his custody, and for safely conducting him from the town of Southampton to the town of Milun, in France, to the King's presence, he at that time being there, viz., from the 26th of August, in the eighth year, to the 28th October, then next following. By writ, &c.,— 10*l.* 12*s.* 7*d.*

To William Percy, esquire. In money paid to his own hands, in discharge of 10 marks which the Lord the King commanded to be paid to the said William, for his costs and expenses, incurred in safely conducting Lord de Tuttevile from the town of Keime to the city of London. By writ, &c.,—6*l.* 13*s.* 4*d.*

18th June.—To Robert Rolleston, clerk of the King's great wardrobe, appointed by the Treasurer of England to order and provide for the reparation, amendment, and preparation of a certain " row barge " of the said Lord the King, called, " Esmond del Toure," ordered to sail to France, to serve the said King in the river Seyne, or elsewhere, at the pleasure of the said King. In money paid to the same Robert, for divers costs and expenses incurred by him for the reparation. amendment, and preparation of the row barge aforesaid, &c.,—21*l.* 14*s.* 8*d.*

4th September.—To the Lord the King in his chamber. In money paid to the same chamber, viz., to the hands of John Bore, of London, harp maker, for a harp purchased of him by the King's command, and sent to the said King into France, 46*s.* 8*d.* ; and for   dozen of cords for the same harp, purchased at the same time ; also for a case for the same harp, 3*s.*, in discharge of 53*s.* 4*d.* which the said Lord the King commanded to be paid, &c.,—2*l.* 13*s.* 8*d.*

ISSUE ROLL, MICHAELMAS, 9 HENRY V.

1st October.—To Master John Boyery, Doctor in Theology, Confessor to the Lady Catherine, Queen of England, to whom the present Lord the King granted 20*l.*, yearly to be received at his Exchequer, during the pleasure of the said King, for his office of Confessor. In money paid to him by the hands of John Langton, chaplain to the said Queen, in part payment, &c.,—5*l.*

6th November.—To the Venerable Father Theodore, Archbishop of Cologn, vassal to the present King, to whom the said Lord the King, by a certain indenture made between the said King and the aforesaid Archbishop, granted a certain fee of 500 marks, yearly to be received at the feast of Easter only, for services by him to be performed, according to a certain form contained in the said indenture. In money paid to him by the hands of Gobellin Clusner and Bertram Cleherst, in discharge of 500 marks for this his fee, &c.,—333*l.* 6*s.* 8*d.*

To Jaquet, Duchess of Holand, to whom the present King, with the assent of his Council, commanded to be paid 100*l.* for every calendar month during the time she was within his kingdom of England, at the King's costs, out of the issues and profits of the lands, tenements, and other possessions, lately assigned in dower to Joan, Queen of England. In money paid to her by the hands of John Frasne, her esquire, &c. By writ, &c.,—50*l.*

21st November.—To the Lord the King, in his chamber. In money paid into the said chamber, by the hands of John Robard, of London, scrivener, for writing twelve books on hunting, for the use of the said Lord the King, and delivered into the chamber aforesaid, by the said King's command,—12*l.* 8*s.*

1st December.—To Ralph Huskard, master of the King's balinger, called the Ann, lately sent by the King's command, and order of his Council, at different times, from this kingdom to Normandy and elsewhere, in the aforesaid balinger, to expedite certain affairs of the King, and from thence returning to the King's presence at the town of Southampton; and afterwards, by the King's command, and order of his Council, sent divers times, as well to Toque and Caan, as to divers other places on this side and beyond sea, safely to conduct the King's servants and friends in a vessel laden with victuals, artillery, and other stores belonging to the King. In money paid to him, &c. By writ, &c.,—40*l.*

To the Lord the King in his chamber, &c., by the hands of Thomas Knolles, for "40 lb. of vertgres and 40 lb. of salarmoniak," purchased from him, and sent to our said Lord the King, in Normandy, in discharge of 6*l.* 17*s.* 5*d.* which the said Lord the King, for certain causes him moving, caused to be paid into the chamber aforesaid, out of the money arising from the issues and profits of the lands and tenements which were lately assigned in dower to Joan, Queen of England, &c.,—6*l.* 17*s.* 5*d.*

4th December.—To Margaret, who was the wife of John Darcy, chevalier, deceased, who held in capite of Lord Henry, late King of England, father of the present Lord the King; the oath of the said Margaret having been first taken, that she would not marry without license of the said Lord the King. The said late Lord the King, on the 11th day of November, in the fourteenth year of his reign, by his writ commanded his escheator in the county of Middlesex, that the said Margaret should have her reasonable dower of all the lands and tenements which had belonged to the aforesaid John, formerly her husband, in his bailiwick, on the day that he died, and which by the death of the said John, by reason of the minority of Philip, his son and heir, had been seized into the said King's hands, &c., according to an extent then thereof made, &c., as by inspection of the Rolls of Chancery, it appeared to the said late King. Thomas Horden, then escheator, &c., assigned to the aforesaid Margaret 20 marks yearly, for dower, out of 40*l.* which the said John had by royal grant, &c.,

2 B

formerly husband of the aforesaid Margaret, as by the said assignment remaining in the Chancery appears, &c.,—20*l.*

To the Lord the King, in his chamber, viz., for money arising
from the issues and profits of the lands and tenements which belonged to Joan, Queen of England. In money paid into the said
chamber by the hands of Eleanor, who was the wife of Sir Almaric
de Sancto Amando, knight, for a zone of gold which belonged to
the said Queen, pledged to the said Eleanor by the said Queen,
and, for non-payment of the money borrowed, forfeited to her, and
delivered to the said Lord the King by the hands of William
Kynwolmerssh, by command of the said Lord the King,—80*l.*

13*th December.*—To the Lord the King, in his chamber. In
money paid to the said chamber by the hands of Thomas Chit-
terne, receiving the money by the hands of Lawrence Lumbard,
for a long chain, weighing by troy weight 28 ounces 1½ quarter,
price the ounce, 30*s.*, purchased from the same Lawrence by the
said Lord the King, and by the said Thomas delivered, by the
King's command, into the chamber aforesaid, as appears by the
bill of the said Thomas, sealed with his seal, &c.,—42*l.* 11*s.* 4*d.*

20*th December.*—To William Bolton, John Sewale, Nicholas
Aunsell, and John Damport, the King's messengers, sent to
different counties of England, to divers lords and ladies, knights
and esquires, with divers letters of privy seal from the King,
directed to them, to be present at Windsor, on the 12th January
next happening, there to attend at the solemnization of the
purification of Catherine, Queen of England. In money paid to
them, &c.,—1*l.* 6*s.* 8*d.*

3*rd February.*—To Elizabeth, who was the wife of Edward
Charleton, chevalier, and John Fitz Piers, esquire, executors of
the will of Edward, late Lord of Powys. In money paid to them
by the hands of Thomas Bradshawe, in part payment of 1000
marks which the Lord the King commanded to be paid to the

said executors for the capture of John Oldecastell, chevalier, late called Lord of Cobham, seized according to a certain proclamation thereof made in each county of England, &c. By writ, &c., 133*l*. 6*s*. 8*d*.

To Sir William Philip, knight, Treasurer at War. In money paid to him by the hands of John Hexham, for payment of the wages of divers masters, mariners, and pages of divers ships and vessels in the ports of Southampton, Melcombe, and other ports and places on the West coast, retained for the passage of the Lady Catherine, Queen of England, and Duke of Bedford, in her retinue, and others of the King's retinue, next to be made to France. In payment, &c.,—266*l*. 13*s*. 4*d*.

18*th February*.—To Bartholomew Goldebeter, of London, goldsmith, John Padesley and others, appointed by the King's commission to provide and order certain weights and " rates," necessary for them, to be made at the King's charge. In money paid to them by the hands of John Darlyngton, viz., as well for 100 small scales, 100 weights, for the noble, 100 weights for the half noble, and 100 weights for a ferling of gold, together with rates for the same weights, provided and ordered by them for the King's benefit, and use of his people, according to an ordinance of the said Lord the King thereon made, in his last parliament, held at Westminster, as for four pair of great and a small balance, together with the weights and rates belonging to the same ; also for 22 pieces of divers weights of latten, for making just weight of the King's gold, from thenceforth to be received at the Receipt of his Exchequer, delivered to the tellers of the said receipt, there to be safely kept for the King's use, by the Treasurer of England and Chamberlain of the Exchequer. By direction of the said Treasurer and Chamberlain of the Exchequer,—10*l*. 7*s*. 4*d*.

In money paid, viz., to John Stone, joiner, for making a chest and a table, covered with a green cloth, ordered for weighing the

King's money at the Receipt of the Exchequer, received by the said tellers, and there to remain for the use of the said King,—13*s.*4*d.* ; also to a certain clothier of London, for a green cloth purchased of him, to cover the table aforesaid,—2*s.* 3*d.* By order of the Treasurer and Chamberlain of the Exchequer,—15*s.* 7*d.*

23rd February.—To Thomas Mareschall and two of his companions, clerks of the King's Chancery. In money paid to them by assignment made this day, by the hands of the said Thomas, for his pains in copying, by direction of the King's Council, for their use, divers transcripts of alliances made between the said Lord the King and the Kings of the Romans, Portugal, and Arragon ; and the Archbishop of Cologn. By writ of privy seal, &c.,—2*l.*

To John Heth, one of the clerks in the office of privy seal of the Lord the King. In money paid to his own hands, in discharge of 66*s.* which the said Lord the King, with the assent of his Council, commanded to be paid to the said John, for 66 great " quaternes " of calf skins, purchased and provided by the said John, to write a Bible thereon, for the use of the said King. By writ of privy seal amongst the mandates of this term,—3*l.* 6*s.*

19th March.—To the Lord the King, in his chamber. In money paid into the said chamber, by the hands of Galeas Goldsmyth, in discharge of 19*l.* which the said Lord the King commanded to be paid to the said Galeas, for a gold collar purchased from him, and sent, by the King's command, by Walter de la Pole, chevalier, to Henry, Duke of Bavaria, to have of the said King's gift, by order of the said King,—19*l.*

ISSUE ROLL, EASTER, 10 HENRY V.

30th April.—To divers messengers, sent to each county of England and the Marches of Wales, with certain letters from the

Duke of Bedford, Lord Keeper of England, directed to each sheriff of the counties aforesaid ; and to the mayors, bailiffs, citizens, and burgesses; also to the keepers of passage boats in all the ports of England, commanding them, on behalf of the King, to seize John Mortymer, Thomas Payne, called Clerk, John Cobham, and divers the King's prisoners, who lately escaped from the Tower of London, to arrest and safely and securely keep them, wheresoever they may be found, within their districts. In money paid to their own hands, for their costs and expenses in going and returning upon the messages aforesaid, &c.,—5*l.*

To Henry Botolf, one of the King's messengers, sent from London to Southampton with a certain letter, to certify the King's Council of the re-capture of Sir John Mortymer, knight, who lately, with other prisoners, escaped from the Tower of London, without the King's licence. In money paid to his own hands, as well for the hire of horses, as for other expenses sustained by him in going and returning on the message aforesaid, &c.,—6*s.* 8*d.*

16*th June.*—To John Stanle, master of the ship called the Peter, of London. In money paid to him by the hands of John Godeston, of the county of Essex, for the passage and conduct of nine master workers of money, who lately came from Roan to England, by command of the King and his Council, to assist other workmen of the same mystery to coin money in the Tower of London, for the more speedy circulation amongst the people of the King's gold and silver taken to the Tower aforesaid,—2*l.*

22*nd June.*—To Margaret, Duchess of Bavaria, Countess of Hainau, Holand, and Zealand, and Lady of Friesland. In money paid to her by the hands of Helung Dornick, her esquire, from money arising out of the dower of Joan, Queen of England, the King's mother, in part payment of 1000 marks which the Lord the King, with the assent of his Council, commanded to be paid to the said Duchess. By writ, &c.,—233*l.* 6*s.* 8*d.*

1st July.—To Bartholomew Goldbeter, master of the King's money in the Tower of London. In money paid to his own hands, in discharge of 80*l.* which the Lord the King, with the consent of his Council, commanded to be paid to the said Bartholomew, as well for the deficiency and waste in 280*l.* of gold, weighed at the Tower of London aforesaid, taken by the Treasurer of England to the said Tower, there to be coined into money for the King's use, as for coining the said money, and other costs, incurred by the said Bartholomew on account of the money aforesaid. By writ, &c.,—80*l.*

To Ralph Makerell, esquire. In money paid to his own hands, for the costs and expenses of 24 of the King's prisoners, committed to his custody, by advice of the King's Council, and taken by the said Ralph from London to Nottingham Castle, there to be safely kept,—64*l.* 13*s.* 4*d.*

To John Bold, chevalier, Constable of Conway Castle. In money paid to him, for the costs and expenses of 12 of the King's prisoners, committed to his custody, by advice of the King's Council, and taken by him from London to the castle aforesaid, there to be safely kept,—13*l.* 6*s.* 8*d.*

To Thomas Barneby, Constable of Carnarvon Castle. In money paid to his own hands, for the costs and expenses of 20 of the King's prisoners, committed to his custody, and by him taken from London to the castle aforesaid, for safe custody, —20*l.*

To Nicholas Saxton, esquire, Constable of Ruthelane Castle. In money paid to him by the hands of Henry Gisson, for the costs and expenses of 20 of the King's prisoners, committed to him by advice of the King's Council, and taken by the said Nicholas from London to the castle aforesaid, there to be safely kept,—20*l.* [Payments for other prisoners, committed to the custody of divers constables of castles, &c., are entered on this Roll.]

10th July.—To John Stourton. In money paid to him, &c., in part payment of 26l. 12s. 4d. which the Lord the King, with the consent of his Council, commanded to be paid to the said John, to hold of his gift, for the costs and expenses incurred by him in the county of Somerset, for capturing Sir John Brakemond, knight, Marselin de Flisc, and Thomas Payne, late clerks and servants of Sir John Oldecastell, knight, who lately escaped from the Tower of London; which said John, Marselin, and Thomas, were taken back to the Tower aforesaid, and delivered to the Constable there, by command of the said Council. By writ, &c., —13l. 6s. 8d.

16th July.—To Richard Maydeston, Controller of the Exchange, in Lumbardstrete, within the city of London. In money paid to his hands, &c., as an especial reward for the continual labour and diligence exercised by him in assiduous pains taken about the faithful controlment of the Exchange aforesaid, as well for the King's benefit, as for the utility, speedy and true delivery to the King's subjects of the sums of money taken by him to the said Exchange, &c.,—13l. 6s. 8d.

29th July.—To Richard Whitegreve, one of the Tellers of the Receipt of the Exchequer. In money paid to his own hands, for divers costs and expenses lately incurred by him, by the King's command, in coming from Paris to London, concerning Oliver Mavue, Guichard de Cesse, captain of Mieux, in Brye; Peter de Lupe, and five other esquires the King's prisoners; and a certain other esquire of the King, of the county of Lincoln, lately committed to the same Robert, by command of the said Lord the King, at Paris aforesaid; viz., for a boat from Paris aforesaid, to Caudebek, and for embarking and safely conducting them from Herfleu to Portsmouth, in England, and from thence, for divers other costs and expenses incurred by the said Robert, for the said prisoners and esquire to London, during five weeks. By direction of the Treasurer, &c.,—32*l.*

26th September.—To John Ardern, clerk of the King's works. In money paid to him by the hands of William Pierson, for 36 ton of stone, from Cane, purchased of him for the tomb of King Henry V., to be made in the church of the Blessed Peter, Westminster, who is there buried,—12*l.*

To Simon Prentot, wax chandler, of London. In money paid to his own hands, at different times, viz., at one time 100 marks; at another time, 50*l.*; at a third time, 100 marks; a fourth time, 117*l.*; in part payment of 310*l.* 1*s.* 6*d.*, paid to him by covenant made in gross, by the Treasurer of England, with the assent of the King's Council, for divers hearses provided by him at Dover, Canterbury, Hosprynge, Rouchester, Dertford, Saint Paul's, London, and Westminster, for the funeral of the most excellent Prince and Lord, King Henry V., so brought from France to England, through the towns and cities aforesaid, to be buried at Westminster aforesaid,—300*l.* 12*s.* 6*d.*

To John Ardern, clerk of the King's works. In money paid to his own hands, for making the tomb of King Henry V., erected in the church of the Blessed Peter, Westminster, who is there buried, 23*l.* 6*s.* 8*d.*

HENRY VI.

ISSUE ROLL, MICHAELMAS, 1 HENRY VI.

21st December.—To Sir John Pelham, knight. In money paid to him by the hands of Thomas Brigges, in discharge of 20*l.* which the present Lord the King, with the advice and consent of his Council, commanded to be paid to the said John Pelham, in advance, for the custody of Sir John Mortymer, knight, confined by the said King's order in Pevensey Castle. By writ, &c.,—20*l.*

27th February.—To Arnald Kent, Esquire, to whom Lord Henry, late King of England, grandfather of the present King, of his especial grace, for the good services by him bestowed, and to be bestowed, as well upon the said grandfather, as to his most dear son, the Prince, and his other infant children, granted by his letters patent 40*l.*, yearly to be received, &c., which the Lord and father of the present King, and the present King himself, confirmed. In money paid, &c. By writ, &c.,—10*l.*

To William Strensale. In money paid to him for fire-wood purchased and provided, burnt and expended, as well during the time of the King's last parliament, held at Westminster, as at divers other times, for the Lords of the King's Council, attending at Westminster aforesaid in winter, upon especial matters and causes intimately concerning the said King and benefit of his kingdom. By direction of the Treasurer and Chamberlains of the Exchequer,—6*s.* 2*d.*

4th March.—To Henry Percy, Earl of Northumberland, sent

as the King's Ambassador to the General Council which met at
Pavy. In money paid to him by the hands of Thomas Stokdale,
in advance, for the wages of the said Earl in going and returning
upon the embassy aforesaid.   By writ, &c.,—100*l.*

ISSUE ROLL, EASTER, 1 HENRY VI.

20th May.—To Edmund, Earl of March, retained in the
King's service by indenture, to be his lieutenant in Ireland from
the 1st of June next happening, during the term of nine years,
fully to be completed, receiving yearly for himself and his men
retained with him for the war and government of the said land
during the nine years aforesaid; viz., for each of the said nine
years, 5000 marks.   In money paid to him by the hands of
William Cotesmore, his esquire, in advance for the safe custody
of the land aforesaid.   By writ, &c.,—400*l.*

2nd June.—To John Sewale, a messenger, sent from London
to Sandwich, as well with letters from the Chancellor and Treasurer of England, directed to the Earl Marshal there, upon certain especial causes contained therein touching the King's benefit;
as also with a writ under the great seal of the said Lord the
King, directed to the Sheriff of Kent, to make proclamation for
preserving the peace lately concluded between the King of England and Duke of Britany.   In money paid to him by the hands
of John Poutrell, for the expenses of the said John Sewale, &c.,
—6*s.* 8*d.*

To James, King of Scotland.   In money paid to his own
hands, in discharge of 100*l.* which the present Lord the King,
with the advice and assent of his Council, ordered to be paid to
the same James of his gift, for his private expenses.   By writ of
privy seal, &c.,—100*l.*

To Sir John Bolde, knight. In money paid to him by the hands of Richard Bolde, his son, in discharge of 11*l.* 3*s.* which the present Lord the King, with the advice and assent of his Council, commanded to be paid to the said John for the carriage, costs, and divers expenses incurred by him about twelve prisoners lately taken at Meaux de Brey, in France, and received by him at London, on the 6th of July, in the 10th year of Lord Henry, late King of England, father of the present Lord the King; and also by the said John safely conducted to the King's castle of Coneway, there to be kept, and from thence taken back to the Tower of London, on the 9th of November last past, as appears as well by the account made with him before the Treasurer and Barons of the Exchequer of money received by him as by virtue of the King's letters of privy seal directed to him for this purpose, &c. By writ, &c.,—11*l.* 3*s.*

21st June.—To Robert Waterton, esquire. In money paid to his own hands, by assignment made this day, in discharge of 276*l.* 6*s.* 10½*d.*, due upon an account made with him before the Treasurer and Barons of the Exchequer, by virtue of the King's letters of privy seal directed to them, and certified to the King's Council, as well for money received by him for the expenses and support of the Duke of York, the government and safe custody of the Earl of Ewe, Arthur de Britany, Marshal Bursigaud, Peter de Lupe, and Guichard de Sesse, prisoners of Lord Henry, late King of England, father of the present King; as also for the expenses of the said Duke and prisoners, in the custody of the said Robert, by order of the said late King and his Council; and also for the costs and expenses of their servants, sent from the county of York to London, at different times, to receive money for the purposes aforesaid, between the 10th October, in the fifth year, and the 24th June, in the tenth year of the said father. By writ, &c.,—276*l.* 6*s.* 10½*d.*

To the Dean and Canons of the King's free chapel of Saint Stephens, within his palace of Westminster, to whom Lord

Edward, late King of England, progenitor of our said now Lord
the King, by his letters patent, amongst other things, granted
184*l*. 14*s*. 7*d*. to be received yearly from his Exchequer, until
they should be provided with certain and perpetual rents to the
value of the said 184*l*. 14*s*. 7*d*. yearly ; and afterwards the same
progenitor, by other letters patent, granted to the said Dean
and Canons a house, with the appurtenances, called the Reole, in
the city of London, to have and to hold to the same Dean and
Canons, and their successors, from the said Lord the King and
his heirs, by services from ancient time due and accustomed for the
same house for ever, to the value of 20*l*. yearly, in part satisfaction of the 184*l*. 14*s*. 7*d*. yearly.   And Lord Richard the second,
late King of England, after the conquest, on the 3rd August, in
the 12th year of his reign, with the assent and advice of his
Council, by his letters patent, gave and granted for himself and
his heirs, &c., to the aforesaid Dean and Canons, all issues, rents,
and profits, of the manors of Asshattesford, Barton, Bukwell,
Eslyng, Meer, Langley near Ledes, Elham, Colbrugge, and a
certain parcel of meadow with the appurtenances, in the county
of Kent, to have and receive to them and their successors yearly,
until by the said late King and his said Council they should be
sufficiently endowed with other possessions, &c. And the said late
King Richard afterwards, viz., on the 6th February, in the 21st
year of his reign, by other letters patent, gave and granted to
the aforesaid Dean and Canons the manors and parcel aforesaid, which were then extended by the escheator of the county
aforesaid, to the value of 111*l*.; and also the reversion of the
manors of Wynchefeld, together with the advowson of the church
of the same manor, after the death of John Kymberley, who
held the same for term of his life, to hold to them and their successors for ever, as in the said letters more fully is contained.   In
money paid to them, &c.   By writ, &c.,—120*l*.

2nd July.—To John Everton, clerk. In money paid to the
same John Everton, by his own hands, with the advice of the
King's Council, in advance, as well for the expenses of the King

of Scotland, from day to day, and month to month, during the whole time he was or should be absent from the King's household, by advice of the said King's Council, as for provisions purchased, carriage, portage, boatage, freightage, and other necessary costs and charges whatsoever, incurred for the expenses of the household of the said King of Scotland : also for the wages of esquires, clerks, valets, and rewards to boys and pages in attendance, during the time aforesaid, upon the said King of Scotland. By writ, &c.,—120*l.*

17*th July.*—To the Venerable Father in Christ, Philip, Bishop of Worcester, ordered and appointed by the King's Council to go to the town of Pountfreyt to confer with other commissioners of the said Lord the King, and to treat with certain commissioners there on behalf of Scotland, of and for the release of the King of Scotland, the King's prisoner. In money paid to him by the hands of William Trefridewe, in discharge of 40*l.* which the said Lord the King, with the advice and consent of his Council aforesaid, commanded to be paid to the said Bishop as a reward for his labour and expenses, &c.,—40*l.*

ISSUE ROLL, MICHAELMAS, 2 HENRY VI.

4*th October.*—To Simon de Teramo, collector in England for the Most Holy Father, the Pope, to whom the lord and father of the present King, for the service which the same Simon had rendered him in the Roman Court, in announcing a certain communication on behalf of the said late King to the said Most Holy Father, granted him 300 marks yearly, to hold so long as the said Simon should remain out of the said kingdom of England. In money paid to him by the hands of Anthony, Francis, and William Freman, in part payment of 255 marks which the present Lord the King, with the advice and assent of his Council, in compliance with the will of his father, commanded to be paid to the said Simon. By writ, &c.,—101*l.* 5*s.* 9½*d.*

18th October.—To John Bernes, of London, goldsmith. In money paid to his own hands in discharge of 20s. which the present Lord the King, with the advice and consent of his Council, commanded to be paid to the said John for his labour, costs, and workmanship in lately riding to the King's castle at Windsor, at his own costs, and there engraving the great seal of the said Lord the King with the privy signet; and also for newly engraving an inscription around the King's privy seal. By writ of privy seal amongst the mandates of this term,—1l.

28th October.—To John Everton, clerk, appointed, by the advice and direction of the Steward and Treasurer of the King's Council, to order and provide for the expenses of the King of Scotland. In money paid to the same John Everton, by the advice of the said King's Council, for the expenses of the household of the said King of Scotland. By writ, &c.,—20l.

3rd November.—To Gokyn Gunner, Walter Lokyer, Walter Hermanson, and Gerard Van Ewe, "gunnemeysters" from Germany, who for a long time remained in the service of Lord Henry, late King of England, father of the present King in France. In money paid to their own hands in discharge of 40l., which the present King, with the consent of his Council, commanded to be paid to the said "gunnemeysters;" viz. to each of them 10l., in part payment of their wages, being due and in arrear from the said late King. By writ, &c.,—40l.

To John Akeland, one of the valets of the King's Crown. In money paid to him, by the hands of Stephen Glover, for the hire of a house at Winchester by the said John for three years, there to place for safe and secure custody six chests containing bows and arrows, of the stock and stuff belonging to the said King, during the said time for the King's use, with divers other costs and expenses incurred by the said John for the carriage of the chests aforesaid, &c.,—13s. 4d.

9th November.—To Sir Thomas Cumberworth, knight, who lately, by command of the King's Council, safely conducted to the King's city of London the Duke of Orleans, and there remained with the said Duke; viz. from the 1st of May last past unto the 1st of June then next following for 32 days, including each day. In money paid to his own hands, by assignment made this day, in discharge of 42*l.* 13*s.* 4*d.* which the Lord the King, with the advice of his Council, commanded to be paid to the said Thomas, &c. By writ, &c.,—42*l.* 13*s.* 4*d.* [On the same day a further payment was ordered to be made to the said Thomas of 114*l.*, in advance for the costs and expenses of the said Duke of Orleans, then in his custody by order of the King's Council at the said King's charge.]

To Robert Watterton, esquire. In money paid to his own hands, by assignment made this day, in advance for the costs and expenses of the Duke of York, the Earl of Ewe, and the King's French prisoners in his custody, by order of the King's Council, at the cost of the said Lord the King,—150*l.*

15th November.—To Sir Robert Babthorp, knight, and others, executors of Lord Henry the Fifth, late King of England, father of the present King. In money paid to them, by the hands of the said Robert and John Wodehouse, in part payment of 1466*l.* 13*s.* 4*d.* which the said now Lord the King, with the advice and assent of his Council, commanded to be paid to the same executors for divers silver vessels and other things purchased from them for the use of the said Lord the King. By writ, &c.,—500*l.*

To John Kyllyngham, Master of the house called the Bell, in Carter Lane, London. In money paid, by the advice and assent of the King's Council, viz. to his own hands, 12*l.* 8*s.*; and by the hands of John Asshefeld, 5*l.* 6*s.* 8*d.*, for the costs and expenses of Sir Gylbyn de Lanvoy, knight, and John de la Roe, esquire, and their servants and horses for 28 days, [which said Sir Gylbyn

and John de la Roe were sent to the Holy Land, by the late
Lord King Henry the Fifth, upon certain important causes and
affairs, &c.] By writ, &c.,—17*l.* 14*s.* 8*d.*

To Sir John Pelham, knight. In money paid to him, by the
hands of Henry Welford, tailor, of London, in part payment of
250*l.* 16*s.* which the present Lord the King, with the advice and
assent of his Council, commanded to be paid to the said John
Pelham, as well for the costs and expenses of the bastard of Bourbon, late in the custody of the said John for two years and a half, as
for the costs and expenses of Sir John Mortymer, knight, also in the
custody of the said John Pelham, from the 29th day of May in
the tenth year of King Henry the Fifth, father of the present
King, until the last day of June last past ; receiving, viz. for
the said bastard, 1*l.* 6*s.* 8*d.* weekly, and for the said John Mortymer weekly, 1*l.* 6*s.* 8*d.*, during the periods aforesaid. By writ of
privy seal, &c.,—40*l.*

22*nd November.*—To Sir John Cornewale, knight. In money
paid to his own hands, by assignment made this day, in discharge
of 600 marks which the present Lord the King, with the assent of
his Council, gave and granted to the same John for costs and expenses by him at different times incurred in prosecuting, as well
for Lord Henry, late King of England, as for the present Lord the
King, for redelivery of his prisoner the Earl of Vendosme. By
writ, &c.,—400*l.*

To Joan Asteley, the present King's nurse, to whom the said
Lord the King, with the advice and assent of his Council, for the
good and laudable service by her bestowed and to be bestowed,
granted her, by his letters patent, 20*l.* yearly, to be received at his
Exchequer, &c., so long as it should please the said Lord the
King. In money paid to her by the hands of John Ardern, in
discharge of 10*l.*, &c. By writ, &c.,—10*l.* [Also an allowance
of 5*l.* yearly is granted to Margaret Brotherman and Agnes

Jakeman, the King's chamber women and laundresses, and to Matilda Fosbroke, the King's daily nurse.]

26th November.—To William Randolf, a citizen and goldsmith, of London. In money paid to him, by the hands of John Goode-felagh, in discharge of 85*l.* 11*s.* 4¾*d.*, which the present Lord the King, with the advice and assent of his Council, commanded to be paid to the said William for divers plate purchased of him for the said King's use; viz. for one large silver spice plate, with a gilt cover; weighing, by troy weight, 24 lbs., price the lb. 40*s.*, and 3 round salt-sellers of silver gilt, with covers, weighing, by troy weight, 10 lbs. 7 oz., price the lb. 33*s.* 4*d.*; 3 candelabras of silver gilt, with their "pykes," weighing, by troy weight, 11 lbs. 11½ oz., price the lb. 33*s.* 4*d.*, which said plate remains for safety in the King's Treasury, for the use of the said Lord the King, in the custody of the Treasurer and Chamberlains of the Exchequer. By writ, &c., —85*l.* 11*s.* 4¾*d.*

1st December.—To Edmund, Earl of March, the King's deputy in Ireland, receiving yearly 5000 marks for the custody of the land aforesaid. In money paid to him, viz. by the hands of Richard Maydeston, 200*l.*, and by the hands of John Carpenter, one of the executors of Richard Whityngton, 500 marks, in advance for the safe custody of the said land. By writ current of privy seal, &c., —803*l.* 6*s.* 8*d.*

15th December.—To Elizabeth Lady of Haryngton, and Thomas Broghton, esquire, executors of the will of the late Lord of Haryng-ton, deceased. In money paid to them, with the advice and assent of the King's Council, by assignment made this day, to the hands of John Ardern, in discharge of 162*l.* 13*s.* 6½*d.*, due to the said John, late Lord of Haryngton, deceased, upon an over-charge, as appears by the account of the said late Lord of Ha-ryngton rendered at the Exchequer for a voyage made by him to foreign parts, in the retinue of Lord Henry, late King of England, father of the present King, in the 3rd year of his

2 c

reign, with a certain number of men at arms and archers, as well
for money by the late Lord of Haryngton to be received, as for the
wages and rewards of himself and the men aforesaid on account of
the said voyage; viz. from the 8th of July in the said 3rd year unto
the 24th of November then next following, for payment of which
sum divers jewels and vessels of gold and silver were, by the said late
King's command, delivered by indenture to the said late Lord of
Haryngton, by the hands of Master Richard Courteney, Treasurer
of the said late King's chamber, as a security for the said wages,
&c., which said jewels are now redelivered to the Treasurer of
England for the King's use, &c.   By writ, &c.,—142*l*.

ISSUE ROLL, EASTER, 2 HENRY VI.

23rd May.—To Catherine, Queen of England, mother of the
present King. In money paid to her, by assignment made this
day, by the hands of Thomas Rokes, Receiver-General of the said
Queen, as an advance upon her certain annual allowance granted
to her for term of life in the name of dower, received at the King's
Exchequer,—300*l*.

29th May.—To Richard, Earl of Warwick. In money paid to
him, by the hands of John Shirley, in advance as well for the
wages and rewards of 1 knight and 29 men at arms, as for the wages
of 90 archers retained with the said Earl to serve the Lord the
King in his wars beyond seas, for half a year in the retinue of the
Duke of Bedford. By writ, &c.,—403*l*. 7*s*. 3½*d*.   [*Note.* This
Roll contains entries of payments to many lords, knights, and
esquires, retained by indentures to serve the King in his wars under
the Duke of Bedford, specifying the number of men each captain
was to provide; amongst other commanders appear the following
names, viz. Sir Geoffrey Fitz Hugh, knight, Lord Robert de
Wyllughby, John Fitz Symond and Giles Burton, esquires, Lord
Robert de Ponynges, William Waller and Thomas d'Ausanger,

Edgar Heton, John Orell, Roland Standissh, esquires, Sir William Oldehall, knight, Robert Treganne, John Bayous, John Walssh, Roger Lowe, esquires, Sir John Klyderowe, knight, Christopher Preston, John Caryngton, Edward Cambre, and Henry Godard, esquires.]

5th June.—To the men of the town of Dover. In money paid them by the hands of John Stratton, viz. in money 20*l.* and by assignment made this day, 60*l.*, for their passage boats and ships called "faircostes," there lately employed by the Treasurer of England, with the advice of the King's Council, for the passage of Lord de Ponynges and others of the King's retinue, to go from the town aforesaid to the town of Calais, and from thence, to serve the Lord the King in his wars in France, taking in gross for the passage of each passage boat every time it made the passage in summer, 73*s.* 4*d.*, being the price the King then was accustomed to pay, as the Council of the said Lord the King was informed, and for the passage of each ship called "faircostes" during the time aforesaid at the King's price of 46*s.* 8*d.*, so sailing from the town aforesaid to Calais, as appears by their parcels delivered to the Treasurer and Chamberlains of the Exchequer, remaining in the hanaper of this term,—80*l.*

8th June.—To Henry Barton, alderman and skinner of London, William Tristour, Cellarer, of London, Thomas Chalton, mercer, of London, and Thomas Stanes, clothier, of London, to whom Lord Henry, late King of England, father of the present King, was indebted for certain goods provided and purchased from them for the King's use. In money paid to them, with the advice and assent of the King's Council and by authority of his last parliament; viz. to the hands of the aforesaid Henry, by assignment made this day,—1200*l.*; to the hands of the aforesaid William, by assignment made on the same day,—1200*l.*; to the hands of the said Thomas Stanes, by assignment on the same day,—81*l.* 6*s.* 8*d.*; and in money to the hands of the aforesaid Thomas Chalton,—100*l.*, in full payment and satisfaction of the sums

2 c 2

aforesaid, for security of which said sums above specified the executors of the will and administrators of the goods of the said late King had delivered to the said persons the moiety of a gold collar, of great price and value, which belonged to the said late King, which said moiety of the collar aforesaid, by the intercession and at the request of the said Council, to the persons aforesaid, was delivered to the Treasurer of England, for the use of the Lord the King, thereon to borrow money, for the present expedition going out for defence of his kingdom of France. By writ of privy seal,—2581*l.* 6*s.* 8*d.* [*Note.* This Roll contains the names of the foreign and British ships retained in the King's service for the wars in France, together with the names of the captains and owners, amount of tonnage, and number of armed men and sailors in each vessel.]

ISSUE ROLL, MICHAELMAS, 3 HENRY VI.

3rd November.—To the venerable father in Christ, Thomas, Bishop of Durham. In money paid to him, by the hands of Thomas Howeden, in discharge of 100*s.* which the present Lord the King, with the assent of his Council, commanded to be paid to the said Bishop for so much money paid by him for the expenses of Master William Doncaster and Master Thomas Ryall, lately sent from the city of Durham to Scotland, there to receive the oath of the King of Scotland to perform those things which he had promised. By writ, &c.,—5*l.*

20th November.—To Joan Beauchamp, Lady of Bergevenny, executrix of the will of Sir Hugh Burnell, knight, late Lord of Holgote and Weoly, deceased. In money paid to the same executrix, by the hands of Brokesby, her esquire, by assignment made this day, in discharge of 200*l.* paid by the Lord the King for restoration of a tally, &c., assigned by the late King Henry, father of the present King, &c., to the said Hugh for his manor called Hame upon Kygeston, in the county of Surrey, with its appurtenances, purchased from him, &c. By writ, &c.,—200*l.*

27th November.—To Richard Hastynges, chevalier, constable of Knaresburgh Castle. In money paid to him, by assignment made this day, in discharge of 10*l.* which the present Lord the King, with the advice and assent of his Council, commanded to be paid as a reward to the said Richard for the labour and costs incurred by him in going, and returning, safely and securely conducting from the castle aforesaid, with four esquires and 20 valets, at his own costs, Gilbert, the son and heir of William Constable, of Scotland, James, Lord Caldore, Robert, the son and heir of Robert Mantalent, chevalier, Robert de Lisle, chevalier, and William Abbernethey, lately in his custody, in the castle aforesaid, from thence to the city of London, and there delivering them to Robert Scot, deputy of the Tower of London. By writ, &c.,—10*l.*

To the Dean and Canons of Windsor College. In money paid to them by the hands of John Chetewyn, esquire, with the advice and assent of the King's Council, viz., for the said Lord the King, 40 marks, and for the King of Denmark, 20*l.*, as is ordered amongst other articles of the statutes of the most honourable order of the garter, viz., that every knight of the said order, according to his estate, on his first entrance, shall give a certain sum of money to the said Dean and Canons, viz., the King of England, 40 marks, and any foreign King, 20*l.*, as in the said statutes more fully is contained. By writ, &c.,—46*l.* 13*s.* 4*d.*

To John Wyntershull, late Sheriff of Surrey and Sussex. In money paid to him by assignment made this day, in advance, for the costs and expenses incurred by him for safely conducting John Mortymer, chevalier, from Pevesey Castle to the Tower of London,—9*l.*

15th January.—To Sir Walter Hungerford, knight, ordered and appointed on the 9th December, in the 1st year of the present King, by authority of the said King's parliament then held at Westminster, to be one of his Council, receiving yearly of the said Lord the King 100*l.* from his Treasury, to be paid at the four principal terms, &c., so long as he should be one of the Council aforesaid ; to have the same as a reward for the great labour and expense which the said Walter had, and in future should sustain, by reason of his attendance upon the aforesaid Council, in like manner as such Councillors, in the time of King Richard II. and Henry IV., grandfather of the present King, for their attendance on the King's said Council, had been accustomed to be allowed, as by inspection and view of divers warrants under the privy seal, and other records, in the time of the said late Kings, for payment of such rewards to the said Councillors, fully doth appear. In money paid to him by assignment made this day, in part payment of 200*l.* which the Lord the King, with the advice and assent of his great Council, ordered as a reward to be paid to the said Walter, viz., from the said 9th day of December, &c. By writ of privy seal, &c.,—100*l.* [*Note.* There are similar payments to the Earl of Warwick and others appointed to be of the King's Council, entered on these Rolls].

To Robert Passemer, one of the King's sergeants at arms, who lately, by command of the Chancellor of England, arrested brother John Grace, and safely conducted him before the said King's Council. In money paid to his own hands, in discharge of 10 marks which the Lord the King, with the advice and assent of his Council, &c., commanded to be paid him, &c. By writ, &c., —6*l.* 13*s.* 4*d.*

To Garter, king of arms, sent, by advice and consent of the King's Council, from the kingdom of England to the Duke of Gloucester, being in his dominion of Hainhalt, upon certain especial causes and matters to be communicated to the said Duke on behalf of the said Council. In money paid, &c., for expenses incurred by him in going and returning upon the business aforesaid, —13*l.* 6*s.* 8*d.*

9th February.—To Henry Lord Fitz Hugh, Lewis Robessart,

Walter Hungerford, Walter Beauchamp, William Porter, Robert Babthorp, John Wodhous, and John Leventhorp, with others, named as executors in the will of Lord Henry, late King of England, father of the present King. In money paid to them by the hands of John Pikeryng, of Calais, by assignment made this day, in part payment of 8266*l.* 13*s.* 4*d.* which the present King, with the advice and assent of his Council, commanded to be paid to the same executors. By writ, &c.,—80*l.*

26th February.—To Simon Blakeburn, the King's sergeant at arms, ordered and appointed by the Treasurer of England to retain divers ships and vessels in the port of London, in the second year of the present King's reign, for the passage of the Lords of Talbot, Clynton, and Ponynges, and others retained with them, to go with the King to Crotey, in Normandy, to recover the castle and town there. In money paid, &c.,—1*l.* 13*s.* 6*d.*

28th February.—To John, Lord of Talbot and Furnevale. In money paid him by assignment made this day, by the hands of John Cantelowe, citizen and mercer of London, in discharge of 244*l.* 3*s.* 4*d.* which the present Lord the King, with the advice and assent of his Council, commanded to be paid him for so much money due to him by Lord Henry, late King of England, grandfather of the present King, for the wages of the said Lord of Talbot and the men of his retinue, during the time he was keeper, under a commission of the said grandfather, of the castle and lordship of Mountgomery, then in the hands of the said grandfather, by reason of the minority of Edward, Earl of March, then within age, and in the custody of the said grandfather, at the time of the Welsh rebellion, as appears of record by the account of the said Lord of Talbot thereof rendered at the Exchequer, in the 9th year of the said grandfather. By writ, &c.,—144*l.* 3*s.* 4*d.*

22nd March.—To Roland, Alexander, James, and Thomas Standyssh, retained in the King's service by indenture made between the said Lord the King and the aforesaid Roland, Alexander, James, and Thomas, to serve the said Lord the King in the war beyond seas for half a year. In money paid to their own hands, in advance, as well for wages and rewards for themselves and six men at arms, as for the wages of 27 archers retained with the same Roland, Alexander, James, and Thomas, &c. By writ, &c.,—122*l.* 7*s.* 6*d.* [This part of the Roll contains a long list of persons retained to serve the King in his wars.]

To Nicholas Bildeston, clerk. In money paid to his own hands, by assignment made this day, in discharge of 50 marks, which the present Lord the King, with the advice and assent of his Council, commanded to be paid to the said Nicholas for "200 duketes," containing the sum of 50 marks, paid by the said Nicholas at the Court of Rome, at the request and command of the Treasurer of England, to a certain Ardesin, the King's advocate in the court aforesaid. By writ, &c.,—33*l.* 6*s.* 8*d.*

ISSUE ROLL, EASTER, 3 HENRY VI.

7th May.—To Garter King of arms, lately sent, by the advice and assent of the King's great Council of London, to the Duke of Burgundy, then in Flanders, 'with a certain letter from the said King, directed to the said Duke, upon certain secret and especial matters therein contained, communicated by the said Council. In money paid to him for going and returning on the business aforesaid,—5*l.*

To John Damport, a King's messenger of the receipt of the Exchequer, sent from London to the Earl Marshal, then in the island of Haxhey, with a certain writ under the King's great seal, directed to the same Earl, to attend at Westminster on the 1st May next happening, at the King's parliament then there to be held. In money paid to his own hands for going and returning upon the message aforesaid,—6*s.* 8*d.*

21st May.—To John Stoute. In money paid to him by the hands of his wife, in discharge of 108s., with 40s., received by him on the 28th February last past, due for making a dozen "quysshons" and five "banqwers," worked with a work called tapestry work, with the arms of the King of England and France on the same, made for the Lords of the King's Council, sitting in the Star Chamber, by direction of the Treasurer and Chamberlains of the Exchequer,—3l. 8s.

26th June.—To John Sewale, one of the King's messengers, sent with two letters directed to John Searle and others, executors of the will of John Wakeryng, late Bishop of Norwich, deceased, to bring, with all possible speed, certain books of account concerning the temporalities of the see of Norwich for the three years last past, before the great Council of the Lord the King, at Westminster, and there to produce the same books, that a true knowledge of the value of the temporalities of the see aforesaid might be had, for the King's benefit, and information of the said Council. In money paid to him for his expenses in going and returning, &c. By direction of the Treasurer, &c.,—6s. 8d.

To Richard Nevile, chevalier, lately dwelling at Braunspath, and attending upon James, King of Scotland, with knights, esquires, and other men, to the number of 160 persons, at the costs and wages of the said Richard for above seven weeks. In money paid to him by the hands of Thomas Stokdale, &c., in discharge of 100l. which the present Lord the King, with the advice and assent of his Council, commanded to be assigned and paid to the same Richard out of the wardship of the lands and tenements, &c., which belonged to Lucy, late Countess of Kent, and out of the wardship of all the lands, &c., which belonged to Elizabeth, one of the daughters of Edmund, late Earl of Kent. By writ, &c.,—100l.

[*Note.*—This Roll contains the names of the lords, knights, and esquires, retained in the King's service, to serve under the Duke of Bedford, the King's uncle, Regent of France.]

ISSUE ROLL, MICHAELMAS, 4 HENRY VI.

10th December.—To Robert Popyngay, executor of the will of Catherine Lardiner. In money paid to him by assignment made this day, to the hands of the said Robert, for a certain gold tabernacle, with a piece of the holy garment without seam, placed in the middle of the said tabernacle, garnished with 27 great pearls, of which 7 are valued at 5 marks each, and 20 at 30*s.* each, weighing in all 61¼ ounces of gold; which said jewel was lately delivered by Richard Courteneye, late Bishop of Norwich, Treasurer and Chamberlain of King Henry V., and keeper of his jewels, to Thomas Dutton, chevalier, lately retained by the said late King, with certain men at arms and archers, to go with him in his service to France, in the third year of his reign, as a security for their wages for the second quarter of the year, and which said jewel was afterwards pledged to the aforesaid Catherine Lardiner for the sum of 80*l.*, and afterwards restored to the Treasurer and Chamberlains of the Exchequer to the King's use, by the said Robert, executor of the will of the said Catherine. Therefore it was adjudged for the King's benefit that the said Robert, executor of the aforesaid Catherine, should have payment assigned him for the said sum of 80*l.*, as is just, by the advice and assent of the Treasurer, Barons, and Chamberlains of the Exchequer, —80*l.*

13th December.—To Thomas Wesenham, esquire. In money paid to his own hands, for a pair of knives, called "kervyng-knyefs," purchased by the said Thomas for the King's use,— 13*s.* 4*d.*

6th February.—To Thomas, Duke of Exeter. In money paid to him by assignment made this day, &c., in discharge of 702*l.* 3*s.* which the present Lord the King, with the advice and assent of his Council, commanded to be paid to the said Duke for two gold cups, garnished with pearls and precious stones, purchased from the same Duke, with the advice and assent of the said Council, by the late Treasurer of England, for the King's use, to be presented to a certain Prince Peter, son of the King of Portugal, who lately arrived in England, given by the said Lord the King, with the advice and assent aforesaid, to the said Prince, &c.,—702*l.* 3*s.*

4th March.—To Nicholas Dixon, clerk of one of the Barons of the Exchequer. In money paid to his own hands for his costs and expenses in going from the city of London to the town of Leicester with divers Rolls, as well from the great Exchequer, as from the receipt thereof, to make declaration to the Lords of the King's Council, in his parliament there, concerning the state of his kingdom, for the benefit of the said Lord the King, paid for going, tarrying, and returning in 15 days, &c.,—10*l.*

ISSUE ROLL, EASTER, 4 HENRY VI.

18th April.—To the Venerable Father in Christ, Henry, Bishop of Winchester, kinsman of the present Lord the King, late his Chancellor of England, to whom the said Lord the King, with the advice and assent of his Council, in consideration of the great labour, charge, costs, and expenses, which the said late Chancellor sustained in the absence of the Dukes of Bedford and Gloucester, the said King's uncles, for the honour of the said King and his kingdom : it was ordered and appointed that he should receive yearly the sum of 2000 marks from his Treasury, so long as the said Bishop should be Chancellor during the absence of his uncles aforesaid ; the time of payment of the sum aforesaid to begin at the feast of Saint Michael, in the third year of the said Lord the King. In money paid, &c. By writ, &c., —666*l.* 13*s.* 4*d.*

11th May.—To Thomas Petit, of the county of York, Thomas Parson, and Thomas de la Howe, one of the tellers of the King's receipt of the Exchequer, severally sent, at divers times, from the

town of Leicester to different parts of England with letters of
privy seal of the said Lord the King, directed to the Earl of
Northumberland, the Abbot of Bury, the Prior of Saint John of
Jerusalem in England, the Bishops of Bangor and Landaff, to
attend with all possible haste at the said King's parliament at
Leicester aforesaid. In money paid to them, &c., for their expenses in going and returning, &c. By direction of the Treasurer, &c.,—11s. 8d. [Several other letters were sent to divers
of the nobility to attend the said parliament at Leicester.]

15th July.—To John Vincent. In money paid to him for so
much money expended by command of the Treasurer of England, for the expenses of 12 jurors of the county of Middlesex,
dining at Westminster, and there attending and waiting to give a
verdict upon a certain inquisition taken between the Lord the
King and Thomas Seyncler, esquire, upon a certain security of
the peace broken by the said Thomas, by which verdict, so delivered by the said jury, before the Treasurer and Barons of the
Exchequer, the same Thomas was convicted for the Lord the
King in 100 marks. By direction of the Treasurer, &c.,—
13s. 4d.

17th July.—To William Hill, one of the clerks of the King's
Chancery. In money paid to his own hands, as an especial reward for writing out a register of all the provinces in Bourdeaux and Gascony, and a certain other book of the fealty and
services of the lords thereof, remaining in the King's Treasury
for safe custody there, for the benefit of the said Lord the King.
By direction of the Treasurer and Chamberlains of the Exchequer,—5l.

To Isabella, late wife of John Dureward, esquire, deceased,
executrix of the will of the said John. In money paid to her by
the hands of Robert Whitegreve, in discharge of 100l., with 50l.,
received by the said executrix, by the kind intercession of Walter,
Lord Hungerford, Treasurer of England, and by agreement be-

tween the said Treasurer and executrix, for a release made to the
King upon payment of the residue of the said 50*l.*, due to the said
Isabella, the executrix; which said 100*l.* the said John lent to the
Lord Henry V., late King of England, father of the present
King, secured upon certain jewels of the said late King, pledged
to the said John for repayment of the said sum, which said jewels appear specified and noted below; viz., a gold tabernacle, with
the image of the Blessed Mary upon a green ground, with the
images of Adam and Eve and four angels at the four corners,
and a cross upon the same tabernacle, with a white crucifix enamelled; and on the top of the said cross a white eagle enamelled,
adorned with 2 rubies, 3 diamonds, 4 other rubies, 3 sapphires, 77
great pearls, and 43 small pearls, weighing by troy weight
42 ounces, price the ounce, 40*s.*:—one cup of beryl, ornamented with gold, 11 great pearls, and 50 small pearls, weighing
by troy weight 21½ ounces; which said jewels aforesaid were delivered into the Receipt of the Exchequer, and remain in the
King's Treasury, &c., there to be kept for the King's use. By
writ, &c.,—50*l.*

26th July.—To William Estfeld, citizen and mercer of London.
In money paid to his own hands, for divers costs by him incurred
by command of the Treasurer of England, as well for the exequies,
as for other expenses about the burial and funeral of Hugh, late
Lord de Camoys, late a minor, and in the King's custody, at
Clerkenwell, deceased, and lately buried in the church of
Clerkenwell aforesaid, as appears, &c.,—7*l.* 10*s.*

To the executors of the will of John Hende. In money paid
to them by assignment made this day, in discharge of 500 marks,
with 148*l.* 6*s.* 8*d.*, paid to the said executors by the kind intercession of Walter, Lord Hungerford, Treasurer of England, and
by agreement had between the said Treasurer and executors, to
release to the King the residue, &c.; which said 500 marks the
same John lent to Lord Henry V., taking for security of repayment
thereof certain jewels, &c., specified below; viz., a pallet, called

" the palette of Spain," garnished with gold and 25 rubies and bastard rubies, 4 sapphires, 15 great emeralds, 103 small emeralds, and 300 pearls, weighing 8 lb. 6 oz., troy weight, the price of the said palette, then valued in the whole at 200*l.* :—one gold coronet, garnished with 10 flowers of gold made in the form of " flourdelice," garnished with rubies, sapphires, emeralds, and pearls, and with 10 other square works, each garnished with a ruby in the middle, with 12 pearls surrounding, weighing by troy weight 18½ ounces and 20 dwts of gold, fully garnished, the price as then valued, 100 marks:—1 other tabernacle with 3 beryls, made for sacred purposes, with three angels, standing upon a tripod, one of which angels is deficient, weighing by the troy weight, 10 lbs. 2½ oz., price the lb. 40*s.*, valued in the whole, as then appraised, at 20*l.* 6*s.* 8*d.*.—1 tablet of gold, garnished in the middle with a great sapphire, engraved with an image of the Trinity, and surrounded by a border, with 4 rubies, 11 pearls, suspended by a gold chain, weighing by troy weight 3 oz. 5*s.* of gold, value of the whole, as then appraised, 20 marks:—2 new silver gilt censers, weighing together 7 lb. 7¾ oz., price the lb., 46*s.* 8*d.*, entire value, as then appraised, 17*l.* 10*s.* :—2 silver candelabras, partly gilt, one of which wants the top and the pyke, and the other a pyke, weighing together 13 lb. 9 oz., price the lb., 30*s.*; the entire value as then appraised, 20*l.* 12*s.* 6*d.* : which said jewels aforesaid were delivered at the Receipt of the Exchequer, and remain in the King's Treasury, &c., for the King's use, &c. By general writ, &c.,—185*l.*

ISSUE ROLL, MICHAELMAS, 5 HENRY VI.

20th March.—To Sir John Radclyff, knight, ordered and appointed by the Lord the King's commission to go to divers counties of England, to search for, take, and arrest, as well within as without the liberties, William Wawe, a public thief and notorious highwayman, and despoiler and robber of churches, who had spoken treason against the royal person of the said Lord the

King, and had been indicted for divers felonies, insurrections, murders, rebellions, errors, and heresies, perpetrated by the said William in divers counties of England; and the said William, together with his accomplices, if any in his company should be found, to bring them before the Lord the King and his Council. In money paid to his own hands, for the costs and expenses of himself and his men, and others riding with him and in his retinue, to take and arrest the aforesaid William Wawe and his accomplices, if they should be found; also for other necessary purposes concerning the advantage of the said Lord the King, and his kingdom. By writ, &c.,—100*l.*

ISSUE ROLL, EASTER, 5 HENRY VI.

12th May.—To Peter Cawode, esquire, ordered and appointed by the King's Council for the safe conduct of divers hostages of James, King of Scotland, from the Tower of London to the city of York, and there to deliver them to Sir Richard Nevyll. In money paid to his own hands, in advance, for divers costs and expenses by him incurred in going, tarrying, and returning upon the business aforesaid,—13*l.* 6*s.* 8*d.*

24th May.—To John, Duke of Bedford, Regent of the kingdom of France. In money paid to him by the hands of Robert Whityngham, in part payment of 2000*l.* which the present Lord the King, with the advice and assent of his Council, commanded to be paid to the said Duke, to have of his gift, in the nature of a reward, as well for the great labour, costs, and expenses incurred and sustained by the said Duke in coming from the said kingdom of France to England, at the instance and request of the said Council; the cause of whose coming was, by God's assistance, chiefly for the good peace and tranquillity of the kingdom of England; as also for the great costs and necessary expenses which he sustained on returning to the said kingdom of France; and also

because the said Duke and family of his household were not
at the King's charge as others were who passed over in his retinue
to France, there to serve the Lord the King in his wars, as was
stated in a petition and request made to the said Lord the King
by the commonalty of his realm of England at his last parliament
held at Leicester, to provide the said Duke with a competent reward for the purposes aforesaid, and also for other great and reasonable causes concerning the said Lord the King respecting this
business, with the assent of his Council. By writ, &c.,—100*l.*

To Gloucester herald, sent to the Duke of Quymbre with
the clothing of the livery of the garter, delivered to the same
Duke. In money paid to his own hands in discharge of 20*l.*
which the Lord the King, with the advice and assent of his
Council, commanded to be paid to the same Gloucester, for his
costs and expenses in going, tarrying, and returning upon the
message aforesaid. By writ of privy seal, &c.,—20*l.*

21*st June.*—To John Talbot, the King's sergeant at arms, at
one time appointed, by a certain commission under the great seal
of the Lord the King, made in the 1st year of his reign, to detain
and seize divers ships and vessels in the ports of London, Sandwich,
Dover, and Winchelsea, to embark Thomas, Duke of Exeter,
John, the Earl Marshal, Robert Lord de Willughby, and other
knights, esquires, and archers of the retinue of our aforesaid Lord
the King in the said ports proceeding to Calais; also at another
time appointed by a like commission of the said Lord the King in
his fifth year, in like manner to detain all and singular ships and
vessels of 20 tons burthen and above, to the number of 140 tons,
within the port of London and Cinque Ports, for the passage of
Lord John, Duke of Bedford, the King's uncle, regent of his
kingdom of France, the Bishop of Winchester, their men, horses,
household, and divers other lords, knights, men at arms, and
archers of the retinue of the said King going to Calais. In money
paid to him, by the hands of John Poutrell, as an especial reward
for his labour, costs, and expenses incurred and sustained, &c.,—5*l.*

3rd July.—To John Copleston, lately appointed, by the King's commission, together with Walter Colles, Clerk, approvers and receivers of all the castles, lordships, manors, &c. which belonged to Hugh Courtenay, late Earl of Devon, which by the death of the said late Earl, and by reason of the minority of Thomas, his son and heir, are now come into the King's hands. &c.   In money paid, &c.,—10*l.*

To the executors of the will of Ralph, late Earl of Westmoreland.   In money paid them by the hands of Thomas Broune, by assignment made this day, in advance for the support of Richard, the son and heir of Richard, late Earl of Cambridge, kinsman and heir of Edward, late Duke of York, being in the King's custody, under the guardianship of the executors of the said late Earl of Westmoreland at the cost of the said Lord the King.   By writ of privy seal, &c.,—66*l.* 13*s.* 4*d.*

11th July.—To Johanicot d'Aguerr, servant to Charles de Beaumont Alferitz, of Navarre, kinsman to the King, who lately brought certain letters to the said Lord the King and his Council from the said Charles.   In money paid to him in discharge of 10*l.* which the present Lord the King, with the advice and assent of his Council, commanded to be paid to the said Johanicot as a reward, &c.   By writ, &c.,—10*l.*   [The end of this Roll contains several entries to provide shipping, &c., for the purpose of taking John Lord de Grey, the King's lieutenant, and his retinue to Ireland].

ISSUE ROLL, MICHAELMAS, 6 HENRY VI.

13th October.—To Paul, Count de Valache, from Greece, to whom the present King, on the 8th of July last past, of his especial grace, in consideration that the same Count was descended from noble blood, and had been nearly destroyed and annihilated by the Turks and Saracens, the enemies of God, and had not wherewith to live or maintain his estate except from the relief of

2 D

good Christians, with the advice and assent of his Council, and
for the sake of charity in these premises, by letters patent, granted
him in aid honestly to support and maintain his estate, 40 marks,
yearly to be received at the Exchequer, &c., so long as it should
please the said King, as in the said letters more fully is contained.
In money paid to his own hands in discharge of 6*l*. 1*s*. 4*d*., paid
to him, &c. from the said 8th of July unto the 29th of September
following, &c. By writ, &c.,—6*l*. 1*s*. 4*d*.

25th November.—To Sir John Juyn, knight, Chief Baron of the
King's Exchequer, appointed, by a commission of the said King,
together with others, to lease all and singular the King's lands and
tenements in the county of Cornwall, being parcel of, or belonging
to his duchy of Cornwall, to fit persons, for a term of seven years,
the term to begin at Michaelmas next following, as well by examination and information obtained from the King's liege subjects
of the counties of Cornwall, Devon, and Somerset, as by all other reasonable means and ways which according to their sound discretion
should be for the King's benefit, &c.; and also to inquire, by the
oaths of good and lawful men of the counties aforesaid, concerning
all and singular merchant ships and merchandize upon the sea-
coast of the said counties, &c., that had not paid the King's customs, &c. In money paid to him for his costs, &c.,—13*l*. 6*s*. 8*d*.

To Richard Crosby, Prior of the cathedral church of the blessed
Mary of Coventry, agent and lawful attorney to the venerable Father
in Christ Thomas Peverell, late Bishop of Worcester, deceased,
the Mayor and Commonalty of the city of Coventry, and William
Waltham, clerk. In money paid to the same Prior, in the names
of the persons aforesaid, by the hands of Thomas Fawkoner, by
assignment made this day of 300*l*. in discharge of 500*l*., with 200*l*.
released by the same Prior, in the names of the said persons, to
the King for payment of the remaining 300*l*. lately borrowed as
well of the said Prior as of the other persons abovenamed by Lord
Henry, late King of England, father of the present King, to prosecute a certain voyage in the third year of his reign; viz. from

the said late Bishop, 300*l.*, from the said Prior 50 marks, from the said Mayor and Commonalty, 200 marks, and from the said William 50 marks; as by the letters patent of the said late King thereon made to the said persons more fully doth appear; for which said 500*l.*, so borrowed from them, the said late King pledged to them his great collar, called Ikelton collar, (during the time he was Prince,) garnished with 4 rubies, 4 great sapphires, 32 great pearls, and 53 other pearls of a lesser sort, weighing 36¼ oz., then valued at 500*l.*, as security for repayment of the said sum so borrowed, &c.; which said collar the said Prior, for this purpose fully empowered, &c. delivered to the Treasurer and Chamberlains, &c., to the King's use. By writ of great seal, &c., —300*l.*

5th December.—To John Iwardeby, Thomas Stokedale, William Baron, and John Poutrell, ordered and appointed by the King's Council to attend and wait at Westminster and London the last autumn during the vacation, to receive 9000 marks granted by the said Lord the King, with the assent of his said Council, to the Duke of Gloucester, his uncle, as a loan to be applied in aid and relief of the Duchess of Gloucester, his wife, the King's kinswoman, then in Holland in great trouble, distress, and adversity, the said sum having been borrowed from divers persons, as well spiritual as temporal, and also of the Mayor and Commonalty of the city of London, &c. In money paid to them for their costs and expenses in attending at Westminster, &c.,— 13*l.* 6*s.* 8*d.*

ISSUE ROLL, EASTER, 6 HENRY VI.

18th May.—To James Polet. In money paid to his own hands in discharge of 50 marks, which the present Lord the King, with the advice and assent of his Council, commanded to be paid to the same James, to have of his gift for the good service by him bestowed as well upon the King's father as to be bestowed upon the present Lord the King; also because the said James, about the month of

August last, between Caen and Bayonne, in France, was taken
prisoner by the enemies and adversaries of the said Lord the
King at Mount Saint Michael in those parts, and by duress
there was extorted from him an excessive ransom, to the amount
of 1800 gold crowns, for payment of which sum the aforesaid
James pledged to divers persons all the lands and tenements
which he had for his ransom aforesaid, so that the said James
had not wherewith to live nor sufficient to pay for his said ransom
without the said King's aid.   By writ, &c.,—33*l.* 6*s.* 8*d.*

To Walter Lucy, citizen and haberdasher of London. In money
paid to his own hands for 12 books of parchment, purchased of
him for certain customers of divers ports within the realm of England, to enter into the same books, and not elsewhere, all and singular the goods and merchandize imported or exported at the said
ports, and by the said books, and not by other documents, to render
their accounts before the Treasurer and Barons of the Exchequer,
for certain necessary causes concerning the King's advantage, &c.,
—4*l.* 7*s.*

To the King of arms, English heralds, and others, foreign
heralds, late in the King's retinue. In money paid to them, by
assignment made this day, by the hands of Garter, king of arms,
in discharge of 200 crowns which the present Lord the King, with
the advice and assent of his Council, commanded to be paid to the
said king and heralds for the good services bestowed by them
upon the said Lord the King, as well at the time when the said
Lord the King received the order of knighthood, as at the time
of the feasts of Easter and Saint George last past, or the value of
the said 200 crowns to be received of his gift, as a reward for the
services aforesaid.   By writ, &c.,—33*l.* 6*s.* 8*d.*

In money paid with the advice and assent of the King's Council,
by the hands of Thomas Broune, for the installation of the Duke de
Quymbre, a kinsman of the said Lord the King, and son of the
King of Portugal, as a knight of the order of the garter, at the

King's castle of Windsor, according to the directions of the statutes of the said order thereupon made and provided. By writ, &c.,—10*l.*

5th July.—To John Sewale, a King's messenger, sent, by command of the Treasurer of England, to Sir Thomas Kyryell, knight, to take a muster of the retinue of the Earl of Salisbury, to be made by the said Thomas and other the King's commissioners, for this purpose appointed, at Berhamdowne, in the county of Kent. In money paid to him for his expenses in going and returning upon the message aforesaid, &c.,—6*s.* 8*d.*

To John, Duke of Norfolk, son of Thomas, late Earl of Nottingham, and Marshal of England, which said Thomas the late Earl, Lord Richard the Second, after the conquest, late King of England, on the 29th day of September, in the 1st year of his reign, by his charter, with the assent of the Prelates, Dukes, nobility, and other peers and commonalty of his kingdom of England, assembled in parliament at Westminster, duly created Duke of Norfolk, with the title, style, name, and honour thereof, and thereupon invested him, by placing the coronet upon his head and delivering to him the golden rod, at the same time discreetly exhorting him to virtue, and so to have and possess the style, title, name, and honour aforesaid to the aforesaid Duke and the heirs male of his body begotten for ever. And that by so exalting his name there would be added greater charge, (as always to such honour is annexed,) with the assent aforesaid, he gave and granted to the same Duke and his heirs aforesaid 40 marks yearly to be received at the Exchequer, &c., as in the charter aforesaid more fully is contained. In money paid to the said present Duke, by assignment made this day, by the hands of Robert Suthwell, as well in discharge of 58*l.* 18*s.* 11½*d.* paid to him for this his allowance, rateably from the 14th day of July in the 3rd year of the present King, upon which day the said Duke did his liege homage as Duke of Norfolk to the said now King, unto the 29th of September then next following, for 77 days, the last day but not the

first day included; as also for Easter Term in the 4th year, and
Michaelmas and Easter Terms in the 5th and 6th years of the
present King. By writ of liberate, &c.,—58*l*. 18*s.* 11½*d.*

17th July.—To Sir William Phelyp, knight, and others,
executors of the will of Thomas, late Duke of Exeter. In money
paid to them, by assignment made this day, &c., in discharge of
600*l.* which the present Lord the King, with the advice and assent
of his Council, ordered to be paid to the same executors for two
jewels; viz. one of Saint George and the other of our Lord Jesus
Christ praying on the mount, garnished with pearls and precious
stones, as they are described and doth fully appear in a certain book
remaining in the King's Remembrancer's Office within the Receipt
of the Exchequer, purchased from them for the King's use, and
with the advice and assent aforesaid ordered to be taken by the
reverend Father in Christ William, Bishop of London, and John
Lord le Scrop, and others the King's Ambassadors, to the most
holy Father the Pope, to have of the said King's gift. By writ of
privy seal, &c.,—600*l.* [This part of the Roll contains payments
of large sums of money to the said Bishop of London and other
Ambassadors, sent to the Pope at this period upon certain important and urgent matters intimately concerning the estate of the
King and his subjects of this kingdom.]

ISSUE ROLL, MICHAELMAS, 7 HENRY VI.

13th October.—To John Snell, clerk, almoner of the King's
household, appointed by the said Lord the King, with the advice
and assent of his Council, to direct the celebration of 10,000 masses
for the souls of those knights of the order of the garter who
had died since the said Lord the King took upon himself the
government of the kingdom, according to a certain ordinance
of the foundation of the order aforesaid, ordered, founded and
established by Lord Edward the Third, after the conquest, late
King of England, progenitor of the present King In money paid

to his own hands in discharge of 41*l*. 13*s*. 4*d*. which the said Lord the King, with the advice and assent aforesaid, commanded to be paid to the said almoner for the purpose aforesaid; viz. for each mass of the 10,000 masses aforesaid so to be celebrated 1*d*.   By writ, &c.,—41*l*. 13*s*. 4*d*.

5*th February*.—To the reverend Father in Christ the King's kinsman, by title of Cardinal of Saint Eusebius, who proceeded by licence and authority of the said Lord the King, from the King's town of York to the Marches between England and Scotland, there personally to confer and treat with the King of Scotland, the King's kinsman, of and upon certain great and weighty matters, especially concerning the honour and benefit of the kingdom of our said Lord the King.   In money paid to him, with the advice and assent of the King's Council, by the hands of John Aysshe, in advance for the costs and expenses of the said Cardinal, for the purpose aforesaid, &c.   By writ, &c.,—333*l*. 6*s*. 8*d*.

ISSUE ROLL, EASTER, 7 HENRY VI.

17*th June*.—To Richard, Earl of Warwick and Albermarle, whom the present Lord the King, on the 1st of June in the 6th year of his reign, with the advice and assent of the Dukes of Bedford and Gloucester, the King's uncles, and of all other Lords of the King's great Council, deputed, ordered, and appointed to be about the person of the said Lord the King for the safe custody thereof, and to exercise all pains and true diligence for the preservation and security of the person of the said Lord the King, and to instruct and inform the said Lord the King, or cause him to be instructed in generous habits, cheerful manners, in literature, and liberal and other useful learning, in the manner and form as in certain the King's letters patent, thereupon made and sealed with his great seal, more fully is contained, receiving yearly for the purpose aforesaid 250 marks at the King's Exchequer, so long as it should please the said King, by equal portions, at the

Michaelmas and Easter Terms. In money paid to him, viz. by
assignment made this day, by the hands of Robert Andrew, 100*l.*
and in money by the hands of John Baysham 100 marks, in discharge of 250 marks paid him for this his allowance; viz. from the
said 1st day of June unto the 1st day of June then next following,
for one whole year. By writ of privy seal, &c.,—166*l.* 13*s.* 4*d.*

2nd July.—To Henry Percy, Earl of Northumberland, whom
the present Lord the King, with the advice and assent of his
Council, by his letters of privy seal, commanded to assist the reverend Father in Christ the King's uncle, by title cardinal of Saint
Eusebius, in Northumberland, upon the coming of the King of
Scotland to the said Cardinal in the parts aforesaid, by virtue of
which command the said Earl went from Semer to the town of
Berwick, attended with 100 horsemen, and returned in sixteen days,
within which time the said Earl provided four days, as he saith,
eight horsemen at his great costs and expense. In money paid, &c.,
in discharge of 50*l.* which the said Lord the King, with the advice
and assent of his Council aforesaid, commanded to be paid to the
said Earl, to have of his gift, as a reward in aid of his costs and
expenses aforesaid. By writ, &c.,—50*l.*

14th July.—To Richard Bukland, Treasurer of the town of
Calais and Marches thereof, whom the present King, with the
advice and assent of his Council, appointed to pay the soldiers of
the castle and town of Calais and of other castles in the Marches
there, out of the sum of 10,000 marks, to be paid by the King of
Scotland by virtue of an appointment made between our Lord the
King and the said King of Scotland heretofore agreed upon, as
was promised by the said King of Scotland; but as the said King
of Scotland had not been able to receive or obtain the said sum of
10,000 marks, the said Lord the King, therefore, with the advice
and assent of his Council, &c., granted a new assignment of 5000
marks, charged upon the first payment to be made by the Duke of
Bourbon to our said King, for payment of the said soldiers, &c.
In money paid to the said Treasurer in discharge of 400*l.* &c., to

satisfy the present necessity of the said soldiers, &c. By writ, &c.,
—400*l*. [The end of this Roll contains many payments for the
fleet and army then proceeding to France under the venerable
Father in Christ, commonly called the Cardinal of England, the
King's uncle.]

Issue Roll, Easter, 8 Henry VI.

1*st May*.—To the Lord Cardinal, by the title of Saint Eusebius.
In money paid to him, by the hands of John Burton, clerk, in discharge of 7233*l*. 6*s*. 8*d*. which the Lord the King, with the assent
of his Council, commanded to be paid to the same Cardinal, his
kinsman, for which said sum certain Lords of the King's Council
were severally bound, by their letters obligatory, as well to the
most holy Father the Pope as to the said Cardinal, for payment
thereof by certain days contained in the said letters, upon which
the said sum was to be paid to his said kinsman, and now paid at
the King's command, for the wages and rewards of certain men at
arms and archers going in his retinue to France, there to resist
the King's enemies and rebels, &c. By writ, &c.,—3616*l*. 13*s*. 4*d*.
[This part of the Roll contains a long list of names of the lords,
knights, and esquires and number of men retained by each to go
with the Lord the King in his retinue to the wars in France, far
too numerous to be inserted here, together with a list of his
household, the names of each officer, servant, artificer, &c., and
names of persons lending money for the said expedition, &c.]

Issue Roll, Michaelmas, 9 Henry VI.

22*nd November*.—To John Collage, one of the King's sergeants
at arms, lately sent, by command of the King's Council, from the
city of London to Windsor with a certain woman, committed to
his care, by assent of the said Council, for him safely and securely to take her to Windsor Castle, and there to deliver her into

safe custody upon certain causes moving the said Council. In money paid to him, &c.,—13s. 4d.

28th November.—To John Talbot, one of the King's sergeants at arms, lately sent, with the advice and assent of the King's Council, from the city of London to Windsor with a certain brother, called brother John Asshewell, Prior of the Holy Trinity, London, committed to his care, by the assent aforesaid, to be by him safely and securely conducted to Windsor Castle, and there delivered to be securely kept for certain causes interesting the said Council. In money paid to him, &c.,—13s. 4d.

16th December.—To John Skelton. In money paid to him for two pair of balances and one great King's beam of iron, also for cords, wooden scales, and other necessaries by him newly purchased and provided, and for divers new weights, made and weighed by the King's weights kept within the receipt of the said King; the same weights to be delivered to divers persons of different counties of England, after having been so regulated and approved according to an ordinance of the King's parliament, &c., 1l. 13s. 8d.

To the same John. In money paid to him for 10 iron stamps engraved, ordered, and provided for the said John, to mark the weights aforesaid so weighed and approved and so to be delivered to certain persons, for which said stamps the said John is answerable. By direction of the Treasurer, &c.,—6s. 8d.

20th February.—To Thomas Curteys, Hugh Prestwyk, John Malmeshill, Thomas Stanford, John Redewell, Nicholas Swaby, John Percevale, and John Story, orators, otherwise called Bedemen, who are orators within the abbey of the blessed Peter, Westminster, to pray as well for the soul of the father of the present Lord the King as for the prosperity and good estate of the said now Lord the King, each receiving daily 2d. of the King's alms. In money paid to them, &c., for 277 days, &c. By writ, &c.,—18l. 9s. 4d.

30th April.—To John Bayons, of Burgh upon Beyne, one of the executors of the will of Sir Thomas Hanley, knight. In money paid to the same John in discharge of 12*l.* 8*s.* 0½*d.*, due to the said Thomas for the wages and reward to himself, a man at arms, and six archers, together with the accustomed reward for the same men at arms, lately retained by Lord Henry, late King of England, father of the present King, to accompany the said late King in person, in the 3rd year of his reign, to France, as in the account of the said Thomas thereof rendered at the Exchequer Roll 33 for this voyage fully appears; for which said money, so remaining due to him, there remained in the hands of the said Thomas the underwritten jewels; viz. a sword ornamented with ostrich feathers of gold, late the sword of Prince Edward, worth 22*l.*; 1 pair of gold spurs, the fastenings of which are of red silk, weighing, by troy weight, 7¾ oz., and deducting therefrom a quarter of an ounce for the said fastenings, half an ounce, price the ounce 1*l.* 6*s.*8*d.*, sum, 9*l.* 13*s.* 4*d.*; 1 ewer of beryl, garnished with silver, gilt, weighing, by troy weight, 30 oz.; which said jewels, &c., were delivered to the Treasurer, &c., for the King's use, &c. By writ of the 4th year of the said King, &c.,—10*l.*

14th July.—To Thomas Haseley, verbally appointed, by the Council of the present King's father, without any other commission thereon had, to take and collect for the use of the said father 2*d.* on every noble exchanged with the Lombards, dwelling in England, by any strangers or clerks, who should go to the court of Rome, or to any other place beyond sea. In money paid to him, &c., as a reward for his office of collector aforesaid, &c. By writ, &c.,—10*l.*

To Richard, Earl of Salisbury. In money paid to him in discharge of 300 marks which the Lord the King, with the advice and consent of his Council, commanded to be paid to the said Earl as well for the expenses which the said Earl had incurred and sustained in assisting the Cardinal of England, who lately, for certain matters touching the good of the said King and his realm of England, travelled together with the King of Scotland in Scotland, as also for the labour and expenses which the same Earl incurred and sustained on the day for the Marches last held at Hawdenstauk; also for the custody of fifteen Scotchmen, called hostages, for the King of Scotland, who dwelt in the kingdom of England in the custody of the said Earl; to have the same, of the King's gift, by way of reward for the causes aforesaid, over and above 100*l.* theretofore paid him for the custody of the fifteen Scotchmen aforesaid. By writ, &c.,—200*l.*

17th July.—To Humphrey, Duke of Gloucester, the King's deputy in his kingdom of England, who, with the advice and assent of the said King's Council, proceeded to different places of the said kingdom to take inquisitions respecting certain heretics, traitors, and rebels, and if any should be found, to take and punish them according to their demerits. In money paid to him, by the hands of John Burdet, clerk, to the Treasurer of his household, in discharge of 500 marks which the Lord the King, with the advice and assent aforesaid, commanded to be paid to the said Duke for his expenses, by way of reward in the business aforesaid, above 500 marks which on a like occasion had been paid him before. By writ of privy seal, &c.,—333*l.* 6*s.* 8*d.*

18th July.—To John Burdet, clerk to the Treasurer of the household of the Duke of Gloucester, keeper of England. In money paid him for the expenses of the Lords of the Council dining at Westminster, and there waiting and in attendance to elect justices to preserve the peace in each county of England at that time appointed. By direction of the Treasurer and Chamberlains of the Exchequer, as appears by the parcels of the said John shown to the same Treasurer and Chamberlains, and allowed by them,—9*l.* 2*s.* 2½*d.*

To Robert Whytegreve, one of the tellers of the Receipt of the Lord the King's Exchequer, lately sent, by advice of the Council of the said Lord the King, to the county of Stafford, there, by commission of the said Lord the King, to arrest Thomas Puttok, chaplain, a thief and a traitor. In money paid to him for his expenses, &c.,—15*l.* 4*s.* 8*d.*

To divers heralds and minstrels at Windsor, attending at the feast of Saint George, last held there by Humphrey, Duke of Gloucester, keeper of England. In money paid them in discharge of 20 marks which the Lord the King, with the assent of his said Council, ordered to be paid to the said heralds and minstrels, to have of his gift, by way of reward. By writ of privy seal,— 13*l.* 6*s.* 8*d.*

ISSUE ROLL, MICHAELMAS, 10 HENRY VI.

3rd November.—To Sir William Iver, knight, who lately took, within the kingdom of England, as his prisoner, as the said William affirms, a Scotchman named Master Thomas Mireton, which said Thomas was then coming with certain letters from the King of Scotland into the kingdom of England, to the Council of our Lord the King of England, and the said Scotchman was manu-captered by a person named John Leman, a citizen of London, by recognizance lately made in the King's Chancery, to answer to the said William in the sum of 100*l.*, if it should be so adjudged. In money paid to the said William in discharge of 40*l.*, which the present Lord the King, with the advice and assent of his Council, commanded to be paid to the said William for the reason afore-said. By writ, &c.,—40*l.*

17th November.—To John Cornwall, chevalier, to whom the present King, on the 29th of December, in the eighth year of his reign, with the assent of his Council, committed the custody of the Duke of Orleans, receiving yearly for the purpose aforesaid 400 marks at the Exchequer of the said Lord the King, so long as the said Duke should be in his custody. In money paid to him, by assignment made this day, in advance for the costs and expenses of the said Duke, whilst in his custody by order of the King's Council. By writ, &c.,—156*l.* 14*s.* 8*d.* [This Roll also contains payments for the costs and expenses of the Duke of Bourbon, in the custody of Sir Thomas Cumberworth, knight.]

11th December.—To Humphrey, Duke of Gloucester. In money paid to him, by assignment made this day, by the hands of John Burdet, in discharge of 2000 marks granted him for his attendance with the King's Council after the coronation of the said King, until the day of the passage of the said King into his kingdom of France, viz., from the 6th of November, in the eighth year of the said King's reign, on which day the said Lord the King was crowned, until the 24th day of April next following, on which day the said Lord the King departed from England to France, deducting therefrom 100 marks for the 21st of April, in the ninth year of the said King; 404*l.* 16*s.* 1*d.* on the 14th of May in the same year; 200 marks on the 16th of May, in the same year; 73*l.* 16*s.* 8*d.* on the 17th of May, in the same year; 64*l.* 18*s.* 8*d.* on the 8th of November, in the tenth year; 200 marks on the 17th of November, in the same year; 200*l.* on the 30th of November, in the same year; and 140*l.* on the 3rd of December, in the same year, such sums having been paid in advance, but now deducted. By writ of privy seal amongst the mandates of Easter Term, in the 8th year of the present King, —116*l.* 8*s.* 7*d.*

18th January.—To Humphrey, Duke of Gloucester, to whom the present King, on the 28th of November last past, with the advice and assent of the Lords spiritual and temporal, then assembled in his great Council at Westminster, considering the great charge, diligence, labour, costs, and expenses which the said Duke, as deputy of his realm of England, had very many times borne and sustained, as well in the presence of the said Lord the King in his kingdom aforesaid as in the absence of the said King ; also for the good government and preservation of the same kingdom against the malice of rebels, traitors, and the King's enemies; and especially of late concerning the taking and execution of the most horrible heretic and impious traitor to God and the said Lord the King, who called himself John Sharp, and of many other heretical malefactors, his accomplices; [for these services, and that he might more ably sustain his burthens in future, there was granted to the said Duke] 6000 marks yearly, to be had in the name of a reward from thenceforth, during the absence of the said Lord the King from his kingdom, and so long as he should continue the said King's deputy in the said kingdom, &c.; and 5000 marks per annum after the said Lord the King, by divine favour, should have returned to his kingdom, to have of the King's gift, by way of reward, so long as it should please the said King, to be paid by the hands of the Treasurer and Chamberlains for the causes aforesaid, for the better maintenance of his estate, and the people retained about him and for defence of the Church, the Catholic faith, and his true liege subjects. In money paid him at different times, &c.,—333*l.* 6*s.* 8*d.*

16*th February.*—To William Werberton, esquire, who lately certified to the Lord the King and his Council, before the proclamation of the said Lord the King thereof made, that William Perkyns, who called himself "Jak Sharp," was making a disturbance at a certain place in Oxford, to which place the said William Werberton sent his servants, to the Chancellor his commissaries and bailiffs of Oxford, commanding them, on behalf of the said King, to seize and place the said William Perkyns under arrest, and safely keep him, without permitting him to be delivered by any bail or manucaption until otherwise it should be ordered by the King's Council for his delivery. In money paid to him, by assignment made this day, in discharge of 20*l.* which the said Lord the King, with the assent of his Council, commanded to be paid to the said William according to the King's proclamation thereon made, to have of his gift by way of reward for the cause aforesaid. By writ of privy seal, &c.,—20*l.*

20th February.—To John Hamden and Andrew Sperlyng. In money paid to them, by the hands of the said Andrew by assignment made this day, in discharge of 8*l.*, paid to them as an especial reward for the labour, costs, and expenses by them incurred and sustained in obtaining 100*l.*, for the King's use, from Sir Thomas Wauton, knight, late Sheriff of Bedfordshire and Buckinghamshire, for permitting the election of knights for the county of Bucks in a manner and form not accustomed, and for returning the said knights to the King's parliament lately held at Westminster, contrary to the form of the statute thereon provided. By direction of the Treasurer and Chamberlains of the Exchequer, —8*l.*

To Anne, Countess of Stafford, to whom the present Lord the King granted and assigned half of 73*l.* 1*s.* 2¼*d.*, as the moiety of the castle and town of Brenles, the lordship of Penkelly and Cantrecelly, the manors and lordships of Langoyt and Alisaundres town, and a third part of the barony of Penkelly, to the Venerable Father in Christ, the Bishop of Bath and Wells, and Sir Roger Aston, knight, upon lease, with the advice and assent of the King's Council, and with the consent of the said Countess, to hold from the feast of Saint Michael, in the 7th year of the said King, until it should be ascertained whether the same castle, town, lordships, manors, and third part, were an entirety in gross by themselves or members and parcels of the said castle and lordship of Brekenoke, &c. In money paid to the said Countess, by assignment, &c., whilst the said matter should remain undecided, &c. By writ, &c.,—109*l.* 11*s.* 10*d.*

23rd February.—To Richard Gatone, late Mayor of the city of New Salisbury, who, by virtue and authority of the King's proclamation, made throughout all the counties of England, viz., that any person whatsoever who should write any seditious bill, or should presume in any place to affix, distribute, or circulate the same, should be seized, and, if convicted before the Lord the King or his Council, and the matter proved, the person procuring such conviction should receive 20*l.* from the said Lord the King, for his labour; and also should have one-half of all the goods of him so taken and convicted :—the said Richard caused to be seized in the said city a person named John Keterige, notoriously suspected, and afterwards convicted of error and heresy, he thus being taken, revealed to the said late Mayor the treason of a person named John Longe, of Abyndon, who lately brought to the said John Keterige divers seditious bills, on account of which information, by the great diligence and personal labour of the said late Mayor, the said John Longe was afterwards taken and imprisoned, as he had a true knowledge whereby to seize John Sharp, the traitor and heretic. In money paid to him by assignment made this day, by the hands of William of Shrewsbury, in discharge of 20*l.* which the said Lord the King commanded to be paid to the said Mayor for the cause aforesaid. By writ, &c., —20*l.*

3rd March.—To Gloucester, herald, and Lancaster, king of arms, who travelled beyond seas with certain letters from the King into his kingdom of France, to the Cardinal of Saint Croix and the Council of the said Lord the King then in his kingdom of France, to treat for a peace between the said Lord the King and the Dauphin, at Cambray. In money paid to them, viz., to the said Gloucester 100*s.*, and to the said Lancaster 5 marks, &c. By writ, &c.,—8*l.* 6*s.* 8*d.*

To Lonure Pursuant, the King's servant, who was lately ordered and appointed by John, Duke of Bedford, the most dear uncle of the said Lord the King, ruler of his kingdom of France, to go into the kingdom of England with certain letters to his most dear uncle Humphrey, Duke of Gloucester, and other Lords of his said Council, in his said kingdom of England, in which said journey the said Lonure was seized in the night by the King's enemies, whilst lying in bed, between Beauvais and Amiens, and from thence, by the said King's enemies, taken into a wood, where the same Lonure remained two- nights and two

2 E

days, in great danger and despair of his life, as the same Lonure informed the King's Council. In money paid to him in discharge of 100*s.* which the Lord the King, &c., commanded to be paid him by way of reward, &c. By writ, &c.,—5*l.*

Issue Roll, Easter, 10 Henry VI.

23rd May.—To Richard Grygge, who lately exposed himself to great danger at sea in a certain boat proceeding from the port of Dover to the town of Calais, to ascertain and obtain a true knowledge of the arrival of the Lord the King in his town aforesaid, and returning from thence to the town of Dover, in the same boat, to inform the Duke of Gloucester, the said King's uncle, and other Lords of his Council, then at Canterbury, of the arrival of the said King in his town aforesaid. In money paid to him, &c., to be had of the King's gift as a reward, &c. By writ, &c.,—5*l.*

23rd June.—To Brother John Lowe, of the order of Augustin Friars, whom the present Lord the King, on the 25th February last past, of his especial grace, with the advice of his Council, appointed his Confessor, continually to reside about his person for the benefit and salvation of his soul, and granted to the said John for the support of himself, his companion, and their servants, in the King's household, 3*s.* per day; and for the wages of four boys and their four horses and a hack, kept in the said household, viz., for each boy, 1½*d.* per day; also for certain small necessary expenses, 160*s.*, yearly to be received, &c., in the same way as Brother William Syward, formerly Confessor of Lord Edward, late King of England, progenitor of the King; and Brother Robert Mascall, late Confessor of Lord Henry, late King of England, grandfather of the King; and Brother Stephen Patryngton, late Confessor of Lord Henry, late King of England, father of the present King, have been accustomed to receive, &c. In money paid, &c. By writ, &c.,—21*l.* 17*s.* 1½*d.*

ISSUE ROLL, MICHAELMAS, 11 HENRY VI.

7th November.—To Sir John de Saint Pey, knight, a native of the country de la Bourt, in the duchy of Acquitaine, who, by the King's command, and with the advice and assent of his Council, by virtue of certain letters to him lately directed, was sent upon a treaty of peace between our said Lord the King and the King of Castile, to the said King of Castile, with a great number of other persons, at the great charge and expense of the said John, so repairing three different times to our said Lord the King, as also to the said King of Castile, which amounted to above the sum of 500*l.* sterling, as he saith. In money paid to him, &c. By writ, &c.,—400*l.*

1st December.—To Giles, the son of the Duke of Britany, being about the King's person, to whom the said Lord the King, with the advice and assent of his Council, commanded to be paid, viz., 125 marks, for the feast of Saint Michael last past, [with other payments] so long as it should please the King; to be had of his gift, for the private expenses of the said Giles and his servants. In money paid to him at different times, &c. By writ current, &c.,—83*l.* 6*s.* 8*d.*

To Gloucester, herald of arms. In money paid to him, in discharge of 25 marks, which the present King, with the advice and assent of his Council, commanded to be paid to the said Gloucester, to have of his gift by way of reward, for the good and acceptable service performed by the said herald for the King, and also in consideration of the same herald having been robbed and put to great and excessive charge when upon certain of the King's messages, in performance of the affairs of the said Lord the King in his kingdom of France. By writ, &c.,—16*l.* 13*s.* 4*d.*

3rd December.—To Robert Rolleston, clerk of the King's great wardrobe. In money paid to him, in advance, as well for providing a certain hearse within the church of Saint Paul, London, as for other costs and expenses incurred by him for the exequies of the Duchess of Bedford, celebrated within the church aforesaid,—40*l.*

27th February.—To Henry Merssh, Constable of Billingesgate ward. In money paid to him, as an especial reward, for the costs and expenses incurred by him in searching for and finding, on the night of the 5th January, in the 11th year of the present King, in two boats, on the river Thames, a certain bale of " bokeram " and other merchandise, which had been unladen from a certain ship of Hayn Bulscamp, an alien, in the port of London, not having paid custom, and without license of the Collectors of the customs, &c., and secretly put the same into boats in a tempestuous night, the customs and subsidies thereon arising not having been paid ; and for this reason they were seized to the King's use by the said Constable, &c., and landed at a certain wharf called Billingesgate, in London, and placed in a certain house there, before any King's officer made any seizure thereof for the King's use, by which said searching and finding, there was answered for to the King 61*l.* 0*s.* 9½*d.*, for the value of the aforesaid merchandise. By order of the Treasurer, &c.,—6*l.*

ISSUE ROLL, EASTER, 11 HENRY VI.

25th April.—To William Wytlesey. In money paid to him as an especial reward, for writing a certain copy of the great truces concluded between the kingdoms of England and France, sent to the Dukes of Bedford and Gloucester and other Lords of the King's Council, at Calais, for certain causes interesting the King's Council. By order of the Treasurer, &c.,—1*l.*

6th May.—To Thomas Collage, one of the King's sergeants at arms, ordered and appointed by the Treasurer of England to safely conduct David Gogh (lately taken for insurrection in South

Wales,) from the city of London to Windsor Castle, where the said
David was delivered to the Lieutenant of the castle aforesaid, by
virtue of the King's writ, under the great seal, directed to
the said Lieutenant. In money paid to the said Thomas, for
his expenses in going and returning upon the business aforesaid.
By direction of the Treasurer, &c.,—13s. 4d.

14th May.—[Payments of 20l. yearly were made to Sir Robert
Roos, knight; Sir Edward Hungerford, knight; Sir William Beauchamp, knight; and Sir John Beauchamp, knight, the King's
carvers, for their services from the 20th October last past.]

25th May.—To the Venerable Father in Christ, Thomas,
Bishop of Worcester, whom the present Lord the King, with
the advice and assent of his Council, lately ordered and appointed
to go as his Ambassador to the general Council, now assembled
at Basyll; and for this purpose the said Lord the King, of his
especial grace, willed that he should be pardoned such sum as
ought to be paid to the said Lord the King for the exchange of
money which was sent to the exchange for this purpose, so, nevertheless, that this remittance should not at another time be taken
as a precedent. In money paid to him by the hands of John
Lavyngton, by assignment made this day, in discharge of 12l. 10s.
which the said Lord the King, with the advice and assent aforesaid, commanded to be paid to the said Bishop, for certain
great causes especially concerning the said Lord the King, and
principally because the said Bishop would have to pay to the said
Lord the King, for exchange upon a certain sum of 500l., payable
to the same Bishop upon the business aforesaid, the said 12l. 10s.,
viz., 2d. upon every noble sent abroad. By writ, &c.,—12l. 10s.

26th May.—To Richard Bukland, Treasurer of Calais. In
money paid to him by the hands of William Estfield, a citizen and
mercer of London, in discharge of 500 marks which the present
Lord the King, with the advice and consent of his Council, commanded to be paid to the said Richard Bukland, therewith to

make payments to divers men at arms and archers, for their wages and rewards for services performed at Saint Valary, beyond seas, and in other places there, held against the said King's will by the enemies of the said King. By writ, &c.,—333*l*. 6*s*. 8*d*.

To Roger Wynter, one of the Tellers of the Receipt of the King's Exchequer, lately sent, by advice of the King's Council, from London to Wynchelse, from thence to Depe, and from thence to Roan, in Normandy, with 2500*l*., there to be delivered to the Lord John, Duke of Bedford, Regent of the said King's kingdom of France, for payment of the wages of divers men at arms and archers, &c. In money paid to him, as well for costs and expenses incurred and sustained by him, for the safe conduct of the said money, as well by land as by sea; as also for divers other costs and expenses incurred by him, in going, tarrying, and returning, for 44 days, upon the business aforesaid. By writ, &c.,—85*l*. 19*s*.

18*th July*.—To the same Roger, to whom the said Lord the King, with the advice and assent of his Council, commanded to be delivered 5000 marks, to be taken in the retinue of John, Lord de Talbot, at the risk of the said Lord the King, by land and by sea, to the most Reverend Father in Christ, the Bishop of Tyrwan, at present the King's Chancellor in his kingdom of France, and to deliver the said 5000 marks to the said Bishop, or his sufficient Attorney in that behalf, at the King's castle of Arkes, to be expended in the King's war there. By writ, &c.,—3333*l*. 6*s*. 8*d*.

ISSUE ROLL, MICHAELMAS, 12 HENRY VI.

7*th October*.—To William Bolton and Nicholas Auncell, the King's messengers, sent at different times to divers parts of England; viz., the aforesaid William Bolton, at one time sent to the Marches of Scotland with divers commissions, directed to divers Earls and other persons, upon especial matters therein contained;

and the aforesaid Nicholas, sent at another time to the Earl of Suffolk, with 34 of the King's letters patent of safe conduct for the Queen of Sicily and other persons coming with her from France to the King's town of Calais. In money paid to them, viz., to the aforesaid William 23*s.* 4*d.*, and to the aforesaid Nicholas 6*s.* 8*d.*, for their costs, &c. By writ, &c.,—1*l.* 10*s.*

13*th February.*—To Henry Jolipas, clerk, executor of the will of Joan, late wife of John Clyff, a minstrel, executrix of the will of the said John Clyff, deceased, with whom an account was made at the Exchequer of Accounts of the receipts of the said John Clyff. who was lately ordered and appointed to go in person with Lord Henry, late King of England, father of the present King, in a certain voyage to France, or elsewhere, which was performed in the third year of his reign, with 17 minstrels his companions, each receiving 12*d.* per day; viz., from the 8th July, in the said third year of the said late King, unto the 24th November then next following; at which time there was due to the said John Clyff upon the account aforesaid, 33*l.* 6*s.*, as appeared by the said account, &c., for security of the payment of which the said John Clyff had the underwritten jewels delivered to him, viz., a silver lantern, gilt, with a foot; a certain tabernacle standing upon four feet; 2 silver ewers, gilt, one engraved with the arms of England and one with stags, with a table standing upon two lions, and divers relicks, weighing together, by troy weight, 26 lb. 6 oz., price the lb., 40*s.*, —sum, 53*l.*: 1 great crater with 3 candelabras of silver with 3 pykes; 1 ladle, 1 stomacher, 1 spice plate, and 1 piece of ivory; 1 small silver cofer, gilt, garnished, and enamelled; 1 silver chafing dish, gilt, weighing, &c., delivered to the Treasurer and Chamberlains to the King's use, &c. By writ, &c.,—10*l.*

25*th February.*—To John Lord de Talbot, to whom the present King, in consideration of the good and acceptable services which the same John had performed, as well for the present King's father, in his kingdom of France, with 24 lancers and archers for 1½ year, without receiving wages and rewards for the same, and in the King's land of Ireland, as also for our said Lord the King in his kingdom of France, for which services a certain sum was due, as the said John fully informed the said King and his Council; and also in consideration of very many other affairs, and chiefly on account of the great necessity in which the said John then was, at which the King was concerned; also because the said John had covenanted that for the said sums, so due to him for the causes aforesaid, he would thereafter make no further claim, but at present entirely acquit the said King for ever. In money paid to him, viz., by the hands of the Treasurer of England, 1000 marks, and by the hands of Richard Leget, 500 marks; in discharge of 1000*l.* which the said Lord the King, with the advice and assent of his Council, commanded to be paid to the said John, to have of his gift, for the causes aforesaid. By writ, &c.,—1000*l.*

ISSUE ROLL, EASTER, 12 HENRY VI.

14th April.—To John Merston, keeper of the King's jewels. In money paid to his own hands, in discharge of 100*l.* which the said Lord the King, with the advice and assent of his Council, commanded to be paid to the said John for having provided divers collars, viz., 6 of gold and 24 of silver, gilt, also other collars of silver; which said collars, with the advice and assent aforesaid, were sent to the Emperor, to be distributed amongst the inhabitants of the town of Basyle and to others, knights and esquires, according to the advice and discretion of the said Emperor and the King's Ambassadors there. By writ of privy seal, &c.,—100*l.*

2nd June.—To John Staunton, clothier, of London. In money paid to him, in discharge of 16*l.* which the present Lord the King, with the advice and assent of his Council, commanded to be paid to the said John for an entire cloth of scarlet, purchased from him, and given, with the advice and assent aforesaid, to

Master Quintin Menart, Reeve of Saint Omers, one of the Ambassadors from the Duke of Burgundy, the King's uncle, lately sent by the said Duke to our said Lord the King and his Council ; to have of his gift.   By writ, &c.,—16*l.*

10*th June.*—To the most Reverend Father in Christ, Henry, Cardinal of England, Bishop of Winchester.   In money paid to him, in discharge of 10,000 marks which he lent to the Lord the King at the Receipt of his Exchequer, on the 2nd day of June last past, &c., for security of repayment of which said sum and certain other sums due to him from the said King, divers jewels of the said King were pledged to him, as appears by a writ remaining upon the file of mandates of this term, testifying the delivery of the jewels aforesaid,—6666*l.* 13*s.* 4*d.*

[To the same Lord Cardinal, from whom divers goods and jewels were lately seized at Sandwich by the King's officers, but restored to him by order of Parliament; the King and his Council acknowledging the great services the said Lord Cardinal had rendered to the said King and the realm.   In money paid, &c.,— 8000*l.*   This entry is too long for entire insertion.]

14*th June.*—To John, Archbishop of York ; John, Bishop of Bath and Wells; Philip, Bishop of Ely; William, Bishop of Lincoln ; William, Earl of Suffolk, and Walter, Lord Hungerford, of the King's Council; who, by their letters obligatory were bound to the most Reverend Father in Christ, Henry, Cardinal of England, Bishop of Winchester, in 5000 marks ; which said sum the said Lord Cardinal lately lent to the said Lord the King at Calais, at the request of the Dukes of Bedford and Gloucester, the King's uncles, and other Lords of the Council ; and which sum, by the advice and assent of the aforesaid uncles and others of the said Council, late at Calais, was delivered to the Venerable Father in Christ, the Bishop of Tyrwen, the King's Chancellor, in his kingdom of France, therewith to make payments for the safe custody of the castles and forts in France, and for the siege of Saint Walleres. In money paid to the said Archbishop, &c. By writ, &c.,—3333*l.* 6*s.* 8*d.*

6th July.—To John, Lord de Curcelles. In money paid to him, in discharge of 100 marks, which the present Lord the King, with the advice and assent of his Council, commanded to be paid to the said John, to have of his gift, for the good and notable service rendered by him to the said Lord the King in his kingdom of France, who, on account of the love he bore the King, had lost the greatest part of his inheritance. By writ, &c.,—66*l.* 13*s.* 4*d.*

ISSUE ROLL, MICHAELMAS, 13 HENRY VI.

5th November.—To John Rodericus, an esquire of the King of Portugal, who brought from thence to our Lord the King letters, announcing his King's coronation and other affairs. In money paid to him in discharge of 25 marks, which our said Lord the King, with the advice and assent of his Council, commanded to be paid to the same Rodericus, to have of his gift, by way of reward, &c. By writ, &c.,—68*l.* 4*s.* 4*d.*

18th February.—To John Iwardeby and Robert Burton, the King's officers at the Receipt of his Exchequer, ordered and appointed by the Treasurer of England to remain and attend at London and Westminster, before the feast of Saint Hilary last past, at the King's court, which, with the advice and assent of his Council, was adjourned, on account of the plague, and they were for divers necessary causes and especial matters, then ordered to attend there for the benefit of the said Lord the King, &c. In money paid to them, by assignment made on the 8th November, for their attendance, &c. By writ, &c.,—13*l.* 6*s.* 8*d.*

19th February.—To Robert Whytyngham, Receiver General

of the duchy of Cornwall; Robert Burton, one of the officers of the Receipt of the Exchequer; and John Somer, one of the auditors of the Exchequer, appointed by the King's commission, together with others, to assess all and singular the lands and tenements in the county of Cornwall, being of his duchy of Cornwall, or to that duchy belonging; because that theretofore the free tenements had been demised by the said Lord the King and his Ministers; as also those which the native tenants held in bondage of our said Lord the King, to beholden of our said Lord the King, by sufficient and fit persons for this purpose, for a term of 21 years, that term to begin at the feast of Saint Michael then next happening for the benefit and advantage of the King, as to them should seem most fit. In money paid to them, &c., for their costs and expenses, &c. By writ, &c.,—28*l.* 10*s.*

Issue Roll, Michaelmas, 14 Henry VI.

9th December.—To John Davy, of London, wax chandler. In money paid to his own hands, at different times; viz., at one time 10*l.*, at another time 31*l.* 13*s.* 4*d.*, in discharge of 41*l.* 13*s.* 4*d.* which the Lord the King, with the advice and assent of his Council, commanded to be paid to the said John for a hearse provided by him at the King's command, in Westminster Abbey, for the exequies and funeral of the Duke of Bedford, the King's uncle, deceased,—36*l.* 13*s.* 4*d.*; and for the expenses of renewing the same hearse for the exequies and the funeral of Anne, late Queen of the King of France, deceased,—100*s.* By writ of privy seal, &c.—41*l.* 13*s.* 4*d.*

To Thomas Daunte, of London, painter. In money paid to his own hands, at different times; viz., at one time 5 marks, at another time 15*l.* 13*s.* 4*d.*, in discharge of 19*l.* which the Lord the King, with the advice and assent of his Council, commanded to be paid to the same Thomas; viz., for 300 shields, with the arms of the Duke of Bedford, deceased, made for the exequies and funeral of the said Duke, the price of each shield, 8*d*.,—sum, 10*l*.; for half a hundred of shields, with the arms of France and of "Berye," departed, price each shield, 6*d*.,—sum, 5*l*.; and for six banners of the said arms, price of each banner, 13*s*. 4*d*., —sum, 4*l*., to place on the hearse aforesaid. By writ, &c.,—19*l*.

16th December.—To Walter Cressever, Captain of the castle and town of Crotey. In money paid to him in advance, for the price of three barrels of gunpowder, purchased and provided by Richard Alrede, by command of the Treasurer of England, containing 1015 lbs. of powder, at 8*d*. per lb.,—sum, 34*l*. 10*s*.; and for the price of two guns, called "foulers," purchased of John Nele,—7*l*.; and for the price of 200 gunstones for the same guns, purchased of William Mason,—5*l*. By writ of privy seal, &c.,—46*l*. 10*s*. [This and the subsequent Roll of Easter, 14 Henry VI. contain many entries of payments made for sending troops, ammunition, and stores, to the said town and castle of Crotey.]

18th January.—To John Flessh, tapestry maker. In money paid to him for a side cushion, or carpet, a bench, and five cushions worked with the King's arms, purchased from him, and ordered and provided by the advice and direction of the Treasurer of England, in honour of the King, to be placed about, and hung at the back of the King's Justice seats, of his Common Bench, within Westminster Hall. By general writ of privy seal amongst the mandates of Easter term, in the 11th year of the present King,—1*l*. 13*s*. 4*d*.

ISSUE ROLL, EASTER, 14 HENRY VI.

24th May.—To Richard, Duke of York, retained in the service of our Lord the King, by indenture between the said Lord the King and the aforesaid Duke, to serve the said Lord the King in the war in his kingdom of France and duchy of Nor-

mandy, during the term of one year.   In money paid to him by
the hands of William Wolston, in advance, for the second quarter
of the year, as well for his wages, at 13*s.* 4*d.* per day ; and to
a Baron and a Banneret, each 4*s.* per day ; 7 Knights, each 2*s.*
per day ; 490 men at arms, each 12*d.* per day, together with the
accustomed reward to the same; as also for the wages of 2200 archers, each at 6*d.* per day, retained by the said Lord the King, to
serve him in his war aforesaid, &c. By writ, &c.,—8506*l.* 7*s.* 6½*d.*

30*th June.*—To John Vampage, the King's Attorney. In
money paid him by assignment made this day, as an especial
reward for the labour, costs, charges, and expenses, incurred and
sustained by him for the Lord the King, as well respecting a plea
late pending in the King's Exchequer between the said Lord the
King and John Blount, junior, of Suddyngton, in the county of
Worcester, esquire, as in the matter of a plea between the Lord the
King and Robert Greyndom, esquire, against whom by his pains
he entirely prevailed for the Lord the King, as fully appears in
the Exchequer, by the Record, &c. By writ amongst the mandates of Easter term, in the 11th year of the present King,—20*l.*

25*th September.*—To divers Masters and Mariners of divers
ships and vessels lately in the port of London, which sailed
from thence to Sandwich with divers ordnance for the King;
viz., mallets of lead, shovels, spades, skopets, and ordnance,
for the King's war, sent to Calais. In money paid to Hugh
Fraunceys, and by him paid to the same masters and mariners ;
viz., to Ralph de Ulton, master of a certain ship, called the Trinity of Barton, for the carriage of 600 mallets of lead and 1625
shovels, spades, and " scopettez," and for other necessary expenses,
59*s.* 4*d.* ; also to John Walson, master of a certain ship, called
Tusewyn, of Newcastle upon Tyne, for the carriage and conduct
of 5400 mallets of lead, and 500 mattocks, 1095 shovels, spades,
and scopettez, and for other necessary expenses,—70*s.* 8*d.*, &c.
By writ, &c., amongst the mandates of Michaelmas term, in the
14th year,—8*l.*

[This Roll contains numerous payments to divers lords, knights, and esquires, specifying the number and quality of the soldiers retained by each, to serve the King in his wars in France and Normandy. Amongst other leaders appear the names of Humphrey, Duke of Gloucester, with 2 earls, 11 barons, 23 knights, 415 men at arms; and Richard, Earl of Warwick, with 1 baron, 3 knights, 55 men at arms, 766 archers, &c.; also the number of guns, bows, arrows, and other weapons supplied, are enumerated, together with their respective prices, and the rate of payment to each rank of soldier, &c.]

ISSUE ROLL, MICHAELMAS, 15 HENRY VI.

16th November.—To Philip de Roy, son of James de Roy, one of the King's subjects, who quitted Paris at the time of the taking thereof, to continue to serve in obedience under our said Lord the King. In money paid to him, in discharge of 10 marks, by command of the King, &c. By writ, &c.,—6*l.* 13*s.* 4*d.*

19th November.—To Matilda, Lady de Saint John, whom the present Lord the King, by his letters of privy seal, commanded to inquire respecting the custody of Humphrey, son and heir of John, late Earl of Arundell, then in the custody of the said Lord the King, as in the said letters doth fully appear; by virtue whereof the said Lady Matilda, with great pains and diligence, executed the command of the said Lord the King, from the day of the death of the said Earl; viz., from the 1st June, in the 13th year of the present King, unto the 14th November, in the 15th year of the said King; with certain persons assisting her, and other necessary attendants suitable to her person and estate, without any payment having been assigned her for costs and expenses, which amounted at least, as the said Matilda saith, to 100*l.* per annum. In money paid, &c., for the costs and expenses of the said Matilda, for the cause aforesaid, &c. By writ, &c.,—80*l.*

24th January.—To John Wynwyke, mason. In money paid to him, as well for divers iron work purchased and provided by him, as for the wages of divers workmen and labourers for repairing and mending the door of a house at the end of Westminster Hall, towards the east, under a certain house or chamber used for the Council of the Duke of Gloucester where the same Council was held and transacted; and also for the safe custody of the King's Records, to be placed therein, in like manner as in the Treasury of the said Lord the King, under the custody of the Treasurer and Chamberlains of the Exchequer, and there to be safely and securely kept. By general writ, &c.,—1*l*. 7*s*. 6*d*. [Another payment for the same purpose was made to John Champaw, smith, in the King's Tower of London.]

4th March.—To John Elkembrogh, a messenger, lately sent from the Emperor to our Lord the King with certain letters from the said Emperor, directed to our said Lord the King, and by the same Lord the King sent back to the same Emperor. In money paid to him, in discharge of 20 marks commanded to be paid to the said John, to have of his gift, by way of reward. By writ, &c.,—13*l*. 6*s*. 8*d*.

18th March.—To Sir John Sutton, knight. In money paid to him, as an especial reward for the costs and expenses incurred by him respecting the escape of John Mayowe, of Neunham, outlawed for felony, &c. ; by whose diligence Simon Simonds, deputy to the Earl of Huntingdon, late Marshal of England, had paid a fine to the Lord the King of 100 marks for the said escape, as appears by the Record in the King's Bench, entered before the Judge there, and afterwards certified into the Exchequer by the said Simon, &c. By writ, &c.,—10*l*.

ISSUE ROLL, EASTER, 15 HENRY VI.

6th July.—To Gilbert Par, esquire, keeper of the King's artillery in the Tower of London. In money paid to him by assignment made this day, by the hands of Robert Large, citizen and alderman of London, for the price of 13 barrels of saltpetre, weighing 5252½ lbs., price each lb. 7*d.*, purchased and provided for the King's use by the Treasurer of England, and paid to the said Gilbert Par by the said Robert in advance for his office. By writ, &c.,—153*l.* 3*s.* 8*d.*

15*th July.*—To Francis Arragonoys, chevalier, captain of the castle and town of Mountarges. In money paid to him by the hands of Gueriner de Romare, in discharge of 994*l.* 3*s.* which the Lord the King, with the advice and assent of his Council, commanded to be paid to the said Francis, for the safe custody of the castle and town aforesaid, as was agreed and settled between the Earl of Suffolk and the said Francis, &c. By writs, &c.,—994*l.* S*s.*

To Peter Rousseau, late a burgess of the town of Paris, who, for the fidelity of the said Peter shown to our Lord the King, on the destruction of the said town, was taken prisoner, by reason whereof he totally lost his goods, and was put to the expense of 160 salutes of gold above the expenses which the enemy exacted from him on account of his ransom. In money paid to him, in discharge of 50 marks, with 10 marks, which at another time he received on this account, which the said Lord the King commanded to be paid to the said Peter, as a reward, &c. By writ, &c.,—26*l.* 13*s.* 4*d.*

17*th July.*—To Lewis of Luxenbergh, Archbishop of Rouen, the King's Chancellor in his kingdom of France. In money paid to him; viz., by the hands of John Belonger, Bertin Lovell, and Henry Moleyn, merchants of Rouen, 3724*l.*, and by the hands of Benedict Boremey, 2000 marks, in advance for those 12,722 marks 2*s.* 11½*d.* appointed by the Lord the King and his Council to be paid to the said Chancellor, for him therewith to pay the wages of 800 men at arms and 2400 archers, lately directed to continue in France and Normandy for the safe custody of the parts aforesaid, &c. By writ, &c.,—5057*l.* 6*s.* 8*d.*

2nd December.—To John Pelestrine, a knight from the Holy Land, who lately came to the Lord the King upon private affairs concerning the said John, which he communicated and declared to our said Lord the King, and again immediately left the kingdom of England for his own country. In money paid to his own hands, in discharge of 25 marks which the said Lord the King, with the advice and assent of his Council, commanded to be paid to the said John, &c. By writ, &c.,—16*l.* 13*s.* 4*d.*

5th December.—To Lewis of Luxenburgh, Archbishop of Rouen, the King's Chancellor in his kingdom of France, to whom the present King, considering the good and acceptable services which the said Archbishop had, and in future intended to bestow upon the said Lord the King, of his especial grace, (in lieu of the deduction from the 1000 marks yearly, which the said Lord the King ordered to be made from the said Bishop at the Receipt of his Exchequer; and also from 1000*l.* ordered to be received of the King's money, to be paid him in Normandy, according to the form of a grant thereof made,) granted to the aforesaid Archbishop all monies arising from the issues and profits of the temporal revenues of the see of Ely, which were then in the King's hands, by reason of the vacancy of the said see, to hold, &c., during the vacancy of the said see, &c. In money paid to him by the hands of Gervase Vulre, the said Archbishop's attorney, for the issues and profits of the temporalties of the see aforesaid, &c.,—500*l.*

7th December.—To Brother John Hayne, who, by the King's command, had been again sent as his messenger with letters directed to the most Holy Father the Pope, at the general council, and also to the Emperor. In money paid to him, in discharge of 20 marks which the said Lord the King, with the advice and assent of his Council, commanded to be paid to the said Brother

2 F

John, to be had of his gift by way of reward, for the cause afore-said. By writ, &c.,—13*l.* 6*s.* 8*d.*

7th December.—To Sir Thomas Rempston, knight, for the good and acceptable services performed by him as well for the King's father, as for the said now Lord the King in his kingdom of France and duchy of Normandy, where he was taken prisoner, and his ransom set at 30,000 salutes, all of which he had paid except 9000 salutes, and also for services intended in future to be performed, for which reasons the said King granted him 1000 marks. In money paid to him in discharge of the 1000 marks aforesaid, which the Lord the King, with the advice of his Council, granted to be had of his gift, &c. By writ of privy seal amongst the mandates of this term,—666*l.* 13*s.* 4*d.*

22nd January.—To Thomas Leuesham, Remembrancer on the King's Remembrancer's side of the Exchequer. In money paid to him, by assignment made this day, as an especial reward for writing out the statutes of Wales in two Rolls for the King's use, by the advice and assent of the Council of the said Lord the King, which were delivered to the Treasurer of England for the King's benefit. By general writ of privy seal amongst the mandates of Easter term in the 11th year,—1*l.*

To Leo, Lord de Welles, retained in the service of the Lord the King by indenture between the said Lord the King and the afore-said Lord de Welles, by which said indenture the said Lord de Welles undertook safely and securely to keep, according to lawful power, to the use and profit of the said Lord the King, during the term of seven years, the King's land of Ireland, under a cer-tain form contained in the said indenture, receiving from the said Lord the King, for this purpose, for the first year of the said seven, 4000 marks; viz. on the day of making the said indenture 1000 marks, and 1000 marks on the 1st of May then next following, on which day the said Lord de Welles should make his muster or show of 300 English archers, at Chester or at Beumarres, in his passage on the sea coast, as in the said indenture more fully is contained. In money paid to him in advance for the safe custody of the land aforesaid. By writ, &c.,—666*l.* 13*s.* 4*d.*

24th February.—To Geoffrey Gawer, Master of a certain balinger called the Catherine of Winchelsea, who, with twenty mariners, was appointed by Thomas Pope and Godard Pulham, by command of the Treasurer of England, to sail in the said balinger to Crotey during the time of the late siege there, and to report the news of the relief of the same, which said master and mariners, when they came to the castle aforesaid, were retained by the deputy of the said castle at wages for the safe custody thereof; viz. at 6*d.* per day to the said master, and 6*d.* to each of the said mariners, so that there was due to him for the 40 days they were at wages, amounting to the sum of 20*l.* and during the time that the same master and mariners were retained at wages in the said castle, his said balinger was burnt by the King's enemies and rebels there, as it lay under the castle aforesaid, to the loss and prejudice of the said Geoffrey Gawer of 40 marks. In money paid to the said Geoffrey by the advice and assent, &c. By writ, &c.,—46*l.* 13*s.* 4*d.*

27th March.—To Thomas Lord de Beaumond. In money paid to him in discharge of 20 marks which the Lord the King, with the advice and assent of his Council, commanded to be paid to the said Lord de Beaumond for all costs and expenses incurred and sustained by him for the custody of, and also for conducting to the King's Council "Oweyn ap Tedre," late a prisoner within the King's prison of Newgate, who had escaped from the said prison, and was afterwards taken and brought to the said Lord de Beaumond; and also for the custody of and conducting to the King's Council a certain priest and a servant of the said Oweyn, who were knowing and consenting to the escape of the said Oweyn. By writ of privy seal amongst the mandates of this term,—13*l.* 6*s.* 8*d.*

2 F 2

26th June.—To John Ardern, clerk of the King's works. In
money paid to him, by assignment made this day, by the hands
of William Marmyon, out of the issues of the lordship of Walyngford, in advance for repairs and for newly making and building the
King's prison there, for the safe and secure custody of the King's
prisoners within his castle of Walyngford. By writ, &c.,—40*l.*

4th July.—To John Santon. In money paid to him, &c., for
the costs and expenses incurred by him, for the King's advantage,
about two juries summoned between John Fray, Nicholas Dixon,
and John Hotoft, the King's patentees, who prosecuted, for
the Lord the King, against Sir Robert Wyngfeld, knight, and
others, feoffees of Thomas, late Lord de Morle, for the manors of
Halyngbury, in the county of Essex, and Walkern, in the county
of Hertford. By writ, &c.,—9*l.* 10*s.*

10th July.—To Garter, King of arms, lately sent abroad as
the King's messenger to the Earl of Warwick, upon which said
message the said Garter was occupied, in the said King's service,
for the space of twenty-six weeks, and was taken prisoner in going
upon the said message by the King's enemies, and his goods taken
from him to the great loss of the said Garter, on which accoun
the said Garter borrowed, to pay his charges in the King's service,
the sum of 30*l.* 13*s.* 4*d.* In money paid to him in discharge of
the said 30*l.* 13*s.* 4*d.*, which the said Lord the King commanded
to be paid to the said Garter of his gift, &c. By writ, &c.,—
30*l.* 13*s.* 4*d.*

15th July.—To Sir Richard Wodevyle, knight, and Jaquette,
late wife of John, late Duke of Bedford, now the wife of the said
Richard. In money paid to them in advance for those 333 marks,
4*s.* 5½*d.* and one-third of a farthing, assigned to the said Richard
and Jaquette as dower of the said Jaquette, to be received yearly
at the receipt of the Exchequer; viz. on the 23rd of March in the

fifteenth year of the present King, as the third part of 1000 marks granted to the said late Duke and his heirs male by Lord Henry, late King of England, father of the present King, &c. By writ, &c.,—88*l.* 17*s.* 9*d.*

ISSUE ROLL, EASTER, 17 HENRY VI.

18*th May.*—To Walter Cressever, esquire, captain of the King's castle of Crotey. In money paid to him, for the price of 3 fothers of lead, with the "shetyng" thereof,—16*l.* 10*s.*; for the price of 100 lbs. of tin,—22*s.*; for the price of 200 lbs. of salt-petre,—66*s.* 8*d.*; for the price of 1000 quarell heads,—33*s.* 4*d.*; for the price of 50 lbs. of coal "de lynde,"—33*s.* 4*d.*; and for 150 sheaves of arrows,—11*l.* 5*s.*; for the price of 4 gross of bowstrings for hand bows,—34*s.*; for the price of 3 casks of vinegar, —12*l.*; for the price of 10 gallons of white wine,—7*s.*; and for the price of 80 lances with points,—10 marks, together with the carriage, tronage, portage, and freightage of the said stuffs from London to Winchelsea, &c., with other necessary expenses, &c. By writ, &c.,—61*l.* 10*s.* 2*d.*

19*thMay.*—To John, Earl of Huntingdon, retained in the service of the Lord the King, by indenture made between the said Lord the King and the said Earl, appointing him his lieutenant of Guyenne for a term of six years, commencing the 8th of June then next happening. In money paid to him in advance for the first quarter of a year, for the wages of himself, at 6*s.* 8*d.* per day; to 2 bannerets, each 4*s.* per day; 16 knights, each 2*s.* per day; 280 men at arms, each at 18*d.* per day; 2000 archers, each at 9*d.* per day; retained by the King to serve him in the manner and form as is fully contained in the said indenture. By writ, &c.,— 8955*l.* 3*s.* 2*d.* [There are many payments entered on the Rolls about this period to the abovenamed John, Earl of Huntingdon.]

16*th July.*—To Catherine de la Pole, Abbess of Berkyng. In money paid her by the hands of Thomas Stokdale, receiving the

money from Sir William Estfeld, knight and alderman of London,
in discharge of 50*l.* which the present Lord the King, with the
advice and assent of his Council, commanded to be paid to the
same Abbess, to be received for all costs and expenses which the
said Abbess had incurred and sustained from the 27th of July, in
the sixteenth year of the present King, until Saturday the last day
of February last past, about "Edmund ap Meredith ap Tydier, and
Jasper ap Meredith ap Todier," lately committed to the custody
of the said Abbess by command of the said Lord the King.   By
writ of privy seal, &c.,—50*l.*

[*Note.* A great portion of this Roll (which is 70 feet in length)
is occupied with the names of shipping retained to take the King's
army to France, specifying who were the commanders, and number
of knights, esquires, men at arms, and archers serving under each
captain, the names of the masters of the ships, number of mariners,
together with an account of the arms and provisions supplied for
this expedition.]

ISSUE ROLL, MICHAELMAS, 18 HENRY VI.

24th November.—To Garter, king at arms, sent, by the advice
and assent of the King's Council, to the county of Somerset, to
confer with the Duke of Orleans, there in the custody of Sir John
Stourton, knight, upon certain especial matters concerning the
Lord the King and his Council.   In money paid to him as an
especial reward for his costs and expenses in going and returning
upon the business aforesaid.   By writ, &c.,—2*l.*

10th December.—To Richard Veer and Thomas Pope, Collectors of the King's customs and subsidies in the port of the town
of Sandwich.   In money paid to them, by assignment made this
day, in discharge of 434*l.* 0*s.* 5*d.* paid by them, as well for the
passage and re-passage of the Lord Cardinal and divers other
lords spiritual and temporal, knights, and clerks, lately sent in
the King's embassy to Calais, to treat for a peace between the said

Lord the King and his adversary of France; also for the passage of the Duke of Orleans, lately going in the retinue of the said lords to the town aforesaid, upon certain affairs, especially concerning the Lord the King and his Council, as also for the passage of Sir Richard Wodewyle, knight, and others in his retinue lately proceeding to France; and also for the safe conduct of the lords aforesaid, and for divers other purposes, as appears by their parcels, together with 50 marks received from Thomas Broun, and 35*l.* received of John Hexham for the affairs aforesaid. By writ, &c.,—345*l.* 13*s.* 9*d.*

24th December.—To John Van Teyndeham, esquire, a Dutchman, who lately gave 4 horses to the Lord the King. In money paid to him, &c., which the King commanded to be paid him of his gift, &c. By writ, &c.,—166*l.* 13*s.* 4*d.*

ISSUE ROLL, EASTER, 18 HENRY VI.

21st June.—To John, Lord of Fawnehope. In money paid to him, by assignment made this day, in discharge of 66*l.* due for 13*s.* 4*d.* per day, granted for the costs and expenses incurred by him for the custody of the Duke of Orleans; viz. from the 29th of January last past, on which day the said Lord of Fawnehope received the custody of the said Duke, until the 8th of May then next following, as appears in his account thereof rendered at the Exchequer of Accounts, inrolled in Roll 16, Roll of Accounts, &c. By writ, &c.,—66*l.*

5th July.—To Hugh Kyngeston, of the King's pantry, lately appointed to wait upon the Chancellor of France during the whole time he was last in England, which said Hugh manucaptured a certain baker of London, called Chester, to supply so much bread to the said Chancellor as amounted to the sum of 52*l.* 16*s.* 8*d.* In money paid to the said Hugh, &c. By writ, &c.,—52*l.* 16*s.* 8*d.*

25th October.—To Sir John Stiward, knight, John Stanley,
nd Thomas Wesenham, esquires, Thomas Pulford, James Grisacre, valets of the King's Crown, John Wattes, valet of the
household, and John Martyn, groom of the said household, to
whom the said Lord the King assigned the safe custody of her
who was lately called Duchess of Gloucester. In money paid to
them in discharge of 40*l.*, which the said Lord the King commanded to be paid for their attendance for the safe custody of
her as aforesaid, unto the feast of the Nativity of our Lord last
past. By writ, &c.,—40*l.*

To divers doctors, notaries, and clerks, lately, by the King's
command, laboriously employed respecting a superstitious sect
of necromancers and persons charged with witchcraft and incantations. In money paid them, by the hands of Master Adam
Moleyns, in discharge of 20*l.* which the said Lord the King commanded to be distributed amongst them, to have by way of reward
for the cause aforesaid. By writ of privy seal amongst the mandates of this term,—20*l.*

27th November.—To Richard, Duke of York, the King's
lieutenant-general and governor in his kingdom of France and
duchy of Normandy. In money paid to him in advance, by the
hands of Peter Bowman, in part payment of 20,000*l.* which the
said Duke ought to have received from the said Lord the King
for the second year of his being retained, according to the force
of certain indentures made between our aforesaid Lord the King
and the aforesaid Duke ; viz. 5000*l.* for the first quarter of the said
second year, for the safe custody and defence of the kingdom and
duchy aforesaid. By writ, &c.,—5000*l.*

28th November.—To John Randolf, one of the Serjeant-
Ushers of the Receipt of the Exchequer. In money paid him for

the costs and expenses of certain jurors in an indictment prosecuted against William Stone, who was lately arrested for falsifying
certain keys of divers chests within the Receipt of the Exchequer,
which said William Stone was convicted of felony, and committed
to the prison of the Abbot of Westminster. By writ, &c.,—10s.

31st January.—To John Stanley and Thomas Wesenham,
esquires, Thomas Pulford, James Grisacre, and John Wattes,
who, by command of the Lord the King, attended to the custody
of Eleanor Cobham, lately called the Duchess of Gloucester. In
money paid to them, by the hands of the said James, for those
10s. daily which the said Lord the King commanded to be paid
them for support of the said Eleanor, and five persons attending for her custody; viz. from the 25th of November last past
unto the 22nd of January then next following. By writ of privy
seal amongst the mandates of this term,—40l.

16th February.—To John Viscount Beaumont, to whom the
present Lord the King, of his especial grace, on the 16th of May,
in the 18th year of his reign, for the support of the estate of the
aforesaid viscount, granted him, by letters patent, &c., 50 marks,
yearly during his life to be received at the Exchequer, &c., as in
the same letters patent more fully is contained. In money paid
to him, by assignment made this day, by the hands of Henry
Lymby, &c. By writ, &c.,—16l. 13s. 4d.

To Ralph Lee, servant of the King's household. In money
paid to him in advance, in discharge of 100l. which the said
Lord the King commanded to be paid him, for the costs and
expenses which, by the King's command, he had incurred and
sustained concerning the reception and conducting Eleanor
Cobham, lately called Duchess of Gloucester, to the city of
Chester. By writ, &c.,—100l.

24th February.—To Bartholomew Hallay, one of the valets
of the Crown, who, by command of the King, attended to the

custody of Roger Bukbroke, upon whom the laws of the said King were executed, and concerning whose custody the said Bartholomew sustained the chief charge and expense, as well for the hire of horses, boats, bed, food, drink, and other necessaries, as well for himself, as for the said Roger, with two attendants for the security of the said Roger during the space of eight weeks and six days. In money paid to his own hands in discharge of 20*l.* which the Lord the King commanded to be paid to the said Bartholomew, to be had as a reward for the business aforesaid. By writ, &c.,—10*l.*

To Sir Philip Boyle, knight, and a baron of Arragon, who lately, upon royal licence granted him, performed certain feats of arms in the presence of the said Lord the King in Smithfield, with John Asteley, a faithful and beloved subject of the said Lord the King. In money paid him in discharge of 100*l.* which the said Lord the King commanded to be paid to the said Philip to be had of his gift. By writ, &c.,—100*l.*

ISSUE ROLL, EASTER, 20 HENRY VI.

27th April.—To Francis de Suriene, called l'Arrogonnoiz, a knight, to whom the present Lord the King, on the 10th of June, in the 19th year of his reign, (for the good services performed and to be performed by him for the said Lord the King, and that he might the more fitly be able to maintain the estate of knighthood, also that the wife and children of the said Francis might not undergo want or poverty,) of his especial grace, and with the advice and consent of his Council, granted him 100 marks yearly to be received at the Exchequer for term of his life, &c., as by the letters patent thereupon made more fully doth appear, &c. In money paid to him, by the hands of Gervase Ulron, in discharge of 50 marks, &c., for this his allowance, viz. for Easter Term, in the 19th year of the present King,—33*l.* 6*s.* 8*d.*

[*Note.* The greater portion of this Roll is occupied with entries of payments to masters and mariners of ships, to take the Duke of York, John Earl of Huntingdon, John Lord Talbot, and other commanders and their retinue to France, Acquitaine, and Calais, specifying the names of the ships, boats, &c., and giving a full account of the preparations for sending this army to France, &c.]

ISSUE ROLL, MICHAELMAS, 21 HENRY VI.

22nd October.—To Owyn ap Tuder. In money paid to his own hands in discharge of 40*l.* which the present Lord the King, of his especial grace, granted to the same Owyn, to be had by way of reward. By writ of privy seal amongst the mandates of this term,—40*l.*

26th October.—To John Hampton, esquire, an attendant upon the King's person. In money paid to him in discharge of 20*l.* which the said Lord the King commanded to be paid for the 40*l.* granted him for certain great employment and costs incurred, and to be incurred by him, by the King's command, for certain labour bestowed upon the King's new college of the blessed Mary, at Eton, committed to the care of the said John by the said Lord the King, viz. for Michaelmas Term last past. By writ of privy seal, &c.,—20*l.*

3rd December.—To Ralph Butler, Lord de Sudeley, the King's Chamberlain. In money paid to him, by the hands of William Beaufitz, for those 100 marks yearly granted him by the present Lord the King for the time he was the said King's Chamberlain, &c.; viz. for Michaelmas Term last past. By writ, &c.,— 33*l.* 6*s.* 8*d.*

31st January.—To Garter, King of arms, who petitioned the Lord the King by bill, that he would vouchsafe to consider that he the said Garter had been constantly employed in the said King's service, about the affairs of obtaining a peace for the space of 21 months, during which period the said Garter had been constrained, on account of his poverty, to borrow 60*l.* 6*s.* 8*d.* In money paid to him, &c. By writ, &c.,—60*l.* 6*s.* 8*d.*

2nd April.—To John Tymperle, esquire, lately sent by the Lord the King upon certain messages to the Duke of Norfolk, which said John safely conducted to the Tower certain persons from the city of Norwich, offenders against and disobedient to the King's laws. In money paid to his own hands in discharge of 5 marks which the said Lord the King commanded to be paid him, to have of his gift by way of reward, &c. By writ, &c.,—3*l.* 6*s.* 8*d.*

2nd April.—To John, Duke of Somerset, retained in the King's service as lieutenant and captain-general of the King's duchy of Acquitaine, in his kingdom of France, which power the Duke of York had previously assumed and exercised by grant from the Lord the King. In money paid to the same Duke of Somerset by the hands of John Daweson, James Gerard, and William Daweson, in advance to make 20 carriages of war, called "ribault-quines," to be conveyed in the present voyage for defence of the said Duke and his retinue, and to resist the adversaries and enemies of the said Lord the King in those parts. By writ, &c.,—100*l.*

ISSUE ROLL, EASTER, 21 HENRY VI.

27th May.—To John, Duke of Somerset, son and heir male of John, late Earl of Somerset, to which said John the Earl, Lord Henry, late King of England, grandfather of the present King, granted 500*l.* yearly, &c. In money paid, &c. By writ, &c.,—40*l.*

18th June.—To William, Bishop of Rochester, sent by the King's command as his Ambassador ; viz., at one time to Frankford beyond seas, to the King of the Romans there, and at

another time to Basile. In money paid to him by assignment
made this day, &c., in discharge of 965*l.* 7*s.* 10*d.* due to him,
&c., for his embassies aforesaid, as appears by his account lately
rendered at the Exchequer, &c., Roll 20, Roll of Accounts. By
writ,—965*l.* 7*s.* 10*d.*

28th June.—To John Dauson, Master of the Ordnance, sent
abroad in the service of the Duke of Somerset. In money paid
to his own hands, in advance; viz., for the price of 1500 bows,
125*l.* 16*s.* 8*d.*; for the price of 1810 sheaves of arrows,
150*l.* 16*s.* 8*d.*; for the price of 200 lances headed with iron, and
200 long "pavys" with iron spikes, 40*l.*; for the price of 96 gross
of cord, 32*l.*; for the price of 200 shovels, 60 "secnons, 80 pekoys," 759 lbs. of ropes, 16*l.* 18*s.* 8*d.*; for the price of a foder of
lead purchased of John Bernewell, to make mallets and other
necessary things, 106*s.* 8*d.*; and for the expense of divers chests,
to contain the bows and arrows aforesaid; also for the expense and
carriage of the said ordnance, as well by land as by sea; and fo
weighing saltpetre and sulphur brought from the Tower of London, also for divers hoops purchased to bind pipes and barrels, to
contain the said saltpetre and sulphur, &c., 10*l.* 12*s.* By writs,
&c.,—381*l.* 9*s.* 8*d.*

2nd July.—To Henry, Earl of Warwick. In money paid to
him by assignment made this day, in advance for 200*l.* yearly
payable to him, by grant of the Lord the King, made at Reading,
appointed for his support so long as he should be within age and in
custody of the said Lord the King; viz., from the last day of
April in the 17th year of the said present King, on which day
Richard, late Earl of Warwick, father of the said Earl, died,
unto the last day of April, in the 21st year of the same King,
viz., for four whole years. By writ, &c.,—800*l.*

6th July.—To John, Duke of Somerset, retained in the King's
service by indenture made between the said Lord the King and
the aforesaid Duke, to serve the said King in his war in France

for one year, and also with his entire force to relieve and succour the King's country of Guyenne by all possible ways and means he could, if the King's enemies should continue their stay there. In money paid to him by the hands of Thomas Gerard, servant to the said Duke, in advance, in part payment of his wages for the second quarter of the year, as well for the wages of the said Duke, at 13*s.* 4*d.* per day; 1 banneret at 4*s.* per day; 6 knights, each at 2*s.* per day; 592 men at arms, to each 12*d.* per day, together with the accustomed reward to the same, as also for the wages of 3949 archers, each at 6*d.* per day; retained by the King to serve him in his wars in the parts aforesaid, for the time aforesaid. By writ, &c.,—11,972*l.* 15*s.* 8*d.*

To John, Duke of Somerset. In money paid him by the hands of John Dauson, receiving the money from William Wytlesey, in advance, for the hire of divers boats, called "showtis," hired by the said John Dauson, for money paid to divers persons for the carriage of the said ordnance, by land, from the house of the Bishop of Salisbury, in Fletestrete, to the house of the Friars Preachers, London, and also carried from the Tower of London to the Thames, and from thence, with the said showtis, to divers ships at Tilbury and in the Pole, there waiting to receive the said ordnance,—6*l.* 15*s.*

22nd July.—To Richard, Duke of York, the King's Lieutenant General and Governor in his kingdom of France and duchy of Normandy. In money paid to him by the hands of John Wygmore, in advance, for the wages of the soldiers remaining for the safe custody of a "bastell" at Diepe. By writ of privy seal, &c.,—1000*l.*

Note. [This long Roll is nearly filled with payments on account of the preparations for the army accompanying the Dukes of York and Somerset in the abovementioned expedition, giving a long list of the shipping, boats, and mariners, &c., employed therein.]

ISSUE ROLL, MICHAELMAS, 22 HENRY VI.

3rd October.—To the Venerable Father in Christ, the Archbishop of Canterbury, Chancellor of England, who, at the time
when he first heard of the death of the Cardinal of Luxenburgh
Archbishop of Rouen, wrote his letters to the most Holy Father
the Pope, and immediately sent the said letters to the said Father
by his own messenger, requesting therein, (so far as the said Pope
could,) that he would be pleased to abstain from promoting any
person to the said Archbishoprick until our Lord the King should
transmit his letters concerning this matter to the said Pope.   In
money paid to him, in discharge of 5 marks which the said Lord
the King, with the advice and assent of his Council, commanded
to be paid to the said Chancellor for so much money by him paid
to the said messenger for the purpose aforesaid.   By writ, &c.,—
3*l.* 6*s.* 8*d.*

28th November.—To Humphrey, Duke of Gloucester.   In
money paid to him by the hands of Ralph Beauford, who received the money from Elizabeth Grey, for the marriage of the
son and heir of Sir Ralph Grey, knight, deceased, in discharge of
196*l.* 13*s.* 4*d.* which the said Lord the King commanded to be
paid to the said Duke, in recompense for certain Alien priories
granted to the said Duke by the same King, and paid by the
said Duke to his college at Eton, as part of 2000 marks for
certain causes granted to the same Duke, as in the letters patent of
the King thereon made, fully is contained.   By writ of privy seal,
&c.,—196*l.* 13*s.* 4*d.*

ISSUE ROLL, EASTER, 22 HENRY VI.

15th May.—To Ralph, Lord de Sudeley, Constable of the
King's castle of Kenelworth, to whom the Lord the King, on the

5th of December last past, committed the custody of Eleanor
Cobham, for whose security and safe custody the said Lord de
Sudeley continually had 12 persons in attendance; viz., one
priest, three gentlemen, one maid, five valets, and two boys, which
said Ralph received daily during the time the said Eleanor was
in his custody, for himself 6s. 8d. per day ; for the said priest,
two gentlemen, and one gentleman, to each of them 8d. per day ;
and for the said maid and each of the said valets, 6d. per day ;
and for each of the said boys, 4d. per day. And moreover the
said Eleanor received for her daily support 100 marks yearly, and
after the same rate during the time aforesaid. In money paid,
&c. By writ, &c.,—33l. 6s. 8d.

9th July.—To Robert Savage, one of the valets of the King's
crown, whom the said Lord the King, by his especial command,
lately appointed to attend upon Master John Batute, a foreigner,
sent to the said Lord the King from the Earl of Armenake, from
the time when the King's city of London adhered to him until
the said Master John departed from England to the city of Bourdeaux, in which city and other parts of Acquitaine the said Robert
continued for a long time, in the service of the said Lord the
King with Sir Robert Roos, knight, without any wages or reward
paid for the great costs of the said Robert Savage, and loss of
his daily wages in the King's household aforesaid. In money
paid to him in discharge of 30l., in recompense of his loss and
reward for his services, &c. By writ, &c.,—15l.

17th August.—To the Marquis of Suffolk, who, by the King's
command, proceeded abroad to bring over and safely conduct
the Queen to the King's presence. In money paid to him by the
hands of Edward Grymeston, in part payment of his wages at
4l. 10s. per day, for two months, for going upon the business
aforesaid, to have by way of reward. By writ, &c.,—146l. 13s. 4d.

To the Countess of Shrewsbury, whom the Lord the King
lately sent abroad to attend upon the Queen on her coming to the

kingdom of England. In money paid to the said Countess by the hands of John Halford, at different times ; viz., at one time 100 marks, and at another time 100 marks, in discharge of 200 marks which said Lord the King commanded to be paid to the said Countess, to be had by way of reward for her costs and expenses. By writ of privy seal, &c.,—133l. 6s. 8d.

[This Roll contains many payments to persons attending upon the Queen upon her coming to England ; amongst others, to Garter King of arms, the Earl of Shrewsbury, John Hampton, Master of the horse to the Queen, &c.]

26th August.—To John Brekenok and John Everdon, clerks in the King's household. In money paid to their own hands at different times; viz., at one time 227l. 10s., at another time 22l. 15s., at another time 207l. 0s. 6d., at another time 427l. 14s., at another time 216l. 17s. 8d., at another time 880l. 0s. 7½d., at another time 200l., another time 691l. 10s., another time 11l. 7s. 6d., and at another time 61l. 8s. 6d., in advance, as well for the wages of 5 barons and baronesses, to each 4s. 6d. per day ; 17 knights, to each 2s. 6d. per day ; 65 esquires, to each 1s. 6d. per day ; and 174 valets, to each 6d. per day ; 4 " charemen and 2 sumpter-men," to each 4d. per day, for one quarter of a year, and for the expenses and necessary charges of the Queen's household ; also for the embarkation, passage, and re-passage, of the Queen and persons aforesaid. By writ, &c.,—2946l. 3s. 9½d.

To Owen Meredith Tudre, esquire. In money paid to him, in discharge of 40l. which the Lord the King, for certain causes him moving, commanded to be paid to the said Owen, to have of his gift. By writ of privy seal amongst the mandates of Michaelmas term last past,—40l.

ISSUE ROLL, MICHAELMAS, 23 HENRY VI.

11th November.—To Reginald, Abbot of Gloucester, whom the present Lord the King sent to the most Holy Father the Pope and to the Apostolic Court, there to exercise the office of King's Orator and Procurator General, to transact such affairs as the present Lord the King now hath, or hereafter may have in the said Court. In money paid to him, &c. By writ, &c.,—100*l.*

To Henry, Lord de Bouchier, lately sent upon a certain journey by the King's command, together with other Ambassadors, to the King's town of Calais, there to conclude a certain treaty of peace between the Lord the King and his adversary of France. In money paid to him, &c., in part payment of 110*l.* 13*s.* 4*d.* due to him, &c. By writ, &c.,—50*l.*

25th November.—To Sir John Stourton, knight. In money paid to him by assignment made this day, by the hands of Hugh Fenn, in part payment of 95*l.* due to him, &c., for the costs and expenses of the Duke of Orleans, late in his custody, at 13*s.* 4*d.* per day, viz., from the 9th July in the 16th year of the present King, on which day the said John first took the said Duke of Orleans into his custody, until the 8th of May in the 17th year of the said King, as appears by his account at the Exchequer, &c., in Roll 20, Roll of Accounts. By writ, &c.,—73*l.* 17*s.* 7*d.*

To Giles Thornton, esquire. In money paid to his own hands at different times ; viz., at one time 10*l.*, at another time 10*l.*, in discharge of 20*l.* which the Lord the King commanded to be paid to the same Giles, in consideration of the costs and expenses incurred by him for the custody of the Prior of Kylmaynan, from the day of Saint James last past unto the 9th November then next following, to be had of his gift for the reason aforesaid. By writ, &c.,—20*l.*

19th January.—To Sir John Fastolff, knight. In money paid to him by assignment made this day, in discharge of 100*l.* which he lent to the Lord the King at the Receipt of the Exchequer, and for the restoration of a tally lately assigned to the same Sir John, &c., as appears in the Roll of Receipts, &c.,—100*l.*

9th April.—To the Lord the King in his chamber. In money paid into the same chamber, by the hands of John Merston, esquire, for a certain jewel called the George, purchased from Sir William Estfeld, knight. By writ of privy seal, &c.,—1333*l.*6*s.*8*d.*

28th April.—To John Damport and his companions, the King's messengers, sent to each county of England with letters of the King's privy seal directed to divers Bishops, Abbots, and other men, respecting the Queen's coronation. In money paid to them by the hands of John Damport, for their costs and expenses in going and returning upon the business aforesaid. By writ, &c., —6*l.* 1*s.* 8*d.*

12th May.—To the Prior of Kilmaynan, in Ireland. In money paid to him by the hands of Giles Thornton, in part payment of 20*l.* which the Lord the King commanded to be paid him in consideration of the costs and expenses sustained by him on attending in the city of London upon a certain matter touching the King's person, pending between the said Prior and the Earl of Ormond. By writ, &c.,—10*l.*

26th May.—To Thomas Parker, armourer. In money paid to him by assignment made this day, &c., in discharge of 20 marks which the Lord the King commanded to be paid him, as well for divers parcels of armour made by him by command of the said King, for the Prior of Kilmaynan, as for other causes. By writ, &c.,—13*l.* 6*s.* 8*d.*

17th June.—To Richard Hakeday, apothecary. In money paid to him by assignment made this day, &c., in part payment of 81*l.* 7*s.* 10*d.* which the Lord the King commanded to be paid to the said Richard, as well for medicines as for other costs by him incurred. By writ, &c.,—49*l.*

18th June.—To five minstrels of the King of Sicily, who lately came to England to witness the state and grand solemnity on the day of the Queen's coronation, and to make a report thereof abroad. In money paid to them in discharge of 50*l.*; viz., to each of them 10*l.*, which the Lord the King commanded to be paid, to be had of his gift by way of reward. By writ, &c.,—50*l.*

To two minstrels of the Duke of Milan, who came to England to witness the solemnization of the Queen's coronation, and report the same to the princes arfd people in their country. In money paid to them by the hands of Edward Grymeston, in discharge of 10 marks; viz., to each of them 5 marks, which the Lord the King, with the advice and assent of his Council, commanded to be paid to the said minstrels, to be had of his gift. By writ, &c.,—6*l.* 13*s.* 4*d.*

To John de Surenceurt, an esquire of the King of Sicily, and steward of the Queen's household abroad, who came previously to the Queen's reception to witness the solemnization of her coronation, and to report the same as above. In money paid to him by the hands of Edward Grymeston, in discharge of 50 marks which the Lord the King, with the advice and assent of his Council, commanded to be paid to the said John, &c. By writ, &c.,—33*l.*6*s.* 8*d.*

To John d'Escoce, an esquire of the King of Sicily, who, as a true subject of the Queen's father, left his own occupations abroad and came in the Queen's retinue to witness the solemnity on the day of her coronation. In money paid to him, &c. By writ, &c.,—66*l.* 13*s.* 4*d.*

19th June.—To Sir Almeric Chaperon, knight, and Charles de Castelion, clerk, Ambassadors from the King of Sicily, lately sent to the Lord the King, in the Queen's retinue, upon certain affairs on behalf of the said Lord the King of Sicily. In money paid to them, in discharge of 200 marks which the said Lord the King commanded to be paid to the said Almeric and Charles;

viz., to each 100 marks, to have of his gift by way of reward. By writ, &c.,—133*l.* 6*s.* 8*d.*

14*th July.*—To Matilda, Lady de Saint John. In money paid to her by assignment made this day, by the hands of Sir Robert Roos, knight, in discharge of 142*l.* 4*s.* 7*d.*, with 80*l.* before received by her, which the said Lord the King commanded to be paid to the said Matilda for those 80 marks yearly granted to the said Matilda for the custody of Humphrey, son and heir of John, late Earl of Arundell, lately being in the custody of the said Matilda; viz., from the 1st June in the 13th year of the present King, to the 30th January in the 16th year of the same King; viz., for 2 whole years one half year and 61 days. By writ, &c.,—62*l.* 4*s.* 7*d.*

20*th July.*—To Alnast d'Alamaa, a knight of Portugal, whom the present Lord the King, on the 13th August, in the 23rd year of his reign, in consideration of the good services and faithful love he showed, as well to the said Lord the King as to his progenitors, created him Earl of Averaunch, and moreover granted to the said Alnast a pension of 500 marks yearly, for his life. In money paid, &c. By writ, &c.,—66*l.* 13*s.* 4*d.*

ISSUE ROLL, MICHAELMAS, 24 HENRY VI.

27*th October.*—To William Gedney, lately sent by the King's command upon certain messages from the castle of Berkhamsted to London, and from thence to the Bishop of Lincoln, then at Sleford, in the county of Lincoln, and to divers other places, to obtain a copy of the last will of Lord Henry the Fifth, father of the present Lord the King. In money paid to him by assignment made this day, by the hands of Richard Lambard, in part payment of 10*l.* 13*s.* 4*d.* which the said Lord the King commanded to be paid him; viz., 6*s.* 8*d.* per day, for the 32 days he was so employed as the King's messenger, to be had as a reward for the business aforesaid. By writ of privy seal, &c.,—5*l.*

7th March.—To John Neuport, esquire, lately taken prisoner by the King's enemies in the town of Depe, to whom the Lord the King, in consideration of 1500 salutes, and for relief of his finances, granted him a certain license to ship by himself, or by his sufficient deputy, 40 pockets of pille wool and lamb wool, and 2000 hides called "shorlyngs and moreyns," in whatsoever port he should please, by which license no other person should receive benefit. In money paid, &c., in discharge of 100*l.* which the Lord the King commanded to be paid him, to be had of his gift by way of reward for the cause aforesaid. By writ, &c.,—100*l.*

Issue Roll, Easter, 24 Henry VI.

18th May.—To Sir John Chalers, knight, late an esquire and sheriff of the counties of Oxford and Berks. In money paid to him by assignment made this day, in discharge of 40 marks which the Lord the King commanded to be paid him, to be had by way of reward, in consideration of the great costs, expense, and labour he had sustained in his office of sheriff, by the King's command, at divers times, for the custody of Thomas Kerver, at that time a traitor to the King, and for conducting the said Thomas to the sessions and other places in the county of Berks, and to London with a great posse, for the safe custody of the person of the aforesaid Thomas. By writ, &c.,—26*l.* 13*s.* 4*d.*

23rd May.—To Margaret Haydok, a virgin or young girl. In money paid to her own hands by assignment made this day, in discharge of 20 marks which the King, being moved with piety, of his especial grace commanded to be paid to the same Margaret, by way of alms. By writ, &c.,—13*l.* 6*s.* 8*d.*

30th May.—To Margaret, Queen of England. In money paid to her by assignment made this day by the hands of John Norys, in discharge of 1000*l.* which the Lord the King commanded to

be paid to the said Queen, as well for the daily expenses of her
chamber as in relief of the great charges which the said Queen
incurred on the day of the Circumcision of our Lord last past.
By writ, &c.,—1000*l.*

To Henry, Duke of Warwick, to whom the present Lord the
King, by the name of Henry, Earl of Warwick, granted 200*l.*
yearly to be received for his support, by the hands of the Treasurer
and Chamberlains of his Exchequer, so long as the said Henry
should remain in the wardship of the said Lord the King. In
money paid to him, by assignment made this day, by the hands
of John Broun, in discharge of all money due to him from the
time of the death of Richard, late Earl of Warwick, his father, for
the 200*l.* aforesaid, unto the 22nd March in the 24th year of the
present King's reign, on which day the said Lord the King delivered to the said Duke the lands and tenements of his inheritance, &c.   By writ, &c.,—578*l.* 9*s.* 10*d.*

9*th July.*—To John Appilton, Keeper of the household of
the Bishop of Salisbury, in Fletestrete, London. In money
paid to him, by the hands of Thomas Birdford, chaplain, for
making of divers resting and other tables, benches, and other
necessary things, there lately destroyed by the King's workmen.
By writ, &c.,—2*l.*

15*th July.*—To John Hampton, one of the esquires of the
King's body, who, by command of the said Lord the King, caused
the bridge to be repaired in his manor within Windsor Park, and
a certain chimney to be made in the great chamber in Windsor
Castle called the Queen's chamber. In money paid to his own
hands in discharge of 36*l.* 13*s.* 4*d.* which the said Lord the King
commanded to be paid to the same John, to be had without
rendering any account therefore. By writ, &c.,—36*l.* 13*s.* 4*d.*

To John le Bousselet, esquire. In money paid to his own hands
in discharge of 50 marks which the Lord the King commanded

to be paid him, in consideration of the continued service the said John had rendered to Lord Henry, late King of England, the present King's father, and also to the said now Lord the King, and for relief of his late necessities and poverty, he having been taken prisoner fourteen times to his great loss. By writ of privy seal, &c.,—33*l*. 6*s*. 8*d*.

19th August —To George Swyllyngton, esquire, who lately proceeded, by the King's command, to his duchy of Guyenne, to receive, in the King's name, the King's town of Blay, then in the custody of the Earl of Longvile. In money paid to him in discharge of 11*l*. which the Lord the King commanded to be paid for so much money by him paid to the said Earl of Longvile, for expenses of the custody of the town aforesaid. By writ, &c., —11*l*.

ISSUE ROLL, MICHAELMAS, 25 HENRY VI.

22nd November.—To Richard Strykelande, for the office of Master of the hounds called " heireres," and to others accustomed to be yearly paid in the said office, viz., for their wages, and for the keep of 1 horse, 36 dogs, called " rennynghoundys," and 9 greyhounds, paid out of the issues and profits of the counties of Bedford and Bucks, by the hands of the Sheriff of the said counties for the time being, at the feast of Saint Michael ; and by reason that the said counties were more charged with divers annuities and other payments than they were formerly accustomed to be, one whole year's arrears were due to the said Richard and others in the same office for their wages and charges aforesaid. &c. In money assigned to them in discharge of 58*l*. 17*s*. 4*d*. due for their wages, &c. By writ, &c.,—58*l*. 17*s*. 4*d*.

3rd December.—To John, Duke of Norfolk. In money paid him, by assignment made this day, by the hands of Richard Almayn, in discharge of 169*l*. 17*s*. 6*d*. which the Lord the King commanded to be paid to the same Duke for the charges and expenses of Thomas Berot, Prior of Kilmaynan, and others gentlemen, valets, and attendants, upon the aforesaid Thomas the Prior, for the safe custody of his person ; viz. from the 23rd December, in the 23rd year of the reign of the present King, unto the 24th December in the 24th year, viz. for one whole year. By writ, &c.,—169*l*. 17*s*. 6*d*.

5th December.—To Oliver Fitz Eustace and Nicholas Berford, of Ireland. In money paid to them, &c., by the hands of John Sheffield, in discharge of 42*l*. 16*s*. 8*d*. which the Lord the King commanded to be paid them, to be had of his gift, as well for embarking as for conducting a person, called Thomas Longman, from the country aforesaid to the King's presence. By writ, &c., —42*l*. 16*s*. 8*d*.

To William Marquis of Suffolk, receiver of the fifteenth part of pure gold and silver within the counties of Devon and Cornwall. In money paid to him, by the hands of John le Maton, in advance for the price of a certain mass of pure silver, weighing, by troy weight, 16¼ lbs. 2¾ oz., price the lb. 34*s*., which said mass Thomas Wyse, attorney to Henry, Cardinal of England, who lately occupied the mines in the counties aforesaid, delivered into the Exchequer of the said Lord the King. By writ of privy seal, &c.,—28*l*. 18*s*.

3rd February.—To Master Lewis de Curtana, who lately came to the Lord the King with divers messages from the Pope, and presented to the same Lord the King a consecrated rose as a present from the said Pope. In money paid to him in discharge of 100 marks, which the said Lord the King commanded to be paid to the said Lewis, to be had of his gift by way of reward. By writ of privy seal, &c.,—66*l*. 13*s*. 4*d*.

17th February.—To Master Thomas Kent, clerk of the King's Council. In money paid to him in part payment of 100*l*., which the said Lord the King commanded to be paid to the same Master

for the great pains taken by him, as well for keeping the privy seal
of the said Lord the King at divers times in the absence of the
Bishop of Chichester, keeper thereof, as also about the Prior of
Kylmaynan and John Davy, lately appealing against certain
persons for treason, to be had of the King's gift, by way of reward
for the causes aforesaid. By writ, &c.,—50*l.*

To Thomas Broun, Clerk to the Treasurer of England, sent
from London to Bury at the time of the parliament held there
with Rolls and other memoranda for the purpose of making known
the state of the realm of England to the Lord the King and nobility
in the same parliament held there.   In money paid to him for his
wages, at 10*s.* per day, from the 10th February, in the 25th year
of the present King, on which day he commenced his journey from
the city aforesaid, unto the 6th March then next following, on
which day he returned to the said city; viz. for 26 days including
each day. By writ, &c.,—13*l.*

ISSUE ROLL, EASTER, 25 HENRY VI.

27th April.—To Thomas Lucy, bailiff of the Queen's lordship
and manor of her town of Enfeld. In money paid to him, &c., in
part payment of 200*l.* which the Lord the King commanded to be
paid to the said Thomas, to be had of the King in recompense for the
costs and expenses incurred by him for victualling two ships, one
called the John of London, and the other Cok John of Chirburgh,
with 500 men sent therein to resist the King's enemies in the
counties of Kent and Suffolk. By writ of privy seal, &c.,—100*l.*

1st May.—To John Penycok, valet of the King's robes. In
money paid to him, by assignment made this day, by the hands
of Thomas Eyo, in advance for repairs done in Byflet Park, and
to a certain bridge within the said park; also for repairing a certain lodge there to keep rabbits within the said park. By writ,
&c.,—64*l.* 7*s.* 4*d.*

To John Stratford, of London, painter. In money paid to him,

by assignment made this day, by the hands of his wife, in discharge
of 10*l.* which the Lord the King commanded to be paid him, as
well for painting the King's barge within and without with the
arms of the King and Queen, as for painting other things in-
trusted to him by Robert Rolleston. By writ, &c.,—10*l.*

15*th July.*—To the Earl of Duinoys, one of the Ambassadors
from France, at present in England, sent to the Lord the King
from his uncle in France to obtain a lasting peace. In money paid
to his own hands in discharge of 101*l.* 2*s.* 3*d.*, which the Lord
the King commanded to be paid him for the price of a pair of
gilt flagons, to be had of his gift. By writ, &c., 101*l.* 2*s.* 3*d.*
[Payments were also made on the same day to the Lord Presseny,
of 79*l.* 8*s.* 10*d.* for the price of a pair of gilt flasks, and 12 gilt
drinking cups; to Master William Cosmont, 40*l.* 4*s.* 6*d.* for the
price of a pair of gilt flasks; and to John Hauard, 25*l.* 11*s.* 7*d.*
for a pair of gilt flasks, who were sent in the same embassy.]

18*th July.*—To Philip Trehere, fishmonger. In money paid
to him, by assignment made this day, in discharge of 20*l.* which
the Lord the King commanded to be paid to the said Philip, in
consideration of the attendance and pains undergone by him, at
the King's especial command, as well in instructing the Prior of
Kilmaynan, who lately appealed the Earl of Ormond of high
treason, in certain points of arms, as instructing and consulting
with John Davy, who appealed John Cateur, armourer, of treason,
to be had by way of reward for the cause aforesaid. By writ, &c.,
—20*l.*

To Thomas Montgomery, esquire, one of the Marshals of the
King's hall, who, at the especial request of the said Lord the King,
attended at different times upon divers persons to his great detri-
ment and charge; viz. first upon the Duke of Norfolk, at Killyngworth and within the Tower of London; secondly, upon John
Astley; thirdly, upon Eleanor Cobham, from Ledys to London and fourthly, upon John Davy, an appellant: also because

he restored into Chancery the King's letters patent, granting him 20*l.* per annum, to be cancelled. In money paid to him, by assignment made this day, &c. By writ, &c.,—40*l.*

24th July.—To Sir Reginald de Fontanes, knight, le Burgeys, Pavyot, le Standard de Milly, John Mercelly, and a secretary accompanying the same, at present on an embassy in England. In money paid to their own hands, viz. to the said Reginald, 10*l.* 13*s.* for the value of a jewel; to the said le Burgeys, 7*l.* 8*s.* for the price of a jewel; to the said Pavyot, 10*l.* for the price of a jewel; to the said le Standard de Mylly, 6*l.* 2*s.* 8*d.* for the price of a jewel; to the said John Mercelly, 111*s.* for the price of a jewel; and to the said secretary, 12*l.* 12*s.* for the price of another jewel, to be had of the King's gift. By writ, &c.,—52*l.* 6*s.* 8*d.*

ISSUE ROLL, MICHAELMAS, 26 HENRY VI.

5th December.—To Master Richard Andrew, the King's secretary. In money paid to his own hands in discharge of 20*l.* which the Lord the King commanded to be paid him, to be applied for certain necessary preparations respecting certain devotions to be made for the King within the royal college of the blessed Mary and Saint Nicholas, in the King's university of Cambridge, at the feast of the Nativity of our Lord next happening. By writ, &c.,—20*l.*

To Francis l'Arrogonoyz, lately made a knight of the garter. In money paid to him, by the hands of Hennage, a servant of Edward Grymeston, in discharge of 20 marks which the Lord the King commanded to be paid to the said Francis, for so much money by him paid for his fee to the college of Saint George, of Windsor, to be had of his gift by way of reward. By writ, &c., —13*l.* 6*s.* 8*d.*

29th April.—To William Postell, gunner, and maker of implements of war, being at present in England with his wife and children, who had for eighteen years past served the Lord the King in his wars, as well in France as Normandy, and because he had truly adhered to the Lord the King lost his inheritance in the bailiwick of Evreux; and also because certain cannon were taken from the house of the said William by persons of the King's Council, in Normandy, during the siege of "Harfflewe," and carried to the said siege, there detained for a long time and used for the purpose of bombarding, and afterwards destroyed, to the damage of the said William of 300*l.* In money paid to him by assignment, &c., which the said Lord the King commanded to be paid to the said William, in recompense for the causes aforesaid. By writ, &c.,—34*l.*

31st May.—To Gwyn Shawson, of Scotland, who lately came from the kingdom of France to see the King in person, in his kingdom of England. In money paid to him, by the hands of William Lumley, in discharge of 100*s.* which the Lord the King commanded to be paid to the said Gwyn to be had of his gift, &c. By writ, &c.,—5*l.*

13th June.—To Edmund Brian, who for his fidelity to the Lord the King, in declaring treasonable matters against the King's person, of which matters the Prior of Kilmaynan appealed the Earl of Ormond, for this and other causes the said Edmund had lost his annuities and fees, all his goods and chattels to a large amount, and also 10*l.* yearly granted him by the said Lord the King for the information aforesaid. In money paid him, &c. By writ, &c.,—26*l.* 13*s.* 4*d.*

16th July.—To Matthew Crompe. In money paid him, by assignment made this day, as well for payment of divers sums of

money, by the King's command, for expediting and obtaining
divers bulls from Pope Eugene, granted for the benefit of the Royal
colleges of the blessed Mary and of Saint Nicholas, Cambridge,
as for his expenses, during the space of 32 months, incurred for
his continued pains for the obtaining and expediting the bulls
aforesaid. By writ, &c.,—101*l.*

To William Boston, clerk of the upper choir of the King's
College, Cambridge, and instructor of the choristers of the same
college. In money paid to him in discharge of 10 marks which
the said Lord the King commanded to be paid to the said William, to be had of his gift by way of reward for the cause aforesaid.
By writ, &c.,—6*l.* 13*s.* 4*d.*

Issue Roll, Michaelmas, 27 Henry VI.

22nd October.—To John Hayne, who from the 18th February,
in the 23rd year, to the 25th June, in the 25th year of the present
King's reign, continued under arrest in the custody of the Constable
of England, and made continued application to the said Lord the
King and his Council for his liberty; and within the said time a great
part of his inheritance as well that in the King's hands as in the
hands of the Duke of York was seized; also a town called Porteseveston, with the castle belonging to the said John, were destroyed and laid waste by the King's rebels and enemies. In
money paid him, by assignment, &c., in discharge of 300*l.* which
the Lord the King commanded to be paid to the said John, as
well for his costs, expenses, and attendance aforesaid, as for the
loss of the profits of his inheritance and the destruction of the town
and castle aforesaid, &c. By writ, &c.,—300*l.*

14th November.—To William Flour, of London, goldsmith.
In money paid to him, by assignment made this day, in discharge
of 20 marks which the Lord the King commanded to be paid to
the said William, to be had by way of reward, because the said

Lord the King stayed in the house of the said William on the day that Queen Margaret, his consort, set out from the Tower of London for her coronation at Westminster. By writ of privy seal amongst the mandates of Michaelmas Term, in the 24th year of the said King,—13*l.* 6*s.* 8*d.*

27th November.—To Sir Richard Vernon, knight, who, by the King's command, as knight-steward, kept the King's Marshal's Court for above the space of three years for divers matters concerning the King's person, as well in the affair between the Prior of Kilmaynan and the Earl of Ormond, at different times, as between others. In money paid to him, &c., in discharge of 200 marks which the Lord the King commanded to be paid him as well in consideration of these premises, as for the cost of 60 men at arms provided, at the charge of the said Richard, for protection of Smithfield during the time of the duels fought there between divers parties. By writ, &c.,—133*l.* 6*s.* 8*d.*

23rd February—To Master John Faceby, the King's physician. In money paid to him in discharge of 150*l.* which the said Lord the King commanded to be paid to the said Master John Faceby, for a certain annuity of 100*l.*, which he had from the same Lord the King for term of his life, paid by the hands of the collector of the small customs in the port of London, &c. By writ, &c.,—150*l.*

ISSUE ROLL, EASTER, 27 HENRY VI.

5th May.—To Gervase Clifton and Alexander Eden, esquires, ordered and appointed by the Lord the King for the protection of the sea. In money paid to them in advance for protecting the sea. By writ, &c.—666*l.* 13*s.* 4*d.*

12th May.—To the Prior and Convent of the house of Preaching Friars, in the town of Beverley, of the King's foundation, in which, by accident, a fire happened, and the dormitory and library were burnt. In money paid to him in discharge of 10 marks which the said Lord the King, of his especial grace, for relief of his great poverty, and to rebuild the house aforesaid, of his alms commanded to be paid him. By writ, &c.,—6*l.* 13*s.* 4*d.*

19*th July.*—To the President and Fellows of Saint Margaret and Saint Barnard's College, in the King's University of Cambridge, founded by Margaret, Queen of England. In money paid to them, by assignment made this day, by the hands of Andrew Docket, in discharge of 200*l.* which the Lord the King commanded to be paid to the said President and Fellows in relief of their poverty, to be had of his gift. By writ, &c.,—200*l.*

19*th July.*—To Brian Holme, esquire, bailiff of the town of Beverley, in the county of York. In money paid to him, by assignment made this day, in discharge of 20 marks which the said Lord the King commanded to be paid him for the costs and expenses of himself and sixteen men riding with him, for the safe conduct of four traitors in his custody, taken from thence by the King's command and given in custody at the prison in the Savoye. By writ, &c.,—13*l.* 6*s.* 8*d.*

21*st July.*—To John Eton, a servant, baker of a bread called " paynman," for the King's eating. In money paid him in discharge of 10*l.* which the said Lord the King commanded to be paid to the said John, as well for the good service bestowed upon the said Lord the King as for the great charge and expenses by him incurred in providing bread for the King's service, &c. By writ, &c.,—10*l.*

To a certain Dutchman, bringing with him a Sarescen to the kingdom of England. In money paid him in part payment of 5 marks which the Lord the King commanded to be paid him, to have of his gift. By writ, &c.,—2*l.*

ISSUE ROLL, MICHAELMAS, 28 HENRY VI.

7th November.—To Robert Honford, esquire, retained in the King's service by indenture, &c., to serve the King in the war in his kingdom of France and duchy of Normandy. In money paid to him, &c. for the first quarter of a year, as well for the wages of himself and 19 men at arms, each at 12*d.* per day, as for the wages of 100 archers, each at 6*d.* per day, with their accustomed reward, &c. By writ, &c.,—362*l.* 18*s.* 10½*d.* [This part of the Roll contains payments to divers captains and their men at arms and archers, &c., retained by indentures in the King's service for his wars in France; amongst others will be found the names of the following commanders; viz. Thomas Drynge, Thomas Keyll, Thomas Davenport, John Clyfton, Ely Longeworth, Cuthbert Colvill, Simon Hammes, Nicholas Morley, Christopher Barton, John Cusac, Henry Angier, esquires, &c.,]

11th December.—To Thomas Maunsell, servant to the Duke of Somerset, the King's lieutenant-general in his kingdom of France and duchy of Normandy. In money paid to the hands of the same Thomas Maunsell, receiving the money at different times; viz. from the Duke of Norfolk,—100*l.*; the Bishop of Winchester,—100*l.*; the Abbot of St. Augustine, Canterbury,—40*l.*; of the Duke of Suffolk,—1773*l.* 5*s.* 8*d.*; of William Porte, and the other executors of Henry, late Cardinal of England,—5000 marks; from the Earl of Oxford,—100 marks; from the Bishop of Carlisle,—200*l.*; from Lord Beauchamp,—50 marks; from John Olney,—20*l.*; from Richard Quartermayns,—50 marks; [with many other sums] received to pay the wages of divers men at arms and archers proceeding to Normandy for defence of those parts, &c. . . . .

ISSUE ROLL, EASTER, 28 HENRY VI.

4th May.—To Morgan Newport, chaplain. In money paid, for his labour, costs, and expenses incurred about executing

2 H

a certain commission, in the nature of a writ of " devenerunt," after the death of Anne, heir of the Duke of Warwick, directed to Sir James de Barkeley, knight, and others in the county of Gloucester and Marches of Wales adjoining. By writ, &c.,—4*l*.

6*th May*.—To Thomas Withiale, the King's engraver, who lately, by the King's command, newly engraved from his own silver, the privy seal of the said Lord the King and made a silver chain thereto, which said seal, with the chain, weighed 15 oz., each oz. at 32*d*., amounting in the whole to 40*s*.; and for the making of the said seal with the chain, 26*s*. 8*d*. In money paid to him, by assignment made this day, in discharge of 8 marks which the said King, &c. By writ, &c.,—3*l*. 6*s*. 8*d*.

29*th June*.—To Lord de Scales, who, by desire and command of the King, was manucaptured to keep and retain together for a certain time such soldiers, liege men, and subjects of the said Lord the King who had lately returned from abroad to England. In money paid to his own hands in discharge of 100 marks which the said Lord the King commanded to be paid to the said Lord de Scales, to be had of his gift, by way of reward for the purpose aforesaid. By writ, &c.,—66*l*. 13*s*. 4*d*.

30*th June*.—To Master Andrew Huls, clerk, keeper of the King's privy seal, who was lately sent, by advice of the King's Council, to communicate with the person who called himself the captain of Kent. In money paid to him in discharge of 10*l*. which the Lord the King commanded to be paid to the said Master Andrew to be had of his gift, by way of reward for his costs and expenses in the business aforesaid. By writ of privy seal, &c.,—10*l*.

To Sir Thomas Tyrell, knight, and Richard Waller, esquire, sent, by the King's command, to Rouchester to seize the goods and chattels which belonged to John Mortymere, the traitor. In money paid to them for their costs and expenses incurred upon the business aforesaid. By writ of privy seal, &c.,—5*l*. 13*s*. 9*d*.

To Brisley, the King's sergeant at arms, sent to Windsor and Sonnyng to seize the goods of William, late Bishop of Salisbury, by command of the King's Council. In money paid to him, &c. By writ, &c.,—1*l.*

To Alexander Eden, Sheriff of Kent, and to divers other persons of the same county. In money paid to them, viz. by the hands of Gervase Clifton, 100*l.*, and by the hands of John Seyncler, 166*l.* 13*s.* 4*d.*, in part payment of 100 marks which the Lord the King commanded to be paid to the same Alexander and others, as well for taking John Cade, an Irishman, calling himself John Mortymer, a great rebel, enemy, and traitor to the King, as also for conducting the person of the said John Cade to the Council of the said Lord the King, after proclamation thereof made in the city of London, to be had of his gift for their pains in the matter aforesaid. By writ of privy seal amongst the mandates of this term,—266*l.* 13*s.* 4*d.*

2nd July.—To Isabella de Lallyng, of the house of Burgundy, who was taken at sea and plundered by the King's subjects. In money paid to the said Isabella in discharge of 40*l.* which the said Lord the King commanded to be paid to her, to be had of his gift for the reason aforesaid. By writ, &c.,—40*l.*

To Adam Blaundyssh and Joan his wife, who lately had a large territory in the duchy of Normandy, and came to England, relinquishing their territory aforesaid on account of their fidelity to the Lord the King. In money paid to them, by the hands of the said Joan, in part payment of 10 marks which the Lord the King, &c. By writ, &c.,—4*l.*

ISSUE ROLL, MICHAELMAS, 29 HENRY VI.

6th October.—To Richard, Duke of York. In money paid to him, by assignment made this day, by the hands of John Wygmore,

2 H 2

in part payment of 114*l.* which the Lord the King commanded to be paid to the said Duke for divers jewels of gold and silver belonging to the said Duke, which said jewels had been stolen by one John Cade, calling himself John Mortymer, a great traitor against the King, out of the house of Philip Malpas, in the city of London, and the said jewels were delivered into the Receipt of the Exchequer, and there sold for the sum aforesaid. By writ of privy seal, &c.,—86*l.* 7*s.*

21*st October.*—To Matthew Phelip. In money paid to him, by assignment made this day, in discharge of 7*l.* 13*s.* 4*d.* which the Lord the King commanded to be paid to the said Matthew, for a seal made by him with his own silver and engraved, by the King's command, for his earldom of Pembrock, and delivered by the same Matthew to the said Lord the King. By writ of privy seal, &c.,—7*l.* 13*s.* 4*d.*

To John Davy. In money paid to him in discharge of 20*l.* which the Lord the King, of his especial grace, commanded to be paid to the said John for the good services lately rendered by him to the said Lord the King, in taking that great traitor and rebel, who called himself John Mortymer, at Hefeld, in the county of Sussex, to be had by way of reward for the reason aforesaid. By writ of privy seal, &c.,—20*l.*

29*th October.*—To Edward, Duke of Somerset, whom the Lord the King sent into the county of Kent to see and direct that peace and tranquillity should be established amongst his peaceable inhabitants there, and to chastise and punish whomsoever should break or disturb such tranquillity or peace. In money paid to him by the hands of Arnold Hostian, goldsmith, in advance for the 20 marks daily allowed him during the time he attended about these premises. By writ, &c.,—200*l.*

27*th February.*—To Garter, king of arms, sent by the King's command to the high seas, there to await the coming of the Earl of Douglas, of Scotland, who was about to arrive in England from the Roman Court, to conduct the said Earl to the King's presence, and continue in attendance upon the said Earl during his stay in England. In money paid to the same Garter, in discharge of 5 marks which the Lord the King commanded to be paid for the costs and expenses incurred by him for the purpose aforesaid. By writ of privy seal, &c.,—3*l.* 6*s.* 8*d.*

Issue Roll, Easter, 29 Henry VI.

27th May.—To Alexander Iden, late Sheriff of Kent. In money paid him by assignment made this day, in discharge of 20 marks which the Lord the King commanded to be paid to the said Alexander, to be had by way of reward, for the costs and expenses incurred by him in taking and conducting to the Lord the King, Robert Spencer, a sworn brother to the great traitor and rebel calling himself John Mortymer. By writ of privy seal amongst the mandates of Easter term, in the 28th year of the present King,—13*l.* 6*s.* 8*d.*

10th June.—To William Neel, one of the grooms of the King's chamber, who had. by the King's command, in his custody John Kyrkeby, of York, appellant ; viz., from the feast of the Nativity of the Blessed Virgin Mary unto the feast of Saint George then next following; and for safely conducting the said appellant from the King's castle of Windsor to York aforesaid, and from thence back again to the castle aforesaid, at his great cost and expense, without any reward having been made him for this purpose. In money paid to him in discharge of 10*l.* which the King, &c. By writ, &c.,—10*l.*

11th June.—To Richard Wodevyle, Lord Ryvers. In money paid to him by assignment made this day, by the hands of Lewis Trees, in part payment of 400 marks which the Lord the King commanded to be paid to the said Richard Lord Ryvers, for the great costs and charges incurred by him in riding and executing the King's commands; viz., at one time in the retinue of the Earl of Oxford, at another time in the retinue of the Earl of Wiltshire and Lord of Molens, upon whose attendance he continued in going and returning for the space of six weeks with 200 men and their horses to his great daily charge, amounting to above the sum of 400 marks. By writ, &c.,—200*l.*

1*st July.*—To John Solers, esquire, lately sent by the King's command to Blackheath, to the great traitor there John Cade, calling himself the Captain of Kent, upon special causes concerning our Lord the King. In money paid to his own hands; viz., 20*s.* in part payment of 10*l.*, which the Lord the King commanded to be paid to the said John in recompense of his services, and for the damage the said John had sustained in his goods. By writ of privy seal amongst the mandates of this term,—1*l.*

9*th July.*—To William Brook, one of the King's valets of his crown, to whom the Lord the King committed the custody of Richard Smyth, appellant, and Philpot Morys, Thomas Bocher, and William Heyley, defendants, for certain treasons, and on this account, by the King's command, they were kept in his custody, in the King's castle of Windsor, for above half a year, he finding them meat and drink, fuel and other necessary things, at his great costs and expense. In money paid, &c. By writ, &c.,—10*l.*

17*th July.*—To Richard Weltden, esquire. In money paid to him by assignment made this day, in discharge of 40 marks which the Lord the King commanded to be paid for the great costs and expenses incurred by him and 12 persons with as many horses, for the period of above a month, for the safe custody and conduct, from Newcastle to the King's presence, of a person called Laweles, who for a long time had been a plunderer and robber at sea, to be had by way of reward, &c. By writ, &c.,— 26*l.* 13*s.* 4*d.*

19*th July.*—To John, Cardinal and Archbishop of York, the

King's Chancellor, who lately rode to the town of Rouchester, (viz., at the time that the great traitor to the King, calling himself John Mortymer, was taken,) for the tranquillity and good government of the King's subjects there, also for the recovery of certain goods seized by the said traitor, then being at the said town of Rouchester. In money paid to him by assignment made this day, in discharge of 20*l.* which the Lord the King commanded to be paid to the same Cardinal for the costs and expenses incurred by him in this behalf, by way of reward, &c. By writ, &c.,—20*l.* [There are several other entries of payments to the same Cardinal on this part of the Roll for having executed certain commissions in the county of Kent directed to him, and also for attending at the King's Council upon this and other important affairs.]

21st July.—To Thomas Kyrkeby, clerk of the Rolls of the King's Chancery, and master of the house of converted Jews. In money paid to him by assignment made this day, by the hands of Robert Waskham, in discharge of 33*l.* 6*s.* 3*d.* due &c., as well for the wages and fees of the said keeper, at 20 marks, as for two chaplains, to each 4*l.*, and to one clerk, at 2 marks yearly, serving the same master there; also for the wages of Martin, the son of Henry Wodstok, John Durdraght, and John Seyt, to each 1½*d.* per day; and to Alice, converted Jews, 1*d.* per day; viz., from the 14th May in the 28th year of the present King, unto the 14th May then next following; viz., for one whole year, reckoning the first but not the last day, as appears in his account thereof lately rendered at the Exchequer, in Roll 28, Roll of Accounts. By writ, &c,—33*l.* 6*s.* 3*d.*

4th August.—To Sir Roger Chamberleyn, knight. In money paid to him by assignment made this day, in part payment of 40 marks which the Lord the King commanded to be paid him, as well for the custody of Queneburgh Castle, at the time when the traitor calling himself the Captain of Kent went from Southwerk, in the county aforesaid, to Rochester with a great mob, as for taking to the King's presence other traitors; viz., Geoffrey Kechyn and another, called "Capitaignes Boucher;" also for other costs and expenses incurred with a fit assemblage of persons retained by him in the said castle, for the reasons aforesaid; and also for repairs done to the same castle. By writ of privy seal amongst the mandates of Easter term, in the 28th year of the present King,—23*l.* 6*s.* 8*d.*

5th August.—To Thomas Waryn, an esquire of the Duke of Somerset. In money paid to him by assignment made this day, by the hands of Nicholas Aves, in discharge of 27*l.* 4*s.* which the Lord the King commanded to be paid for his costs and expenses, at 12*d.* per day, and for 24 persons, to each of whom was paid 8*d.* per day, for the space of 32 days, for the custody of William Parmenter, calling himself a Captain of Kent, with other principals his companions or allies within the said county, also being in his custody during the time aforesaid, by the King's command, and afterwards, by virtue of the King's letters, conducted to the castles of Windsor and Wynchester. By writ, &c.,—27*l.* 0*s.* 4*d.*

ISSUE ROLL, MICHAELMAS, 30 HENRY VI.

11th December.—To Garter, king of arms, sent, by the King's command, at different times, as well to the Duke of Burgundy as to the King of Scotland, with certain messages upon which he was occupied, and engaged for the space of 147 days. In money paid to him by assignment made this day, in discharge of 13*l.* 3*s.* 4*d.* which the Lord the King, &c. By writ, &c.,—13*l.* 3*s.* 4*d.*

To the same Garter, lately sent, by the King's command, to travel with Sir James Dowglas, knight, on his coming to the Lord the King, and to bring the said James to the King's presence at Winchester, Salisbury, or elsewhere; and to conduct him to Scotland; also for presenting certain letters from our said King to the King of Scotland during which time he continued his stay, for 78 days. In money paid to him, &c. By writ, &c.,—13*l.*

17th February.—To John Hampton, an esquire of the King's body. In money paid to him by assignment made this day, in discharge of 24*l.* 6*s.* 8*d.* which was paid to the same John by the King's command, at different times, for the purposes under-written ; viz., at one time incurred for plays and recreations for the same Lord the King, at the feast of the Nativity of our Lord, in the 28th year of his reign, 12*l.* 6*s.* 8*d.* ; and also at another time, 11*l.* 19*s.* 7*d.*, for certain expenses incurred for the feast of Saint George, held at Windsor, in the same 28th year. By writ, &c.,— 24*l.* 6*s.* 8*d.*

ISSUE ROLL, EASTER, 30 HENRY VI.

18th July.—To John Nanfan, esquire, whom the Lord the King ordered and appointed to be Keeper and Governor of the islands of Jersey and Gernesay, with the appurtenances, and of the castles, and other places within the same, retained in the King's service, by indenture made between the said Lord the King and the said John, for him to have continually in the said islands, for the security and safe custody of the said islands, castles, and places, 130 archers, well and sufficiently arrayed, as to them doth belong, for and during the time and term of half a year, to begin on the day of the muster of the archers made by the said John ; viz., the 9th August, in the 30th year of the present King, &c., for the first quarter of the said half year. By writ, &c.,—295*l.* 15*s.*

4th August.—To a certain messenger of the Lord the King, sent with the King's writs directed to Lord Grey, Sir William Oldehale, and Sir John Fastolff, knights, upon certain matters therein contained concerning the Lord the King and his Council. In money paid to him for his costs and expenses in going and re-turning upon the business aforesaid. By writ, &c.,—10*s.*

26th October.—To Clarencieux, king of arms, whom the Lord
the King sent as his messenger with John Newport, esquire, to
the Kings of Arragon and Poland, to invest and admit them, on
behalf of the Lord the King, to the order of the garter. In money
paid to him in discharge of 20*l.* which the said Lord the King
commanded to be paid to the same Clarencieux, to be had of his
gift, &c.; also in consideration of the good services performed by the
said Clarencieux for the said King during a period of 19 years, not
having had any wages or fees granted him. By writ, &c.,—20*l.*

3rd November.—To Thomas Vaghan, esquire, master of the
King's ordnance. In money paid him by assignment made this
day, in discharge of 46*l.* 13*s.* which the Lord the King commanded to be paid, for divers pieces of ordnance ordered and
provided by the said Thomas, and on the 20th June, in the 28th
year of the said King, taken to the said King's presence to his
camp; viz., for two " serpentynes and one colveryn," with 9
chambers; and for 200 stones, and lead provided for darts for
the said serpentynes and culverynes, to the value of 100*s.*; and for
5 great "rybaudekyns," prepared, with 10 chambers, for the said
camp, price 4*l.*; and for two great " rybawdekyns," with four
chambers, price of each 100*s.*; also two carriages for the said
ordnance, with 30 persons, gunners, carpenters, smiths, and
lantern (or match bearers,) attending with the ordnance aforesaid
for three days and for one cade of fine powder, weighing 30 lbs.,
price the lb. 20*d.*; and for two barrels of gunpowder, containing
103 lbs., price the lb. 12*d.* By writ of privy seal amongst the
mandates of Easter term, in the 38th year of the present King,—
46*l.* 13*s.*

2nd December.—To John Styvecle, attending at Westminster
for the safe custody of John Halton, seized for treason. In money
paid to him for his costs and expenses, &c. By writ, &c.,—
6*s.* 8*d.*

8th December.—To John Baker, esquire, retained in the service of our Lord the King by indenture made between the said Lord the King and the aforesaid John, to serve the said King with 10 men at arms, each at 8*d.* per day, himself included; and 10 archers, each at 4*d.* per day, for the safe custody of the King's castle of Carisbrok, in the Isle of Wight. In money paid to him by assignment made this day, by the hands of Thomas Loge, in part payment of 263*l.* due to him, &c.; viz., from the 21st April, in the 29th year, unto the feast of Saint Michael, in the 31st year of the present King, for one whole year and 161 days, &c. By writ, &c.,—66*l.* 13*s.* 4*d.*

28th February.—To Thomas Est and John Beaufitz. In money paid to them by assignment made this day, by the hands of William Beaufitz, in discharge of 7*l.* 9*s.* 4*d.* which the Lord the King commanded to be paid to the said Thomas and John, &c., for costs and expenses incurred and sustained by them for the safe custody of Robert Ardern, esquire, and John Mattys, in Kyllyngworth Castle, by the said King's command; and also for conducting the said Robert and John from the said castle to the city of Hereford, and for keeping them there 3 days; also for fetters purchased for their safe and secure custody, &c. By writ, &c.,— 7*l.* 9*s.* 4*d.*

ISSUE ROLL, EASTER, 31 HENRY VI.

8th May.—To Richard, Earl of Salisbury, who, by the King's command, in the month of September, in the 30th year of his reign, commenced his journey to the said Lord the King, then at his castle of Kynelworth, where, and at the King's city of Coventry, he attended with a numerous retinue, at his great costs and charges about the King's person during the whole time that the said Lord the King remained there; and also the said Earl, with diligent attention, for a long time was in attendance about the King's person in his last journey from his palace at Westminster to

Northampton, and from thence into Kent, with a great number of persons likewise at his own great costs and charges. In money paid to him by assignment, &c., in discharge of 333*l*. 6*s*. 8*d*. which the Lord the King commanded to be paid him, &c. By writ, &c.,—333*l*. 6*s*. 8*d*.

14*th May*.—To Thomas Yerde, esquire, who, to his great loss, was constituted and appointed, by the King's command, Sheriff of Surrey and Sussex, and served that office from the feast of Saint Michael in the 30th year of the present King, unto the feast of Saint Michael then next following, for one whole year, who, during the said period, at his own costs and expenses, assembled together a considerable number of able persons of the counties aforesaid, and brought them to the same Lord the King, then at Blackheath, to resist, with other forces, the rebels there assembled against the said Lord the King. In money paid to him, &c., in discharge of 50*l*. which the Lord the King commanded to be paid him as a reward, &c. By writ, &c.,—50*l*.

17*th May*.—To Lancaster, king of arms, who, by the King's command, in the 28th year of his reign, during the time of the insurrection of the great traitor John Cade, calling himself the Captain of Kent, with great speed rode from Leicester to London, Daventry, and divers other places, in which journey he injured two horses worth 8*l*., and moreover paid for the hire of other horses to the amount of 40*s*., by which riding he was a loser. In money paid to him, &c., in discharge of 40 marks which the Lord the King, of his especial grace, ordered to be paid to the same Lancaster, as well for his costs in these premises, &c., amounting to 100*s*., as for a certain coat of arms for the King, price 20*l*., delivered by him to the said Lord the King, &c. By writ, &c.,— 26*l*. 13*s*. 4*d*.

18*th May*.—To Thomas Harper, valet of the King's crown, ordered and appointed by the said Lord the King to attend upon the person of Sir William Oldehale, knight, for the safe and secure custody of the same William within the royal chapel of Saint Martin le Grand, London. In money paid, &c., for the purpose aforesaid. By writ, &c.,—2*l.*

12*th June.*—To John Halton, who, in the King's cause, appealed Robert Noreys, and with him joined battle, to be decided by them, in their own persons, at Smithfield, on a certain day appointed. In money paid to him by the hands of Averey Crambroke, in part payment of 50 marks which the Lord the King ordered to be paid to the same John Halton for divers necessaries and other things ordered for him, to be provided for the cause aforesaid. By writ, &c.,—26*l.* 13*s.* 4*d.*

30*th July.*—To George of Judea, who lately arrived in England from the Patriarch of Jerusalem. In money paid to his own hands, in discharge of 10 marks which the Lord the King ordered to be paid to the said George, &c. By writ, &c.,—6*l.* 13*s.* 4*d.*

ISSUE ROLL, MICHAELMAS, 32 HENRY VI.

19*th February.*—To John Smert, Garter king of arms, who was lately sent by the King's commands to the Marches of Scotland, there to request certain appointments to be made with the Earl of Douglas, and also for attending upon the Lord of Hamelton, at London and other places, for more than five weeks; also attending upon our Lord the King from Sherborne, in the county of Dorset, to Kenelworth, for the space of six weeks, to obtain an answer from the Lord the King to the Commissioners and the said Earl of Douglas, then being in those parts. In money paid, &c. By writ, &c.,—16*l.* 13*s.* 4*d.*

23*rd February.*—To Richard Neville, Earl of Warwick, one of the Chamberlains of the Exchequer, in right of Anne, his late wife, sister and heir of Henry, late Duke of Warwick, deceased, who was lately one of the Chamberlains of the same Exchequer. In money paid to him, &c., for his wages, at 8d. per day; viz., from the 6th December, in the 29th year of the present King, unto the 13th January then next following, &c. By writ, &c.,—1l. 6s.

ISSUE ROLL, EASTER, 32 HENRY VI.

To Humphrey, Duke of Buckingham, who, by the King's command, in the month of September, in the 29th year of his reign, went to the said Lord the King at his castle of Kyllyng-worth, and to his city of Coventry, with a strong guard; also attended at great costs and expenses about the King's person. In money paid to him by assignment made this day by the hands of John Andrew, 400l. which the Lord the King commanded to be paid him, &c. By writ, &c.—400l.

17th July.—To Margaret, Queen of England. In money paid to her by assignment made this day by the hands of Robert Tanfield, for divers sums of money paid by the said Queen, for an embroidered cloth, called "crisome," for the baptism of the Prince the King's son, and for 20 yards of russet cloth of gold, called "tisshu," and "540 broun sable bakkes," worth altogether 554l. 16s. 8d.; the said Queen to have the same by the King's command of his gift. By writ, &c.,—554l. 16s. 8d.

ISSUE ROLL, MICHAELMAS, 33 HENRY VI.

19th February.—To the Prior and Convent of the Blessed Peter, Westminster. In money paid to them by the hands of John Wode, in discharge of 10l. which the Lord the King, with the advice of his Council, commanded to be paid to the said Prior and Convent, for the wax lights burnt at the baptism of Edward, the son of our Lord the King. By writ of privy seal amongst the mandates of this term,—10*l.*

21*st February.*—To Margaret, Duchess of Somerset, who, by the King's command, resided and remained in attendance in the city of London and suburbs thereof, from the feast of Lent, in the 31st year, to the 11th August then next following, at her great cost and charge. In money paid to her, &c., in discharge of 100*l.* which the said Lord the King commanded to be paid to the said Duchess, of his gift, &c. By writ of privy seal,—100*l.*

ISSUE ROLL, EASTER, 33 HENRY VI.

16*th April.*—To Thomas Thorp, one of the Barons of the Exchequer, receiving yearly 40 marks for his fee in his office aforesaid. In money paid to his own hands in discharge of 20 marks, &c. By writ, &c.,—13*l.* 6*s.* 8*d.*

15*th July.*—To William Welden and Hugh Fenne. In money paid to them by assignment made this day; viz., for themselves 40 marks, and for their clerks 5 marks, as an especial reward for their labour and attendance in compiling and writing out a declaration of the state of the office of Treasurer of England, reported and pronounced in the King's present parliament to be for the advantage of the King and benefit and utility of his kingdom of England. By writ, &c.,—30*l.*

To James, Earl of Douglas. In money paid to him by the hands of Richard Symson, in part payment of 400 marks which the Lord the King, with the advice of his Council, granted to the same James, for succour, provisions, relief, and rescue of the castle of Treve, which said castle the said Earl gave to the King. By writ, &c.,—100*l.*

To the same James, Earl of Douglas, to whom the present

Lord the King, with the advice of his Council, on the 4th August, in his 33rd year, granted 500*l.* yearly for the services performed by the said Earl to the said Lord the King, to be received, &c., until the said Earl should have recovered or be restored to his inheritance, or to the great property taken from him by the person who calls himself the King of Scotland. In money paid to him by the hands of John Shaw, in advance, &c. By writ, &c.,—100*l.*

<hr>

Issue Roll, Michaelmas, 34 Henry VI.

22nd October.—To Matthew Philip, of London, goldsmith In money paid to his own hands, in part payment of 100 marks, for a certain gilt garter ornamented with pearls and flowers, purchased from the same Matthew, and delivered to John Feteplace, esquire, for him to take the said garter and present it to the King of Portugal. By writ of privy seal, &c.,—40*l.*

To John Feteplace, esquire. In money paid to his own hands in discharge of 40*l.* which the Lord the King commanded to be paid to the said John for his costs and expenses in carrying the said garter to the King of Portugal, &c. By writ, &c.,—40*l.*

8th November.—To John Andrew. In money paid to him by assignment made this day, as an especial reward for the great pains and diligence exercised by him for the King's advantage, in prosecuting certain matters in the King's Bench against John Wyngfeld, esquire, late sheriff of the county of Norfolk. By writ, &c.,—10*l.*

<hr>

Issue Roll, Easter, 34 Henry VI.

12th July.—To Lancaster, herald, sent by the Lord the King and the Lords of his Council to the Duke of York, to attend the said Duke on his going to Scotland to resist the King of Scotland

and others coming with him to the kingdom of England. In
money paid, &c.   By writ, &c.,—6*l.* 13*s.* 4*d.*

15*th July.*—To a certain Esquire of the King of Denmark, who
lately came to England and received the military order at Windsor.
In money paid to him in discharge of 20*l.* which the said Lord
the King commanded to be paid him for his costs and expenses,
by way of reward, of the King's gift.   By writ, &c.,—20*l.*

To John Agiropulus, from Constantynople.   In money paid to
his own hands, in discharge of 10*l.* which the Lord the King
commanded to be paid to the said John of his gift, by way of reward.   By writ, &c.,—10*l.*

ISSUE ROLL, MICHAELMAS, 35 HENRY VI.

20*th October.*—To Walter Ingham.   In money paid to him by
assignment made this day, as an especial reward for the labour,
costs, and expenses, incurred by him in obtaining information for
the Treasurer of England that Thomas Denys and Richard
Plonkes, who were manucaptors for John Roswell to keep the
peace, had not produced the aforesaid John before the Lord the
King on the day appointed them, and that the aforesaid Thomas
had pleaded the death of the aforesaid John, whereby he intended
that the Lord the King, for this reason, should not be able to demand
against them; but the aforesaid Walter proved that the aforesaid
John was alive, and gave the Court of the Lord the King full
proof thereof.   By writ, &c.,—10*l.*

21*st October.*—To Stephen Clampard, esquire, sent by the
King's command to Kyllyngworth, with guns and other implements of war.   In money paid him for his costs and expenses, for
the things so sent for the purpose aforesaid.   By writ, &c.,—5*l.*

ISSUE ROLL, EASTER, 35 HENRY VI.

30th April.—To Philip Reynold, one of the clerks of the King's chapel. In money paid to his own hands in discharge of 20 marks which the Lord the King commanded to be paid him, to be had of his gift, as well for the sake of piety and alms, as because the same Philip was accidentally maimed, on account of which, and other great infirmities, he was not able to attend to his duties for the said Lord the King, nor to gain his living until God should restore him to health. By writ, &c.,—13*l.* 6*s.* 8*d.*

19th May.—To John Judde. In money paid to him by assignment made this day, in discharge of 133*l.* 8*s.* 5½*d.* which the said Lord the King commanded to be paid to the said John for 26 new cannon called serpentynes, with their apparatus for the field, weighing 700 lbs., price the lb. 3*d.* ; for two hogsheads of sulphur, weighing 12 cwt. 14 lbs., price the lb. 1½*d.* ; and for two cades of gunpowder, weighing 13 score 14 lbs., price the lb. 6*d.* ; and for 7 cades of saltpetre, weighing 18½ cwt., price the lb. 5*d.* ; and for a certain cannon called a " culveryne ;" also for an iron and a leaden mortar, price 17*s.* 8½*d.* ; and for carriages and two carts from London to Kenelworth Castle, 24*s.* 8*d.*, &c. By writ, &c.,—133*l.* 8*s.* 5½*d.*

30th May.—To Robert Tomelynson, who informed the Lord the King of certain horrible treasons, conspiracies, and intentions against the said King's Majesty and his person, and also against the persons of the Queen and the Lord the Prince, the said King's son, by John Atte Wode, of the county of Norfolk ; which said treasons the said Robert was ready to prove, as might be required or demanded by the King's laws. In money paid to the said Robert, in discharge of 10*l.* which the Lord the King commanded to be paid him of his gift by way of reward, for his great costs and charges in a certain appeal made by him against the said John Atte Wode. By writ, &c.,—10*l.*

To Thomas Poleyn, "brigandermaker." In money paid to
him, in part payment of 8*l.* 16*s.* 8*d.* which the Lord the King
commanded to be paid to the said Thomas, as well for making a
pair of "brigandiers," as for the stuff thereof, price 11 marks,
to serve the said Lord the King in his journey to Leicester to
the King's last parliament held there, also for enlarging and
making new gauntlets to the same brigandiers, 30*s.* By writ,
&c.,—7*l.* 13*s.* 4*d.*

ISSUE ROLL, EASTER, 36 HENRY VI.

24th April.—To the Bishop of Durham. In money paid
him by assignment made this day, in discharge of 126*l.* 13*s.* 4*d.*
paid to him, with 100*l.*, on the 20th February last past, as
an especial reward, for divers labour, costs, and expenses, incurred by his servants and officers on collecting and levying
710*l.* 8*s.* 10¼*d.*, due to the Lord the King for the issues and profits
of the temporalties of the see of Durham, void by the death of
Robert, late Bishop there, and in the King's hands from the
9th July in the 35th year, unto the 18th October then next following, during which period the officers and ministers of the Lord the
King were not permitted to enter without writs, warrants, or
other precepts of the said present Bishop, under his seal, from
his Chancery, &c. By writ, &c.,—26*l.* 13*s.* 4*d.*

6th June.—To Mary de la Sparr, daughter of John, late
Duke of Bedford, to whom the present King, on the 12th
August, in the 35th year of his reign, of his especial grace,
granted 25 marks yearly so long as it should please the King, to
be paid at the Receipt of the Exchequer, by the hands of the
Treasurer and Chamberlains there for the time being. In money
paid, &c., in discharge of 8*l.* 6*s.* 8*d.*, &c., from the said 12th
August to the 10th February, in the 36th year of the present
King, for half a year. By writ, &c.,—8*l.* 6*s.* 8*d.*

Issue Roll, Easter, 37 Henry VI.

23rd April.—To John Brekenok, esquire, late Treasurer of the King's household. In money paid to him by the hands of Thomas Eyre, parson and clerk of the said King's chapel in his household, for wages due to him receiving the money from the fines of those persons who would not accept the order of knighthood according to the King's proclamation made in the 36th year of the King's reign. By writ, &c.,—10*l.* 13*s.* 4*d.*

9th May.—To Andrew, Abbot of Melros, and the Rotyssey herald, who lately came to our Lord the King with certain messages from the King of Scotland. In money paid them; viz., to the said Andrew 20 marks, and to the said Rotyssey 5 marks, in discharge of 16*l.* 13*s.* 4*d.* which our said Lord the King commanded to be paid to the same Andrew and Rotyssey, to be had of his gift by way of reward. By writ, &c.,—16*l,* 13*s.* 4*d.*

Issue Roll, Michaelmas, 39 Henry VI.

15th October.—To Henry Assheborne. In money paid to him by the hands of John Leynton, as an especial reward, for writing out divers copies of a certain act of parliament for the King's household. By general writ, &c., amongst the mandates of Michaelmas term, in the 37th year of the said present King,—7*s.* 4*d.*

31st October.—To Master Robert Stillyngton, Dean of Saint Martin's, London, whom the Lord the King, with the advice of his Council, on the 28th July, in the 39th year of his reign, ordered, constituted, and appointed keeper of his privy seal, receiving in the same office, for support of the charge thereof, 20*s.* per day, as other keepers of the said privy seal had been accustomed to receive, &c. By writ, &c.,—100*l*

5th December.—To Richard Symson, one of the Chamberlain's clerks of the Exchequer, keeper of the foils in the said Exchequer. In money paid him by assignment made this day, as an especial reward, as well for labour, costs, and expenses incurred by him for divers searches made at different times, by command of the Treasurer of England, in divers foils remaining in his office, as for writing out on paper and delivering the same to the said Treasurer, for certain especial causes moving the said Treasurer. By writ, &c.,—10*l.*

27th January.—To John Godyn and John Lambe, wardens of the Company of Grocers, of the city of London. In money paid them by assignment made this day, by the hands of Thomas Pound, in discharge of 200*l.* which they lent to the Lord the King at the Receipt of his Exchequer, on the 5th December last past, as appears in the Roll of Receipts of that day,—200*l.*

APPENDIX.

11th December.—To Richard Wydevyle Lord Rivers, and Jaquette, Duchess of Bedford, his wife, who lately received and enjoyed the dower of the said Jaquette, arising after the death of John, late Duke of Bedford, her former husband, amongst other things, a certain annual rent of 333 marks 4*s.* 5¾*d.* and one-third of a farthing, assigned to the said Richard and Jaquette, payable as the dower of the said Jaquette, at the Receipt of the Exchequer, in the town of Westminster, in the county of Middlesex, which said rent, amongst other things, was assigned to the said Richard and Jaquette, as fully appears by a certain Record assigning such dower, remaining in the King's Chancery, &c.;— and the Lord the King, on the 10th of December last past, affectionately considering the state and benefit of the said Duchess and Richard, of his especial grace, by letters patent, granted to the same Richard and Jaquette the said annual rent, to have, receive, and enjoy the same, to the said Richard and Jaquette, for the life of the said Jaquette, from the time of the said assignment and grant of the dower, &c., as in the said letters patent fully doth appear. In money paid them by assignment made this day, by the hands of John Hulcote, in advance for this annual payment. By writ, &c.,—100*l.*

25th February.—To Richard Whethill, who, by command of the Earl of Warwick, Captain of the town of Calais, and deputy of the Marches there, exercised great diligence to reduce the

castle of Guysnes to the King's obedience, and to drive away
the rebels and other disaffected persons who for a long time had
occupied the same in opposition to the desire and command of the
Lord the King, and contrary to their allegiance, intending to surrender the same place into the hands of the King's enemies; but
for preservation of the said castle, the aforesaid Richard Whethill
paid and expended the sum of 632*l*. 16*s*. 11½*d*. for the expulsion
of a certain company of soldiers who then had the guard and
custody of the castle aforesaid; and to avoid further danger and
inconvenience which might have shortly happened, took the said
castle for the King into his own possession and governance; and
the said Richard Whethill delivered to other soldiers the said
castle, to be kept for the King's use, and paid them for provisions and other necessaries above the sum of 400*l*., which
sums in the whole amounted to 1032*l*. 16*s*. 11½*d*. In money paid
to him by assignment made this day, by the hands of Richard
Sherwyn, his servant, in part payment of 1032*l*. 16*s*. 11½*d*. By
writ, &c.,—666*l*. 13*s*. 8½*d*.

To John Toller, of London, grocer. In money paid to his
own hands, for wax purchased of him for supplying a hearse
for the Duke of York, in the cathedral church of Saint Paul,
London. By writ of privy seal,—44*l*.

17th March.—To John Talbot, of London, waxchandler. In
money paid to his own hands, for supplying a hearse in the
cathedral church of Saint Paul, London, for the obsequies of the
late Duke of York there performed. By writ of privy seal, &c.,
—74*l*. 17*s*. 2*d*.

To John Toller, of London, grocer. In money paid to his
own hands, for providing wax purchased of him for the said
hearse in the church aforesaid, for the obsequies of the said late
Duke. By writ of privy seal, &c.,—37*l*. 16*s*. 10*d*.

Issue Roll, Easter, 4 Edward IV.

9th May.—To John Clerk, the King's Apothecary. In money paid to his own hands by assignment made this day, in discharge of 87*l.* 18*s.* 7½*d.* which the Lord the King commanded to be paid to the said John for certain physic supplied for the said King's use, and administered to him under the advice of the said King's physicians. By writ, &c.,—87*l.* 18*s.* 7½*d.*

11th June.—To Nicholas Rawle, chaplain, who, by the King's command, celebrated and performed divine service in the chapel of the Blessed Mary of Berkyng, near the Tower of London, by praying to God and the Blessed Mary for the prosperity and good success of the said Lord the King, and for the salvation of the soul of the most noble and famous Prince of worthy memory the Duke of York, the King's father. In money paid him, by assignment made this day, by the hands of Richard Warner, in advance for the 10*l.* yearly granted him by the present Lord the King until the said Lord the King should otherwise provide for the said yearly salary of the said Nicholas. By writ, &c.,—2*l.* 10*s.*

Roll of Accounts, Easter, 5 Edward IV.

To Sir Henry Percy, knight, to provide for his table and four persons attendant upon him in the King's prison of the Flete, during two months and four days, taking for each week 1*l.* 6*s.* 8*d.*,—11*l.* 3*s.* 8*d.*

To John Wilson, Roger Hall, and Walter Wynter, attending upon the said Henry Percy during the said period, in the prison aforesaid, by way of reward, each taking 6*d.* per day,—4*l.* 16*s.*

And for the costs and expenses incurred for Henry of Windsor, late de facto et non de jure King of England, being in the Tower of London, paid to the hands of William Gryffith and Edmund Glace,—10*l*.

To Sir Thomas Talbot, Sir James Haryngton, and Sir John Tempest, knights, for the costs and charges incurred by themselves and their companions upon taking Henry, late de facto et non de jure King of England,—66*l*. 13*s*. 4*d*.

To the same Sir Thomas Talbot, as his own reward for the purpose aforesaid, paid to his own hands,—100*l*.

To Sir John Tempest, knight, as a reward for the same purpose, —66*l*. 13*s*. 4*d*.

To John Levesey, as a reward for the like purpose,—20*l*.

To William Rogers, of Serne, and David Colinley, valets of the King's chamber, as a reward for the cause aforesaid, paid to the hands of Edmund Glace, receiving the money from Lord Randulph Hethcote,—6*l*. 13*s*. 4*d*.

To James Haryngton, for the like purpose, paid to his own hands,—66*l*. 13*s*. 4*d*.

ROLL OF ACCOUNTS, MICHAELMAS, 5 EDWARD IV.

In money paid at different times for the costs and expenses of Henry Wyndsore, late de facto et non de jure King of England, being in the Tower of London; by the hands of Thomas Grey and Richard Hatfield; viz. at one time 5 marks, by the hands of Thomas Grey; at a second time 10 marks by the hands of Richard Hatfield; at ten times 32*l*. 13*s*. 4*d*., by the hands of William Griffith, at another time 5 marks, and at another time 5 marks, by the hands of Hugh Courtenay,—49*l*. 6*s*. 8*d*.

To James Rose, Speaker of the King's parliament in Ireland, paid to his own hands, as a reward, by the King's command,— 10 marks.

To Richard, Earl of Warwick, for costs and expenses incurred by him for the Lord Duke of Gloucester, the King's brother, and for an exhibition, &c., of the wardship and marriage of the son and heir of the Lord de Lovell,—1000*l.*

To William Alayn, sent by the King's command to Scotland, to observe and inform himself of the intentions and proposals of the King's rebels and enemies there, and thereof to certify to the Lord the King and his Council,—3*l.*

ISSUE ROLL, MICHAELMAS, 7 EDWARD IV.

To a certain private person whom the Lord the King wished not to be named. In money paid to his own hands, for certain secret and especial purposes interesting the said Lord the King. By writ of privy seal,—34*l.*

ISSUE ROLL, EASTER, 8 EDWARD IV.

13th *May.*—To William Kymberley, a chaplain, attending, by the King's command, in the Tower of London, there daily performing divine service before Henry, late de facto et non de jure King of England, from the feast of Saint James the Apostle, in the 5th year of the said present King, unto the 4th November, in the 6th year of the same King, without any fee or reward for his said attendance. In money paid to him by assignment made this day, by his own hands, in discharge of 14*l.* 10*s.* 7½*d.* which the Lord the King commanded to be paid to the said William of his gift, by way of reward, after the rate of 7½*d.* per day, for his attendance aforesaid, &c. By writ, &c.,—14*l.* 10*s.* 7½*d.*

13th May.—To Roger Ponsbury, of the town of Shrewsbury. In money paid to him by assignment made this day, by the hands of Roger Lathebury, in discharge, as well of 20l. which he lent to the Lord the King before he was deprived of his royal majesty, whilst he remained with the Earl of March, as for 13l. 4s. in like manner paid to the same Lord the King, for the value of divers cloths of silk and wool supplied for the King's use. By writ, &c., amongst the mandates of Easter term in the 6th year of the present King,—33l. 4s.

1st June.—To the Lord the King in his chamber. In money paid into his said chamber, for the value of 8 chargers, 15 platters, 13 plates, 6 dishes, 6 saucers, 12 small saucers, 4 plates, 2 candelabras for the chapel, partly gilt; one chafing dish, partly gilt; 3 candelabras, with sockets; 2 bowls, 2 washing basins, partly gilt; 2 basins, with entwined roses; 2 basins, with the arms of Salisbury; 1 spice plate, gilt; 1 drinking cup, with a cover; 12 gilt spoons, 1 gilt washing basin, and 1 gilt "solar voc' aman," weighing in all 152½ lbs., for the King's private use in his chamber. By writ, &c.,—397l. Also paid by the hands of Richard Willy, for the value of four pieces of arras, with a representation of the history of "Nabugodonoser;" 9 pieces of arras, of the history of Alexander; and 3 valences for a bed; 6 pieces of arras, with a representation of the Passion; one piece of arras, of the Judgment; 28 pieces of green velvet; 15 pieces of valence, for the green bed; two dozen of green cushions; paid to the same Richard out of part of the fine of Sir Thomas Cook, knight. By writ, &c.,—984l. 8s. 8d.

To Gerard Van Rye, goldsmith. In money paid to him for a gold ring, set with a diamond, purchased by the Lord the King, and sent to the Duke of Burgundy in the name of Lady Margaret, the King's sister. By writ, &c.,—20l.

To Capo, a herald from the King of Sicily, who lately came to the Lord the King upon a certain message from the said King of Sicily; also to Stephen Ranvers, of Burgundy, who lately came from the Duke of Burgundy to the Lord the King upon certain affairs; and to a certain stranger, called the bastard of Yorke, who lately came to England to our Lord the King. In money paid to them; viz., to the said Capo 10*l.*; to the said Stephen 50 marks; to the said bastard 20 marks, which the said Lord the King commanded to be paid them by way of reward. By writ, &c.,—60*l.*

2nd September.—To Lewis de Gremaldys and others, merchants of Genoa. In money paid to their own hands, by assignment made this day, in discharge of 2000*l.* which they lent to the Lord the King, at the Receipt of the Exchequer, on the 9th August last past, as appears in the Roll of Receipts of that day,—2000*l.*

12th September.—To Walter Lord Mountjoy, who was, by an indenture dated the 10th September last past, retained to serve the King with 3000 men, of whom 60 were to be men at arms and the rest archers, with captains to the number aforesaid, well and sufficiently found and armed for service; of which said number of 3000 men, 1200 were to be horse and the remainder foot soldiers, to proceed to the most potent prince, the Duke of Britany, cousin of our said Lord the King, for the war of the said Duke, and there to continue in the war against Lewis, the said King's enemy, &c.,—600*l.*

ISSUE ROLL, EASTER, 9 EDWARD IV.

13th May.—To Thomas Grey, esquire. In money paid to his own hands, in advance, as well for the expenses and diet of Henry VI., late de facto et non de jure King of England, being within the Tower of London, as for the expenses and diet of the said Thomas and others dwelling within the said Tower for the safe custody of the said Henry. By writ of privy seal amongst the mandates of Michaelmas term in the 7th year of the present King—106*l.* 13*s.* 4*d.*

ISSUE ROLL, EASTER, 11 EDWARD IV.

1st May.—To the Lord the King in his chamber. In money paid in the same chamber by his own hands, for divers oblations and alms bestowed by the said Lord the King at Westminster, and also given to the prisoners of Newgate and Ludgate, in the city of London. By general writ, &c.,—2*l.*

To the Lord the King in his chamber. In money paid in the same chamber, by the hands of Hugh Brice, for the impression of a precious stone, and for repairing one of the King's garters. By general writ, &c.,—1*l.* 15*s.* 0*d.*

16th May.—To the same Lord the King in his chamber. In money paid in the same chamber, by the hands of Thomas Vaughan, for so much money given by the said Lord the King to his heralds and minstrels on the day of the creation of the Lord the Prince, at Westminster. By general writ, &c.,—20*l.*

For various sums of money paid in the said chamber at different times; viz., at one time to William Harding, goldsmith, of London, for 6 gold collars delivered to the King, weighing 9¼ oz., price of each ounce 36*s.*; at another time 10*l.*, to John Clerk, apothecary, for divers medicines provided against the plague; at another time 10*l.*, to Thomas Wegewode, for the price of a horse called a "jenet," of Spain, purchased of him for the Lord the King; also 2*l.* 13*s.* 4*d.* for a "gestron and braice of mayle;" and 9*l.* 6*s.* 8*d.* for 3½ yards of cloth of gold, to make a "jaquette" for the King's person; also 20*s.* for 8 yards of fustian and 3 yards of satin to braid and plait the King's said jaquette, and 2*l.* 8*s.* 4*d.* for 2 ells of linen cloth and 3 yards of damask for the said "jaquette," and for points and laces purchased for the King; also 6*s.* 8*d.* for making the said jaquette, and 5*s.* paid for horse hire to carry a pair of "brigganders and the said jaquette" from the city of London to the Lord the King at Chichester; also 14*l.*0*s.*10*d.*

for 8½ timbers and 4 ermyn skins, and ½ a tymber of ermyns' "wombes," and 78*s.* for 2½ tymber and 5 ermyn skins, and 12 skins called "ermyns' bakkes," purchased to ornament the trappings of the King's horses; also 50*s.* for a pair of "leggeharnes" and for a pair of "gauntelettx" for the King; also 16*l.* 6*s.* 4*d.* for 5¼ yards of gilt cloth, to make a "jaquette" for the King, at 2*l.* 13*s.* 4*d.* per yard; and for 5½ yards of satin, to make plaits and brades for the same, at 6*s.* per yard; also 5*l.* 12*s.* for 14 yards of black damask, to make a robe for the King's person, at 8*s.* per yard; and 6*s.* 4*d.* for half a yard of black velvet for the same robe; also 23*l.* 2*s.* for 15 yards of crimson velvet and 14 yards of black damask for the King's person; and 20*l.* for the apparel of the King's "heuxmen;" 23*l.* 0*s.* 8*d.* for half a yard of black velvet for double "cuffys," and 15 yards of crimson velvet for a cloak for the King's person, and 15 yards of black satin to line the same; also 32*l.* 6*s.* 8*d.* for 14 yards of tawny satin, gilt, at 33*s.* 4*d.* per yard, for a robe for the King; and 15 yards of velvet to line the said robe, at 12*s.* a yard. [With many other payments for the King's wardrobe.]

To Anthony Earl Rivers, sent, by advice of the King's Council, to the county of Kent, to suppress divers rebels there assembled against the King. In money paid to him for the wages of 30 armed horsemen, at 12*d.* per day,—15*l.*; and 20 marks for the wages of 40 foot soldiers, at 8*d.* per day; 22*l.* 6*s.* for a barrel of gunpowder, and 1 firkin of "serpentyne powder," and 50 bows, at 2*s.* each; 100 sheaves of arrows, at 2*s.* the sheaf, and 3 gross of bowstrings, at 18*s.* per gross. [Many payments are entered on this part of the Roll, to persons sent into Kent and Essex to suppress the rebellion there, amongst whom are to be found the names of Lord Durasse, Robert Radclyff, esquire, Sir John Scotte, Lord Bourghchier, Lord Dynham, together with the names of the persons retained to ride with and attend the King in person in his journey, &c.; also payments to Lord Hastings and his soldiers, to take possession of Calais and Ruysbanke in the King's name.]

29th May.—To John Stokes. In money paid him by command of the King and Lords of his Council, receiving the money with his own hands, for two casks of red wine purchased from him and distributed to the citizens and inhabitants of the city of London after the conflict by the said inhabitants with the King's rebels at Milende and elsewhere. By writ, &c.,—11*l.* 14*s.* 4*d.*

To John Belle. In money paid to him for the value of a horse, a saddle, and bridle purchased of him, to conduct Nicholas Faunte, late mayor of the city of Canterbury, from the Tower of London to the Lord the King, then in the county of Kent. By writ, &c.,—1*l.* 3*s.* 4*d.*

To William, Earl of Pembroke, sent by the King's commission to South Wales, there to hold the sessions in the King's name, and to seize the rebels and traitors, also to reduce the castles there to the King's obedience. In money paid, &c. By writ, &c.,— 333*l.* 6*s.* 8*d.*

[Several payments are entered on this Roll to provide gun-powder, arms, and ammunition for defence of the Tower of London and other places in England and Wales then in a state of insurrection; also payments to workmen for building walls and other fortifications at the Tower of London aforesaid; with a list of the names of the carpenters, masons, soldiers, engineers, and workmen, who came from Calais, to fortify and defend the said Tower.]

24th June.—To Richard Radclyf, esquire. In money paid to his own hands, for the expenses of Henry, late de facto et non de jure King of England, then within the Tower; viz., on the 23rd day of April last past. By writ,—2*l.*

To Hugh Brice. In money paid to his own hands, for so much money expended by him, as well for wax, linen, spices, and other ordinary expenses incurred for the burial of the said Henry of

Windsor, who died within the Tower of London; and for wages and rewards to divers men carrying torches from the Tower aforesaid to the cathedral church of Saint Paul's, London, and from thence accompanying the body to Chertesey. By writ, &c., —15*l*. 3*s*. 6½*d*.

To Master Richard Martyn. In money paid to him at different times; viz., at one time to his own hands 9*l*. 10*s*. 11*d*., for so much money by him expended for 28 yards of linen cloth from Holland, and for expenses incurred, as well within the Tower aforesaid, at the last valediction of the said Henry, as also at Chertesey on the day of his burial; and 'for a reward given to divers soldiers from Calais guarding his body, and for the hire of barges, with masters and sailors rowing the same on the river Thames to Chertesey aforesaid; also at another time 8*l*.12*s*. 3*d*., for so much money paid by him to four orders of brethren within the city of London; and to the brethren of the Holy Cross therein; also for other works of charity; viz., to the Carmelite brethren 20*s*., to the Augustine Friars 20*s*., to the Friars Minors 20*s*., and to the Friars Preachers, to celebrate obsequies and masses, 40*s*.; also to the said brethren of the Holy Cross, 10*s*.; and for obsequies and masses said at Chertesey aforesaid, on the day of the burial of the said Henry,—52*s*. 3*d*. By writ, &c.,—18*l*. 3*s*. 2*d*.

To William Sayer, esquire. In money paid to him at different times; viz., at one time 6*s*. 8*d*., for the daily allowance of Henry, called Duke of Exeter, for 7 days, commencing on the 26th May in the 11th year of the present King; at another time 15*s*., for the daily allowances of Nicholas Leventhorp, Richard Goteley, one chaplain, one cook and his page, and one valet of the said Duke; also for 3 servants of the said William, Nicholas, and Richard, attending at Westminster upon the said Duke during the time aforesaid, &c. By writ, &c.,—1*l*. 1*s*. 8*d*. [With several other payments on this Roll for the said Duke.]

To Bawder Herman. In money paid to him in advance, at

different times, for the expenses and daily allowances to Margaret, lately called the Queen, and to other persons attendant upon the said Queen ; viz., at one time 100s., at another time 10 marks, at another time 8l., at another time 10l., at another time 10l., at another time 10 marks, at another time 8l., for such expenses and allowances.   By general writ current, &c.,—54l. 6s. 8d.

To William Mulsho, esquire. In money paid to his own hands, for the ordinary costs and expenses of the said Margaret, from the 22nd of September, in the 11th year of the present King, unto the 6th October then next following, for two weeks, after the rate of 5 marks for each week.   By writ, &c.,—6l. 13s. 4d.

To Robert Cosyn, to provide robes, beds, and other necessaries, for Henry of Windsor, in the Tower of London ; paid to his own hands,—10l.

To Robert Radclyff and William Sayer, esquires. In money paid, &c., as well for their wages and daily provision, as for the diet and wages of 36 other persons, each of them receiving 6d. per day, attending at the Tower for the safe custody of the said Henry ; viz., for 7 days, the first day commencing on the 29th day of April, in the 11th year of the present King ; paid to the hands of the said Robert and William, &c. By writ,—6l. 9s. 6d.

To William Sayer, esquire. In money paid him in advance, for the diet of the said Henry and eleven persons attending in the Tower for his safe custody,—2l. 10s.

To William Sayer, esquire. In money paid him for the expenses and diet of the said Henry and ten persons, attending in the Tower for the custody of the said Henry; viz. for 14 days, the first day beginning the 11th May last past,—4l. 5s.

[There are several other payments on this Roll for attendance, &c., upon King Henry VI. during his confinement in the Tower of London.]

2 κ

ROLL OF ACCOUNTS, MICHAELMAS, 11 EDWARD IV.

To Thomas, the Cardinal, for the King's jewels; viz. for a drinking cup called "the Cup of Alaunson," and for two books called "a Gospeler and Epistoler," covered with gold and jacinths, in pledge to the same Cardinal,—200*l.*

To the Lord the King, in his chamber, for a certain jacinth called a ruby, put in the "knopp" of a certain drinking cup, called "the Cup of Alaunson," together with gold placed around the setting of the same jacinth, receiving the money from Henry Brice,—20*s.*

———

ROLL OF ACCOUNTS, EASTER, 15 EDWARD IV.

To Richard, Duke of Gloucester, for the wages of 116 men at arms, including himself; viz. as Duke, at 13*s.* 4*d.* per day,—60*l.* 13*s.* 4*d.*; 6 knights, to each of them 2*s.* per day,—54*l.* 12*s.*; and to each of the remainder of the said 116 men at arms, 12*d.* per day and 6*d.* per day as a reward,—743*l.* 18*s.* 6*d.*; and to 950 archers in his retinue, to each of them 6*d.* per day,—2161*l.* 5*s.* [This and the preceding Roll contain other payments to Richard, Duke of Gloucester, afterwards King Richard the Third, and is also interesting and important in containing a list of the commanders and captains in the King's service at this period, with the number of men at arms, archers, and other soldiers under their command, specifying their quality, and the amount of wages and rewards, &c. paid to each.]

To Richard Haute, esquire, paid as a reward for the costs and expenses incurred by him for conducting Margaret, lately called the Queen, from London to the town of Sandwich, by the King's command, paid by the hands of Thomas Leventhorp,—20*l.*

Issue Roll, Easter, 19 Edward IV.

15th June.—To William Caxton. In money paid to his own hands in discharge of 20*l.* which the Lord the King commanded to be paid to the same William for certain causes and matters performed by him for the said Lord the King. By writ of privy seal amongst the mandates of this term,—20*l.*

Roll of Accounts, Easter, 20 Edward IV.

To Master Thomas Langton, one of the King's Council, sent by the King as Ambassador to Lewis, calling himself King of France; paid for his costs and expenses, by the hands of Robert Langton,—40*l.*

To Richard, Duke of Gloucester, in part payment of 500*l.* for the manor and lordship of Hoton Panyll, otherwise Hoton upon the Hill, with all and singular its appurtenances, in the county of York, and for 200 acres of land, 80 acres of meadow, 200 acres of pasture, 20 acres of wood, and 6*l.* rent, with the appurtenances, in Hoton Panell, in the county aforesaid, purchased and acquired by the Lord the King from the same Duke, receiving the money from Nicholas Leventhorp, receiver-general of the duchy of Lancaster; besides 200*l.* paid by John Fitzherbert to the same Duke at Michaelmas Term, in the 18th year, &c.; also besides 20*l.* paid by the said Nicholas Leventhorp,—240*l.*

To Richard, Duke of Gloucester, keeper of the West Marches of England, near Scotland, for the safe custody of the said Marches, paid by the hands of Thomas Leynham, his servant,—6*l.* 13*s.* 4*d.*

To John What, for wine purchased for the King's Council, at the Cardinal's hat without Newgate, they being there in attendance for the King's advantage; paid to his own hands,—1*s.* 6*d.*

To the Lord the King in his chamber, on the 3rd May, for the value of 129 of half crusats, 17½ of castellans, 18 ducats and salutes, and 7 old gold nobles, weighing in all 1 lb. 10 oz. 1 qr. ; paid by the hands of Master William Daubenay. By writ,— 41*l.* 0*s.* 5½*d.*

To William Elys, brickmaker, in part payment of a greater sum assigned to him by the King for making twenty hundred thousand bricks to repair Dover Castle; paid to his own hands,—33*l.* 6*s.* 8*d.*

To William Fedreston, master of the King's ship called the Fawcon, in part payment of 64*l.* 3*s.* 4*d.* for the wages and victuals of 140 mariners, appointed by the said Lord the King to the said ship, as well for the safe conduct of divers ships laden with wool and woolfells, going from the ports of Saint Botolph and London to the port of the town of Calais, as for his attendance with the aforesaid ship upon the Lady Margaret, Duchess of Burgundy, the King's sister, coming from beyond sea to England, retained for one month commencing . . . day of June last past, each mariner receiving for his wages per week 15*d.* ; and to each of them for victuals per week, 12½*d.* ; paid to his own hands,—20*l.*

ROLL OF ACCOUNTS, MICHAELMAS, 20 EDWARD IV.

To John Barker, of London, goldsmith, in full payment of 273*l.* 6*s.* 8*d.* for 80 butts of malmsey, purchased by him for the use of the army of the Lord the King, going as well by land as by water against his Scotch enemies, price the butt, 3*l.* 8*s.* 4*d.*, besides 100*l.* received by him from William Daubeney, 173*l.* 6*s.* 8*d.* [There are several other payments entered on this Roll to supply the army with provisions, &c., then proceeding to Scotland, with many other matters relating to this war, for the settling of which dispute John, Earl of Douglas, and others, were sent by the King and his Council to the Scotch Marches.]

To Richard, Duke of Gloucester, for the purchase of the manors of Southwelles and Roke, in the parishes of Odyam and Crondale, with the appurtenances, and other lands and tenements with their appurtenances, in the county of Southampton, which lately belonged to John Grenefeld of Southwelles, lately purchased of him by the Lord the King, by command of the said Lord the King, paid by the hands of Thomas Leynham, servant of the said Duke, —200*l.*

To Richard, Duke of Gloucester, for those sums of money assigned him by the King, for repairing the walls of the city of Carlisle, above 100 marks formerly given him by the King for the same purpose, and received by the same Duke by the hands of Richard Poole on the 12th December,—50 marks.

ROLL OF ACCOUNTS, EASTER, 22 EDWARD IV.

To Sir John Elryngton, knight, the King's Treasurer at War, by the hands of Richard, Duke of Gloucester; viz. for the wages of 1700 fighting men, retained by the said Duke to accompany him in the war against the Scotch; viz. from the 11th August until the end of fourteen days then next following,—595*l.*

To Peter Curteys, Keeper of the King's great wardrobe, for the purchase of divers stuffs and making thereof, at the King's command, for the Duke of Albany, for the journey of the said Duke, who accompanied the Duke of Gloucester in his expedition to the kingdom of Scotland, receiving the money from Thomas Shelley, merchant of London,—50*l.*

To Richard Boteler, sent, by the King, to the town of Berwick, with 800*l.* in money counted, to be delivered to the King's Treasurer at War then being there; also sent upon other affairs concerning the preservation of the said town for the Duke of Gloucester and other nobility collected there on the part of the Lord the King; paid him for costs and expenses sustained for the purpose aforesaid during the space of five weeks,—12*l.* 19*s.* 4*d.*

To Lewis, of Naples, as a reward for rose and divers other waters presented by him to the King; paid to his own hands by the King's command,—10*l*.

To the Duke of Gloucester, in full payment of 2000 marks due from the King to the same Duke, at the feast of the Nativity of Saint John the Baptist, according to the form of a certain indenture thereon made between the King and the said Duke; paid by the hands of Thomas Lynham,—164*l*. 15*s*.

To Sir John Elryngton, knight, the King's Treasurer at War, in part payment of the wages of 20,000 men at arms, going upon a certain expedition with the Duke of Gloucester against the Scots; paid to his own hands,—4504*l*. 11*s*. 8½*d*.

To the same Treasurer, as a reward given to divers soldiers, as well in the retinue of the Duke of Gloucester as in the retinue of the Earl of Northumberland and others, for their expenses in going from the town of Berwick to their own homes; viz. by the hands of the aforesaid Duke, 350*l*., and by the hands of the aforesaid Earl, 94*l*. 13*s*. 6*d*., and by the hands of John Broun, of the King's household, 16*s*.,—345*l*. 9*s*. 6*d*. [This Roll contains very many payments for preparations made for the army proceeding against the Scotch enemy.]

To William, ... of the town of Campens, in Eastland, as a reward directed by the King to be given him for 3 lions, lately brought by him to the said Lord the King from beyond sea as a present from the merchants of the said town called the "Steds;" paid by the hands of Richard Hyll,—10*l*.

To John Crowcher, for the reparation and amendment of a certain crane at London, called the "Heydox Crane," damaged by the weight of the King's tomb there landed, paid to his own hands by command of the Under Treasurer,—10*s*. 10*d*.

To Alexander, Duke of Albany, brother to the King of Scotland, who lately came from France to the Lord the King in England, to serve the said Lord the King of England, as his liege subject, against his Scotch enemies and rebels, directed by the said Lord the King to be given him as a reward to be distributed amongst the soldiers and mariners, who conducted the said Duke, in a certain Scotch carvell, from the parts aforesaid to the port of the town of Southampton; paid by the hands of John Rotherford, his servant,—100*l.*

To Alexander, Duke of Albany, brother to the King of Scotland. In money paid him, by the hands of George Cheynewe, one of the valets of the King's crown, by especial command of the said Lord the King, for the costs and expenses of the said Duke and others his servants, attending him at London in the house called the "Erber," from the 2nd May to the 4th day of the same month this term,—5*l.* 15*s.* 7½*d.*

To James Douglas, master of a certain carvell, who lately conducted the Duke of Albany, brother to the King of Scotland, from France to the town of Southampton, now appointed by the Lord the King to serve him in the war against the King's enemies, with 100 men in his retinue, for the space of eight weeks, each man receiving weekly for his wages and victuals, 2*s.* 3½*d.*, and for the wages and victuals of the said master during the time aforesaid, 18*s.* 4*d.* By writ, &c.,—92*l.* 11*s.* 8*d.*

To Master William Hobbes, the King's physician and surgeon, sent by the King to the North to attend upon the Duke of Gloucester, in the King's service against the Scotch, with eight surgeons in his retinue, paid for their wages for one month, receiving for himself per day, 2*s.*, and for each of the other seven surgeons aforesaid, 12*d.* per day, and for the other of the aforesaid persons, 6*d.* per day, by the hands of Simon Cole and Alexander Slye,—13*l.* 6*s.*

To John Clerk, the King's apothecary, for divers medicines,

504

" ciripp, alexaundrines, botellis, electuary," and other necessaries,
provided and purchased of the same, delivered, by the King's
command, to the Duke of Gloucester, by the hands of Thomas
Lynham, his servant, of the King's gift, for the use of the said
Duke in his service against the Scotch; paid to his own hands,
—13*l.* 16*s.* 9½*d.*

To Richard, Duke of Gloucester, by command of the King and
the Lords of his Council, in money sent him by Henry Sambroke, one of the grooms of the King's chamber, to pay the wages
of divers fighting men upon the western sea, proceeding against
the Scotch, according to the discretion of the said Duke; paid to
the hands of the said Henry,—133*l.* 6*s.* 8*d.*

To Henry Sambroke, for his costs and expenses, ordered to be
paid him by the Lords of the King's Council for the safe conduct
of the sum of 200 marks, taken to the said Duke in the North;
paid to his own hands,—3*l.* 6*s.* 8*d.*

To Henry Hansom, of Lynton, in the county of Hereford,
esquire. In money paid to him, by the King's command, by way
of reward for letters obligatory containing 699*l.*, late in his custody,
and by him delivered to the Lord the King, by which the Abbot
of the house of the blessed Peter, of Gloucester was bound for
Jasper, Earl of Pembroke, and Thomas Fitz Henry, esquire,
attainted as rebels and traitors against the present King, by
reason of which attainder the same belongs to the King; paid to
his own hands,—99*l.*

ROLL OF ACCOUNTS, MICHAELMAS, 22 EDWARD IV.

To James Lydell, a Scotch knight, sent from the Duke of
Albany to the King as Ambassador, given by the King as a
reward for his expenses, and paid to his own hands,—40*l.*

To John Oter, servant to the Duke of Gloucester, an attendant, and in waiting upon the said James Lydell, on his coming from the North to London, and on his return back, given him by the King, as a reward for his expenses, and paid to his own hands,—2*l.*

To Peter Curtes, Keeper of the King's great wardrobe, for his office, viz. for the burial of Mary, the King's daughter, and Duchess of York, paid to the hands of John Doket, of London, draper,—25*l.* 4*s.*

To John Grene, of Calais, Master of the ship called the Little Jesus, appointed as a reward for him, by the advice of the King's Council and by command of the Lord Treasurer, for the passage of a servant of Lord Hastyngs from Dover to Calais, sent to Lord Dynham then being there, to convey to him the first information and news of the demise of the most excellent and dread Prince, of happy memory, Edward the Fourth, which he performed on the 10th day of April, being the day after his death, receiving the money from the collectors of the subsidies in the port of Sandwich, paid to his own hands,—3*l.* 6*s.* 8*d.*

To Sir John Wode, knight, speaker in the parliament began at Westminster the 21st day of January, in the 22nd year of the present King, given him as a reward by the King for the great labour exercised by him in the said parliament for the benefit of the King and his kingdom, receiving the money from the King's coffer, &c.,—100*l.* ; [also paid 9*l.* 1*s.* 3*d.* to Edward Tankard for the value of 3 pieces of worsted of the great assize, 3 pieces of worsted of the middle assize, 1 hammer, 1 pair of pincers, half a hundred of " crochetts," half a hundred of " tapet hoks," 2 lbs. of cotton thread, and 100 " trasshes," purchased *for the chamber called the Parliament Chamber.*]

ROLL OF THE JEWS OF SAINT HILARY AND EASTER TERMS
IN THE 17TH YEAR OF KING HENRY III.

NORTHAMPTON.

Of Samuel, the son of Abraham, half a mark, as a fine for
many debts.

NOTTINGHAM AND DERBY.

Of Rachael, the daughter of David, 11s. 4d., for an aid to
marry the King's sister.

OXFORD.

Of Copinus, of Oxford, 50s., for debts purchased from the
Treasury.

Of Bonamy, son of Copinus, 9s., as a fine for many debts.

Of David, of Oxford, 40d., for the chattels of Bone of Nottingham.

WILTSHIRE.

Of Isaac, the son of Josces Wilton, 10s. 6d., for an account of
6000 marks.

Of the same, 15d., for an account of 2500 marks.

LONDON AND MIDDLESEX.

Of Margery, for a chyrograph, 2 marks, for an account of
6000 marks.

Of Ely Blunde, 20d., for an account of 2500 marks.

Of James Crespin, 10s., for a fine for the chattels of Deudon,
the son of Bonevie.

Of the same, half a mark for the same, for Abraham the son of
Benedict of Oxford.

Of Leon, the son of Isaac, 20s., for the same for many debts.

Of Belacez, wife of Sampson Kokeman, 1 mark, for the same.

Of Benedict Levesque, 50s. for the same.

Of Ely Levesque, 10s., for the same.

Of Aaron le Blund, 20s., for the same.

Of Abraham, the son of Muř. as a fine for pleas.

LINCOLN.

Of Josceus, the son of Mosse, 3d., for an account of 5000 marks.

Of the same, 3d., for an account of 6000 marks.

GLOUCESTER.

Of Juetta, a widow, 11½d., for an account of 4000 marks.

Of Mirable, of Gloucester, for many debts, 10s.

Of Bouenfaut, her son, 10s., for the same.

Of Salomon, the Turk, 40d., for the same.

Of Juetta, a widow, 5s., for the same.

Of Belina, daughter of Mirable, 5s., for the same.

Of Fluria, of Gloucester, 4s., for the same.

---

m. 2. ## OF SAINT HILARY TERM IN THE 17TH YEAR OF THE REIGN OF KING HENRY III.

NORFOLK AND SUFFOLK, KENT, YORK, BEDFORD, BUCKINGHAM, SOUTHAMPTON, GLOUCESTER, OXFORD, DEVON, LONDON, MIDDLESEX, ESSEX, HERTFORD, BERKSHIRE, SURRY, LANCASTER, LEICESTER, WARWICK, AND ON THE DORSE OF THE ROLL, ALSO YORK, CUMBERLAND, NORTHAMPTON, WILTSHIRE, DORSET, SOMERSET, NOTTINGHAM, DERBY, SUSSEX, LINCOLN, STAFFORD, SHROPSHIRE, CAMBRIDGE, HUNTINGDON.

NORFOLK, SUFFOLK.
Robert de Brus, Sheriff.

Of Robert Moracho, 32 marks, for a fine.

Of the same, 10 marks, for two palfreys.

Of T., Bishop of Norwich, 166l. 1 mark, for a fine to have his liberties.

Of William de Kentewell, 100s., for a fine and scutage.

Of William de Blunde, 46s. 8d., in advauce for Ireland.

> The liberty of the Abbot of Saint Edmund.

Of Walter de Bertun, 1 mark, for a jury.

Of Henry Hache, 9s. 4d., for the same.

Of William Truve, 10s. 4d., for the same.

Of Josceline de Hereswell, 14s. 4d., for the same.

Of William de Muncheneby, 100s., for a fine.

Of Nicholas, the son of Hugh, and his brethren, half a mark, to have a jury.

Of Robert de Tybotot, 40d., for pledges.

Of Robert de Cokfelt, half a mark, for a false claim.

Of William, parson of Trenchetune, 5s., to have an aid.

Of Henry de Meleford, 40d., for a false claim.

Of Everard, brother and heir of Walter Pichard, 20s., to have seisin.

Of Nicholas le Merveillus, 10s. for licence to grant.

Of Thomas de Muletun, 2 marks, for the horses of Thomas Maletake.

> The liberty of the Abbot of Saint Edmund.

Of the men of Luddingeland, 11l., for their farm.

Of Robert Plonch, half a mark, for a fine.

Of William de Totstok, half a mark, for a judgment.

Of Cecilia le Arblaster, half a mark, for the same.

Of Adam de Whelevetham, 2s. 6d., for the same.

Of William Bigod, 2s., for the arrears of Hugh Rufus.

> The liberty of Saint Edmund.

Of Robert de Briwes, 333l. half a mark, for the issues of the lands of the Earls of Arundel and Clare.

Of the citizens of Norwich, 4l., for tallage.

Of the men of Ipswich, 100s., for increase of their farm.

Of Robert de Aldewartun, 1 mark, to have an inquisition.

Of William de Pinkeny, 20s., as a fine for judgment.

Of the men of Yarmouth, 34l., for their farm.

Of the men of Dunewich, 10l., for their farm.

Of Philip de Eya, 40s., for the farm of Combes, for Bartholomew de Crek.

Of the same, 60s., for the fines of many Jews for the same Bartholomew.

Of Bartholomew de Crek, 30s., for the yearly scutage of Combes.

Of the same, half a mark, for the farm of Combes.

LONDON AND MIDDLESEX.

Of Peter, the son of Alulfus, 20s., for a judgment.

Of Robert de Basmeurt, half a mark, for the debt of Alan le Burser.

Of the same, 20d., for wine sold contrary to the assize.

Of John Camerarius, 5s., for the land which belonged to John Bukointe.

Of Peter, the son of Alan, 20s., for a promise.

Of Ralph de Wilinton, 15s., for the debt of John Bukointe, for a judgment.

Of Geoffrey, of Saint Edmunds, half a mark, for tallage.

Of Thomas, of Durham, 2 marks, for the tallage of London.

Of Richard le Bacheler, 20s., for the tallage of London.

Of Richard de Craneford, 27s. 6d., for the scutage of Poitou.

Of Richard de Stanmere, 5s., for a fine.

Of William Iwode, half a mark, for the tallage of London.

Of Hugh le Tanur, 10s., for the same.

Of Eustace, the mercer, 20s., for the same.

Of John Hanin, 10s., for wine sold.

Of Richard de Crankford, half a mark, for licence to agree.

Of Osbert de Northbroc, 2s. 6d., for Peter, the son of Alulfus, for a judgment.

Of Walter de Kyrkeham, keeper of the archives, 25l. 0s. 4½d., for the issues of the manor of Herewes.

Of the same, 117s. 11½d., for the issues of the manor of Hese.

Of the same, 45s., for the scutage of Elveyn in Herewes.

Of Michael, of Saint Elens, 24l., for the farm of London.

Of Isaac, of Norwich, 2 marks, for the debt of Matthew Blunde.

Of Walter, Bishop of Carlisle, 18l. 16s. 7½d., for the issues of the manors of Herewes and of Hese.

Of Peter, the son of Alulfus, 8s. 4d., as a fine for a judgment.

Of Laurence le Linekere, 40d., for the debt of Peter, the son of Alulfus, for a judgment.

Of Stephen, the son of Andrew, 40d., as a fine for his father's debt.

Of Walter, Bishop of Carlisle, 10l. 18s. 4d., for the issues of the manors of Herewes and Hese.

Of the same, 24l., for the issues of the same manors.

Of Roger le Crik, 100s., as a fine for Richard de Buterewik.

Of the same, 20s., for Ingulfus le Gorterer, for the tallage of London.

Of John de Wuburne, 2 marks, as a fine for tallage.

Of Master Alexander de Dorsette, 39l. 10s. 10½d., for the arrears of the Exchange of London.

Of Stephen, of the Strand, 1 mark, by John Richeman, for a pledge.

Of Seherus, the son of Henry, half a mark, by Ely, his son, for a fine.

Of Michael, of Saint Elens, 32d., for his ward for tallage.

Of the same, and of Walter Bussle, 14d., for the remainder of the farm of London.

Of Robert, the son of John, and Walter of Winchester, 15s. 7½d., for the remainder of the farm of London.

Of the heirs of Robert of Winchester, 1 mark, for his father's debt.

[*Note.* The remaining portion of this membrane consists of similar entries to the above for the other counties enumerated at the head of the Roll, which payments are the same as are usually found on the Pipe Rolls in the Exchequer.]

m. 3. WRITS OF SAINT HILARY TERM, IN THE 17th YEAR OF THE
REIGN OF KING HENRY, SON OF KING JOHN.

Henry, by the grace of God, King of England, Lord of Ireland, Duke of Normandy, Acquitaine, and Earl of Anjou, to his
Treasurer and Chamberlains greeting. Pay, from our Treasury,
to Robert de Sablolio, 500 marks of our gift, for his ransom.
Witness ourself at Wudestok, 11th January, in the 17th year of
our reign. By the King himself, before the Bishop of Winchester, the Justices, and Earl Marshal.

Henry, by the grace of God, &c. Pay, from our Treasury, to
Geoffrey de Tannay, 500*l*., of our gift, and 25 marks, for the arrears
which we owed him at Michaelmas term in the 15th year of our
reign, for his annual fee of 100 marks. Witness ourself at
Wudestok, 8th January, anno 17°. By the King himself, (ut
supra.)

Henry, by the grace of God, &c. Pay, from our Treasury, to
Aumaricus de Sancto Amando, going as our messenger beyond
seas, 40 marks, for his expenses, of our gift. Witness ourself at
Wudestok, 12th January, anno 17°, (ut supra.)

Henry, by the grace of God, &c. Pay, from our Treasury, to
Sir William Fucher, knight, for Hugh de Vivoñ, our Steward, in
Gascony, 200 marks, to be taken to the said Hugh, to stock our
castle in those parts. Witness, &c. 10th January, (ut supra.)

Henry, by the grace of God, &c. Pay, from our Treasury, to
William Perdriz, going as our messenger to Hugh, Bishop of Ely,
9*d*., for his expenses. Witness P., Bishop of Winchester, at Westminster, 18th January, anno 17°.

Henry, by the grace of God, &c. Pay, from our Treasury, to
Ranulph Bonpar, 10*l*., for the 16th year of our reign, for his

yearly fee, and 5 marks of our gift, for his expenses. Witness
ourself at Wudestok, 8th January, anno 16°.

Henry, by the grace of God, &c.   Pay, from our Treasury, to
Master Roger, clerk to Bishop "Walsatansis," 15 marks, for the
use of William de Pimbus, the said Bishop's nephew, for the
one year's 15 marks which we granted him to be received at our
Exchequer, until we should provide him with an ecclesiastical
benefice.   Witness, &c., 12th January, anno 17°, (ut supra.)

Henry, by the grace of God, &c.   Pay, from our Treasury, to
Bernard de Acra, of our city of Burgundy, 10 marks, to the use
of Stephen, his son, for the one year's 10 marks which we
granted him, yearly to be received at our Exchequer, until we
should provide him with an ecclesiastical benefice. Witness, &c.,
12th January, anno 17°, (ut supra.)

Henry, by the grace of God, &c.   Pay, from our Treasury, to
Seginus de Regula, for the use of the citizens of Regula, 100 marks,
in part payment of 1010 marks, for which we made a fine with
them, for their houses destroyed on building our castle at Regula.
Witness, &c., 8th January, anno 17°., (ut supra.)

Henry, by the grace of God, &c.   Pay, from our Treasury, to
Master Philip de Ardern, 100 marks, of our gift, for his expenses
incurred in our service at the Court of Rome.   Witness, &c.,
12th January, anno 17°, (ut supra.)

Henry, by the grace of God, &c.   Pay, from our Treasury, to
Bonacursus Ingelesk, Amery Chosse, and their companions,
Florentine merchants, 1000 marks, for the use of the Lord the
Pope, for his yearly tax ; viz., for Easter term, in the 16th year,
and Michaelmas term in the same year.   Witness, P., Bishop of
Winchester, 23rd January, anno 17°.

Henry, by the grace of God, &c.   Pay, from our Treasury, to

Godfrey Spigurnel, servant of our chapel, 10*s.*, which he expended by our command, for 20 lbs. of wax to seal our writs. Witness, &c., 24th January, anno 17°, (ut supra.)

Henry, by the grace of God, &c. Pay, from our Treasury, to William Hardel, our clerk, 100*s.*, which he paid to the soldiers who carried 1000 marks from London to Worcester, against the feast of the Nativity of our Lord, in the 17th year of our reign, &c.; which said 1000 marks we caused to be taken there from our Treasury at London. Witness ourself at Westminster, the 3rd day of February, in the 17th year of our reign.

Henry, by the grace of God, &c. Pay, from our Treasury, to Walter de Lenz and his companions, clerks of our chapel, 25*s.* for chanting " Christ hath conquered," which they sung before us at Worcester, on the day of the Nativity of our Lord, in the 17th year of our reign; and 25*s.* for chanting " Christ hath conquered," which they sung before us at Westminster, on the day of the Purification of the Blessed Mary. Witness ourself at Westminster, the 4th February, anno 17°, &c.

Henry, by the grace of God, &c. Pay, from our Treasury, to Pandulf and Reginald, Nuncios from the Lord the Pope, 1 mark, for their expenses, of our gift. Witness ourself at Westminster, the 8th February, anno 17°., &c.

Henry, by the grace of God, &c. Pay, from our Treasury, to Master Simon Norman, for going in our service to the Roman Court, 20 marks, for his expenses, of our gift. Witness ourself at Westminster, (ut supra.)

Henry, by the grace of God, &c. Pay, from our Treasury, to Brother Lawrence, a messenger from the King of Norway, returning to his home, 40*s.*, for his expenses, of our gift. Witness &c., (ut supra.)

2 L

Henry, by the grace of God, &c. Pay, from our Treasury, to Simon de Bassingeshawe, a chaplain serving in the chapel of the Blessed Mary, in the Jewry, London, 30s., for Michaelmas term in the 16th year, and at the Nativity of our Lord, in the 17th year of our reign, of the 60s. which he receives yearly at our Exchequer for his support, of our gift. Witness ourself at Westminster, the 8th of February, in the 17th year of our reign.

Henry, by the grace of God, &c. Pay, from our Treasury, to Josceus, the son of Peter, and Stephen, of the Strand, 20l., for the works done to the church of the converted Jews, and for the clothing of those Jews so converted. Witness, &c., (ut supra.)

Henry, by the grace of God, &c. Pay, from our Treasury, to Brother Geoffrey, or to Brother John, our almoners, 44 marks, to pay for 11 lasts of herrings which they bought by our command, to be distributed to the poor; viz., for each last 4 marks. Witness P., Bishop of Winchester, at Westminster, the 21st February, anno 17°. By letters under the privy seal.

Henry, by the grace of God, &c. Pay, from our Treasury, to Brother William, keeper of Saint Thomas's hospital, Southwerk, 40s., to buy fire-wood for the use of the poor of the hospital there, of our gift. Witness, &c., 23rd February, anno 17°. By the King himself.

Henry, by the grace of God, &c. Pay, from our Treasury, to Sir Richard de Burun, knight, 104l. 10s., to pay for the liveries of the knights and soldiers who, during the time of Richard, Earl of Chester and Lincoln, were in the garrison of the castle of Saint James upon Beveron; viz., from the day of Saint Martin, in the 17th year of our reign, unto Saturday, next following after the feast of Saint Matthew the Apostle, in the same year, including each day. Witness ourself at Westminster, the 27th day of February, anno 17°. By the King himself, before the Bishop of Winchester and the Justices.

Henry, by the grace of God, &c. Pay, from our Treasury, to Robert Passelewe, and Odo, the goldsmith, 100 marks, for our works done at Westminster; and to Stephen, of the Strand, and Josceus, the son of Peter, 20 marks, for work done to the church of the converted Jews, London, and for enclosing their court; and to Walter, chaplain of the same converts, 10 marks, in part payment of 30 marks which he receives yearly at our Exchequer for his support. Witness ourself at Westminster, the 27th day of February, anno 17°.

MICHAELMAS TERM, 2 HENRY VII.

To John Serle, the King's painter, as a reward for painting divers figures, beasts, and armed men, upon the King's stairs (or landing bridge), at Westminster, besides 8*l.* before paid him by Thomas Stoks for the same purpose; paid to his own hands, —2*l.*

MICHAELMAS TERM, 9 HENRY VII.

To Richard Daland, for providing certain spectacles, or theatres, commonly called scaffolds, in the great hall at Westminster, for performance of "the disguisyngs," exhibited to the people on the night of the Epiphany, as appears by a book of particulars; paid to his own hands,—28*l.* 3*s.* 5¾*d.*

MICHAELMAS TERM, 10 HENRY VII.

To John Englissh, Edward Maye, Richard Gibson, and John Hamond, "lusoribus Regis," otherwise called in English the players of the King's interludes, for their fees; viz. to each of them 5 marks yearly. By the King's writ of privy seal, paid to their own hands.

[*Note.* In the 19th year of King Henry VII. is a similar entry, omitting the name of Edward Maye, and inserting those of William Rutter and John Scott.]

EASTER, 12 HENRY VII.

To Sir Henry Willoughby and Sir Edward Stannap, knights, and to Edward Belknap, esquire, as a reward for taking Nicholas

Joseph, chief leader of the Cornish rebels, as appears by warrant
dated   .   .   .   .   .   ,—40*l.*

[*Note.* This Roll contains the names of the different leaders
of the royal army, and number of their retinue, who fought the
rebels at the battle of Blackheath; also a list of the army sent
to Scotland under Lord Daubeney.]

EASTER TERM, 11 ELIZABETH.

To George, Earl of Shrewsbury.   In money paid to him for
the diet of the Queen of Scotland, by virtue of writs of privy seal,
dated 17th April, in the 11th year of Queen Elizabeth,—500*l.*
[Other entries for the same purpose are contained on this Roll.]

To Valentine Browne, esquire, Treasurer of the town of Berwick.
In money paid to him for payment of divers soldiers attending
upon the Queen of Scotland, as appears by writ of privy seal,
dated 7th March, in the 11th year of Queen Elizabeth, —400*l.*

EASTER TERM, 40 ELIZABETH.

29th June.—To William Davison, esquire, late one of the
principal secretaries of the Lady the Queen, for his fee at 100*l.*
per annum, due to him for the quarter of the year ending at the
feast of the Nativity of Saint John the Baptist, in the 40th year
of Queen Elizabeth.

[*Note.* It appears by the Issue Rolls that the late Secretary
Davison enjoyed this annuity during the remainder of this reign,
and even subsequent to the time of Queen Elizabeth.]

Easter, 43 Elizabeth.

1st September.—To Sir Thomas Lucy, knight, sheriff of the county of Warwick, paid him by the hands of William Cleve, for the safe conduct of money and other charges for fifty soldiers, raised in the said county, and sent to Bristol to be embarked for Ireland, with 40*d.*, allowed to the aforesaid William Cleve, for portage to the city of London of the money raised for furnishing the said soldiers in the county aforesaid. By writ dated 20th July, 1601, &c.,—24*l.*

Michaelmas, 44 & 45 Elizabeth.

14th March.—To Thomas Hutton and others, clerks of John Coniers, one of the auditors of the prests, for divers labours in attending commissioners at various times for determining the account of Lady Margaret Hawkins and Thomas Drake, esquire, executors of John Hawkins and Sir Francis Drake, knight, lately deceased, for their expedition to the West Indies. By way of reward by general writ,—6*l.* 13*s.* 4*d.*

INDEX.

2 N

Bysshopesten, Robert, a prisoner, 251, 252.

Cade, John, an Irishman and a traitor, taken before the Council, 467 — seized at Hafield, in Sussex, 468 — calls himself Mortymer, steals the jewels of Richard, Duke of York, 468, 469 — heads the insurrection at Blackheath, calling himself the Captain of Kent, 470, 471, 476. See Kent, and Eden, Alexander.

Cadurcis, Henry de, *vel* Cadurco, Hervey de, remunerated for the loss of his forge in Dean Forest, 78, 89, 90.

Caernarvon Castle, Constable of, prisoners sent to, 365, 374.
———————— County of, archers from, 231.

Caieswell, Manor of, 161.

Calabria, messenger sent from a Lady of, 40.

Calais, 156, 157, 211, 219, 221, 268, 282, 291, 325, 418, 496 — battle at, 158 — rings sent to, for John, King of France, 176 — treaty of peace concluded at, 179, 450 — ransom paid at, for John, King of France, 181, 182 — Earl of Saint Paul sent to, 210 — duel at, with John Grey, a traitor, 216 — traitors captured at, 216 — knights and esquires sent to, to receive the Queen of King Richard II., 217 — William, Earl of Salisbury, captain of, 218 — fortified with cannon, 229, — town of, garrisoned by Matthew de Gournay, 238 — soldiers at, paid on vacating the town, agreeably to a truce, 239 — Treasurer of, 253, 420 — duel fought at, 262, 263 — Earl of Nottingham Captain of, 263 — Queen Isabella's passage to, 282 — Emperor of Constantinople at, 284 — new tower made at, 287, 315 — Treasurer and Comptroller of, 287 — Captain of the town and castle there, 298 — castle of, fortified, 298 — proclamation for the rescue of, and an army sent to, 304 — Captain of the tower of, 315 — Mayor of the staple there, 322 — medicines sent to, for King Henry V. and his army, 342 — tents of cloth of gold taken to, for King Henry V. and the Emperor to dwell in, 347 — King Henry V. proceeds to, with his army, to meet the Emperor, 347 — money taken to King Henry V. at, 348 — Lord de Ponynges' passage to, 387 — army proceeds to, 400 — soldiers of the town, castle, and marches, to be paid by the King of Scotland, 408 — council at, 420 — Queen of Sicily arrives at, 423 — ships sail to, with ordnance and stores for King Henry VI., 429 — Ambassadors sent to, to obtain peace, 438 — shipping sent to, 443 — town taken possession of by Lord Hastings, 494 — workmen and engineers come from to fortify the tower of London, 495 — information of the death of King Edward IV. taken to, 505.

2 N 2

2 Q

ELY, profits of the see of, granted to the Archbishop of Rouen, 433.
ELY, BISHOP OF, 5—dines with Edward the Prince, 107.
—— HUGH, BISHOP OF, 511.
—— PHILIP, BISHOP OF, 425.
—— SIMON, BISHOP OF, and Chancellor of England, 182.
ELYNGEHAM, JOHN, Sergeant at Arms, 234, 237, 239, 249, 260.
ELYOT, THOMAS, Mayor of Corf, 176.
ELYS, ROGER, a chandler of London, 211, 265.
—— WILLIAM, a brickmaker, 500.
EMELIAN, SAINT, Reeve of, 33.
EMPEROR, THE, at the General Council at Constance, 335, 433—Letters sent
        to, by the Agincourt Herald, 345—shipping detained for, to take
        him to France, 347—expenses of, at Eltham, 348—a messenger
        sent from, 431.
ENEFEUD, WILLIAM DE, 51.
ENEOR, JOHN, Esquire, 269.
ENFIELD MANOR, bailiff of, 458.
ENGAYN, LORD D', sends a charger to King Edward III., 176.
ENGERAM, 2.
ENGLAND, 244, 260, 278 — messengers sent to divers parts of, 26 — a tenth
        granted from the churches of, for the Holy Land, 105—arms
        of, 145 — King of, (Edward III.) ratifies a peace with Scot-
        land, 183 — marshal of, 207—money not to be taken out of, 243,
        [et passim.]
ENGLISH, ROBERT, 47.
ENGLISSH, JOHN, a player, 516.
ERBER, house so called in London, 503.
ERDINGTON, GILES DE, 28.
EREMYN, WILLIAM, treasurer of Calais, 211.
ERMIN, SAINT WILLIAM OF, 33.
ERMINA, SANCTA, WILLIAM DE, 40.
ERMYN SKINS, purchased for the robes of King Edward IV., 494.
ERNALD, the Chaplain, 33.
ERPYNGHAM, SIR THOMAS, Chamberlain, and Steward of the Household,
        280, 303 — fetters, &c. sent to, 330.
ERYON, JOHN, 152.
ESCHEATORS OF ENGLAND, writs to, 268.
ESCHEP, RICHARD DE, 48.
ESCOCE, JOHN D', an Esquire of the King of Sicily, arrives to witness
        Queen Margaret's Coronation, 452.
ESHFORD MANOR, farm of, 124.
ESKYN, SIR ROBERT DE, a Scotch Knight, 183.

2 Q 2

2 R

GILES, son of the Duke of Britany, 419.
———— WILLIAM, of Essex, 54.
———— SAINT, London, chaplain to the hospital of, 82.
GINGER, JOHN, 54.
GISSON, HENRY, 374.
GLACE, EDMUND, 489.
GLAMORGAN LORDSHIP, seal ordered for, 201.
GLANVILL, HUGH DE, paid for the removal of the body of Edward II. from
       Berkeley Castle to Gloucester Abbey, 139, 140, 141, 142.
GLASTON, EUSTACE DE, 164.
GLENDURDY vel GLENDOURDI, vel GLENDOUR, OWEN, with other Welsh
       rebels, resisted, 287 — besieges Hardelagh Castle in North
       Wales, 290 — information given respecting him, 332.
———————— GRIFFIN, the son of Owen, 306, 312.
———————— the wife of Owen, 321.
GLOUCESTER, 81, 306, 466, 507—lampreys obtained from, for King Edward
       II.^{d's}. coronation, 122 — council at, 209 — courier sent to, 220 —
       King Henry IV. at, 317.
——————— ABBEY OF, or St. Peter's Church, Edward II.^{d's} body removed
       to, from Berkeley Castle, 140, 141— King Edward buried at,
       259, 264 —money borrowed from the Abbot of, 315.
——————— CASTLE, a clerk imprisoned in, for anti-popery, 209—Nicholas
       Brembre, a prisoner in, 234.
——————— DUKE OF, 420, 425, 505 — charges Nicholas Brembre with
       treason, 234—Garter, King of arms, sent to him, at Hainhalt, 390.
————————————— uncle to Henry VI., 407 — his absence from Eng-
       land, 395 — at Canterbury and Westminster with the Lords of
       the Council, 418, 431.
——————— HUMPHREY, DUKE OF, keeper of England, King Henry V^{th's}
       brother, 350, 366, 413, 414, 417 — takes inquisitions respecting
       heretics, traitors, &c., 412—his services as Lord Deputy of Eng-
       land during the King's absence, 414, 415—his exertions in taking
       the traitor John Sharp, 415,— retained to serve the King in
       France and Normandy, 430 — alien priories granted to, 447.
——————— RICHARD, DUKE OF, (afterwards Richard III.) his expenses,
       490, 502 — persons retained to serve under his command, 498 —
       appointed keeper of the west marches of Scotland, 499 — pay-
       ment to, for the Manor of Hoton Panyll, &c., 499, 501 — pay-
       ments to, for repairing the walls of Carlisle, 501 — fighting men
       retained by him for the Scotch war, 501, 502 — at the town of
       Berwick, with other lords, 502 — attended to Scotland by the

GUNNER, GOKYN, a German-gunsmith, 382.

GUNPOWDER provided, 277, 474 — supplied to Earl Rivers to suppress the rebels in Kent, 494.

GUNS and gunpowder provided, 277, 346.

GUNSMITHS, payments to, 382.

GUNSTEDE, SIMON, the Originalia written by, 293.

GURGENY AP ITHELL AP EIGNON, 231.

GUYDICOIS, RICHARD, a Merchant of the Society of Ricardoz, 102.

GUYENNE, vel GUYNES, vel GUYENES, relieved by John, Duke of Somerset, 445, 446 — John, Earl of Huntingdon, Lieutenant of, 437 — town of Blay, in, given up to King Henry VI., 456.

———— CASTLE, Captain of, 287 — defence of, by Richard Whethill, 487.

GWYLL, PETER DE MONTE ALBANO, 92.

GYNEWELL, JOHN DE, 144.

GYNGER, JOHN, 47.

GYSELHAM, WILLIAM DE, a Justice, 100.

HACHE, HENRY, 508.

HADDAM, PHILIP DE, 10, 11.

HADDELE, STEPHEN DE, 199.

HADDON, JOHN DE, brings David de Bruys from Odiham Castle to London, 166.

HADHAM, ROBERT DE, 179.

HADLE, in Suffolk, 255.

HAGGE, ANDREW, and BLANCH, his wife, kinswoman to Richard II., 248.

HAIA, THOMAS DE, 7, 9.

HAINAU, MARGARET, COUNTESS OF, 373.

HAINAULT, 140 — arms of, 145 — Duke of Gloucester in the dominions of, 390.

———— EARL OF, contract of marriage with his daughter and King Edward III., 140.

HAINFIELD, ADAM DE, payments by, to divers couriers, 28.

HAKE, RICHARD, 162.

HAKEDAY, RICHARD, an apothecary, paid for medicines, 451.

HAKEFORD, ROBERT DE, 65.

HAKEN, WALTER DE, fishmonger, 121.

HALDANBY, ROGER, 281.

HALE, SIR FRANK DE, 190, 191.

HALES, ROBERT, Prior of the hospital of Saint John of Jerusalem, appointed Treasurer of England, 215.

———— THOMAS DE, 121.

HALFORD, JOHN, 449.

HALL, ROGER, an attendant on Sir Henry Percy, 488.

2 s

2 s 2

2 T

2 T 2

2 U

2 x

MATTYS, JOHN, expenses for the custody of, in Kenilworth Castle, 475 — taken to Hereford, 475.

MAUDELYN, ROBERT, Clerk, 266.

MAULEVERER. ROBERT, 307, 322.

MAUNSELL, JOHN, Treasurer of York, 39.

———— THOMAS, 465.

MAUTRAVERS, JOHN, payments to, for expenses of King Edward II., 139.

———————— SIR JOHN, the daughters and heirs of, to be taken in wardship, 231.

MAVUE, OLIVER, a prisoner, 375.

MAYE, EDWARD, a player, 516.

MAYDESTON, RICHARD, 311, 312, 385 — Comptroller of the Exchange in Lombard-street, 375.

MAYHEU, JOHN, Master of the ship Trinity, offers a small ship made of silver to the image of the Holy Mother at the town of Aques, 267 — presents a stone of adamant to King Henry IV., 277.

MAYN, JOHN, 169.

MAYOWE, JOHN, of Neunham, outlawed for felony, his escape, 431.

MEAUGRE, JOHN LE, called Burcigald, Marshal of France, pays for the ransom of John, King of France, 189, 190.

MEAUX DE BREY, in France, expenses for prisoners taken at, 379.

MEDICI, ALBERT, Clerk, sent to Gascony concerning the affairs of Aquitaine, 129.

MEDIOLANNEN, Chancellor of, 36.

MEER, Manor of, 380.

MELBOURN, PETER, Esquire, 269.

MELCOMBE, Port of, 371.

MELEFORD, HENRY DE, 508.

MELETONE, ELY DE, 54 bis.

MELKSHAM, 112.

MELOUN, VISCOUNT DE, Ambassador from France, 253.

MELROS, ANDREW, ABBOT OF, brings a message from the King of Scotland, 484.

MELTON, JOHN, 237, 256 —Clerk in the Exchequer, 254.

———————— WILLIAM DE, Comptroller of the Wardrobe, 118, 126.

MELVER, CONUS, a goldsmith, 357, 358.

MEMORANCY, CHARLES, LORD DE, of France, debt due to, from Joan, Queen of Scotland, 180.

MEMORANDA BOOK of the Receipt of the Exchequer, 189 — Rolls of the Exchequer and Pell Office, 181, 300.

MENART, QUINTIN, Reeve of Saint Omers, and Ambassador from the Duke of Burgundy, scarlet cloth given to, 424, 425.

MENDIEU, BISHOP OF, 162.

2 z

3 A

3 A 2

STAMFORD FAIR, horses purchased at, 291.

STAPOLYN, WILLIAM, his account of the defective government of Ireland, 199.

STAR CHAMBER, a kalendar, cushions, tapestry, and rich cloth provided for the Lords of the Council in, 237, 274 — tapestry work made for, 393. [See Council.]

STAUNFORD, WILLIAM DE, Usher of Queen Eleanor's chapel, 87—Clerk to Robert de Beverley, 91.

STAUNTON, HERVEY DE, Chancellor of the Exchequer, his fee, 135.

———— JOHN, clothier, cloth purchased of, 424.

STEBENHEATH, 102, 103.

STEDS, Merchants of, present three lions to King Edward IV., 502.

STEPHEN, the King's painter, 79 bis.

———— Clerk of Sir Thomas Beaufort, 315.

———— the son of Andrew, 510.

STEPHEN'S, SAINT, CHAPEL, Westminster, chaplain of, 11, 13 — wax-light, &c., provided for, by the King's command, 13, 62 — advowsons of Dewsbury and Walkefield appropriated to, 167 — payments and grants to the Dean and Canons of, 379 — grant to, by King Richard II., 380. [See Westminster.]

———— Chaplain of, 11, 13.

STEVENES, JOHN, 299 — inspects the making of cannon at Bristol, 332.

STEWARD of King Edward I^st's Household, 111.

———— of the King of Scotland, his clerk, 183.

STEYNTON, lands in, 89.

STILLYNGTON, ROBERT, Dean of Saint Martin's, London, Keeper of the Privy Seal, 484.

STIWARD, SIR JOHN, hath the custody of the Duchess of Gloucester, 440.

STOCKBRUGG, NICHOLAS DE, Usher of the King's kitchen, 36.

STOCKTON, HUGH DE, Treasurer of the Templars, London, 18.

STOK, RALPH DE, 124.

STOKDALE, THOMAS, 354, 359, 378, 393, 403, 437 — sent to Normandy, 360.

STOKE, RICHARD, a Courier, 210, 220.

STOKES, ALAN DE, Clerk of the Wardrobe, 209, 226, 233, 252.

———— SIR ALAN DE, 196.

———— JOHN, 495.

———— RALPH DE, 133.

STOKEWELL, JOHN DE, 79.

———————— WILLIAM, paid for painting a ship built at Southampton, 339— indicted for making false keys to chests in the Receipt of the Exchequer, 441.

STORTEFORD, WILLIAM, 247.

3 D

3 E 2

THE END.

LONDON : Printed by W. CLOWES and Sons, Stamford street.

Lightning Source UK Ltd.
Milton Keynes UK
UKHW020639270922
409514UK00005B/275